[illegible] Studies

Volume [illegible]

Edited by [illegible]

V&R unipress

Mamluk Studies

Volume 20

Edited by Stephan Conermann and Bethany J. Walker

ANNEMARIE SCHIMMEL KOLLEG
History and Society during the Mamluk Era (1250 - 1517)

Abdelkader Al Ghouz (ed.)

Islamic Philosophy from the 12th to the 14th Century

With 17 figures

V&R unipress

Bonn University Press

UNIVERSITÄT BONN

MIX
Papier aus verantwortungsvollen Quellen
FSC www.fsc.org FSC® C083411

Bibliographic information published by the Deutsche Nationalbibliothek
The Deutsche Nationalbibliothek lists this publication in the Deutsche Nationalbibliografie; detailed bibliographic data are available online: http://dnb.d-nb.de.

Publications of Bonn University Press
are published by V&R unipress GmbH.

Sponsored by the DFG-funded Annemarie Schimmel Institute for Advanced Study "History and Society during the Mamluk Era, 1250–1517".

Cover image: Portrait of Avicenna by an Uzbek artist, bought by Y. Michot in Bukhara's market in September 2005.
Printed and bound by CPI books GmbH, Birkstraße 10, 25917 Leck, Germany
Printed in the EU.

Vandenhoeck & Ruprecht Verlage | www.vandenhoeck-ruprecht-verlage.com

ISSN 2198-5375
ISBN 978-3-8471-0900-6

Contents

Acknowledgements

The present volume grew out of the international conference "Islamic Philosophy from the 12th to the 14th Century" which took place on 24–26 February 2016 in Bonn. The conference was sponsored by the Annemarie-Schimmel-Kolleg of the University of Bonn, Centre for Advanced Studies, "History and Society during the Mamluk Era (1250–1517)".

First, I would like to express my deep gratitude to the Annemarie-Schimmel-Kolleg, which in turn is funded by the German Research Foundation (DFG), for offering financial support and making this international event possible. I am deeply indebted to Professor Dr. Stephan Conermann (Bonn University, Germany) as well: The idea of publishing this edited volume is the outcome of a fortunate brainstorming between Professor Conermann and myself, who encouraged me while I was a *junior fellow* at the Annemarie-Schimmel-Kolleg to organize an international conference with a focus on my own research areas. I am also immensely grateful to Professor Dr. Frank Griffel (Yale University, New Haven, USA) for his valuable comments and remarks concerning the initial concept of the conference. I am also indebted to the senior and junior fellows of the Annemarie-Schimmel-Kolleg at that time. Many thanks are due to the staff members of the Annemarie-Schimmel-Kolleg – previous and current – who lent me tremendous support with administrative and organizational aspects before, during and after the conference: Dr. Mohammad Gharaibeh, Sebastian Wißdorf, Sarah Spiegel, Fabian Falter, Dr. Claudia El Hawary, Wencke Uhl, Sherihan Inalo, Esther Schirrmacher, Ann-Kathrin Pfeiffer and Jan Hörber. My thanks to the Editorial Board of the *Mamluk Studies Series* for accepting the publication of this edited volume: Prof. Dr. Stephan Conermann (Bonn, Germany), Prof. Dr. Bethany J. Walker (Bonn, Germany), Prof. Dr. Thomas Bauer (Münster, Germany), Prof. Dr. Albrecht Fuess (Marburg, Germany), Dr. Thomas Herzog (Bern, Switzerland), Prof. Dr. Konrad Hirschler (London, Great Britain), Prof. Dr. Anna Paulina Lewicka (Warsaw, Poland), Prof. Dr. Linda Northrup (Toronto, Canada), Prof. Dr. Jo Van Steenbergen (Gent, Belgium). My gratitude also goes to the publisher *Vandenhoeck & Ruprecht* (V&R unipress, Göttingen, Germany), especially to Ms. Laura Haase, Ms. Anke Moseberg and Mr. Oliver Kätsch for their highly professional and friendly handling as well as for their great patience and constructive feedback.

Abdelkader Al Ghouz, Bonn, August 2018

Abdelkader Al Ghouz

Introduction

Brief introductory remarks on the narratives of the supposed disappearance of *falsafa* after al-Ghazālī

Through the end of the 20th century, some historians of philosophy, such as Salomon Munk (1805–1867) and Ernest Renan (1823–1892), considered al-Ghazālī and his condemnation of the *falāsifa* in his work *The Incoherence of the Philosophers* (*Tahāfut al-Falāsifa*) a turning point in the history of "Islamic"[1]

1 Characterising philosophy in the Islamic world as "Arabic" or "Islamic" is a very difficult question that has been the object of controversial debates among historians of philosophy. Indeed, the Arabic language was the common link between all philosophers and translators who contributed to the genesis and development of philosophy in Islam. These were not only Muslims, but Christians, Jews and Pagan. However, because the 13 articles submitted to the this edited volume focus only on philosophers and theologians of Muslim belief, and because the leading question of this volume concerns "what Islamic philosophy was all about from the 12th to the 14th century", it seems to be more appropriate to use the adjective "Islamic" rather than "Arabic". This follows Ayman Shihadeh, who states: "This gap was to be filled by al-Rāzī, who, by his gradual synthesis of *kalām* and *falsafa*, presents, for the first time, an 'Islamic philosophy'. This timely development was exactly what the milieu required: a mature philosophy, or philosophical theology, that was seen not to conflict with orthodoxy, and that did not approach *falsafa* in an essentially negativist manner" (Ayman Shihadeh, "From al-Ghazālī to al-Rāzī: 6th/12th Century Developments in Muslim Philosophical Theology," *Arabic Sciences and Philosophy*, vol. 15 (2005), 178). Furthermore, the focus of all 13 articles revolves *a priori* around the process of naturalising the Avicennian philosophy in Islamic theology from the 12th to the 14th century. Engaging with philosophy as discussed by Muslim as well as by Christian, Jewish and pagan scholars should be characterised as "Arabic philosophy" in order to avoid dismissing the role of the non-Muslim scholars. For the controversial debate on the use of "Islamic" or "Arabic", cf. Michael F. Marmura, "The Islamic Philosophers' Conception of Islam," in: Richard G. Hovanissian and Speros Vryonis, Jr. (Eds.), *Islam's Understanding of Itself*, Malibu: Undena Publications, 1983, 87–88; Oliver Leaman, "Introduction," in: Seyyed Hossein Nasr (Ed.), *Encyclopaedia of Islamic Philosophy*, Lahore: Suhail Academy, 2002, 1; Dimitri Gutas, "The Study of Arabic Philosophy in the Twentieth Century: An Essay on the Historiography of Arabic Philosophy," *British Journal of Middle Eastern Studies*, 29, 2002, 16–19; for a detailed discussion of this debate, see also Shahab Ahmed, *What is Islam? The Importance of Being Islamic*, Princeton: Princeton University Press, 2016, 5–109.

philosophy. Munk, for instance, coined the idea that the philosophical tradition in Islam underwent a deep change as a consequence of al-Ghazālī's critics of philosophy in his work the *Tahāfut.* Munk's interpretation of the Ghazālian impact on the reception of the Avicennian philosophy by Muslim scholars found a sympathetic ear by some of his contemporaries (e.g., Ernest Renan), who further elaborated on and expanded Munk's interpretation to a Ghazālian turn in the study of philosophy in Islamic civilizations. In his work *Averroès et l'Averroïsme: Essai historique,* Renan claimed that al-Ghazālī was one of the "intolerant enemies" of the philosophers because he completely rejected rationalism and converted to Sufism.[2] Furthermore, Renan introduced the Andalusian Muslim philosopher Ibn Rushd (Averroes, d. 595/1198) as the last philosopher whose death marked the end of philosophy in medieval Islam. In addition to Renan and Munk, other historians adopted the narratives of the disappearance of medieval philosophy in Islamic East after the death of al-Ghazālī, and in the Islamic West after the death of Ibn Rushd, e.g., Tjitze J. de Boer (1866–1942) and Ignaz Goldziher (1850–1921).[3]

Over the last 20 years, the study of the post-Avicennian philosophy has attracted the attention of historians of Islamic intellectual history. Generally speaking, most historians of *falsafa* and *kalām* have now broken epistemologically with the narratives revolving around the assumption that al-Ghazālī's condemnation of the philosophers was a "death blow" to *falsafa.*[4] For instance, Frank Griffel writes:

> The same applies to philosophy. Certain intellectual circles in Islam have frowned upon, shunned, and stigmatized the study of philosophy. Other circles, however, favoured it, encouraged philosophers to write books, and rewarded them for it. There is clear evidence that even after al-Ghazālī there were enough of the latter circles to safeguard that philosophy in Islam did not disappear after 1100. At the beginning of this chapter, I tried to show that after al-Ghazālī there were still quite a number of philosophers, who were Muslims, who followed Avicenna, and who taught, for instance, the pre-eternity of the world. If my field of study, that is Islamic studies, has given a wrong impression

2 Renan, *Averroès et l'Averroïsme: Essai historique*, Paris: Librairie August Durand, 1852, 97.

3 For a detailed survey of how these opinions developed in the 19th and 20th centuries, cf. Griffel, *Apostasie und Toleranz im Islam. Die Entwicklung zu al-Ġazālīs Urteil gegen die Philosophie und die Reaktionen der Philosophen,* Leiden: Brill 2000, 3–16; idem, *Al-Ghazālī's Philosophical Theology*, New York: Oxford University Press, 2009, 3–7.

4 See, for instance, Dimitri Gutas, *Greek Thought, Arabic Culture*, London and New York: Routledge, 1998; Robert Wisnovsky, "Towards a Genealogy of Avicennism," *Oriens* 42 (2014), 323–363; Tzvi Y. Langermann (Ed.), *Avicenna and his Legacy: A Golden Age of Science and Philosophy*, Turnhout: Brepols, 2009; Heidrun Eichner, *The Post-Avicennian Philosophical Tradition and Islamic Orthodoxy: Philosophical and Theological Summae in Context* (Habilitation Thesis, Halle, 2009); Griffel, *Al-Ghazālī's Philosophical Theology*, Oxford: Oxford University Press, 2009.

about this in the past one-hundred and sixty years since the appearance of Ernest Renan's 'Averroès et l'Averroïsme' it is now high time to rectify this mistake.[5]

Why choose the period from the 12th to the 14th century?

Why from the 12th century?

It is widely recognised in the academia nowadays that *kalām* underwent a historical turning point as a reaction to the intense engagement with the philosophical legacy of Ibn Sīnā (Avicenna, d. 428/1037). This interaction of *falsafa* and *kalām* was one result of naturalising philosophy/science in Islam during Ibn Sīnā's lifetime. It is also the reason why Wisnovsky speaks of an "Avicennian turn" initiated by the Ašʿarite theologian and the *Imām al-Ḥaramayn* al-Juwaynī (d. 487/1085):

> Some in fact are coming to the conclusion that al-Ġazālī's importance in the history of Islamic philosophy and theology derives as much from his assiduous incorporation of basic metaphysical ideas into central doctrines of Sunnī *kalām*, as from his far more celebrated bashing of the *falāsifa*. What is less well known is that al-Ġazālī's role in the "philosophizing" of Sunnī theology was not a lonely struggle by a single genius, but part of a broader trend that seems to have begun during Avicenna's lifetime and that picked up speed in the first and second generations after Avicenna's death in 1037, with the work of al-Ġazālī's teacher, the Ašʿarite al-Ǧuwaynī (d. 1085), as well as of the Māturīdite al-Bazdawī (d. 1099), work that was carried forward by dozens of subsequent members of those two major Sunnī theological schools. It is clear, in fact, that the dividing line between the Sunnī theologians commonly referred to in the later Islamic tradition as *mutaqaddimūn* ("early" or "ancient"), and those referred to as *mutaʾaḫḫirūn* ("late" or "modern"), lies not with al-Ġazālī but with Avicenna himself, and that the turn in Sunnī *kalām* was therefore Avicennian, not Ġazālian.[6]

Historians of medieval Islamic intellectual history mostly highlight two different timeframes as two different tuning points in the history for the interaction between philosophy/science and *kalām*.[7] The first turning point took place during

5 Frank Griffel, "'… and the killing of someone who upholds these convictions is obligatory!' Religious Law and the Assumed Disappearance of Philosophy in Islam," in: Andreas Speer und Guy Guldentops (Eds.) *Miscellanea Mediaevalia 39:* Das Gesetz, Berlin and Boston: de Gruyter, 2014, 226.

6 Wisnovsky, "One Aspect of the Avicennian Turn in Sunnī Theology," in: *Arabic Sciences and Philosophy* 14 (2004), 65.

7 For the interaction of *falsafa* and *kalām* after Ibn Sīnā, see, for instance, Abdelhamid Sabra, "The Appropriation and Subsequent Naturalization of Greek Science in Medieval Islam: A Preliminary Statement," *History of Science* 25 (1987), 223–243; idem, "Science and Philosophy in Medieval Islamic Theology: The Evidence of the Fourteenth Century," *Zeitschrift für Geschichte der arabisch-islamischen Wissenschaften* 9 (1994), 1–42; idem, "*Kalām* Atomism as an

the phase from Ibn Sīnā to al-Ghazālī, and the second one between al-Ghazālī and Fakhr al-Dīn al-Rāzī (d. 606/1210). The Aristotelian/Avicennian philosophical thought was introduced into Sunnī *kalam* during the first phase. After this introductory period, Muslim theologians were characterised in the second phase (from the 12th century onwards) by their very familiarity with philosophy/science.[8] The process of naturalising philosophy/science in *kalām* reached its zenith in the 12th century[9] in the context of what Yahya Michot calls the "Avicennian pandemic" affecting the development of Islamic theology from the 12th century onwards.[10] Concerning the time from al-Ghazālī to al-Rāzī, Shihadeh states:

> Al-Rāzī transformed Islamic theology to the extent that previous *kalām* seemed irrelevant and obsolete. Perhaps this partly explains the scarcity of information on the 6th/12th century intellectual activity examined here. Even Abū al-Barakāt al-Baghdādī takes a step to the background, as his direct influence on later Islamic thought diminishes. Al-Rāzī's place in later Muslim theology is somewhat comparable to that of Ibn Sīnā in *falsafa*. For it appears that almost all later theology, that of proponents and opponents alike, was done *vis-à-vis* his philosophical theology. This, however, is another story.[11]

For his part, Wisnovsky points out:

> (…) In this sense, Rāzī stood in relation to Avicenna as Avicenna stood to Aristotle: as a sometimes critical but nevertheless deeply indebted appropriator of the srcinal author's theories. Ṭūsī, by contrast, stood in relation to Avicenna as Averroes (Ibn Rushd, d. 595/1198) stood to Aristotle: as an energetic defender stamping out the corruptions of previous (mis)interpreters.
>
> Partly as a result of his broader understanding of exegetical practice, Rāzī came to be presented in subsequent narratives of post-classical Islamic philosophy as one of Avicenna's greatest opponents, while Ṭūsī was portrayed as Avicenna's greatest defender. One slogan of such narratives was that Rāzī was 'Leader of those who raise objections' (*imām al-mushakkikīn*), whereas Ṭūsī was 'Leader of those who establish the

---

Alternative Philosophy to Hellenizing *Falsafa*," in: James E. Montgomery (Ed.), *Arabic Theology, Arabic Philosophy. From the Many to the One: Essays in Celebration of Richard M. Frank*, Leuven: Peeters, 2006, 199–272; Dominik Perler and Ulrich Rudolph (Eds.), *Logik und Theologie: Das Organon im arabischen und im lateinischen Mittelalter*, Leiden and Boston: Brill, 2005; Sabine Schmidtke (Ed.), *The Oxford Handbook of Islamic Theology*, Oxford: Oxford University Press, 2016.

8 Shihadeh, "From al-Ghazālī to al-Rāzī: 6th/12th Century Developments in Muslim Philosophical Theology," *Arabic Sciences and Philosophy*, vol. 15 (2005), 141–179, cf. Eichner, *The Post-Avicennian Philosophical Tradition and Islamic Orthodoxy*, 8, n. 5.

9 Cf. Griffel, *Al-Ghazālī's Philosophical Theology*, 7; Adamson, "Philosophical Theology," in: Sabine Schmidtke (Ed.), *The Oxford Handbook of Islamic Theology*, Oxford: Oxford University Press, 2016, 309.

10 Michot, "La pandémie avicennienne au VIe/XIIe siècle," *Arabica* 40 (1993), 287–344.

11 Shihadeh, "From al-Ghazālī to al-Rāzī: 6th/12th Century Developments in Muslim Philosophical Theology," 179.

truth' (*imām al-muḥaqqiqīn*). In other words, Rāzī's way of construing *taḥqīq* – as including a critical engagement with the theories being interpreted – was rejected and relabeled as *tashkīk*, whereas Ṭūsī's more restrictive view of *taḥqīq* was embraced and came to predominate, at least in the context of Avicennian exegetical practice.[12]

Why to the 14th century?

The present volume limits itself to the 14th century in agreement with the programmatic article by Dimitri Gutas entitled "The Heritage of Avicenna: The Golden Age of Arabic Philosophy, 1000–ca. 1350", which he conceptualizes as a catalogue of criteria to be examined to show – in terms of case studies – the extent to which the timeframe under consideration in this volume was philosophically significant.[13]

The present volume

In order to make a comprehensive contribution to the ongoing research challenges concerning the question of how *falsafa* and *kalām* interacted with each other in the context of naturalising philosophy/science in Islam, this volume centres on the following questions: What was philosophy all about and which reactions did it create especially in *kalām* works from the 12th to the 14th century? The present volume comprises 13 articles that tackle these questions from various different angles. It is structured around six main sections reflecting the topics and the approaches of the contributions.

Section 1, "Historical and Social Approaches to Philosophy", consists of two contributions that present a social approach to studying intellectual history. *Dimitri Gutas* traces the role of prominent scholars who contributed tremendously to the genesis of new genres of writing after Ibn Sīnā. He asks whether the period under consideration was indeed a "golden age" of philosophy/science or

12 Wisnovsky, "Towards a Genealogy of Avicennism," 326. Dimitri Gutas, for his part, refutes Wisnovsky's interpretation quoted above and argues: "Avicenna had no pre-determined (or revealed) doctrine to which he tried to make Aristotle fit, whereas ar-Rāzī did, his criticism by and large tending to make Avicenna conform to Ashʿarite views." Gutas, "Avicenna and After: The Development of Paraphilosophy," in: Abdelkader Al Ghouz (Ed.), *Islamic Philosophy from the 12th to the 14th Century*, Göttingen: Bonn University Press and V&R unipress, 2018, 51, n. 73.

13 Gutas, "The Heritage of Avicenna: The Golden Age of Arabic Philosophy, 1000–ca. 1350," in: Jules Janssens and Daniel De Smet (Eds.), *Avicenna and His Heritage.* Acts of the International Colloquium, Leuven – Louvain-la-Neuve, September 8–11, 1999, Leuven: Leuven University Press, 2002, 81–97.

rather of "paraphilosophy". *Maribel Fierro* examines the nature of the relationship of Averroes, a harsh critic of the Ash'arite theology, with both the Mu'minid caliphs of his times and the Almohad movement founded by Ibn Tūmart (d. 524/1130), who was a strong adherent of Ash'arism. This approach is crucial for contextualising Averroes' "disgrace", both socially and scholarly.

The two articles presented in Section 2, "Knowing the Unknown", are centred on occultism and its interpretations by prominent philosophers and theologians. *Yahya Michot* examines how Ibn Taymiyya (d. 728/1328) read Ibn Sīnā's interpretation of the prophetic faculties as described in the *namaṭ* of the *Ishārāt* in a Mamluk context. In order to let Ibn Taymiyya speak for himself, Michot includes in his article an English translation of the passages quoted by Ibn Taymiyya in his work the *Ṣafadiyya. Luis Xavier López-Farjeat* tackles the question of how Ibn Bājja (Avempace, d. 533/1138), Ibn Rushd (Averroes, d. 595/1198) and Ibn Khaldūn (d. 808/1406) interpreted Ibn Sinā's doctrine of veridical dreams and prophecy described in his epistle *al-Risāla al-Manāmiyya.* Using a comparative approach, López-Farjeat examines how each of the above-mentioned scholars explained the acquisition of particular forms and how they conceived the dimensions of veridical dreams and prophecy.

Section 3, "God, Man and the Physical World", presents some views of prominent scholars concerning the world's creation and creation itself. Basing his contribution on the scholarly milieu of the $6^{th}/12^{th}$-century Bagdad, *Andreas Lammer* analyses al-Shahrastānī's (d. 548/1153) and Abū l-Barakāt al-Baghdādī's (d. 560/1164–5) doctrines concerning God's priority over the world and the question of *when* God brought the world into being. *Davlat Dadikhuda* sheds lights on the issue of how Fakhr al-Dīn al-Rāzī (d. 606/1210) and Nāsīr al-Dīn al-Ṭūsī (d. 672/1274) engaged with and reacted to Ibn Sīnā's philosophy of the human soul and the latter's relationship to the body, basing the analysis on *Kitāb al-Ishārāt* VII.6. *Peter Adamson* tackles one of the crucial points where philosophy/science and *kalām* meet up in the context of the above-mentioned process of naturalization. Adamson presents al-Rāzī's conception of the void, aiming to explain the extent to which al-Rāzī accepted the Avicennian arguments in the *Shifā'* and, consequently, Aristotle's arguments in the fourth section of the *Physics.*

In Section 4, "Universals", *Fedor Benevich* describes Muḥammad b. ʿAbd al-Karīm al-Shahrastānī's (d. 1153) metaphysics. He argues that al-Shahrastānī found a way to combine the *aḥwāl* theory of traditional Ash'arism with the Avicennian metaphysics of universals. *Yuki Nakanishi* sheds light on the controversy surrounding the reality of existence (*wuǧūd*) as discussed by the early Timurid philosopher-theologian Sa'd al-Dīn al-Taftāzānī (d. 792/1390) and the early Ottoman Akbarian mystic Shams al-Dīn al-Fanārī (d. 834/1431).

In the first article of Section 5, "Logic and Intellect", *Hanif Amin Beidokhti* first outlines the epistemic basis used in debating the categories up to the 13th century and then addresses the question of what al-Suhrawardī (d. 586/1191) criticised in the peripatetic classification of categories. Furthermore, Beidokhti briefly discusses the philosophical benefits of the categories for al-Suhrawardī's *Ḥikmat al-Ishrāq*. *Nariman Aavani* looks at the philosophical reflections of the (understudied) philosopher-theologian Afḍal al-Dīn Muḥammad Ibn Ḥasan Kāshānī (known as Bābā Afḍal, d. 610/1214) and exposes Bābā Afḍal's epistemic arguments for the unification of the intellect, the intellector and the intelligible, contextualising them within the broader scholarly context of the Aristotelian and Avicennian philosophy.

Section 6, the final section of the present volume, "Anthropomorphism and Incorporealism", consists of two articles that shed light on debating God's attributes in Ḥanbalite theology. *Livnat Holtzman* focuses on Ibn Taymiyya's tolerant attitude towards answering theological questions that fall in the category of *bi-lā kayfa*, such as questions related to anthropomorphism. *Jon Hoover* addresses the question of how Ibn Taymiyya uses Averroes' philosophy in order to criticise Fakhr al-Dīn al-Rāzī's incorporealist concept of God.

Bibliography

Adamson, Peter, "Philosophical Theology." In: Sabine Schmidtke (Ed.), *The Oxford Handbook of Islamic Theology*, Oxford: Oxford University Press, 2016, 297–312.

Ahmed, Shahab, *What is Islam? The Importance of Being Islamic*, Princeton: Princeton University Press, 2016.

Eichner, Heidrun, *The Post-Avicennian Philosophical Tradition and Islamic Orthodoxy: Philosophical and Theological Summae in Context* (Habilitation Thesis, Halle, 2009).

Griffel, Frank, *Apostasie und Toleranz im Islam. Die Entwicklung zu al-Ġazālīs Urteil gegen die Philosophie und die Reaktionen der Philosophen*, Leiden: Brill, 2000.

–, *Al-Ghazālī's Philosophical Theology*, New York: Oxford University Press, 2009.

–, "'… and the killing of someone who upholds these convictions is obligatory!' Religious Law and the Assumed Disappearance of Philosophy in Islam." In: Andreas Speer und Guy Guldentops (Eds.), *Miscellanea Mediaevalia 39: Das Gesetz*, Berlin and Boston: de Gruyter, 2014, 201–226.

Gutas, Dimitri, *Greek Thought, Arabic Culture*, London and New York: Routledge, 1998.

–, "The Study of Arabic Philosophy in the Twentieth Century: An Essay on the Historiography of Arabic Philosophy." *British Journal of Middle Eastern Studies*, 29, 2002, 16–19.

–, "The Heritage of Avicenna: The Golden Age of Arabic Philosophy, 1000 – ca. 1350." In: Jules Janssens and Daniel De Smet (Eds.), *Avicenna and His Heritage. Acts of the International Colloquium, Leuven – Louvain-la-Neuve*, September 8–11, 1999, Leuven: Leuven University Press, 2002, 81–97.

–, "Avicenna and After: The Development of Paraphilosophy." In: Abdelkader Al Ghouz (Ed.), *Islamic Philosophy from the 12th to the 14th Century*, Göttingen: Bonn University Press and V&R unipress, 2018, 19–71.

Langermann, Tzvi Y. (Ed.), *Avicenna and his Legacy: A Golden Age of Science and Philosophy*, Turnhout: Brepols, 2009.

Leaman, Oliver, "Introduction." In: Seyyed Hossein Nasr (Ed.), *Encyclopaedia of Islamic Philosophy*, Lahore: Suhail Academy, 2002.

Marmura, Michael F., "The Islamic Philosophers' Conception of Islam." In: Richard G. Hovanissian and Speros Vryonis, Jr. (Eds.), *Islam's Understanding of Itself*, Malibu: Undena Publications, 1983, 87–88.

Michot, Yahya, "La pandémie avicennienne au VIe/XIIe siècle." *Arabica* 40 (1993), 287–344.

Perler, Dominik and Rudolph, Ulrich (Eds.), *Logik und Theologie: Das Organon im arabischen und im lateinischen Mittelalter*, Leiden and Boston: Brill, 2005.

Renan, Ernest, *Averroès et l'Averroïsme: Essai historique*, Paris: Librairie August Durand, 1852.

Sabra, Abdelhamid I., "The Appropriation and Subsequent Naturalization of Greek Science in Medieval Islam: A Preliminary Statement." *History of Science* 25 (1987), 223–243.

–, "Science and Philosophy in Medieval Islamic Theology: The Evidence of the Fourteenth Century." *Zeitschrift für Geschichte der arabisch-islamischen Wissenschaften* 9 (1994), 1–42.

–, "*Kalām* Atomism as an Alternative Philosophy to Hellenizing *Falsafa*." In: James E. Montgomery (Ed.), *Arabic Theology, Arabic Philosophy. From the Many to the One: Essays in Celebration of Richard M. Frank*, Leuven: Peeters, 2006, 199–272.

Schmidtke, Sabine (Ed.), *The Oxford Handbook of Islamic Theology*, Oxford: Oxford University Press, 2016.

Shihadeh, Ayman, "From al-Ghazālī to al-Rāzī: 6th/12th Century Developments in Muslim Philosophical Theology." *Arabic Sciences and Philosophy*, vol. 15 (2005), 141–179.

Wisnovsky, Robert, "One Aspect of the Avicennian Turn in Sunnī Theology." *Arabic Sciences and Philosophy* 14 (2004), 65–100.

–, "Towards a Genealogy of Avicennism." *Oriens* 42 (2014), 323–363.

Historical and Social Approaches to Philosophy

Dimitri Gutas

Avicenna and After: The Development of Paraphilosophy. A History of Science Approach*

Mais que foutait Dieu avant la création?
Samuel Beckett[1]

Introduction: The Terms of the Discussion

With Avicenna now demonstrably situated at the center of the philosophical tradition in the Islamic world, it has become apparent that philosophy after him was mostly in reaction to his philosophy. What at first started as a working hypothesis, that the different reactions to Avicenna's philosophy in the three centuries after him (1050–1350) as either supporting, or rejecting, or reforming his theories constituted a "golden age of Arabic philosophy," has opened up a very fruitful period of research on the post-Avicenna developments which partly substantiates the hypothesis: this period did witness an unprecedented and committed engagement with Avicenna's philosophy at various levels of sophistication and participation.[2] But what this engagement consisted in, and what its essence, motivation, and function were – or "what philosophy was all about" after

* This is a revised and expanded version of the keynote speech delivered at the conference on February 24th, 2016. The relatively informal tone of the lecture has been retained, as was the sketchy format, given the broad spectrum covered, which also necessitated that the added annotation, with a certain well-meaning didactic edge to it, be kept to the essential minimum. I wish to thank Peter Adamson, Asad Ahmed, Dag Hasse, Matthew Melvin-Koushki, and Ayman Shihadeh for their very helpful comments and suggestions on earlier drafts, while I assume responsibility for all interpretation of the historical record and for errors that may remain.

1 *Molloy*, Paris: Editions de Minuit, 1951, 227. Beckett's own English translation, in collaboration with Patrick Bowles, has a different twist, and inexplicably (to me) leaves out the crucial objection in *mais:* "What was God doing with himself before the creation?" (*Three Novels by Samuel Beckett. Molloy. Malone Dies. The Unnamable*, New York: Grove Press, 1965, 167). The irreverence – if irreverence it is – is twentieth century, but the question itself with its sea of implications, and the exasperation in the tone, are dead serious, and old (Augustine put it as follows: *Quid faciebat deus, antequam faceret caelum et terram? Confessiones* XI,10); they are also the subject of paraphilosophy in Islam after Avicenna.

2 Gutas, "The Heritage of Avicenna," which the present essay re-focuses by providing the historical and ideological context.

Avicenna until the Timurids, as the question is put in the program of our conference, and whether this golden age was a golden age of *philosophy* – is a different matter, and is the problem at hand, which I propose to discuss historically.

First, it is necessary to be precise about what is meant by "philosophy" historically in the Islamic world – not what we mean by it today but what the medieval scholars understood by it, and indeed at different times. Because this is a serious part of the problem. For us moderns (or post-moderns, if you will, and leaving aside the professors of philosophy – *not* the historians of philosophy – in academic departments today), philosophy is a fuzzy concept, basically meaning deep thoughts about life and the world in general, and at best including ethics of a non-religious character.[3] Even logic, modern logic, and the philosophy of language, may be considered border-line philosophy. For the ancient and medieval philosophers, though, and especially for thinkers from late antiquity onward, with whom we are concerned here, philosophy was something quite concrete: it meant all the rational sciences, so basically what we broadly term science nowadays.[4] This must be obvious to anyone who has had a look at the classification of the sciences in medieval Islam, or, at the very least, at the contents of Avicenna's *ash-Shifāʾ*: it includes logic, the theoretical sciences – namely physics, whose eight parts range from the principles of physics and cosmology to psychology, zoology, and botany (we do not call these subjects "philosophy" today) – then mathematics – the ancient quadrivium of arithmetic, geometry, astronomy, and music – and then metaphysics, or the investigation into the principles of being and the ultimate, or necessary, being itself. Avicenna also treats what were classified as the practical sciences – ethics, oeconomics, and politics – briefly at the end of the metaphysics: these were no less scientific studies insofar as they investigate human behavior in individuals, in families, and in the city or state. So, the philosophers were doing science, and so was Avicenna, and once we stop using the (for us) fuzzy word "philosophy" we can acquire a better tool with

3 The fuzziness of the concept, even as used by historians of philosophy, at times verges on meaninglessness when it is claimed that "philosophy is where you find it," or "philosophy is, ultimately, whatever philosophers think it is" (which is tautological, for it raises the circular question who a philosopher is – one who does philosophy!). See note 57 below and the references cited there.

4 I hardly need to cite authorities to support this historical fact, but it helps to provide the broader context of the discussion: "When we study ancient philosophy, we are guided by our contemporary conception of the philosophical enterprise. This makes it easy for us to overlook the fact that the ancient philosophers had a very different conception of their philosophical activity;" Michael Frede, "The Philosopher," in Brunschwig and Lloyd, 2. And more to the point, the statement of the two editors of this volume in their "Introduction," p. xii: "[T]his division [in "contemporary parlance"] between science and philosophy does not correspond at all to the conceptual frameworks of antiquity."

which to gauge what Avicenna as well as his predecessors and successors were doing.

Our investigation is thus the history of *science*, as understood by the medieval thinkers themselves (and the ancients, of course, as I will soon mention), and not by us and our categories and definitions;[5] henceforth I will be using the word science (and at times also science/philosophy) to refer to what we usually call philosophy or science and philosophy. But before we can talk about what Avicenna did in his science, it is necessary to discuss briefly what had previously been done in science in Greek, since science in the Islamic world is partly the extension and partly the revival of Hellenic science,[6] and we can best understand what Avicenna was doing by reference to this background. But having said that, two more terminological clarifications are needed before we proceed, first about the Hellenes and second about science.

I will be talking about the Hellenes to refer to what we normally call ancient Greeks, that is, the Greek speaking peoples of the first millennium BC and following in the southern Balkans and the Aegean, with their culture and ethnic Olympian religion. The reason why I make this disctinction is that they tend to be confused with the Greek speaking peoples in the eastern Roman empire, whom we normally, and again, ill-advisedly, call Byzantines, because of the identity of their language. But the Hellenes *as historical agents* through their societies, institutions, beliefs, and ideas were quite different from the Roman Orthodox (whom I will so name instead of "Byzantines")[7] in almost every aspect except the language, and calling everybody indiscriminately Greek confuses the issues – sometimes deliberately.[8] I also hope this distinction will stave off a misunderstanding that I am arguing on racial grounds, race not being a category that is, or can be, of use in historical hermeneutics.

5 There is a lot of discussion nowadays on these subjects, on what science is, among historians and philosophers of science; there are even those who maintain that science begins with Newton and that everything that went before him is not science: it is "nature-knowledge" or "mathematical knowledge," etc. But such a priori definitions and theoretical ruminations are hardly relevant, or of benefit, to historical investigations such as the present one.

6 In general, see Gutas, "The Rebirth of Philosophy."

7 Byzantium was a Megarian colony at the mouth of the Bosporus inhabited by Hellenes. The Roman emperor Constantine chose it as the site of his residence, and the name, Christian this time, was changed to Constantinople. Thus Byzantines refers to the pre-Constantine Hellenic inhabitants of the city and their culture. Under Christianity the term "Byzantines" referred only, if at all, to the inhabitants of the capital city, not to all the subjects of the eastern Roman empire, as the term does today. The empire itself, like its culture, was called, knew itself as, and was, always Roman; see the extensive discussion by Kaldellis, *Hellenism*.

8 In a way I am following the medieval Arab usage, which was historically correct in the discrimination it makes: they called the Hellenes *Yūnān*, and the Roman Orthodox, very properly, *Rūm*, or Romans.

When it comes to the Hellenic science I will be discussing next, it must be emphasized, again to avoid misunderstanding, that I (or any of my sources, particularly Lloyd) am not *defining* what Hellenic science or any science was, is, or should be, but simply describing what it historically was according to the best scholarship available, and the reason is that it was precisely this science that was transmitted into early Islam, which is my subject. The late David Pingree wrote an excellent article warning against the symptoms of the disease he called "Hellenophilia," which are, thinking that the Hellenes invented science, that they discovered the scientific method, that their sciences are the only real sciences, and that true science is only what scientists, following the Hellenes, are doing now. I am doing none of this but describing what Hellenic science was, and saying that it was followed and applied in early Islam not because Muslims (and Christians, and Jews, and Zoroastrians, and polytheists in the early ʿAbbāsid and Būyid periods) *had* to follow it if they wanted to do science, but because they in fact *did*. The historical specificity of my argument throughout is essential to investigating and understanding what philosophy was before, for, and after Avicenna.

1. Hellenic Science in History

The Hellenes, then, did science, but in addition they talked about its methods and what it means to do science. Hellenic science can be defined by the following three characteristics it exhibited: it was (a) an open-ended and rational inquiry into reality (all reality and not only the physical world, but also the cosmos as well as social products: ethics, politics, literature); (b) an investigation and explanation of first principles and causes; and (c) a continuous discussion and reevaluation of the methods used in the inquiry both by oneself and by others. These characteristics of Hellenic scientific inquiries as well as their origin, progression, causes, and social context have been examined in great detail by a number of scholars and in particular in the publications by G.E.R. Lloyd, which provide a precise historical understanding of science as practiced by the Hellenes.[9]

The progression of this science can be seen from the sixth century BC to the sixth century after Christ. It was, however, very uneven, and its rate depended on a number of historical factors, which need to be stated, examined, and studied in

9 Primarily Lloyd, *Magic, Reason and Experience*; *Science, Folklore and Ideology*; and *The Revolutions of Wisdom*, with many others being of relevance. They are highly recommended, for their methodology and approach, to students of all history of science and not only Hellenic, and certainly also "Islamic."

each case. For our purposes, I will mention three major aspects or characteristics of the *practice* of this science, which will also help us as we move forward to science in the Islamic world.[10]

The first is the development of *research science:* it is the basic function of the scientific approach to reality, whose rational investigation aims to find out, explain, and prove how things – all things – work or are set up. Among the Hellenes, these developments start with the first pre-Socratics and continue apace throughout antiquity. The different fields of inquiry are established: physics, astronomy, mathematics, medicine, metaphysics (inquiry into first principles and being as being), ethics, politics, etc., and, with Aristotle's *Poetics*, even literature.[11] This initial period is analyzed in great detail by Lloyd who shows, step by step, how the shift was made from a mythological view of reality at one end of the ideological spectrum, closer to a scientific one at the other end – from mythos toward logos, as it has often been described, but with the understanding that mythos and logos are the two extremes of the ideological continuum that is socially constructed, not two absolute and incommensurable modes of being in binary opposition. The shift was piecemeal, very gradual, and of course never complete (it still isn't), but it itself was real and revolutionary; as Lloyd puts it,

> The distinction between science and myth, between the new wisdom and the old, was often a fine one, and the failures of ancient science to practise what it preached are frequent; yet what it preached was different from myth, and not *just* more of the same, more myth. The rhetoric of rationality was powerful and cunning rhetoric, yet it was exceptional rhetoric, not so much in that it claimed not to be rhetoric at all, ... as in supplying the wherewithal for its own unmasking.[12]

The major nodal point in this process which Lloyd's analysis reveals, and which demands continuous attention, is the confrontation between the results of scientific research and the traditional beliefs of society, religious and otherwise –

10 P.R. Blum drew a useful distinction in his 1998 book between two types of doing philosophy, what he called "philosopher's philosophy" (*Philosophenphilosophie*) and "school or curricular philosophy" (*Schulphilosophie*). The first refers to a philosopher's independent and open-ended thinking outside of institutionally and socially imposed modes of thought, and the latter to scholasticized philosophy as an academic subject that is to be taught. His analyses refer to the early modern period, but the distinctions are actual and historically accurate and can be applied to philosophizing of all periods. Niketas Siniossoglou (to whom I am indebted for bringing Blum's study to my attention) and I used it with reference to philosophy in the later Roman Empire ("Philosophy and 'Byzantine Philosophy'"). In what follows I expand upon the concept for application to philosophy in antiquity and Islam.

11 In his introduction (1447b9), with a word preserved only in the Syriac and then its Arabic translation, Aristotle expressly says that this field had not been recognized until his day and remains "anonymous" (*bi-lā tasmiyatin*).

12 Lloyd, *The Revolutions of Wisdom*, 336.

some of which the titles of Lloyd's books specify as magic, folklore, and ideology. At each such point of discovery and the research that led up to it, the question is which side the scientist himself will take, and why, as well as what the factors are that will allow or hinder the acceptance and reception of this discovery within society in general. This confrontation and the research that leads up to it constitute the major conflict in the social history of science and the basic criterion by which we can judge scientific developments. This makes scientific research a highly political act, and political analysis can never be dissociated from the history of science (as unfortunately is still very much the case).[13] I will come back to the issue of traditional beliefs later (in section 2).

The second is the development, already by the end of the fourth century BC, of *curricular* or *school science,* that is, the formation of a collection of scientific doctrines as a body of teachings already achieved, usually following the views of an authority scientist, for the purpose of their study and dissemination. This leads to what may be called the *scholasticization* of science, in both meanings of the term scholastic, referring to teaching and also to pedantic adherence to a set of teachings. This is a prerequisite for research science, insofar as each scientist has to advance to the level of his predecessors before he can move forward, but the scholasticization of a body of knowledge also led to its use for social and political purposes. This process started with, or at least was fully put deliberately in place by, Aristotle, both in his personal method of research and in the practice of his school. Aristotle as a rule gave a survey of his predecessors' opinions on any given subject before he proceeded to its investigation, and to that end he and his school were the first to start collecting source material for all their studies – today we would say that they compiled data bases: opinions of mathematicians, of physicists, constitutions of the Greek city states, etc.[14]

Through an amazing confluence of historical events, this procedure of scholasticized science, of forming a body of scientific knowledge for the purposes of studying it, teaching it, and progressing beyond it, acquired a manifest social and political function, even if previously implicit, right after the death of Aristotle, because of Alexander's conquests. Some of Aristotle's and Theophrastus's

13 The political and socially anchored dimension of scientific research, which is often crucial to its survival, should be easier to comprehend and appreciate in 2017 when climate change and a host of other scientific results find little purchase among Western governments, let alone the rest of the world.

14 The concise formulation of the Peripatetic project under Aristotle, which was to record what has been called the history of science until his day and collect the opinions of his predecessor scientists, remains that by Jaeger, *Aristotle*, 334–336, followed by numerous studies that provide the details and explore the ramifications. For Eudemus, one of Aristotle's students most active in this area, see the illuminating collection of articles edited by Bodnár and Fortenbaugh. A recent comprehensive study of the ancient historiography of science is by Zhmud.

students, notably Demetrius of Phaleron, moved to Alexandria under the first Ptolemies and were instrumental in the foundation of the Museum and the Library there at the very beginning of the Hellenistic period (323–31 BC). The Museum and the Library, as repositories of all knowledge – that is, by this time, of both research and school science – became symbols of the majesty of the Ptolemies and henceforth an indispensable tool of royal glory, used by all rulers in centuries to come. Augustus in particular, the first Roman emperor, had a cultural policy, for political purposes, of extolling classical Hellenic civilization.[15] The significance of this development for our purposes is that it adds yet another political angle in our analysis of scientific work. In this context, the engagement of each scientist has to be assessed for whether it was directed to research science or school science, or both, and why: what was the social inducement, or reward, or impediment for each scientist and at each historical context to engage in one or the other, or in both?

The third is what can be called the *dogmatization of school science:* by late antiquity, the corpus of Hellenic school teachings became rationalized and consolidated to assume a doctrinaire quality; this consolidation, whatever its negative effects on research science scince by definition it would not allow improvements, nevertheless makes this now well-defined body of Hellenic school science exportable, and as a result we see its international acknowledgment as universally valid science and its attendant translation into other languages in the West (of India), notably Syriac and Middle Persian at first and eventually Arabic and other languages. This had far-reaching implications, depending on the circumstances, on research science in each historical context.

Briefly, the historical course of this development can be traced as follows. Until the fourth Christian century, research science and school science were heavily engaged in in the Greek speaking world in the eastern Mediterranean and the Near East, with the scientific view of reality spreading among the educated elites and without noteworthy resistance from traditional forms of belief and proponents of the Greaco-Roman mythological world-view. This is true even for the non-Greek speaking populations, whose elite, educated in Greek, participated in the scientific activities *in Greek.* Latin speakers who were educated enough as to be interested in these subjects read or studied them in Greek – or bought educated Greek slaves; while Aramaeans themselves contributed mightily in Greek: the two most notable thinkers being Iamblichus from Apamea in Syria (d. ca. 325) and Porphyry from Tyre in today's Lebanon (d. ca. 305). Plotinus (d. 270) provides the most striking example: a Greco-Egyptian, or most likely a native Latin speaker from upper Egypt (Plotinus is a Latin name – Plotina was the

15 Of the many studies on the Ptolemies and the early Empire, particularly revealing of cultural policies is the study by Spawforth.

emperor Trajan's wife – and he was the protégé of the Roman emperor and Roman aristocracy), he taught philosophy in Rome *in a defective Greek* whose written expression had to be corrected by Porphyry,[16] whose native tongue was Aramaic!

But the emergence of Christianity as a social force in the fourth century proclaimed and championed the mythological approach to reality in a form more vehement than anything that Hellenic traditional forms of belief could produce. The defining characteristic of late antiquity, certainly from the viewpoint of the history of science, but also more generally, was the conflict between Hellenism and Christianity, the ensuing defeat of the former, and the complete change in outlook and approach to reality that this brought about. This was of huge consequence to science: truth was no longer what was discovered at the end of open-ended inquiry into reality by rational – including logical and mathematical – means, but what is encoded and revealed once and for all in a book: in the case of Christianity, the mythological narrative of the Bible.[17] Others scholars have more charitably called this change in outlook a change from the anthropocentric to the theocentric.[18] This, though perhaps true from a certain viewpoint, softens the contrast; but it is necessary to be explicit about its stark and vehement nature.

After Constantine established Christianity as the state religion of the Roman Empire early in the fourth century, the pressure on the Hellenes was thus to conform – the pressure being exerted by social, administrative, and violent means: the lynching of the woman scientist Hypatia in Alexandria by a Christian mob, instigated by the bishop Cyril, later sanctified for his efforts; Justinian's edict prohibiting Hellenes to teach, thus effectively shutting down the Academy in Athens in 529; and a host of other measures and activities, all well documented, aiming at suppressing, delegitimizing, and ultimately killing or converting the adherents of the Olympian religion (and other religions as well).[19] The effect on

16 Porphyry, *Life of Plotinus*, §§ 19–20.

17 In a chapter in which he discusses the interplay and dialectic between tradition and innovation (or mythos and logos, traditional beliefs and science) in Hellenic societies until late antiquity, G.E.R. Lloyd makes the following assessment of the change that came about at the end of that process: "What in some areas of thought was to alter the balance [between tradition and innovation] irrevocably – indeed by the sixth century A.D. had already done so in those areas – was the appeal to a particular text, the Bible, as revealed truth. The shift from reference to the 'divine Hippocrates,' the 'divine Plato,' and so on, to reference to the word of God may seem not so great in verbal terms, but it reflects fundamental differences not least in the underlying institutional realities: the creation of a church, the constitution of Christianity as the official religion of empire, and the availability of a new battery of sanctions that could be deployed against the deviant;" *Revolutions of Wisdom* 107.

18 Athanassiadi in *Mutations*, p. ix, and throughout the Introduction.

19 A recent publication edited by Marie-Françoise Baslez, on the persecutions conducted *by* Christians in the fourth century alone, offers nuanced and sensitive studies of their history, even if at times apologetic for the stark presentation of Christian cruelty. In one of the articles,

the progression of science of such relentless persecution from the fourth century onwards was accordingly for Hellenic science to consolidate and rationalize its teachings and establish a corpus of Hellenic doctrine and eventually dogma, as the line of defense against Christian dogma. This trend can be documented in most fields of Hellenic endeavor. Up until the third century the various schools of ancient science/philosophy were active; after that they gradually fade out and only Platonists and Aristotelians remain to contest the center of general scientific activity. The same applies to particular fields like medicine: in the second century Galen was energetically arguing against the other approaches to medicine which were antagonistic to his own; in the following centuries we hear less and less of them. And the most explicit acknowledgment of this effort to consolidate, rationalize, and dogmatize the results of Hellenic learning comes from the field of medicine: the emperor Julian, himself in mortal combat against Christianity in the fourth century, asked the physician Oribasius to collect "all that is most important from all the best doctors" in a comprehensive *Medical Collection*, which Oribasius did, in seventy volumes.[20] Similar developments can be seen in astronomy with and after Ptolemy (second century), whose work was eventually frozen as the undisputed authority in that field, and in other sciences: a body of doctrine became standardized, consolidated, and dogmatized, usually on the authority of a key figure or figures, for the purposes not only of teaching at home but, more importantly, of projecting persuasive respectability abroad in the contest with rival dogmas.

The doctrine of science itself was what we call Neoplatonism, a system with an Aristotelian body capped by a rather incongruous Platonic head, while the curriculum of scientific teaching was Aristotelian throughout, with the Platonic dialogues forming the culmination of philosophical training.[21] Aristotle himself had already, and famously, established the classification of the different parts of philosophy/science, in *Metaphysics* E.1 and K.7, into the various fields I enumerated above. This classification was used by Andronicus of Rhodes for editorial purposes when he put the extant school treatises of Aristotle in a certain se-

"Les maisons de la cachette" (pp. 395–402), Yann Le Bohec begins his study (p. 395) by stating that the task of the historian is not to judge what is good and what evil in history but to establish the facts, and that the practices revealed by these facts should not be explained, much less judged, as if they were taking place today. This is well and good, and applies to the present study as well, which is why I cite it, but at the same time it must also be emphasized that such practices of curtailing and denying, by whatever means, freedom of speech, religion, and thought, even if we do not condemn them by modern standards, had historical consequences which should be equally explicitly stated and not swept under the rug.

20 *Corpus Medicorum Graecorum* 6.1.1.4.7f., cited in Lloyd, *The Revolutions of Wisdom*, 332n152.

21 A brief survey of late antique developments in the conduct and instruction of science/philosophy in Greek is conveniently offered by Rudolph, "The Late Ancient Background."

quence in his edition in the first century BC, and was later further elaborated upon by the Neoplatonists for the purposes of instruction in their numerous introductions to the study of Aristotle. But the Neoplatonists went even beyond that and erected an elaborate schema of classification of Aristotle's works in which individual treatises corresponded to a discrete field of study. The result of this process was that the classification of *Aristotle's* works became, in effect, a classification of all the sciences, and hence of *all human knowledge*. Thus a curricular classification of the sciences whose function was initially descriptive and later preponderantly pedagogical, eventually was dogmatized to acquire normative value on the assumption that it reflected ontological reality as well: as the last Neoplatonist teachers in Alexandria insisted, science/philosophy – that is, all rational human knowledge – is so divided because inherently and by its very nature can be only so divided.[22]

The system thus codified for pedagogic and ontological – or factual – reasons represented the sum total of Hellenic science and offered the scientific view of the world in contradistinction to the mythological narratives of religions – not only Christianity, but potentially all religions. It was thus eminently teachable, but also, not being culture- and religion-specific, exportable. And it was this essentially Aristotelian system that was adopted and translated, in the pre-Renaissance era, into the languages of the various peoples in the West (of India).

I do not know (or I do not know yet, if I live long enough) the historical reasons behind this momentous change in cultural attitudes – from engaging in science *in Greek* to *translating* it into one's own language – but the evidence we have all points to the fact that at the beginning of the sixth century, in a period of amazing historical synchronicity, there are programmatic efforts to translate the Greek Aristotelian curriculum into national languages. Boethius in Italy conceives the plan to translate Aristotle into Latin, his contemporary Sergius of Rēshʿaynā in northern Mesopotamia starts on a similar project in Syriac, while *their* contemporary, the Sasanian emperor Chosroes I (Anūshirwān) is clearly sponsoring the translation of some of the logical and physical works of Aristotle into Middle Persian. Although the progress and outcome of these beginnings varied as time went by, the fact is that the Hellenic scientific body of learning in the form of the Aristotelian curriculum as developed and dogmatized by the last Hellenes, the Neoplatonists, was internationally acknowledged throughout the West even before Islam appeared.

22 See Gutas, "Paul the Persian," 255–259.

2. The Historical Agency of Traditional Beliefs and Religion

Before we proceed with Islam, let me discuss a bit more explicitly the main conflict between science and traditional beliefs and religion. A very significant subject, it is usually misunderstood and misapplied in discussions of the history of science.

Briefly, traditional beliefs and religion can be understood as the account of reality provided in a mythological narrative endorsed by a society at large. This mythological narrative is generally considered sacrosanct and, in monotheistic religions, immutable and unnegotiable. But scientific research discovers ways in which reality works that are inconsistent with this narrative. At this point the real issue is not whether religion in general, or any specific religion, as it is mostly taken, is essentially for or against science, but the political, social, and cultural factors that are powerful enough to determine whether, and the extent to which, the scientific discovery is to be accommodated to the mythological narrative or upheld independently. Accordingly, there is *a scale of adherence to the mythological narrative* of a religion, from none to total, which is the discriminating factor in this case. If no adherence at all on one end of the scale would be atheism, the minimal might be that of the Epicureans, for example, who made gods responsible for the universe but then abstain completely from running it. Descartes (1596–1650) also did the same: as Blaise Pascal (1623–1662) said in his *Pensées*, complaining about him,

> To write against those who plunge too deeply into science. Descartes.
> I cannot forgive Descartes. He would gladly have left God out of his whole philosophy. But he could not help making Him give one flip to set the world in motion. After that he had no more use for God.
> Descartes, useless, and questionable.[23]

Around the middle of the scale would be most likely the majority of medieval scientists: while adhering to and even believing in the mythological narrative of their respective religions, they nevertheless found different ways to accommodate it to the superior scientific truth, usually by allegorizing it and making it express symbolically what the scientists say, as the early Muslim philosophers did (about whom more later in section 3). There are thus numerous positions that were historically adopted by different peoples at different times and which register at different points on the scale.

So when one discusses religion as inhibitor of scientific progress one should be careful to discriminate as I have just described. For frequently religion is the motivating factor for scientific research. An excellent example is provided by the

23 J.M. Cohen, translator, 82.

development of the science about the age of the earth.[24] The early scientists who began investigating the subject, including Newton (1642–1727), started from the position of the Biblical dating which they sought to verify. Scores of scientists in the succeeding centuries, with different approaches (in astronomy, geology, biology: evolution, and physics: radioactive measuring) came up with different answers up until we have reached the point we have today. The crucial issue at each new discovery about the age of the earth that was inconsistent with the Biblical mythological narrative was, which side the scientist would support – the Bible or his scientific discovery – and the answer in each case depends on the confluence of forces, attitudes, and consequences, and this is broadly speaking the *political context*. What determines the position of a scientist, or a part or the entirety of the intellectual class, on the scale of adherence to the mythological narrative is the political and ideological context in each case, which has to be carefully scrutinized for its specific effect on scientific activity. The question is not, what a specific religion says in general or in a particular revealed text about science or any given scientific issue – the age of the earth, for example, or the creation – but what political authority (ruler), entity, or class supported, promoted, or enforced a particular religious position on these subjects at a specific time and place, and why they felt that such a position was beneficial for their hold on and projection of power, for their finances, and for their legitimacy.

The dominant ideology of the eastern Roman and the Islamic empires was the Biblical revealed religion which was used as their major source of legitimacy and social and political organization. In the case of the Roman Orthodox of the eastern Roman Empire, which initiated the confrontation with Hellenism, we see that with few exceptions, they placed themselves on the scale at the literalist and unnegotiable extreme of total adherence to the mythological narrative. They did this legally, in Justinian's code; ecclesiastically, in the two *synodicons* (ninth and twelfth centuries) anathematizing Hellenic learning; and socially, both through physical violence against Hellenes and through public opprobrium and displacement against them. The historical reasons for this, scholars of the Roman Orthodox religion have been (benignly?) negligent in investigating, but surely two reasons were preponderant: the extreme closeness of the emperor to the church, whose organization was an effective means of control and support, and the self-identification of the Roman Orthodox elites as the anti-Hellenes: because Greek-speaking Orthodox Christianity in the eastern half of the Roman Empire developed within a Greek-speaking Hellenic population, it had to define itself for its very essence as the correction, transformation or simply *negation* of Hellenism as a worldview. In the zero-sum game that ensued in the centuries from late antiquity onward, any concession to Hellenism would inevitably mean a diminu-

24 Described with a light touch by Krivine, 13–46.

tion of the essence of Orthodoxy. Thus, at the intellectual level all aspects of Hellenism as a worldview had to be fought against to the bitter end, and certainly the science and scientific worldview, the very embodiment of Hellenism. What the Roman Orthodox thus retained of Hellenic science was school science, which was preserved in the copying of some scientific manuscripts (certainly not all – the amount that was lost is stupendous).[25]

To proceed next to the historical agency of religion as it relates to science beyond the Greek-speaking context and in translation, there is the case of Syriac. With the Arameans in the Near East by the sixth century, the situation had changed. What had changed, of course, was that they had converted to Christianity. Whereas until well into the fourth century they had participated in research science in Greek as adherents of their ethnic religion, like Porphyry and Iamblichus I cited earlier as examples, once Christianized they produced no more research scientists. The revealed truth of Christianity which they had adopted left no room for independent investigations into reality; at most they could use and translate parts – quarantined parts – of school science. The educated could read the Hellenic scientific canon in Greek, but in the confrontation of their mythological narrative of reality with Hellenic science they opted for the former, and on the scale of adherence to the mythological narrative they registered quite close to the "right" extreme: they accommodated school or dogmatic science to fit their mythology. Let me cite two examples among many.

Jacob of Edessa (ca. 630–708), an ecclesiastic and bishop of that city, was without doubt one of the most learned Syriac scholars, who knew Greek intimately. In his *Hexaemeron*, a description of the world from its beginning, Jacob uses scientific sources, including Aristotle's *Physics* (which he had manifestly read in the original), seeking to prove that Hellenic philosophy is in agreement with Moses. But in the course of his argumentation, he dismisses or corrects whatever in Hellenic science does not agree with the Mosaic account, and describes it as foolish and godless speculation.[26]

In a recent article, Henri Hugonnard-Roche studied in detail the discussion of the human soul in the Syriac philosophical tradition. Not surprisingly, he found that it was completely dominated by Christological concerns and was alien to the psychology of Aristotle and the Aristotelian tradition.[27] The *De anima*, which was

25 This fact is not commonly known and even less appreciated: of the two thousand four hundred and fifty (2450) names of Hellenic philosophers/scientists about whose activity between the sixth century BC and the end of the sixth century AD we have certain evidence, there survive the texts of only a very small fraction of them in any significant amount. See the statistics and tables given by Richard Goulet and Ulrich Rudolph in their Introduction in Derron, pp. xi–xxxvii.

26 Wilks, "Jacob of Edessa's Use of Greek Philosophy," 223.

27 Hugonnard-Roche, "La question de l'âme."

the foundation of Western scientific psychology until the 19th century (and arguably down to Freud), was of no interest to Syriac scholars.

However, Syriac speakers were not as viscerally antagonistic to Hellenism as such, or to Hellenic science, as the Roman Orthodox. They did translate selectively the Hellenic scientific corpus – primarily logic and some popular and paraenetic literature, and almost no physics and metaphysics – but this was curricular or school science, translated for paedagogic purposes, material that at best could be adopted for theological purposes.[28] What was studied of this material was studied mostly in digest form, as part of a holistic education which had to include Hellenic science because of its fame, rather than as a higher discipline which had to be engaged in for research purposes.[29] Daniel King reports that on occasion some Hellenic science was studied even for the purpose of "name-dropping," of showing oneself off as educated and hence superior to one's interlocutor.[30] In such cultural context research science can hardly exist, let alone flourish, and the Christian Syriac scholars did not have any science. Faced with this fact, Ernest Renan famously said back in 1852 that Syriac speakers were by nature of mediocre abilities.[31] Perhaps today we can be less racist and explain this fact in social and political terms. The center of the Syriac communities after their conversion to Christianity was the church and the monastery, around which their social life revolved, since they did not have an independent state of their own that would provide civil or administrative institutions; church ideology was thus necessarily dominant, and conformity to it rewarded members of the society. Accordingly, they registered high on the "right" extreme on the scale of adherence to their mythological narrative.

3. Science in Early Islam

With the Muslims of the early period until Avicenna (d. 1037), the situation was different. As the new kids on the international block, it was advantageous to the Muslim rulers, especially after the ʿAbbāsid revolution, to adopt the body of knowledge of their time, and this was the Hellenic school science. For many

28 Cf. Hugonnard-Roche, "Traductions syriaques."

29 See the assessment, on the basis of a study of the manuscript materials actually used for instruction, by Arzhanov and Arnzen, "Die syrische Rezeption der aristotelischen *Physik*," 438: "Die syrische Schultradition dazu neigte, philosophische Texte der aristotelischen Tradition entweder in verkürzter Form oder in Form von Sammelwerken zu tradieren, in denen Zitate von Aristoteles mit der Kommentarliteratur eng verwoben wurden."

30 Daniel King, "Why were the Syrians Interested in Greek Philosophy?" 77–78.

31 *De philosophia peripatetica apud Syros* 3. For fuller discussion see Gutas, "Historical and Ideological Dimensions," 336–339.

reasons that I have discussed elsewhere, the scientific curriculum was translated.[32] Among these reasons I could briefly cite primarily the development of a climate of rationalism among the elites that was both politically advantageous and conducive to scientific research, something that was the case neither with the Roman Orthodox across the Islamic frontier nor with the Syriac communities inside it, as just summarily described, but was rather akin to what we can estimate to have been the climate fostered by the last Sasanians, notably Anūshirwān: one is reminded of the introduction to the *Kalīla wa-Dimna*, a product of Anūshirwān's time, that extols rationalism.[33] But in any case, this subject of early ʿAbbāsid rationalism is in need of extensive study and explanation.

On its basis, then, it was possible under the early ʿAbbāsids to engage in research science; the mythological narrative of Islam at that point was accommodated to the needs of science, and it was politically feasible for the Muslim scientists to position themselves, for the most part, at some middle point on the scale of adherence to that narrative. Al-Kindī (d. after 866), who also introduced formally the discipline of philosophy/science into Arabic as an integrated thought system, from metaphysics to mathematics and astrology, did this in a wonderfully inventive way.

In his listing of the books of Aristotle and their aims, al-Kindī indulges in a few asides to emphasize the significance of a point he is making. When talking about the significance of Aristotle's logical works, especially the *Categories*, he mentions their importance for the acquisition of knowledge by humans, which is different, he says, from the way that prophets acquire knowledge. He says, in effect,

> Human knowledge … [is] below the rank of divine knowledge: divine knowledge comes about without seeking and exertion, without any human technique (*ḥīla*), and without time, like the knowledge possessed by prophets. God has granted them exclusively this knowledge which comes about without seeking, or exertion, or research, or any technique – be it the mathematical sciences or logic – or time, but rather it comes simultaneously with His will through the purification of their souls and their illumination toward truth by means of His support … . For this knowledge is proper to prophets to the exclusion of all other humans … since those among mankind who are not prophets have no access to … knowledge … except through seeking and .. through logic and the mathematical sciences we mentioned, and in time.[34]

32 Gutas, *Greek Thought, Arabic Culture.*

33 See for a brief review of these developments, Gutas, "The Rebirth of Philosophy," 108–121, with references.

34 Al-Kindī, *Fī kammiyyat kutub Arisṭū*, I,372–373 (Abū Riḍā ed.). Cf. the full passage in Adamson and Pormann, *The Philosophical Works of al-Kindī*, 286.

Very cleverly, al-Kindī puts the requirements of the Islamic mythological narrative beyond the concern of humans, leaving the field open for scientific inquiry. God gives supreme knowledge to prophets and only to prophets, he says, thus conceding the mythological narrative, but since the rest of humanity are not prophets – nor can we expect to have another one, given the Islamic belief about Muḥammad's being the last – they can only acquire knowledge by scientific means: logic, mathematics, and the methods and techniques (he uses the word *ḥiyal*) of scientific investigation.

This attitude toward scientific inquiry, which was widely shared among the elite in Baghdadi circles and in other major provincial capitals in the Islamic world (Avicenna, it should be remembered, grew up in Bukhara, and Averroes in Cordoba), enabled the Arabic reception through translations of the Hellenic school science to proceed to research science. As a result, we witness in the first three centuries of ʿAbbāsid rule a kaleidoscope of research avenues pursued in Baghdad and beyond, which is indicative of the absence of dogmatic science. The al-Kindī line of scientists are largely ignored by the Aristotelians of Baghdad, who set up their own research methods and priorities, and all are shunned by Abū Bakr ar-Rāzī (d. 925), who comes up with his own account of reality, and in whose arguments against the Ismāʿīlī Abū Ḥātim ar-Rāzī (d. 934) we see a description of scientific research with which all scientists could identify. When Abū Ḥātim blames Abū Bakr and the scientists for not speaking with one voice and for disagreeing with each other (as opposed to the followers of revealed truth who all believe in one thing), Abū Bakr tries to explain that this is precisely how open-ended scientific research is conducted, with each scientist progressing beyond the findings of his predecessor with his new discoveries.[35]

Avicenna represents the culmination of this approach. He improves and corrects Aristotelian science in many areas (as he himself expressly records), notably in logic, metaphysics, and the theory of the soul, he develops an empiricist approach to knowledge, and completely accommodates religion to scientific truth by *explaining* it, and not merely explaining it away, in symbolic and allegorical terms. He makes no concessions whatsoever to the Islamic mythological narrative, explaining everything by constant reference to scientific positions in natural science, and thus improves upon al-Kindī. His position is that prophets are not special people who were mythically and inexplicably given special knowledge by God, unattainable by the rest of humanity, as al-Kindī would have it, but regular humans who happen to have extraordinarily developed

35 A much translated and discussed debate, see the translation and references in Gutas, *Avicenna*, 235–240.

the two major faculties of their soul, intellect and imagination, basing his explanation on a far-ranging development of Aristotle's theory of the soul.[36]

Here it is important to note that in the areas in which Avicenna worked during his politically turbulent career – Transoxiana, Khurasan, and Iran – the cultural attitudes of the power structures (the rulers and their courts, and the *ʿulamāʾ*) continued to be receptive to and appreciative of scientific research, which Avicenna was able to conduct. The ruling elites who were dispensing patronage to scientists like Avicenna were genuinely interested in scientific research, and if not for the science itself, then certainly for the prestige that accrued to them for having a scientist of the caliber of Avicenna in their court: this prestige translated into legitimation, projection of power, and (posthumous?) fame. This is clearly indicated by the controversies in which Avicenna was embroiled while in Iran, notably with the philosophaster from Hamaḏān, Abū l-Qāsim al-Kirmānī. His defense consisted of writing letters to the philosophers in Baghdad, and to viziers, in which he discussed at length scientific points, expecting to be vindicated on the basis of the soundness of his science, and not on his probity, character, innocence, or, especially, orthodoxy. It is even more telling that his opponents (possibly Abū l-Qāsim himself) tried to accuse him of having imitated the style of the Qurʾān, thus bringing Avicenna's religious standing into question; Avicenna naturally wrote a letter defending himself, but nothing of import happened: the affair appears to have been of no consequence.[37] In the Būyid century, and certainly in the two centuries preceding it, strict adherence to the mythological narrative of Islam was not an instrument which the ruling elites thought they could use to their advantage to bolster or secure their power.

The achievement of Avicenna in historical terms is that he presented an entire, integrated, self-consistent, and rational view of all reality, based on school science and his own research science, which incorporated and explained, but also respected, religions, revelation, and the Islamic tradition. This is what made it immensely successful and irresistible, but at the same time it potentially set itself up, and eventually was set up by others having specific political agendas, as the opposite and contradictory world-view to that presented by the Islamic mythological narrative. This constituted the major ideological conflict in Islamic societies in the East after Avicenna (and even beyond Timurid times), and the ensuing intellectual history is largely a record of the ways in which this conflict played itself out. The contest in the various reactions to Avicenna was between the defense, with the occasional additional arguments and materials, of the school science view of reality as presented in his work on the one hand, and the attempts

36 Gutas, *Avicenna*; Adamson, *Interpreting Avicenna.*

37 For the personal writings of Avicenna relating to these controversies see Gutas, *Avicenna* 503–504 and the literature cited there.

against science aiming to rehabilitate, endorse, and enforce the literal validity of the Islamic mythological narrative on the other. These anti-scientific attempts, though united in their ultimate aim as just described, were nevertheless of various colorings, and generated, both directly and indirectly, sundry positions and traditions that characterize the intellectual and ideological landscape after Avicenna. These positions evolved and developed gradually over the following few centuries and were pursued with impressive sophistication and expertise. The most siginificant of them are discussed below.

4. Anti-Scientific Developments in Islam after Avicenna

The very first and most important anti-scientific step that was taken by all factions was in the epistemological domain, aiming to reject the primacy, indeed the unique relevance, of reason in science, and postulate, or rather assert as fact, an extra- or supra-rational means of acquiring knowledge that was variously described as illumination (*ishrāq*), "unveiling" (*kashf*), "tasting" (*dhawq*), inspiration, etc.

Al-Ghazālī (d. 1111) was the first major thinker to take this approach, in a specific manner. In a very public document – a self-serving apologia and justification of his actions, allegedly concerned about orthodoxy, in the service of political authorities – he discusses the very central question of epistemology, how we know. In the *Munqidh* he divides the acquisition of knowledge into four separate and graded stages (*aṭwār*),[38] and assigns to each its own specific objects: sense-perception (*ḥiss*), discernment (*tamyīz*), intellection (*ʿaql*), and what he calls only metaphorically the "eye of prophecy" (*ʿayn an-nubuwwa*), by which one "beholds the unseen, what is to be in the future, and other things which are beyond the ken of intellect." He takes great pains to emphasize the absolute distinction between the last two stages: the intellect (*ʿaql*), he says, acknowledges "its own inability to apprehend what is apprehended by the eye of prophecy," and prophecy, he repeats, constitutes "a stage (*ṭawr*) beyond reason."[39] Eventually al-

38 The choice of words is typical of al-Ghazālī's procedure of replacing scientific terminology with vague concepts that have no specific referents, only rhetorical effect and, frequently, religious resonance. Here he substitutes the term *ṭawr*, a stage, phase, or state that something is in, for what philosophers had always called the "faculties" of the soul, *quwwa*, pl. *quwan*, a scientifically specific component of organic life. *Ṭawr*, of course, is a Qurʾānic term (71:14). See on this subject Treiger, *Inspired Knowledge* 22–23, and more generally, for al-Ghazālī's "camouflaging" (p. 6) of Avicennan technical terminology.

39 Al-Ghazālī, *Al-Munqidh min aḍ-ḍalāl*, 110–11, 116–117, 124 (ed. J. Ṣalībā and K. ʿAyyād); English translation by Watt, *Al-Ghazālī*, 63–64, 70, 78 (in this last passage Watt translates *ṭawr* inconsistently as "sphere," which I corrected). The same four stages of the acquisition of knowledge are repeated by al-Ghazālī in his *Mishkāt*; see Treiger, *Inspired Knowledge*, 53.

Ghazālī also used the word *dhawq* (taste), another Avicennan term misappropriated by him, to refer to the same stage of supra-rational cognition by non-prophets.[40] Thus, in direct contrast to Avicenna's epistemology, which has the prophet's intellect alone grasping the highest truths through logical means, al-Ghazālī restricts the function of the intellect and logic to the acquisition of the inferior part of knowledge (the intelligibles, necessary truths, etc.), and postulated only a mythical "eye of prophecy" as the means to the highest part (the "unseen," i.e. the nature of the deity, future events, etc.). What Avicenna with scientific rigor had clarified and incorporated into a rational system of scientific explanation is obfuscated by al-Ghazālī and mystified once more.[41]

Radically compromising the very foundation of scientific research as al-Ghazālī's actions were, they were nevertheless conducted by an insider, or by one who posed (and was perceived) as an insider of the scientific tradition, and accordingly his epistemological positions affected that tradition. Suhrawardī, the executed (*maqtūl*, d. 1191) Master of Illumination, came from outside and declared his personal supra-rational acquisition of knowledge from the outset. In the introduction to his *Ḥikmat al-ishrāq* he emphasizes that the philosophy of illumination (manifestly both the book and the philosophy itself) "came at first upon me not by means of a thought process, but its setting in was by means of something else,"[42] and then proceeds to divide philosophers into a number of classes or ranks (*ṭabaqāt*) according to the degree to which they combine in their method "research" (*baḥth*) and "auto-apotheosis" (*ta'alluh*, self-deification). According to this, it becomes clear that this "something else" in the previous quotation was his "self-deification." Suhrawardī's primary promoter and enthusiast in the succeeding century, Shamsaddīn ash-Shahrazūrī (d. after 1288), specifies in his commentary on *Ḥikmat al-ishrāq* that the sciences which investigate reality are of two sorts, those conducted on the basis of "taste" (*dhawq*) and "unveiling" (*kashf*) and those conducted on the basis of "research and theoretical investigation,"[43] and concludes by naming Suhrawardī as the "quintessence of the self-deified philosophers" (*lubb al-falāsifa wa-l-ḥukamā' al-muta'allihīn*).

40 Treiger, *Inspired Knowledge*, 55, and the entire chapter for the transformation of Avicennan *dhawq* into supra-rational knowledge.

41 Gutas, "Ibn Ṭufayl", 238–239.

42 In Arabic, *lam yaḥṣul lī awwalan bi-l-fikr, bal kāna ḥuṣūluhū bi-amrin ākhara* (Corbin, *Oeuvres*, 10,9; Walbridge and Ziai 2,6–7 (Arabic)). One is to note the use of the impersonal and intransitive verb *ḥaṣala* here, which indicates that the knowledge in question was not actively acquired by Suhrawardī as the result of inquiry and investigation but that it was something that came or happened to him from outside.

43 In Arabic, *al-ʿulūm al-ḥaqīqiyya tanqasimu ilā qismayni, dhawqiyya kashfiyya wa-baḥthiyya naẓariyya*, in Corbin, *Oeuvres*, 5,8 and 6,14.

After Suhrawardī and al-Ghazālī, the theory, now taken as fact, of the existence of a supra-rational mode of knowledge becomes ubiquitous, both within the traditional scientific/philosophical tradition and outside it, in the newly launched Illuminationist tradition. There is hardly a thinker, of any affiliation, who did not subscribe to it. This includes even staunch followers of Avicenna, like Naṣīraddīn aṭ-Ṭūsī (d. 1274), the great scientist who managed to convince even the Mongol Hülegü to fund the Marāgha observatory and research center. One would have expected Ṭūsī to stay true to the foundations of scientific thought espoused by Avicenna, but in a crucial epistemological passage in his commentary of the *Ishārāt* he blazes the way for supra-rational perception. At the end of that work, *Namaṭ* X, section 9, Avicenna says that "those thoroughly versed in the philosophy of the supernal [world]" (*ar-rāsikhūna fī l-ḥikma al-mutaʿāliya*)[44] know that the supernal spheres, in addition to having corporeal souls and separate intellects, also have non-corporeal rational souls which are able to perceive universals and particulars simultaneously. His phrase *al-ḥikma al-mutaʿāliya* in context thus means "philosophical doctrine relating to the supernal spheres." In his commentary, ar-Rāzī takes this understanding of the phrase as self-evident and has little to say about the passage other than to point to this doctrine of non-corporeal rational souls by Avicenna. Ṭūsī, however, inexplicably – or rather, surprisingly – mystifies the term and says that it refers to knowledge through "unveiling" and "tasting," using the two words *kashf* and *dhawq*, which by then had become among the most commonly used expressions for supra-rational cognition.[45] Avicenna does not say anything about either of these two words in this passage, or even hint at anything remotely relating to extra-rational perception, and so Ṭūsī's interpretation is completely gratuitous; what is worse, the phrase as interpreted by Ṭūsī had a notorious afterlife in Islamic thinking.[46] Now one may speculate about the motivations behind Ṭūsī's interpretation – whether he really believed it, or was following a trend he did not wish to resist, or felt compelled to toe a line consonant with the political and ideological inclinations of his sponsors (given his turbulent career amid Ismāʿīlīs, Twelvers, shamanistic Mongols, and various shades of Sunnīs) – but the incident shows precisely how politically motivated the positions taken by thinkers were in the confrontation of science with the mythological narrative of Islam.

In later centuries, the existence of supra-rational cognition, which by then had been elevated to the status of scientific fact, becomes entrenched in self-styled philosophical discourse and indeed one of the means used to criticize the scientists (i. e., Avicenna) for disregarding it. As one example among many I could

44 *Al-Ishārāt wa-t-tanbīhāt* 375 (Zāreʿī).
45 *Sharḥ al-Ishārāt* IV, pp. 122–124 (Dunyā).
46 See Gutas, "*Al-Ḥikma al-mutaʿāliya*" for full discussion of this passage and references.

cite Mīr Ḥusayn al-Maybudī (d. 1504), one of the major scholars straddling the pre-Safavid and early Safavid era in Iran, where "philosophy" was most actively engaged in. In his works which best represent his philosophical thinking, *Sharḥ-i Dīwān-i ʿAlī* and *Jām-i gītī-numā*, "he is outspoken in his criticism of Ibn Sīnā's rejection of God's knowledge of particulars and of the latter's rejection of bodily resurrection" (obviously the reach of the long arm of Ghazālī's condemnation of the philosophers, to be discussed below, stretched throughout the centuries). "He blames the Aristotelian philosophers for having restricted the sources of knowledge to the intellect (*ʿaql*), and shows his sympathy with Suhrawardī's philosophy of Illumination. According to him the path of Illumination is a middle way (*barzakh*) between intellectual thought (*tafakkur*) and Sufism (*taṣawwuf*)."[47]

The establishment of the theory of the existence of supra-rational cognition in scientific thinking had momentous consequences for the development of science/philosophy in the eastern Islamic world in the period from Avicenna's death to the Timurids (and also beyond). If science/philosophy is the open-ended *rational* investigation into reality, which all who possess reason, as all humans do, can follow, then it can be easily seen that asserting one's superior knowledge through some unspecified and mysterious "inspiration" etc. negates the entire scientific enterprise. Not only does this justify the Islamic myth of prophecy through *waḥy* – this would be the least problematic aspect of its adoption, as thoroughgoing rationalism could be maintained even when Muḥammad's prophecy can be interpreted as the last miraculous exception to the rule of reason (as al-Kindī did, discussed above) – but it opens the way to arbitrary proclamations of higher truths attained through "tasting," inspiration, etc., by any self-appointed seer, visionary, or wiseman.

The second grievous anti-scientific development after Avicenna was in the social and legal domain, with the criminalization of heterodox thought, which was defined as unbelief (*kufr*) and accorded the legal status of "clandestine apostasy", *zandaqa*, punishable by death under certain circumstances. At the forefront of these legal developments, al-Ghazālī in particular was effective in the equation of unbelief as apostasy and in the identification as unbelief of the three philosophical tenets he singles out in the *Tahāfut*.[48] It is important to ascertain al-Ghazālī's specific agency and personal responsibility in this matter, in order to understand precisely how and in what sense he can be absolved (as the current scholarly trend has it), if at all, of the charge that he brought about the downfall of

47 Pourjavady, *Nayrizī*, 36–37.

48 Griffel, *Apostasie und Toleranz*, who discusses the historical development of the concept of apostasy, with briefer accounts in his *Al-Ghazālī*, 104–105, and "Apostasy" in *EI*³, with further references.

science/philosophy. The legal developments concerning *zandaqa* and *kufr* in Shāfiʿī and Ḥanafī circles came about in the mid-eleventh century and subsequently, during the political struggles of the Baghdad caliphate and the encroaching Sunnī Saljuqs against the increasing influence of the Fāṭimid Ismāʿīlīs (al-Ghazālī's book against the Ismāʿīlīs, *Faḍāʾiḥ al-bāṭiniyya*, was commissioned by the caliph al-Mustaẓhir). In this context, tightening legal definitions of apostasy to include political opponents of the state is understandable and explicable. But scientific knowledge and ideas were never actually, nor were they considered until that time as being, seditious against established authorities; as a matter of fact, exactly the opposite was the case throughout the first three ʿAbbāsid centuries, when scientists were sponsored and patronized by various rulers in the central and eastern Islamic lands, as we just saw above in the case of Avicenna. Disagreements and bitter feuds among the various disciplines and even within a single discipline certainly did exist, and they were sometimes accompanied by rhetorical charges of impiety or unbelief,[49] but this is quite different from relegating one's ideological but *not* political opponents to a legal status in which one can demand their execution by the state. But this is precisely what al-Ghazālī did, deliberately and gratuitously, and without any precedent: he selected three scientific theories of Avicenna, branded them as unbelief, and demanded the capital punishment for those who upheld them. In other words, al-Ghazālī made literal adherence to the mythological narrative of Islam at the extreme right end of the scale I mentioned above a *legal* and *political*, not scientific issue.[50] That no one took al-Ghazālī's *fatwā*, if *fatwā* it was, seriously, and that no thinker after him was executed on these charges, indicates precisely that al-Ghazālī was personally responsible for taking this position and that he was not simply expressing the political climate and mainstream religious sensibilities of his time. At the same time, however, that no one was executed on these charges would also tend to show that no one dared to hold explicitly and unambiguously the condemned opinions lest the very charges be brought against him. In other words, the condemnation worked.

49 Griffel, *Al-Ghazālī* 104, reminds us of the case of the ninth century Muʿtazilite Abū Mūsā al-Murdār who accused of unbelief all people who did not share his beliefs, and of his colleague's witty repartee that "according to al-Murdār's view only he and three people who agreed with him" would enter paradise.

50 The unique and gratuitous nature of al-Ghazālī's action is also brought out when compared with other refutations of the philosophical positions, like that of his younger contemporary al-Malāḥimī: "Al-Ghazālī combines his theological and philosophical refutations with a legal condemnation. His willingness to adopt so much from Ibn Sīnā coincided with a forcefully intolerant, one can even say violent attitude toward those elements he regarded as dangerous. Ibn al-Malāḥimī's refutation lacks that kind of intolerance. As … a Muʿtazilite he did not think that unbelief (*kufr*) should or could be punished by state authorities or leading members of the Muslim community" (Griffel, "Theology Engages" 453).

The extraordinary nature of al-Ghazālī's actions and their chilling effect on science cannot be easily overlooked (or sugarcoated), and the question of his motivations remains. Political and religious reasons would seem to be operative here, though it is difficult to see, now that we have better accounts of his life, whose political interests he served, and what benefits he himself would reap, not so much from scapegoating the scientists (if it is assumed that such an animus against scientists was representative of a more general attitude), as particularly from threatening them with capital punishment, especially when it is seen that up until a generation or two before him, in Syria and Iraq with the Baghdad Aristotelians, and in central Asia and Iran with Avicenna, science/philosophy had been a well established and respected theoretical discipline in social life. Religious motivations should be discounted as well, if only because there were just as many pious Muslims like al-Ghazālī before him who felt no need to go to the extremes that he did in order to "save" or "revive" Islam. Personal, or rather, personality considerations may be just as operative.

Avicenna's greatness and reputation, also as they found expression in his Autobiography, were an object of envy to all posterity and proved to be an irritant and a challenge, calling for response and one-upmanship. Avicenna famously says in the Autobiography that he learned all of science/philosophy on his own, when he was about sixteen years old, in a year and a half. In the *Munqidh*, al-Ghazālī retorts that he learned science/philosophy in about the same time that it took Avicenna to do it, but he goes one better by mentioning that he did it under extreme circumstances: while Avicenna devoted himself day and night to his studies, al-Ghazālī says he had to do it in stolen moments from between writing and lecturing three hundred students! Al-Ghazālī's mention of the number – rounded out, to be sure – has no other function than to highlight the difference between Avicenna's study of philosophy in tranquillity and his own under stress, and to show himself, al-Ghazālī, to be the superior thinker.[51] But al-Ghazālī's motivations aside, his identification of three scientific tenets as unbelief, along with his condemnation of many others as unproven, limited necessarily the area of scientific operation, as these subjects were pronounced off limits to scientific investigation.

The third major anti-scientific development was that the Avicennan corpus of school science pertaining to metaphysics and some of the physics, now subject to supra-rational methods of analysis and treated with the theological aim of accommodating al-Ghazālī's inquisition and Islamic doctrine more generally, was re-formulated, re-packaged, and regurgitated in a new genre of writing that we are at pains to identify. This process took some time to reach maturity, and it also took a variety of forms, the motor driving it being al-Ghazālī's intervention that

51 Gutas, "Graeco-Arabic Philosophical Autobiographies" 53–56.

changed the terms of the discussion by making religion the arbiter of science at both the intellectual and legal plane. The new genre that was developed was neither science/philosophy nor the traditional theology/*kalām* because the exigencies to which it responded were different from those that had generated the other two disciplines.

> In a situation w[h]ere the same people were interested in both *falsafa* and orthodox theology, what was most needed was an Islamic *falsafa*, not variations of anti-*falsafī* dialectical *kalām*. ... This gap was to be filled by [Fakhraddīn] al-Rāzī, who, by his gradual synthesis of *kalām* and *falsafa* presents, for the first time, an 'Islamic philosophy'. This timely development was exactly what the milieu required: a mature philosophy, or philosophical theology, that was seen not to conflict with orthodoxy, and that did not approach *falsafa* in an essentially negativist manner.[52]

In other words, what "the milieu", the Muslim intellectual tradition in the East, wanted was to eat their cake and have it too, a manifestly impossible situation (what Abū Sulaymān as-Sijistānī, cited below in section 7, called "an aspiration on the way to which there are insurmountable obstacles") that can only lead, and did lead to paralysis.[53]

5. Paraphilosophy: The New Discipline

This new discipline that emerged and the new genre of writing it generated, what Shihadeh calls "Islamic philosophy," had primarily theological aims, in that its principal intention was to argue in favor of Islamic doctrine in philosophical terms, but it was different from the traditional theology, *kalām*, it was not theology in that sense. It has been broadly recognized, as Gerhard Endress aptly put it, that philosophy after Avicenna was "reduced to an instrument of religious hermeneutic"[54] (with the emphasis, I might add, on "reduced" being no less significant than on the other words), and there is need to understand the precise nature of this new discipline before we see it as a continuation of philosophy as

52 Shihadeh, "From al-Ghazālī to al-Rāzī" 156, 178. Shihadeh's insightful appellation of this new genre as "Islamic philosophy" is now corroborated by historical evidence from Bāyezīd II's librarian ʿĀṭūfī, to be discussed below in section VI.

53 In another essay ("Arabic into Byzantine Greek" 249), I called the Roman Orthodox attitude to Hellenic science "cultural schizophrenia," in that those whom the Roman Orthodox considered barbarians (the Muslims in general) "had adopted ancient Greek learning, to which the Byzantines had access in the original language which they could read, but which they did not wish to, because it represented the hated Hellenic learning." I am not sure that the Muslim case under discussion here is exactly analogous, but the Roman Orthodox certainly did display the same attitude of wanting to eat their cake and have it too, and it did lead to scientific paralysis.

54 In G. Endress and J.A. Aertsen, eds., *Averroes and the Aristotelian Tradition*, p.vii.

practiced before. Traditional theology had its own methods, procedures, and technical terminology, and it did not try to pass them off as philosophy; the new genre of writing did. But then it was neither philosophy, that is, science, as discussed (section 1), in that it violated all the basic principles of what historically had meant to do science, which was the open-ended rational investigation of all reality. It was not open-ended, in that it strove to argue for one pre-determined thesis, the Islamic mythological narrative; it was not completely rational, in that it admitted selectively supra-rational modes of acquisition of knowledge; and it was not an investigation of all reality in that it narrowed the discussion to certain subjects, those of interest to religious doctrine (essentially, metaphysics, cosmology, and psychology, as will be discussed below). Accordingly, it cannot be called "philosophical theology," since it was neither. The expression "philosophical theology," whatever rhetorical value it might have in granting the discipline enhanced status because of the very presence of the valorized word "philosophy" in it, does so merely because of the fuzzy and inchoate notion of philosophy that we moderns have as something intellectually profound, as I mentioned at the very outset. But if we understand philosophy as science, as it was understood in antiquity and the Middle Ages, then it will be seen that the expression "philosophical theology" actually means "scientific theology," which is an oxymoron and hardly intelligible (unless it is meant ironically in order to ridicule the concept). The same applies to the expression "Islamic philosophy," if we now understand it as equivalent to "Islamic science," intended to mean not science done by Muslims, which would be fine (though in need of explicit mention), but science that somehow reflects and is based on particularly Islamic doctrinal positions, which would be absurd.[55] For this reason I suggest that we call this sort of clandestine theologizing that *simulates* and presents itself as philosophy "paraphilosophy," and understand the term to mean, "doing what appears to be philosophy/science in order to divert attention from, subvert, and substitute for philosophy/science, and as a result avoid doing philosophy/science."[56]

---

55 Some people find it difficult to see the distinction. The determination of the *qibla*, for example, is a problem that was generated in Muslim societies for doctrinal reasons, and thus the problem itself is Islamic. But the mathematics that solves the problem is just mathematics, universally valid and applicable, and can be used for the determination of any geographical directions on the globe. Hence the absurdity of "Islamic mathematics" and accordingly of "Islamic science" in that sense.

56 The term thus covers and applies to most of the uses to which the Greek preposition *para* is put in such compounds in English: parajournalism is "subjective journalism that uses some of the techniques or license of fiction" (incidents of which have been quite proliferating in the United States in 2016 and 2017); a parasite is "an organism that grows, feeds and lives on or in another organism to whose survival it contributes nothing;" something paranormal is "beyond the range of normal experience or scientific explanation;" parapsychology is "the study

The problem in contemporary scholarship of confusing theological discourse with philosophical discourse and calling both indiscriminately philosophy is not confined to Islam alone, but it exists also for Christian theology, both Roman Catholic and, recently, also Roman Orthodox, which are called "Christian philosophy." The supporting argument that is most frequently made is that rational argumentation exists in all these enterprises, which are then called accordingly philosophical.[57] But what fails to be appreciated and acknowledged is that the rationality of an argument, decontextualized from the intent, epistemic basis, and function of the entire discourse, cannot by itself define it as philosophical. Sophistry is not science/philosophy (Aristotle wrote a book about it). And if discourses are not discriminated on the basis of their intent, epistemic basis, and function, then the ability to understand them substantively through their causes, as Aristotle would say, but also historically, is abdicated; they become mere exercises in argumentation without referents, as the percipient Ibn Khaldūn remarked (cited below in this section). Arguing along the lines I adumbrated above about the internal incongruity of the term "Islamic philosophy," "Martin Heidegger considered the coupling of the words 'Christianity' and 'philosophy' as unfair to both Christianity and philosophy. The expression 'Christian philosophy,' one reads in a recently published volume of his notebooks, consists of two halves that do not make up a whole.[58] Neither the confessional implications of the word Christian nor any necessary prerequisites of the word philosophy are seriously and honestly acknowledged in it; rather, both words are conveniently reoriented toward more loose and hazardless (*harmlos*) concepts in order precisely to authorize the (feel-good) term Christian philosophy."[59]

Recent scholarship is coming to an understanding of the post-Avicenna transformations in theology and philosophy and has begun the process of de-

of the evidence for psychological phenomena, such as telepathy, that are inexplicable by science;" etc. (all definitions from *The American Heritage College Dictionary*, [4]2004).

57 Most recently (2017) by Peter Adamson, admittedly in a popular forum, though quite representative: "[M]y view is that philosophy is where you find it, and that it is narrow-minded to ignore philosophical argumentation put forward by thinkers simply because they have a religious agenda, whether that agenda grows out of Christianity (as with Aquinas), Judaism (as with Maimonides), Hinduism (as with Nyāya epistemology or Vedānta philosophy of mind), or Islam;" in Adamson's essay, "If Aquinas is a philosopher then so are the Islamic theologians." In reality, the argument in his title should be reversed to say, "If the Islamic theologians are not philosophers then neither is Aquinas." As for the statement that "philosophy is where you find it," it is relativist and tautological, and can hardly form the basis of rational scholarly discussion of historical problems (see also above, note 3). Something similar is claimed by those who maintain the existence of a Byzantine "philosophy", for which see Siniossoglou and Gutas, "Philosophy and 'Byzantine philosophy'," 274.

58 Martin Heidegger, *Gesamtausgabe IV. Band 96*, 214.

59 Siniossoglou in Siniossoglou and Gutas, "Philosophy and 'Byzantine Philosophy'," 292–293, with full discussion of the problem of "Byzantine philosophy."

scription and analysis of this new genre of high intellectual endeavor,[60] but we are not the first or the only ones to come to this realization. In the past, Muslim scholars were well aware of the methodological hybridity and therefore theoretical invalidity of works in this new genre. Averroes in particular discussed how al-Ghazālī mixed approaches and methods for his theological ends and suggested that his books, which mix "poetical, rhetorical or dialectical methods" in scientific (demonstrative) research should be banned because they confuse and disorient people who are not of a caliber to do science. What Averroes says, in effect, is that

> al-Ghazālī wished by this [procedure] to increase the number of those engaged in science (*ahl al-ʿilm*), and yet he increased thereby only those engaged in obscurantism (*ahl al-fasād*),[61] without increase in the number of those engaged in science at all![62] As a result, some people found a way to challenge philosophy as false, others to challenge religious law as false, and yet others to conflate the two. It seems that this was [precisely] one of his objectives in his books![63]

The imputation of dishonest motivations to al-Ghazālī in Averroes' text here is interesting, and may well be due to the titanic antagonism between the two, but it is not unfounded and worth keeping in mind.

Two centuries after Averroes, Ibn Khaldūn made similar observations about the new genre of theologizing after Avicenna. In the section on *kalām* in his *Muqaddima*, he described accurately the distinction between philosophy/science and theology and said the following:

> The philosophical study of [bodies] differs from the theological. The philosophers study bodies in so far as they move or are stationary [i.e., they try to find out what their

60 Notably Shihadeh, "From al-Ghazālī to al-Rāzī" (2005) and Eichner "Dissolving the Unity of *Metaphysics*" (2007), and especially her fundamental work, *The Post-Avicennian Philosophical Tradition* (2009).

61 Averroes uses the term *fasād* as the opposite of *ʿilm*, knowledge or science, which would be in English "obscurantism" rather than the more ethically tinged "corruption". *Webster's New Dictionary of Synonyms* (1978) defines obscurantist as someone "who is precluded (as by prejudice, traditionalism, or bigotry) from intellectual candor and open-minded inquiry and who is opposed to the introduction of new and enlightened ideas and methods," i.e., exactly someone opposed to philosophy/science as understood in antiquity and early Islam, as I have been arguing, or al-Ghazālī, as Averroes is arguing.

62 Following the text of ʿEmāra (Cairo 1972), *bi-dūna kathrati ahli l-ʿilmi*. According to ʿEmāra's apparatus, two MSS read, *laysa bi-dūna* … (a reading taken into the text by Butterworth, p. 22), which is clearly an apologetic and clumsy addition to the text by a pro-Ghazalian scribe or redactor. It makes no sense for Averroes to have said that al-Ghazālī wanted to increase the number of scientists and yet he increased the number of obscurantists, and then to go on and say, but he increased the number of scientists anyway! The force of the prepositional phrase *bi-dūna* is precisely to say that al-Ghazālī did not increase the number of scientists *at all*, he fell short of (*dūna*) doing that.

63 *Faṣl al-maqāl* 52 (ʿEmāra).

essential characteristics are and how they work]. The theologians, on the other hand, study them in so far as they serve as an argument for [*yadullu ʿalā*] the Maker. In the same way, the philosophical study of metaphysics [*ilāhiyyāt*] studies absolute being[64] as such and what it requires because of itself [i. e., Aristotle's definition of metaphysics as the study of being *qua* being]. The theologians, on the other hand, study (in metaphysics) being (*al-mawjūd*) in so far as it serves as argument for Him who causes being. …

However, the two approaches have been mixed up by recent scholars. *The problems of theology have been confused with those of philosophy to the point that the one discipline is no longer distinguishable from the other, and the student cannot learn (either discipline) from the books of (the recent scholars).* Such mixing (of theology and philosophy) was done by al-Bayḍāwī, in the *Ṭawāliʿ*, and by later, *non-Arab* [*Persian: al-ʿajam*] *scholars, in all their works.* However, some students have occupied themselves with the (mixed) approach (in spite of its uselessness for the study of theology) *in order to learn the different school opinions and to become versed in the knowledge of argumentation* (*li-l-iṭṭilāʿ ʿalā l-madhāhib wa-l-ighrāq fī maʿrifat al-ḥijāj*), which is amply represented in (the works of the mixed approach).

The approach of the early Muslims can be reconciled with the beliefs of the science of *kalām* only if one follows the old approach of the theologians (and not the mixed approach of recent scholars). In general, it must be known that this science – *the science of* kalām – *is not something that is necessary to the contemporary student* since heretics and innovators have been destroyed, and the orthodox [*ahl as-sunna*] religious leaders have given us protection against heretics and innovators in their systematic works and treatments.[65]

Ibn Khaldūn was a contemporary of Tamerlane, and he was looking back at the theological and philosophical tradition precisely in the period between Avicenna and the Timurids, with which we are concerned. From this vantage point, which affords us the benefit of his historical insight, he clearly identified the new genre of writing and the implied new hybrid discipline between theology and philosophy, and he properly localized it in the Iranian east – indeed, the vast majority of paraphilosophers from al-Ghazālī onward were Iranians. This is not so much intended by Ibn Khaldūn to malign the Iranians as to show up, again, the novelty of the new genre and discipline in comparison with the theology of the older theologians. And the real problem, as he went on to state indirectly, is that he could see no purpose or discern no function to this new mixed approach. It is not theology insofar as representing Islamic doctrine is concerned, he said, because Muslim beliefs cannot be reconciled with it but only with the old style theology; and it is not theology in the sense of defending Islamic doctrine against heretics and innovators because that had already been done satisfactorily, and (Sunnī)

64 Reading *al-mawjūd*, as in what follows regarding the theologians, for *wujūd* in the text.
65 Ibn Khaldūn, *al-Muqaddimah*, III,35–36 (ash-Shaddādī); translation adapted from F. Rosenthal, *The Muqaddimah*, III, 52–54, with added emphasis.

Islamic beliefs were no longer in danger. We can also infer from his statements about the aims of philosophy and his tone later in the argument in that passage that he would not characterize the new genre as philosophy either. His conclusion can hardly be avoided: the new genre of writing representing this hybrid discipline has no purpose, no epistemic basis, and no social value except possibly as a school exercise. Students become engaged in it, he stated, not to learn either philosophy or theology, but "to learn the different school opinions and to become versed in the knowledge of argumentation." In other words, it was a school exercise that was elevated to the status of a discipline.

It is not accidental that the two thinkers I just cited who present their objections to and doubts about the new hybrid discipline are Mālikī scholars. They were outside the Shāfiʿī/Ḥanafī and Ashʿarī/Twelver Shīʿite intellectual consensus that had developed in eastern Islam by the thirteenth century, and as such present a critical perspective on it which, even if it may deceptively appear as not wholly objective in its tone, is nevertheless accurate and provides an insight that is illuminating to historical investigation. Because the perplexity about the purpose, goals, and results of the new genre of writing, as it was practiced by theologians, philosophers, and sufis following Ibn ʿArabī (d. 1240), was prevalent among leading laymen and possibly among the practitioners themselves. For this we have the evidence of no less a leading layman than the Ottoman Conqueror (*fātiḥ*) of Constantinople, Meḥmed II (d. 1481). He was confronted with the same perplexity about the respective fields of inquiry of the three disciplines, philosophy, theology, and mysticism, and requested from the poet and scholar al-Jāmī (1414–1492) to compose a treatise adjudicating (*muḥākama*) among the positions of these three disciplines. Al-Jāmī did this, in a treatise entitled *The Precious Pearl* (*ad-Durra al-fākhira*), which presents the views of the three disciplines on the questions of God's existence and unity, his attributes, and the emanation of the world from Him – the subjects, essentially, dealt with in paraphilosophy. Al-Jāmī is partial to the mystics, given his background and training, but he is also fair in his representation of the respective positions on these issues. The different positions of the three disciplines are seemingly identical and expressed in a highly technical philosophical language and argumentation that in itself cannot be distinguished on any formal level.[66] The final conclusion which these largely identical arguments reach varies in the three cases, which leads one to question the existence of an independently verifiable basis for the differentiation beyond mere word-play, or their relation to reality, and ultimately their validity.[67]

66 Translated in an exemplary fashion by Nicholas Heer, *The Precious Pearl*.

67 Typical is al-Jāmī's summary of the three positions regarding the eternity or creation of the world in time, which entails the question whether God freely chose to create or not: "The theologians affirmed the free choice of the agent [God] and denied [the existence of] an eternal effect, whereas the philosophers affirmed [the existence of] an eternal effect and

We do not know what Meḥmed II's reaction to all this was and what he made of it because he died before he actually received al-Jāmī's treatise which was sent to him in Constantinople from Herat. We do have, however, the views on the subject of the Muslim *ʿulamāʾ* of the time, at the end of the fifteenth century, from a project that was started by his son and successor to the Ottoman throne, Bāyezīd II (reigned 1481–1512). In 1502, this Sultan asked his librarian, a scholar named ʿĀṭūfī,[68] to draw up a catalogue of his imperial library, which happily survives in a manuscript in the Oriental Collection of the Library of the Hungarian Academy of Sciences.[69] ʿĀṭūfī lists all manuscripts under the various subject categories, Qurʾān, *ḥadīth*, law, etc., as one would expect. When it comes to theology and philosophy, though, he uses subject headings, and lists books under each, in explicit ways which reflect precisely the understanding of these disciplines and their contents according to the Shāfiʿī/Ḥanafī and Ashʿarī/Twelver Shīʿite consensus prevalent in the eastern half of the Islamic world.[70]

Separately from books on theology (*ʿilm al-kalām*), ʿĀṭūfī divides books on philosophy (*ḥikma*) into two, what he calls "Islamic philosophy" (*ḥikma islāmiyya*) and "philosophical philosophy" (*ḥikma falsafiyya*). His categories of classification in this case are clearly based on the degree of adherence to Islamic doctrine which the books exhibit. Works which are considered to defend or follow Islamic doctrine are categorized under *ḥikma islāmiyya*, and those which do not, or present an account without reference to specific Islamic doctrine, are categorized under *ḥikma falsafiyya*. This is expressly stated by ʿĀṭūfī himself in a

denied the free choice [of the agent]. As for the Ṣūfīs ..., they allowed the dependence of an eternal effect on a free agent and combined affirmation of [the agent's] free choice with belief in the existence of an eternal effect" (Heer 57). My thanks to Ulrich Rudolph for unveiling with taste the inner meaning and structure of *The Precious Pearl* in a lecture delivered at Yale on April 1, 2017 (now published as "ʿAbd al-Raḥmān al-Jāmī (d. 898/1492) on the Eternity of the World," *The Muslim World* 107 (2017) 537–548), though the following assessment is mine: Properly worded, with terms/concepts taken from diverse disciplines and used deliberately outside their original discourse context (cf. the examples in Rudolph 543–544), any thesis or conclusion is both possible at this level of highly abstract sophistication and beyond the reach of rational criticism, especially when, as al-Jāmī goes on to say about the Sufis, it is acquired by means of supra-rational *al-kashf aṣ-ṣarīḥ*, "clear [mystical] unveiling "(Heer), or "pure unveiling" (Rudolph).

68 A brief biography is given in Taşköprüzade, *al-Shaqāʾiq al-nuʿmāniyya fī ʿulamāʾ al-Dawla al-ʿuthmāniyya*, ed. Ahmed Subhi Furat, Istanbul: İstanbul Üniversitesi Edebiyat Fakültesi Yayınları, 1985, 416–17.

69 Magyar Tudományos Akadémia Könyvtára Keleti Gyüjtemény, MS Török F. 59. My thanks to my Ottomanist colleagues Gülru Necipoğlu, Cemal Kafadar, and Cornell Fleischer who introduced me to this precious document and invited me to participate in its forthcoming edition and study.

70 For the significance of the classification of the sciences, whether in theory or practice, as in this case, for an understanding of the nature, aims, and social and political context of sciences see Melvin-Koushki, "Powers of One," 143–179.

comment defining *al-ḥikma al-islāmiyya* which he inserted in the catalogue, where he says (p. 339, lines 9–10), *wa-hiya llatī yubḥathu fīhā ʿalā qānūn ash-sharʿ ash-sharīf an-nabawī*, that is, "[Islamic philosophy,] which is the one in which research is conducted in accordance with the rules of the noble Prophetic Law." If that is the case, then *ḥikma falsafiyya* would mean its opposite, "non-Islamic philosophy," which ʿĀṭūfī clearly meant to be taken as meaning "heretical philosophy." After the titles of some books on "philosophical philosophy" he inserts comments indicating their heretical nature: thus al-Ghazālī's *Tahāfut* is described as "invalidating philosophical philosophy" (*fī ibṭāl al-ḥikma al-falsafiyya*), and some of Suhrawardī's works are said to be "leaning toward truth" (*al-māʾila ilā l-ḥaqq*), with the implication that Avicenna's books are devoid of truth.

The identity and number of the books that are listed under these categories provide further information about their nature. The section on works of theology (*kalām*) presents nothing extraordinary. Although the holdings in Bāyezīd II's library are not comprehensive, they nevertheless include major works in the field from the ninth century onward until ʿĀṭūfī's own lifetime, as well as texts and commentaries by Ottoman scholars manifestly used for instruction. The books listed under *ḥikma islāmiyya* and *ḥikma falsafiyya,* on the other hand, present a different picture. Those under the former heading, to begin with, are few: mainly some works by Fakhraddīn ar-Rāzī , notably his *al-Mulakhkhaṣ fī l-ḥikma,* with commentaries,[71] and his commentary on Avicenna's *Ishārāt* (along with at-Taḥtānī's *Muḥākamāt*); al-Abharī's *Kashf al-ḥaqāʾiq*; al-Urmawī's *Maṭāliʿ al-anwār* with his own commentary on it, *Lawāmiʿ*, and his *Bayān*; al-Ḥillī's *al-Asrār al-khafiyya*; and two other unidentified treatises – all authors who lived within slightly more than a century of each other, the oldest being ar-Rāzī (d. 1210) and the youngest al-Ḥillī (d. 1325), with nobody else listed for the fourteenth and fifteenth centuries. ʿĀṭūfī did not identify works composed during the two centuries before the compilation of his catalogue that he could catalogue under the heading of "Islamic philosophy".

The books listed under *ḥikma falsafiyya* are more numerous and present a slightly more varied picture, but it is essentially analogous to the preceding one in that there are no works on this subject listed from the two centuries preceding the catalogue either: the youngest author included in the list who is not a commentator on Avicenna or Suhrawardī is Ibn Kammūna, who died in 1284. In addition, this section is dominated by Avicenna (d. 1037), for whom there are

71 Thus providing historical evidence, unbeknownst to Eichner, for her perceptive recognition of the particular significance of this work: "[H]is *al-Mulakhkhaṣ fī l-ḥikma* can be identified as one decisive mediator between the philosophical and the theological traditions from the early 13th century onwards. The influence of the *al-Mulakhkhaṣ* can be traced throughout a variety of philosophical and theological works," in "Dissolving the Unity of *Metaphysics*", 152.

listed thirty-seven works, together with their commentaries. Suhrawardī (d. 1191) comes next as a distant second, with nine titles to his name, also with commentaries, followed by Ibn Kammūna, for whom seven works are registered, three with known titles and four unspecified. The philosophers before Avicenna who are represented are those one would expect – Plato, Aristotle, al-Kindī, Ḥunayn b. Isḥāq, al-Fārābī, Ikhwān aṣ-ṣafā', and Miskawayh – while those who came later, other than Suhrawardī, Ibn Kammūna, and commentators, are all the well known names from the twelfth and thirteenth centuries, each represented, for the most part, by his most famous book: al-Abharī (d. 1264), Abū l-Barakāt al-Baghdādī (d. 1165), al-Ghazālī (d. 1111; the *Maqāṣid* and the *Tahāfut*), al-Kātibī (d. 1277), al-Mas'ūdī (d. before 1204), Nāṣir Khusraw (d. 1078), Fakhraddīn ar-Rāzī (d. 1210; *al-Mabāḥiṯ* only other than the commentaries), 'Umar b. Sahlān as-Sāwī (d. ca. 1145), ash-Shahrazūrī (thirteenth century), Naṣīraddīn aṭ-Ṭūsī (d. 1274), and al-Urmawī (d. 1283).

The librarian 'Āṭūfī's classification and listing of philosophical works offer further and prime evidence, and indeed from the perspective of all Muslim scholars themselves when we add Averroes' and Ibn Khaldūn's testimonies, for the development of the new genre of paraphilosophy in the eastern Islamic lands after Avicenna, as I have been adumbrating.

Avicenna's scientific system, which consisted of the Hellenic school science he had received and the research science developed by his predecessors in early Islam and by himself (and massively represented in the extensive holdings in Bāyezīd II's library), was perceived and presented as constituting science/philosophy as such in the centuries immediately following his death. It was given the name "philosophical philosophy," that is, non-Islamic philosophy, since it was distinguished from "Islamic philosophy" which was understood to be conducted on the basis of Islamic doctrines, and it was criticized as not being conducive to, or representing truth. Theologians after Avicenna engaged in attempts to fashion what could be perceived as a philosophical approach that would avoid those aspects of his philosophy that were contrary to Islamic principles. These efforts came to a head in the work of Fakhraddīn ar-Rāzī,[72] who reorganized both the contents and the terms of the discussion and perfected the new genre of writing that was generated, something that could be called – and was called by 'Āṭūfī (and Ayman Shihadeh) – "Islamic philosophy" as distinct from Islamic theology, *'ilm al-kalām*. The intention was to provide philosophical argumentation for Islamic doctrinal positions by using whatever elements of school science could be effectively harnessed to that end without explicitly acknowledging the nature of the

72 As it is being now amply demonstrated in recent research, notably the work of Heidrun Eichner; see her *The Post-Avicennian Philosophical Tradition*, and "Dissolving the Unity of Metaphysics."

enterprise.[73] As ʿĀṭūfī put it, "Islamic philosophy is the one in which research is conducted in accordance with the rules of the noble Prophetic Law" (cited above). Even logic was tweaked with this intention,[74] but the undertaking was very skillfully done, with a masterly blend of defense of the school science[75] with variations aiming at supporting the mostly unacknowledged doctrinal (Ashʿarite) positions, and was conducted with ever higher degrees of sophistication by thinkers beginning with Fakhraddīn ar-Rāzī.

To begin with, the subjects dealt with in this reorganization by ar-Rāzī of the contents and terms of discussion in the new discipline of paraphilosophy were restricted only to physics and metaphysics (with the mathematical and practical sciences excluded), and of physics only material treated in Aristotle/Avicenna's principles of physics, cosmology, and psychology (i. e., *Physics, On Heaven, Generation and Corruption*, and *On the Soul*, with zoology and botany as well as the derivative sciences of physics, like medicine, excluded), all subjects of relevance to Islamic doctrine. In essence, these are the very subjects treated in the second book of Avicenna's *Ishārāt*, and there would hardly appear any reasonable doubt that it was the reception of this book that determined the contents and parameters of paraphilosophy. It may be thought that ironically, Avicenna himself provided (unwittingly?) the means, inspiration, and field of action for the transmogrification of his scientific system into what he strove to avoid.

Ar-Rāzī's reorganization involved additionally a break-up of the Aristotelian/ Avicennan classification of the sciences as epistemologically interconnected fields of inquiry, and propagated instead the study of reality based on a comprehensive classification of existents (substances, accidents, etc.). As expressed by Eichner,

> This classification, however, leaves no space to integrate more specialized scientific disciplines of the Greek canon. Paradoxically, we may identify the comprehensive and systematic character of these encyclopaedic expositions as a considerable obstacle for developing an epistemological theory that can integrate specialized scientific disciplines into a coherent framework. Disciplines like ethics, political science, or mathematics and

73 I would thus disagree with Robert Wisnovsky's assessment: "Rāzī stood in relation to Avicenna as Avicenna stood to Aristotle: as a sometimes critical but nevertheless deeply indebted appropriator of the original author's theories;" in "Genealogy of Avicennism" 326. Avicenna had no pre-determined (or revealed) doctrine to which he tried to make Aristotle fit, whereas ar-Rāzī did, his criticism by and large tending to make Avicenna conform to Ashʿarite views.

74 The modifications that ar-Rāzī effects on Avicenna's modal logic are "congenial with … the controlling modal notion of the Ašʿarites, which is, roughly, that what is always the case, here or in the heavens, does not have to be the case;" Street, "Faḫraddīn ar-Rāzī's Critique of Avicennan Logic" 110–111.

75 See, for example, Shihadeh's exposition of the procedures used by ar-Rāzī in his commentary on the *Ishārāt*, "Al-Rāzī's (d. 1210) Commentary on Avicenna's *Pointers*."

> astronomy, or medicine are not integrated in the framework of the program of Post-Avicennian philosophical disciplines.
>
> In the case of some disciplines, rudimentary basics are dealt with in this encyclopaedic context. However, *the encyclopaedic character prevents a more detailed investigation of these topics. Thus, rudimentary cosmological sketches form part of most expositions, likewise the theory of the elements and the basics of humoral pathology.* The presence of these topics in philosophical works and, from the 13th century onwards, in *kalām* works is typically interpreted as pointing to a close relation between rationalist traditions among Islamic theologians and science. The relation, however, is to be evaluated in a more nuanced way: When theological expositions mention some basic information on scientific theories this certainly may show that theologians were not hostile towards discussing these theories, but this did not necessarily imply that they possessed a serious scientific command of the relevant disciplines.[76]

Eichner sees the reorganization of contents by ar-Rāzī as being followed in most later works but not all, some of which – the encyclopaedic works she refers to in the passage above, notably al-Abharī's *Hidāya* and al-Kātibī's *Ḥikmat al-ʿayn* – follow the Avicennan classification of sciences into metaphysics and physics with its subdivisions. The terms of discussion, though, were the same in both kinds, following ar-Rāzī's exposition.[77] That the context and purpose of the whole enterprise is theological is thus seen also from the subjects in physics and metaphysics that have been selected for discussion, all of relevance, as mentioned, to theological issues broadly perceived. In essence, paraphilosophy dealt principally, if not solely, and over the centuries obsessively, with the myriad implications of the question asked by Beckett in the epigraph above. It changed the orientation and method of science/philosophy from open-ended research into apologetics, and it restricted its compass to the subjects just mentioned, with only perfunctory, if any, treatment of other subjects. The rest of the sciences developed discretely and independently, their purpose and progression to be studied separately and assessed in connection with the social and ideological environment in which they found themselves.[78]

The task, then, in the future study of paraphilosophy is to investigate the precise ways in which it functioned by examining all philosophical arguments and determining their underlying *reason and motive.* In many cases the theological aim is transparent, but not always. A discussion in physics of the nature of time, for example, seems innocuous enough, and can be considered as a discussion intended to advance school science beyond the works of Avicenna, which

76 Eichner, *The Post-Avicennian Philosophical Tradition*, 420; emphasis added.

77 Eichner, "Dissolving the Unity of Metaphysics," 166–167.

78 See, for example, the questions asked by Melvin-Koushki, "Powers of One," 182, about mathematics and astronomy in their Timurid and Safavid context, or the progression of certain problems of logic in various historical periods described by El-Rouayheb, *History of Arabic Logic.*

it may well be. But the nature of time, of course, is a key element in the discussion of the eternity of the world or its creation in time, and the approach taken by the thinker would thus be compromised as being directed to finding philosophical ways to accommodate the Islamic mythical narrative either by arguing for it or by arguing for a theory of time that might have implications for revising the literal understanding of it but never for directly opposing it. The second alternative is precisely what was intended by Mīr Dāmād (d. 1631) with his abstruse theory of perpetual creation, an insight, he claims, which was "a divine revelation received on the night of 13 Shaʿbān 1014 / 5 December 1604." This theory, which Mīr Dāmād equally claims "requires an act of grace and the practice of spiritual exercises" in order to be understood,[79] was received unfavorably in India, where Mīr Dāmād's younger contemporary Maḥmūd Jawnpūrī (1606–1651) called him on his ruse and commented as follows about it:

> Know that one of the excellent ones who attaches himself to specialists of the past [Mīr Dāmād] – despite his penetrating journeys into the land of reality and his intimacy with swimming in the waters of philosophy… – since his Hashimite vein beats to protect the blood of the religion that is its surface [reality] and to defend the zeal of the mass of co-religionists who subscribe to [the doctrine of] of the generation of the world (*ḥudūth al-ʿālam*)…and [since, at the same time,] his critical insight and his blazing genius did not allow him to embrace the doctrine of the temporal generation of time (*al-ḥudūth al-zamānī li-l-zamān*) and of the contingents that precede it…he invented the doctrine of perpetual generation (*al-ḥudūth al-dahrī*) and perpetual priority (*qabliyya dahriyya*). And he contrived subtle rules regarding this [doctrine] and put together elegant pages [about it]."[80]

Jawnpūrī, who actually refuted Mīr Dāmād's theory in this work,[81] is politely castigating him here for conducting his science not in an open-ended way but tailoring it to please the religious sensibilities "of the mass of co-religionists;" or, if what he says about Mīr Dāmād not allowing himself to accept the generation of time in time is sincere, then he is equally castigating him for tailoring his science so as not to displease the said sensibilities by writing elegant but vacuous pages. Jawnpūrī's comments describe perfectly the nature of paraphilosophy: it has theological intent and motivation, it consists of abstruse arguments of little or no scientific substance, and, from what we know from Mīr Dāmād himself, it was acquired through supra-rational means.

The abstruseness of the arguments in paraphilosophy also had another function other than the display of perceived wisdom for fame and fortune. It

79 Both quotations in Rizvi, "Mīr Dāmād" 457 and 461. For Mīr Dāmād's otherwise occultist and lettrist approach to "philosophy" see Melvin-Koushki, "Powers of One," 186–187.

80 Maḥmūd Jawnpūrī, *al-Shams al-bāzigha* (al-Maṭbaʿ al-Muṣṭafāʾī, 1288 AH), p. 130. I am indebted to Asad Ahmed for drawing my attention to this passage and offering its translation.

81 Rizvi, "Mīr Dāmād", 460.

allowed scholars of an independent mind to argue in favor of the condemned theories of science, or the disapproved ones, in oblique and complex ways that led to positions very near to the desired goal but not at it – the final step was never taken, though one had the feeling or satisfaction that the alternatives to the condemned theories were being discussed. For example, again on the question of the eternity of the world vs. creation (the paraphilosophical subject par excellence), one of the arguments used was whether the eternity of possibility required the possibility of eternity, that is, whether the existence of the world as eternally possible before its existence necessitates the possibility of the world's eternity. This was argued up and down, with very complex arguments, over the centuries from al-Ghazālī onward. By the time of ʿĀṭūfī, his contemporary Kamālpashazāda (d. 1534), an accomplished Ottoman scholar, wrote on this subject trying to ascertain the merits of the opposing positions, but in the end he could not decide, finding al-Sharīf al-Jurjānī's (d. 1413) position both right and wrong.[82] This indicates that scholars had the feeling of being able to discuss the taboo subject of the eternity of the world, but it also reveals the inconsequential nature of whatever conclusions, negative or positive, were reached, since there seemed to be no discernible criteria for evaluation. The arguments were just arguments, and the step from these conclusions to the position challenging the mythological narrative was not (or was not even intended to be) taken – the possibility of the eternity of the world never became the fact of the eternity of the world.

As these last examples indicate, by the end of the fifteenth century, if not a century earlier, paraphilosophy established itself at the center of scientific discussion as "Islamic" philosophy, and its practitioners, conscious of the novelty of the discipline, described its development as a move away from and partly antithetical to Avicenna, who remained the paradigmatic exponent of science/philosophy (*falsafa*), and also as a differentiation from traditional theology, *kalām*. Their scholarly tradition had devised means and a set of criteria whereby the distinctions could be made,[83] and the librarian ʿĀṭūfī, who was schooled in this tradition, relies on it to enable him to assign a philosophical work accordingly to its proper category, even if in some cases doubts persist.

---

82 I am indebted to the paper by Ömer Mahir Alper, "Does the Eternity of Contingency Require the Contingency of Eternity? Kamālpashazāda's Approach to the Question," delivered at Yale on April 1, 2017.

83 The problem of distinguishing among these disciplines was evidently discussed in scholarly circles. Al-Urmawī wrote an essay on the subject, *Risāla fī l-farq bayna nawʿay al-ʿilm al-ilāhī wa-l-kalām* ("Treatise on the Distinction between the Genres of Metaphysics and Theology"), discussed by Eichner in *The Post-Avicennian Philosophical Tradition*, chapter XI, along with other authors.

ʿĀṭūfī's classification, however, is evidence also for further developments, as it shows both streams of philosophical activity, the "Islamic" and the "philosophical" (or non-Islamic), petering out by the middle of the fourteenth century, for he finds no works to register in these fields from that time until his days early in the sixteenth century. "Islamic philosophy" thus eventually blends both with *kalām*, as the latter increasingly adopts philosophical terminology and argumentation for those parts of the subject that do not deal with specific Islamic doctrine and law (the *sharʿiyyāt*), and with thought systems developed in Timurid and Safavid times that are increasingly based on newly legitimized occult sciences (discussed further below). Science/ philosophy (ʿĀṭūfī's *al-ḥikma al-falsafiyya*) itself just dies out in *this* tradition (though its apparent resurgence and actual nature in the newly organized occult tradition remains to be investigated), and *falsafa*, that is science, is discussed only as a *historical* body of work, mainly the works of Avicenna, with no contemporary representatives of the discipline. References to philosophy and philosophers (usually to the "Peripatetics," *al-mashshāʾūn*) are to the frozen corpus of Avicenna's works.[84]

Avicenna was indeed the last major philosopher in the sense of philosophy as research science – al-Qūnawī (d. 1274) even calls him "the seal of the philosophers (*khātam al-ḥukamāʾ*)[85], meaning that no philosopher came, or could come, after him – even if we can follow the last vestiges of philosophy/science in the works of some twelfth and thirteenth century thinkers like Abū l-Barakāt al-Baghdādī and Ibn Kammūna, and possibly in between the chapters of the famous paraphilosophical works of the great twelfth century scholars, which have yet to be fully analyzed for the presence of such material. Al-Qūnawī's clever re-application of the Prophetic epithet to Avicenna is emblematic of the awareness exhibited by the paraphilosophers that *ḥikma falsafiyya* (corresponding to the historical *jāhiliyya* in this analogy) had expired and *ḥikma islāmiyya* (corresponding to the historical advent if Islam) was in effect in its stead. In historical terms, the achievement of paraphilosophy in the ideological continuum in society between the scientific worldview and the mythical one was to usurp the place of the scientific worldview and, by presenting itself as "Islamic" science (about which more in the next section) against the mythical worldview, leave no space for science in this tradition in which it had been practiced before.

84 Gutas, "Philosophical Manuscripts."
85 Todd, *The Sufi Doctrine of Man*, 54.

6. Paraphilosophy and Its Aftereffects. The Formation of Islamic Science

Related developments that accompanied and followed upon the generation of paraphilosophy, as roughly delineated, include the following. Most significant for the delegitimization of the scientific outlook and the dissolution of a unified scientific worldview, elements which promoted and were responsible for research science in antiquity and early Islam, was the fragmentation of science that took place in the centuries following Avicenna. The various branches of science that constituted the scientific/philosophical approach to reality and were included, following the classificatory schemes I mentioned at the outset, as an integrated and interrelated whole in Avicenna's scientific summa *ash-Shifāʾ*, began slowly to be decoupled from the entire scientific edifice and were atomized. Most importantly for the issue at hand, metaphysics and some parts of physics were quarantined into a field unto themselves, as already mentioned, and this was now given exclusively the name *ḥikma*, with *ilāhiyyāt* and *ṭabīʿiyyāt* referring respectively to metaphysics and physics. The term *falsafa* came now to refer not so much to the contents of the discipline as to the method used in investigating it, that is, the non-Islamic (heretical) method used essentially by Avicenna, just as the term *al-falāsifa*, in a process of reverse metonymy in the works of paraphilosophy, came to signify Avicenna. In essence, this is also abundantly clear from ʿĀṭūfī's two terms, *ḥikma islāmiyya* (and his definition of it cited above) and *ḥikma falsafiyya*, which now can be properly seen to mean, respectively, "Islamic physics and metaphysics" and "philosophical/Avicennan physics and metaphysics."

Just as clearly, logic also was separated from "philosophy", both *ḥikma* and *falsafa*, and listed separately from them, not as a part, reflecting long established practice. Following Avicenna's characterization of logic as both a science in itself and an instrument for the other sciences, this position, classically formulated in al-Kātibī's *ash-Shamsiyya*, led to the establishment of logic as an independent discipline, decoupled from the exegesis of Arisotle's logic, which continued its existence well into the nineteenth century.[86] The mathematical sciences also went their individual way. Astronomy, now renamed as "the science of the configuration [of the stars]" (*ʿilm al-hayʾa*), "freed" itself from both philosophy and astrology (*nujūm, aḥkām an-nujūm*).[87] Of the natural sciences, zoology descended to the level of the miraculous, with books on "the marvels of creation" *ʿajāʾib al-makhlūqāt*. As for the practical sciences, ethics and politics also stopped being part of *ḥikma* and *falsafa* and continued their existence independently, not

86 Street, "Kātibī (d. 1277)" 353–355; El-Rouayheb, *History of Arabic Logic*, 8, and throughout.
87 Ragep, "Freeing Astronomy."

as philosophical/scientific subjects, but primarily in the form of *akhlāq* books that functioned essentially as mirrors for princes.[88]

By fragmenting the scientific worldview into separate compartments, one was free to accept wholesale the Islamic mythological narrative while working on one part of school science that was in any case theologically indifferent. But the example of Islamization that paraphilosophy set forth as acceptable (and only) science affected also the practice of sciences that contained doctrinally sensitive parts. In astronomy, for example, now renamed *ʿilm al-hayʾa*, as just mentioned, ʿAlāʾaddīn al-Qūshjī (d. 1474) argued

> that *ʿilm al-hayʾa* could stand on its own without relying on philosophical metaphysics. Such awareness of critiques of Hellenic philosophy explains reports of astronomy being studied as late as the nineteenth and early twentieth centuries within a *madrasa*, a foundation for the study of Islamic subjects, most notably Islamic law.… *ʿIlm al-hayʾa*'s success within a tradition of religious scholarship was due in part to the fact that criticisms of astronomy emphasised the weaknesses of its foundations in Hellenic philosophy *and not the value of its findings.* Inasmuch as *ʿilm al-hayʾa* texts ceased to situate themselves within a Hellenic taxonomy of the sciences, in which astronomy was connected to Hellenic philosophy, *ʿilm al-hayʾa* became *an Islamic science.*[89]

Similarly in medicine, the growth of what is called "Prophetic medicine" (*ṭibb nabawī*) is certainly an instance of the Islamization of the sciences, even if at the vulgar level at which it operated it may not command or demand (or have commanded and demanded) serious attention, but the process of accommodating science to fit the Islamic mythological narrative affected mainstream medicine as well, as can be seen in the case of the celebrated physician Ibn an-Nafīs (d. 1288), who is well known for his new theory, against the authority of Galen and Avicenna, of the pulmonary transit (not circulation) of the blood between heart and lungs. In a recent study, Nahyan Fancy examined in detail Ibn an-Nafīs's life and works, and in particular his new theory. He was able to unearth that one of the motivations of the physician for this new theory was his desire to uphold the Qurʾānic doctrine of the resurrection of the body, and accordingly *posited* the new theory, without any discernible grounds, which in the end enabled him to support the Qurʾānic doctrine. This raises the question of what the approach to science was, by Ibn an-Nafīs himself and his society, and how it was seen as acceptable to tweak at will scientific data to serve a religious purpose. This half-and-half approach to science – toggling reason on and off depending on the circumstances – would seem to be a basic operating principle in paraphilosophy

88 Gutas, "Ethische Schriften". For developments in religious ethics see Shihadeh, "Theories of Ethical Value."

89 Brentjes and Morrison, "The Sciences" 611–612, emphasis added. I also changed the misused word "Hellenistic," repeated in the text, to "Hellenic." "Hellenistic" refers to the period of 323–30 BC, which is not what the authors are referring to.

and in all the sciences where a process of Islamization began to take place, something that will have to be studied case by case.

For the Mamlūk period (1250–1517), whose very beginning is straddled by Ibn-an-Nafīs who marked indelibly its medical tradition, the Islamization of the medical *profession* is now being documented. From recent research it emerges that "the founding *waqfiyya* [instrument] for the [Manṣūrī] hospital [in Cairo], dated 12 Ṣafar 685/9 April 1286, forbids the employment or even the treatment of non-Muslims at the hospital. … [T]he hospital was to function as a center of medical learning, education, and treatment for Muslims alone."[90] It may well be that such formally and legally stated policies had no "serious effects on the ground, whether in general or in relation to medicine," as it has recently been argued,[91] but the effect on attitudes and the general social and scientific climate was just as severe, very much like al-Ghazālī's condemnation of the philosophical positions which, though never legally enforced, had nevertheless the chilling effect that it did on research science (discussed above in section 4). As a consequence of such policies of religious segregation in medical culture, the theologians gave medicine a religious attribute which it lacked before. In addition, they engaged themselves in theoretical medicine, replacing the earlier scientist-philosophers, but they did not actually practice medicine: that was left to those excluded from the hospitals and theoretical medicine, mostly Christian and Jewish physicians.

Ibn-an-Nafīs lived in Cairo exactly when these developments were taking place, and he died two years after the foundation of the Manṣūrī hospital which formally excluded non-Muslims from its functions. The real question then is not whether these exclusions were actually followed through in practice, as just mentioned, but what the position, function, and attitude of Ibn an-Nafīs was in this socio-political and medical context which included an avowedly religiously correct "medicine of the Prophet" (*ṭibb nabawī*). If, as we are informed, "he was attached" to this hospital, prima facie it appears that he condoned its exclusionary policy, with all that this would imply for his understanding of what it means to do scientific research as a rational endeavor, when manifestly it is not only Muslims that are endowed with reason. And most significantly, what comes into question in this very context is his scientific method when he *posits* a "new" physiology to accommodate the doctrine that the dead are bodily resurrected.[92]

The anti-rationalistic stand for the acquisition of knowledge that para-philosophy adopted as a legitimate form of scientific work affected all sciences

90 Northrup, "Al-Bīmāristān al-Manṣūrī – Explorations," 121–122, and related articles in the same volume.

91 Ragab, *Islamic Hospital,* 167–168.

92 See the complete review of Nahyan Fancy's book by D. Gutas in *Nazariyat* 4/1 (2017), 139–145.

and eventually led to the development of fantastic (and at times illusionary) intellectual constructs that presented themselves as philosophical/scientific systems, adopting all the terminology and mode of argumentation of philosophical/scientific discourse.

One of the earliest, longest lived, and arguably most influential, was the brand of mysticism developed by Ibn ʿArabī (1165–1240), dubbed *ash-shayḫ al-akbar* (the Greatest Master) to surpass and outshine Avicenna, a mere *ash-shayḫ ar-raʾīs* (the Leading Master), who transformed Sufi discourse into philosophical discourse[93] (much as al-Ghazālī and ar-Rāzī had transformed *kalām* discourse into philosophy discourse), and further disseminated and popularized by his star pupil, Ṣadraddīn al-Qūnawī. In this new and "improved" formulation, anti-rationalism gained formal legitimacy as a philosophical stand. "Qūnawī's critique of rational inquiry is an integral part of his teachings, and one ... that would seem to have exerted an influence on the intellectual orientation of later generations in both the Ottoman and Persian lands."[94]

Rational control over science thus relaxed, and the authority of non- or supra-rational, "inspired" knowledge thus enhanced, the floodgates were opened for the influx of all forms of esotericism and the appearance of various occult sciences (*al-ʿulūm al-ġarība*, or, literally, *al-khafiyya*) as formally reorganized thought systems framing or incorporating whatever elements of school science were convenient for the purposes at hand (ʿĀṭūfī has a separate section for them in his catalogue). At the same time, the political usefulness of these new intellectual configurations was eagerly seized upon – or was the motivation behind them. If in the early ʿAbbāsid and Būyid periods sponsorship of science was seen, and therefore functioned, as a major legitimating factor of the power of the rulers, and if after the middle of the eleventh century rulers saw their legitimacy validated through strict adherence to the Islamic mythological narrative made intellectually respectable by paraphilosophy, then the Timurid, Safavid, Ottoman, and Mughal rulers claimed the right to rule (*wilāya*, "sacral power") through the authority of occult sciences, notably lettrism (*ʿilm al-ḥurūf*), geomancy (*ʿilm ar-raml*), and astrology.

> [L]ettrism, by the early fifteenth century, was widely considered to be not only the most Islamic of all the occult sciences, but also the most Islamic, and the most universal, of *all* sciences in its status as both the chiefest branch of the 'science of divine unity' (*ʿilm al-tawḥīd*) and the 'science of the saints' (*ʿilm al-awliyāʾ*) *par excellence.* So argued the 'Greatest Master' Ibn ʿArabī (d. 1240), foremost theoretician of *walāya*, and his argument was first formalised in Ilkhanid courtly circles by Shams al-Dīn Āmulī (d. 1352). ... By the sixteenth century, then, ... these three occult sciences – lettrism, astrology and

93 Rosenthal, "Ibn ʿArabī".

94 Todd, *The Sufi Doctrine of Man*, 51

> geomancy – were promulgated among and eagerly seized upon by the ruling elites throughout the Persianate world as philosophically-scientifically rigorous means of harnessing *walāya*. Their intellectual cachet and complementarity is testified to by Safavid-era philosophers like Shams al-Dīn Khafrī (d. 1535), … who authored treatises on geomancy and lettrism both. … Likewise, Mīr Dāmād (d. 1630), a founding member of the so-called philosophical school of Isfahan and intimate of Shah ʿAbbās, declared the basis of his metaphysical system as a whole to be emanationist-lettrist neo-pythagoreanism: word as (Arabic) text. … [S]uch lofty (occult-)philosophising had very immediate political applications. The greatest thinkers of sixteenth- and seventeenth-century Iran, including Mīr Dāmād and his peers, feature in some contemporary sources as practicing occultists in service to the Safavid state, master talismanists responsible for protecting the realm and letter-magically directing its political course. … Iranian scholar-occultists were even more in demand at the neighbouring Mughal and Ottoman courts, both far wealthier and more cosmopolitan than the Safavid, and many accordingly decamped to seek their fortunes abroad.[95]

With the Timurids and later with the Ottomans, Safavids, and Mughals, and the ascendancy of the occult sciences, further developments in paraphilosophy and intellectual history are in evidence. With the old Avicennan paradigm of science defunct and transformed into paraphilosophy, and following upon the attendant atomization of the sciences, as described, individual sciences were (free to be) incorporated into the new paradigm of "neoplatonic and neopythagorean" orientation espoused by the occult sciences, which involved their mathematization, as recent research indicates.[96] This is a new era in the intellectual history of the Islamic east, and the course of philosophy as research science, which ran dry in the paraphilosophical tradition, as well as the further advancement of "Islamic" philosophy in the new intellectual environment dominated by occultism, are now the focus of much needed research.

7. Review

The long view of the history of science/philosophy presented above, despite the necessarily abbreviated treatment of the main points made and discussed, has the advantage of granting historical perspective to the analysis, with regard to both the nature and kinds of scientific thought in various times and places, and the vital significance of the political and social context in understanding how science advances in concrete terms. In the first place, such an approach helps to

95 Melvin-Koushki, "Astrology, Lettrism, Geomancy" 144–146, with references to related new literature by him and others. For a study of one of the masters of lettrism, (Ibn) Turka Iṣfahānī (d. 1432), see his *The Quest for a Universal Science*.

96 Melvin-Koushki, "Powers of One."

resolve, or rather to remove from the discussion, the conundrum, endlessly repeated in histories of science, "why did the scientific revolution not take place in ancient Greece" or in medieval Islam?[97] If we understand the historical processes in the given societies that determine the back and forth shift in the ideological continuum between the mythological worldview and the scientific one, as (necessarily) very sketchily adumbrated above, the question loses its meaning.

The history of science approach also provides a gauge, by means of rationalism, to measure and assess the various intellectual formations that developed in Islam over the centuries without the risk of floundering in relativism in the assessment of thought systems, for if all such systems are valid and to be respected equally (certainly insofar as they are historical realities), they are, nevertheless, not all equal in their motivations, essential natures, epistemic bases, and functions or historical agencies. This does not mean to judge them, but to discriminate among them.

In this light, it becomes clear that to what is now broadly recognised as the three major distinct historical periods in eastern Islam – the formative period through the early ʿAbbāsids with the Būyids in tow (beginnings to 1050), the later ʿAbbāsids as eclipsed and exterminated by the incursions of the "steppe peoples" (the Turkic and Mongol invasions) and their Ilkhanid and Timurid aftermath (1050–1500), and the pre-modern period of the "gunpowder" empires, the Ottomans, Safavids, and Mughals (1500 and after)[98] – there roughly correspond three major distinct phases in the development of philosophical/scientific thought – as they must, if we acknowledge that distinct historical periods generate their own distinct ideologies. The politically and socially eventful middle period, from the advent of the Saljuqs in Iraq in the middle of the eleventh century to the long aftermath of the Mongol invasions until about the rise of the Timurids after the middle of the fourteenth, is to be coordinated with the development, or saw the generation, of paraphilosophy, with the characteristics described above, and exhibits an amazing degree of intellectual vivacity – irrespective of its being a "golden age" of paraphilosophy rather than of philosophy/science, it was certainly vivacious. The effervescence is due to the strong reactions that were elicited by the worldview demonstrated in Avicenna's scientific system which was made to be seen as contradicting the Islamic mythological narrative, reactions which aimed primarily at its refutation and/or cooptation along with its occasional defense in religiously non-sensitive areas. The form of reaction that eventually gained wide acceptance was the cooptation of philosophical discourse

97 As in, for example, among many others, Cohen, *The Scientific Revolution*, 241–260, 384–417.

98 See the widely held consensus view regarding the analysis of this periodisation expressed by Morgan and Reid in their Introduction to vol. 3 of *The New Cambridge History of Islam.*

for religious ends in a new genre of writing best described as paraphilosophy. At the same time, this shift in the ideological continuum, from a mostly scientific worldview that was espoused by most literate urban classes to a mythological one, signalled the end of research science in *this* particular tradition, with school science partially surviving as a frozen body of doctrines in the work of Avicenna. In the fragmentation of the sciences that followed, it remains to be seen to which extent various sciences – now independent, or affiliated with the new philosophical paradigm provided by the resurgent occultism – developed beyond the stage at which they were left after the demise of research science, as it appears to have happened notably in logic and astronomy. Paraphilosophy itself restricted the subjects of discussion mainly to metaphysics, now termed the "divine science" (*al-ʿilm al-ilāhī*), to the basic principles of physics such as time and motion, and to cosmology, the theory of the elements, and the theory of the soul, with emphasis in this last area again on the question of its survival and ultimate destination in the afterlife.

This new discipline and new genre of writing were paraphilosophy for the reasons I listed above, but what the new name is intended to emphasize is the fact that they were different from anything that had preceded. This was recognized and remarked upon by the Muslim scholars themselves, also as discussed above, and notably by ʿĀṭūfī, the librarian of Bāyezīd II, who called the new discipline "Islamic philosophy." Thus beyond the issue of its mere appellation, what is significant about the acknowledgment of the new discipline with a new name is that it indicates a shift in cultural attitudes regarding scientific knowledge, in that it was now possible to view it as exclusively *Islamic* scientific knowledge as opposed to the scientific knowledge of others. This development parallels the emergence of *Islamic* medicine in the form of "Prophetic medicine" (*ṭibb nabawī*, no matter that the actual contents of this medicine were watered down snippets pilfered from Avicenna's *Qānūn* and elsewhere), and the development of *Islamic* astronomy as anti-Hellenic astronomy. Thus, before about 1050, science was understood to be common to all humanity (which, in any case, was the very rationale for the translations and the importation of "foreign" science into Arabic), with the variations from the mythological narrative of Islam either explained (away) in metaphorical and allegorical terms, or disregarded as belonging to two distinct and disparate spheres of human and social experience, and hence not in mutual conflict, as aptly expressed by Abū Sulaymān as-Sijistānī in his castigation of the Ikhwān aṣ-Ṣafāʾ:

> They claim that perfection is achieved when Greek philosophy and Arab [Islamic] law [*ash-sharīʿa*] are brought together in an orderly arrangement. … They thought they could insert philosophy into Islamic law and attach Islamic law to philosophy. This, however, is an aspiration on the way to which there are insurmountable obstacles

> [*marāmun dūnahu ḥadadun*]: ... Islamic law is derived from God, by means of an ambassador between Him and humans, by way of revelation.[99]

The cognitive obstacles to which Abū Sulaymān is referring here are clear: science is science, and applicable to all, whereas revealed laws are multiple, with each nation having its own. Thus it is possible to have alternative laws, but not alternative sciences, in which case it was preferable to have science and the law to be applicable to different spheres of activity respectively, lest they be brought into conflict and one have to choose between the two, creating the insurmountable obstacles. After about 1050, the process is set into motion which culminates in the creation of paraphilosophy, in which the obstacles Abū Sulaymān is talking about are rhetorically surmounted and the two disparate spheres are joined so that an alternative science is created which belongs not to all humanity but to Muslims alone: "Islamic" philosophy, "Prophetic" medicine, "Islamic" astronomy. In other words, Sunnī and Shīʿa Muslims accomplished that for which Abū Sulaymān was criticizing the Ikhwān aṣ-Ṣafāʾ. The purpose then of paraphilosophy is seen not to be so much to make science/philosophy, or Avicenna's scientific system and world-view, acceptable to Muslims by sanitizing it, but to create this alternative Islamic science.

The historical and social factors that contributed to and generated this shift in cultural orientation in the Islamic East are certainly related to the incoming of the Saljuqs and the "Sunnī restoration" that historians discuss, as a result of which society shifted to the extreme right end on the scale of adherence to the mythological narrative of Islam, a position that found its most effective expression in al-Ghazālī, as discussed above (in section 4). The processes by which this shift occurred, and why it occurred and was widely accepted by society, remain obscure, as do the questions why the Saljuqs should have chosen to champion this extreme form of Sunnism and why it was in their particular political interest to do so.[100] The historical problem so described needs further study and elucidation, for this is how we may begin to understand the development of processes that led to the Islamization of science.

That said, the precise nature of the paraphilosophical structure and its application and function also remain to be investigated, beyond its original purpose of creating an alternative "Islamic" philosophy to usurp the functions of "philosophical" philosophy, or science, as just mentioned. Because its theological

99 In Abū Ḥayyān at-Tawḥīdī, *al-Imtāʿ wa-l-muʾānasa* II,5–6 (az-Zayn and Amīn, eds.), cited in Gutas, *Greek Thought, Arabic Culture*, 163–164.

100 Cf. Morgan and Reid 5: "[T]he Saljuqs had become Muslim before they crossed the frontier: though precisely what kind of Muslims is not as obvious as is sometimes assumed. ... If they had in fact been converted to a syncretic, Shamanism-like form of Sufi Islam, it is not immediately obvious why they should have become, once in power in Iran and Iraq, fervent champions of hardline Sunnī orthodoxy."

function of providing arguments apart from revelation in order to justify revelation – if indeed it had such a function – must certainly have been accomplished already by the twelfth century, if not earlier, in that there were no scientists around who were producing fresh scientific arguments discordant with revelation that had to be refuted. Avicenna's religiously controversial positions, even those condemned by al-Ghazālī, had long been disposed of in a number of ways that were deemed acceptable, something that in any case was not hard to do once extra-rational argumentation by way of an individual's "taste" or "unveiling" was made into, and was accepted as, a legitimate form of paraphilosophical procedures. Thus the function could hardly have been the defense of revelation, as Ibn Khaldūn astutely observed, in which case the question of the reason for which ever more rococo arguments were produced and proffered remains.

There are considerations, first, of the various disciplines with which individual scholars were associated, as we can witness from al-Jāmī when he presents the arguments of philosophers, theologians, and mystics on the same set of questions asked in paraphilosophy. It is to be observed, though, that none of the adherents of any of the three disciplines is disputing the veracity of revelation; it is merely a matter of presenting an argument, in support of a doctrinal position, which can be judged to be better, though the criteria by which this would be established are not expressed; and in any case, it is doubtful that any of the three would accept arguments coming from another discipline as superior. So what was important was the adherence to a particular school and the championing of its dogmatized positions rather than any functional dialogue. As Ibn Khaldūn observed, students engaged in paraphilophy "in order to learn the different school opinions."

There are then personal and professional considerations, which should be seriously taken into account. Being a scholar in these disciplines and having a reputation as excelling in them were matters of social and financial advancement, and scholars were in stiff competition for royal or princely favors and emoluments, to say nothing of their (secret?) ambitions to prove themselves superior even to Avicenna in an one-upmanship game, as the biographies and autobiographies of these scholars indicate.[101] But in this case, too, scholars were arguing against each other as to who would produce the "best" argument about already accepted basic religious doctrines, not scientific positions dismissed as being heretical. Hence it was an intra-theological discussion both between and among theologians of various colorings, Ashʿarites and "neo-Ashʿarites" and Māturīdites and Twelver Shīʿites, etc. It is thus that we see certain subjects and arguments endlessly repeated and recycled in ever more elaborate forms, giving paraphilosophy its obsessive character mentioned above (section 5). Another prime example, in addition to the one on the eternity of the world discussed

101 See Gutas, "Graeco-Arabic Philosophical Autobiographies."

above (section 5), would be the question whether existence is superadded to essence or is identical with it, a question which was debated from Avicenna onward, through al-Jāmī (it is the first question he discusses in *ad-Durra al-fākhira*) and the bitter conflict between ad-Dawānī (d. 1502) and ad-Dashtakī (d. 1498), all the way down to Muḥammad ʿAbduh (d. 1905).[102] If the problem was to find scientifically acceptable arguments enabling one to make the transition "from the necessary existent to the God" of the Qurʾān[103] (was it?), one would have expected this to have been resolved after 900 years, from Avicenna to ʿAbduh. We thus have to be able to understand both the intellectual and social/political reason and motivation of the endless repetition of these arguments, and how they relate to reality, if we are to avoid the assessment that this recycling was merely a lot of activity on a treadmill pursued for sundry professional, political, and personal reasons, not what the activity was aiming at intellectually. Again as Ibn Khaldūn observed, students engaged in paraphilosophy in order "to become versed in the knowledge of argumentation."

There are also political considerations, which are equally, if not more, significant. The scholars producing paraphilosophy were organic intellectuals in the service of political authorities and were helpful to them in a number of ways. As scholars of repute, they continued to provide the courts with which they were associated the same services in the post-Avicenna period as they did before it, scientific authority and cultural legitimation. But beyond this they expressed political and religious policy consonant with the rulers' agenda and shaped public opinion in favor of their policies. Al-Ghazālī is arguably the one scholar who was most deeply involved in political intrigues[104] and most obviously mouthed elegantly composed propaganda on behalf of the Saljuqs and the Baghdad caliphs, but most, if not all, prominent paraphilosophical scholars, by dint of their very prominence, led lives close to the political elites and functioned politically as just described. Alternatively, if not directly involved in promoting a ruler's policies and image, well paid and honored intellectuals who were recycling hackneyed and inconsequential arguments actually supported the established order and did not pose the threat of coming up with new ideas – but were there in these arguments subversive or reformist elements that were expressed most inconspicuously through the repetitions of the arguments? And to whom were they addressed? The works of the post-Avicennan paraphilosophers need to be analyzed to detect how their writings reflect – directly or indirectly, or subversively, if

102 See Wisnovsky, "Essence and Existence," Eichner, "Essence and Existence," and Pourjavady, "Jalāl al-Dīn al-Dāwānī (d. 908/1502)," along with Heer, *The Precious Pearl*, 33–36. For the debate continuing down to Muḥammad ʿAbduh see Wisnovsky "Avicenna's Islamic Reception," 210–213.

103 As Adamson put it in an article by that title.

104 See his biography in Griffel, *Al-Ghazālī*, chapter 1.

at all – theological and other ideological positions of interest and benefit to, or criticism of, political authorities.

All these reasons, singly and in combination, have to be assessed and evaluated for each scholar in order to understand the processes that generated a scholastic culture in which paraphilosophy functioned as the safety valve that both contained it within Islamic parameters and protected it against ruptures. Overall it can be observed that, in the subjects cultivated in paraphilosophy, metaphysics and the principles of physics along with its cosmological and psychological parts, Avicennan school science was scholastically adhered to – literally: it was integrated into the *madrasa* system[105] – to the extent that parts of it were theologically neutral. But the question that has to be answered by future investigations is whether, and where, there was any research science in the interstices to burst the scholastic coccoon, and if there was, on what basis the new material was presented. In our studies we should not only describe what each thinker did, or what new arguments he brought, but on what basis and why he did it: the question of motive is paramount. "It is now time to investigate the horizontal axes of Islamicate intellectual history with the same vigor as has been devoted to the vertical."[106] We have to understand the entire paraphilosophical enterprise better in order to describe with some accuracy the interplay between tradition and innovation, or Islamic science and science, in Islamic societies after Avicenna.

Bibliography

Muḥammad Abū Riḍā, ed., *Rasāʾil al-Kindī al-falsafiyya*, Cairo 1950.

Peter Adamson, ed., *Interpreting Avicenna. Critical Essays,* Cambride: Cambridge University Press, 2013.

–, "From the Necessary Existent to God," in Adamson, ed., *Interpreting Avicenna*, 170–189.

–, "If Aquinas is a philosopher then so are the Islamic theologians," https://aeon.co/ideas/if-aquinas-is-a-philosopher-then-so-are-the-islamic-theologians, accessed March 2017.

Peter Adamson and Peter E. Pormann, *The Philosophical Works of al-Kindī*, Karachi: Oxford University Press, 2012.

Yuri Arzhanov and Rüdiger Arnzen, "Die Glossen in Ms. *Leyden Or. 583* und die syrische Rezeption der aristotelischen *Physik*," in Elisa Coda and Cecilia Martini Bonadeo, eds., *De l'Antiquité tardive au Moyen Âge. Études de logique aristotélicienne et de philosophie grecque, syriaque, arabe et latine offertes à Henri Hugonnard-Roche*, Paris: Vrin, 2014, 416–463.

105 See the fundamental essay for these developments by Endress, "Reading Avicenna."

106 Melvin-Koushki, "Powers of One," 183, citing Daniel Stolz in his forthcoming *The Lighthouse and the Observatory.*

Polymnia Athanassiadi, *Mutations of Hellenism in Late Antiquity*, Farnham, Surrey: Ashgate, 2015.

Marie-Françoise Baslez, *Chrétiens persécuteurs. Destructions, exclusions, violences religieuses au IVe siècle*, Paris: Albin Michel, 2014.

P.R. Blum, *Philosophenphilosophie und Schulphilosophie: Typen des Philosophierens in der Neuzeit*, Stuttgart: Franz Steiner, 1998.

István Bodnár and William W. Fortenbaugh, eds., *Eudemus of Rhodes* (*Rutgers University Studies in Classical Humanities,* Vol. XI), New Brunswick / London: Transaction, 2002.

Sonja Brentjes and Robert G. Morrison, "The Sciences in Islamic Societies," in Robert Irwin, ed., *The New Cambridge History of Islam*, Vol. 4, Cambridge: Cambridge University Press, 2010, 564–639.

Jacques Brunschwig and Geoffrey E.R. Lloyd, eds., *The Greek Pursuit of Knowledge*, Cambridge, Mass. and London: Harvard University Press, 2003.

Charles E. Butterworth, *Averroës. Decisive Treatise & Epistle Dedicatory*, Provo, Utah: Brigham Young University Press, 2001.

H. Floris Cohen, *The Scientific Revolution. A Historiographical Inquiry*, Chicago & London: The University of Chicago Press, 1994.

J.M. Cohen, translator, *Pascal. The Pensées*, Harmondsworth, Middlesex: Penguin Books, 1961.

Henry Corbin, *Œuvres philosophiques et mystiques de Shihabaddin Yahya Sohrawardi*, Tehran: Institut Franco-Iranien and Paris: Adrien-Maisonneuve, 1952.

Pascale Derron, *Entre Orient et Occident: La philosophie et la science gréco-romaines dans le monde arabe*, [Fondation HARDT, Entretiens sur l'antiquité classique, Tome LVII], Genève: Fondation Hardt, 2011.

Sulaymān Dunyā, ed., *al-Ishārāt wa-t-tanbīhāt li-Abī ʿAlī b. Sīnā*, Cairo: Dār al-Maʿārif bi-Miṣr, 1968.

Heidrun Eichner, "Dissolving the Unity of *Metaphysics:* From Fakhr al-Dīn al-Rāzī to Mullā Ṣadrā al-Shīrāzī," *Medioevo* 32 (2007) 139–197.

–, *The Post-Avicennian Philosophical Tradition and Islamic Orthodoxy: Philosophical and Theological Summae in Context,* unpublished *Habilitation*, Halle 2009.

–, "Essence and Existence. Thirteenth-Century Perspectives in Arabic-Islamic Philosophy and Theology," in Hasse and Bertolacci, 123–151.

Khaled El-Rouayheb, *Relational Syllogisms and the History of Arabic Logic, 900–1900*, Leiden / Boston: Brill, 2010.

Khaled El-Rouayheb and Sabine Schmidtke, eds., *The Oxford Handbook of Islamic Philosophy*, New York: Oxford University Press, 2017.

Muḥammad ʿEmāra, ed., *Ibn Rushd, Faṣl al-maqāl,* Cairo 1972.

Gerhard Endress, "Reading Avicenna in the *Madrasa.* Intellectual Genealogies and Chains of Transmission of Philosophy and the Sciences in the Islamic East," in James E. Montgomery, ed., *Arabic Theology, Arabic Philosophy. From the Many to the One: Essays in Celebration of Richard M. Frank*, Leuven: Peters, 2006, 371–422.

Gerhard Endress and J.A. Aertsen, eds., *Averroes and the Aristotelian Tradition*, Leiden: Brill, 1999.

Nahyan Fancy, *Science and Religion in Mamluk Egypt. Ibn al-Nafīs, Pulmonary Transit and Bodily Resurrection,* London and New York: Routledge, 2013.

Michael Frede, "The Philosopher," in Brunschwig and Lloyd, *The Greek Pursuit of Knowledge*, 1–17.
Frank Griffel, *Apostasie und Toleranz im Islam. Die Entwicklung zu al-Ġazālīs Urteil gegen die Philosophie und die Reaktionen der Philosophen*, Leiden: Brill, 2000.
–, "Apostasy," in *Encyclopaedia of Islam Three.*
–, *Al-Ghazālī's Philosophical Theology*, Oxford: Oxford University Press, 2009.
–, "Theology Engages with Avicennan Philosophy," in Sabine Schmidtke, ed., *The Oxford Handbook of Islamic Theology*, Oxford: Oxford University Press, 2016, 435–455.
Dimitri Gutas, "Paul the Persian on the Classification of the Parts of Aristotle's Philosophy: A Milestone between Alexandria and Baġdād," *Der Islam* 60 (1983) 231-67; repr. in Gutas, *Greek Philosophers*, no. IX.
–, "Ethische Schriften im Islam," in W. Heinrichs, ed., *Neues Handbuch der Literaturwissenschaft*, Band 5: *Orientalisches Mittelalter*, Wiesbaden: Aula-Verlag, 1990, 346-365.
–, "Ibn Ṭufayl on Ibn Sīnā's Eastern Philosophy," *Oriens* 34 (1994) 222-241; repr. in Gutas, *Orientations*, no. XVI.
–, *Greek Thought, Arabic Culture. The Graeco-Arabic Translation Movement in Baghdad and Early ʿAbbāsid Society (2nd-4th/8th-10th c.)*, London: Routledge, 1998.
–, *Greek Philosophers in the Arabic Tradition* [Variorum Collected Studies Series: CS 698], Aldershot: Ashgate, 2000.
–, "The Heritage of Avicenna: The Golden Age of Arabic Philosophy, 1000 - ca. 1350," in Jules Janssens and Daniel De Smet, eds., *Avicenna and His Heritage. Acts of the International Colloquium, Leuven - Louvain-la-Neuve, September 8 -September 11, 1999*, Leuven: Leuven University Press, 2002, 81-97.
–, "Arabic into Byzantine Greek: Introducing a Survey of the Translations," in Andreas Speer and Philipp Steinkrüger, eds., *Knotenpunkt Byzanz. Wissensformen und kulturelle Wechselbeziehungen* [*Miscellanea Medievalia* 36], Berlin: Walter de Gruyter, 2012, 246–262.
–, *Avicenna and the Aristotelian Tradition. Introduction to Reading Avicenna's Philosophical Works. Second, revised and enlarged edition, including an inventory of Avicenna's authentic works*, Leiden: Brill, 2014.
–, *Orientations of Avicenna's Philosophy. Essays on His Life, Method, Heritage* [Variorum Collected Studies Series CS 1050], Farnham, Surrey: Ashgate, 2014.
–, "The Author as Pioneer[ing Genius]: Graeco-Arabic Philosophical Autobiographies and the Paradigmatic Ego," in Lale Behzadi and Jaakko Hämeen-Anttila, eds., *Concepts of Authorship in Pre-Modern Arabic Texts*, Bamberg: University of Bamberg Press, 2015, 47–62.
–, "The Rebirth of Philosophy and the Translations into Arabic," in Rudolph, Hansberger, and Adamson, eds., *Philosophy in the Islamic World*, 95–142.
–, "Avicenna's *al-ḥikma al-mutaʿāliya.* Meaning and Early Reception," in Dag Nikolaus Hasse and Amos Bertolacci, eds., *The Arabic, Hebrew, and Latin Reception of Avicenna's Physics and Cosmology*, Berlin / Boston: Walter de Gruyter, forthcoming 2018.
–, "Philosophical Manuscripts: Two Alternative Philosophies", in Gülru Necipoğlu, Cemal Kafadar, and Cornell Fleischer, eds., *Treasures of Knowledge: An Inventory of the Ottoman Palace Library Commissioned by Sultan Bayezid II from His Librarian ʿAtufi*, Leiden and Boston: Brill, forthcoming 2019.

Dag Nikolaus Hasse and Amos Bertolacci, eds., *The Arabic, Hebrew, and Latin Reception of Avicenna's Metaphysics*, Berlin/Boston: Walter de Gruyter, 2012.
Nicholas L. Heer, *The Precious Pearl. Al-Jāmī's al-Durrah al-Fākhirah, with the Commentary of ʿAbd al-Ghafūr al-Lārī*, Albany: State University of New York Press, 1979.
Martin Heidegger, *Gesamtausgabe IV. Abteilung: Hinweise und Aufzeichnungen. Band 96, Schwarze Hefte 1939–1941*, Tübingen 2014.
Henri Hugonnard-Roche, "Le mouvement des traductions syriaques: Arrière-plan historique et sociologique," in Derron, ed., *Entre Orient et Occident*, 45–86.
–, "La question de l'âme dans la tradition philosophique syriaque (VIe-IXe siècle)," *Studia Graeco-arabica* 4 (2014) 17–64.
Werner Jaeger, *Aristotle. Fundamentals of the History of His Development*, Oxford: Oxford University Press, ^{2}1948.
Anthony Kaldellis, *Hellenism in Byzantium. The Transformations of Greek Identity and the Reception of the Classical Tradition*, Cambridge and New York: Cambridge University Press, 2007.
Daniel King, "Why Were the Syrians Interested in Greek Philosophy?" in Philip Wood, ed., *History and Identity in the Late Antique Near East*, Oxord: Oxford University Press, 2013, 61–82.
Hubert Krivine, *The Earth. From Myths to Knowledge*, London / New York: Verso, 2015.
Geoffrey E.R. Lloyd, *Magic, Reason and Experience. Studies in the Origin and Development of Greek Science*, Cambridge: Cambridge University Press, 1979.
–, *Science, Folklore and Ideology. Studies in the Life Sciences in Ancient Greece*, Cambridge: Cambridge University Press, 1983.
–, *The Revolutions of Wisdom. Studies in the Claims and Practice of Ancient Greek Science*, Berkeley: University of California Press, 1987.
Matthew Melvin-Koushki, *The Quest for a Universal Science: The Occult Philosophy of Ṣāʾin al-Dīn Turka Iṣfahānī (1369–1432) and Intellectual Millenarianism in Early Timurid Iran*, Ph.D. diss., Yale University, 2012.
–, "Astrology, Lettrism, Geomancy: The Occult-Scientific Methods of Post-Mongol Islamicate Imperialism," *The Medieval History Journal* 19 (2016) 142–150.
–, "Powers of One: The Mathematicalization of the Occult Sciences in the High Persianate Tradition," *Intellectual History of the Islamicate World* 5 (2017) 127–199.
David O. Morgan and Anthony Reid, eds., *The New Cambridge History of Islam*, Vol. 3, Cambridge: Cambridge University Press, 2010.
Linda S. Northrup, "Al-Bīmāristān al-Manṣūrī – Explorations: The Interface Between Medicine, Politics, and Culture in Early Mamluk Egypt," in Stephan Conermann, ed., *History and Society during the Mamluk Period (1250–1517)*, Göttingen: V&R Unipress; Bonn University Press, 2014, 107–142.
David Pingree, "Hellenophilia versus the History of Science," *Isis* 83 (1992) 554–563; reprinted in his *Pathways into the Study of Ancient Sciences*, Isabelle Pingree and John M. Steele, eds., Philadelphia: The American Philosophical Society Press, 2014, 3–12.
Reza Pourjavady, *Philosophy in Early Safavid Iran: Najm Al-Dīn Maḥmūd Al-Nayrīzī and His Writings*, Leiden: Brill, 2011.
–, "Jalāl al-Dīn al-Dawānī (d. 908/1502), Glosses on ʿAlāʾ al-Dīn al-Qūshjī's Commentary on Naṣīr al-Dīn's *Tajrīd al-iʿtiqād*," in El-Rouayheb and Schmidtke, eds., 415–437.

Ahmed Ragab, *The Medieval Hospital. Medicine, Religion, and Charity*, Cambridge: Cambridge University Press, 2015.

F. Jamil Ragep, "Freeing Astronomy from Philosophy. An Aspect of Islamic Influence on Science," *Osiris* 2001, 49–71.

Ernest Renan, *De philosophia peripatetica apud Syros*, Paris: A. Durand, 1852.

Sajjad Rizvi, "Mīr Dāmād's (d. 1631) *al-Qabasāt. The Problem of the Eternity of the Cosmos*," in El-Rouayheb and Schmidtke, *The Oxford Handbook of Islamic Philosophy*, 438–464.

Franz Rosenthal, *Ibn Khaldūn. The Muqaddimah. An Introduction to History*, 3 vols., Princeton: Princeton University Press, ²1967.

–, "Ibn ʿArabī between Philosophy and Mysticism," *Oriens* 31 (1988) 1–35.

Ulrich Rudolph, "The Late Ancient Bakground," in Rudolph, Hansberger, and Adamson, eds., *Philosophy in the Islamic World*, 29–73.

Ulrich Rudolph, Rotraud Hansberger, and Peter Adamson, eds., *Philosophy in the Islamic World. Volume 1: 8th – 10th Centuries* [Handbuch der Orientalistik, I, 115/1], Leiden / Boston: Brill, 2017.

J. Ṣalībā and K. ʿAyyād, eds., *Al-Ghazālī, Al-Munqidh min aḍ-ḍalāl*, Beirut ⁷1968.

Sabine Schmidtke, ed., *The Oxford Handbook of Islamic Theology*, Oxford: Oxford University Press, 2016.

ʿAbdassalām ash-Shaddādī, ed., *Ibn Khaldūn. Al-Muqaddima*, ad-Dār al-Bayḍāʾ: Bayt al-Funūn wa-l-ʿulūm wa-l-ādāb, 2005.

Ayman Shihadeh, "From al-Ghazālī to al-Rāzī: 6th/12th Century Developments in Muslim Philosophical Theology," *Arabic Sciences and Philosophy* 15 (2005 141–179.

–, "A Post-Ghazalian Critic of Avicenna," *Journal of Islamic Studies* 24:2 (2013) 135–174.

–, "Theories of Ethical Value in *Kalām:* A New Interpretation," in Schmidtke, ed., *Islamic Theology*, 384–407

–, "Al-Rāzī's (d. 1210) Commentary on Avicenna's *Pointers:* The Confluence of Exegesis and Aporetics," in El-Rouayheb and Schmidtke, *The Oxford Handbook of Islamic Philosophy*, 296–325.

Niketas Siniossoglou and Dimitri Gutas, "Philosophy and 'Byzantine Philosophy'," in Anthony Kaldellis and Niketas Siniossoglou, eds., *The Cambridge Intellectual History of Byzantium*, Cambridge: Cambridge University Press, 2017, 271–295.

A.J.S. Spawforth, *Greece and the Augustan Cultural Revolution*, Cambridge: Cambridge University Press, 2012.

Tony Street, "Faḫraddīn ar-Rāzī's Critique of Avicennan Logic," in Dominik Perler & Ulrich Rudolph, eds., *Logik und Theologie. Das* Organon *im arabischen und im lateinischen Mittelalter*, Leiden: Brill, 2005, 99–116.

–, "Kātibī (d. 1277), Taḥtānī (d. 1365), and the *Shamsiyya*," in El-Rouayheb and Schmidtke, 348–374.

Richard Todd, *The Sufi Doctrine of Man*, Leiden: Brill, 2014.

John Walbridge and Hossein Ziai, *Suhrawardī. The Philosophy of Illumination*, Provo, Utah: Brigham Young University Press, 1999.

Marina Wilks, "Jacob of Edessa's Use of Greek Philosophy in His *Hexaemeron*," in Bas ter Haar Romeny, ed., *Jacob of Edessa and the Syriac Culture of His Day*, Leiden: Brill, 2008, 223–238.

Robert Wisnovsky, "Essence and Existence in the Eleventh- and Twelfth-Century Islamic East (*Mašriq*): A Sketch," in Hasse and Bertolacci, 27–50.
–, "Avicenna's Islamic Reception," in Adamson, *Interpreting Avicenna*, 190–213.
–, "Towards a Genealogy of Avicennism," *Oriens* 42 (2014) 323–363.
Mojtabā Zāreʿī, ed., *Al-Išārāt wa-t-tanbīhāt li-š-Šayḫ ar-Raʾīs Ibn Sīnā*, Qum: Būstān-e Ketāb-e Qom, 1381Š/2002.
Leonid Zhmud, *The Origin of the History of Science in Classical Antiquity*, Berlin / New York : Walter de Gruyter, 2006.

Maribel Fierro

Ibn Rushd's (Averroes) 'Disgrace' and his Relation with the Almohads*

Ibn Rushd and the Almohads

Was Ibn Rushd al-Ḥafīd (also known as Averroes) a member of the *ṭalaba?* The *ṭalaba* were Almohad-trained scholars who served the Mu'minid caliphs in their doctrinal and religious policies.[1] Specialists in the history of philosophy have studied Ibn Rushd's thought together with the textual tradition of his *oeuvre*[2] and the impact that it had in Christian and Jewish circles. Some scholars have also dealt with the political implications of his *oeuvre* as well as Ibn Rushd's relations with those in power. The scholars who have directly addressed Ibn Rushd's relationships with the rulers of his times tend to conclude that he was not a member of the *ṭalaba*. For example, Josep Puig Montada – who has written a series of articles on Ibn Rushd and on what he calls 'Averroes' 'circle', i.e., his teachers and pupils and his contemporaries with whom he shared scholarly interests – states that although Ibn Rushd had very close links with the Almohad caliphs and their court, he was not a member of the Almohad *ṭalaba* (or, as he

* Previous versions of this paper were read at Marquette University (2011), at the *Séminaire* directed by Pierre Bouretz at the EHESS, Paris (2012) and at the International Conference *Islamic Philosophy from the 12th to the 14th Century*, University of Bonn (2016). I wish to thank Professor Richard Taylor, Professor Maurice Kriegel and Dr. Abdelkader Al Ghouz for offering me these opportunities to present my research. I am also grateful to those who responded to it with comments and suggestions. The version presented here has been finalized for the project "Practicing Knowledge in Islamic Societies and Their Neighbours," Anneliese Maier Award 2014 (Humboldt Foundation). I wish to thank Luis Molina for his help.

1 The most recent study on the *ṭalaba* is by Émile Fricaud, "Les *ṭalaba* dans la société almohade (le temps d'Averroés)," *Al-Qanṭara* XVIII (1997), pp. 331–388. A study that is still relevant today is J.F.P. Hopkins, *Medieval Muslim Government in Barbary until the Sixth Century of the Hijra*, London: Luzac, 1958.

2 Gerhard Endress, "Le projet d'Averroès: constitution, réception et édition du corpus des oeuvres d'Ibn Rushd," in Gerhard Endress and Jan A. Aertsen (ed.), *Averroes and the Aristotelian Tradition: Sources, Constitution and Reception of the Philosophy of Ibn Rushd (1126–1198). Proceedings of the Fourth Symposium Averroicum (Cologne, 1996)*, Leiden, 1999, pp. 3–32.

puts it, a member of their doctrinal corporation). Puig continues by stating that while Ibn Rushd did make use of the Almohad doctrine in his writings, he was not an official exponent of such doctrine himself[3] due to the fact that the founder of the Almohad movement, Ibn Tūmart (d. 524/1130), was an Ashʿari, and Ibn Rushd wrote against Ashʿarism in his theological works. In other words, Puig concludes that Ibn Rushd was not what we may now call 'an organic intellectual'[4] of the Almohads. What was then the nature of Ibn Rushd's relations with the Almohad movement and with the Mu'minid caliphs?

The Almohad period has often been portrayed as a period of religious fanaticism and barbarian rule. The Almohad movement, led by the Mahdī Ibn Tūmart, had started among non-Arabic speaking Berbers in the mountains of southern Morocco. The leadership of a charismatic and Messianic figure who claimed knowledge of the truth allowed the Almohads to condemn those who opposed them as non-believers and to justify the massacre of their enemies.[5] The Mahdī's successors then upheld a *retour aux sources* (the Qur'ān and the Prophet's Tradition) that allowed them to dispense with the religious establishment of the lands they conquered. As the representation of the Almohads as violent fanatics and conservative believers does not correspond with the flourishing philosophy of their times, the connection between their rule and this philosophical booming has often been ignored as an issue of study. Only a small number of scholars have considered Almohad intellectual and cultural life worthy of discussion, among them William Montgomery Watt and, most importantly, Dominique Urvoy.[6] In fact, many of the relevant figures of the period were studied in isolation of the context in which they lived.[7] Traditional Spanish

3 Josep Puig Montada, "Ibn Rušd and the Almohad Context," in Resianne Fontaine, Ruth Glasner, Reimund Leicht, and Giuseppe Veltri (eds.), *Studies in the History of Culture and Science: A tribute to Gad Freudenthal*, Leiden/Boston: Brill, 2011, pp. 189–208; "El pensamiento de Averroes en su contexto personal y social," *Miscelánea de Estudios Arabes y Hebraicos* XXXVIII (1989–90), pp. 307–324; "Materials on Averroes' circle," *Journal of Near Eastern Studies*. 51/4 (1992), pp. 241–60; "Averroes, vida y persecución de un filósofo," *Revista Española de Filosofía Medieval* 6 (1999), pp. 217–232; "Abū ʿAbd al-Raḥmān b. Ṭāhir," *Revista Española de Filosofía Medieval* 7 (2000), pp. 181–5.

4 An expression coined by Antonio Gramsci (*Selections from the Prison Notebooks*, New York: International Publishers, 1971) to refer to those intellectuals whose mission was to give support (through their writings) to the aims of the party with which they aligned themselves.

5 Yassir Benhima, "Du *tamyīz* à l'*iʿtirāf*: usages et légitimation du massacre au début de l'époque almohade," *Annales Islamologiques* 43 (2009), pp. 137–153.

6 William Montgomery Watt, "Philosophy and Theology under the Almohads," *Actas del Primer Congreso de Estudios Arabes e Islámicos (Córdoba, 1962)*, Madrid, 1964, pp. 101–7 (also in *The Islamic Quarterly* VIII (1964), pp. 46–51); Dominique Urvoy, *Pensers d'al-Andalus. La vie intellectuelle à Cordoue et Sevilla au temps des Empires Berberes (fin XIe siècle-début XIIIe siècle)*, Toulouse: Editions du CNRS, Presses Universitaires du Mirail, 1990.

7 An overview of the most important bibliographical references can be found in Maribel Fierro, "Almohads," *Oxford Bibliographies in Islamic Studies*, ed. Andrew Rippin, New York: Oxford

Arabism held a particularly negative view of the Almoravids and Almohads as foreign invaders of the Iberian Peninsula, invaders who had put an end to what was seen as the vibrant intellectual and cultural life of the Umayyad and Taifa periods. Given their proximity to the pre-Islamic past, these periods were the main object of studies looking for continuities with that past, while later periods led to al-Andalus being ruled by North African dynasties and thus, as it was believed, to political and cultural decay. This attitude obscured the fact that of the most innovative and original thinkers of al-Andalus – and more generally of the Islamic West, given that the Almohads ruled over both the Iberian Peninsula and North Africa – many were active under the Almohads: Ibn Ṭufayl (d. 581/1185), Ibn Rushd (d. 595/1198), Maimonides (d. 1204) and Muḥyī l-dīn Ibn ʿArabī (d. 638/1240). Is it a coincidence that such original thinkers lived in such close proximity? Lawrence Conrad's analysis of Ibn Ṭufayl's career serving the Almohads was an illuminating contribution that departed from the usual viewpoint of scholars, as it is the more recent book on Maimonides by Sarah Stroumsa that shows the Jewish thinker's close links to his Almohad background.[8] Studies that deal with Ibn Rushd's thought in the Almohad context, such as those by Dominique Urvoy and Marc Geoffroy, have indicated that there was no clear-cut incompatibility between Ibn Rushd's theological views and those of the Almohads, especially if 'Almohadism' was analysed by taking into account its evolution through time, from the Messianic and revolutionary origins to the eventual renunciation of such origins.[9] The general lack of attention to the Almohad context (in which the above-mentioned thinkers –Ibn Ṭufayl, Ibn Rushd, Maimonides and Muḥyī l-dīn Ibn ʿArabī – were active for most or part of their lives) was also influenced by an event in Ibn Rushd's life, his persecution, understood as proving how inimical such context was to rational thought and this since E.

University Press, 2016 http://www.oxfordbibliographies.com/browse?module_0=obo-9780195390155.

8 Lawrence I. Conrad, "An Andalusian Physician at the Court of the Muwaḥḥids: Some Notes on the Public Career of Ibn Ṭufayl," *Al-Qanṭara* 16.1 (1995), pp. 3–13; see also L. I. Conrad (ed.), *The World of Ibn Tufayl: Interdisciplinary Perspectives on Ḥayy ibn Yaqẓān*, Leiden: Brill, 1996. Sarah Stroumsa, *Maimonides in His World: Portrait of a Mediterranean Thinker*, Princeton: Princeton University Press, 2009.

9 Dominique Urvoy, "La pensée almohade dans l'oeuvre d'Averroès," *Multiple Averroès. Actes du Colloque Internationale organisé à l'occasion du 850e anniversaire de la naissance d'Averroès, Paris 20–23 septembre 1976*, ed. J. Jolivet, Paris: Les Belles Lettres, 1978; idem, *Ibn Rushd (Averroes)*, transl. O. Stewart, London / New York, 1991 (proving that Ibn Tūmart and Ibn Rushd followed similar methods and had similar aims); Marc Geoffroy, "L'almohadisme théologique d'Averroès (Ibn Rushd)," *Archives d'Histoire Doctrinale et Littéraire du Moyen Age* 66 (1999), pp. 9–47. The contrast between the Almohad creed and Ashʿarism is discussed by Jan Thiele in "Facing the Mahdī's True Belief: Abū ʿAmr al-Salālijī's Ashʿarite Creed and the Almohads' Claim to Religious Authority," forthcoming.

Renan's influential work.[10] Ibn Rushd's 'disgrace' (*nakba*), the trial and persecution he underwent, took place towards the end of his life, during the reign of the third Mu'minid caliph al-Manṣūr (r. 580/1184–595/1198). After this trial, Ibn Rushd was expelled from the mosque of Cordoba and exiled to nearby Lucena. There were also other indications that philosophy was not easily accepted in Almohad society, although, at the same time, it enjoyed official support under the first Mu'minid caliphs. Ibn Rushd was charged with writing his commentaries on Aristotle by the second caliph Abū Yaʿqūb Yūsuf when he was still a prince. Ibn Ṭufayl, who had introduced Ibn Rushd to Abū Yaʿqūb Yūsuf and who as noted was a member of the *ṭalaba*, had written a novel (*Ḥayy b. Yaqẓān*, the 'self-taught philosopher') in which he illustrated the limits of the philosopher's activity in society, eventually advocating his isolation from the rest of the population given the basic incompatibility between his way of thinking and aspirations and that of society's.[11] The forced conversion of Jews under the Almohads, the suspicion towards those converts, the discriminatory measures taken against them (due to the impossibility of knowing what they really believed and the desire of some to return to their previous faith) moved some intellectuals among the converted Jews to emigrate from Almohad lands, as Maimonides did. Philosophical Sufis such as Ibn ʿArabī also emigrated for reasons that have yet to be fully explored. These factors all contributed to modern scholars being generally uninterested in a deeper understanding of the link between the Almohad context and those who were devoted to rational speculation.

At the same time, it could not be ignored that Ibn Rushd – despite his 'disgrace' – had close ties to the Mu'minid caliphs. As a jurist, he was named judge of Seville and Cordoba by the caliphs, and his career as a philosopher started under their influence as well. Parts of his literary output were also explicitly written under their command or were dedicated to them. A famous text describes how a young Ibn Rushd was presented to the future second caliph, Abū Yaʿqūb Yūsuf (r. 558/1163–580/1184), then still a prince, by his mentor Ibn Ṭufayl, and the future caliph then instructed Ibn Rushd to provide a commentary on Aristotle.[12] As previously mentioned, Ibn Ṭufayl is now accepted to have been a member of

10 Ernest Renan, *Averroès et l'averroéisme*, Paris, 1882, pp. 15–42.

11 For a useful overview of *Ḥayy b. Yaqẓān* see Taneli Kukkonen, *Ibn Tufayl*, London, 2014. For my own understanding of this work as a way to indicate the limits of the Almohad revolution in its efforts to educate the masses, see "The Islamic West in the Time of Maimonides: The Almohad Revolution," in Lukas Muehlethaler (ed.), *'Höre die Wahrheit, wer sie auch spricht'. Stationen des Werks von Moses Maimonides vom islamischen Spanien bis ins moderne Berlin*, Herausgegeben im Auftrag des Jüdischen Museums Berlin, 2014, pp. 21–31.

12 'Abd al-Wāḥid al-Marrākushī (d. after 621/1224), *Kitāb al-mu'jib fī talkhīṣ akhbār al-Maghrib*, ed. R. Dozy, 2ª ed., Leiden, 1881, pp. 353–4. The encounter and its date has been analyzed by Nemesio Morata, "La presentación de Averroes en la corte almohade," *La Ciudad de Dios* 153 (1941), pp. 101–122.

the Almohad doctrinarians or learned elites, the *ṭalaba*, and more specifically of the *ṭalabat al-ḥaḍar*, those directly linked to the ruler.[13] In the text on Ibn Rushd's presentation to the future caliph, Ibn Ṭufayl – a renowned doctor and a *ṭālib* known for his interest in both mysticism and philosophy – introduces a young Ibn Rushd, praising his capability to carry out the intellectual project (a commentary of Aristotle's works) suggested by the Mu'minid prince. Sarah Stroumsa has expressed doubt regarding the veracity of the story on the basis that it is a single report, stating that it is found in a relatively late source and that there are chronological inconsistencies.[14] In addition to these factors, there is also the issue of the extent of Mu'minid agency in charging the young Ibn Rushd with commenting on Aristotle, an enterprise that Stroumsa sees more as originating with the young Ibn Rushd himself as an internal development in his philosophical training and not as a duty carried out for a paying master. However, if we look at this event within the general context of the times, it adds to what we know about the recruitment of young bright men into the Almohad 'doctrinal corporation' begun under the first caliph ʿAbd al-Mu'min (r. 524/1130–558/1163), as well as what we know regarding Ibn Rushd's own writing on how he entered Almohad service.[15] It also fits the educational aims of the Almohad revolution and the need on the part of the Almohad caliphs to find a substitute for Messianism after the Mahdī's death, and for this philosophy was of help.

The last twenty years have seen an important advancement of studies related to the Almohads, with Émile Fricaud greatly contributing to this expansion by reviving the study of the Almohad religious and political elites, the *ṭalaba* and *ḥuffāẓ*. In this study, Fricaud provides insight into the use of the term *al-amr* and *al-amr al-ʿazīz* among the Almohads (they use this term to speak of their rule),[16] and thoroughly analyses the Arabic sources on Ibn Rushd's 'disgrace' (*nakba*).[17] In this study, Fricaud returns to a source that was previously relatively neglected – *al-Dhayl wa-l-takmila* by Ibn ʿAbd al-Malik al-Marrākushī (d. 702/1302) –, yet one that is full of precious information on Almohad times, as highlighted in 1999

13 See Notes 1 and 8 above.

14 Sarah Stroumsa, "Philosophes almohades? Averroès, Maïmonide et l'idéologie almohade," in M. Fierro, P. Cressier and L. Molina (eds.), *Los almohades: problemas y perspectivas*, Madrid, CSIC/Casa de Velázquez, 2005, pp. 1137–1162. Morata has already proposed a solution for the chronological inconsistencies. ʿAbd al-Wāḥid al-Marrākushī's *Kitāb al-muʿjib* is often our only source for other events during the Almohad period.

15 See Note 101 below.

16 Émile Fricaud, "Origine de l'utilisation privilégiée du terme *amr* chez les Mu'minides almohades," *Al-Qanṭara* XXIII (2002), pp. 93–122; Salvador Peña, "El término de origen coránico *amr Allāh* ('Disposición de Dios') y el linguocentrismo trascendente islámico, en torno al siglo XII," *Anaquel de Estudios Arabes* 22 (2011), pp. 197–224.

17 Émile Fricaud, "Le problème de la disgrâce d'Averroès," in A. Bazzana et al. (eds.), *Averroès et l'averroïsme (XIIe–XVe siècle) : un itinéraire historique du Haut Atlas à Paris et Padoue*, Lyon, 2005, pp. 155–189.

by the Moroccan scholar Muḥammad Ibn Sharīfa in a book in which he collected the Arabic source materials on Ibn Rushd's life.[18] This information will be discussed in more detail in the following section.

1. Ibn Rushd's 'Disgrace': The Reasons for this Disgrace and Extant Interpretations of the Topic

In the Arabic sources, we find a number of disjointed data to be considered for an appraisal of Ibn Rushd's 'disgrace' in the year 593/1197. These data are listed below in an attempt at chronological order (though approximate). They are also numbered in order to facilitate references to the data in the interpretation provided in the following section. A chronology is provided at the end of this article to help the reader place Ibn Rushd's 'disgrace' in a more general context.

1) *Good relations with the Mu'minid prince (sayyid) Abū Yaḥyā, governor of Cordoba, later suspect of rebellion (?):* Ibn Rushd was on very good terms with a brother of Abū Yūsuf Yaʿqūb al-Manṣūr (r. 580/1184–595/1198) before the latter became the third Mu'minid caliph. This brother, called Abū Yaḥyā, had been named governor of Cordoba by his father Abū Yaʿqūb Yūsuf, the second caliph (r. 558/1163–580/1184), around the same time (year 579/1183) as when Ibn Rushd was named judge of the town, and on the suggestion – it seems – of Ibn Rushd himself. Abū Yaḥyā is normally understood as having been the caliph's brother who later attempted to take power (year 587/1191) and who was put to death by al-Manṣūr.[19] Three years before, the caliph's brother Abū Ḥafṣ ʿUmar al-Rashīd, governor of Murcia, and his uncle Abū l-Rabīʿ Sulaymān had been executed in Salé for disaffection, an event that reveals the internal tensions within the Mu'minid family. These tensions, which had previously been checked, would prove to be decisive in the fall of the dynasty.

2) Relations with other scholars: Ibn Rushd was on good terms with several of the scholars of Cordoba, the town where he was born and where his grandfather Ibn Rushd al-Jadd (d. 520/1126) had been a very important figure under the Al-

18 Ibn ʿAbd al-Malik al-Marrākushī (m. 702/1302), *al-Dhayl wa-l-takmila*, especially in the entry on Ibn Rushd (vol. VI, ed. Iḥsān ʿAbbās, Beirut, 1973, number 51, pp. 21–31), but also in other entries; Muḥammad Ibn Sharīfa, *Ibn Rushd al-ḥafīd: sīra wathā'iqiyya*, al-Dār al-Bayḍā': Maṭbaʿat al-Najāh al-Jadīda, 1999. Ibn ʿAbd al-Malik al-Marrākushī's information was already known – although in a truncated form – to Renan who quoted this author under the name 'al-Anṣārī'.

19 Ibn Sharīfa, *Ibn Rushd al-ḥafīd*, p. 64; Fricaud, "Le problème de la disgrâce d'Averroès," pp. 158–160, referring to Ibn ʿAbd al-Malik al-Marrākushī, *Dhayl*, vol. VI, p. 26.

moravids (both as a judge and as a 'reformed' Maliki jurist).[20] When Ibn Rushd was named judge of Cordoba in 579/1183, he replaced Ibn al-Ṣaffār.[21] This judge of Cordoba was a member of a family of notables who had counted with influential scholars in past years. A member of the Banū l-Ṣaffār married Ibn Rushd's daughter and they had at least one child together.[22] There is no indication that Ibn al-Ṣaffār held any grudge against Ibn Rushd for having replaced him in the qāḍiship.

However, Ibn Rushd did run into problems with a number of other scholars.[23] While we know that one of these scholars was ʿAbd al-Raḥmān b. Zakariyyā' al-Rajrājī (judge of Ecija, near Cordoba), we do not know what caused the problems between the two men.[24] Another scholar with whom Ibn Rushd had problems was the Sevillan Abū ʿAbd Allāh Ibn Zarqūn, who died in 586/1190, before the 'disgrace' took place. His son Abū l-Ḥusayn Muḥammad Ibn Zarqūn (d. 621/1224) was also an influential Maliki scholar who was persecuted when the caliph al-Manṣūr (r. 580/1184–595/1198) ordered the burning of Maliki writings.[25] Ibn Zarqūn's (the father) enmity towards Ibn Rushd is revealed in his accusation that Ibn Rushd had plagiarized another book in his legal work *Bidāyat al-mujtahid wa-nihāyat al-muqtaṣid*.[26] Ibn Zarqūn – like his son – was a staunch Maliki who

20 On Ibn Rushd al-Jadd, see Delfina Serrano, "Ibn Rushd al-Jadd (d. 520/1126)," in Ousamma Arabi, David S. Powers and Susan Spectorsky (ed.), *Islamic Legal Thought: Jurists and Their Work*, Leiden: Brill, 2013, pp. 295–322. For the 'reformed' Malikis, see Maribel Fierro, "Proto-Mālikīs, Mālikīs and Reformed Mālikīs," in P. Bearman, R. Peters, F. E. Vogel (eds.), *The Islamic School of Law: Evolution, Devolution, and Progress*, Cambridge, Mass.: Harvard University Press, 2005, pp. 57–76.

21 He was the grandson of Abū l-Ḥasan Yūnus b. Mughīth al-Anṣārī (d. 532/1138): see J. M. Vizcaíno Plaza, "Ibn al-Ṣaffār, Abū l-Ḥasan Yūnus," *Biblioteca de al-Andalus*, vol. 5: *De Ibn Saʿāda a Ibn Wuhayb*, ed. Jorge Lirola Delgado, Almería: Fundación Ibn Tufayl, 2007, pp. 66–8, nº 1040. He belonged to an important Cordoban family, the Banū Mughīth or Banū l-Ṣaffār.

22 On Ibn al-Ṣaffār see *Prosopografía de los Ulemas de al-Andalus (= PUA)*, ID 10984 http://www.eea.csic.es/pua/ [consulted 29/12/2016]; Manuela Marín and Maribel Fierro, *Sabios y santos musulmanes de Algeciras*, Algeciras, 2004, pp. 122–23, nº 76.

23 See also below, number 7) regarding his relations with the Cordobans according to the historian Ibn ʿUmar/Ghamr.

24 On ʿAbd al-Raḥmān b. Zakariyyā' al-Rajrājī see *Prosopografía de los Ulemas de al-Andalus (= PUA)*, ID 4356 http://www.eea.csic.es/pua/ [consulted 29/12/2016]. Ibn Sharīfa, *Ibn Rushd al-ḥafīd*, p. 71; Fricaud, "Le problème de la disgrâce d'Averroès," p. 162.

25 Fricaud, "Les *ṭalaba* dans la société almohade," p. 357; Janina Safran, "The Politics of Book Burning in al-Andalus," *Journal of Medieval Iberian Studies* 6 (2014), pp. 148–168.

26 On the father, see his biography in Ibn al-Abbār, *al-Takmila li-kitāb al-Ṣila*, ed. F. Codera, 2 vols., Madrid, 1886 (*BAH*, t. V–VI), nº 824; Ibn ʿAbd al-Malik al-Marrākushī, *al-Dhayl wa-l-takmila*, ed. I. ʿAbbās, Beirut, 1973, VI, 203–8, nº 597; [Documentación con la colaboración de Brahim ben Abella], "Ibn Zarqūn, Abū ʿAbd Allāh," *Biblioteca de al-Andalus*, vol. 6: *De Ibn al-Ŷabbāb a Nubḏat al-ʿaṣr*, ed. Jorge Lirola Delgado, Almería: Fundación Ibn Tufayl, 2009, pp. 275–7, nº 1436. On the son, see D. Serrano Ruano, "Ibn Zarqūn, Abū l-Ḥusayn," *Biblioteca de al-Andalus*, vol. 6, pp. 277–80, nº 1437. On the issue of plagiarism, see M.ʿA. Makkī,

had defended the Maliki legal school when the Almohads, under the first caliph ʿAbd al-Mu'min, had tried to substitute the Maliki doctrines prevalent in the Islamic West by insisting that legal regulations had to be directly linked to the Qur'ān and the Tradition of the Prophet, a policy that made Ẓāhirism – and especially Ibn Ḥazm's methodology and doctrine – attractive for the new rulers of the Maghreb and al-Andalus. The strong anti-*madhhab* spirit of the Almohad revolution which was very useful for getting rid of the former religious establishment and allowing for the creation of new scholarly elites oriented their legal policy towards Ẓāhirism and especially towards Ibn Ḥazm's Ẓāhirism. This form of Ẓāhirism was the most important anti-*madhhab* current in the Islamic West, and Ibn Ḥazm's vitriolic attacks were very helpful in discrediting the Malikis.[27] In a text found in al-Burzulī's *Nawāzil,*[28] ʿAbd al-Mu'min, the first Almohad caliph, is said to have wanted to replace Malikism with Ibn Ḥazm's doctrines. The vizier and secretary Abū Jaʿfar b. ʿAṭiyya accused the Maliki jurists of having abandoned the Qur'ān and the *sunna* of the Prophet and of following the legal casuistry books (*kutub al-furū', kutub al-masā'il*), such as Saḥnūn's (d. 240/854) *Mudawwana.* The vizier cited the case of the repetition of the invalid prayer as an example, a case which had been the object of controversy between Ibn Ḥazm and the Malikis.[29] The Maliki jurist Abū ʿAbd Allāh Ibn Zarqūn (d. 586/1190) then intervened, arguing that Maliki doctrine in this case corresponded to the Prophetic Tradition and that the contents of the *Mudawwana* concerning that case were in agreement with the Qur'ān and *sunna.* Thus, according to al-Burzulī's text, Ibn Zarqūn was able to convince the caliph ʿAbd al-Mu'min that Maliki doctrine did not depart from the truth. According to Saʿd Aʿrāb, this success

"Contribución de Averroes a la ciencia jurídica musulmana," *Al encuentro de Averroes*, ed. A. Martínez Lorca, Madrid, 1993, pp. 15–38.

27 For such vitriolic attacks, see Camilla Adang, "Restoring the Prophet's Authority, Rejecting *Taqlīd:* Ibn Ḥazm's *Epistle to the One who Shouts from Afar,*" in D. Ephrat and M. Hatina (ed.), *Religious Knowledge, Authority and Charisma: Islamic and Jewish Perspectives*, Salt Lake City: The University of Utah Press, 2014, pp. 50–63. The following passages are taken from Maribel Fierro, "The Legal Policies of the Almohad Caliphs and Ibn Rushd's *Bidāyat al-mujtahid,*" *Journal of Islamic Studies* 10/3 (1999), pp. 226–248 (repr. in Carool Kersten (eds.), *The Caliphate and Islamic Statehood: Formation, Fragmentation and Modern Interpretations*, 3 vols., Berlin-London: Gerlach Press, 2015, vol. III, pp. 252–271).

28 Al-Burzulī (d. 841/1438), *Fatāwā al-Burzulī: jāmi' masā'il al-aḥkām li-mā nazala min al-qaḍāyā bil-l-muftiyyīn wa-l-ḥukkām*, ed. Muḥammad al-Ḥabīb al-Hīla, Beirut: Dār al-Gharb al-Islāmī, 2002, VI, 376–379. Before these *Fatāwā* were edited, Saʿd Aʿrāb edited this text in his "Mawqif al-muwaḥḥidīn min kutub al-furūʿ wa-ḥaml al-nās ʿalā l-madhhab al-ḥazmī," *Da'wat al-ḥaqq* 249 (1985), pp. 26–30.

29 This example also coincides with one of the precepts imposed by Ibn Yāsīn, the founder of the Almoravid movement: Nehemia Levtzion, "ʿAbd Allāh b. Yāsīn and the Almoravids," in J.R. Willis (ed.), *Studies in West African Islamic History*, vol. I, London, 1977, pp. 78–112, p. 86, which allows one to think that the case was probably chosen as a direct attack against Almoravid Malikism.

proved that the Maliki jurists were well prepared to defend their doctrine with the same weapons (the traditions of the Prophet) used by their opponents.[30]

Abū l-Ḥusayn ʿAbd al-Raḥmān Ibn Rabīʿ al-Ashʿarī (d. 585/1189), who claimed descent from the Companion of the Prophet Abū Mūsā al-Ashʿarī and who was also a follower of Ashʿari theology, had hoped to be named judge in Cordoba, but instead received the position in the less important Ecija. His son Abū ʿĀmir Yaḥyā (d. 640/1242) wrote several tracts refuting Ibn Rushd's theological writings, including the *Kashf 'an manāhij al-adilla fī 'aqā'id al-milla.*[31] The famous traveller Ibn Jubayr (d. 614/1217) also had no sympathy for Ibn Rushd, whom he attacked for his occupation with philosophy after returning from his second *riḥla* that had taken place between 585/1189–587/1191.[32]

3) *Doubting the historicity of the people of 'Ād:* One of Ibn Rushd's pupils, Abū Muḥammad ʿAbd al-Kabīr b. Muḥammad b. ʿĪsā al-Ghāfiqī (d. 616/1220), was his secretary while Ibn Rushd was judge in Cordoba and acted as delegate judge in his name in certain villages.[33] ʿAbd al-Kabīr b. Muḥammad al-Ghāfiqī reported that he could testify that Ibn Rushd was a reliable Muslim in performing his religious duties (such as ablutions and prayer), a testimony that must have taken place during Ibn Rushd's trial and that showed what other sources confirm – that Ibn Rushd was a practicing and devout Muslim. The only 'religious' fault that he witnessed – no date is indicated – was the following. The governor (*walī*) of Cordoba (perhaps Abū Yaḥyā?) consulted the *ṭalaba* regarding the rumour announcing the arrival of a violent wind (*rīḥ 'ātiya*) that would destroy humanity. This rumour had spread in both the East and al-Andalus. When Ibn Rushd and his friend Ibn Bundūd[34] *left the presence of the governor* [the italics are mine: MF]

30 In fact, by the sixth/twelfth century, such Maliki *aggiornamento* had already taken place: see Fierro's article quoted above in Note 20.

31 On the father and son, see B. Boloix Gallardo, "Ibn Rabīʿ al-Ašʿarī, Abū l-Ḥusayn/l-Ḥasan," *Biblioteca de al-Andalus*, vol. 4: *De Ibn al-Labbāna a Ibn al-Ruyūlī*, ed. Jorge Lirola Delgado, Almería: Fundación Ibn Tufayl, 2006, pp. 435–6, nº 974 and "Ibn Rabīʿ al-ʿAšʿarī, Abū ʿĀmir," *Biblioteca de al-Andalus*, vol. 4, pp. 431–5, nº 973; Ibn Sharīfa, *Ibn Rushd al-ḥafīd*, pp. 69–73, 179–183; Fricaud, "Le problème de la disgrâce d'Averroès," pp. 161–2.

32 Ibn Sharīfa, *Ibn Rushd al-ḥafīd*, pp. 81–2, 99, quoting Ibn ʿAbd al-Malik al-Marrākushī, *al-Dhayl wa-l-takmila*, VI, p. 30–31 and V, 608–612.

33 On ʿAbd al-Kabīr b. Muḥammad al-Ghāfiqī see Documentación, "al-Gāfiqī al-Mursī, Abū Muḥammad," *Biblioteca de al-Andalus*, vol. 1: *De al-'Abbādīya a Ibn Abyaḍ*, ed. Jorge Lirola Delgado and José Miguel Puerta Vílchez, Almería: Fundación Ibn Tufayl, 2012, p. 351–2, nº 114 with no mention of this event; Ibn Sharīfa, *Ibn Rushd al-ḥafīd*, pp. 237–9, 275–6. The event quoted here is found in Ibn ʿAbd al-Malik al-Marrākushī, *Dhayl*, VI, 29 and in vols. IV–V, ed. Iḥsān ʿAbbās, Beirut, s.d., number 407, pp. 233–4. See Ibn Sharīfa, *Ibn Rushd al-ḥafīd*, pp. 174–5; Fricaud, "Le problème de la disgrâce d'Averroès," pp. 163–164.

34 See Documentación, "Bundūd, Abū Bakr," *Biblioteca de al-Andalus, Apéndice*, ed. Jorge Lirola Delgado, Almería: Fundación Ibn Tufayl, 2013, p. 36, nº 1937, entry on Bundūd as the scholar who transmitted the first encounter between Ibn Rushd and the second Almohad

whose *majlis* they had attended, they continued discussing such a possibility from the viewpoint of nature (*ṭabī'a*) and by discussing the influence of the stars. ʿAbd al-Kabīr b. Muḥammad al-Ghāfiqī mentioned that if such a wind would appear, this would be the second time that God had similarly intervened in the lives of men, as there had previously been the episode of the 'roaring wind' (*rīḥ ṣarṣar*) that destroyed the people of ʿĀd, according to the Qur'ān.[35] Ibn Rushd retorted that he doubted the historical existence of the people of ʿĀd and the story of their destruction, causing much concern and astonishment to those who were present. For them, such a comment was *kufr* (infidelity), as it meant the rejection (*takdhīb*) of what the Qur'ān states.[36]

4) *Ibn Rushd under attack (590/1194):* In 590/1194, opponents of Ibn Rushd went to Marrakech to protest against him. The caliph paid no attention to these protests, although those opponents seem to have thought that the caliph intended to execute the philosopher.[37]

Besides the fact that Ibn Rushd was disliked by several of his contemporaries, the caliph himself was also unhappy with the philosopher for two main reasons. According to the judge Abū Marwān al-Bājī (564/1168–635/1237),[38] the caliph disliked the fact that every time Ibn Rushd attended his *majlis* and discussed something regarding *'ilm*, the philosopher would address him, saying: 'Listen, oh, brother' (*tasma' yā akhī*). The same judge claimed that the philosopher had treated the caliph disrespectfully, referring to him as *malik al-barbar* in a book he had written on animals, in the section dealing with the giraffe that he had seen in the court of the 'king of the Berbers'. Ibn Rushd would have tried to refute this by explaining that what he had meant was to call the caliph *malik al-barrayn*, meaning the king of the two lands (North Africa and al-Andalus).[39]

---

caliph, and where mention is made of his son (?) Abū l-Ḥasan ʿAlī b. Bundūd, likely the one meant here; see also Ibn Sharīfa, *Ibn Rushd al-ḥafīd*, pp. 147, 233–4.

35 Such wind is mentioned in Qur'ān 41:16, 54:19, 69:6–7.

36 That Ibn Rushd was not alone in doubting the historicity of the Qur'ānic narrative is shown by the case of ʿAbd al-Qahhār b. Mufarrij (b. ʿAbd al-Qahhār) b. Hudhayl b. Muḥammad al-Fazārī/al-Fāzāzī al-Gharnāṭī (alive in 590/1193–4) who wrote a *Qaṣīda shi'riyya radda bihā 'alā l-qā'il bi-ihlāk al-rīḥ al-arḍ*; see H. M. Hajjaj Lahsen, "Ibn Huḏayl al-Fazārī, Abū Muhammad," *Biblioteca de al-Andalus, Apéndice*, nº 2188.

37 Fricaud, "Le problème de la disgrâce d'Averroès," pp. 164–5, quoting Ibn ʿAbd al-Malik al-Marrākushī, *Dhayl*, VI, p. 25, and Ibn ʿIdhārī (d. 695/1295), *al-Bayān al-mughrib*, part on the Almohads, ed. M. I. al-Kattānī et al., Beirut-Casablanca, 1985, p. 226.

38 On Abū Marwān al-Bājī, see Manuela Marín, "El viaje a Oriente de Abū Marwān al-Bāŷī (m. 635/1237)," *Estudios Onomástico-Biográficos de al-Andalus. VI*, ed. Manuela Marín, Madrid: CSIC, 1994, pp. 273–304.

39 Ibn Abī ʿUṣaybiʿa (d. 668/1270), *'Uyūn al-anbā' fī ṭabaqāt al-aṭibbā'*, entry on Ibn Rushd: see the edition and translation by H. Jahier and A. Noureddin, *Médecins de l'Occident musulman*, Alger: Librairie Ferraris, 1377/1958, p. 134/135.

5) *The caliph publicly shows his respect for Ibn Rushd (591/1195):* In 591/1195, the Almohad army defeated the king of Castile Alfonso VIII at Alarcos. During the campaign, the third Almohad caliph – called al-Manṣūr because of that victory – stopped in Cordoba and had a long conversation with Ibn Rushd. The caliph awarded Ibn Rushd great respect at this meeting, as he placed him in the position where Abū Muḥammad ʿAbd al-Wāḥid normally stood. Abū Muḥammad ʿAbd al-Wāḥid was the son of Abū ʿUmar Ḥafṣ Intī (Hintātī), one of the most powerful of the Almohad shaykhs, those who had been Ibn Tūmart's companions. With their tribal followings, these shaykhs were instrumental in helping ʿAbd al-Mu'min become the first Mu'minid caliph.[40] It is not clear if Abū Muḥammad ʿAbd al-Wāḥid was relegated to another position or if he was not present on that occasion. Did the fact that the caliph granted such a high position (close to him) to someone recruited into Almohadism at a late stage provoke the jealousy and anger of the Almohad shaykhs, for whom such a position was usually reserved? Were the Almohad shaykhs and their followers those who had sought Ibn Rushd's 'disgrace' in the previous year?

When Ibn Rushd heard of the victory of Alarcos, he performed a prostration of thanksgiving (*sajdat al-shukr*), a ritual which I will discuss in more detail at a later point.

6) *The year of the 'disgrace' (593/1197):* In 593/1197, the caliph named Abū Zayd Ibn Yūjjān al-Hintātī as vizier in Seville,[41] where Ibn Yūjjānm ran into the famous doctor Abū Bakr Ibn Zuhr al-Ḥafīd (507/1113–595/1198 or 596/1199), a member of an Andalusī family who had reached high positions in both the Almoravid and the Almohad courts due to their medical expertise.[42] The Hintāta was one of the Berber tribes who had adhered to the Almohad cause very early. The Almohad shaykh whose position near the caliph had been given to Ibn Rushd also belonged to this family (as seen in Number 5).

40 Fricaud, "Le problème de la disgrâce d'Averroès," p. 165, quoting Ibn Abī ʿUṣaybiʿa (d. 668/1270), *'Uyūn al-anbā' fī ṭabaqāt al-aṭibbā'*. See Ibn Abī ʿUṣaybiʿa's on Ibn Rushd in the text edited and translated by H. Jahier and A. Noureddin, *Médecins de l'Occident musulman*, Alger: Librairie Ferraris, 1377/1958, pp. 131–141, at pp. 132/133. The Almohad shaykh Abū Muḥammad ʿAbd al-Wāḥid was named governor of the province of Ifrīqiya and would eventually rule there independently (r. 603/1207–618/1221).

41 Luis Molina, "Instituciones administrativas: visires y secretarios," in *Historia de España Menéndez Pidal*, vol. VIII/2 (*El retroceso territorial de al-Andalus. Almorávides y almohades. Siglos XI al XIII*), coord. M.J. Viguera, Madrid: Espasa Calpe, pp. 147–167.

42 On Ibn Zuhr, see R. Valencia, "Ibn Zuhr, Abū Bakr," *Biblioteca de al-Andalus*, vol. 6, 350–2, nº 1495.

The 'disgrace' of Ibn Rushd and the persecution of the philosophers took place in this same year. Abū Bakr Ibn Zuhr was charged with supervising the burning of logic and philosophy books.[43]

7) *Ibn 'Umar/Ghamr, Almohad historian, on the reasons for the 'disgrace':* The Almohad historian Ibn ʿUmar/Ghamr[44] mentioned that enmity existed between Ibn Rushd and several Cordobans, enmity caused by envy and rivalry (*waḥsha, muḥāsada*) that had resulted from living together for a long period of time. He also stated that the main accusation against Ibn Rushd was that he had departed from the norms (*sunan*) of the Revealed law (*sharī'a*), instead preferring the rule (*ḥukm*) of nature, thus giving priority to nature (*ṭabī'a*) over the *sharī'a.* Ibn Rushd's Cordoban enemies had collected, albeit in a distorted fashion, sayings and expressions that Ibn Rushd had uttered, writing them down on pieces of paper, some of which had allegedly been written by him.[45] They demonstrated – according to Ibn Rushd's Cordoban enemies – that Ibn Rushd had fallen into error (*hafawāt*) and that he followed a damaging methodology.[46]

8) *Ibn Rushd put under trial and expelled from the Cordoban Great Mosque:* The accusations led to a session of debate (*mudhākara*) in the presence of the caliph: 'The caliph ordered the *ṭalaba* of his council and the jurists (*fuqahā'*) of his government to go to the congregation of the Muslims and to explain to the people that Ibn Rushd was a heretic (*bi-annahu maraqa min al-dīn*).' With the unanimity of the *plenum (ijtimā' al-mala')*, the caliph condemned Ibn Rushd, but not to death, only to an exemplary punishment. The punishment started with a session held in the Great Mosque of Cordoba organized by the *ṭalaba* and the *fuqahā'* (the caliph was not present) in which both Ibn Rushd and Abū ʿAbd Allāh b. Ibrāhīm al-Uṣūlī[47] (a scholar also devoted to philosophy) were publicly con-

---

43 Fricaud, "Le problème de la disgrâce d'Averroès," pp. 185–187. On the relationship between Ibn Rushd and the Banū Zuhr, see Ibn Sharīfa, *Ibn Rushd al-ḥafīd*, pp. 212–5.

44 On Ibn ʿUmar/Ghamr, see Muḥammad Ibn Sharīfa, "Abū l-Ḥajjāj Yūsuf b. Ghamr, mu'arrikh dawlat Yaʿqūb al-Manṣūr. Taʿrīf wa-taṣḥīḥ taṣḥīf," *Majallat al-Ākādimiyya* 10 (1993), pp. 83–107; Documentación, "Ibn ʿUmar al-Umawī, Abū l-Ḥaŷŷāŷ," *Biblioteca de al-Andalus*, vol. 5, pp. 530–1, nº 1284 and Apéndice, 446, nº 1284.

45 One case involved Ibn Rushd mentioning Venus (al-Zuharat) as 'one of the divinities': Fricaud, "Le problème de la disgrâce d'Averroès," p. 175, quoting ʿAbd al-Wāḥid al-Marrākushī, *Kitāb al-mu'jib.*

46 Ibn Sharīfa, *Ibn Rušd al-ḥafīd*, pp. 141–4; Fricaud, "Le problème de la disgrâce d'Averroès," pp. 169–173, quoting Ibn ʿAbd al-Malik al-Marrākushī, *Dhayl*, VI, p. 25–6, and Ibn ʿIdhārī, *al-Bayān al-mughrib*, section on the Almohads, p. 226.

47 On Abū ʿAbd Allāh b. Ibrāhīm al-Uṣūlī see J. Haremska, "al-Uṣūlī, Abū ʿAbd Allāh," *Biblioteca de al-Andalus*, vol. 7: *De al-Qabrīrī a Zumurrud*, ed. Jorge Lirola Delgado, Almería: Fundación Ibn Tufayl, pp. 584–5, nº 1827. On the scholars condemned with Ibn Rushd, see Fricaud, "Le problème de la disgrâce d'Averroès," pp. 178–182.

demned. Both of these men were made to stand while the attendants passed in front of them, damning them and spitting on their faces. But after this, our sources comment that the two accused were perfect in their knowledge, and that they had benefitted many with their pedagogy and their teachings. They also add that the students of Ibn Rushd spread all over.[48]

9) *Public statements on why Ibn Rushd was condemned:* During the session in the Great Mosque of Cordoba, the judge Abū ʿAbd Allāh b. Marwān intervened, stating that philosophy (*falsafa*) was like fire which can be used for good or for bad; when the useful aspect of philosophy is superior to the bad, it is acceptable to take advantage of it; but when the bad is superior to the good, then philosophy should not be used. An anti-falsafa *khuṭba* followed, written by Abū Ḥafṣ ʿUmar al-Sulamī al-Aghmātī.[49] The *khaṭīb* Abū ʿAlī Ibn Ḥajjāj then stated that the two men were heretics (*annahum maraqū min al-dīn*) and transgressors of the creeds of the believers (*wa-khālafū 'aqā'id al-mu'minīn*).[50] The official letter of condemnation calls the accused 'hypocrites'.[51]

10) *Exile to Lucena:* Ibn Rushd was exiled to Lucena, a town inhabited by the Jews, as he was purported to be from the Banū Isrā'il without any tribal affiliation in al-Andalus. Ibn ʿIdhārī does not mention this exile, only stating that Ibn Rushd was imprisoned.[52]

---

48 Ibn ʿAbd al-Malik al-Marrākushī, *Dhayl*, VI, p. 26, and Ibn ʿIdhārī, *al-Bayān al-mughrib*, section on the Almohads, p. 226; Fricaud, "Le problème de la disgrâce d'Averroès," p. 172.

49 Ibn Sharīfa, *Ibn Rušd al-ḥafīd*, p. 81; Fricaud, "Le problème de la disgrâce d'Averroès," pp. 183–4. His biography in Ibn ʿAbd al-Malik al-Marrākushī, *Dhayl*, vol. VIII, ed. Muḥammad b. Sharīfa, Rabat, 1984, pp. 222–232, nº 26 (including the text of the *khuṭba*).

50 Ibn ʿAbd al-Malik al-Marrākushī, *Dhayl*, vol. VI, p. 26. On Abū ʿAlī, see Ibn Ḥajjāj Ibn Sharīfa, *Ibn Rušd al-ḥafīd*, pp. 35, 61, 144, 185–6. Due to the accusation of being a heretic, Ibn Rushd was threatened with the death penalty. Ibn Rushd's views on heresy are worth paying attention to. On the one hand, at the end of his *Tahāfut al-Tahāfut*, he states that the best philosophers do not allow for controversies on the principles of religion and thus, for them, heretics should be condemned to death (Maurice-Ruben Hayoun, "L'averroïsme dans les milieux intellectuels du judaïsme: Moïse de Narbonne (1300–1362) et Eliya Delmédigo (v. 1460–1493)," in Bazzana et al. (eds.), *Averroès et l'averroïsme*, p. 292). On the other hand, in his *Faṣl al-maqāl*, he advocates great caution in using *takfīr* against one's opponents when dealing with the theoretical sciences in which consensus is difficult to reach contrary to what happens in the natural sciences: Makkī, "Contribución de Averroes a la ciencia jurídica musulmana," p. 26; Fred R. Dallmayr, "Reason, Faith, and Politics: A Journey to Muslim Andalusia," *The Maghreb Review* 25, 3–4 (2000), 194–216, p. 207.

51 The text of the letter in Ibn ʿAbd al-Malik al-Marrākushī, *Dhayl*, vol. VI, pp. 26–28. See Fricaud, "Le problème de la disgrâce d'Averroès," p. 183.

52 The election of Lucena, known for its predominantly Jewish population, was related to the alleged Jewish origins of the Banū Rushd: Delfina Serrano, "Explicit Cruelty, Implicit Compassion: Judaism, Forced Conversions and the Genealogy of the Banū Rushd," *Journal of Medieval Iberian Studies* 2/2 (2010), pp. 217–33 and Maribel Fierro, "Ibn Rushd al-Hafid

11) *The causes for the 'disgrace'*: The close relationship (*ikhtiṣāṣ*) between the philosopher and the caliph al-Manṣūr's brother Abū Yaḥyā was considered by some – according to Ibn ʿAbd al-Malik al-Marrākushī – to have been the cause of Ibn Rushd's 'disgrace' (*nakba*) (Number 1). If the brother was the man executed in 587/1191 due to suspicions regarding his loyalty, such *ikhtiṣāṣ* may have led the caliph to distrust the philosopher, in addition to the fact that Ibn Rushd had also upset him (Number 4). However, by 591/1195, the two appeared to be on good terms once again (Number 5).

The Almohad historian Ibn ʿUmar/Ghamr deemed the engagement with philosophy to be the main reason for the 'disgrace' of Ibn Rushd, which is a common viewpoint many historians have of this 'disgrace'. However, Ibn ʿUmar/Ghamr also suggested that the accusation of engagement with philosophy was the weapon used by Ibn Rushd's enemies who held grudges against him for other reasons. For Ernst Renan, Ibn Rushd's case was yet one more example of the persecution of philosophy and the philosophers that had been part of the Islamic world since the sixth/twelfth century, with al-Ghazālī as its main proponent.[53] George Vajda famously said that although Ibn Rushd was a sincere Muslim in his own way, he was condemned by the orthodox scholars of his religion because of his preference for philosophy.[54]

In modern times, the 'disgrace' has been linked to the *jihad* against the Christians, as the Almohad caliph would have wanted to gain the support of the orthodox jurists in order to maintain the cohesion of society.[55] Some Muslim scholars also tend to look for contextual political explanations. In his book on Ibn Rushd, published in 1998, Al-Jābirī mentions the estrangement between the

(Averroes) and his exile to Lucena: Jewish ancestry, genealogy and forced conversion," *Al-Qantara* XXXVIII (2017), pp. 131–152.

53 Renan, *Averroès et l'averroèisme*, pp. 15–42. On the complex engagement of Ibn Rushd with al-Ghazālī's thought see J. Puig Montada, "Ibn Rushd versus al-Ghazālī: Reconsideration of a Polemic," *The Muslim World* LXXXII (1992), pp. 113–131, and Frank Griffel, "The Relationship between Averroes and al-Ghazālī as it Presents Itself in Averroes' Early Writings, especially in his Commentary on al-Ghazālī's *al-Mustaṣfā*," in John Inglis (ed.), *Medieval Philosophy and the Classical Tradition in Islam, Judaism and Christianity*, Richmond: Curzon Press, 2002, pp. 51–63.

54 George Vajda, *Isaac Albalag Averroïste juif traducteur et annotateur d'Al-Ghazali*, Paris, 1960, p. 264. This attitude brings to mind Charles Hirschkind's article in which he argues that the thought of the modern Egyptian scholar Nasr Hamid Abu Zayd, accused of *zandaqa* and condemned for his views on the Qur'ān, can be considered to be more on the side of heresy than of hermeneutics: Ch. Hirschkind, "Heresy or Hermeneutics: The Case of Naṣr Ḥāmid Abū Zayd," *The American Journal of Islamic Social Sciences* 12/4 (1995), pp. 463–77.

55 On this view, see Pierre Guichard, *Les musulmans de Valence et la Reconquête (XIe–XIIIe siècles)*, 2 vols., Damascus, 1990–1991, I, 130–1; J. C. Bürgel, "Ibn Ṭufayl and his *Ḥayy Ibn Yaqẓān:* A Turning Point in Arabic Philosophical Writing," in S. Jayyusi (ed.), *The Legacy of Muslim Spain*, Leiden, 1992, pp. 830–846, p. 843.

caliph and the philosopher, and also the envy and the grudges held by the Cordobans. Al-Jābirī considers these factors to be pretexts, not true causes for the 'disgrace'. In his opinion, the true cause was Ibn Rushd's commentary on Plato's *Republic*. The book was dedicated to Abū Yaḥyā, the caliph's brother, and the accusations raised against Ibn Rushd were based on his opinions expressed in the book, such as his criticism of the situation in the country:

> Thus men will be of two categories: a category called the masses, *hamon*, and another called the mighty, as is the case of the people in Persia and in many of our own states. In such a situation, the masses will be plundered by the mighty. The mighty commit excesses by seizing property from them, until this leads them at times to tyranny, just as happens in our own time and our own state.[56]

Al-Jābirī believes that Ibn Rushd is attacking the caliph al-Manṣūr in this passage. However, Puig notes that Rosenthal had suggested that Ibn Rushd likely composed the book during the reign of Abū Yaʿqūb Yūsuf. Ibn Sharīfa, however, believes that Ibn Rushd's 'disgrace' should be understood within a political context that responded to specific circumstances and should not be understood as the condemnation of philosophy, thus taking into account the changeability over time of Almohad policies.[57]

2. Revisiting the Evidence on Ibn Rushd's 'Disgrace'

Given his close relationship with the philosopher, ʿAbd al-Kabīr b. Muḥammad al-Ghāfiqī's report (Number 3) is especially relevant. First, he highlights the fact that Ibn Rushd's behaviour was, externally, that of a scrupulous Muslim. Secondly, he explains that while Ibn Rushd did make comments regarding the rhetorical or 'imaginative' character of the Sacred Scripture and the need to 'interpret' it, he only did so outside the official setting of the meeting with the governor of Cordoba when he must have felt that he was among like-minded scholars capable of understanding his rationalistic thinking. In other words, he did not say in public what he felt he could safely say in a more private context. Thirdly, ʿAbd al-Kabīr b. Muḥammad al-Ghāfiqī's report suggests that either Ibn Rushd had a faulty understanding of his secretary's grasp of philosophical inquiry or he was trying to educate him, introducing him to more subtle ways of thinking without realizing that he was unable to acquire demonstrative reasoning

56 Puig Montada, "Ibn Rušd and the Almohad Context," p. 193, quoting Muḥammad ʿĀbid al-Jābirī, *Ibn Rushd. Sīra wa-fikr*, Beirut, 1998, second ed. 2001, and *Averroès Commentary on Plato's Republic*, edited with and introduction, translation and notes by E.I.J. Rosenthal, Cambridge: The University Press, 1969, p. 214.

57 Ibn Sharīfa, *Ibn Rushd al-ḥafīd*, p. 101.

or that his student was opposed it. Ibn Rushd's and, more generally, the Almohad educational aims – which deserves more attention – are in the background,[58] together with the limitations they faced, which were already a cause of concern for his teacher Ibn Ṭufayl.[59]

Ibn Rushd's comment regarding scripture can be linked to similar statements by Maimonides, on which Stroumsa writes: 'When Maimonides rejects out of hand some of the recognized Talmudic *midrashim* as idle fantasy, he is thus going further against religious literary tradition than any of the Muslim thinkers did.'[60] However, Ibn Rushd not only dismissed the veracity (*ḥaqq*) of both the people of ʿĀd and their destruction, but also claimed that the story about Abraham sacrificing his son was a fable (*figmentum*) with the purpose of inducing men to worship God.[61] The following story told by the Muḥyī l-dīn Ibn ʿArabī indicates that such views were not uncommonly discussed in Almohad times. In 586/1190, Muḥyī l-dīn Ibn ʿArabī met a philosopher in al-Andalus (Ibn Rushd himself?) who denied that miracles (*karāmāt*) could be performed. The encounter took place in winter, in front of a fire. The philosopher explained that the common people believed that Abraham was thrown into the fire without being affected by it, whereas fire by its nature burns all matter susceptible of combustion. In fact, the philosopher said, the fire mentioned in the Qur'ān in the story of Abraham was meant to be understood as the symbolic expression of Nimrod's anger. Among those present was a Sufi endowed with *karāmāt* (Ibn ʿArabī himself?) who, pointing to the fire in the room, asked if that fire belonged to those that burnt matter. The philosopher answered 'yes' and threw him some of the coals,

58 For Ibn Rushd, it was acceptable to teach fables to the children, but theologians should be criticised because some of their teachings – transformed into beliefs by way of imitation – were wrong, such as saying that God is the cause of both good and evil. For more on his educational views, see Louis Lazar, "L'éducation politique selon Ibn Roshd (Averroes)," *Studia Islamica* 52 (1980), 135–166 (reference to the above quotation in p. 151). I have dealt with Ibn Rushd's views on education and with the pedagogical outlook of his whole oeuvre in Maribel Fierro, "Education for the People? The Case of the Almohad Revolution," paper presented at the Near and Middle East History Seminar, SOAS, February 7, 2011, at the *Séminaire* organized by Maurice Kriegel, EHESS, May 22, 2012 and at the Workshop ARC1"Al-Andalus, un carrefour de cultures", *Speculum Arabicum project*, Université Louvaine-la-Neuve (2011), December 5, 2013. Its publication is forthcoming.

59 As noted by L. Conrad, "Through the Thin Veil: On the Question of Communication and the Socialization of Knowledge in Ḥayy b. Yaqẓān," in Lawrence I. Conrad (ed.), *The World of Ibn Tufayl: Interdisciplinary Perspectives on Ḥayy ibn Yaqẓān*, Leiden: E.J. Brill, 1996, pp. 238–266, pp. 244–5.

60 Stroumsa, *Maimonides in his World*, p. 124.

61 Wim van Dooren, "Ibn Rušd's Attitude towards Authority," in A. Hasnawi, A. Elamrani-Jamal and M. Aouad (eds.), *Perspectives arabes et médiévales sur la tradition scientifique et philosophique grecques: actes du colloque de la* SIHSPAI, Paris, 1993, Leuven, 1997, pp. 623–33, p. 631.

only to witness with astonishment that the Sufi was unaffected.[62] Van Dooren points out that in Ibn Rushd's view, philosophers do not discuss the issue of miracles '*coram populo*', but instead take them for granted because of their value for the common people, as they help people to lead a virtuous life. However, the philosophers know that God does not allow any aberration and supernatural miracles are therefore impossible. When the Qur'ān is called a miracle in Ibn Rushd's *Tahāfut al-tahāfut*, such 'miracle' is understood as referring to its inimitability (*i'jāz*) on the assumption that it does not contain any interruption of the course of nature.[63]

The belief that the main accusation against Ibn Rushd was that he gave priority to rational speculation over Revelation can be clearly seen in other Almohad sources, such as Ibn ʿUmar/Ghamr (Number 7) and in the statements produced during the trial and 'disgrace' (Number 9). Natural and rational sciences acquired a central position in the Almohad world of scholarship,[64] and the issue of *ṭabīʿa* versus *sharīʿa* appears in a variety of sources.[65] For example, the judge Abū Mūsā ʿĪsā b. ʿAbd Allāh al-Lakhmī al-Ḍujjī al-Sharīsī (d. after 615/1218)[66] reported that one day he heard a poem written in the style of Ibn Khafāja. In this poem, there was a verse about a horse that read: 'The hand of nature (*yad al-ṭabīʿa*) shaped it by iron and fire / using for this gold and silver.' Abū Mūsā liked the verse so much that he kept repeating it in his mind while he was studying an issue from the science of the 'principles of religion' (*uṣūl al-dīn*). That night, he went to bed, and in his dreams he saw a man whom he thought to be one of the four orthodox caliphs. He was correct, as that man was ʿAlī b. Abī Ṭālib. Abū Mūsā approached him and started to greet him, but ʿAlī rejected Abū Mūsā: 'How dare you recite

62 Claude Addas, *Ibn 'Arabī ou La quête du Soufre Rouge*, París: Editions Gallimard, 1989, pp. 135–6.

63 van Dooren, "Ibn Rušd's Attitude towards Authority," p. 631. However, the Prophet's miracles continued to be taught in Almohad times. In the *Risālat al-fuṣūl*, a letter by ʿAbd al-Mu'min written in 556/1161, it is stated that Ibn Tūmart's *'Aqīda* had to be learned 'from its beginning to its last word on Prophetic miracles (*min awwālihi ilā ākhir al-qawl fī l-muʿjizāt*):" Évariste Lévi-Provençal, *Trente-sept lettres officielles almohades*, Collection des textes arabes publiée par l'Institut des Hautes Études Marocaines, Rabat, 1941, p. 132 and *Documents inédits d'histoire almohade (Fragments manuscrits du "legajo" 1919 du fonds arabe de l'Escurial)*, París, Librairie Orientaliste Paul Geuthner, 1928, pp. 22–24.

64 Urvoy, *Pensers d'al-Andalus*; Miquel Forcada, "Las ciencias de los antiguos en al-Andalus durante el periodo almohade: una aproximación biográfica," *Estudios Onomástico-Biográficos de al-Andalus*, volume X. *Biografías almohades, II*, eds. M.L. Avila and M. Fierro, Madrid-Granada, 2000, pp. 359–411 and "Síntesis y contexto de las ciencias de los antiguos en época almohade," in P. Cressier, M. Fierro and L. Molina (eds.), *Los almohades: problemas y perspectivas*, 2 vols., Madrid: CSIC/Casa de Velázquez, 2005, II, pp. 1091–1135.

65 Pierre Guichard, "La situation de la philosophie et des sciences dans les mondes chrétien latin et arabo-musulman vers 1212," in P. Cressier and V. Salvatierra (eds.), *Las Navas de Tolosa 1212–2012*, Jaén, 2014, pp. 277–290.

66 M. Á. Borrego Soto, "al-Ḍuŷŷī, Abū Mūsà," *Biblioteca de al-Andalus*, vol. 1, pp. 336–7, nº 103.

'The hand of nature shaped it' while studying *uṣūl?*' Abū Mūsā answered that he had done so because the poet had written the verse in that way. But ʿAlī replied that it would be more correct to say: 'The hand of the Omnipotent (*yad al-qadīr*) shaped it with His power.' Abū Mūsā agreed with him, as the verse now included a reference to the Creator.[67] Moralizing stories such as this, in which the protagonist role accorded to nature is resisted because it undermines religious belief, must have been helpful in increasing resistance to the promotion of philosophical views.

If we read such stories against their moralizing message, what they reveal is the existence of a trend to change 'habituation' to certain beliefs and practices in favour of a philosophically-oriented view of both nature and God -an attempt that was possible because it had caliphal support.[68] Such an endeavour, however, exposed those engaged in it – including the caliph – to criticism and rejection. In the report on the trial of Ibn Rushd that took place in the palace (Number 8), the term *al-mala'* is Qur'ānic and means an assembly of the notables. In the Qur'ān, the idea is conveyed that the majority of the peoples addressed by prophets rejected them, with their leaders (*al-mala'*) singled out for particular blame. The leading citizens in a town or tribal assembly (*al-mala'*) always constitute the biggest obstacle to the success of a prophet's mission (Qur'ān 7:60, 75–7).[69] The use of the term *al-mala'* when describing Ibn Rushd's trial implies a negative judgement of those who condemned him, and in fact compares the philosopher to a prophet. Recently, Diego Sarrió Cucarella has interpreted Ibn Rushd's career as an attempt to claim the inheritance of the Prophet Muḥammad for the philosophers.[70] This is a suggestion worth pursuing for its implications in terms of how political and religious authority was conceptualized under the Almohads.[71] During the public exposure of Ibn Rushd in the Great Mosque of

67 Miguel Angel Borrego Soto, *Gala del mundo y adorno de los almimbares. El esplendor literario del Jerez andalusí*, Jerez, 2011, p. 71, quoting Abū ʿAbd Allāh Ibn ʿAskar and Abū Bakr b. Khamīs, *A'lām Mālaqa*, Beirut, 1999, pp. 327–8, number 146.

68 I have dealt with the changes brought by the Almohads to the doctrinal and ritual domains in Maribel Fierro, "Doctrina y práctica jurídicas bajo los almohades," in P. Cressier et al. (eds.), *Los almohades: problemas y perspectivas*, vol. II, pp. 895–935, and in the paper mentioned in Note 58. See also Maroun Aouad and Frédérique Woerther, "Le commentaire par Averroès du chapitre 9 du livre X de *l'Éthique à Nicomaque:* pédagogie de la contrainte, habitudes et lois," *Mélanges de l'Université Saint-Joseph* LXII (2009), pp. 353–80. For similar educational concerns in Maimonides, see Carlos Fraenkel, "Legislating Truth: Maimonides, the Almohads and the 13th Century Jewish Enlightment," in R. Fontaine et al. (eds.), *Studies in the History of Culture and Science presented to Gad Freudenthal*, Leiden, 2010, pp. 209–231.

69 M. H. Fadel in *Encyclopaedia of the Qur'ān*, vol. I, 297.

70 Diego R. Sarrió Cucarella, "The Philosopher as the Heir of the Prophets: Averroes' Islamic Rationalism," *Al-Qanṭara* XXXVI (2015), pp. 45–68.

71 Another suggestive approach – but one which suffers from a faulty knowledge of Almohad history – is Vanessa Martin, "A Comparison Between Khumainī's Government of the Jurist

Cordoba, the judge Abū ʿAbd Allāh b. Marwān showed a relativistic acceptance of philosophy when he said that *falsafa* was like fire which could be used for good or for bad: when the useful aspect of the fire was superior to the bad, it was acceptable to take advantage of it, but when the bad was superior to the good, then the fire should not be used (Number 9). This statement by a delegate of the Almohad caliph implies that philosophy had previously been given a place in Almohad society and thus confirms caliphal support for its study, a support that was rationalized as providing something useful and good for society. Moreover, the judge's intervention suggests that the caliph himself was affected by Ibn Rushd's condemnation and had to be saved from it by pointing that philosophy was not entirely bad thus, the caliph had not been mistaken in promoting it initially, but also that it could not be accepted in absolute terms. This goes directly against Ibn Rushd's defence of philosophy as an obligatory duty. In his *Faṣl al-maqāl*, written between 575/1179–576/1180, Ibn Rushd had said that the study of philosophy was not merely allowable but 'obligatory' (*wājib*), employing Islamic classical legal terminology to defend something that many found indefensible. In the same work, Ibn Rushd had also provided ingenious and innovative arguments for the eternity of the world, using proof-texts from the Qur'ān itself.[72] According to the judge's intervention, the dismissal of philosophy was not complete (as the caliph had promoted the study of it), but it was now underlined that philosophy could not be taken as being more important than religion.

The criticism against Ibn Rushd also involved other aspects. The statement that those condemned were transgressors of the creeds of the believers (Number 9) could be a reference to the Almohad profession of faith.[73] Dominique Urvoy has studied the points of concordance and contrast between Ibn Rushd's theological positions and those found in Ibn Tūmart's professions of faith.[74] There was a specific 'transgression' that had previously caused trouble for Ibn Rushd. In the first version of the *Kashf 'an manāhij al-adilla*, Ibn Rushd had pointed out that a staunch opposition to *tashbīh* – the position attributed to Ibn Tūmart which had

and *The Commentary on Plato's Republic* of Ibn Rushd," *Journal of Islamic Studies* 7 (1996), pp. 16–31.

72 Eric Ormsby's review on Majid Fakhry, *Averroes (Ibn Rushd): His Life, Works and Influence* (Oneworld 2003) https://networks.h-net.org/node/8330/reviews/8936/ormsby-fakhry-averroes-ibn-rushd-his-life-works-and-influence [consulted 26/12/2016]; Taneli Kukkonen, "Averroes and the Teleological Argument," *Religious Studies* 38/4 (2002), pp. 405–428.

73 On the *'aqīda* and its popular versions, see Henri Massé, "La profession de foi (*'aqīda*) et les guides spirituels (*morchida*) du Mahdi Ibn Toumert," *Mémorial Henri Basset*, t. II, Paris, 1928, pp. 105–121.

74 See Note 9 above and Dominique Urvoy, "Les professions de foi d'Ibn Tūmart. Problèmes textuels et doctrinaux," in P. Cressier et al. (eds.), *Los almohades: problemas y perspectivas*, vol. II, pp. 739–52.

allowed for de-legitimization of the previous dynasty (the Almoravids, accused of being anthropomorphists) –[75] could lead to dangerous consequences because the 'anthropomorphist' Qur'ānic expressions were helpful for maintaining the faith of the common people. As Marc Geoffroy has proved, Ibn Rushd was forced to recant and to change the corresponding passages.[76] Ibn Rushd had written the *Kashf* between 575/1179–576/1180[77] and, although we do not know for sure when Ibn Rushd corrected the text in order to avoid overtly criticizing Ibn Tūmart's anti-anthropomorphic doctrine, perhaps this could be related to the events of 590/1194, when his Cordoban opponents went to Marrakech to denounce him to the caliph. It could also have caused Abū ʿĀmir Yaḥyā al-Ashʿarī to write his refutation of the *Kashf* (Number 2).

The role accorded to philosophy and the issue of how to cater the understanding of correct belief to the needs of different types of people clearly seem to have been the arguments used in Cordoba to bring about Ibn Rushd's 'disgrace' and, most especially, to justify it to wider audiences. This is what I would call the 'religious' explanation: religion *versus* philosophy.

However, there is also the 'ethnic' explanation. According to Abū Marwān al-Bājī, Ibn Rushd would have referred to the Almohad caliph as *malik al-barbar* (Number 4). The Almohad movement was closely linked to Berber claims to political and religious authority, especially in its origins. The founder Ibn Tūmart was a Masmuda Berber and the Mu'minids, the Almohad caliphs, were Zanata Berbers. Their lands in the Maghrib were considered to be those in which religious knowledge (*ʿilm*) now resided, so that its inhabitantes no longer had any need to travel to the East in search of knowledge.[78] The Almohads also used the Berber language (*al-lisān al-gharbī*) in many ways, such as in the call to prayer and for the creeds that those living under Almohad rule were required learn by heart. Among the Andalusis, however, there was a long history of antagonism towards the North African Berbers, an antagonism born out of a mixture of need and admiration for their military power, resentment of their rule over al-Andalus and contempt for their illiteracy, their ignorance of Arabic and their lack of intellectual sophistication. The derogatory appraisal of he who claimed the title

75 Delfina Serrano, "¿Por qué llamaron los almohades antropomorfistas a los almorávides," in Cressier et al. (eds.), *Los almohades: problemas y perspectivas*, vol. II, 451–76.

76 Marc Geoffroy, "À propos de l'almohadisme d'Averroès: l'anthropomorphisme (*tağsīm*) dans la seconde version du *Kitāb kašf ʿan manāhiğ al-adilla*," in P. Cressier et al. (eds.), *Los almohades: problemas y perspectivas*, vol. II, pp. 853–94; Di Donato, Silvia, "Le Kitāb al-Kašf ʿan manāhiğ al-adilla d'Averroès: les phases de la rédaction dans les discours sur l'existence de dieu et sur la direction, d'après l'original arabe et la traduction hébaïque." *Arabic Sciences and Philosophy* 25/1 (2015), pp. 105–133.

77 The *Tahāfut* and the *Faṣl al-maqāl* were written in the same period.

78 This was especially so in the early Almohad period. Ibn Rushd, like many other of his contemporaries, did not perform any *riḥla*.

of 'Commander of the Faithful' as *malik al-barbar* on the part of an Andalusi such as Ibn Rushd was plausible, although of course dangerous to be made in public.[79] Offering such an explanation for Ibn Rushd's 'disgrace' seems to provide an easy answer without having to go too much into contextual detail, and this explanation was also appealing to audiences for which *barbar* had a negative meaning – which is what the term conjured, be it in al-Andalus or in the East. It also excludes philosophy as the cause of Ibn Rushd's 'disgrace'. A variant of the 'ethnic' accusation is the accusation that Ibn Rushd addressed the caliph as 'brother'. The use of this term suggests that Ibn Rushd was too familiar with the caliph and did not show enough respect for his high status, proving the Andalusis' sense of superiority over the non-Andalusis. But another interpretation is possible, one in which philosophy re-enters the picture. Such an expression was in fact common among philosophically-oriented scholars, including the Brethren of Purity (Ikhwān al-Ṣafā'). Ibn Ṭufayl also uses it at the end of his *Risālat Ḥayy b. Yaqẓān.*[80] In his *Commentarium magnum in Aristotelis. De anima libros*, Ibn Rushd says: 'I have believed adequate to write my opinion on this matter. Even if my opinion were not perfect, it would serve as the beginning for the perfect opinion. For this I ask the *brothers* [the italics are mine: MF] when they see this writing to write their doubts and perhaps in this way truth will be found, if by then I have not yet found it.'[81] From this passage, it is clear that Ibn Rushd used the expression to address his readers, those who he felt were his equals in rational understanding, and he must have used the same expression when addressing those engaged in the study of philosophy who were his contemporaries. The caliph must have been among them.

There is also the 'political' explanation (Numbers 1, 2, 5) which has a number of variants that are not necessarily mutually exclusive. Ibn Rushd would have been too close to a brother of the caliph, a brother whom the caliph could have

79 For how Andalusis viewed the Berbers, see Emilio García Gómez, *Andalucía contra Berbería*, Barcelona, 1976; Göran Larsson, "The Berber as a Symbolic Epitome in the History of al-Andalus", in Bo Isaksson and Marianne Laanatza (eds.), *About the Berbers – History, Language and Culture and Socio-Economic Conditions*, Uppsala 2004, pp. 90–98; Ramzi Rouighi, "The Andalusi Origins of the Berbers," *Journal of Medieval Iberian Studies* 2/1 (2010), pp. 93–108; Maribel Fierro, "The Maghreb and the Maghrebis in the Medieval Muslim Imaginaire," paper presented at the *28th Congress of the Union Européenne des Arabisants et Islamisants (UEAI 28)*, Palermo 12–16 September 2016. See also Ibn Sharīfa, *Ibn Rushd al-ḥafīd*, p. 60, quotation from Ibn Rushd in his *Talkhīṣ al-khiṭāba:* "We hate the Berbers and they hate us," using the root b.gh.ḍ, which, according to him, refers to *jins* and not to individuals.

80 "And I beg of God Mercy and Forgiveness, and that he would please to lead us to the Well of the pure Knowledge of himself, for he is gracious and liberal of his Favours. Peace be to thee, my Brother, whom 'tis my Duty to assist, and the Mercy and Blessing of God be upon thee": Abu Bakr Ibn Tufayl, *The History of Hayy Ibn Yaqzan*, transl. Simon Ockley, revised by A.S. Fulton, 1929 (repr., 1986), p. 179.

81 Puig, "EI proyecto vital de Averroes," p. 45.

seen as a possible rival.[82] Ibn Rushd was resented and envied by other scholars for the high position he had achieved in the Almohad political system. Ibn Rushd was singled out by the caliph, who gave him the place normally reserved for the descendant of one of Ibn Tūmar's closest companions. This would have displeased the Almohad shaykhs, who already were ill-disposed against the *ṭalaba.* This was due to the fact that the *ṭalaba* had joined the movement at a later time and their loyalty tended to be directed towards those who recruited them, the Mu'minid caliphs, and not as much to the original doctrines of the Almohads.[83] Modern scholars have also added other variants to these possibilities. Christian threat – in spite of the victory of Alarcos – would have made the caliph look for internal cohesion and thus he allowed the philosopher, whom he had defended until then, to be persecuted. Ibn Rushd was too critical of Almohad policies and that which he wrote in his *Commentary to Plato's Republic* was used against him. However, we still lack a close analysis in such *Commentary* of the references to the Andalusi case and to the situation in Ibn Rushd's own times carried out from a deep understanding of Almohad history and politics.[84] In any case, Ibn Rushd's critical views on Almohad policies are not surprising in themselves. In fact, there was no lack of internal criticism among the Almohads[85] nor lack of awareness of the need to stop corrupt practices. In 586/1190, the caliph Abū Yūsuf Yaʿqūb had arrived in al-Andalus. While part of his army besieged Silves, the caliph attacked the king of Portugal in the area north of Santarem. Lack of provisions and illness caused him to return to Seville, where he punished corrupt Almohad officials, personally administered justice and forbade music. In that same year, ʿAlī al-Jazīrī, a member of the Almohad religious and intellectual elite (*ṭalaba*), rebelled in the Maghreb as a reviver of the Almohad original doctrine. He gained a wide following during this time. In the fight against him, Abū Yūsuf Yaʿqūb ordered the judge of Málaga to be flogged because of corruption. Thus, when Ibn Rushd says in his *Commentary to Plato's Republic* that 'The mighty commit excesses by seizing property from them, until this leads them at times to tyranny, just as happens in our own time and our own state'[86], it could very well have been a

82 Later on, in 584/1188–89, the caliph ordered two family members to be executed because of disaffection: his brother Abū Ḥafṣ ʿUmar al-Rashīd, governor of Murcia, and his uncle Abū l-Rabīʿ Sulaymān.

83 An exception, that of ʿAlī al-Jazīrī, below. Some *ṭalaba* may have been recruited among the descendants of the Almohad shaykhs.

84 In my lecture at the *Séminaire* directed by Pierre Bouretz at the EHESS, Paris (2012), I proposed such analysis on which I am preparing a study. See also Francisco Pérez Ruiz, "Averroes y la República de Platón," *Pensamiento 50* (1994), pp. 25–46.

85 Manuela Marín, "Dulces, vino y oposición política: un ejemplo biográfico de época almohade," *Estudios Onomástico-Biográficos de al-Andalus.* VIII, *Biografías y género biográfico en el Occidente islámico*, Madrid, 1997, pp. 93–126.

86 See Note 56 above.

reflection of contemporary events, as there is no consensus on when the *Commentary* was written, with some scholars believing it was written in the final part of Ibn Rushd's life.

3. Returning to Ibn Rushd's Relation to the Almohads

For Urvoy, there is no doubt that Ibn Rushd was decidedly in favour of 'Almohadism', as proven by the fact that he follows the Mahdī Ibn Tūmart's doctrines in most of the *Kashf 'an manāhij al-adilla* and that he mentions him in his commentary on the poem of medicine by Ibn Sīnā (Avicenna). In the *Faṣl al-maqāl*, Ibn Rushd praised Almohadism for having liberated the spirits of mental depravities and having opened the path for the people of rational speculation. Contrary to what was claimed by Vincent Cornell, Almohad thought was truly an intellectual doctrine for Ibn Rushd, and was not limited to practice.[87] In a previous study, Urvoy had paid special attention to other works, mainly the *Kashf*, to conclude that Ibn Tūmart and Ibn Rushd followed similar methods and had similar purposes. For Urvoy, although Ibn Rushd cannot be considered a disciple of Ibn Tūmart in the proper sense, he was an Andalusi defender of the essential dogmas of the Almohad doctrine. Urvoy states that there was no relationship between Ibn Tūmart and al-Ghazālī, not even at the level of doctrinal influences, although from a very early point in time – as early as in the time of ʿAbd al-Mu'min – an attempt was made to connect both. This was an attempt that Ibn Rushd tried to counteract so that it would not become a fixed trait of Almohadism. Urvoy believes that the Almohad doctrine underwent changes and evolution and that we should be careful of accepting what later sources say about the various aspects of Almohadism. Thus, for Ibn ʿAsākir, Ibn Tūmart was an Ashʿari; for Ibn Taymiyya, he was an anti-Ashʿari, closer to *falsafa* and Ismaʿilism, and al-Subkī described him as syncretistic.

On his part, F. Griffel points out that Ibn Rushd was a high-ranking figure who had great influence on the formation of Almohad politics and ideology. What Renan interpreted as the persecution of Ibn Rushd was actually a mere falling into disgrace, which was to some extent due to anti-philosophical tensions within the circle of religious scholars in al-Andalus. Al-Ghazālī did inspire the movement of the Almohads, but his attitude towards philosophy was far from being hostile. Al-Ghazālī should more accurately be called a champion of the philo-

87 Dominique Urvoy, "Les professions de foi d'Ibn Tūmart. Problèmes textuels et doctrinaux," in P. Cressier et al. (eds.), *Los almohades: problemas y perspectivas*, vol. II, pp. 739–52, quoting Vincent J. Cornell, "Understanding is the Mother of Ability: Responsibility and Action in the Doctrine of Ibn Tūmart," *Studia Islamica* 66 (1987), pp. 71–103.

sophical method. Although he rejected a number of philosophical propositions, he never rejected philosophy as a whole. His own teachings are deeply influenced by the ontology of Ibn Sīnā. Ibn Tūmart – according to Griffel – was influenced by a pupil of al-Ghazālī, al-Kiyā' al-Harrāsī, who succeeded al-Ghazālī at the Niẓāmiyya school in Baghdad. The writings of Ibn Tūmart would reveal a profound influence from the philosophy of Ibn Sīnā in particular, and thus it should not come as a surprise that the Almohad movement was not hostile to philosophy, but instead just the opposite.[88] Griffel concludes that Ibn Rushd belonged to the new generation of religious scholars who had a vivid interest in the philosophical methods and the teachings of the philosophers. This new brand of religious scholars all emerged from the critical examination of philosophy in Ashʿari *kalam*, which began with al-Juwaynī at the Niẓāmiyya school in Nishapur and followed al-Ghazālī to Baghdad. Ibn Rushd was – via Abū Jaʿfar al-Turjālī and Abū Bakr b. al-ʿArabī – a pupil of al-Ghazālī in the third generation. This would explain why he found himself at ease with the Almohads, as Ibn Tūmart would have come from the same background.

Geoffroy agrees with Urvoy in the view that Ibn Rushd closely follows Ibn Tūmart's theological doctrines, while he shows how Ibn Rushd was trying to tone down Ibn Tūmart's absolute denial of divine anthropomorphism and was obliged to recant under the pressure of the more traditional followers of Ibn Tūmart.[89] For Puig, the fact that Ibn Rushd – according to him – 'was not an official exponent of the Almohad doctrine does not exclude the possibility of his intellectual involvement with it in his writings,' allows him to conclude that there is radical discrepancy between the Almohad doctrine and Ibn Rushd's philosophy given that, for Puig, Ibn Tūmart was an Ashʿari.[90] Asking if Ibn Rushd pursued a coherent, continuous policy of influencing the Almohad ideology, he concludes that this was perhaps the case with the *Kashf* and the *Faṣl*, where Ibn Rushd wrote that the Almohad doctrine was 'a middle way of knowing God the Glorious, which is placed above the low level of the followers of authority but is below the turbulence of the theologians'. However, in regards to the *Tahāfut* and his major writings, such as the *Long Commentary on the Metaphysics*, 'we find no traces of any further attempt to influence the Almohad doctrine.' After all, says Puig, it was in these texts that Ibn Rushd refuted fundamental Ashʿari doctrines, for example, on the temporal creation of the universe. Vindicating Aristotle meant refuting al-Ghazālī and the Ashʿari school, these being – according to Puig- pillars of the

88 Frank Griffel, "The Relationship between Averroes and al-Ghazālī as it Presents Itself in Averroes' Early Writings, especially in his Commentary on al-Ghazālī's *al-Mustaṣfā*," in John Inglis (ed.), *Medieval Philosophy and the Classical Tradition in Islam, Judaism and Christianity*, Richmond: Curzon Press, 2002, pp. 51–63, p. 51–2.

89 See Note 76 above.

90 Puig Montada, "Ibn Rušd and the Almohad Context," p. 202.

Almohad ideology. Puig does not consider the extent to which Ibn Rushd's works and activities represent explorations of possible ways of evolving from within Almohadism. Puig maintains that it is not only Ashʿarism that separated Ibn Rushd and the Almohads, but also religion. The philosopher is obligated to choose the best religion of his period, even when these religions are equally true for him, but at the same time he must believe that the best religion will be abrogated by the introduction of a still better doctrine (i.e. philosophy). In his long *Commentary on the Metaphysics*, referring to the gratitude owed to the philosophers and especially to Aristotle, Ibn Rushd stated: 'We devote ourselves to the study of his doctrines and we comment on them and explain them to all people. The religion (*sharī'a*) exclusive of the learned men (*ḥukamā'*) is the enquiry about all beings because the noblest form to adore the Creator is knowledge of His creatures that leads to the true knowledge of His essence.'[91] At the same time, Puig writes, the philosopher should not scorn the religion in which he has been brought up, as he is obligated to adopt it. On the contrary, he should explain the universal character of religion, which brings us back to philosophy.

For Alfred Ivry, Ibn Rushd's view of political philosophy developed from a theoretical perspective that only tangentially addressed the practical needs and concerns of his society, as the philosopher's obligation is to be true to the life of the mind and the pursuit of the ideal. For Ivry, Ibn Rushd's philosophical activity was a private affair. Ivry is convinced that as a philosopher, Ibn Rushd would have preferred not to be a public figure at all and that he wrote his commentaries mostly for himself, his students and the few philosophical colleagues he may have had, and that just as he had inherited a rich tradition of theoretical philosophical inquiry, so too was he passing it on to those who came after him.[92] The philosopher cannot enlighten the masses for whom the revealed truth – which, properly interpreted, corresponds to the teachings of philosophy –[93] is the one best adapted to their understanding and needs; the philosopher's only task in regards to the masses is to save them from being confused by the theologians and their dialectical methods, while also avoiding exposing the masses to the logical ar-

91 Puig Montada, "Ibn Rušd and the Almohad Context," p. 203, quoting *Tafsīr mā ba'd aṭ-ṭabī'at (Grand Commentaire de la Metaphysique)*, ed. M. Bouyges, Bibliotheca Arabica Scholasticorum vol. 2, Beirut, 1938, p. 10.

92 Alfred L. Ivry, "Averroes' Understanding of the Philosopher's Role in Society," in Anna Akasoy and Wim Raven (eds.), *Islamic Thought in the Middle Ages: Studies in Text, Transmission and Translation, in Honour of Hans Daiber*, Leiden, Boston, 2008, pp. 113–122.

93 Richard Taylor, "Truth Does Not Contradict Truth: Averroes and the Unity of Truth," *Topoi, An International Review of Philosophy* 19/1 (2000), pp. 3–16. Ibn Rushd believed that both philosophy and religion represented the truth and there was no disharmony between them, and he worked to show how apparent contradictions could be reconciled. Indeed, philosophy, in his view, supported the law of Islam. It does not contradict religion, but rather confirms it, and both provide a means for grasping the truth of the physical and the metaphysical world.

guments and allegorical interpretations which philosophers adopt. At the same time, Ibn Rushd did think the masses should be taught true beliefs and moral practices, but that this should be done resorting to those means – i. e. rhetorical – that are fit for their comprehension. Philosophers should avoid public debate with non-philosophers because such debate could only end with having to discuss allegorical interpretation and by exposing the elitist nature of philosophers.

W. Montgomery Watt, in an article published in 1964,[94] was the rare case among modern scholars in directly addressing the connection of philosophy with the Almohad society in al-Andalus; for Watt, the philosophical doctrines of Ibn Ṭufayl and Ibn Rushd reflected aspects of the social structure of al-Andalus. Watt starts by pointing out three characteristics of Ibn Tūmart, the founder of the Almohad movement: a) his opposition to anthropomorphism that linked him to Ashʿarism, Muʿtazilism and the Neo-platonic philosophers; b) his attack against those theologians and jurists who relied on mere opinion (*ẓann*) even if this was probable opinion;[95] c) his rejection of Malikism, although – in his opinion – Ibn Tūmart's claim to be the Mahdī does not seem to have been intended as a practical basis for legal reforms, but rather as an attempt to meet the religious need of the Berbers for a divinely-inspired and supported leader. For Watt, the Almohads lacked the intellectual vitality to produce a new corpus of law or perhaps did not feel the need of any far-reaching changes in the substance of the law, simply being content with the attainment of Berber sovereignty.[96] In regard to the *ṭalaba,* Watt makes an important point: the Almohads believed that the final decisions in legal matters had to be in the hands of men friendly with the government and not in the hands of Maliki scholars, those who represented the religious establishment inherited from the time before the Almohad rise to power.[97] For Watt, there were two rival groups of intellectuals under the Almohads: those who supported the Almohad movement on its intellectual side and then the Malikis. This situation underwent changes between two periods, that of Ibn Ṭufayl and that of Ibn Rushd. Ibn Ṭufayl lived for eighty years, forty under the Almoravid and forty under the Almohads. In his *Ḥayy b. Yaqẓān,* Watt sees someone who stands for pure philosophy (in Ibn Ṭufayl's understanding, it was Neo-Platonic philosophy

94 William Montgomery Watt, "Philosophy and Theology under the Almohads," *Actas del Primer Congreso de Estudios Arabes e Islámicos (Córdoba, 1962),* Madrid, 1964, pp. 101–7; also in *The Islamic Quarterly* VIII (1964), pp. 46–51 ("Philosophy and Social Structure in Almohad Spain").

95 Robert Brunschvig has shown how Ibn Tūmart accepts the inevitability of *ẓann* in the practical application of legal principles, while insisting that the principles themselves must have objective validity: "Sur la doctrine du Mahdī Ibn Tūmart," *Arabica* 2 (1955), pp. 137–49 and "Encore sur la doctrine du Mahdī Ibn Tūmart," *Folia Orientalia* (1970), pp. 33–40.

96 I will discuss my objections to this point below.

97 For Watt, these Maliki scholars were mostly of Arab descent contrary to the scholars who worked for the Almohads, thus pointing to an ethnic dimension in the world of scholarship.

that culminated in mystical ecstasy). This pure philosophy of Ḥayy is essentially identical with the rational theology of Absāl that Watt equates with the official theology of the Almohads. For Watt, Absāl differs from the Almohads in that he seeks solitude, which is significant 'since it would be unusual for a militant religious movement to encourage withdrawal into solitude.' This expresses a deep sense of frustration motivated by the fact that, for Ibn Ṭufayl, in spite of his high position at the Almohad court, the system of ideas he held true was incapable of bringing about any superior ordering of the society in which he lived.[98] Ibn Ṭufayl seems to have given up on actual society as hopeless. The people of Absāl's island are unable to rise above anthropomorphism and unable to learn philosophical religion. This was likely a reflection of the fact that the relation between jurists and 'philosophical theologians' was not clear in al-Andalus during Ibn Ṭufayl's times. Not much later, Ibn Rushd wrote that the conflict between philosophy and revealed religion was only apparent and not real. His famous threefold scheme as presented in the *Faṣl al-maqāl* (people are of three classes according to the methods of acquiring truth which they are capable of employing: rhetorical, dialectical and demonstrative) enables Ibn Rushd to link philosophical religion with popular religion.[99] For Ibn Rushd, there was an essential continuity between his own philosophical religion and that of the masses. Unlike Ibn Ṭufayl, Ibn Rushd does not seem to try to distinguish between pure philosophy and philosophical theology, and, according to Watt, this is perhaps an indication that it was the same persons who practised both disciplines in Ibn Rushd's time.

Contrary to what most scholars have considered until now, the available evidence points to the fact that Ibn Rushd was a member of the *ṭalaba* (more specifically, of the *ṭalabat al-ḥaḍar*) or more precisely, that given such evidence, the task for modern scholars is to prove that he was not a member of the *ṭalaba*. In any case, let's review the evidence.

Ibn Rushd wrote a book explaining how he entered the service of the Almohads (*Maqāla fī kayfiyyat dukhūlihi fī l-amr al-ʿazīz wa-taʿallumihi fīhi wa-mā fuḍḍila min ʿilm al-Mahdī*), a work that is not usually mentioned when discussing Ibn Rushd and the Almohads. Nevertheless, this book – unfortunately lost –

98 Watt points out that in Ibn Bājja (d. 533/1139), there are traces of an attempt to show that the philosopher, in trying to live out his philosophy in an imperfect state, is making some contribution to its well-being; however, nothing of this kind is found in Ibn Ṭufayl. On Ibn Bājja's position, see now Ibn Bāǧǧa (Avempace), *La conduite de l'isolé et deux autres épîtres*, introduction, édition critique du texte arabe, traduction et commentaire par Charles Genequand, Paris: Vrin, 2010, pp. 183–203, 351–81.

99 In his *Faṣl*, Ibn Rushd deals with the Qur'anic verse 16:125 ("Summon to the way of your Lord by wisdom and by good preaching and debate with them in the most effective manner") where he finds the three categories of the demonstrative, the dialectical and the rhetorical people.

proves that Ibn Rushd entered the Almohad 'doctrinal corporation' and served the caliphs: *al-amr al-'azīz* was the standard way to refer to Almohad rule.[100] This 'service' included economic compensation; after the meeting in which Ibn Ṭufayl introduced him to Abū Yaʿqūb Yūsuf, Ibn Rushd received money, a robe of honour and a mounting animal. In other words, Ibn Rushd was being paid by the Almohads. Moreover, Ibn Rushd appears to be regularly taking part in sessions devoted to intellectual matters in which the Almohad rulers (caliphs, governors) are present, sessions that were reserved for the intellectual and religious elites of the dynasty.

Ibn Rushd also wrote a commentary on Ibn Tūmart's profession of faith.[101] His theological treatise *Kashf* shows a basic agreement with Ibn Tūmart's creed. The main divergence that had created a problem between Ibn Rushd and the Almohad purist doctrinarians, regarding the usefulness of anthropomorphic views for the masses,[102] can be explained in the following way: Ibn Rushd wrote the *Kashf* when the initial Almohad revolutionary impulse that had focused on taking power from the previous religious establishment was a thing of the past and the Almohads were in need of winning the masses to their side, rather than alienating them by letting the Malikis give them a type of religion that was better suited to their needs. Ibn Rushd also wrote a work on teaching Islam to the deaf. Puig states that this work is probably not by Ibn Rushd's, but does not explain why he thinks so. After all, this work is mentioned by al-Marrākushī in his list of Ibn Rushd's works, a list that Puig previously praised for its exactitude.[103] There is no reason to doubt that Ibn Rushd wrote the work, as it is a book that reveals his deep pedagogical concerns,[104] views which are also shown in his commentaries on Aristotle commissioned by the second Almohad caliph. Such commentaries take the form of *jawāmi'*, *talākhīṣ* and *shurūḥ*,[105] with the *talākhīṣ* written between 563/1168–570/1175 and the *shurūḥ* in the 1180s. They are of course not directed to the masses, but to those with the intellectual capabilities to pursue rational inquiry; they are also adjusted to meet different needs, as Ivry has

100 See Note 16 above.

101 On these works by Ibn Rushd, see Maribel Fierro (dir.), *Historia de los Autores y Transmisores de al-Andalus (= HATA)*, s.v. Ibn Rušd al-Ḥafīd, IV, 174.1 [consulted 06/01/2017]. Ibn Sharīfa has suggested that the commentary on Ibn Tūmart's creed, considered lost, might be extant in a Moroccan library.

102 See Note 76 above.

103 Puig, "El proyecto vital de Averroes," Note 8 and cf. p. 12.

104 Maribel Fierro, "Notes on Reason, Language and Conversion in the 13th century in the Iberian Peninsula," *Quaderns de la Mediterrània* 9 (Ramon Llull and Islam, the Beginning of a Dialogue), 49–58 (repr. in Nicole Koulayan and Mansour Sayah (eds.), *Synoptikos. Mélanges offerts à Dominique Urvoy*, CNRS/Université de Toulouse Le Mirail, 2011, pp. 169–182).

105 Puig, "El proyecto vital de Averroes," p. 26.

shown.[106] According to the famous passage in al-Marrākushī's *Kitāb al-mu'jib* describing how Ibn Ṭufayl introduced Ibn Rushd to Abū Yaʿqūb Yūsuf[107] the prince had complained about the difficulties of the expressions used by Aristotle and his commentators, as well as the obscurity of meaning. Abū Yaʿqūb Yūsuf had hoped that someone would clarify and synthesize (*talkhīṣ*) the Greek philosopher's books, making them accessible and understandable to the people (*al-nās*). This passage implies that Abū Yaʿqūb Yūsuf had already become interested in philosophy, perhaps through Ibn Ṭufayl's mentoring, and also that the 'people' were likely the intellectuals being trained by the Almohads, meaning the *ṭalaba*.

Puig states that 'in spite of his distance from Zahirism, Ibn Rushd was helpful to the Almohads by creating a balance among the various legal schools. However, Ibn Rushd was not permanently engaged in a project of legal reform and we do not find any juridical works such as *fatwās* besides the *Bidāya*. His purpose was only to supply the independent jurist with a handbook enabling him to form his own legal conclusions.'[108] In my view, this is in itself a project of legal reform, in the sense of striving for the formation of a new type of jurist who needed to be educated in a different way. Although this did not lack precedent, it was still revolutionary. Moreover, Ibn Rushd's *Bidāyat al-mujtahid wa-nihāyat al-muqtaṣid* may have actually been something more, that is, the first step towards the production of a legal code.[109] It does not seem to have been a coincidence that exactly the same year in which the work was finished (584/1188), the caliph ordered the burning of *furū'* works. Around the same time, a member of the *ṭalabat al-ḥaḍar*, al-Dhahabī (554/1159–601/1204), an expert on *'ulūm al-awā'il* active in Ibn Rushd's circle, was entrusted with the supervision of the *qāḍīs* and their legal opinions (*shūrā wa-fatwā*).[110] It may also be that the initiative taken against Ibn Rushd by several Cordoban scholars in 590/1194 was motivated by what may have been the beginning of a legislative reform that would have shattered the area where the Malikis still preserved their power: the application of the law. The caliph stood by Ibn Rushd in 590/1194. In 591/1195, when Ibn Rushd heard of the victory of Alarcos – he previously had preached *jihād* in the mosque

106 Ivry, "Averroes on the Philosopher's Role in Society," p. 114.

107 See Note 12 above.

108 Puig, "Almohad Context," p. 206. I have dealt with the absence of *fatāwā* during the Almohad period in Maribel Fierro, "*Fatāwā* Compilations and Legal Codification: The Case of the Islamic West (8th-15th Centuries)", paper read at the conference *New Approaches to World Islamic and Middle East Studies*, Institute of Islamic Studies, McGill University, May 16–18, 2014, forthcoming in *Jerusalem Studies in Arabic and Islam.*

109 Fierro, "The Legal Policies of the Almohad Caliphs and Ibn Rushd's *Bidāyat al-mujtahid*," quoted in Note 27 and "Codifying the Law: The Case of the Medieval Islamic West," in John Hudson and Ana Rodríguez (eds.), *Diverging Paths? The Shapes of Power and Institutions in Medieval Christendom and Islam*, Leiden: Brill, 2014, pp. 98–118.

110 Puig, "Materials," p. 248.

of Cordoba, which is another performance by Ibn Rushd usually omitted in modern scholarship –he performed a prostration of thanksgiving (*sajdat al-shukr*) and taught those who were with him the *ḥadīth* found in Abū Dāwūd's canonical collection, according to which the Prophet had performed the *sajdat al-shukr.* In this teaching, Ibn Rushd was explaining a ritual to his fellow Cordobans, a ritual that until then had been censored by the Andalusi Malikis.[111]

4. Placing Ibn Rushd in the Almohad Context

Robert Brunschvig and Catarina Belo have written on the coherence of the Averroist corpus and the problematic consequences of differentiating between his 'original' works, such as the *Kashf 'an manāhij al-adilla*, the *Faṣl al-maqāl* and *Tahāfut al-Tahāfut* that are addressed to the educated general public, and his commentaries on Aristotle, which were inaccessible to most of his contemporaries. Theological issues are discussed in the commentaries while Aristotelian doctrines such as causality appear in the other works. His legal work *Bidāyat al-mujtahid* also very clearly shows his overall philosophical/rationalistic approach with his insistence that the general principles precede and dominate particular cases, and the same is evident in his work on medicine, the *Kitāb al-kulliyyāt.*[112]

Early Almohad teachings[113] had spoken against the *mujassima*, those who gave a literal reading of the anthropomorphic passages of the Qur'an and therefore were guilty of *tashbīh*, assimilation of the Creator to his creatures. As previously noted, such condemnation had profound political implications as it legitimized the Almohads and their substitution of Almoravid rulers and their intellectual elites. Decades later, Ibn Rushd, in the first version of his *Kashf*, showed his disagreement with such teachings, as in the anthropomorphic passages he saw

111 On the *sajdat al-shukr* and its rejection by the Malikis, see Maribel Fierro, "The Treatises against Innovations (*kutub al-bida'*)," *Der Islam* 69 (1992), 204–46, p. 231, and Roberto Tottoli, "The Thanksgiving Prostration (*sujūd al-shukr)* in Muslim Traditions," *Bulletin of the School of Oriental and African Studies* 61/2 (1998), pp. 309–13. For how the Almohads introduced changes in traditional practices, see Note 68 above.

112 Robert Brunschvig, "Averroès juriste," *Études d'Orientalisme dédiées à la memoire de Lévi-Provençal*, París, 1962, vol. I, pp. 35–68; Catarina Belo, "Some Considerations on Averroes' Views Regarding Women and Their Role in Society," *Journal of Islamic Studies* 20 (2009), pp. 1–20, pp. 13–4.

113 I prefer to speak of 'early Almohad teachings' instead of 'Ibn Tūmart's teachings' as I am deeply skeptical of the possibility of separating between what it is attributed to Ibn Tūmart and what were in fact developments taking place under 'Abd al-Mu'min's reign: see Maribel Fierro, "El Mahdī Ibn Tūmart: más allá de la biografía oficial," in Miguel Angel Manzano and Rachid El Hour (ed.), *Política, sociedad e dentidades en el Occidente islámico (siglos XI–XIV)*, Salamanca, 2016, pp. 73–98.

symbols intended for the people of rhetoric who were incapable of reaching rational knowledge and who thus needed them.[114] Doing otherwise was to risk having them believe in nothing. In other words, for Ibn Rushd there was no explicit statement in the Qur'an or the *sunna* regarding whether or not God had a body. By pointing to this fact, Ibn Rushd was following the pedagogical programme supported by Ibn Ṭufayl in his *Ḥayy b. Yaqẓān*, a book on the limits of the Almohad revolution. In this book, Ibn Ṭufayl had shown that certain types of knowledge were above the degree of understanding of most people and therefore should be restricted to an elite, leaving the majority of the population to their old beliefs – although education should be provided to those capable of more complex ways of thinking.

By trying to re-direct the early Almohad teachings from their revolutionary context to the needs of present-day society, Ibn Rushd was met with opposition. As his doctrine could be understood as undermining the Almohad basis for legitimacy (showing himself to be in favour of 'anthropomorphist leniency' with the masses could be taken as an attack on the impeccability of the founder of Almohadism, the Mahdī Ibn Tūmart), Ibn Rushd was made to retract his views. In this retraction, Ibn Rushd said that in his anti-anthropomorphist stance, Ibn Tūmart had acted according to his *khāṣṣa* that allowed him to put an end to the diverging views of the Muslims.[115] Ibn Rushd did not use the term *'iṣma* (impeccability, infallibility) that is normally used to refer to Ibn Tūmart (as in *al-imām al-ma'ṣūm al-mahdī al-ma'lūm* found on coins and in official letters), but instead adopted a term found in Ibn Tūmart's *Kitāb*.[116] In other words, Ibn Rushd justified his departure from early Almohad doctrine by saying that Ibn Tūmart had been forced to insist on anti-anthropomorphism because of the disputes regarding this issue in his time and in order to put an end to the divergences with knowledge that completed and illuminated the text of Revelation. Ibn Tūmart had eliminated the ambiguity found in the sources of Revelation –an ambiguity that, according to Ibn Rushd and his teacher Ibn Ṭufayl, it would be better to maintain in order to better rule the new society that had emerged thanks to the intransigent belief of Ibn Tūmart's followers.[117]

Taking place more than fifty years after the Mahdī's death, Ibn Rushd's 'disgrace' should be understood in relation to the problem of the place to be

114 See Note 76 above.

115 Geoffroy, "À propos de l'almohadisme d'Averroès," p. 874.

116 Chapter on *al-imāma wa-'alāmāt al-Mahdī: Le livre de Mohammed Ibn Toumert, Mahdi des Almohades*, ed. D. Luciani, Algiers, 1903 p. 251, ls. 7–18.

117 Maribel Fierro, "The religious policy of the Almohads," *The Oxford Handbook of Islamic Theology*, ed. Sabine Schmidtke, online publication date March 2014 http://www.oxfordhandbooks.com/browse?jumpTo=f&page=8&pageSize=50&sort=authorsort&t1=ORR%3AAHU03020.

accorded to Ibn Tūmart in Almohad thought and society. Ibn Rushd's 'disgrace' would have been the result of the opposition of those who rejected that philosophy and its practitioners was accorded a central place in the new society with the support of the political power.[118] This was so not so much out of opposition to philosophy *per se*, but because the legitimacy of those religious and political elites that had been created by the victory of the Almohad movement (most especially the Almohad shaykhs and in a lesser degree the Almohad *ṭalaba,* as they had come into existence at a later stage) depended on Ibn Tūmart's *'iṣma*. Their status was in danger due to the educational and reformist programme developed by Ibn Rushd (himself a member of the *ṭalaba),* a programme which eroded Messianism while elevating rational inquiry.

Ibn Rushd was -most probably from 548/1153 - a member of the Almohad *ṭalaba*. The Almohad *ṭalaba* were the creation of the Mu'minids, made to support the dynasty and check the power of the Almohad shaykhs. On the one hand, the *ṭalaba* had to follow the doctrines attributed to Ibn Tūmart (his creed in particular), but on the other hand, they also had to give the caliphs a new doctrinal basis to enhance their right to rule. Philosophy was a substitute to Mahdism: if Ibn Tūmart was able to know the truth because of his charisma, the Mu'minid caliphs would also able to reach the truth due to the demonstrative method. Apart from being trained in philosophy - as Abū Yaʿqūb Yūsuf and Abū Yūsuf Yaʿqūb were - they had philosophers in their entourage and also promoted the study of philosophy themselves. The relationship between the caliph and the philosophers was one of need. This was a relationship that had already been articulated by Ibn Rushd's friend and contemporary Ibn Ṭāhir. Muḥammad b. ʿAbd al-Raḥmān b. Aḥmad b. ʿAbd al-Raḥmān b. Ṭāhir al-Qaysī (d. 574/1178) belonged to an important family in Murcia who had ruled the town during the Taifa period. He himself ruled for some months in 540/1145, at the time when several Andalusi towns were trying to rid themselves of Almoravid rule. In 542/1147, Murcia came under the control of Ibn Mardanīsh (d. 567/1172), a man of the sword who carved a reign for himself during the period of the disintegration of the Almoravid Empire. Ibn Ṭāhir continued to live in the town under Ibn Mardanīsh's rule. When the Almohads conquered Murcia in 567/1172, after Ibn Mardanīsh's death, Ibn Ṭāhir eventually joined them and was named its governor. He died in Marrakech in 574/1178.[119] As Ibn Ṭāhir felt the need to explain why he had joined the Almohads, he wrote a short tract in which he discussed the proofs that certified

118 Alain de Libera, introduction to *Averroes, Discours décisif*, transl. by Marc Geoffroy, Paris, 1996, p. 73.

119 Josep Puig Montada, "Abū ʿAbd al-Raḥmān Ibn Ṭāhir. Addenda a 'Averroes, vida y persecución de un filósofo'," *Revista Española de Filosofía Medieval* 7 (2000), pp. 181–6; A. J. Martín Castellanos-M. Forcada, "Ibn Ṭāhir al-Qaysī, Abū ʿAbd al-Raḥmān (nieto)," *Biblioteca de al-Andalus*, vol. 5, pp. 461–3, nº 1235.

that Ibn Tūmart, the founder of the Almohad movement, had been the Mahdī, the rightly guided one or Messiah.[120] In his work, Ibn Ṭāhir compares the previous political and religious situation in al-Andalus with the 'perfect city' brought by the Almohads. He applies the philosophical category of *al-madīna al-fāḍila* developed by al-Fārābī (d. 339/950) to the Almohad polity.[121] Ibn Ṭāhir explains that before he had felt himself to be a 'stranger' (*gharīb*) among his contemporaries, but when he was informed of what the Prince of the Believers ʿAbd al-Mu'min – the first Almohad Caliph – stood for, he then realized that the end had come for the cities of ignorance. This was thanks to the Mahdī and his successors, the Mu'minid caliphs, who illuminated the lawful path in this life and also the path to the afterlife.[122] In Almohadism, Ibn Rushd also saw a chance for the Muslims of al-Andalus to obtain a better government and follow a truer version of their religion, and philosophy was the path to both. Philosophical reasoning would always remain the domain of an intellectual elite, because any attempt to popularize difficult concepts and ideas entailed known dangers, as Ibn Ṭufayl had warned. However, being aware of the limits of philosophy and the lines its practitioners could not cross did not exclude expanding true knowledge through education or the training of those in positions of power. Disaffection of the masses had to be avoided, and Ibn Rushd seems to have succeeded in this. His 'disgrace' was not caused by those in the lower strata of society but came from the reduced circles of the educated and those close to the caliph.

Sarrió Cucarella has highlighted a statement by Ibn Rushd that he found remarkable 'given the pervasive intellectual elitism that dominated the culture and which he himself shared', a statement in which 'Averroes says that whoever comes to acknowledge God's existence by means of these arguments proposed by Scripture 'becomes one of the learned scholars''.[123] Ibn Rushd's main concern was that everybody should feel that they were part of the same community and that difference of understanding, while unavoidable, should not lead to alienation. It was also important to elevate such understanding in those who could not attain the highest level represented by philosophy. Education was necessary at all levels. Ibn Rushd seems to have succeeded remarkably well at the highest and the lowest levels of society. His problems came from those who had more to lose in

120 The short tract is referred to as *Maqāla 'ilmiyya yuqarrir fīhā ṣiḥḥat amr al-mahdī al-qā'im bi-amr Allāh* or *al-Kāfiya fī barāhīn al-imām al-mahdī*. It has been preserved in Ibn al-Qaṭṭān (*ca.* 580/1184-d. after 650/1252), *Naẓm al-jumān fī akhbār al-zamān*, ed. Maḥmūd ʿAlī Makkī, 2nd ed., Beirut: Dār al-Gharb al-Islāmī, 1990, pp. 101–122.

121 Richard Walzer, *Al-Farabi on the Perfect State*, Oxford: Clarendon Press, 1985.

122 On the *ghurabā'* (sing. *gharīb*), see Maribel Fierro, "Spiritual Alienation and Political Activism: The *Ghurabā'* in al-Andalus during the Sixth/Twelfth Century," *Arabica* XLVII (2000), pp. 230–260.

123 Sarrió, "The Philosopher as the Heir of the Prophets," p. 61.

the expansion of knowledge and in the ruler's support to the claim that philosophers were those best entitled to the legacy of the Prophet. The traditional scholars (the *fuqahā'*) saw the danger of the legislative reform proposed by Ibn Rushd, and the Almohad shaykhs saw the danger of pushing Ibn Tūmart and his creed to the side. Several of the *ṭalaba* were also in favour of retaining the early teachings: the *ṭālib* ʿAlī al-Jazīrī had rebelled in 586/1190, claiming the revival of Almohadism, perhaps an indication of resentment that philosophy was not accessible to all of them. It was within these circles where Ibn Rushd's 'disgrace' was planned, among those who were close to the philosopher and could therefore collect evidence in order to damage his reputation once they felt he had gone too far in what he represented. And what he represented was the 'new man' made possible by the Almohad revolution: a member of the new religious and intellectual elite (the *ṭalaba*), a philosopher, legislator, educator and political reformer. As professor Endress so aptly describes, Ibn Rushd's works in their totality illustrate 'thought in action during his whole life in permanent exchange with a society in transformation.'[124]

Chronology

520/1126	Birth of Ibn Rushd al-Ḥafīd (Averroes); Death of his grandfather, Ibn Rushd al-Jadd, the jurist, commentator and reformer of Malikism, judge of Cordoba under the Almoravids
524/1130	Death of Ibn Tūmart, the founder of the Almohad movement
535/1140	Andalusi revolts against the Almoravids; The judges, as representatives of the urban elites, come to power in towns such as Córdoba, Jaén, Málaga, Murcia and Valencia; Local soldiers trained in the frontier areas, such as Sayf al-Dawla Ibn Hūd, make their bid for power; Rebellion of the Bāṭinī thinker Ibn Qasī in the Algarve (southern Portugal)
536–37/1141–42	Death of the Sufi/Bāṭinī Ibn Barrajān and of the Sufi Ibn al-ʿArīf
540/1146	Death of Sayf al-Dawla Ibn Hūd
541/1147	Conquest of Marrakech by ʿAbd al-Mu'min, one of the Companions of the Mahdī Ibn Tūmart and his successor; Massacre of the Almoravids; An Almohad army successively takes Jerez, Niebla, Silves, Beja, Badajoz, Mertola and Seville; Cordoba conquered two years later
542/1147	King of Portugal conquers Lisbon and Santarem; Almería falls into Christian hands (until 552/1157)

124 Endress, "Le projet d'Averroès," p. 30: "Il vaut toutefois la peine de considérer l'oeuvre intégrale du philosophe, comme le témoignage d'une pensée en action durant toute sa vie et en échange perpétuel avec une société en transformation."

543/1148	Ebro Valley lost to the Christians
540–58/1146–63	Ibn Ṭāhir from Murcia dedicates a tract defending Ibn Tūmart's Mahdism, imamate and his legitimacy to rule to the Almohad caliph ʿAbd al-Mu'min using philosophical arguments
546/1151	Assassination of the rebel Ibn Qasī in the Algarve
548/1153	Ibn Rushd in Marrakech: possible connection with the recruitment of young men as *ṭalaba* to serve the Mu'minid dynasty; Caliph ʿAbd al-Mu'min defeats the Arabs at Sétif
550–58/1155–63	Ibn Rushd presented by Ibn Tufayl to the Mu'minid prince Abū Yaʿqūb Yūsuf (then governor in Seville, later second Mu'minid caliph); On the latter's suggestion, Ibn Rushd starts writing commentaries on Aristotle in order to spread the demonstrative method in al-Andalus by paraphrasing and commenting the Aristotelian *corpus*
552/1157	Ibn Rushd writes *al-Ḍarūrī fī l-fiqh* (based on al-Ghazālī); The pledge of obedience of the original Almohad tribes is renewed and the caliph ʿAbd al-Mu'min pays his traditional visit to Tinmal where Ibn Tūmart was buried
553/1158	Campaign against Ifrīqiya is finally launched; Tunis is conquered in 554/1159, as are Mahdiyya, Sfax and Tripoli
ca. 555/1160	Ibn Tufayl writes *Ḥayy b. Yaqẓān* in which he describes the limits of the Almohad revolution
556/1161	Transfer of the Arab tribes from Ifrīqiya and the central Maghreb to the extreme Maghreb (Morocco), marking the beginning of Arabization in the countryside
556–65/1162–69	Ibn Rushd writes the *Kulliyyāt* (on medicine)
558/1163	Death of ʿAbd al-Mu'min
558/1163–580/1184	Reign of Abū Yaʿqūb Yūsuf
560–62/1165–66	The Almohads fight and defeat the rebel Mazizdag al-Ghumārī and his son in northern Morocco
560/1165	Abū Yaʿqūb Yūsuf sends letter to the Almohad governors forbidding them to impose death sentences without his approval; Maimonides arrives in Egypt
561/1166	Death of the Eastern Sufi ʿAbd al-Qādir al-Jilānī
563/1168	Ibn Rushd starts writing his legal work *Bidāyat al-mujtahid* and finishes his *talkhīṣ* or Middle Commentary on the Topics (fourth book of the *Organon*)
564–65/1169–71	Ibn Rushd is judge in Seville
563/1168–570/1175	Ibn Rushd writes the *talākhīṣ* or 'Middle Commentaries' on Aristotle, directed to the *non-cognoscenti*
565/1170	Plague in Marrakech
567/1171	End of the Fatimid caliphate by Saladin; Abū Yaʿqūb Yūsuf arrives in al-Andalus; Between this year and 571/1176, construction on the mosque of Seville is begun
567/1172	Ibn Rushd accompanies the caliph Abū Yaʿqūb Yūsuf during his failed campaign against the fortress of Huete; Study sessions with the *ṭalabat al-ḥaḍar* (the *ṭalaba* who accompanied the caliph) are con-

	ducted during the campaign; Death of Ibn Mardanīsh, the Andalusi ruler who had resisted the Almohads in Murcia; After this date, Ibn Ṭāhir writes his *Maqāla 'ilmiyya yuqarrir fīhā ṣiḥḥat amr al-mahdī al-qā'im bi-amr Allāh* or *al-Kāfiya fī barāhīn al-imām al-mahdī*
569/1173	Castilians from Avila lay waste to the area of Ecija and Cordoba
571/1176	Death of Abū Ḥafṣ ʿUmar Intī (Hintātī), the last of Ibn Tūmart's companions and the most influential
572/1176	Ibn Rushd writes his *Talkhīṣ Kitāb al-akhlāq li-Aristū* and perhaps his *Commentary on Plato's Republic* (for some modern scholars, this writing was written in the final part of Ibn Rushd's life)
574/1178	Death of Ibn Ṭāhir
575–76/1180–81	Abū Yaʿqūb Yūsuf leads a successful expedition against Gafsa; The defeated Arabs are sent to al-Andalus to wage jihad against the Christians; Ibn Rushd starts writing the Long Commentaries (*shurūḥ*)
575/1179–576/1180	Ibn Rushd writes *Tahāfut, Faṣl al-maqāl, Kashf*; He also writes the Long Commentary on the *Analytica Posteriora*
578/1182	Alfonso VIII of Castile camps in front of Cordoba and his raids reach Algeciras near the sea; Ibn Rushd visits Marrakech (illness of the caliph) and Tịnmal
578/1183	First *riḥla* of Ibn Jubayr
579/1183	Caliph names his son the *sayyid* Abū Yaḥyā as governor of Cordoba; Also names Ibn Rushd judge of the town
580/1184	Death of Abū Yaʿqūb Yūsuf
580/1184–595/1198	Reign of Abū Yūsuf Yaʿqūb (al-Manṣūr); Ibn Rushd writes most of his Long Commentaries
580/1184–587/1191	Campaigns of al-Manṣūr in Ifriqiya and al-Andalus
581/1185	Death of Ibn Ṭufayl
583/1187	Saladin's victory at Ḥattīn, followed by Muslim conquest of Acre and Jerusalem; Dinar issued by Saladin in Damascus to celebrate the victory over the Franks
584/1188–89	Ibn Rushd finishes the *Bidāyat al-mujtahid*, adding the chapter on pilgrimage; Burning of *furū'* works, including the *Mudawwana*, takes place under the supervision of Abu Bakr Ibn Zuhr; The caliph's brother Abū Ḥafṣ ʿUmar al-Rashīd, governor of Murcia, and his uncle Abū l-Rabīʿ Sulaymān are executed in Salé for disaffection
585/1189	Third crusade; Death of Abū l-Ḥusayn ʿAbd al-Raḥmān Ibn Rabīʿ al-Ashʿarī; His son Abū ʿĀmir Yaḥyā (563/1168–639/1241 or 640/1242) writes tracts against Ibn Rushd, especially against his *Kashf 'an manāhij al-adilla*
585/1189–587/1191	Second *riḥla* of Ibn Jubayr
586/1190	An ambassador sent by Saladin asks the Almohad caliph's help to halt the crusaders in the East by sea; The caliph arrives in al-Andalus and signs a truce with the king of Castile; While part of his army besieged Silves, the Almohad caliph attacks the King of Portugal in the area north of Santarem; Lack of provisions and illness cause him to return to Seville, where he punishes corrupt Almohad officials, personally

	administers justice and forbids music. Destruction of a statue (*ṣūra*) in Madinat al-Zahra'; Rebellion of ʿAlī al-Jazīrī, a member of the *ṭalaba*, in the Maghreb as a reviver of the Almohad original doctrine; ʿAlī al-Jazīrī gains a wide following in al-Andalus; Al-Manṣūr orders the judge of Málaga to be flogged because of corruption; Muḥyī l-dīn Ibn ʿArabī has a discussion on miracles with a philosopher
587/1191	A brother of the caliph (the *sayyid* Abū Yaḥyā?) is executed; Acre conquered by the Crusaders; Al-Suhrawardī executed in Aleppo on Saladin's orders
589/1193	Death of Saladin
590/1194	Cordoban opponents of Ibn Rushd go to Marrakech to protest against him; Caliph pays no attention, although the opponents seem to think that the caliph wants to execute Ibn Rushd
591/1195	Almohad army defeats Alfonso VIII at Alarcos; In Cordoba, al-Manṣūr has Ibn Rushd sit close to him in the place normally reserved for the son of Abū Ḥafṣ ʿUmar Intī (Hintātī), thus honouring him greatly; When Ibn Rushd hears of the victory of Almohad army, he performs the *sajdat al-shukr*; he had previously preached jihad in the mosque.
593/1197	Caliph named Abū Zayd Ibn Yūjjān al-Hintātī as vizier in Seville; Some time later, the 'disgrace' of Ibn Rushd takes place; Caliph orders the *ṭalaba* of his council and the jurists of his government to go to the congregation of the Muslims and to explain to the people that Ibn Rushd is a heretic; Books of logic and philosophy are burnt under the supervision of Ibn Zuhr
594/1198	Rehabilitation of Ibn Rushd and of *falsafa* once the caliph returns to Marrakech
595/1198–99	Death of Ibn Rushd (December 1198); Death of al-Manṣūr (January 1199)

Bibliography

Primary Sources

'Abd al-Wāḥid al-Marrākushī, *Kitāb al-mu'jib fī talkhīṣ akhbār al-Maghrib*, ed. R. Dozy, 2nd ed., Leiden, 1881.

Averroès Commentary on Plato's Republic, edited with and introduction, translation and notes by E.I.J. Rosenthal, Cambridge: The University Press, 1969.

al-Burzulī, *Fatāwā al-Burzulī: jāmi' masā'il al-aḥkām li-mā nazala min al-qaḍāyā bil-l-muftiyyīn wa-l-ḥukkām*, ed. Muḥammad al-Ḥabīb al-Hīla, Beirut: Dār al-Gharb al-Islāmī, 2002.

Ibn al-Abbār, *al-Takmila li-kitāb al-Ṣila*, ed. F. Codera, 2 vols., Madrid, 1886.

Ibn ʿAbd al-Malik al-Marrākushī, *al-Dhayl wa-l-takmila*, ed. Iḥsān ʿAbbās, Beirut, 1973.

Ibn Abī ʿUṣaybiʿa, *ʿUyūn al-anbāʾ fī ṭabaqāt al-aṭibbāʾ*, ed. and trans. by H. Jahier and A. Noureddin, *Médecins de l'Occident musulman*, Alger: Librairie Ferraris, 1377/1958.
Ibn ʿAskar, Abū ʿAbd Allāh and Abū Bakr b. Khamīs, *Aʿlām Mālaqa*, Beirut, 1999.
Ibn Bāǧǧa (Avempace), *La conduite de l'isolé et deux autres épîtres*, introduction, édition critique du texte arabe, traduction et commentaire par Charles Genequand, Paris: Vrin, 2010.
Ibn ʿIdhārī (d. 695/1295), *al-Bayān al-mughrib*, part on the Almohads, ed. M. I. al-Kattānī *et al.*, Beirut-Casablanca, 1985.
Ibn al-Qaṭṭān, *Naẓm al-jumān fī akhbār al-zamān*, ed. Maḥmūd ʿAlī Makkī, 2nd ed., Beirut: Dār al-Gharb al-Islāmī, 1990.
Ibn Rushd, *Tafsīr mā baʿd aṭ-ṭabīʿat (Grand Commentaire de la Metaphysique)*, ed. M. Bouyges, Bibliotheca Arabica Scholasticorum, 3 vols, Beirut, 1938–48.
Ibn Tufayl, Abu Bakr, *The History of Hayy Ibn Yaqzan*, transl. Simon Ockley, revised by A.S. Fulton, 1929 (repr., 1986).
Ibn Tūmart, *al-Imāma wa-ʿalāmāt al-Mahdī: Le livre de Mohammed Ibn Toumert, Mahdi des Almohades*, ed. D. Luciani, Algiers, 1903.

Secondary Sources

ʿĀbid al-Jābirī, Muḥammad, *Ibn Rushd. Sīra wa-fikr*, Beirut, second ed., 2001.
Adang, Camilla, "Restoring the Prophet's authority, rejecting *taqlīd:* Ibn Ḥazm's *Epistle to the one who shouts from afar*," in D. Ephrat and M. Hatina (ed.), *Religious knowledge, authority and charisma. Islamic and Jewish perspectives*, Salt Lake City: The University of Utah Press, 2014, pp. 50–63.
Addas, Claude, *Ibn ʿArabī ou La quête du Soufre Rouge*, París: Editions Gallimard, 1989.
Aouad, Maroun and Frédérique Woerther, "Le commentaire par Averroès du chapitre 9 du livre X de *l'Éthique à Nicomaque:* pédagogie de la contrainte, habitudes et lois," *Mélanges de l'Université Saint-Joseph* LXII (2009), pp. 353–80.
Aʿrāb, Saʿd, "Mawqif al- muwaḥḥidīn min kutub al-furūʿ wa-ḥaml al-nās ʿalā l-madhhab al-ḥazmī," *Daʿwat al-ḥaqq* 249 (1985), pp. 26–30.
Belo, Catarina, "Some Considerations on Averroes' Views Regarding Women and Their Role in Society," *Journal of Islamic Studies* 20 (2009), pp. 1–20.
Ben Abella, Brahim, "Ibn Zarqūn, Abū ʿAbd Allāh," *Biblioteca de al-Andalus*, vol. 6: *De Ibn al-Ŷabbāb a Nubḏat al-ʿaṣr*, ed. Jorge Lirola Delgado, Almería: Fundación Ibn Tufayl, 2009, nº 1436, pp. 275–7.
Benhima, Yassir, "Du *tamyīz* à l'*iʿtirāf:* usages et légitimation du massacre au début de l'époque almohade," *Annales Islamologiques* 43 (2009), pp. 137–153.
Boloix Gallardo, Bárbara, "Ibn Rabīʿ al-Ašʿarī, Abū l-Ḥusayn/l-Ḥasan," *Biblioteca de al-Andalus*, vol. 4: *De Ibn al-Labbāna a Ibn al-Ruyūlī*, ed. Jorge Lirola Delgado, Almería: Fundación Ibn Tufayl, 2006, nº 974, pp. 435–6.
–, "Ibn Rabīʿ al-ʿAšʿarī, Abū ʿĀmir," *Biblioteca de al-Andalus*, vol. 4: *De Ibn al-Labbāna a Ibn al-Ruyūlī*, ed. Jorge Lirola Delgado, Almería: Fundación Ibn Tufayl, 2006, nº 973, pp. 431–5.

Borrego Soto, Miguel Ángel, *Gala del mundo y adorno de los almimbares. El esplendor literario del Jerez andalusí*, Jerez, 2011.

–, "al-Ḏuŷŷī, Abū Mūsà," *Biblioteca de al-Andalus*, vol. 1: *De al-'Abbādīya a Ibn Abyaḍ*, ed. Jorge Lirola Delgado and José Miguel Puerta Vílchez, Almería: Fundación Ibn Tufayl, 2012, nº 103, pp. 336–7.

Brunschvig, Robert, "Sur la doctrine du Mahdī Ibn Tūmart," *Arabica* 2 (1955), pp. 137–49.

–, "Averroès juriste," *Études d'Orientalisme dédiées à la memoire de Lévi-Provençal*, París, 1962, vol. I, pp. 35–68.

–, "Encore sur la doctrine du Mahdī Ibn Tūmart", *Folia Orientalia* (1970), pp. 33–40.

Bürgel, J. C., "Ibn Ṭufayl and his *Ḥayy Ibn Yaqẓān:* a turning point in Arabic philosophical writing," in S. Jayyusi (ed.), *The legacy of Muslim Spain*, Leiden, 1992, pp. 830–846.

Conrad, Lawrence I., "An Andalusian Physician at the Court of the Muwaḥḥids: Some Notes on the Public Career of Ibn Ṭufayl," *Al-Qanṭara* 16.1 (1995), pp. 3–13.

–, "Through the thin veil: on the question of communication and the socialization of knowledge in Ḥayy b. Yaqẓān," in Lawrence I. Conrad (ed.), *The World of Ibn Tufayl. Interdisciplinary perspectives on Ḥayy ibn Yaqẓān*, Leiden: E.J. Brill, 1996, pp. 238–266.

–, *The world of Ibn Tufayl. Interdisciplinary Perspectives on Ḥayy ibn Yaqẓān*, Leiden: Brill, 1996.

Cornell, Vincent J., "Understanding is the Mother of Ability: Responsibility and Action in the Doctrine of Ibn Tūmart," *Studia Islamica* 66 (1987), pp. 71–103.

Cressier, P. Fierro, M. and Molina, L. (eds.), *Los almohades: problemas y perspectivas*, Madrid: Casa de Velázquez, 2005, 2 vols.

Dallmayr, Fred R., "Reason, faith, and politics: a journey to Muslim Andalusia," *The Maghreb Review* 25, 3–4 (2000), pp. 194–216.

De Libera, Alain, "Introduction", in Marc Geoffroy (trans.), *Averroes, Discours décisif*, Paris, 1996.

Di Donato, Silvia, "Le Kitāb al-Kašf ʿan manāhiǧ al-adilla d'Averroès: les phases de la rédaction dans les discours sur l'existence de dieu et sur la direction, d'après l'original arabe et la traduction hébaïque." *Arabic Sciences and Philosophy* 25/1 (2015), pp. 105–133.

Documentación, "Ibn ʿUmar al-Umawī, Abū l-Ḥaŷŷāŷ," *Biblioteca de al-Andalus*, vol. 5: *de Ibn Sa'āda a ibn Wuhayb*, ed. Jorge Lirola Delgado, Almería: Fundación Ibn Tufayl, 2007, nº 1284, pp. 530–1.

Documentación, "Ibn ʿUmar al-Išbīlī, Abū l-Ḥaŷŷāŷ", *Biblioteca de al-Andalus, Apéndice*, ed. Jorge Lirola Delgado, Almería: Fundación Ibn Tufayl, 2012, nº 1284, p. 446.

Documentación, "Bundūd, Abū Bakr," *Biblioteca de al-Andalus, Apéndice*, ed. Jorge Lirola Delgado, Almería: Fundación Ibn Tufayl, 2012, nº 1937, p. 36.

Documentación, "al-Gāfiqī al-Mursī, Abū Muḥammad," *Biblioteca de al-Andalus*, vol. 1: *De al-'Abbādīya a Ibn Abyaḍ*, ed. Jorge Lirola Delgado and José Miguel Puerta Vílchez, Almería: Fundación Ibn Tufayl, 2012, nº 114, p. 351–2.

Endress, Gerhard, "Le projet d'Averroès: constitution, réception et édition du corpus des oeuvres d'Ibn Rushd," in Gerhard Endress and Jan A. Aertsen (ed.), *Averroes and the Aristotelian tradition: sources, constitution and reception of the philosophy of Ibn Rushd (1126–1198). Proceedings of the Fourth Symposium Averroicum (Cologne, 1996)*, Leiden, 1999, pp. 3–32.

Fadel, M. H., "Chastisement and Punishment," *Encyclopaedia of the Qur'ān, Index Volume*, Brill, Leiden-Boston-Köln, 2001, vol. I, pp. 294–298.
Fierro, Maribel, "The treatises against innovations (*kutub al-bida'*)," *Der Islam* 69 (1992), pp. 204–46.
–, "The legal policies of the Almohad caliphs and Ibn Rushd's *Bidāyat al-mujtahid*," *Journal of Islamic Studies* 10/3 (1999), pp. 226–248; repr. in Carool Kersten (ed.), *The Caliphate and Islamic Statehood. Formation, Fragmentation and Modern Interpretations*, Berlin-London: Gerlach Press, 2015, vol. III, pp. 252–271.
–, "Spiritual alienation and political activism: the *ghurabā'* in al-Andalus during the sixth/twelfth century," *Arabica* XLVII (2000), pp. 230–260.
–, "Proto-Mālikīs, Mālikīs and reformed Mālikīs," in P. Bearman, R. Peters, F. E. Vogel (eds.), *The Islamic School of Law: Evolution, Devolution, and Progress*, Cambridge, Mass.: Harvard University Press, 2005, pp. 57–76.
–, "Doctrina y práctica jurídicas bajo los almohades," in P. Cressier et *al.* (eds.), *Los almohades: problemas y perspectivas*, Madrid: Casa de Velázquez, 2005, vol. II, pp. 895–935.
–, "Notes on Reason, Language and Conversion in the 13th century in the Iberian Peninsula," *Quaderns de la Mediterrània* 9 (Ramon Llull and Islam, the Beginning of a Dialogue), Barcelona: IEMed, 2008, pp. 49–58; repr. in Nicole Koulayan and Mansour Sayah (eds.), *Synoptikos. Mélanges offerts à Dominique Urvoy*, CNRS/Université de Toulouse Le Mirail, 2011, pp. 169–182.
–, "The Islamic West in the time of Maimonides: the Almohad revolution," in Lukas Muehlethaler (ed.), *'Höre die Wahrheit, wer sie auch spricht'. Stationen des Werks von Moses Maimonides vom islamischen Spanien bis ins moderne Berlin*, Herausgegeben im Auftrag des Jüdischen Museums Berlin, 2014, pp. 21–31.
–, "Codifying the law: the case of the Medieval Islamic West," in John Hudson and Ana Rodríguez (eds.), *Diverging paths? The shapes of power and institutions in Medieval Christendom and Islam*, Leiden: Brill, 2014, pp. 98–118.
–, "Almohads," in Andrew Rippin (ed.), *Oxford Bibliographies in Islamic Studies*, New York: Oxford University Press, 2016.
–, "The Maghreb and the Maghrebis in the Medieval Muslim imaginaire," paper presented at the *28th Congress of the Union Européenne des Arabisants et Islamisants (UEAI 28)*, Palermo 12–16 September 2016.
–, "Ibn Rushd al-Ḥafīd (Averroes) and his exile to Lucena: Jewish ancestry, genealogy and forced conversion", *Al-Qantara* XXXVIII (2017), pp. 131–152.
–, (2016) "El Mahdī Ibn Tūmart: más allá de la biografía oficial," in Miguel Angel Manzano and Rachid El Hour (ed.), *Política, sociedad e dentidades en el Occidente islámico (siglos XI–XIV)*, Salamanca, pp. 73–98.
–, "Education for the people? The case of the Almohad revolution," forthcoming.
Forcada, Miquel, "Las ciencias de los antiguos en al-Andalus durante el periodo almohade: una aproximación biográfica," in M.L. Avila and M. Fierro (eds.), *Estudios Onomástico-Biográficos de al-Andalus*, volume X. *Biografías almohades, II*, Madrid-Granada, 2000, pp. 359–411.
–, "Síntesis y contexto de las ciencias de los antiguos en época almohade," in P. Cressier *et al.* (eds.), *Los almohades: problemas y perspectivas*, 2 vols., Madrid: CSIC/Casa de Velázquez, 2005, vol. II, pp. 1091–1135.

Fraenkel, Carlos, "Legislating truth: Maimonides, the Almohads and the 13th century Jewish Enlightment," in R. Fontaine et al. (eds.), *Studies in the History of Culture and Science presented to Gad Freudenthal*, Leiden, 2010, pp. 209–231.

Fricaud, Émile, "Les *ṭalaba* dans la société almohade (le temps d'Averroés)," *Al-Qanṭara* XVIII (1997), pp. 331–388.

–, "Origine de l'utilisation privilégiée du terme *amr* chez les Mu'minides almohades," *Al-Qanṭara* XXIII (2002), pp. 93–122.

–, "Le problème de la disgrâce d'Averroès," in A. Bazzana *et al.* (eds.), *Averroès et l'averroïsme (XIIe–XVe siècle): un itinéraire historique du Haut Atlas à Paris et Padoue*, Lyon, 2005, pp. 155–189.

García Gómez, Emilio, *Andalucía contra Berbería*, Barcelona, 1976.

Geoffroy, Marc, "L'almohadisme théologique d'Averroès (Ibn Rushd)," *Archives d'Histoire Doctrinale et Littéraire du Moyen Age* 66 (1999), pp. 9–47.

–, "À propos de l'almohadisme d'Averroès: l'anthropomorphisme (*taǧsīm*) dans la seconde version du *Kitāb kašf 'an manāhiǧ al-adilla*," in P. Cressier *et al.* (eds.), *Los almohades: problemas y perspectivas*, Madrid: Casa de Velázquez, 2005, vol. II, pp. 853–94.

Gramsci, Antonio, *Selections from the Prison Notebooks*, New York: International Publishers, 1971.

Griffel, Frank, "The relationship between Averroes and al-Ghazālī as it presents itself in Averroes' early writings, especially in his commentary on al-Ghazālī's *al-Mustaṣfā*," in John Inglis (ed.), *Medieval Philosophy and the classical tradition in Islam, Judaism and Christianity*, Richmond: Curzon Press, 2002, pp. 51–63.

Guichard, Pierre, *Les musulmans de Valence et la Reconquête (XIe–XIIIe siècles)*, 2 vols., Damascus , 1990–1991.

–, "La situation de la philosophie et des sciences dans les mondes chrétien latin et arabo-musulman vers 1212," in P. Cressier and V. Salvatierra (eds.), *Las Navas de Tolosa 1212–2012*, Jaén, 2014, pp. 277–290.

Hajjaj Lahsen, H. M., "Ibn Huḏayl al-Fazārī, Abū Muhammad," *Biblioteca de al-Andalus, Apéndice*, ed. Jorge Lirola Delgado, Almería: Fundación Ibn Tufayl, 2012, nº 2188, pp. 245–246.

Haremska, J., "al-Uṣūlī, Abū 'Abd Allāh," *Biblioteca de al-Andalus*, vol. 7: *De al-Qabrīrī a Zumurrud*, ed. Jorge Lirola Delgado, Almería: Fundación Ibn Tufayl, nº 1827, pp. 584–5.

Hayoun, Maurice-Ruben, "L'averroïsme dans les milieux intellectuels du judaïsme: Moïse de Narbonne (1300–1362) et Eliya Delmédigo (v. 1460–1493)," in Bazzana *et al.* (eds.), *Averroès et l'averroïsme, un itinéraire historique du haut Atlas à Paris et à Padoue*, Lyon: Presses Universitaires de Lyon, 2005, pp. 275–305.

Hirschkind, Charles, "Heresy or Hermeneutics: the case of Naṣr Ḥāmid Abū Zayd," *The American Journal of Islamic Social Sciences* 12/4 (1995), pp. 463–77.

Historia de los Autores y Transmisores de al-Andalus (= HATA), Maribel Fierro (dir.), online: http://kohepocu.cchs.csic.es/register/to/hata_kohepocu/

Hopkins, J.F.P., *Medieval Muslim government in Barbary until the sixth century of the hijra*, London: Luzac, 1958.

Ibn Sharīfa, Muḥammad, "Abū l-Ḥajjāj Yūsuf b. Ghamr, mu'arrikh dawlat Ya'qūb al-Manṣūr. Ta'rīf wa-taṣḥīḥ taṣḥīf," *Majallat al-Ākādimiya* 10 (1993), pp. 83–107.

–, *Ibn Rushd al-ḥafīd: sīra wathā'iqiyya*, al-Dār al-Bayḍā': Maṭbaʿat al-Najāh al-Jadīda, 1999.

Ivry, Alfred L., "Averroes' Understanding of the Philosopher's Role in Society," in Anna Akasoy and Wim Raven (eds.), *Islamic Thought in the Middle Ages. Studies in Text, Transmission and Translation, in Honour of Hans Daiber*, Leiden, Boston, 2008, pp. 113–122.

Kukkonen, Taneli, "Averroes and the teleological argument," *Religious Studies* 38/4 (2002), pp. 405–428.

–, *Ibn Tufayl*, London, 2014.

Larsson, Göran, "The Berber as a symbolic epitome in the history of al-Andalus", in Bo Isaksson and Marianne Laanatza (eds.), *About the Berbers – History, Language and Culture and socio-economic conditions*, Uppsala 2004, pp. 90–98.

Lazar, Louis, "L'éducation politique selon Ibn Roshd (Averroes)," *Studia Islamica* 52 (1980), pp. 135–166.

Lévi-Provençal, Évariste, *Documents inédits d'histoire almohade (Fragments manuscrits du "legajo" 1919 du fonds arabe de l'Escurial)*, Paris, Librairie Orientaliste Paul Geuthner, 1928.

–, *Trente-sept lettres officielles almohades*, Collection des textes arabes publiée par l'Institut des Hautes Études Marocaines, Rabat, 1941.

Levtzion, Nehemia, "ʿAbd Allāh b. Yāsīn and the Almoravids," in J.R. Willis (ed.), *Studies in West African Islamic History*, vol. I, London, 1977, pp. 78–112.

Makkī, M.ʿA., "Contribución de Averroes a la ciencia jurídica musulmana," *Al encuentro de Averroes*, ed. A. Martínez Lorca, Madrid, 1993, pp. 15–38.

Marín, Manuela, "El viaje a Oriente de Abū Marwān al-Bāŷī (m. 635/1237)," in Manuela Marín (ed.), *Estudios Onomástico-Biográficos de al-Andalus. VI*, Madrid: CSIC, 1994, pp. 273–304.

–, "Dulces, vino y oposición política: un ejemplo biográfico de época almohade," *Estudios Onomástico-Biográficos de al-Andalus.* VIII, *Biografías y género biográfico en el Occidente islámico*, Madrid, 1997, pp. 93–126.

Marín, Manuela and Maribel Fierro, *Sabios y santos musulmanes de Algeciras*, Algeciras, 2004.

Martin, Vanessa, "A Comparison between Khumainī's Government of the Jurist and *The Commentary on Plato's Republic* of Ibn Rushd," *Journal of Islamic Studies* 7 (1996), pp. 16–31.

Martín Castellanos, A. J. and Miquel Forcada, "Ibn Ṭāhir al-Qaysī, Abū ʿAbd al-Raḥmān (nieto)," *Biblioteca de al-Andalus*, vol. 5: *de Ibn Sa'āda a ibn Wuhayb*, ed. Jorge Lirola Delgado, Almería: Fundación Ibn Tufayl, 2007, nº 1235, pp. 461–3.

Massé, Henri, "La profession de foi (*ʿaqīda*) et les guides spirituels (*morchida*) du Mahdi Ibn Toumert," *Mémorial Henri Basset*, t. II, Paris, 1928, pp. 105–121.

Molina, Luis, "Instituciones administrativas: visires y secretarios," in M.J. Viguera (coord.), *Historia de España Menéndez Pidal*, vol. VIII/2 (*El retroceso territorial de al-Andalus. Almorávides y almohades. Siglos XI al XIII*), Madrid: Espasa Calpe, pp. 147–167.

Morata, Nemesio, "La presentación de Averroes en la corte almohade," *La Ciudad de Dios* 153 (1941), pp. 101–122.

Ormsby, Eric, "Review of Fakhry, Majid, *Averroes (Ibn Rushd): His Life, Works and Influence*", *H-Mideast-Medieval, H-net Reviews*, December (2003).

Pérez Ruiz, Francisco, "Averroes y la República de Platón," *Pensamiento 50* (1994), pp. 25–46.

Puig Montada, Josep, "El pensamiento de Averroes en su contexto personal y social," *Miscelánea de Estudios Arabes y Hebraicos* XXXVIII (1989–90), pp. 307–324.

–, "Materials on Averroes' circle," *Journal of Near Eastern Studies* 51/4 (1992), pp. 241–60.

–, "Ibn Rushd versus al-Ghazālī: reconsideration of a polemic," *The Muslim World* LXXXII (1992), pp. 113–131.

–, "Averroes, vida y persecución de un filósofo," *Revista Española de Filosofía Medieval* 6 (1999), pp. 217–232

–, "Abū ʿAbd al-Raḥmān Ibn Ṭāhir. Addenda a 'Averroes, vida y persecución de un filósofo'," *Revista Española de Filosofía Medieval* 7 (2000), pp. 181–8.

–, "Ibn Rušd and the Almohad context," in Resianne Fontaine, Ruth Glasner, Reimund Leicht, and Giuseppe Veltri (eds.), *Studies in the History of Culture and Science. A tribute to Gad Freudenthal*, Leiden/Boston: Brill, 2011, pp. 189–208.

Renan, Ernest, *Averroès et l'averroéisme*, Paris, 1882.

Rouighi, Ramzi, "The Andalusi origins of the Berbers," *Journal of Medieval Iberian Studies* 2/1 (2010), pp. 93–108.

Peña, Salvador, "El término de origen coránico *amr Allāh* ('Disposición de Dios') y el linguocentrismo trascendente islámico, en torno al siglo XII," *Anaquel de Estudios Árabes* 22 (2011), pp. 197–224.

Safran, Janina, "The politics of book burning in al-Andalus," *Journal of Medieval Iberian Studies* 6 (2014), pp. 148–168.

Sarrió, D. R., "The philosopher as the heir of the Prophets: Averroes' Islamic Rationalism," *Al-Qanṭara* XXXVI (2015), pp. 45–68.

Serrano, Delfina, "¿Por qué llamaron los almohades antropomorfistas a los almorávides," in Cressier *et al.* (eds.), *Los almohades: problemas y perspectivas*, Madrid: Casa de Velázquez, 2005, vol. II, 451–76.

–, "Ibn Zarqūn, Abū l-Ḥusayn," *Biblioteca de al-Andalus*, vol. 6, *De Ibn al-Ŷabbāb a Nubḏat al-ʿaṣr*, ed. Jorge Lirola Delgado, Almería: Fundación Ibn Tufayl, 2009, nº 1437, pp. 277–80.

–, "Explicit cruelty, implicit compassion: Judaism, forced conversions and the genealogy of the Banū Rushd," *Journal of Medieval Iberian Studies* 2/2 (2010), pp. 217–33.

–, "Ibn Rushd al-Jadd (d. 520/1126)," in Ousamma Arabi, David S. Powers and Susan Spectorsky (ed.), *Islamic Legal Thought: Jurists and Their Work*, Leiden: Brill, 2013, pp. 295–322.

Stroumsa, Sara, "Philosophes almohades? Averroès, Maïmonide et l'idéologie almohade," in P. Cressier *et al.* (eds.), *Los almohades: problemas y perspectivas*, Madrid, CSIC/Casa de Velázquez, 2005, pp. 1137–1162.

–, *Maimonides in his world: portrait of a Mediterranean thinker*, Princeton: Princeton University Press, 2009.

Taylor, Richard, "Truth does not contradict truth: Averroes and the unity of truth," *Topoi, an international review of philosophy* 19/1 (2000), pp. 3–16.

Thiele, Jan, "Facing the Mahdī's True Belief. Abū ʿAmr al-Salālijī's Ashʿarite Creed and the Almohads' Claim to Religious Authority," forthcoming in *Formulating the caliphate in the Islamic West* to appear in *al-Usur al-wusta*.

Tottoli, Roberto, "The thanksgiving prostration (*sujūd al-shukr)* in Muslim traditions," *Bulletin of the School of Oriental and African Studies* 61/2 (1998), pp. 309–13.

Urvoy, Dominique, "La pensée almohade dans l'oeuvre d'Averroès," in J. Jolivet (ed.), *Multiple Averroès. Actes du Colloque Internationale organisé à l'occasion du 850e anniversaire de la naissance d'Averroès, Paris 20–23 septembre 1976*, Paris: Les Belles Lettres, 1978.

–, *Pensers d'al-Andalus. La vie intellectuelle à Cordoue et Sevilla au temps des Empires Berbères (fin XIe siècle-début XIIIe siècle)*, Toulouse: Editions du CNRS, Presses Universitaires du Mirail, 1990.

–, *Ibn Rushd (Averroes)*, transl. O. Stewart, London / New York, 1991.

–, "Les professions de foi d'Ibn Tūmart. Problèmes textuels et doctrinaux," in P. Cressier *et al.* (eds.), *Los almohades: problemas y perspectivas*, Madrid: Casa de Velázquez, 2005, vol. II, pp. 739–52.

Vajda, George, *Isaac Albalag Averroïste juif traducteur et annotateur d'Al-Ghazali*, Paris, 1960.

Valencia, Rafael, "Ibn Zuhr, Abū Bakr," *Biblioteca de al-Andalus*, vol. 6, *De Ibn al-Ŷabbāb a Nubḏat al-'aṣr*, ed. Jorge Lirola Delgado, Almería: Fundación Ibn Tufayl, 2009, nº 1495, 350–2.

Van Dooren, Wim, "Ibn Rušd's attitude towards authority," in A. Hasnawi, A. Elamrani-Jamal and M. Aouad (eds.), *Perspectives arabes et médiévales sur la tradition scientifique et philosophique grecques: actes du colloque de la* SIHSPAI, Paris, 1993, Leuven, 1997, pp. 623–33.

Vizcaíno Plaza, J. M., "Ibn al-Ṣaffār, Abū l-Ḥasan Yūnus," *Biblioteca de al-Andalus*, vol. 5: *De Ibn Sa'āda a Ibn Wuhayb*, ed. Jorge Lirola Delgado, Almería: Fundación Ibn Tufayl, 2007, nº 1040, pp. 66–8.

Walzer, Richard, *Al-Farabi on the perfect State*, Oxford: Clarendon Press, 1985.

Watt, William Montgomery, "Philosophy and theology under the Almohads," *Actas del Primer Congreso de Estudios Arabes e Islámicos (Córdoba, 1962)*, Madrid, 1964, pp. 101–7.

–, "Philosophy and social structure in Almohad Spain", *The Islamic Quarterly* VIII (1964), pp. 46–51.

Knowing the Unknown

Yahya M. Michot

Ibn Taymiyya's Commentary on Avicenna's *Ishārāt, namaṭ* X*

Introduction

In the two last parts *(namaṭ)* of his famous *Ishārāt* – *The Stations of the Knowers (maqāmāt al-ʿārifīn)* and *The Secrets of the Signs (asrār al-āyāt)* –, Avicenna approaches prophethood and the prophetic miracles through the lens of the spiritual journey of ecstatics, from asceticism to gnosis, and their psychic capacities. This philosophical reading of mysticism can legitimately be seen as one more manifestation of the widespread effort to normalize Sufism that followed the execution of al-Ḥallāj in 309/922 and gave birth to the great classical doctrinal treatises on the subject, from the *Kitāb al-lumaʿ fī l-taṣawwuf* of Abū Naṣr al-Sarrāj (d. 378/988) to the *Iḥyāʾ ʿulūm al-dīn* of al-Ghazālī (d. 505/1111). Another type of religious literature with regard to which it is worth situating the last parts of the *Ishārāt* consists of several relatively contemporaneous works concerning prophethood and its signs, i. e., most often, miracles: *Kitāb al-bayān ʿan al-farq bayn al-muʿjizāt wa l-karamāt wa l-ḥiyal wa l-kiḥāna wa l-ṣihr wa l-nāranjāt – The Book Showing the Difference between Miracles, Prodigies, Trickery, Divination, Magic, and Illusionism* of Abū Bakr al-Bāqillānī (d. 403/1013), *Tathbīt dalāʾil al-nubuwwa – The Establishment of the Proofs of Prophethood* of Qāḍī ʿAbd al-Jabbār al-Hamadhānī (d. 415/1025), *Dalāʾil al-nubuwwa – The Proofs of Prophethood* of Abū Nuʿaym al-Iṣfahānī (d. 430/1038), *Aʿlām al-nubuwwa – The Tokens of Prophethood* of ʿAlī al-Māwardī (d. 450/1058), *Dalāʾil al-nubuwwa wa maʿrifat aḥwāl ṣāḥib al-sharīʿa – The Proofs of Prophethood and the Knowledge of the States of the Author of the Law* of Abū Bakr al-Bayhaqī (d. 458/1066)...[1] Avicenna's explanation of the prophetic miracles by the mere powers, or forces, of human souls effectively meant two things: (a) the Prophets are not so different from other humans; (b) every human can, with the adequate training, hope to

* I am greatly indebted to Jamil Qureshi for editing the English of the present article.

1 See A. B. AL-BĀQILLĀNĪ, *Bayān*; ʿA. al-J. AL-HAMADHĀNĪ, *Tathbīt*; A. N. AL-IṢFAHĀNĪ, *Dalāʾil*; ʿA. AL-MĀWARDĪ, *Aʿlām*; A. B. AL-BAYHAQĪ, *Dalāʾil*.

become some sort of Prophet and to acquire extraordinary, miraculous, powers. These were strong, controversial, statements in a time when ulema were spreading both a mythological image of the uniqueness of prophethood and ballooning collections of Muḥammadan miracles.

As his *Qāʿida sharīfa fī l-muʿjizāt wa l-karamāt – Noble Rule Concerning the Miracles and Prodigies*[2] shows, the Damascene theologian-mufti Ibn Taymiyya (d. 728/1328) was himself interested in this aspect of prophetology. He could therefore be expected to have reacted against Avicenna's views on the matter and he indeed did so on more than one occasion, including about the last pages of the *Ishārāt.* Several recent studies have paved the way towards a more accurate understanding of his importance as a post-*falāsifa* philosophizing *(mutafalsif)* theologian *(mutakallim).* I have translated and studied a number of Taymiyyan texts relating to, or commenting on, the Ikhwān al-Ṣafā', Abū Ḥāmid al-Ghazālī, Fakhr al-Dīn al-Rāzī, Naṣīr al-Dīn al-Ṭūsī and, also, Avicenna, more precisely his *Risālat Aḍḥawiyya.*[3] Ibn Taymiyya was surely right when he wrote that al-Ghazālī's "disease was *The Healing (maraḍu-hu al-shifā'),* i.e., *[The Book of] the Healing* [composed] by Avicenna in philosophy."[4] But so too Shams al-Dīn al-Dhahabī (d. 748/1348) was right when he accused the theologian-mufti of having "repeatedly swallowed the poison of the philosophers and their works," and then explained: "the body becomes addicted to the frequent use of poison so that it is secreted, by God, in the very bones."[5] Ibn Taymiyya was actually well acquainted with the central themes of the Shaykh al-Ra'īs' philosophy and, beside the *Aḍḥawiyya,* knew a number of other important works of the Avicennan *corpus.* The titles that he quotes, as surveyed by R. Y. al-Shāmī,[6] are the following:

- *Aḥwāl al-nafs*
- *al-Risālat al-Aḍḥawiyya*
- *al-Najāt*
- *al-Ishārāt*
- *al-Shifā'*
- *al-Ḥikmat al-mashriqiyya*
- *al-Mabda' wa l-maʿād*

Al-Shāmī very helpfully provides references to the texts in which Ibn Taymiyya mentions these titles, but his survey is not exhaustive. Moreover, it does not reveal that the Damascene theologian-mufti sometimes quotes verbatim lengthy excerpts from these works and comments on them in various ways. The *Ishārāt* seems to be the book he was the most interested in. He calls it "the holy writ *(muṣḥaf)* of these philosophers"[7] and refers to it in works as diverse as his *Bayān*

2 See Ibn Taymiyya, *Muʿjizāt,* trans. Michot, *Textes N.S. XXI.*
3 See Y. Michot, *Misled, Reader, Esotericism, Textes N.S. XI, Vizir, Mamlūk I* & *II*; also, *Textes N.S. XIV, Historiography.*
4 See the Taymiyyan text translated in Y. Michot, *Reader,* p. 136.
5 See Y. Michot, *Vanités,* p. 600; *Mamlūk I,* p. 166, n. 39.
6 See R. Y. al-Shāmī, *Maṣādir,* p. 235–236.
7 Ibn Taymiyya, *Dar',* vol. ix, p. 254.

talbīs al-Jahmiyya – Exposition of the Deceit of the Jahmīs, Dar' al-ta'āruḍ – Averting the Conflict between Reason and [religious] Tradition, al-Istiqāma – The Book of Rectitude, Minhāj al-sunnat al-nabawiyya – The Way of the Prophetic Sunna, *al-Nubuwwāt – On Prophethood, al-Radd 'alā l-manṭiqiyyīn – Refutation of the Logicians, Kitāb al-Ṣafadiyya – Book of Safed.*[8]

Ibn Taymiyya also knows, and comments on, the *Commentaries on the Ishārāt* by Fakhr al-Dīn al-Rāzī and Naṣīr al-Dīn al-Ṭūsī.[9] For example, he totally disagrees with their exaltation of "what Avicenna said in the *Stations of the Knowers*, which is the Seal of their holy writ *(muṣḥaf)*," i.e., the ninth part *(namaṭ)* of the book:

> "'This part,' al-Rāzī said,[10] 'is the most sublime *(ajall)* of what there is in this book. [Therein, Avicenna] indeed organized the science of the Sufis in a manner about which none of his predecessors had thought before him and which has remained unsurpassed after him.' Al-Ṭūsī approved him for such words and said: 'The eminent **[56]** commentator mentioned that this part was the most sublime of what there is in this book and that, [therein, Avicenna] had indeed organized the science of the Sufis in a manner about which none of his predecessors had thought before him and which has remained unsurpassed after him.'[11] This is the utmost degree of what those [thinkers] have of the knowledge of the Sufis. When it is pondered by one knowledgeable of what God sent His Messenger with and of what is [known] by the shaykhs of the Sufis *(al-qawm)* who believe in God and in His Messenger, who follow the Book and the *Sunna*, it is clear for him that what [Avicenna] mentioned in [that] book, [even] after it is perfectly made into a reality *(taḥqīq)*, a man does not become a Muslim thereby, not to speak of being a Friend of God. The Friends of God, they are the believers who fear [Him], whereas the utmost degree, for [Avicenna], is the extinction *(fanā')* in the proclamation of [God's] oneness *(tawḥīd)* which he described, i.e., the proclamation of [God's] oneness of the Jahmī exaggerators, which includes denying the [divine] attributes together with speaking of the pre-eternity of the [celestial] spheres and saying that the Lord is necessitating by essence, not acting by His will, and that He does not know the particulars."[12]

---

8 Neither G. C. ANAWATI (*Essai*, p. 4–12, no 3) nor Y. MAHDAVI (*Bibliographie*, p. 32–38, no 27) mention Ibn Taymiyya among the authors of commentaries or refutations of the *Ishārāt*. The Damascene theologian-mufti is also absent from the pages devoted by G. ENDRESS (*Reading*, p. 410–415) to the reading of the *Ishārāt* "in commentary, refutation, and arbitration."

9 See for example several Taymiyyan texts translated in Y. MICHOT, *Vizir*.

10 See F. D. al-Rāzī, *Sharḥ*, vol. ii, p. 100, l. 35–36.

11 See N. D. AL-ṬŪSĪ, *Sharḥ*, vol. ii, p. 101, l. 1–2 (commentary on IBN SĪNĀ, *Ishārāt*, IX, i, ed. FORGET, p. 198; ed. DUNYĀ, vol. iv, p. 47; trans. INATI, *Mysticism*, p. 81; trans. GOICHON, *Directives*, p. 483).

12 IBN TAYMIYYA, *Dar'*, vol. vi, p. 55–56. Similar ideas are also present in IBN TAYMIYYA, *Ṣafadiyya*, vol. ii, p. 339: "The Sufizing ones of the philosophers thread on the path of Avicenna concerning the stations of the knowers which he mentioned in the last part of the *Ishārāt*. This was extensively spoken about elsewhere and it was then made clear that the utmost degree of this, despite al-Rāzī's praise of it, is a deficient extinction *(fanā')*, with a

In another work, Ibn Taymiyya's opinion about the penultimate part of the *Ishārāt* is expressed in a shorter phrase but is as clearly negative: "Avicenna spoke about the stations[13] of the knowers according to a corrupt Sufism *(bi-taṣawwuf fāsid)*!"[14]

As for the tenth, and last, *namaṭ*, *The Secrets of the Signs*, the mixed feelings it sometimes inspires in the Damascene theologian-mufti provide another example of what I have called, about some aspects of his commentary on Avicenna's *Aḍḥawiyya*, "the pecularity of the great Mamlūk theologian's love–hate relationship with the ideas of the Shaykh al-Ra'īs."[15] The following three passages from his *al-Nubuwwāt – On Prophethood* are most illustrative in this regard:

> "The [more] astute *(ḥādhiq)* of the philosophers who spoke about [prophethood], like Avicenna – the most eminent of their group but, also, the most ignorant of those who have spoken on this topic – considered it all as pertaining to the forces *(quwwa)* of the soul, the difference [between the Prophet and the magician] being that the soul of the Prophet and the righteous man is pure and seeks the good whereas the soul of the magician is wicked. As for the difference between the Prophet and the righteous man, it is imperceptible according to what these say."[16]

> "Avicenna built up the affair of prophethood [by saying] that it pertains to the forces *(quwwa)* of the soul, the forces *(quwwa)* of the soul being dissimilar *(mutafāwit)* [in humans]. All this is the words of someone who does not know prophethood but, rather, is estranged from it, and more deficient than someone who would want to affirm that there are in this world jurists and physicians, would not know anything except poets, and would use the existence of poets as a proof that jurists and physicians exist! Or, rather, this image would even be closer [to the truth]! The distance of prophethood from non-prophets is indeed greater than the distance of the jurist and the physician from the poet! But these [philosophers] are among the people the most ignorant of prophethood. They saw that the mentioning of the Prophets was spreading, and they wanted to bring that out *(takhrīj)* according to the principles of people who had not known the Prophets."[17]

> "This is Avicenna's astuteness *(ḥidhq)* and his way of disposing of things *(taṣarruf)*: as he was informed of strange affairs [happening] in the world which it was not possible for him to pronounce as lies, he wanted to bring them out *(ikhrāj)* in accordance to the principles of the [philosophers] and stated it openly in his *Ishārāt*. He said: 'We have not established these affairs from the start. Rather, when we realized that there are in the world affairs of this genus, we wanted to make their causes clear.'"[18]

---

deficiency in the proclamation of the oneness of the [divine] lordship *(tawḥīd al-rubūbiyya)* and in the affirmation [of the divine attributes]."

13 maqāmāt : maqālāt **N** *the discourses*

14 Ibn Taymiyya, *Nubuwwāt*, p. 634.

15 See Y. Michot, *Mamlūk I*, p. 160, n. 34.

16 Ibn Taymiyya, *Nubuwwāt*, p. 137–138.

17 Ibn Taymiyya, *Nubuwwāt*, p. 196–197.

18 Ibn Taymiyya, *Nubuwwāt*, p. 702.

Another work in which Ibn Taymiyya looks into the last *namaṭ* of the *Ishārāt* is the *Kitāb al-Ṣafadiyya – Book of Safed.* This work is named after the Northern Palestinian city from which the question it addresses was sent. Anterior to, or contemporaneous with, *al-Radd ʿalā l-manṭiqiyyīn – Refutation of the Logicians* in which it is explicitly mentioned a number of times,[19] the *Ṣafadiyya* is considered by its editor, M. R. Sālim, as also contemporaneous with the *Darʾ al-taʿāruḍ – Averting the Conflict between Reason and [religious] Tradition*, and thus dated by him from Ibn Taymiyya's very productive years in Damascus, 713/1313–717/1317.[20]

> "In the name of God, the Merciful, the Compassionate. There is no might and no force *(quwwa)* except in God, the High, the Sublime. The shaykh, the imām, the very knowledgeable ulema, the shaykh al-Islām, the remainder of the [prophetic] age, the model of the late comers, Taqī al-Dīn Abū l-ʿAbbās Aḥmad, son of the shaykh, the imām, the ulema, Shihāb al-Dīn ʿAbd al-Ḥalīm, son of the shaykh, the very knowledgeable imām, Majd al-Dīn ʿAbd al-Salām b. Taymiyya, God be pleased with him and please him, was asked about a Muslim man who says that the miracles of the Prophets, God bless them and grant them peace, are [due to] psychic forces *(quwwa)*.[21] Give us a fatwa and rewarded you will then be."[22]

Safed in the early 20th century

Technically speaking, beginning as it does, the *Ṣafadiyya* is thus another one of these extensive fatwas which Ibn Taymiyya devoted to questions, not of jurisprudence *(fiqh)*, but of philosophizing *Kalām* theology. In M. R. Sālim's edition, it covers more than six hundred pages. It could of course have been much shorter but, as often in his books, the Damascene theologian-mufti approaches some

19 See M. R. Sālim's introduction to his edition of Ibn Taymiyya, *Ṣafadiyya*, vol. i, p. 3–4, 11–12.

20 See M. R. Sālim's introduction to his edition of Ibn Taymiyya, *Ṣafadiyya*, vol. i, p. 9–10.

21 *Muʿjizāt al-anbiyāʾ [...] quwā nafsāniyya.* The translation "miracle" for *muʿjiza* does not convey the active sense of the Arabic; hence the addition of "due to". A more literal translation would be: "the dispowering [abilities] of the Prophets [...] are psychic forces."

22 Ibn Taymiyya, *Ṣafadiyya*, vol. i, p. 1.

questions from a multitude of viewpoints, including their sources and consequences, doctrinal or socio-historical, in reference to every imaginable author or group, without concern about repeating himself. As for an internal structure, there might be several thoughtfully devised mini-ensembles but the general aspect of the whole work remains, to say the least, loose and fluid. Somehow, the first few pages of the Damascene theologian-mufti's answer say it all:

> "'– Praise belongs to God, the Lord of the worlds!'[23] he answered. Such words – i. e., the saying of whosoever says that the miracles of the Prophets, God bless them and grant them peace, are [due to] psychic forces *(quwwa)* – are vain or, even, they are unbelief. Someone saying them will be called to repent and the truth shall be made clear to him. If he persists in believing it after the Legal justification has been notified to him, he is an unbeliever. And if he persists in holding this [opinion] publicly after having been called to repent, he shall be killed.
>
> This is among the things said by a group of the philosophizers, the esotericist *(bāṭinī)*[24] Qarmaṭīs,[25] **[2]** the Ismā'īlīs, and those similar to them, such as Avicenna and his like, the authors of the *Epistles* of the Ikhwān al-Ṣafā',[26] the 'Ubaydids[27] who were in Egypt – the Ḥākimīs[28] and those resembling them. These people were making out as if they were Shī'īs but were inwardly heretics (*mulḥid*). They are called the Qarmaṭīs, the esotericists, etc. **[3]** The members of Avicenna's household were among the followers of these, his father only being among the adherents of their missionary movement *(da'wa)*,[29] and this is why he engaged in the doctrines of the philosophers. These make out as if they were following the [various] religions *(milla)* and claim that the religion has an inward [reality] which contradicts its outward [appearance].
>
> In this missionary movement, [these people] occupy [different] degrees. Those of them who have reached the major attainment and the supreme *nomos*,[30] like the Qar-

23 Qur'ān, *al-Fātiḥa* – i, 1.

24 To Ibn Taymiyya, all those who, Shī'īs, Sufis or philosophers, reject the manifest meaning of the Scripture in favour of an esoteric meaning *(bāṭin)*; see M. G. S. Hodgson, *EI2*, art. *Bāṭiniyya.*

25 One of the Ismā'īlī sects; see W. Madelung, *EI2*, art. *Ḳarmaṭī.*

26 For Ibn Taymiyya's opinion on the Ikhwān al-Ṣafā', see Y. Michot, *Misled*, in which the two first paragraphs of the present fatwa are also translated.

27 I.e., the Fāṭimids, whose movement was founded by the Ismā'īlī 'Ubayd Allāh al-Mahdī (d. 322/934). Jawhar, general of the fourth Fāṭimid caliph, al-Mu'izz, conquered Egypt and begun building Cairo in 358/969–359/970; see M. Canard, *EI2*, art. *Fāṭimids.*

28 The followers of al-Ḥākim bi-Amr Allāh, the sixth Fāṭimid caliph (b. 375/985; r. 386/996–411/1021). He disappeared in Cairo and was divinized by some of his partisans, including the Druzes; see M. Canard, *EI2*, art. *al-Ḥākim bi-Amr Allāh.*

29 See Avicenna's autobiography, trans. W. E. Gohlman, *Life*, p. 19: "My father was one of those who responded to the propaganda of the Egyptians and was reckoned among the Ismā'īliyya…" See also the Taymiyyan text translated in Y. Michot, *Astrology*, p. 180. According to D. Gutas (*Avicenna*, p. 333), Avicenna was in reality a Ḥanafī Sunnī.

30 According to al-Ghazālī (*Faḍā'iḥ*, p. 32), "the major attainment" *(al-balāgh al-akbar)* is the highest degree esotericists seek to reach; they then throw off all form of obedience to Islām. *Al-balāgh al-akbar wa l-nāmūs al-a'ẓam* is also the title of an important pseudo-Ismā'īlī work that was already known in the 4th/10th century; see W. Madelung, *Fāṭimids*, p. 43–45, 66–68. Ibn Taymiyya analyzes its content in his fatwa against the Nuṣayrīs; see S. Guyard, *Fetwa*, p. 191–192.

maṭīs [4] of Baḥrayn,[31] the followers of al-Jannābī,[32] the masters of Alamūt,[33] Sinān[34] who was in Syria, and their like, do not believe in the obligatoriness of the five prayers, nor of almsgiving, nor of fasting the month of Ramaḍān, nor of making the pilgrimage of the antique House, nor of prohibiting what God and His Messenger have prohibited – wine, games of chance, fornication, etc. They claim that for these texts there is [5] an interpretation *(ta'wīl)* and an inward [meaning] that is at variance with the outward [meaning] known to the Muslims. Praying, for them, consists in knowing their secrets; fasting, in concealing their secrets; making the pilgrimage, in visiting their shaykhs, and similar things. They may also say that for the elite these obligations are dropped, not for the commonalty. As for the texts concerning eschatology *(ma'ād)*, the names of God, His attributes, and His angels, their claims concerning them are [even] broader and more numerous! A group of those who relate themselves to Sufism and *Kalām* theology engaged in many of the things which these [esotericists] were saying about the sciences, or about the sciences and actions. The words of Ibn 'Arabī,[35] Ibn Sab'īn,[36] and their like among the heretics of the Sufis go back to what such [esotericists] say.

These heretics – the philosophizers, the Qarmaṭīs and those agreeing with them – say that prophethood consists of three properties [which are such that] anyone in which they exist is a Prophet. Moreover, for them, prophethood does not come to an end. Rather, after every Prophet, God sends out [another] Prophet, continuously. Many of them also say that [Prophethood] is acquirable *(muktasab)*. Al-Suhrawardī[37] [6] – the one of them who was killed – was seeking to become a Prophet. Likewise, Ibn Sab'īn was seeking to become a Prophet. Of magic and phantasmagoria *(sīmā')*[38] they used to

---

31 Region of Eastern Arabia, including the homonymous archipelago, ruled by Qarmaṭīs from *c.* 267/890 until *c.* 462/1070; see G. Rentz & W. E. Mulligan, *EI2*, art. *al-Baḥrayn.*

32 Qarmaṭī leader who controlled Eastern Arabia, defeated the army of the caliph al-Mu'taḍid, and was assassinated in 301/913; see B. Carra de Vaux & M. G. S. Hodgson, *EI2*, art. *al-Djannābī, Abū Sa'īd.*

33 Fortress in the Alburz mountains, North-North-East of Qazwīn. The Ismā'īlī propagandist Ḥasan-i Ṣabbāḥ (d. 518/1124) took it from the Saljūqs in 483/1090 and made it the headquarters of the Nizārī sect (the "Assassins"). The Mongols destroyed it in 654/1256; see M. G. S. Hodgson, *EI2*, art. *Alamūt.*

34 Rashīd al-Dīn Sinān b. Salmān b. Muḥammad Abū l-Ḥasan al-Baṣrī, the "Old Man of the Mountain" of the Crusaders' chronicles, the most important Nizārī Ismā'īlī leader in medieval Syria (d. 589/1193); see F. Daftary, *EI2*, art. *Rashīd al-Dīn Sinān.* See also the Taymiyyan text translated in Y. Michot, *Mamlūk I*, p. 185.

35 Muḥyī l-Dīn Abū 'Abd Allāh Muḥammad b. al-'Arabī (Murcia, 560/1165 – Damascus, 638/1240), theosophist and mystic.

36 Quṭb al-Dīn Abū Muḥammad 'Abd al-Ḥaqq b. Sab'īn (Murcia, 613/1217 – Makka, 668/1269), philosopher and mystic; see A. Akasoy, *Philosophie, Muḥaqqiq.*

37 Shihāb al-Dīn Yaḥyā l-Suhrawardī, theosophist and mystic (Suhraward, 549/1154 – Aleppo, 587/1191); see H. Ziai, *EI2*, art. *al-Suhrawardī.* See also the Taymiyyan texts translated in Y. Michot, *Mamlūk I*, p. 183–184.

38 *Sīmā'* or *sīmiyā'*; see D. B. Macdonald & T. Fahd, *EI2*, art. *Sīmiyā'*; E. Doutté, *Magie*, p. 173, who translates it "science des lettres et des mots." "The eminences among the adepts of alchemy *(kīmiyā')* attach to it what they call 'phantasmagoria' *(sīmiyā')* – something like that which Ibn Sab'īn, al-Suhrawardī – the one who was killed –, al-Ḥallāj, and their like were fabricating. It is however well known that this is prohibited *(muḥarram)* by the Book of God, the *Sunna* of His Messenger, and the consensus *(ijmā')* of the community. Or, even, most of

practise things by which they led astray those whom they were deluding.

The first property is that [the Prophet] has a holy force *(quwwa qudsiyya)*, i. e., the force *(quwwa)* of intuition *(ḥads)*, so that something comes easily to him, in the matter of knowledge, which does not come to others than him except with great trouble. They may express this [by saying] that he perceives the middle term [of a syllogism] without needing that which is needed by someone who is not like him. The outcome of the matter is that he is more clever *(adhkā)* than the others and that knowledge is easier for him than for the others than him.

The second property is the force *(quwwa)* of imagination *(takhyīl)* and internal sense, so that what the Prophet knows gets represented *(tamaththala)* for him in his soul; he sees it, and he hears it. He thus sees in his soul luminous forms which, according to them, are the angels of God, and he hears in his soul sounds which, according to them, are the word of God, of the genus of what happens to someone sleeping in his dream *(manām)*, of the genus of what happens to some of the adepts of [spiritual] exercise *(riyāḍa)*, and of **[7]** the genus of what happens to some of the bilious *(mamrūr)* individuals having an epileptic fit. They also say that what the Messengers inform of, concerning the affairs of the [divine] lordship and the Last Day, are only an imaginal representation *(takhyīl)* and things given as similitudes *(amthāl maḍrūba)*, and not that they are informations about the realities *(ḥaqā'iq)* as they are in themselves.

The third property is that [the Prophet] has a psychic force *(quwwa)* by which he freely disposes *(taṣarrafa)* of the hylè of the world just as the individual giving the evil eye *('ā'in)* has a psychic force *(quwwa)* by which he has an influence on the one given the evil eye *(ma'īn)*. They claim that the extraordinary phenomena *(khāriq al-'āda)*[39] linked to the Prophets and the Friends [of God] are of this type.

The basis of the affair of these is that they do not affirm the Artisan of the world to have a will, a choice, a power *(qudra)* by which He is capable *(qadara)* of changing the world and making it pass from one state to another. Their imāms do not even affirm that He knows the details of the states of the world. On the contrary, there are among them some who say that He knows nothing, there are some who say that He does not know [anything] except Himself, and there are some who say that He knows the particulars from a universal viewpoint – this is Avicenna's choice, and it is the best of what they say, despite the self-contradiction of such a saying and its corrupt nature. **[8]** Every existent in the outside is indeed an identifiable *(mu'ayyan)*, particular existent, whereas the universals are only universals in the minds, not in the concrete *(a'yān)*. The Artisan Himself is a necessary, identifiable, existent, He is not universal. Likewise, also, [for] what emanates from Him, such as the [celestial] spheres and such as the intelligences and the souls which they affirm [to exist]. If He does not know [anything] except a universal, He does not know Himself, nor what emanates from Him, nor the spheres. Also, nothing exists except something which is particular. So, if He does not know [anything] except universals, He does not know any of the existents.

These [people] moreover say that He is a complete cause necessarily entailing

---

the ulema are of the opinion that the magician is an unbeliever *(kāfir)* who must be killed" (Ibn Taymiyya, *MF*, vol. xxix, p. 383–384).

39 More literally, *khāriq al-'āda* means a thing, or an event, breaking the ordinary pattern of things.

> *(mustalzim)* the world and that the world is generated *(mutawallid)* from Him through a necessarily concomitant *(lāzim)* generation, such that it is not possible for Him to be disjoined from it[40] as a complete cause necessarily entails what is caused by it."[41]

As already manifest in these first pages of the *Ṣafadiyya*, Ibn Taymiyya is convinced that it is to Avicenna that one must trace back the *nubuwwāt* that have become the standard Islamic prophetology in his time, and more specifically to the *Ishārāt*. For him, this philosophical prophetology is not to be rejected as a whole. Indeed,

> "true *(ḥaqq)* is the description which the [philosophers] have given of the Prophets by [saying] that they have properties – about knowledge, power *(qudra)*, hearing, and seeing – by which they stand out. But vain is the [philosophers'] claim that the utmost limit of the properties of the [Prophets] is what they have mentioned. We, we do not deny that God, Exalted is He, specially distinguishes *(khaṣṣa)* the Prophet by a holy force *(quwwa qudsiyya)* by which he knows what others than him do not know. Nor do we deny that which, of the truthful things congruent with the realities, God strikes likenesses *(maththala)* of for [the Prophet], either while he is awake or in his sleep. We also do not deny that God might put in the souls forces *(quwwa)* by which [some] influence takes place in the existence."[42]

Rather than being black and white, matters of prophetology, especially concerning the specific faculties and powers of the Prophets, must thus be examined in depth and with all the required distinctions. Coming back at some point in the *Ṣafadiyya* to the question at the start of the book – are the miracles of the Prophets due to psychic forces? –, Ibn Taymiyya approaches it within two wider contexts: one, the various theories of causality opposing different *Kalām* schools and the philosophers; the other, the question of the actual capacity of human souls to have some influence in the world. This in turn leads him to revisit some of Avicenna's statements in the last *namaṭ* of the *Ishārāt*, his most influential book, to quote them verbatim, and to comment on them.[43] One should not, however, expect from the Damascene theologian-mufti a systematic commentary of the kind Averroes, for example, offers of Aristotle's *Metaphysics*. He might at some point develop his refutation of Avicenna's ideas from ten explicitly numbered angles but his approach to the last *namaṭ* of the *Ishārāt* remains essentially free,

---

40 Or: "for it to be disjoined from Him."

41 Ibn Taymiyya, *Ṣafadiyya*, vol. i, p. 1–8.

42 Ibn Taymiyya, *Ṣafadiyya*, vol. i, p. 135.

43 The *Ishārāt* is not the only text quoted and commented on in the *Ṣafadiyya*. Other important texts are *al-Arbaʿīn* of Fakhr al-Dīn al-Rāzī (quoted in vol. i, p. 29–33, with a reference to al-Urmawī and to al-Rāzī's *al-Maṭālib al-ʿāliya*; p. 60–62) and his *al-Sirr al-maktūm* (quoted in vol. i, p. 66–70), *al-Iftikhār* of Abū Yaʿqūb al-Sijistānī (quoted in vol. ii, p. 3–4), *al-Najāt* of Avicenna (quoted in vol. ii, p. 181–186), *al-Muʿtabar* of Abū l-Barakāt al-Baghdādī (quoted in vol. ii, p. 253–256, 332–334).

as he goes back and forth through its text. Moreover, quite thin is the relation which some passages, despite their particularly fascinating character, have to the main object of the commentary, as is the case with a description of a shamanic séance, a denial that Mary is a Prophetess, and an analysis of the miraculous nature of the Kaʿba. But how would the Damascene theologian-mufti ever resist the pleasure of an excursus? With the consequence that his prose, like the *Arabian Nights*, is sometimes there to be enjoyed rather than investigated. That being said, it is obvious that he has pondered deeply the passages he comments on. For example, the way he summarizes the first twenty-six sections of the tenth *namaṭ* gives them a clear structure somehow lacking in Avicenna's text.[44]

Two principal elements of Avicenna's treatment of strange *(gharīb)* and extraordinary *(khāriq)* phenomena in the last *namaṭ* of the *Ishārāt* capture Ibn Taymiyya's attention. First, there is his distinction of three types "of strange affairs arising in the world of nature" and his linking them to three specific principles: (i) magic and, "even" *(bal)*, the miracles of the Prophets and the prodigies of the saints are a matter of psychic disposition;[45] (ii) white magic *(nīranjiyyāt)* is based on the properties of elementary bodies; (iii) talismans are to be explained by celestial forces having a particular relation to terrestrial bodies or souls with specific dispositions or states. The second element is Avicenna's selection of the following four feats as special powers of the "knowers" *(ʿārif)*: abstaining from food for a long time, having the bodily strength to perform particularly toilsome actions, informing of unknown matters by dreams or

---

44 See *infra*, p. 176–177 of the Arabic text. The lack of transparency of the *Ishārāt* is a feature of the book about which we have a complaint by the young noble Bahmanyār b. al-Marzubān himself for whom Avicenna had written it as a manual of philosophy, in Isfahān sometime between 415/1024 and Dhū l-Ḥijja 420 / Dec. 1029. In a letter to his famous mentor, Bahmanyār wrote: "I would also ask his munificence [i. e., Avicenna] to kindly facilitate the learning of the intermediate [student], so that he does not get annoyed by [speaking from behind] a veil, thus asks to be excused *(istaʿfā)* from [explaining] what remains [to be explained], while I get lost in the middle!" (Ibn Sīnā, *Mubāḥathāt*, VI, p. 145–146). In an earlier letter (Isfahān, March-April 421/1030) to his beloved student, Avicenna had indeed declared pursuing a pedagogical purpose when writing in a relatively opaque manner, i. e., "from behind a veil:" "What it was possible for me to uncover, I have done so, either openly or from behind a veil *(warāʾ ḥijāb)* in which there is a sort of stimulus *(taḥrīk)* and training *(tadrīb)*. What it was not possible for me [to uncover], I ask to be excused *(istaʿfā)* [for not uncovering it] and I acknowledge [it]. What is known by humans is indeed finite" (Ibn Sīnā, *Mubāḥathāt*, II, p. 5–54). In *Making* (p. 234–237), D. Reisman gave a completely wrong translation and interpretation of Bahmanyār's complaint and was thus unable to recognize in it an answer to Avicenna's letter of March-April 421/1030; see Y. Michot, *Riz*, p. 91–92.

45 The translations of this passage of the *Ishārāt* by Sh. Inati (*Mysticism*, p. 107) and A.-M. Goichon (*Directives*, p. 524) both ignore *bal* and therefore make the serious mistake of attaching miracles and the saints' prodigies to the second category of strange affairs distinguished by Avicenna.

otherwise, exercising an influence on the elements of the world as on one's own body.

For Ibn Taymiyya, Avicenna differs from other philosophers – he calls them "naturalists" *(ṭabī'ī)* – in that he is a "theologizing" *(ilāhī)* thinker affirming against them, on the basis of experience and truthful reports, the existence, not just the possibility, of a number of strange, extraordinary, things and phenomena, offering a typology of these and finding their causes in three different principles. The problem, the theologian-mufti adds, is however that the argument used by the Shaykh al-Ra'īs to invite naturalists to believe in the phenomena they deny can itself be turned against him about things which he himself seems to refuse as he does not mention them among the sources of unusual events, namely jinns, spirits, angels, demons, whose existence and actions are observed and reported in every human community. Avicenna's typology of strange phenomena and their causes is thus far too restrictive from two viewpoints: (i) keeping silent about many extraordinary existents that should also have been taken into account; (ii) limiting their causes to the three principles already mentioned. For Ibn Taymiyya, the restrictiveness of this approach results from mistakes of both epistemological and metaphysical nature. A particularly unacceptable aspect of the second viewpoint is the Shaykh al-Ra'īs' gross overestimation of the powers of the human soul by making it the cause of nothing less than magic, plus saintly prodigies, plus prophetic miracles. Aren't books of magic replete with references to the role of the spiritual beings attached to the planets in magical operations? Also, how could one not involve in all this the angels "administering the affairs of the sky, the earth, the clouds, the rain, etc."?

Ibn Taymiyya thereafter sees two problems in the way Avicenna presents the four feats mentioned above as special powers of the knowers. A first, serious, problem is the confusion which the philosopher, in the tenth *namaṭ*, entertains on the one hand between the knowers and the Prophets, on the other hand between the signs *(āya)* of the first and the miracles of the second, as if they formed one same continuum, or belonged to one same genus. For Ibn Taymiyya, the truth is rather that there are powers that exclusively belong to the Prophets and thus differ *generically* from the capacities of other humans, not just in intensity or scope. In other words, there is a generic peculiarity of prophethood that forbids diluting it into gnosis. As for the examples of extraordinary deeds of knowers which Avicenna gives in the tenth *namaṭ*, section xxv – from making rain fall to causing a plague, etc. –, for the theologian-mufti they belong in no way, despite appearances, to the genus of prophetic miracles. A second problem is that, once again, Avicenna unduly inflates the powers of the human soul to the detriment of the other effective agents of extraordinary events and things.

The limits which Ibn Taymiyya sets to psychologization in the explanation of signs, wonders, and other extraordinary phenomena and his doctrine of the generic difference of miracles are major components of the prophetology inspiring the ten viewpoints from which he then starts refuting Avicenna's idea that a human soul may dispose freely of other bodies than its own.

In viewpoint I, Ibn Taymiyya wonders what proof philosophers like Avicenna have that the influences they attribute to human souls on the elements effectively come from them rather than, for example, from jinns. Quoting the Qur'ān, he judges that "they follow nothing but an opinion…"

Viewpoint II presents the core of the Taymiyyan doctrine of the generic uniqueness of miracles. The signs of the knowers mentioned by Avicenna in the tenth *namaṭ*, section xxv, belong to a genus of affairs due to causes that are in no way unusual or extraordinary. As for the sea being parted into twelve parts, a rod being turned into a snake, the manna and the quail coming down, twelve springs gushing out from the rock, etc., these are signs of another genus, truly extraordinary phenomena, real miracles, belonging exclusively to Prophets. Although Avicenna does not mention them in the tenth *namaṭ*, Ibn Taymiyya does not liken him to the thinkers who purely and simply deny the existence of all types of strange things: he indeed accepted a species of the latter "and considered the prodigies and the miracles as being of that sort."

Viewpoint III in some sense completes viewpoint II. Coming back to the four feats presented at the beginning of the tenth *namaṭ* as special powers of the knowers, Ibn Taymiyya reaffirms that the "people" ready to explain their cause – he is probably thinking of Avicenna and his like – did not go further than that. As for the genus of the real miracles, exclusive to prophethood, they denied their possibility and they could not assign their cause "to the forces of the soul."

Viewpoint IV draws from the Qur'ān a long list of the real miracles which, according to Ibn Taymiyya, the philosophers and other intellectuals cannot link to any force in the created world, be they forces of the human soul or "any of the forces known in the world, superior and inferior." In order to explain many strange phenomena, there is no need to resort to anything other than ordinary natural causes – planetary conjunctions, active celestial forces, passive terrestrial ones, forces of the human soul and body, etc. What about the real miracles? For Ibn Taymiyya, they "diverge from the natural law" and only God's free will can explain them. A collateral theological benefit of accepting the reality of such miracles is to confirm that God is indeed a choosing and freely willing agent, not "one necessitating by essence." It similarly proves the possibility of the resurrection. As for attributing these real miracles to the forces of the soul, the theologian-mufti concludes, philosophers themselves acknowledge that it is not possible.

Viewpoint V deals with the "capacity to inform of unknown matters" considered by Avicenna a special power of the knowers. Ibn Taymiyya starts by acknowledging the reality of such uncoverings *(kashf)* of the soul. According to him, an individual's capacity to inform of unknown matters may nevertheless also have other causes, wicked, demonic or not, or angelic. Jinns speak by the tongue of epileptics or inform diviners; demonic spirits speak by the tongue of adepts of demonic rituals – be they Hindus, Mongol shamans or some types of Sufis –; angels inform Prophets. Contrary to the claims of some, demons and angels have a concrete existence outside of human souls, with the evil or righteous forces of which they cannot be identified. Angelic informing of the Prophets is of course the highest type of uncovering and the theologian-mufti blames the philosophers for not realizing how generically different it is from the other, inferior, types of *kashf* through which they approach it.

Viewpoint VI should be of great interest to anthropologists of Muslim religious practices under the Mamlūks. Referring to his own experiences as well as to reports from others, Ibn Taymiyya relates a number of extraordinary events orchestrated by jinns and demons: people being carried in the air over long distances, people dancing in the air during Sufi concerts, people receiving stolen food from demons, jinns informing some individuals about this or that, etc. As already alluded to *supra*, he even describes a Mongol shamanic séance. His only purpose, in all this, is to convince his reader that such "extraordinary phenomena are not due to the powers of the souls but, rather, to the action of the jinns" and the demons. To deny this would be foolish and, he adds, most of the philosophers are on this topic in agreement with the adepts of the various religions. Aren't a number of their books explicitly explaining how to benefit from the jinns or to tap the energy of the planets?

Viewpoint VII is only three lines long. It follows up on the previous one by adding to its survey of jinns-operated and demonic feats the well known collaboration that existed, in pre-Islamic Arabia, between the jinns and the diviners.

Viewpoint VIII, the longest of the ten, occupies more than twenty-five pages in M. R. Sālim's edition. At the beginning, Ibn Taymiyya turns the prophetology of philosophers whom he calls "Ṣābi'ans" and "esotericists" against those who claim that the prophetic miracles are due to powers of the human soul. His reasoning develops as follows: these philosophers consider the Prophets truthful; now, the Prophets have told us about the concrete, extra-mental, visible, existence of the angels and the jinns and about their informing humans concerning unknown matters or performing "actions outside of the power of mankind;" the prophetic reports are thus true and the achievements of the angels and jinns cannot be attributed to psychic powers of humans. To support his argument, the theologian-mufti feels it necessary to remind his reader of the prophetic reports he has in mind and he gives long quotes from the Qur'ān where they can be found. These quotes mostly relate to Abraham, Lot, Moses, Mary, and Muḥammad. Revisiting the Qur'ān in this way leads Ibn Taymiyya to make some quick remarks on topics like the correspondence between the Book and the Torah, or the question of Mary's prophethood. More importantly, it also leads him to reassess whole philosophical – often Avicennan – doctrines, particularly in metaphysics and cosmology, angelology and prophetology. He does so mostly in the light of the Qur'ān, from which he then quotes a number of other passages.

Here are the main points which he tackles: the angels involved in the process of revelation are neither faculties of the Prophet's soul (imagination, etc.), nor the heavenly souls and intelligences of the philosophers' cosmography; the first, unique, existent caused by God from which the philosophers make the rest of the creation emanate is an invention of their mind, without concrete reality in the outside; the angels and other creatures described in the Qur'ān as serving and fearing God cannot be likened to the intelligences "or, rather, the whole world," which the philosophers consider "generated from God through a preeternal, eternal, generative process *(tawallud)* necessarily accompanying His essence;" if the world was caused by God through such a process of generation, which is what the philosophers effectively say when they speak of emanation, God would have a partner, as "there is no generation except from two principles – philosophers are thus worse than those who give God an associate or a child;" what occurs in the world cannot "emanate from a complete, eternal cause;" the Throne is not the ninth celestial sphere and the angels, who are scripturally known to be "ranged in ranks," cannot be assimilated to the ten intelligences, who are not so; Gabriel is not the agent intellect (which, by the way, "has no wings") and he can indeed come down to the earth; the forces at work in the world are not exclusively psychic or natural, but also angelic; the philosophers cannot, simultaneously, affirm the perfect knowledge, piety, truthfulness, of the Prophets and claim that they do not inform people of the "true natures of things" for reasons of socio-political pragmatism; the philosophical concept of "holy force," or "holy faculty," *(quwwa qudsiyya)* is too narrow to encompass all the types of revelation, divine speaking, and inspiration, alluded to in the Qur'ān; the philosophers' concept of intercession does not correspond to the Islamic understanding of prophetic and angelic intercession; al-Ghazālī adopted the philosophers' prophetology, was therefore duly criticized by many scholars but eventually recanted his errors. So, whereas philosophers find in the revealed scripture images of the views they develop independently from it, Ibn Taymiyya reads the Qur'an literally, notably its angelology, and therefore judges such philosophical interpretations seriously inadequate.

To conclude this eighth viewpoint, Ibn Taymiyya highlights its major inputs: a properly Islamic angelology, a confirmation that the philosophers' theology, angelology and prophetology contradict the Scriptures, an invalidation of their doctrine assimilating miracles to forces of the human soul. Possibly afraid to be misunderstood about this last input, he directly adds: "We nevertheless do not deny that the forces that are in the souls and the rest of the bodies have some effects in the world commensurate with them, but to relate the extraordinary phenomena to that" would be as vain as assimilating them to some sort of white magic *(nīrānjiyyāt)*.

Viewpoint IX makes an argument that holds in the following syllogism: for a soul to have an influence, it needs to be there, living, conscious, willing and acting; now, a number of extraordinary phenomena linked to the Prophets take place without them being conscious of them, before their birth, or after their death; such phenomena can thus not be explained by forces of the prophetic souls. In order to establish the minor premise, Ibn Taymiyya examines a number of such extraordinary phenomena. From the time preceding the birth of Muḥammad, the theologian-mufti brings up the three following "prodigies of the Prophet:" the failure of the attack of the people of the elephant against Mecca, the information given by jinns to diviners about his prophethood, the passages of the Jewish and Christian scriptures announcing his coming.

The people of the elephant attacking Mecca[46]

The prodigious nature of the Ka'ba, with the veneration it commands and its unparalleled appeal since Abraham built it, "thousands of years ago," is even more impressive. For Ibn Taymiyya, who then writes beautiful things, there is in the Ka'ba-prodigy something which is "outside of the power of mankind, of the

46 Popular lithograph, Tunis, Maṭba'at al-Manār, *c.* 1975 (author's collection).

forces of their souls and bodies," including those of the Prophets, as well as "outside of the gauge of the intellects and the canons of the sciences" of all the baffled philosophers, astrologers and naturalists who have tried to explain it, sometimes by means of the most fanciful elucubrations. Considering, for example, the Kaʿba as some kind of talisman designed by Abraham does not make sense for a number of reasons which the theologian-mufti expounds. To sum up, just as the Kaʿba-prodigy cannot be explained by human forces, it is not the effect of "forces of the natural bodies, nor of the astral forces mixed with elementary forces. It is rather an affair outside of all this." That being said, the Qur'ān reports that Abraham prayed God for Mecca.[47] It could thus be argued that by doing so he was at the origin of the Kaʿba-prodigy or, in other words, that the latter was somehow influenced by his soul. Ibn Taymiyya imagines such an objection and answers it by clarifying the respective parts played by humans and God in an answered invocation. In this case, acknowledging that "extraordinary phenomena happen by God answering invocations" does in no way mean that it is simply the force of the soul of the invoker which disposes freely and independently of the world.

As for extraordinary phenomena, unexplainable by psychic powers, either human or prophetic, that followed the death of Muḥammad, Ibn Taymiyya mentions first the preservation of the Qur'ān and of Islamic Law *(sharīʿa)* longer than any royal or philosophical laws; then the spontaneous love and veneration hearts had for the Prophet through the centuries, as well as their knowledge of his august status; finally, "the cursing and hatred put by God in the hearts of the believers toward the unbelievers and their followers." Similar prodigies, he adds, had of course already been witnessed in relation to earlier Prophets, as mentioned in a number of Qur'ānic verses which he quotes.

Viewpoint X explores the nature of prophethood in relation to what philosophers and some theologians say about it. Quoting a number of Qur'ānic verses, Ibn Taymiyya has no difficulty acknowledging to the Prophet God-given "eminent qualities, beautiful traits, noble morals" and some special psychic powers that "are causes of extraordinary phenomena by which God honours him and which are miracles and prodigies." This being so, he feels it necessary to finely tune his ideas about three points. First, these prophetic qualities and psychic powers are not the cause of "*all* the extraordinary phenomena" reported about the Prophets. Second, prophethood does not consist in these qualities and psychic forces alone. The three properties defining prophethood according to the philosophers are true, but prophethood cannot be limited to possessing these three properties. Third, prophethood is not something humans can acquire by their own endeavour *(iktisāb)*. Wrong is thus the philosophers' idea that pre-

47 See Qur'ān, *Ibrāhīm* – xiv, 35.

paredness through self-purification is enough to receive, automatically, a flow of knowledge from some "agent intellect just as the rays flow on a polished mirror when it is cleansed and the sun is faced by it." In reality, it is God's will and power that make prophethood appear, through revelation. Hence the criticisms often addressed to partisans of the doctrine of "acquirable prophethood" like al-Ghazālī, Ibn Qasī, Ibn 'Arabī and Ibn Sab'īn; even more so when they start claiming some superiority over the Prophets.

The ten viewpoints developed by Ibn Taymiyya against Avicenna cover far more ground than just the ideas of the Shaykh al-Ra'īs and offer a good illustration of the breadth of interests, depth of exploration of Islamic thought – philosophical and other –, Qur'ānic literacy, and loose methodology, that give a very particular, unconventional, character to his commentary of the tenth *namaṭ* of the *Ishārāt.* He himself does of course not present these pages as a commentary and, when one considers them as such, it becomes difficult to decide where such a commentary precisely ends in the flowing text of the *Ṣafadiyya.* "This is the amount of writing which these sheets of paper have capacity for to answer this question." The nature of the question alluded to in this sentence appearing on p. 236 of M. R. Sālim's edition is a mystery. This sentence could even raise puzzling questions about the composition of the *Ṣafadiyya* as a book. For the present article, it nevertheless provides a useful point where to end our translation.

Where Ibn Taymiyya ends his tenth viewpoint is also unclear, and the decision we took thereabout by dividing the translation into two new sections might have been arbitrary. These last two sections of the translation may however, in some sense, serve as concluding remarks on his part. The theologian-mufti starts the first of these two sections with a strong judgement: people considering the prophetology of the philosophers faithful to the Qur'ān must inevitably be either ignorants or hypocrites. Reviewing the various groups forming the society of his time, religious and profane, he finds many people ignoring both "the perfection of prophethood and messengership" and the true nature of the affirmations of the philosophers. Quoting the Qur'ān, he invites them not to renegade Islām. As for the hypocrites, they are free-thinkers deceiving the believers. Sometimes, things might be more complicated and Ibn Taymiyya also speaks of people who do not really intend to be free-thinkers or hypocrites, are venerating the Prophet but are themselves, out of ignorance, misguided by the philosophers' prophetology. Approaching once again the matter from a sociological angle somehow foreshadowing Ibn Khaldūn, he explains the appearing of a great number of such people by what he calls "places of religious lukewarmness" *(amākin al-fatarāt)* where the traces of prophethood are weak," as is the case under regimes of the Age of Ignorance like the Fāṭimids in Avicenna's time or, in his own time, under the Mongols. As God does not expect more from anyone than what they can deliver, the theologian-mufti thereafter writes that He will forgive whomever, among these misguided people, will have done his best to have faith in the Messenger, even if what such a person then says would have to be considered unbelief from the point of view of orthodoxy once he would be informed of the latter.

These theological explanations might not appeal to Avicennan scholars specializing in commentaries on the *Ishārāt.* For a history of the Shaykh al-Ra'īs' impact on later Islamic thought, these explanations are however of great value. Implicitly but nevertheless obviously, it is indeed people like Avicenna, or al-Ghazālī, who are their object. Now, what they imply is that, despite the strong condemnation by which Ibn Taymiyya began his fatwa[48] and despite the serious objections he formulates against many of their views, he is ready to find excuses for their shortcomings and speaks of God forgiving their like! To the Taymiyyan specialist, this theology of mercy commanded by historical realism does not come as a surprise. The leniency which the theologian-mufti now shows about well-intentioned but theologically deficient philosophizers is the same one which he displays in other texts or fatwas concerning the Mamlūks and their military music, the Qalandars and their antinomianism, the Rāfiḍīs and their extremist views.[49] For each of these groups, following what he calls his "*Rule for Accusing of Unbelief*," he considers that the general condemnations he is expected to pronounce as a jurist cannot be applied to particular cases except by also fulfilling two conditions: first, having all the reasons to apply such general judgements to these cases; second, and more importantly, having refuted all the objections against applying them in these particular instances. To justify this position, Ibn Taymiyya repeatedly speaks of times or places "of religious lukewarmness," where almost no trace is left of the prophetic teachings, or quotes, as he does in this passage of the *Ṣafadiyya*, the *ḥadīth* of God's pardon to a man doubting of His power to resuscitate and punish him if his children incinerated his body after his death.

The last section of the pages of the *Ṣafadiyya* translated in this article starts with the typically Taymiyyan phrase: "What is aimed at here is…" As if he feared having drifted too far from his main subject, the theologian-mufti comes back to his assessment of philosophical prophetology in the tenth viewpoint. Appraising elsewhere the views of the Mu'tazilīs and the Ash'arīs concerning the divine attributes and human agency, he judges them right in what they affirm and wrong in what they deny. Using the same criterion here, he judges the philosophers right in what they say of "the confirmed eminent qualities of the Prophets" and wrong in what they do not acknowledge: God's power and will to create what He wants of

48 See the text translated *supra*, p. 118–121.
49 See Y. Michot, *Mamlūks*; *Extremisms*, p. 34–82.

extraordinary phenomena, the existence and actions of the angels, the jinns, etc, the *generic* difference separating the Prophets from the "knowers" of the *Ishārāt*'s last *namaṭs*. The philosophers are also right to speak of the presence of a form of prophethood among some eminent people who are not Prophets, through dreams or otherwise. This is indeed acknowledged in various authentic prophetic traditions mentioning "parts" of prophethood and "branches" of faith which Ibn Taymiyya quotes. Moreover, according to his wife 'Ā'isha, Muḥammad's career as a Prophet started with "a right dream vision in his sleep." Between a part and the whole of prophethood there is however, for the theologian-mufti, a *generic* discontinuity that obliges him to reiterate his total refusal of the view that prophethood could simply be acquired through some human effort. This being so, Ibn Taymiyya finally writes, what the philosophers "mention in the matter of vain things is to be thrown back at them. It is clear, the miracles of the Prophets are outside of the psychic and natural forces existing in the world, superior and inferior. It is also clear, God is the Creator of everything by His will and His power, and He creates what He wills by the causes which He makes occur, for the wise purpose which He wills."

Three remarks will conclude this presentation of Ibn Taymiyya's commentary on the *Ishārāt*'s last *namaṭ*.

When looking at the history of classical Islamic thought, some modern scholars speak of two main, clearly distinct, trends: philosophical research on the one hand, mythological religious narratives on the other. In such a divided ideological landscape, where does a work like Avicenna's *Ishārāt* belong? Written by a *faylasūf*, it indeed became, as noticed by Ibn Taymiyya, a sort of "Holy Book" *(muṣḥaf)* among philosophers. More precisely, the Shaykh' al-Ra'īs' distinction of three types of strange phenomena, his linking of the prophetic miracles and the saints's prodigies to magic and, especially, his psychologization of prophethood with its three properties soon acquired a religious-like authoritativeness. As for Ibn Taymiyya, his weltanschauung was even more deeply marked by *merveilleux* than that of Avicenna: his God's action was not bound by any natural law and spirits, jinns, angels and demons were omnipresent actors in his universe. This being so, there are more questions, doubts *(shukūk)*, both theological and philosophical, in the pages of his *Ṣafadiyya* concerning the last *namaṭ* of the *Ishārāt* than in the Avicennan text itself. A philosopher is not always immune from narratives of a religious-like mythological type and inquisitive research can very well be conducted by a theologian-mufti.

As alluded to earlier on, Ibn Taymiyya's relationship to Avicenna is a love-hate one. In his commentary on the last part of the *Ishārāt*, this relationship is also affected by a serious misunderstanding of the Shaykh al-Ra'īs conception of man. For the philosopher, the human soul is constrainted despite appearing having a choice: *"Al-nafs muḍṭarra fī ṣūra mukhtāra."*[50] "All our actions, our wills and the dispositions we take are by a divine decree *(qadar)* and we are coerced *(mujbar)*."[51] From some viewpoint *(bi-wajh mā)*, man is a *Cogito* and an agent in the world; in reality however *(fī l-ḥaqīqa)*, his thoughts and actions are less his than God's, through a long chain of secondary causes of course, but essentially in a manner reminiscent of the Ash'arite monism of divine agency. When, commenting on the *Ishārāt* in the *Ṣafadiyya*, Ibn Taymiyya repeatedly accuses Avicenna of attributing too much power to the human soul in his explanation of miracles and other extraordinary phenomena, it is as if this soul was some kind of autonomous principle, independent from God, which is in no way a fair representation of the Shaykh al-Ra'īs' psychology. This being so, paradoxically, there seems to be more religion in the philosopher's view of man and, if the word involves less dependence on the divine, more humanism in the theologian-mufti's approach.

Like many ulema of his time, Avicenna got interested in magic, some prodigies and miracles, white magic and talismans. By attempting to provide a philosophical explanation of their reality, did he himself contribute to the rise of obscurantism and occultism in later Muslim societies? And what about Ibn Taymiyya who expected the philosophers to take into account an even broader spectrum of extraordinary phenomena, like generically different prophetic feats and wonders operated by jinns, demons, and angels? Also, if the rise of occultism played a role in drawing away later Muslim societies from properly facing the challenges of history, were the responsibilities of the philosopher and the theologian-mufti much different? Rather than trying to answer here these complex, and possibly controversial, questions, I would prefer to highlight a fact of cultural history that should not trigger any dispute: the striking similarity of some of the extraordinary phenomena interesting both Ibn Taymiyya and Avicenna with those we are repeatedly told about, and entertained with, by Scheherezade in the *Arabian Nights*. For example, jinns bringing food to people or carrying them in the air to distant places feature in *Aladdin's Lamp* as well as in Ibn Taymiyya's commentary. And how to explain Ali Baba's "Open , O sesame!" except by the psychic force freely disposing of the hylè of the world theorized by Avicenna in his prophetology? This being so, the time has now come to let the Damascene theologian-mufti tell us his own tale…

50 Ibn Sīnā, *Ta'līqāt*, p. 53, trans. Michot, *Réfutation*, p. 71*, no 10.

51 Ibn Sīnā, *Ta'līqāt*, p. 131, trans. Michot, *Réfutation*, p. 66*, no 5. See also the other Avicennan texts translated in Y. Michot, *Réfutation*, p. 61*–71*.

Translation[52]

[Avicenna's restrictive approach to strange things and extraordinary phenomena]

Avicenna sealed his *Ishārāt* by saying:

> • Strange *(gharīb)* affairs arise in the world of nature from three principles. One of them is the psychic[53] disposition. The second is the properties of the elementary bodies, for example the fact that the magnet attracts iron by a force *(quwwa)* which is special to it. The third one is a celestial force *(quwwa)*[54] between which and the complexions of terrestrial bodies with special position-related dispositions, or between which and the forces *(quwwa)* of terrestrial souls with special astral[55] states – active or passive – there is a correspondence[56] demanding to be followed[57] by the occurrence of strange effects *(athar)*.[58]

He [then] said:

> • Magic is of the first category, and even *(bal)* the miracles and the prodigies [of the saints]. The operations of white magic[59] are of the second category. The talismans are of the third category.[60]

[Avicenna] thus claimed that the causes of extraordinary phenomena *(khāriq al-'āda)* in this world are these three causes: either the psychic forces *(quwwa)*, or the bodily elementary forces *(quwwa)*, or the astral forces *(quwwa)* [together] with the bodily or psychic forces *(quwwa)*. **[166]**

He did not mention any proof of [the validity of] this denial [of other causes] and he has no proof of it. Now, it is incumbent upon the denier to provide the proof [of the validity of his denial] just as it is incumbent upon the affirming one to provide the proof [of the validity of his affirmation]. He says:

> • The stupidity *(khurq)* that there would be in you calling a lie something of which the wisdom[61] has not become evident would not be less than the stupidity that there would be in you assenting to something[62] of which the evidence has not arisen before you.[63]

---

52 Ibn Taymiyya, *Ṣafadiyya*, vol. i, p. 165–236.

53 al-nafsiyya **Ṣ** : al-nafsāniyyat al-madhkūra **F** *the [above-]mentioned psychic*

54 quwwa **Ṣ** : quwā **F** *is celestial forces*

55 falakī **Ṣ** : malakī **F** *angelic*

56 munāsabat^{un} + **F** : infi'āliyya **Ṣ**

57 tastatbi'u **Ṣ** : tastabi'u **F**

58 Ibn Sīnā, *Ishārāt*, X, xxx, ed. Forget, p. 221, l. 8–13 (trans. Inati, *Mysticism*, p. 106–107; trans. Goichon, *Directives*, p. 523–524).

59 al-nīranjiyyāt **Ṣ** : al-nīranjāt **F**. On the various meanings of this term and the diversity of operations it covers, see T. Fahd, *EI2*, art. *Nīrandj*; Ch. Burnett, *Ṯābit*, p. 17.

60 Ibn Sīnā, *Ishārāt*, X, xxx, ed. Forget, p. 221, l. 13–15 (mistaken trans. Inati, *Mysticism*, p. 107; mistaken trans. Goichon, *Directives*, p. 524).

61 ḥikmatu-hu **Ṣ** : la-ka ba'du jaliyyatu-hu **F** *the clarity has not yet become evident to you*

62 mā **Ṣ** : bi-mā **F**

This [denying of other causes] is like their denying of the jinns and the angels. It is imperative that these people furnish the proof of [the validity of] their denying. Now they have no proof [of it]! They nevertheless call a lie what they have no comprehensive knowledge of and that whose interpretation has not[64] reached them. This is however among the things which it would be appropriate to know. What these people rely on, in their corrupted restrictive approach *(ḥaṣr)*, is denying [things] and calling [them] lies, without any knowledge at all.

Moreover we – ourselves and others than us – know the vain nature of such a restrictive approach, for having witnessed [it], from abundantly recurrent reports, and by the proofs providing certainty. [We know] that many affairs happen in this world [that result] from other rational living [beings] than the souls of the sons of Adam, from other [things] than the elementary bodies and from other things than the astral sphere and its forces *(quwwa)*.

Avicenna mentioned the possibility of that which, of the strange things,[65] he assented to, when he spoke about establishing [the existence of] the extraordinary phenomena according to the principles of his brothers the philosophers who claim that the Originator of the world is necessitating *(mūjib)* by an essence having neither power *(qudra)* nor will and that the splitting of the astral spheres is impossible, as well as the changing of this world. Those [philosophers] indeed call lies – or many of them call lies – many of the strange things that Avicenna and his like acknowledge: the theologizing ones *(al-ilāhiyyūn)* among the philosophers acknowledge many affairs that the naturalists *(al-ṭabīʿiyyūn)* among them deny.

When [Avicenna] mentioned the possibility of that which, of the strange things, he assented to, and mentioned the proof of [**167**] its possibility according to the principles of his brothers, he said:

> • Know that what is said of these [strange] things, as well as the testimonies given about them, are not[66] just possibility-related opinions to which one is led by matters rational only – even though that would be something reliable if it was taking place. These [strange things], rather, are [the object of] experiences *(tajriba)* [which are such that], when they are evident,[67] their causes are sought. One of the happy things[68] that happen to the lovers of intelligence *(istibṣār)* is that such states occur to them in themselves or that they observe them time after time in others. This is thus an experience, as far as

63 Ibn Sīnā, *Ishārāt*, X, xxxi, ed. Forget, p. 221, l. 17–19 (trans. Inati, *Mysticism*, p. 107; trans. Goichon, *Directives*, p. 524).

64 lam : lammā Ṣ

65 imkān mā ṣaddaqa bi-hi min al-gharā'ib + : sīnā Ṣ. I correct this obvious lacuna on the basis of the last line of p. 166 (the first line of the next paragraph).

66 laysa Ṣ : sabīl + F *Know that the way to speak of these [strange] things, as well as the testimonies given about them, are not*

67 buyyinat Ṣ : thubbitat F *established*

68 al-saʿādāt F : al-ʿādāt Ṣ *the habits*

establishing [the existence of] an amazing affair is concerned, so that it is a proof[69] and invites to search for its cause. And when it is clear, the benefit from it is complete;[70] the soul becomes certain of the existence of these causes, the estimative [faculty] submits and does not oppose the intellect concerning what the latter appreciates doing or seeing[71] of [these things], and this is among the most enormous[72] benefits and the major preoccupations. Myself, if I was telling the particular [aspects] of this sort [of affairs] concerning things which we have observed and concerning things related by people who have spoken to us about it,[73] talking would become too long. [Moreover], to someone not assenting to a summary it would also be of little importance, [a fortiori], not to assent[74] to the detailed presentation![75]

This is what [Avicenna] said. It is evident that what[76] he mentioned of the causes of strange things like[77] informing about unknown matters *(mughayyabāt)*, he did not mention it because of this simply being a possible opinion, whose possibility would be known by means of rational proofs but, rather, due to the fact that such strange things are known through observation [**168**] and by truthful information, their causes being then sought. Now, this shall identically be said to him concerning what others than him [also] know to be established through observation and by truthful informations [whereas he denies it]. Some people have observed the existence of the jinns and seen them as living rational [beings] distinct from humans; or this is established for them by truthful informations; or, of the proofs providing certainty, they know something that proves it, just as whomever God wills knows that. They therefore know with certainty that the jinns are not psychic forces *(quwwa)* and they know that, among the strange things, there are some that result from the actions of the jinns and from the informations which they provide.

69 li-yakūna ḥujjat^an Ṣ : la-hu kawn wa ṣiḥḥa F *affair having a reality, an authenticity, and something inviting to*
70 ḥasamat Ṣ : jussimat F *magnified*
71 qaddara fi'la-hu aw ru'yā-hu Ṣ : yarba'u rab'a-hu F *latter esteems highly of*
72 ajamm Ṣ : ajsam F *greatest*
73 ḥaddatha-nā-hu Ṣ : ṣaddaqnā-hu F *people whom we deemed credible*
74 ayḍ^an an lā yuṣaddiqa Ṣ : an lā yuṣaddiqa ayḍ^an F *would be of little importance, [a fortiori], not to assent also to*
75 Ibn Sīnā, *Ishārāt*, X, xxiv, ed. Forget, p. 218, l. 9–219, l. 2 (trans. Inati, *Mysticism*, p. 103–104; trans. Goichon, *Directives*, p. 519). Both Inati and Goichon mistranslate the beginning of this paragraph.
76 mā : inna-mā Ṣ
77 ka-l-ikhbār : al-ikhbār Ṣ

Jinn, Demon (Iblīs), Angel[78]

[What about the jinns, the angels, the demons?]

This is a matter which is well known to all the communities – the Arabs, the Turks,[79] the Indians, etc. The affairs abundantly reported in the [various] communities about the diviners *(kāhin)* are too many to be numbered. Also, what we have known in our time – people whom the jinns carry and make fly in the air, for whom they steal [different] species of food (sweets, etc.) which they bring to them, and whom they inform of some matters unknown to them – these are many affairs[80] which it would be too long to describe in this section *(bāb)*. As for the affair of the angels, it is more sublime, more august, and the informations [given by] them are abundantly reported among the people of the Books, whereas their effects in the world are known through seeing with one's own eyes *(muʿāyana)* and observation.

The allegation of whoever, after that, alleges that the miracles, the prodigies and magic are psychic forces *(quwwa)* is thus among the vainest of the vain [affirmations]. Much magic is indeed [performed] by the demons, as God Most High said: "They followed that which the demons uttered against Solomon's

78 Right: *Angel*, detail from a miniature of the MS Munich, Bayerische Staatsbibliothek, Cod. ar 464, of Zakariyyā' b. Muḥammad AL-QAZWĪNĪ (d. 682/1283), *ʿAjā'ib al-makhlūqāt wa gharā'ib al-mawjūdāt*, fol. 36 r. (Iraq, 679/1280). Centre: *Iblīs*, detail from a miniature of the MS Paris, Bibliothèque Nationale, Suppl. turc 242, of Sayyid Muḥammad b. Amīr Ḥasan AL-SUʿŪDĪ, *Maṭāliʿ al-saʿāda wa yanābiʿ al-siyāda*, fol. 89 v. (Turkey, 990/1582). Left: *Jinn*, detail from a caricature showing Aladdin's lamp by the contemporary Palestinian Hishām Shamālī; see *http://www.ejaaba.com/490774*.

79 I.e., the Mongols.

80 fa-umūr : bi-umūr Ṣ

reign. Yet Solomon did not disbelieve, but the demons disbelieved, teaching people magic. Nothing was sent down *(wa mā unzila)*[81] to the two kings[82] at Babylon, Hārūt and Mārūt, and these two did not teach anyone until they had said: 'We are only a temptation; therefore do not disbelieve!' From these two, people would learn things by which they would cause a split between a man and his wife. They would however not harm anyone thereby except with God's permission. They would also learn things that would harm them and not benefit them; though they surely knew that he who bought that would have no share in the Hereafter. Surely, evil is that for which they sold their souls; had they known!"[83] **[169]**

The books of magic are replete with oaths and incantations against the jinns, appealing to their masters, whom they revere. This is also why humans were seeking refuge with the jinns, as God Most High said: "Indeed there were individuals among the humans who used to take refuge with individuals among the jinns; they thus increased them in folly."[84] Humans used to say, when an individual among them stopped over in a wadi: "I take refuge with the lord of this wadi from its fools." God thus sent down this verse.[85] Also, the Prophet, God bless

81 The three words following "magic" in the Qur'ānic verse *al-Baqara* – ii, 102 are usually translated "and that which was sent down;" see for example S. H. NASR (ed.), *Study Quran*, p. 48. The translation favoured here is based on the grammatical possibility of *mā* being a negation rather than a pronoun, as indicated by F. D. AL-RĀZĪ, *Tafsīr*, vol. iii, p. 218. This choice gives the verse a much clearer sense, based on three successive negations aimed at insisting on God's condemnation of the satanic nature of magic: Solomon did not disbelieve… Nothing was sent down… These two did not teach anyone until… Nothing is said about the matter in S. H. NASR (ed.), *Study Quran*, p. 48. Why this more transparent understanding of the verse didn't become the most widely accepted one would however be worth an investigation. Here, it is not possible to know how Ibn Taymiyya himself understood the verse.

82 Translations usually have "the two angels" *(al-malakayn)*; see for example S. H. NASR (ed.), *Study Quran*, p. 48. It is however "authentically recorded (see Ṭabarī, Zamakhsharī, Baghawī, Rāzī, etc.) that the great Companion of the Prophet, Ibn 'Abbās, as well as several learned men of the next generation – e. g., al-Ḥasan al-Baṣrī, Abu 'l-Aswad and Aḍ-Ḍaḥḥāk – read […] *malikayn* ('the two kings')" (M. ASAD, *Message*, p. 21, n. 83). This reading does not involve angels in the teaching of magic and thus fits better with the general aim of the verse as explained in the preceding footnote. The three remarks ending this preceding footnote are also valid here. On Hārūt and Mārūt, see G. VAJDA, *EI2*, art. *Hārūt wa-Mārūt*; W. M. BRINNER, *EQ*, art. *Hārūt and Mārūt*.

83 Qur'ān, *al-Baqara* – ii, 102. Ibn Taymiyya only quotes the first part of this verse and adds: "to the end of the verse."

84 Qur'ān, *al-Jinn* – lxxii, 6.

85 See IBN KATHĪR, *Tafsīr*, vol. iv, p. 429: "I.e., we, [the jinns], thought that we had [some] proeminence over the humans because they used to take refuge with us when they stopped over in a wadi or in a desolate place in the desert, etc. It was indeed the custom of the Arabs, in the age of their ignorance, to take refuge with the lord of the jinns of that place so that they would not hit them with something that would hurt them. Likewise, each of the [Arabs] used to enter the country of his enemies in the vicinity of a great man, under his protection and

him and grant him peace, used to seek refuge for al-Ḥasan and al-Ḥusayn, saying: "I seek refuge for you both, with the perfect words of God, from every demon and vermin, and from every evil eye."[86] [The Prophet] thus made a distinction between the demon, vermin and the eyes of humans. This, correspondingly, proves the existence of harm from these three viewpoints: the humans, the jinns, and vermin.

The Most High said: "That is how for every Prophet We appointed an enemy: the demons from among the humans and the jinns, who reveal flowery sayings to each other, deceptively."[87] The Most High also said: "Say: 'I take refuge with the Lord of mankind, the King of mankind, the God of mankind, from the evil of the sneaking whisperer who whispers in the breasts of mankind, of the jinns and mankind.'"[88] [God] thus commanded [the Prophet] to seek refuge from the evil of the whisperer of the jinns and mankind, who whispers in the breasts of mankind. **[170]**

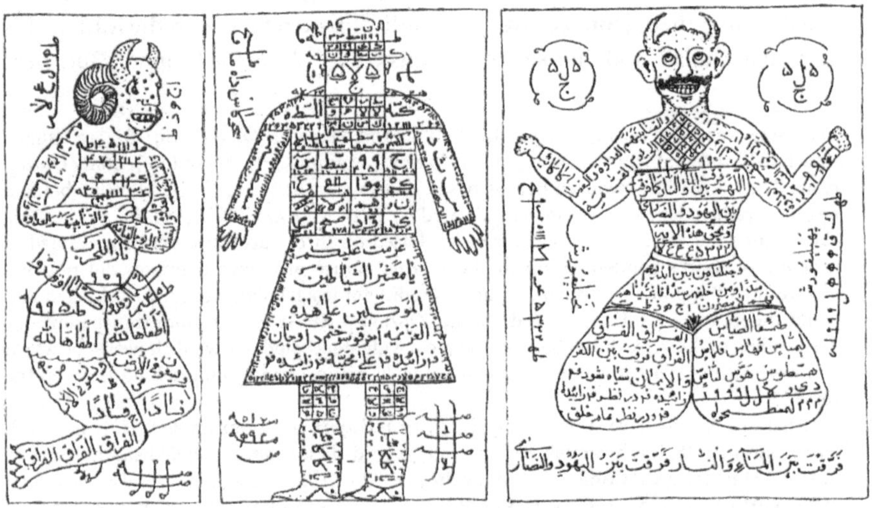

Three amulets with demons[89]

guardianship. So, when the jinns saw the humans taking refuge with them because of their fright of them, they increased them in folly, i.e., in fright, terror, and panic, with the consequence that they remained more frightened than them and took even more refuge with them."

86 See AL-BUKHĀRĪ, *Ṣaḥīḥ*, *Anbiyā'*, vol. iv, p. 147; ABŪ DĀ'ŪD, *Sunan*, *Sunna*, vol. iv, p. 235, no 4737; IBN ḤANBAL, *Musnad*, vol. i, p. 236; IBN MĀJA, *Sunan*, *Ṭibb*, vol. ii, p. 1164–1165, no 3525.

87 Qur'ān, *al-An'ām* – vi, 112.

88 Qur'ān, *al-Nās* – cxiv. Ibn Taymiyya only quotes the first verse of this *sūra* and adds : "to its end."

89 From ṬUMṬUM AL-HINDĪ, *Ṭelesmāt*, p. 37, 44, 88.

In His Book, God informed [us] of His address to the Jinns and of the command[s] and prohibition[s] He gave them. So He said: "O company of jinns and humans! Did there not come to you messengers from yourselves?"[90] The Most High also said: "O company of jinns and humans! If you are able to pass through the confines of the heavens and the earth, then do pass through. But you will not pass through except with [some] power *(sulṭān).*"[91] He also said: "And when we dispatched toward you a group of the jinns listening to the Qur'ān. When they were in its presence they said: 'Be silent!' When the [recitation] was over, they went back to their people as warners. They said: 'O our people! Indeed we have heard a Book which has been sent down after Moses, confirming what was before it. It guides toward the Real and to a straight road. O our people! Respond to God's summoner and believe in him. He will forgive you [some] of your sins and shelter you from a painful punishment.'"[92] And He said: "Say: 'It has been revealed to me that a group of the jinns listened [to the Qur'ān], and said: 'Indeed we heard a wonderful Qur'ān…'''"[93]

And if we ourselves were to mention what we have seen and heard of the states of the jinns – their states with the righteous believers and their states with the adepts of lying and depravity –, it would be speaking too long. God Most High thus so said: "Shall I inform you on whom the demons descend? They descend on every sinful falsifier. They eavesdrop and most of them are liars."[94]

[God's power, causality, and magic]

Those people restricted existence and its causes to what they knew and they did not have any knowledge of the inexistence *(intifā')* of that which they knew not. The ultimate point one of them [reached] was to deny a thing because of the inexistence of a precise *(mu'ayyan)* proof. Now, this is ultimate ignorance! They are ignorants from two points of view: one of the two is the absence *('adam)* of knowledge of many of the species of existents and of their states; the second is the absence of knowledge of the causes of the things happening *(ḥādith).* As they did not establish the power *(qudra)* of the Lord to change the world and denied His will by which the things happening happen, they came to reject the occurrence of

90 Qur'ān, *al-An'ām* – vi, 130.

91 Qur'ān, *al-Raḥmān* – lv, 33.

92 Qur'ān, *al-Aḥqāf* – xlvi, 29–31. The edition only quotes the beginning of verse 29 and the end of verse 31, with, in between, the self-contradictory indication: "to the end of the *sūra*, until He says."

93 Qur'ān, *al-Jinn* – lxxii, 1. Ibn Taymiyya only quotes the beginning of the first verse of this *sūra* and adds : "to the end of the *sūra.*"

94 Qur'ān, *al-Shu'arā'* – xxvi, 221–223.

extraordinary phenomena *(kharq al-ʿādāt)*. In order to [171] establish [the existence of] strange things *(gharāʾib)*, they therefore needed to make them happen according to that vain law *(qānūn)*. This is why we expounded the corrupt nature of the principle upon which they built their doctrine, i. e., the fact that the world is generated *(mutawallad)* from a cause *(ʿilla)* necessitating *(mūjib)* by essence, necessarily entailing *(mustalzim)* its effect *(maʿlūl)*. If indeed this principle is vain, vain is their claim that the things happening do not come to be except by these causes and it is possible that God is the one who makes them happen by His will and His power *(qudra)*, Praised and Exalted is He, even if what He wills and creates comes to be by causes which He creates and with a wise purpose *(ḥikma)* which He wills, Praised and Exalted is He.

Among the things making evident their ignorance in their restrictive approach and the corrupted nature[95] of what they mention – i. e., that the causes of the miracles, the prodigies and magic are psychic forces *(quwwa)* –, there is the fact that they are in error about the agent of magic. Their error about the agent of the miracles and the prodigies is, a fortiori, more serious.

Indeed, the people of knowledge about magic are agreed about that, [the agent of] magic is not simply the forces *(quwwa)* of the soul as [Avicenna] mentioned. Rather, the magicians seek help from spirits linked to them. The books of magic inherited from the Kasdaeans[96] *(kashdāniyyūn)*, the Indians, the Greeks, the Copts and other communities are replete with mentions [172] of that; for example the books of Ṭumṭum[97] the Indian and of Tinkalūshā[98] the Babylonian, the books of Thābit b. Qurra,[99] Abū Maʿshar al-Balkhī[100] and the others who com-

95 fasād : anna Ṣ

96 See Ibn Kathīr, *Bidāya*, vol. i, p. 132: "Abraham was not born in Ḥarrān. His birth took place in the land of the Chaldeans *(kaldāniyyūn)*, i. e., the land of Babylon and what surrounds it. Then they moved toward the land of the Cananeans *(kanʿāniyyūn)*, i. e., the regions of Jerusalem. They then settled in Ḥarrān, which was in that time the land of the Kasdaeans *(kashdāniyyūn)*, and similarly also the land of High Mesopotamia *(al-jazīra)* and Syria. They were worshipping the seven planets." On the Kasdaeans, see also the text translated in n. 102 and Y. Michot, *Textes N.S. XI*, p. 2, n. 5.

97 The identity of Ṭumṭum al-Hindī is unclear; see M. Ullmann, *Natur*, p. 298–299, 381. A number of astrological and magical treatises are attributed to him, some of whom are still reprinted today, e. g., *The Indian Talismans, the Subjugation of Spiritual Beings and the Secrets of Incenses*; see Ṭumṭum al-Hindī, *Ṭalāsim, Ṭelesmāt.*

98 Tinkalūshā – from Tinkalūs, or Ṭīnqarūs, etc. – al-Bābilī, i. e., pseudo-Teukros of Babylon (the Egyptian Memphis; d. first century before, or after, 0 CE?), author of a *Treatise on the Configurations of the Degrees of the Ecliptic and the Indications they Give Concerning the Situations of those Born under Them (Ṣuwar daraj al-falak wa mā tadullu ʿalay-hi min aḥwāl mawlūdīn bi-hā)*; see M. Ullmann, *Natur*, p. 278–279, 329–330.

99 Abū l-Ḥasan Thābit b. Qurra b. Zahrūn (Ḥarrān, 221/836 – Baghdād, 288/901), mathematician, astronomer, physician and philosopher; see R. Rashed & R. Morelon, *EI2*, art. *Thābit b. Ḳurra.* To him is attributed an important treatise on talismanic magic, mostly known through two twelfth century Latin versions as *Liber Prestigiorum Elbidis secundum*

posed in this field. Abū 'Abd Allāh b. Muḥammad b. al-Khaṭīb[101] mentioned many affairs about this in his book which he called *The Concealed Secret Concerning Magic, Talismans, and Addressing the Stars (al-Sirr al-maktūm fī l-siḥr wa-l-ṭilasmāt wa-mukhāṭabat al-nujūm).*[102] **[173]**

These [people] worship the planets by [various] species of acts of worship and sacrifices *(qurbān)*, and upon them come down the demons whom they themselves call the "spiritual beings" *(rūḥāniyyāt)* of the planets. These are persons distinct from them. Even if they don't see them, they hear them talking. They thus inform them [of things], speak to them about many matters and, for them, answer [various] species of needs. Such a [situation] frequently exists today in the countries of the Turks, the Kitai *(khiṭā)*,[103] the Iranians *('ajam)*, the Indians and, even, in the countries of Egypt, Yemen, Iraq, Syria, etc.

I know a number of these [people]. They are as the Most High said: "The magician will not be successful, wherever he may go."[104] The Most High also said: "Though they surely knew that he who bought that would have no share in the Hereafter. Surely, evil is that for which they sold their souls; had they known!"[105] The Most High also said: "They followed that which the demons uttered against Solomon's reign…"[106] and the [rest of the] verse, which was mentioned previously.

Ptolomeum et Hermetem and under other titles. An important part of the original Arabic text was recently discovered in two twelfth or thirteenth century manuscripts copied in Hebrew characters; see Ch. Burnett, *Ṯābit*; Ch. Burnett & G. Bohak, *Version* (I am grateful to Ch. Burnett for providing me with copies of these two articles); R. Lemay, *Books*, p. 169–170.

100 Abū Ma'shar Ja'far b. Muḥammad b. 'Umar al-Balkhī (Balkh, *c.* 170/186 – Wāsiṭ, 272/886), Albumasar for the medieval Latins, the greatest medieval astrologer, author of a number of pivotal treatises on astrology, notably a *Great Introduction to Astrology* (see A. M. al-Balkhī, *Mudkhal*), and to whom various occult treatises are also attributed (see for example A. M. al-Balkhī, *Kitāb*); see J. M. Millás, *EI2*, art. *Abū Ma'shar al-Balkhī*; D. Pingree, *Abū Ma'shar*; Y. Michot, *Astrology*, p. 148, 185, 208.

101 Fakhr al-Dīn, Abū 'Abd Allāh Muḥammad b. 'Umar b. al-Ḥusayn al-Rāzī (Rayy, 543/1149 – Herāt, 606/1209), the Ash'arī theologian and commentator of Avicenna and of the Qur'ān, also called Ibn al-Khaṭīb; see G. C. Anawati, *EI2*, art. *Fakhr al-Dīn al-Rāzī*.

102 See F. D. al-Rāzī, *Sirr*. "After [al-Ghazālī] came the author of the book *The Concealed Secret Concerning Magic and Addressing the Stars.* He spoke therein of pure associationism: worshipping the planets, the jinns and the demons, the invocations to [address to] them, the incense [fitting] them, their seals and the idols to make for them according to the doctrine of the associators – the Chaldeans *(kaldāniyyūn)* and the Kasdaeans *(kashdāniyyūn)* – towards whom Abraham, the Friend [of the Merciful] was sent" (Ibn Taymiyya, *Radd*, p. 544; trans. Michot, *Textes N.S. XI*, p. 2).

103 Nomadic people originating from the north and north-east of China (*K'i-tan*, or *Liao*, in the Chinese medieval sources); see C. E. Bosworth, *EI2*, art. *Ḳarā Khiṭāy.*

104 Qur'ān, *Ṭā Hā* – xx, 69.

105 Qur'ān, *al-Baqara* – ii, 102.

106 Qur'ān, *al-Baqara* – ii, 102.

These people are agreed with the adepts of the religions *(milla)* concerning what they witness and hear of the existence of these living, rational, beings distinct from the human species, [174] the four elements, and the astral spheres, and concerning the multitude of the strange things emanating from them. How therefore would it be said that the causes of strange things are only the three [forces mentioned by Avicenna]? It is thus clear, one who makes magic come only from simple psychic forces *(quwwa)* is among the people of the gravest ignorance and erring. As for someone saying that about the miracles, he is [even] more ignorant and erring than him.

Moreover, these people might speak of the preeternity of the world or of its origination *(ḥudūth)*. Together with the origination, they might also speak of the permanence *(dawām)* of the action of the Lord, or of its renewing after it is not. Together with the preeternity of the world, they might also say that it has a cause creating [it] or not say that. Whatever the case, they don't have to hand anything that would deny the existence of the things – the astral spheres and the spirits, superior and inferior – of whose existence they have no knowledge. They openly declare not having to hand anything proving that the astral spheres are nine.[107] Or, rather, they affirm something which they believe to have been established by a proof. As for denying that there might be more [astral spheres than nine], they have no proof for negating that.

This being [the situation] as to the astral spheres, which are perceptible by the senses and about whose number proofs are provided by the eclipses that the stars [produce] of one another and by the diversity of the movements of the seven planets, other[108] things than that it is even more true that they have no proof to deny it. At this moment, they don't have any proof to deny the [existence of] angels many many times more numerous than the ten intellects,[109] nor to deny the [existence of] angels administering the affairs of the sky, the earth, the clouds, the rain, etc. If someone informed [us] of the existence of such [things], of whom it would be known neither whether he is veracious nor whether he is lying, it would not be permitted to accuse him of lying except with a proof. How then, [a fortiori], will [things be] when the veracious and reliable Prophets inform [us] of that? The actions of these [angels] are then among the major causes for the

107 I.e., the spheres of the seven Ptolemaic planets, of the fixed stars, sometimes assimilated to the footstool *(kursī)* of God, and of the "sphere of the spheres" *(falak al-aflāk)*, sometimes assimilated to the Throne *('arsh)* of God – a view refused by Ibn Taymiyya; see *infra*, p. 201 of the Arabic text.

108 fa-ghayr : wa ghayr Ṣ

109 I.e., the ten superior intelligences moving the heavens in the Avicennan cosmography, from the first caused existent down to the agent intellect.

existence of the strange things. How will it thus be said that the latter have no cause except these three causes?[110]

And also, the proofs proving the existence of the angels that are other than the informations [provided by] the Prophets are multiple. Among them is the fact that it is said that the movements existing in the world [175] are three: compelled, natural, and voluntary. The motive for this restriction [of the movements to three] is that the principle of the movement either comes from the [thing] moving or from an external cause. If its movement is not possible except by a cause external to it – as [when] a stone rises up –, this is the compelled movement. If [its movement] is by a cause [coming] from it, either the [thing] moving has a perception *(shu'ūr)* or it has none. If it has a perception, it is the voluntary movement; if not, it is the natural [one]. The natural movement in the elements might be due to the fact that the body has come out from its natural place *(markaz)*. If it is not [the case], when earth is in its [natural] place, it is not in its nature to move. The [things] generated from the elements do not move except because of some compulsion *(qāsir)* which compels the elements to move to each other. As the natural and compelled movements are in need of a [cause] moving *(muḥarrik)* from outside, it is known that the origin of all movements is the will. Therefrom it necessarily follows *(lazima)* that the principle of all the movements of the superior and inferior world is the will.

At this moment, if the Lord is what moves everything without an intermediary, it is established that He is a choosing agent; the basis of what they say is thus vain and it is permissible that the miracles originate from His volition without cause. If, [on the contrary], He moves [things] by means of other wills, these are the angels. Now, it is known by many proofs that God is creating the things by the causes. It is [moreover] known that the angels are the intermediaries in what God Most High creates, as the Most High has said: "By those who administer affairs!"[111] – "By those who distribute by [His] command!"[112] As the angels are existing, it is possible that the things occurring *(ḥādith)* originate from them and vain is the saying of someone claiming that [these things] are due to nothing but the three causes mentioned previously. [176]

110 I.e., the three principles distinguished in Ibn Sīnā, *Ishārāt*, X, xxx; see *supra*, p. 165 of the Arabic text.

111 Qur'ān, *al-Nāzi'āt* – lxxix, 5.

112 Qur'ān, *al-Dhāriyāt* – li, 4.

[Back to the *Ishārāt*]

Moreover, those people say that what obligatorily brings *(muqtaḍī)* the extraordinary phenomena is either psychic forces *(quwwa)* or bodily ones, and that if [these forces] are bodily, they are either bodily elementary or bodily astral. The extraordinary phenomena coming from the psychic influences are, according to them, miracles, prodigies and magical phenomena *(siḥriyya)*. The ones coming from the elementary forces *(quwwa)*, like the attraction of the magnet, are[113] white magic *(nīranjiyyāt)* and the ones coming from the astral forces *(quwwa)* are the talismans. The astral forces *(quwwa)* have no influence on an extraordinary phenomenon except when the receptive elementary forces *(quwwa)* or the active psychic terrestrial forces *(quwwa)* join *(inḍimām)* with them, and this is the talismans.

Avicenna is among those of them who most [clearly] establish [the existence] of the extraordinary phenomena. He spoke of the causes of the extraordinary phenomena about four matters.

[The first] concerns the cause of the capacity *(tamakkun)* to abstain from food for a period of time and it is that the soul is kept so distracted by that which happens to it – [some] knowledge, love, fear, etc. – that it is not hungry, because[114] the digesting faculties are distracted from dissolving the food.[115]

[The second] concerns the cause of the capacity *(tamakkun)* to perform toilsome actions. The knower *(ʿārif)* is for example capable of an action or movement that is outside the aptitude of his like. This is just as, when it happens to the soul to be angry, or joyful, or to be somehow intoxicated with a moderate inebriety, or similar things, a strength *(quwwa)* happens to it which was not [there] before that. Similarly when something of the states of the knowers happens to it that fortifies it.[116]

113 fa-hiya : wa hiya Ṣ

114 bi-sabab : bi-sab Ṣ

115 See Ibn Sīnā, *Ishārāt*, X, i–iv, ed. Forget, p. 207, l. 8–208, l. 16 (trans. Inati, *Mysticism*, p. 92–94; trans. Goichon, *Directives*, p. 503–505).

116 See Ibn Sīnā, *Ishārāt*, X, v–vi, ed. Forget, p. 208, l. 17–209, l. 12 (trans. Inati, *Mysticism*, p. 94; trans. Goichon, *Directives*, p. 505–506).

Majnūn in the desert[117]

[The third] concerns the cause of the capacity *(tamakkun)* to inform of unknown things *(ghuyūb)*. What it involves is that one might [177] know the unknown while awake as he knows it while asleep. They have claimed that the cause thereof is that the knowledge of occurring [things] is inscribed in the agent intellect or the astral soul. When the rational soul is connected therewith, it learns that. Then, the imagination sometimes represents it in a simile *(mithāl)* and sometimes does not represent it. The cause necessitating *(mūjib)* the connection of the soul is the weakness of its bond to the body. [This] weakness is sometimes due to madness *(junūn)* or disease – similarly to what afflicts the people with black bile[118] –, sometimes due to the excess of hunger, or tiredness, or some other states, and sometimes due to [some] exercise of the soul.[119]

These three divisions – patiently abstaining from food for a period of time, the strength of the body, warning [of things] by dreams and what follows their course – is something that happens to the Muslim and the unbeliever, the pious and the depraved, and is the cause of extraordinary phenomena.

117 Lower part of a tile panel attributed to Mīrzā ʿAbd al-Razzāq (Shiraz, first half of the 20th c.; digitally reformatted); see H. Seif, *Tiles*, p. 122. Maddened by his love for Laylā, Majnūn lived a long time in the wilderness without hardly taking any food.

118 *Mirra sawdā'*, one of the four humors of Hippocratic medicine. I.e., the people suffering from melancholy.

119 See Ibn Sīnā, *Ishārāt*, X, vii–xxiii, ed. Forget, p. 209, l. 13–218, l. 8 (trans. Inati, *Mysticism*, p. 95–103; trans. Goichon, *Directives*, p. 506–518).

[The fourth] concerns the cause of[120] [the soul's] disposing freely *(taṣarruf)* of the elements. Just as it has an influence in its own body by making [it] move and mutate *(taḥwīl)* from a state to another, it is permissible that it has an influence in the element[s] of the world, so that the latter is for it like a body.[121] The [soul] then influences [things] by [causing] earthquakes, making rain come down, etc.[122]

[Avicenna said]:

• He to whom this[123] occurs in the original nature *(jibilla)* of [his] soul, who[124] is well guided, and keeps his soul pure, is one of the Prophets performing miracles and[125] one of the Friends [of God] performing prodigies.[126]

• He to whom this occurs,[127] is evil, **[178]** and uses it for evil, is a wicked magician.[128]

He [also] said:

• Giving the evil eye could be of this sort [of influence].[129]

He [also] said:

• This is only considered far-fetched by someone who assumes that what has an influence in the bodies is in contact [with them], or emits a part [of itself] and[130] dispatches [some] property through an intermediary.[131] Whoever meditates what we have described[132] drops such a condition from the degree of what to take into consideration.[133]

This is a summary of what they say on this subject. It is known that all that they have mentioned is something ordinary, frequent. It is not among the extra-

120 fī sabab + : wa Ṣ
121 See Ibn Sīnā, *Ishārāt*, X, xxvi, ed. Forget, p. 219, l. 11–220, l. 10 (trans. Inati, *Mysticism*, p. 104–105; trans. Goichon, *Directives*, p. 520–522).
122 Ibn Sīnā, *Ishārāt*, X, xxv, ed. Forget, p. 219, l. 3–10 (trans. Inati, *Mysticism*, p. 104; trans. Goichon, *Directives*, p. 519–520), quoted *infra* by Ibn Taymiyya (see p. 178–179 of the Arabic text).
123 I.e., the power of the soul to have an influence in bodies other than its own.
124 wa yakūnu Ṣ : thumma yakūnu khayr[an] **F**, *who is then good*
125 wa Ṣ : aw **F** *or*
126 Ibn Sīnā, *Ishārāt*, X, xxviii, ed. Forget, p. 220, l. 15–17 (trans. Inati, *Mysticism*, p. 106; trans. Goichon, *Directives*, p. 522).
127 wa Ṣ : thumma **F**, *who is then evil*
128 Ibn Sīnā, *Ishārāt*, X, xxviii, ed. Forget, p. 220, l. 18–19 (trans. Inati, *Mysticism*, p. 106; trans. Goichon, *Directives*, p. 522–523).
129 Ibn Sīnā, *Ishārāt*, X, xxix, ed. Forget, p. 221, l. 3 (trans. Inati, *Mysticism*, p. 106; trans. Goichon, *Directives*, p. 523).
130 wa Ṣ : aw **F** *or*
131 bi-wāsiṭa Ṣ : fī wāsiṭa **F** *in an intermediary*
132 waṣafnā-hu Ṣ : aṣṣalnā-hu **F** *that of which we have laid the principles*
133 Ibn Sīnā, *Ishārāt*, X, xxix, ed. Forget, p. 221, l. 5–7 (trans. Inati, *Mysticism*, p. 106; trans. Goichon, *Directives*, p. 523).

ordinary phenomena and it is not of the genus of the miracles. This is why Avicenna, after[134] having mentioned that and having mentioned what was told previously, said that:

• To someone who[135] does not accept [a matter] as true on the whole, [its] detail is of little importance.[136]

Thereupon he said:

• Informations have perhaps reached you[137] about some[138] of the knowers that might entail an inversion[139] of custom *('āda)* [and] which you would rush to call a lie. It will for example be said that a Prophet sometimes[140] asked [God] for rain for people and that they received it, **[179]** or that he asked for them[141] to be healed and that they were healed, or that he invoked [God] against them and that they were swallowed up into the ground, struck by earthquakes, or perished in another way; and[142] also, that he invoked [God] for them and that an epidemic and a plague were turned away from them, or a torrential stream,[143] or a flood. Or [it will be said] that lions submitted to one of them, or that birds were not fleeing from him, or similar things that you shall not take[144] the way clearly impossible things [are taken]. So, halt and do not rush! Things similar to these have causes that are part of[145] the mysteries of nature. Perhaps I will have the opportunity[146] to tell[147] you about some of them.[148]

Thereafter [Avicenna] mentioned that the cause of such [things] might come from the force *(quwwa)* of the soul: as it is disposing freely of its [own] body, it is indeed permissible for it to dispose freely of other ones.[149]

---

134 In fact, *before* having mentioned it.

135 anna-hu man : min anna-hu [man] Ṣ

136 Ibn Sīnā, *Ishārāt*, X, xxiv, ed. Forget, p. 219, l. 1–2 (trans. Inati, *Mysticism*, p. 104; trans. Goichon, *Directives*, p. 519).

137 balagha-ka Ṣ : tablughu-ka F *are perhaps reaching you*

138 ba'ḍ Ṣ : — F *about the knowers*

139 bi-taqallub Ṣ : bi-qalb F

140 nabiyy^{an} rubba-mā Ṣ : 'ārif^{an} F *a knower*

141 la-hum + F : istashfā Ṣ

142 wa Ṣ : aw F *or*

143 al-sayl Ṣ : al-sa'īr F *a fire*

144 ta'khudhu : ya'khudhu ṢF

145 min Ṣ : fī F *causes in*

146 yata'attā F : ta'attā Ṣ

147 aqtaṣṣa F : aquṣṣa Ṣ

148 Ibn Sīnā, *Ishārāt*, X, xxv, ed. Forget, p. 219, l. 3–10 (trans. Inati, *Mysticism*, p. 104; trans. Goichon, *Directives*, p. 519–520).

149 See Ibn Sīnā, *Ishārāt*, X, xxvi–xxvii, ed. Forget, p. 219–220 (trans. Inati, *Mysticism*, p. 104–105; trans. Goichon, *Directives*, p. 520–522). Inati's translation (*Mysticism*, p. 105) of *Ishārāt*, X, xxvii (ed. Forget, p. 220, l. 11–14) is grammatically incorrect and thus unclear. As for Goichon's translation (*Directives*, p. 522), it is mistaken and leads to a wrong understanding of Avicenna's doctrine of the soul's individuation. Here is a more accurate translation of this section xxvii: "This force *(quwwa)* may belong to the soul in virtue of the

[Refutation of Avicenna from ten viewpoints]

[FIRST VIEWPOINT.] It is known that what these [people] have mentioned does not provide an apodictic confirmation *(jazm)* of what they say but only [provides], at the most, the possibility thereof and its permissibility; [and this], by [their] saying: "As it is permissible for a human to see a dream indicating unknown things, it is [also] possible that the knowledge of all unknown things be of that type. As it is permissible for the soul to have an influence in its body and in something small, it is [also] permissible for it to have an influence in the whole of air, water, earth and fire. As it is permissible for the soul to have the strength to [perform] some actions, it is [also] permissible for it to fly in the air and to walk on water, to turn upside down the cities of the people of Lot[150] and to part the sea,[151] to make the manna and the quail come down[152] and to make twelve springs gush out from the rock,[153] to turn a rod into a snake[154] and to bring out lice and frogs,[155] **[180]** to make a table on which there is bread, fish and olives come down,[156] and things similar to that."

---

fundamental complexion which is such that, because of what it provides as psychic disposition, its individuation* comes to belong to the individual soul. [This force] may also come to be because of a complexion that comes to be and it may come to be through a sort of endeavour *(kasb)* that makes the soul as if it were denuded due to the intensity of [its] purity**, as happens to the pious Friends of God" (* tashakhkhuṣu-hā : tashakhkhuṣa-hā **F**; ** al-zakā' **F ap. cr.** : al-dhakā' **F**). According to Goichon's translation (which follows Forget's reading *tashakhkhuṣa-hā*), it is the "fundamental complexion" which "becomes, for the individual soul, [the cause itself of] its individuation." Such a material origin of the soul's individuation is too Aristotelian, or Fārābian, to be Avicennan. In the Shaykh al-Ra'īs' Ash'arizing philosophy, the fundamental complexion does not provide anything more than some preparation *(isti'dād)* – what he calls here "a psychic disposition." As for the individuation *(tashakhkhuṣ)* itself of the soul, it is an immaterial quality that must necessarily emanate from a superior principle. In other words, individuation comes from the Giver of forms *(wāhib al-ṣuwar)*, not from the complexion, but comes to be when the inferior dimensions (the complexion and the "psychic disposition") are in harmony with this emanating of the individuation and constitute some kind of preparation to it (a *wasaṭ, aw mā bi-ḥukmi-hi*). On this, see also the Avicennan texts translated by S. PINÈS, *Conception*, p. 206: "Le fait que la cause d'un individu soit, sous un certain rapport, la matière et une chose matérielle ne serait pas, à ce point de vue, une objection valable, pourvu que la caractéristique qui se rattache à lui et qui l'individue ne soit pas elle-même matérielle, mais fasse partie des caractéristiques qui particularisent ce qui n'est pas un corps dans son individuation;" p. 212: "En notre ipséité nous aurons [après la séparation du corps] l'aperception des caractéristiques par lesquelles elle a reçu l'individuation qui lui est propre."

150 See Qur'ān, *Hūd* – xi, 82.

151 See Qur'ān, *al-Shu'arā'* – xxvi, 63.

152 See Qur'ān, *al-Baqara* – ii, 57.

153 See Qur'ān, *al-Baqara* – ii, 60.

154 See Qur'ān, *al-A'rāf* – vii, 107.

155 See Qur'ān, *al-A'rāf* – vii, 133.

156 See Qur'ān, *al-Mā'ida* – v, 114.

Hippocrates[157]

Among the things known is the fact that this does not prove undoubtedly that such possible [things] are taking place.[158] So, why did you say that this is what takes place? Your words concerning this are similar to your words relating the rest of the species of epilepsy *(ṣarʿ)* to the black and phlegmatic humor, although this would only be valid[159] if the jinns did not exist. The physicians have no proof to deny the jinns and, in their art, there is nothing forbidding the existence of the jinns. The ancient physicians like Hippocrates[160] and others acknowledge that but say that there is nothing, in their art, proving that there are *(thubūt)* jinns. Now, the non-existence of knowledge is not knowledge of a non-existence, and the non-existence of a proof is not knowledge of the non-existence of its object.

157 Miniature from the *Fālnāmeh* of the Ottoman sultan Ahmed I (r. 1012/1603–1026/1617), MS Istanbul, Topkapı Palace Museum, H. 1703, fol. 38 v.; see M. FARHAD (ed.), *Falnama*, p. 164–165.

158 wuqūʿ: nawʿ Ṣ

159 — : an Ṣ

160 The most famous Greek physician (*c.* 460 – *c.* 375 BCE).

Indeed, the non-existence of something proving a concrete *(muʿayyan)* thing does not imply its absence *(intifāʾ)*. How [will the matter be, a fortiori], when it is known by many proofs that the jinns can make people have epileptic fits. ʿAbd Allāh,[161] the son of Aḥmad b. Ḥanbal said for example: "I said to my father that the physicians say that no jinn enters into the body of a human and he said: 'O my son, they lie! That one [even] speaks by his tongue!'" **[181]** And this is something which we have experienced more than once, ourselves and others. As to sensorial knowledges – seeing and hearing – concerning that, we have had [experiences] with which it is not possible [any more] to doubt.

What is aimed at here is to make clear that they deny something without knowledge. It is incumbent upon the denier [to provide] the proof as it is incumbent upon the affirmer [to provide] the proof. Now, in order to [affirm] that these signs come about from the psychic forces *(quwwa)*, they have nothing with them except simply [speaking of] permissibility and possibility. "They follow nothing but an opinion and they do nothing but surmise."[162] Also, they have fundamentally no proof of the possibility for the souls to have an influence in things like this, except simply using an improbable analogy *(qiyās)* which does not imply that.

This was the first of the viewpoints, [which consisted] in saying: "You, you have no proof that these effects come from the forces *(quwwa)* of the souls."

SECOND VIEWPOINT. It is to say that these effects are multiple affairs for which, yourselves acknowledge it, it is impossible to be among the effects of the souls, as previously pointed out. Your statement that the effects known by the Muslims, the Jews and the Nazarenes are among the effects of the souls is thus vain. In the ensemble of things which they have mentioned, there is nothing that might depart from being analogous to ordinary affairs, except occurring events like the coming down of the rain, the healing of the sick, an earthquake, being swallowed up into the ground, the turning away of a torrential stream and an epidemic, the submissiveness of lions and birds. The genus *(jins)* of these affairs is [nevertheless] due to ordinary causes[163] and this **[182]** [is] unlike the sea being parted into twelve parts that are each like a huge mountain, a rod being turned into a snake, the manna and the quail coming down, and twelve springs gushing out

161 Abū ʿAbd al-Raḥmān ʿAbd Allāh b. Aḥmad b. Ḥanbal (d. 290/903), traditionist and transmitter of his father's work; see H. LAOUST, *EI2*, art. *Aḥmad b. Ḥanbal*, p. 273.

162 Qurʾān, *al-Anʿām* – vi, 116.

163 — : fa-inna l-maṭar… muʿtāda Ṣ *The rain comes down due to numerous causes and, similarly, the healing of the sick, the occurrence of being swallowed up into the ground and destruction are due to ordinary causes, just as its species is due to ordinary causes.* M. R. Sālim draws this sentence (with various words added by him) from a marginal note in the manuscript Istanbul, Pertev 358 he bases his edition on. It does not seem to be part of the original text of Ibn Taymiyya.

from the rock. Also, for example, water gushing forth from between fingers,[164] the multiplication of food and drinks so as to suffice many more than those they were sufficing,[165] the unrooting of a tree and, thereafter, its return to its place, firmly standing,[166] the genus of these affairs and their like does not emanate from an ordinary cause. These are indeed extraordinary phenomena, unlike that which is extraordinary in its measure *(qadr)*, not in its genus. Now, this genus [of phenomena], they refuse its occurring in the world, either by forces *(quwwa)* of the soul or by other [forces]. However, the knowledge [one has] of the occurrence of

164 See AL-BUKHĀRĪ, *Ṣaḥīḥ, Wuḍū'*, vol. i, p. 45, 51; *Manāqib*, vol. iv, p. 192, 194; *Ashriba*, vol. vii, p. 114; MUSLIM, *Ṣaḥīḥ, Faḍā'il*, vol. vii, p. 59; *Zuhd*, vol. viii, p. 235–236. See also A. N. AL-IṢFAHĀNĪ, *Dalā'il*, p. 405–409, 413, nos 311–318, 321; M. al-QURṬUBĪ, *I'lām*, p. 351–352.

165 See AL-BUKHĀRĪ, *Ṣaḥīḥ, Manāqib*, vol. iv, p. 193–194; MUSLIM, *Ṣaḥīḥ, Faḍā'il*, vol. vii, p. 60. See also A. N. AL-IṢFAHĀNĪ, *Dalā'il*, p. 407–430, nos 313–336; M. al-QURṬUBĪ, *I'lām*, p. 351–356. "God informed us that the afreet said to Solomon: 'I will bring it to you before you rise from your place' (Q., *al-Naml* – xxvii. 39). This is freely disposing *(taṣarruf)* of the accidents of a living [individual]. Death, disease, moving are accidents, and a living being ordinarily receives the like of these accidents. In this, there is no turning of a genus into [another] genus; nor is there, in this, anything that would exclusively be *(ikhtaṣṣa bi-)* in the power *(qudra)* of the Lord, nor anything of which the angels would have the exclusivity. Similarly for supplying what is [sometimes] supplied of food, or money, or clothes, or other things, from an unknown [source] *(ghayb)*: this* only consists in transferring some good from a place to [another] place; now, humans and jinns do this – the jinns do it and people do not see that. This is different from a small [quantity of] water flowing [by] itself to the point of becoming abundant, by gushing forth from between fingers, without any [other quantity of water] being added to it. This, neither human nor jinn is capable *(qadara)* of it." * fa-hadhā : wa hadhā **N** (IBN TAYMIYYA, *Nubuwwāt*, p. 145). "The Prophet, God bless him and grant him peace, was only putting his hand in the water and water was gushing forth from between his fingers. This, neither a human nor a jinn are capable *(qadara)* of it. Similarly [for] a small [quantity of] food becoming abundant: this, neither a jinn nor a human are capable *(qadara)* of it. The Prophet, God bless him and grant him peace, never brought food from an unknown [source], nor drinks. This was only happening to some of his Companions, just as Khubayb b. 'Adī, while he was detained in Mecca, brought some picked grapes [from an unknown source]. This genus of [actions] is not among the things that the Prophets have the exclusivity of. Mary, peace be upon her, was not a Prophetess and she was brought food. This might **[526]** [come] from a licit [source] – it is then a prodigy *(karāma)* and it is brought either by an angel or by a Muslim jinn – and it might be prohibited. Every [deed] which is among the signs of the Prophets will not be, [as such], a prodigy of the righteous" (IBN TAYMIYYA, *Nubuwwāt*, p. 525–526).

166 See IBN ḤANBAL, *Musnad*, vol. iii, p. 113; AL-DĀRIMĪ, *Sunan, Muqaddima*, vol. i, p. 12–13; IBN MĀJA, *Sunan, Fitan*, vol. ii, p. 1336, no 4028: "One day Gabriel, peace be upon him, came to the Messenger of God, God bless him and grant him peace, while he was sitting, grieved, covered with blood because some of the people of Mecca had beaten him. He said: 'What is the matter with you?' He said: 'These people did such and such to me.' [Gabriel] said: 'Would you like me to show you a sign?' He said: 'Yes, show me.' He looked at a tree on the other side of the wadi and said: 'Call that tree.' So [the Prophet] called it and it came walking until it stood before him. [Gabriel] said: 'Tell it to go back.' So [the Prophet] told [the tree] and it went back, returning to its place. Then the Messenger of God said, God bless him and grant him peace: 'This is enough for me.'" See also A. N. AL-IṢFAHĀNĪ, *Dalā'il*, p. 389–394, nos 290–298; M. al-QURṬUBĪ, *I'lām*, p. 356–358.

[affairs] like that, either for having seen [them] with one's own eyes *(mu'āyana)* or through veracious reports, makes the corrupt nature of their principle clear.

This is among the things that someone intelligent *('āqil)* ought to ponder. Indeed, the measure *(qadr)* of strange things whose cause they have expounded does not belong to the genus of the extraordinary phenomena but, rather, belongs to the genus of ordinary affairs and, on the basis of this, they deny [the existence of] the genus of extraordinary phenomena. This is their corrupt principle, whose corrupt nature is known by multiple proofs. Avicenna, however, took a road in which he wanted to bring together their corrupt principles and acceptance as true a species of strange things, and to consider the prodigies and the miracles as being of that sort *(namaṭ)*. Magic comes from ordinary affairs, like the causes by which disease, death, etc. occur. Belonging to [magic], there are also affairs that go against custom *('āda)* and nature but are amongst the things that are ordinarily produced by the demons – in connection, however, with things that prove their deceptive and depraved nature. It doesn't thus bear a resemblance to the prodigies of the righteous, let alone to the miracles. It is spoken extensively about this elsewhere and what is aimed at here is to make clear the corrupt nature of what is said by someone considering the miracles as [due to] psychic forces *(quwwa)*. **[183]**

THIRD VIEWPOINT. It is to say that the extraordinary phenomena are of three species. [One] of them is that which belongs to the genus of independence *(ghanā')* from human needs. [Another one] of them is that which belongs to the genus of the knowledge exceeding the forces *(quwwa)* of humans. [A third one] of them is what belongs to the genus of capacities *(maqdūrāt)* exceeding the power *(qudra)* of humans.[167] This is why Noah, peace be upon him, i. e., the first Messenger whom God sent to the people of the earth, said: "I do not say to you that I possess the treasures of God, nor do I know the unknown, and I do not say that I am an angel."[168] And God, Exalted is He, said of[169] the Seal of the Messengers that he said: "I do not say to you that I possess the treasures of God, nor do I know the unknown, and I do not say to you that I am an angel."[170] [People]

---

167 In his *Noble Rule Concerning the Miracles and the Prodigies*, Ibn Taymiyya also distinguishes three types of extraordinary phenomena relatively to what he then calls the "attributes of perfection:" knowledge, power and richness (*ghanā'*, translated here as "independence"); see IBN TAYMIYYA, *Mu'jizāt*, p. 312, trans. MICHOT, *Textes N.S. XXI*, p. 1.

168 Qur'ān, *Hūd* – xi, 31.

169 'an khātim : li-khātim Ṣ

170 Qur'ān, *al-An'ām* – vi, 50. "God, Exalted is He, commanded to Noah and Muḥammad to say: 'I do not say to you that I possess the treasures of God, nor do I know the unknown, and I do not say that I am an angel.' The ignorants nevertheless want from the one followed [by them] that he be knowledgeable about everything he is asked about, capable of everything which is demanded from him, and exempt of human needs like the angels. Such a requirement *(iqtirāḥ)* from the holders of command is like the Khārijites requiring from the community

have only mentioned the cause of things like the independence *(ghanā')* belonging to the genus of the ability to dispense *(istighnā')* with food and drink for a period of time, the knowledge belonging to the genus of informing about unknown things *(ghuyūb)*, the power *(qudra)* belonging to the genus of the toilsome actions which [one performs] with one's body and of the free disposition *(taṣarruf)* of the elements by a permutation *(istiḥāla)*, an earthquake, etc. As for the cause for which a rod is turned into a snake, a she-camel comes out from the ground[171] and the like of that, they acknowledge that it is not possible and it is not possible for them to assign its cause to the forces *(quwwa)* of the soul.

FOURTH VIEWPOINT. It is to say that the species of [extraordinary phenomena] about which they say that it is due to the forces *(quwwa)* of the soul,[172] they do not pretend that the influence of the [soul responsible for these phenomena] goes as far as to make come down the water of the flood which drowned the people of the earth,[173] nor [as far as] to send during seven nights and eight days in succession[174] the fatal wind[175] which made 'Ād perish, nor [as far as] to exterminate the cities of the people of Lot and to turn them upside down so that all those who [**184**] were in them perished, pursued by stones that were pursuing the fugitive among them, nor [as far as] to send flocks of birds with stones of shale coming down upon the masters of the elephant one by one, each bird having with it three little stones – one stone in its beak and two stones in its feet – until the masters of the elephant perished: their stratagem thus went awry to the point that He sent against them stones of shale "and made them like chewed-up straw."[176] Nor is it in the forces *(quwwa)* of the soul that in the morning of every day it makes come down[177] the manna and the quail sufficing the army *('askar)* of Moses, that it overshadows them with the white cloud[178] wherever they march to and makes this [white cloud] stay immobile with them every time they lengthen [their stay somewhere], and that it makes water gush out every day from the rock as twelve springs – one spring for each tribe.[179] Nor is it [in the soul's forces] that the sea is parted[180] into twelve parts that are each like a huge mountain, until the

in general that none of its [members] have any sin, whoever having a sin being, according to them, an unbeliever who shall be kept eternally in the fire. This is all vain, contrary to what God has created, and contrary to what God has legislated" (IBN TAYMIYYA, *Minhāj*, vol. vi, p. 367–368).

171 See Qur'ān, *al-A'rāf* – vii, 73.

172 — : yu'aththiru ta'thīr[an] Ṣ. *Yu'aththiru* is added by M. R. Sālim.

173 See Qur'ān, *al-A'rāf* – vii, 64.

174 See Qur'ān, *al-Ḥāqqa* – lxix, 7.

175 See Qur'ān, *al-Dhāriyāt* – li, 41.

176 See Qur'ān, *al-Fīl* – cv. See also A. N. AL-IṢFAHĀNĪ, *Dalā'il*, p. 143–151, nos 84–88.

177 tunazzilu : yunazzilu Ṣ

178 See Qur'ān, *al-A'rāf* – vii, 160.

179 See Qur'ān, *al-A'rāf* – vii, 160.

180 tafarruq : yufarriqu Ṣ

moment when the army of Moses comes out from it and the army of Pharaoh enters into it, it closes itself over them and drowns them all.

Similarly, revival of the dead – Adamic beings and animals – is also among the extraordinary phenomena that are outside of the forces *(quwwa)* of the souls. God has mentioned that in more than one place of His Book. He has [notably] mentioned it in five places in the *sūra The Cow.* The Most High said: "And when you said, 'O Moses, we will not believe in you until we see God openly,' a thunderbolt seized you while you were looking on. Then We raised you up after your death, so that you might give thanks."[181] The Most High also said: "We said, 'Strike him with a piece of it!' Thus does God revive the dead, and He shows you His signs, so that you might reason."[182] The Most High also said: "Have you not looked at those who came out of their homes in thousands, apprehensive of death? God said to them, 'Die!' Thereafter He revived them. **[185]** Indeed God is bountiful to humans but most of the humans do not give thanks."[183] The Most High also said: "Or [bethink] of the like of him[184] who passed by a city as it lay fallen on its trellises. He said, 'How will God revive this after its death?' God made him die a hundred years, then raised him up and said, 'How long have you remained?' Said he, 'I have remained a day or part of a day.' [God] said, 'Rather you have remained a hundred years. Yet look at your food and drink: they have not rotted! And look at your donkey! We will make you a sign for the humans. And look at the bones, how We adjust them and then clothe them with flesh!' When [the matter] became clear to him, he said, 'I know that God is powerful over everything.'"[185]

God, Glorified is He, also mentioned the reviving of the dead by the Messiah with the permission of God.[186] He also mentioned, Glorified is He, the story of the companions of the cave and their staying asleep, without eating and drinking, for three hundred solar years, corresponding to three hundred and nine lunar years. "So it was that We let [people] come upon them,[187] so that they might know that God's promise is true and that concerning the Hour there is no doubt."[188]

181 Qur'ān, *al-Baqara* – ii, 55–56.
182 Qur'ān, *al-Baqara* – ii, 73.
183 Qur'ān, *al-Baqara* – ii, 243.
184 I.e., Ezra.
185 Qur'ān, *al-Baqara* – ii, 259.
186 See Qur'ān, *al-Mā'ida* – v, 110.
187 I.e., the sleepers. See Qur'ān, *al-Kahf* – xviii, 9–22.
188 Qur'ān, *al-Kahf* – xviii, 21.

Jeremiah, two baskets with a hundred years old, but still fresh, food and his donkey being resurrected[189]

The reviving of Adamic beings after their death time after time, the reviving of the donkey, the preservation of the food and drink for a hundred years with no change, the preservation of the sleepers for three hundred nine years, tearing the four birds to pieces, placing them in four parts on the mountains and, then, their coming running when Abraham, the Friend [of God], peace be upon him, called them…[190] In these stories that God tells there are various species of things to draw a lesson from *(i'tibār)*.

One of them is to confirm that the Prophets perform miracles **[186]** and that they are outside of the forces *(quwwa)* of the soul. The philosophers and the rest of the people using their intellect *('āqil)* are agreed on that neither the forces *(quwwa)* of the souls do anything like this, nor, even, any of the forces *(quwwa)* known in the world, superior and inferior.

A second [lesson] is that, in [all] that, there is an affirmation that God is an agent, choosing, Who acts by His will and His power *(qudra)*. He makes occur

189 Miniature from Rashīd al-Dīn Faḍl Allāh (d. 718/1318), *Jāmi' al-Tawārīkh*, Edinburgh University, Or. MS 20, fol. 13 v. (714/1314, Tabriz, Iran); see D. Talbot Rice, *Illustrations*, p. 72–73.

190 See Qur'ān, *al-Baqara* – ii, 260.

what He wills according to His will and His wisdom. He is not necessitating *(mūjib)* by [His] essence. One necessitating *(mūjib)* by [His] essence is indeed necessarily entailing *(mustalzim)* His effects and it is impossible that His actions diverge from the natural law *(qānūn)*. Even if various species of strange things *(gharība)* occur in this world by the configurations of the astral sphere and the planetary conjunctions, there must inevitably be a preparation of the receptacles and these conjonctions must inevitably take place according to the law *(qānūn)* which, for these [philosophers], is ordinary *(mu'tād)*. Now, both [things] are denied in these extraordinary phenomena *(khāriqa)*: the inferior matter does not ordinarily accept anything like this and something like this does not occur from the astral conjunctions. This is why what occurs of the strange things because of the mingling of the active celestial forces *(quwwa)* or of the passive terrestrial forces *(quwwa)* is not of this type. It is rather among the things to the like of which one is used; for example repelling some animals from a place or attracting them into it, the diseases of some of the bodies or their death, or other affairs.

A third [lesson] is that these [Qur'ānic stories] are among the greatest proofs of the possibility of the coming back *(ma'ād)* of the bodies and of the return *(i'āda)* of the spirits into them. There is indeed no better proof of the possibility of a thing than its taking place or the taking place of something similar to it: as this takes place, it is known that it is possible.

Similarly, **[187]** Jesus, peace be upon him, making come down every day from heaven the table on which there were olives, fish, etc. was among the things that are outside of the forces *(quwwa)* of the soul. Indeed, the influence of the soul in the hylè of the world is only proportionate to what the hylè accepts. Now, to suspend such [a table] in the air is not among the things that the air accepts. Moreover, the influence of the soul in what is simple is simple; it does not include any composition similar to that. Likewise, it is not in the forces *(quwwa)* of the soul to generate an animal from the womb of its mother without sexual intercourse, and similar examples of the extraordinary phenomena [that are such] that, they recognize it, the influence of the forces *(quwwa)* of the soul does not attain any such scope *(ḥadd)* even if they have an influence in the superior genus thereof. This is just as the forces *(quwwa)* of the body are well known – walking, hastening, etc. – whereas it is not in the forces *(quwwa)* of anyone's body to carry a mountain, nor six cities, on his back. Neither is it in the forces *(quwwa)* of his body to fly in the air, and similar things. It is thus clear, the [philosophers] acknowledge that it is not possible to attribute such affairs to the forces *(quwwa)* of the soul.

FIFTH VIEWPOINT. It is to say that we do not contest that a species of uncovering *(kashf)* happens for the soul, either awake or asleep, because of the tenuity of its bond with the body, either by means of [some] exercise or by other means. This is the psychic uncovering *(kashf nafsānī)*.

It has nevertheless also been established, by proofs both rational *('aqlī)* and coming from the Law *(shar'ī)*, that the jinns exist and that they inform the humans about matters unknown *(ghā'ib)* to them, as it happens to the diviners *(kāhin)* struck with epilepsy *(maṣrū')* and others. From someone struck with epilepsy people hear various species of utterance, informations about unknown matters, and a strange language [which is such] that, they obligatorily know it, it is not in the capacity *(quwwa)* of this man [to speak it. The situation] is similar with the adepts of demonic acts of worship **[188]** – the Brahmins,[191] the *bakhsis*,[192] and their like among the associationist worshippers –, with whoever is similar to them from among those who affiliate themselves with the people of the *Qibla*, like the various sorts of the Yūnusiyya,[193] the Aḥmadiyya,[194] the Khālidiyya,[195] the

191 The Brahmins are the members of the Hindu sacerdotal caste. For Muslim classical authors, the term becomes a label for anyone refusing all type of prophethood; see AL-SHAHRASTĀNĪ, *Religions II*, trans. MONNOT – JOLIVET, p. 527–537; IBN TAYMIYYA, *Qubruṣ*, trans. MICHOT, *Roi croisé*, p. 144.

192 *Al-bakhshiyya.* Originally designating the Mongol shamans, *bakhsi* or *bakshi* was sometimes used for Buddhist holy men; see J.-P. ROUX, *Religion*, p. 64; *Histoire*, p. 561; R. AMITAI-PREISS, *Sufis*, p. 41; Y. MICHOT, *Mamlūk II*, p. 430; *Vizir*, p. 469–470. "At the court of the Il-khans and the other western khanates, divination and astrology seem to have been monopolized by the *baqshis* (teacher), a name usually used for Buddhist monks, and the shamans were not very important. With Islamization these *baqshis* disappeared or, in the Golden Horde and its successor states, left the court to practice among ordinary herders" (C. P. ATWOOD, *Encyclopedia*, p. 495). In the manuscript of the *Epistle on the Spiritual Way* of Ibn Taymiyya's Ḥanbalī student al-Ba'labakkī (d. 734/1333) which A. Post edits and translates, a word devoid of initial dots appears which he reads *baḥriyya* (A. POST, *Glimpse*, facsimile of the MS on p. 171; edition on p. 173). In a footnote of his translation, A. Post then writes: "The word 'Baḥriyya' seems out of place in this context and is likely an error of the copyist. Perhaps it was meant to say 'Aḥmadiyya,' in which case it would most likely be a reference to the Rifā'i Sufi order" (p. 180, n. 66). *Bakhshiyya*, I suggest, could be a better reading, as it is closer to the drawing of the word in the manuscript. The translation of the passage concerned would thus become: "There are [also] people who realize renunciation without realizing piety. They are numerous among those who are associated with [the way of] poverty *(faqr)*, such as the Bakhshiyya and others. That is because they renounce this world, as there is no beneficial purpose for them in it and their hearts have no attachment to it. However, they do not realize piety and do not observe the [divine] commands and prohibitions. They are thus afflicted by distance [from God] and the door [to Him] is locked to them. They do not achieve any benefit with their spiritual method *(sulūk)* due to the fact that they place a barrier between themselves and that which the Messenger (may God bless him and grant him peace) has brought" (A. POST, *Glimpse*, p. 180, modified). Like a number of his teacher's writings, al-Ba'labakkī's epistle would thus have an anti-Mongol flavour, which would make it even more fascinating.

193 The followers of Yūnus b. Yūsuf b. Musā'id al-Shaybānī l-Makhāriqī (m. 619/1222); see IBN KHALLIKĀN, *Wafayāt*, vol. vii, p. 256–257. "He was the shaykh of the Yūnusiyya sect which is foremost [known for its] ecstatic utterances, paucity of intellect, and abundance of ignorance, may God do away with their evil. He was the possessor of a [spiritual] state and uncovering, and prodigies *(karāma)* are told about him" (IBN AL-'IMĀD, *Shadharāt*, vol. v, p. 87).

194 The followers of Abū l-'Abbās Aḥmad b. 'Alī l-Ḥusaynī, known as al-Sayyid al-Badawī (Fās,

Dasūqiyya,[196] and with the like of those among the adepts of associationist acts of worship that go against the Book and the *Sunna.* One hears from them, in [their] state of [ecstatic] audition *(samā')*, species **[189]** of talking and strange language which it is not possible for that person to speak and [which are such] that it becomes known that the one speaking by his tongue[197] is someone other than him, or that the one dictating to him such utterance is someone other than him, and not that his soul alone has done that without a distinct cause from among the spirits. As this is among the things that are observed in the wicked souls and as many of the informations which they provide come from the information given to them by demonic spirits, the information provided by the Prophets [must] a fortiori *(bi-ṭarīq al-awlā)* come from the information [given to them] by the spirits of the angels.

– According to us, [the philosophers] say, the demons are the forces *(quwwa)* of the wicked soul and the angels are the forces *(quwwa)* of the righteous soul.

– It was said earlier on, we say, that most *(jumhūr)* of the Muslims do not contest the existence of these forces *(quwwa)*, as said earlier on. What is aimed at here is however that the existence of things distinct, other, than these forces *(quwwa)* be known, like the jinns informing many of the diviners of many matters. This is indeed obligatorily known to every person who is in direct contact with them or who has been informed by someone happening to know what they inform about. Ourselves, we have indeed known that, obligatorily, more than once. This is a species of the uncoverings *(mukāshafa)* and the informing about the unknown which is other than psychic.

As for the third division, i. e., what the angels inform about, this is the noblest of [these three] divisions, as proven by the many *ex auditu (sam'ī)* and rational *('aqlī)* proofs.

It is [now] established that informing about unknown matters *(mughayyabāt)* can be due to psychic causes, can be due to wicked causes, demonic and non-demonic, and can be due to angelic causes. What [the philosophers] mention is therefore one species among the three species, and it is the weakest of them. The utmost degree of their faith in prophethood consists in giving the Prophet the same status as a man among the weakest of the righteous people! **[190]**

596/1199 – Ṭanṭa, 675/1276), one of the most influential Sufi masters of Egypt until today; see K. Vollers & E. Littmann, *EI2*, art. *Aḥmad al-Badawī.*

195 It was not possible to identify the shaykh of this Sufi group.

196 The followers of Burhān al-Dīn Ibrāhīm b. Abī l-Majd 'Abd al-'Azīz al-Dasūqī (d. 696/1296), important Sufi master of Egypt; see W. Khalidi, *EI2*, art. *al-Dasūḳī, Burhān al-Dīn.*

197 lisāni-hi : lisān Ṣ

Demonic uncovering[198]

Afreet carrying a man[199]

SIXTH VIEWPOINT. It is to say that we know, obligatorily and from abundantly recurrent sources *(tawātur)*, that the jinns carry a man from one place to another where his [own] power *(qudra)* is unable to reach. Ourselves, we have known this in more than one form, and others than us know, as particular cases of that, things which we do not know. Whoever doubts about the root *(aṣl)* of this, let him refer to whosoever has the knowledge thereof. Otherwise, it does not belong to a man to treat as a lie what he does not know. Ourselves, we know thereof many many affairs. We know a great number [of people] who were carried in the air from their cities to ʿArafāt and to Mecca at another time than [the day of] ʿArafāt. Some of them were unbelievers who had not converted to Islam. Some of them were hypocrites not confessing the obligatoriness *(wujūb)* of prayer. Some of them were ignorants believing that their standing at ʿArafāt without being in the state required for the pilgrimage *(iḥrām)* and their return to their country without [having performed] the circumambulation [of the Kaʿba] *(ṭawāf)* and the run [between al-Ṣafā and al-Marwa] *(saʿy)*, nor having been in the state required for the pilgrimage *(iḥrām)*, was an act of worship and a prodigy among the prodigies of the righteous. [Another] example is the great number [of people] who were carried to somewhere else than Mecca. If I were to mention what I know of this, it would be a long discourse!

I know a person from among our companions whom the jinns carried in the air from the lowest [part] of a house to its highest [part], whom they advised on the affairs of the religion, who repented, and to whom something good happened.

198 Detail from the cover of A. AL-JAZĀʾIRĪ B. ḤAMDĀN, *Kawākib*.
199 Drawing from ANONYMOUS, *Majmūʿa*, p. 20.

Another had with him a demon who was carrying him in front of the people in the city of al-Shawbak[200] and who was ascending in the air to the summits of the mountains. Another was carried by his demon from the mountain of al-Ṣāliḥiyya[201] to the village of Yaldā,[202] about **[191]** one parasang [away]. Demons carried a group [of people] from the city of Palmyra to Jerusalem and commanded them to pray towards the north. They prayed towards it for days and [the demons] informed them that this [Islamic] Law *(sharīʿa)* had changed and been abrogated. As, [after their return from Jerusalem], they were living in a grotto, the Muslims demanded that they come to the mosque of Palmyra and asked them to repent. They did not repent but, rather, kept on praying toward the north for three days. Then, thereafter, they repented and it became clear to them that this had come from Satan. Another [individual] came to people who were dancing during an [ecstatic] concert *(samāʿ)* and kept up dancing in the air above their heads. Someone saw him and shouted at him, so that he fell. This was taking place in the presence of shaykh Shabīb al-Shaṭṭī.[203] "This [individual] deprived me of my [spiritual] state," [the one who had fallen] said to the shaykh.[204] [The shaykh] interrogated the [person who had shouted], who then said: "He did not have any [spiritual] state.[205] [What happened was] only this: a demon carried him from al-Raḥba[206] to here; I shouted at him, so he dropped him and fled." Something similar to this story has happened to more than one.

Among the things widely known, for which there are abundantly recurrent reports among the Turks,[207] there is what their magicians and their diviners do –

200 Fortress in the South of Jordan, between ʿAmmān and ʿAqaba, near al-Karak; see M. A. Bakhit, *EI2*, art. *al-Shawbak.*

201 Suburb of Damascus, on the slopes of Mount Qāsiyūn.

202 Yaldā or Yaldān, village, at three miles from Damascus; see Yāqūt, *Muʿjam*, vol. v, p. 504, no 12902.

203 I have been unable to identify this shaykh.

204 li-l-shaykh : al-shaykh Ṣ

205 On this incident, see also Ibn Taymiyya, *Istiqāma*, vol. I, p. 310: "There was once an [ecstatic] concert attended by shaykh Shabīb al-Shaṭṭī. While they were busy dancing*, an afreet was dancing in the air above their heads. They were amazed at it and the shaykh interrogated his disciple *(murīd)*, shaykh Abū Bakr b. Fīnān, who [enjoyed a spiritual] state and was knowledgeable. When he saw the [afreet], he shouted at him and he fell. When they ended the [concert], [the one who had fallen] asked him to treat him fairly and said: "This [individual] deprived me of my [spiritual] state!" The shaykh [Abū Bakr] then said: "He did not have any [spiritual] state! He was in al-Raḥba, his demon carried him to here, and started make him dance. When I saw the demon, I shouted at him, he fled, and this one fell!" * raqṣi-him : [samāʿ] aḥadi-him I

206 According to Yāqūt (*Muʿjam*, vol. iii, p. 37–41), a number of places are called "al-Raḥba," the most famous of which is a city on the right bank of the Euphrates (today's al-Mayādīn), between Dayr al-Zūr and the Iraqi border; see E. Honigmann – Th. Bianquis, *EI2*, art. *al-Raḥba.* The one alluded to here might also be Raḥba Dimashq, one of the villages surrounding the Syrian capital; see Yāqūt, *Muʿjam*, vol. iii, p. 38, no 5418.

207 I.e., the Mongols.

the *bakhsis*, the *toyins*[208] and their shaykh who is called the *böö*.[209] For them, a condition he has to fill is to be an effeminate fellow *(mukhannath)*, a catamite to have sex with *(ma'būn yunkaḥu)*.[210] They put up for him a yurt[211] during darkness, slaughter a sacrificial animal for Satan and sing for him. The demons then come and speak to them about some unknown matters like the situations *(ḥāl)* of those of them who are absent, their thefts,[212] etc. The *böö* is carried [up] and made to stand in the air and they see him.[213] At that moment, there is no Muslim among

208 *Al-ṭūyiniyya*. A *toyin* is a Buddhist monk; see J.-P. Roux, *Histoire*, p. 563; Y. Michot, *Mamlūk II*, p. 430; *Vizir*, p. 472.

209 *Al-būwā (?)*. This non-Arabic name given by Ibn Taymiyya to the shaykh of the *bakhsis* and *toyins* and the description he offers of his office seem to refer to what is now called in Mongolian a *böö*, i.e., a shaman – *böö* or *böge*, the latter's *g* being purely graphic and the pronunciation being *bö'e* or *bö*; see J.-P. Roux, *Religion*, p. 64, 71; J. A. Boyle, *Genghis Khan*, p. 518, n. 9; F. D. Lessing (ed.), *Dictionary*, p. 123, *bøge*. "Under the Mongol Empire the khans kept a whole college of male shamans (Mongol, *bö'e*; Turkish, *qam*) who specialized in various functions. Some made astrological observations and could predict eclipses. Scapulimancy and astrology were used to appoint favorable and unfavorable days for nomadizings, make decisions about wars, and divine the sources of troubles [...] Only some shamans performed the meat offering and drummed the famous shamanic seances that are now essential for any shaman" (C. P. Atwood, *Encyclopedia*, p. 494–495).

210 On transvestism and androgyny in shamanism, see M. Stutley, *Shamanism*, p. 8–15; J.-P. Roux, *Religion*, p. 65.

211 *Khurqāt*, from the Persian *khurqāh*, "pavilion," "tent." According to Ibn Baṭṭūṭa (*Riḥla*, trans. Mackintosh-Smith, *Travels*, p. 109), "a tent of the kind which is called by them *kharqah* [...] consists of wooden laths put together in the shape of a cupola and covered with pieces of felt. The upper part of it can be opened to admit light and air, like a ventilation pipe, and can be closed when required."

212 According to J.-P. Roux (*Religion*, p. 64), a shamanic séance has very precise purposes: "Il s'agit fondamentalement d'interroger les esprits sur les secrets qu'ils possèdent, c'est-à-dire de prédire l'avenir, de rechercher l'âme des malades, âme dérobée par des êtres invisibles ou vagabonde et menacée par eux d'enlèvement, c'est-à-dire de procéder à la guérison magique." It might also aim at obtaining from spirits news about boys or girls kidnapped by sorcerers or devils; see J.-P. Roux, *Religion*, p. 70.

213 The main phases of the séance alluded to by Ibn Taymiyya are comparable to those of an Altaic, mostly Tatar, shamanic ceremony of the nineteenth century, as described by M. Eliade, *Shamanism*, p. 190–197: "The first evening is devoted to preparation for the rite. The *kam*, having chosen a spot in a meadow, erects a new yurt there, setting inside it a young birch stripped of its lower branches and with nine steps *(tapty)* notched into its trunk [...] Then a light-colored horse is chosen [...] He blesses the horse and, with the help of several of the audience, kills it in a cruel way [...] On the following evening [...] the shaman offers horse meat to the Masters of the Drum, that is, the spirits that personify the shamanic powers of his family, and sings [...] Putting on his shamanic costume, the *kam* sits down on a bench, and while he fumigates his drum, begins to invoke a multitude of spirits, great and small, who answer, in turn: 'I am here, *kam!*' [...] The kam suddenly takes his place on the first notch *(tapty)* in the birch, beating his drum violently and crying 'Čok! Čok!' He also makes motions to indicate that he is mounting into the sky [...] The shaman climbs the notches in the birch one after the other, thus successively entering the other celestial regions [...] When he has gone as high as his power permits, he stops and humbly addresses Bai Ülgän [...] The shaman learns from Bai Ülgän if the sacrifice has been accepted and receives predictions

them, nor is there any writing with [some] Qur'ān in it. This has been widely known among them until this time. More than one person has informed us of it. [192]

To others, the demons were bringing food which they had stolen from people's shops. This has happened to more than one in our time and in other periods than our time. People brought sweets from the air and these stolen sweets were recognized, as their owner had lost them and the vessels in which they were had been described. Their price was thus given back to him. Such affairs, and similar ones, are well known to us, obligatorily and from abundantly recurrent reports.

As the jinns carry a man in the air from one place to another, far away, carry goods to him from a far away place, and inform him of matters unknown to the people present, one knows that these extraordinary phenomena are not due to the forces *(quwwa)* of the souls but, rather, to the action of the jinns. And though the jinns do such things, the angels are [still] superior to them and more powerful, more perfect and more eminent.

Just as the people of the [different] religions – the Muslims, the Nazarenes, and the Jews – pronounce these affairs to be true, most *(jumhūr)* of the philosophers also pronounce them to be true. The books on the spiritual beings *(rūḥāniyyāt)* which they have are loaded with mentions of the like of these affairs. The [various] sorts of incantations *('azīma)* and spells *(ruqya)* which they mention are loaded with assignments *(qism 'alā)* to the jinns, oaths sworn by *(qasam bi-)* them, invocations to them and demands from them. Those among them who address the planets and the one upon whom the spiritual being of the planets comes down, it is[214] a demon who comes down upon him, informs him of [some] affairs, and freely disposes [some of his] affairs for him. These things are known from abundantly recurrent sources among them. Whoever says that these extraordinary phenomena are among the effects of the [human] souls only and contests that the jinns and the demons exist and that they have an influence on [such] transmissions of information *(ikhbār)* and extraordinary phenomena is thus talking idly *(mubṭil)* – the people of the [various] religions are agreed on this, and so are most of the philosophers – and that [this person] is lying is

concerning the weather and the coming harvest [...] This episode is the culminating point of the 'ecstasy': the shaman collapses, exhausted." In one of his fetwas on al-Ḥallāj, Ibn Taymiyya gives another description of a Mongol shamanic séance, less detailed than the present one but including some aspects absent from it; it is translated in Y. Michot, *Sang.* Ibn Taymiyya's description has also various elements in common with that by the Franciscan missionary William of Rubruck (d. *c.* 1293); see J.-P. Roux, *Religion*, p. 75–76. For earlier descriptions of shamanic séances by Muslim authors (including Avicenna), see J.-P. Roux, *Religion*, p. 68–70.

214 fa-hiya : hiya Ṣ

obligatorily known by anyone who knows these affairs through observation or reports known to be true. **[193]**

SEVENTH VIEWPOINT. It is that relevant to this topic is what is reported, from abundantly recurrent sources concerning this topic, of the informations [provided by] the diviners of the Arabs and of what they were informing these [Arabs] of unknown matters because the jinns had informed them of it.

EIGHTH VIEWPOINT. It is that someone claiming that the extraordinary [actions] which the Prophets have performed by informing about the unknown – [one] of the affairs outside of the power *(qudra)* of mankind – are due to the forces *(quwwa)* of the soul is either pronouncing the Messengers to be truthful concerning what he knows they informed about, or is pronouncing them to be liars. If he is pronouncing them to be liars, one will firstly speak with him in order to establish prophethood and to affirm it. Now, these philosophers, the Ṣābi'ans, and their followers – the esotericists *(bāṭinī)* from among the people of the [various] religions and their like –, attach great importance to the affair of the Prophets and affirm the perfection of their knowledge, of their religion, of their truthfulness, and claim that what the Prophets brought does not contradict the principles of philosophy – and this is the road [followed by] those who say that the miracles of the Prophets are psychic forces *(quwwa)*. As this is so, the words of the Prophets are thus true, [the philosophers] being agreed thereon with the rest of the people of the (various] religions.

As this is so, the [following] shall be said: it is obligatorily known, the Messengers have informed [us] about the angels and the jinns and [told us] that they are living rational *(nāṭiq)* [beings], subsisting by themselves, not accidents subsisting by something other than themselves. They also informed [us] that they bring informations about unknown matters and that they accomplish actions outside of the power *(qudra)* of mankind.

God Most High notably informed [us], about the angels, that they came to Abraham, [His] Friend, peace be upon him, then went from him to Lot. The Most High said: "Has the story of Abraham's honoured guests reached you? When they entered upon him and said, 'Peace!' 'Peace!' he said, 'an unfamiliar folk!' Then he retired to his family, brought **[194]** a fattened calf, and placed it close to them, saying: 'Will you not eat?' Then he conceived a fear of them. They said, 'Do not fear!' and they gave him the good news of a knowledgeable son. Then his wife came forward with a loud cry, smote her face, and said, 'A barren old woman!' They said, 'So has your Lord said. Indeed He is the Wise, the Knowing.' [Abraham] said, 'What is your errand, O messengers?' They said, 'We have been sent toward a guilty people, to send upon them stones of clay, marked with your Lord for the profligate.'"[215] The Most High said also: "Our messengers came to

215 Qur'ān, *al-Dhāriyāt* – li, 24–34.

Abraham with the good news. They said, 'Peace!' 'Peace!' he said, and delayed not to bring a roasted calf. But when he saw their hands not reaching for it, he took them amiss and conceived a fear of them. They said, 'Do not fear! We have been sent unto the people of Lot.' His wife, standing by, laughed as We gave her the good news [of the birth] of Isaac and, after Isaac, of Jacob. She said, 'Oh woe unto me! Shall I, an old woman, bear a child, and this my husband is an old man?! That would indeed be an amazing thing!' They said, 'Are you amazed at the commandment of God? [This is] the mercy of God and His blessings upon you, members of the household! Indeed He is Laudable, Glorious!' So when the awe had departed from Abraham, and the good news had come unto him, he pleaded with Us concerning the people of Lot. Truly Abraham was clement, tender-hearted, penitent. 'O Abraham! Keep out of this! Your Lord's commandment has certainly come, and an irrevocable punishment shall come unto them.' When Our messengers came to Lot, **[195]** he was distressed on their account and in a predicament for their sake. He said, 'This is a terrible day!' His people came to him, running towards him – and, before then, they used to commit evil deeds. He said, 'O my people! These are my daughters! They are purer for you. Beware of God, and disgrace me not with regard to my guests. Is there not among you any upright man?' They said, 'You certainly know that we have no right to your daughters, and surely you know what we want.' He said, 'If only I had some force *(quwwa)* against you or could seek refuge in some mighty support!' [The messengers] said, 'O Lot, we are the messengers of your Lord. They shall not reach you. Set out with your family in a part of the night, and none of you should turn round, except your wife; indeed what strikes them shall strike her. Their tryst is the dawn. Is not the dawn nigh?'"[216]

This story is mentioned in the Torah and in other books of the people of the Book just as it is mentioned in the Qur'ān, although it is known that neither of the two Prophets – Moses and Muḥammad – took it from the other. Now, this is among the things that make it necessary *(awjaba)* to acknowledge its authenticity before, [even], the prophethood of the two of them is established. Indeed, an agreement on something like such a narrative, without connivance *(tawāṭu')*, is ordinarily impossible. [Moreover], it is ordinarily impossible that two [persons] **[196]** be agreed on lying, when [telling] something like such a long story, without being in connivance. As the reports of the two [persons] reporting this [story] are agreeing with each other, one thus knows that it is true, and the fact that both are reporting it is a proof of the prophethood of each of them.

[God] said also: "And tell them of the guests of Abraham, when they entered unto him and said, 'Peace!' He said, 'We are afraid of you.' They said, 'Do not be afraid! We bring you the good news of a knowledgeable son.' He said, 'Do you

216 Qur'ān, *Hūd* – xi, 69–81.

bring me the good news [of a son] when old age has befallen me? Of what then are you bringing me good news?' They said, 'We bring you good news in truth. So do not be of those who despair.' He said, 'Who despairs of the mercy of his Lord except those who are astray?' He said, 'What is your errand, O messengers?' They said, 'We have been sent toward a criminal people, except the family of Lot. We shall surely save them, all together, except for his wife, [who], We have determined, shall indeed be of those who lagged behind.' So when the messengers came to the family of Lot, he said, 'You are indeed an unfamiliar folk.' They said, 'Rather we bring you that concerning which they used to dispute. We have brought you the truth, and surely we are truthful. Set out with your family in a part of the night and follow in their rear. None of you should turn round, and proceed wherever you are commanded.'"[217] In this story it is established that the angels exist and that they are living, rational, beings, distinct from the Adamic beings, who address these and whom these – the Prophets and others than the Prophets – see in the forms *(ṣūra)* of the Adamic beings. Sarah, the wife of the Friend [of God], upon him the peace, notably saw them, just as the Companions also used to see Gabriel when he was coming. He was indeed coming in **[197]** the form of a bedouin[218] and, sometimes, in the form of Daḥya l-Kalbī.[219]

Also related to this topic are these words of [God] in the story of Mary: "We sent to her Our Spirit and it assumed for her the likeness of a well-proportioned human. She said, 'I seek refuge in the Merciful from you, should you be God-fearing!' He said, 'I am only the messenger of your Lord, that I may give you a pure son.'"[220] **[198]** The Most High said also: "And Mary, daughter of 'Imrān, who preserved the chastity of her womb, We breathed therein of Our Spirit."[221] This spirit presented itself in the form of a well-proportioned human, addressed Mary, and breathed in her. It is well known, the psychic forces *(quwwa)* that are in the soul of a Prophet, or of someone other than a Prophet, are not seen by those present, and the like of these states, sayings, and actions do not come from them.

217 Qur'ān, *al-Ḥijr* – xv, 51–65.

218 See al-Bukhārī, *Ṣaḥīḥ, Bad' al-waḥy*, vol. i, p. 6; Muslim, *Ṣaḥīḥ, Īmān*, vol. i, p. 30–31.

219 Daḥya (or Diḥya) b. Khalīfa l-Kalbī, bedouin from the tribe of the Banū Kalb who, according to the tradition, was so handsome that Gabriel borrowed his appearance more than once to appear to the Prophet and the Companions; see H. Lammens & Ch. Pellat, *EI2*, art. *Diḥya*. See al-Bukhārī, *Ṣaḥīḥ, Manāqib*, vol. iv, p. 206; Muslim, *Ṣaḥīḥ, Īmān*, vol. i, p. 106. See also A. N. al-Iṣfahānī, *Dalā'il*, p. 222, no 170.

220 Qur'ān, *Maryam* – xix, 17–19.

221 Qur'ān, *al-Taḥrīm* – lxvi, 12.

The Annunciation[222]

Mary was not a Prophetess *(nabiyya)*. She was rather, at the most, a truthful woman *(ṣiddīqa)* as [God] has said: "The Messiah, son of Mary, was naught but a Messenger – Messengers [the like of whom] had passed away before him – and his mother was a truthful one."[223] The Most High said also: "We did not send before you [any Messengers] except men to whom We revealed, from among the people of the towns."[224] A consensus on the inexistence of a Prophetess among women is reported by more than one [scholar], for example the *qāḍī* Abū Bakr b. al-Ṭayyib,[225] the *qāḍī* Abū Ya'lā,[226] Abū l-Ma'ālī al-Juwaynī,[227] and the opposing view of Ibn Ḥazm[228] is an exception, surpassed by the consensus. His claim that the mother of Moses was a Prophetess, and Mary as well, is a saying unknown from any of the ancients *(salaf)* and the imāms. The number of those of the women

222 Miniature from Rashīd al-Dīn Faḍl Allāh (d. 718/1318), *Jāmi' al-Tawārīkh*, Edinburgh University, Or. MS 20, fol. 22 r. (714/1314, Tabriz, Iran); see D. Talbot Rice, *Illustrations*, p. 84–85.

223 Qur'ān, *al-Mā'ida* – v, 75.

224 Qur'ān, *Yūsuf* – xii, 109.

225 Abū Bakr Muḥammad b. al-Ṭayyib al-Bāqillānī (d. 403/1013), Ash'arī theologian and Mālikī *qāḍī*; see R. J. McCarthy, *EI2*, art. *al-Bāḳillānī*.

226 Muḥammad b. al-Ḥusayn b. al-Farrā' (d. 458/1066), better known as *qāḍī* Abū Ya'lā, Ḥanbalī theologian from Baghdād; see H. Laoust, *EI2*, art. *Ibn al-Farrā'*.

227 Abū l-Ma'ālī 'Abd al-Malik al-Juwaynī (d. 478/1085), Imām al-Ḥaramayn, Ash'arī theologian, professor of al-Ghazālī; see C. Brockelmann & L. Gardet, *EI2*, art. *al-Djuwaynī*.

228 Abū Muḥammad 'Alī b. Aḥmad b. Ḥazm (d. Manta Līsham, 456/1064), famous Andalusian poet, historian, philosopher, theologian and ẓāhirī jurist; see R. Arnaldez, *EI2*, art. *Ibn Ḥazm*. For Ibn Ḥazm's acceptance of female prophethood, see his *Fiṣal*, vol. v, p. 17–19.

who were perfect is established in the *Ṣaḥīḥ* and the mother of Moses is not among them. Rather, [the Prophet], God bless him and grant him peace, said in the authentic *ḥadīth*: "Of the men many were perfect. Of the women, none was perfect except Mary, daughter of [199] 'Imrān, and Āsiya, daughter of Muzāḥim."[229] The[230] Prophets are more eminent than the other [humans]. If there was a Prophetess, someone other than a Prophet would thus be more eminent than the latter, or someone other than perfect would be more eminent than someone perfect.

Moreover, God described the angels with attributes implying that they are living, rational, beings exterior to the forces *(quwwa)* of humans and to the intellects and the souls whose [existence] the philosophers establish. One thus knows that the angels about whom the Prophets inform [us] do not correspond to what is said by these [philosophers] who say that the miracles of the Prophets are [due to] psychic forces *(quwwa)*. **[200]**

This is just as He said: "The one of mighty forces *(quwwa)* has taught him, the one vigorous. He stood upright when he was upon the highest horizon. Then he drew nearer and came close, till he was within two bows' length or nearer. Then He revealed to His servant whatever He revealed. The heart lied not in what it saw. Will you then dispute with him as to what he saw?! Certainly he saw him yet another time, at the Lote Tree of the Boundary, near which lies the Garden of the Refuge, when there covered the Lote Tree that which covered. The gaze did not swerve, nor did it transgress. Indeed, he saw one of the greatest signs of his Lord."[231] He said also: "It is indeed the speech of a noble messenger, forceful *(dhū quwwa)*, before the Lord of the Throne, of high rank, obeyed there, trustworthy. Your companion is not mad. Surely he saw him upon the clear horizon, and he does not withhold grudgingly the unknown. Nor is this the speech of a demon worthy to be stoned."[232]

God thus informed [us] that the one who brought the Qur'ān was "a noble messenger, forceful *(dhū quwwa)*, before the Lord of the Throne, of high rank," and that he was "obeyed there, trustworthy." Now, it is impossible that this be the attribute of accidents subsisting by the souls of humans; especially according to

229 See AL-BUKHĀRĪ, *Ṣaḥīḥ, Anbiyā'*, vol. iv, p. 158; MUSLIM, *Ṣaḥīḥ, Faḍā'il*, vol. vii, p. 133; IBN ḤANBAL, *Musnad*, vol. iv, p. 394; IBN MĀJA, *Sunan, Aṭ'ima*, vol. ii, p. 1091, no 3280; AL-TIRMIDHĪ, *Sunan, Aṭ'ima*, vol. iii, p. 179–180, no 1894. Āsiya is the name given by the commentators to the wife of Pharaoh mentioned in the Qur'ān; see A.J. WENSINCK, *EI2*, art. *Āsiya*.

230 —: ya'nī… wa ghayru-humā Ṣ *I.e., among those who [lived] before us and are remembered. Who brought up Moses. Among those who were perfect, of those who were not Prophets, were also Khadīja, Āsiya the wife of Pharaoh, and others than them.* These two lines following the *ḥadīth* just quoted appear to be marginal notes erroneously added to the main text.

231 Qur'ān, *al-Najm* – liii, 5–18.

232 Qur'ān, *al-Takwīr* – lxxxi, 19–25.

those philosophers who declare it to be impossible for the invocations of humans to have an influence on the supreme assembly.[233] He also informed [us] that the [Prophet] had seen him "at the Lote Tree of the Boundary, near which lies the Garden of the Refuge" and had seen him "upon the clear horizon." Now, what occurs in the soul of the Messenger is [taking place] neither here nor there.

The utmost degree they [reach] is to say that this is [some] imagining *(takhayyul)* in the soul of the [Prophet], although it is not existing in the outside. At that moment, the Messenger is thus [belonging] to the genus of the exceptional **[201]** Muslims who see in their sleep that they are in the heavens, that the angels address them, and similar things that exceptional people see. Someone like this would however be deemed a liar neither by the Quraysh, nor by any of the creatures. Someone like this would moreover neither be "forceful *(dhū quwwa)*, before the Lord of the Throne, of high rank," nor "obeyed there, trustworthy."

Among the [philosophers] there are also some who say that Gabriel is the agent intellect which overflows *(fāḍa)* and is not stingy *(ḍanīn)*, i. e., niggardly, in flowing. This [idea] is also vain from many viewpoints.

One of them is that such an [intellect] does not presents itself in the form either of a bedouin, or of Daḥya, or of the guest of Abraham – the Friend [of God] –, or of [the interlocutor of] Lot, or in the form of a well-proportioned human, breathing in Mary.

One of these [viewpoints] is also that [God] said "forceful *(dhū quwwa)*, before the Lord of the Throne, of high rank, obeyed there." Now, the agent intellect is not obeyed there. The utmost degree it [reachs], according to them, is that the lowest [celestial] sphere moves by assimilating *(tashabbuh)* itself to it.[234] As for what is above that, it has no influence on it. They might also say that the Throne is the ninth sphere. What is to be said against that was explained extensively elsewhere and it was made clear that the Throne is above the ninth sphere, it is not that [sphere].

Moreover, [the Qur'ān] informed [us] that [the Prophet] saw [Gabriel] "at the Lote Tree of the Boundary" and that he saw him "upon the clear horizon," twice. In the *Ṣaḥīḥ*, it is also established that he saw Gabriel in his [own] form, in which he had been created, twice, and that he saw him having six hundred wings, two of which were such that he covered by them what is between the orient and the occident.[235] Now, this description **[202]** does not fit the agent intellect: the latter is not visible in two places and it has no wings.

---

233 *Al-mala' al-a'lā*. See Qur'ān, *al-Ṣaffāt* – xxxvii, 8.

234 This statement is actually incorrect. In the Avicennan cosmography, the lowest celestial sphere, i. e., that of the moon, moves by assimilation to the ninth intelligence, not the tenth, i. e., the intellect agent, from which it is the earth that emanates, not a celestial sphere.

235 See AL-BUKHĀRĪ, *Ṣaḥīḥ*, *Bad' al-khalq*, vol. iv, p. 115–116; MUSLIM, *Ṣaḥīḥ*, *Īmān*, vol. i,

These people might say that the Prophets inform people, in their interest *(maṣlaḥa)*, of things that are, as far as the matter itself is concerned, lies. They may also express themselves in a better way and say that the [Prophets] did not inform of the true natures of things *(ḥaqīqa)* but rather mentioned, by striking likenesses *(tamthīl)* and providing imaginal representations (*takhyīl*) related to the faith in God and in the last Day, things from which the commonalty would benefit. As for the true nature of things, they did not inform of it and it is not possible to inform the commonalty thereof.[236] This is something whose vanity is obligatorily known by the religion of the Envoys and we have spoken extensively elsewhere to prove it vain.[237] **[203]** Whoever knows the doctrine of these [philosophers] and knows what the Messengers have said obligatorily knows that what the [philosophers] say goes against what the Messengers say, is not consistent with it. The necessary consequence *(lazima)* shall thus be either judging the Messengers truthful and pronouncing these people to be liars, or pronouncing the Messengers to be liars and judging these people truthful. Now, these people believe in the Messengers from one point of view and disbelieve in them from another. They do not say that they are liars, nor ignorants, and they do not deem them truthful in every thing of which they inform. It is nevertheless well known, when the information given by someone informing of something does not match what he informs about, either he is deliberately lying or he is mistaken. They however admit that the Messengers are among the creatures the most knowledgeable of the true natures of things, that they are specially endowed *(makhṣūṣ)* with holy faculties *(quwā qudsiyya)* by which they know things that it is not possible for others to know, and that they are among the most pious humans and the most truthful of them. As they confess that the [Prophets] possess the ultimate perfection as to knowledge and truthfulness, this contradicts what they mention concerning the [Prophets'] informations. It consequently requires, necessarily *(istalzama)*, to pronounce these [philosophers] either to be liars or to be ignorants.

This is why these people were contradicting themselves concerning matters prophetic. Neither were they pronouncing the [Prophets] to be liars the way these are pronounced to be so by those pronouncing matters prophetic to be lies absolutely, nor were they judging them truthful the way they are judged to be so by the believers who believe in them absolutely. Rather, they were like those who

---

p. 109–111; Ibn Ḥanbal, *Musnad*, vol. i, p. 395. See also A. N. al-Iṣfahānī, *Dalā'il*, p. 215–216, no 163.

236 The philosophical ideas expressed "in a better way" Ibn Taymiyya refers to here are almost certainly those of Avicenna in his *Epistle on the Return for the Feast of the Sacrifice*; see Ibn Sīnā, *Aḍḥawiyya*, p. 43–47; trans. Lucchetta, *Epistola*, p. 42–46.

237 See Ibn Taymiyya's commentary on Avicenna's *Aḍḥawiyya* translated in Y. Michot, *Mamlūk I & II.*

believe in some things and disbelieve in some others. Now, those people are among the unbelievers, verily, while they are among the hypocrites swinging neither toward those nor toward these. Moreover, there are among them some whose hypocrisy and free-thinking *(zandaqa)* abound, and there are among them some whose hypocrisy is less [serious] than the hypocrisy of others.

Moreover, God Most High says: "It is not for any human that God should speak to him except by revelation or from behind a veil, [**204**] or that He should send a messenger in order to reveal by His permission whatever He wills."[238] He thus distinguished, Praised is He, between the revelation and the sending of the messenger who reveals by His permission whatever He wills, just as He distinguished between that and speaking *(takallum)* in His saying, Exalted is He: "We have revealed to you as We revealed to Noah and the Prophets after him. We also revealed to Abraham and Ishmael, Isaac and Jacob, and the Tribes, Jesus and Job, Jonah, Aaron, and Solomon – and We gave David the Psalms – and Messengers We have recounted to you before, and Messengers We have not recounted to you – and God spoke directly to Moses."[239] [God] also distinguished between the general revealing *(īḥā')*, which is shared between the Prophets, and His speaking *(taklīm)* to Moses, peace be upon him, just as He distinguished between revealing and sending a messenger who reveals "by His permission whatever He wills." Now, this contradicts these [philosophers'] doctrine concerning the two principles. They indeed do not establish [the existence of anything] except what is of the genus of revelation and inspiration *(ilhām)*, like the [thing] which they call[240] "the holy force *(quwwa)*." The revelation and inspiration whose [existence] God establishes is however above that whose [existence] they establish of the holy force *(quwwa)*. It is thus proven that the states of the messengers whom God sends to the Prophets are outside of the forces *(quwwa)* of the soul and outside of the genus of general revealing and shared inspiration, just as God Most High said: "God elects from among the angels messengers, and from among mankind."[241] It is clear that He elects Messengers from among mankind and messengers from among the angels.

[God] likewise informed [us] that He speaks to humans "from behind a veil," as He informed [us] that He "spoke directly to Moses" and as He said, Exalted is He: "Those are the Messengers, some of whom We gave a preeminence over others. Among them are those to whom God spoke."[242] He also said: "When Moses came to Our tryst and his Lord spoke unto him, he said, 'My Lord, show

238 Qur'ān, *al-Shūrā* – xlii, 51.
239 Qur'ān, *al-Nisā'* – iv, 163–164. Ibn Taymiyya only quotes the beginning and the end of this Qur'ānic passage and writes between the two: "until the Most High says."
240 yusammūna-hu : yusammūna-hā Ṣ
241 Qur'ān, *al-Ḥajj* – xxii, 75.
242 Qur'ān, *al-Baqara* – ii, 253.

me, that I may look upon You.' He said, 'You will not see Me.'"[243] This implies that [God] speaks directly to some of His servants, outside of **[205]** the genus of what occurs by revelation and inspiration – the things that the holy force *(quwwa)* and other [faculties] deal with.

God also said, Praised is He: "O you who believe! Remember God's blessing upon you when hosts came at you, and We sent against them a wind and hosts whom you did not see. And God sees whatsoever you do."[244] He thus informed [us] that He had sent with the wind hosts whom the believers did not see. The Most High said also: "And on the day of Ḥunayn,[245] when your great number amazed you but it availed you naught, and the earth, despite its breadth, became narrow for you; whereupon you turned your backs. Then God sent down His Tranquility upon His Messenger and upon the believers. He also sent down hosts whom you did not see, and punished those who disbelieved. Such is the reward of the disbelievers."[246] He thus informed [us] that He had sent down the Tranquility upon His Messenger and upon the believers. Therewith He also sent down hosts whom they did not see. The Most High said also: "When you said to the believers, 'Is it not enough for you that your Lord should aid you with three thousand angels sent down?' Yes, if you are patient and God-wary, and should they come at you suddenly, your Lord will aid you with five thousand angels bearing marks."[247] He also said, Exalted is He: "When you sought succour from your Lord, He answered you, 'I shall aid you with a thousand of the angels rank upon rank.' God made it not but as a good news, and that your hearts thereby be reassured. Victory comes only from God. Indeed God is Mighty, Wise. When He covered you with sleepiness, security from Him, and sent down upon you water from the sky to purify you thereby, to remove from you the defilement of Satan, to fortify your hearts, and to make firm [your] steps thereby. When your Lord revealed to the angels, 'I am with you. So make firm those who believe.'"[248] He thus **[206]** informed [us] that He aided them with hosts from among the angels who helped them to victory. In those verses, He informed [us] that the angels come down with knowledge and revelation, and in these verses, He informed [us] that they come down with victory and power *(qudra)*. This makes it clear, what was occurring to the Messenger as knowledge and power – [spiritual] uncovering and influence in the world – was occurring to him thanks to something which was outside of the

243 Qur'ān, *al-A'rāf* – vii, 143.

244 Qur'ān, *al-Aḥzāb* – xxxiii, 9.

245 Name of a famous battle (8/630) where the Prophet, after initial problems, eventually defeated the Meccans; see H. LAMMENS & A. KAMAL, *EI2*, art. *Ḥunayn*.

246 Qur'ān, *al-Tawba* – ix, 25–26.

247 Qur'ān, *Āl 'Imrān* – iii, 124–125.

248 Qur'ān, *al-Anfāl* – viii, 9–12. Ibn Taymiyya only quotes the beginning and the end of this Qur'ānic passage and writes between the two: "until He says."

forces *(quwwa)* of his soul: the knowledge with which the angels come down and the victory with which the angels come down.

The angels helping the Muslims fighting at Badr[249]

God Most High moreover said: "Were you to see when the angels take back those who disbelieve, striking their faces and their backs, and [saying], 'Taste the punishment of the burning!'"[250] The Most High also said: "Indeed, those whom the angels take back while they wrong themselves, [the angels] say, 'What state were you in?' They say, 'We were reduced to weakness in the land.'"[251] The Most High also said: "Those whom the angels take back while they are good, they say [to them], 'Peace be upon you! Enter the Garden for that which you used to do.' Do they await aught but that the angels should come to them or that your Lord's command should come?"[252] In these verses, [God] informs [us] that the angels take back the souls, address the dead [to tell them something] either good or bad,

249 Detail from a popular under-glass painting, Senegal, *c.* 1936; see M. Renaudeau & M. Strobel, *Peinture*, p. 44–45.
250 Qur'ān, *al-Anfāl* – viii, 50.
251 Qur'ān, *al-Nisā'* – iv, 97.
252 Qur'ān, *al-Naḥl* – xvi, 32–33.

and do what they do to them in the matter of bliss and punishment. He said likewise: "Truly those who say, 'Our Lord is God!' and afterward are upright, the angels descend upon them, [saying], 'Do not fear, nor be grieved! Receive the good news of the Garden which you have been promised. We are your friends in the life of this world and in the Hereafter, and you will have in it whatsoever your souls desire, **[207]** and you will have in it whatsoever you call for, as a hospitality from One Forgiving, Merciful.'"[253] The Most High also said: "Do they await aught but that the angels should come to them, or that your Lord should come, or that some of your Lord's signs should come?"[254] He also said: "Do they await anything but that God should come to them in the shades of the clouds, and the angels, and the matter be decreed?"[255] These texts and their like explicitly establish [the existence of] the angels, of their actions, of their speaking, and of their influence in the world, by saying and acting. Now this makes vain the saying of these [philosophers] that what has an influence in the world is the psychic forces *(quwwa)* or the natural forces *(quwwa)*. Indeed the angels are outside of these and outside of those. At that moment, what occurs of the extraordinary phenomena through the actions of the angels is greater than what simply occurs through the psychic forces *(quwwa)*. Also, the Prophets are the humans who most deserve that the angels help them and that God Most High support them, as God, Praised is He, informed [us] thereof.

God Most High moreover said: "By those ranged in ranks, and the ones rebuking vigorously, and the readers of a reminder!"[256] And He said in the last part of the *sūra:* "So ask them, 'Has your Lord the daughters while they have the sons? Or did We create the angels female, while they were witnesses?' Lo! It is out of their mendacity that they say, 'God has begotten.' Verily they tell a lie. Has He elected the daughters over the sons? What ails you? How do you judge? Will you not take admonition? Or have you a manifest authority? Then produce your writ, if you are truthful. They have set up a kinship between Him and the jinns – yet the jinns certainly know that they will be presented before [Him]. Praised be God above that which they ascribe. Not so for the consecrated servants of God. For truly neither you nor that which you worship tempts [anyone] against Him, except someone who is bound to the Gehenna. 'There is none among us but has a known station. **[208]** Indeed, it is we who are the ranged ones. Indeed, it is we who are those who celebrate His praise.'"[257] He has thus informed [us] that the angels are ranged, praising, and that they are ranged in ranks, drivers driving. Now, this

253 Qur'ān, *Fuṣṣilat* – xli, 30–32.
254 Qur'ān, *al-An'ām* – vi, 158.
255 Qur'ān, *al-Baqara* – ii, 210.
256 Qur'ān, *al-Ṣāffāt* – xxxvii, 1–3.
257 Qur'ān, *al-Ṣāffāt* – xxxvii, 149–166. Ibn Taymiyya only quotes the beginning and the end of this Qur'ānic passage and writes between the two: "until He says."

contradicts what these [philosophers] say. The ten intelligences are indeed not standing in ranks. They are rather one above the other in degree and dependence, with the impossibility for them to be in ranks *(maṣāffa)*, according to these [philosophers]. It is also impossible to describe the accidents subsisting by the soul by means of that which He, Praised and Exalted is He, has mentioned: standing in ranks, rebuking, reading, and the other attributes.

The Most High said likewise: "We do not come down except by the command of your Lord. To Him belongs whatsoever is before us and whatsoever is behind us and whatsoever is in between that, and your Lord is not forgetful."[258] It is established that the Prophet, God bless him and grant him peace, said to Gabriel: "What forbids you to visit us more often than you visit us?"[259] God then sent down this verse. This makes it clear, Gabriel comes down to the earth and he does not come down except by the command of God. Now, according to these [philosophers], it is impossible for an angel to come down to the earth and it is impossible for God to command Gabriel to come down [to it].

The Most High said also: "They say, 'The Merciful has taken a son.' Be He Praised! Rather they are honoured servants. They do not precede Him in speech, and they act by His command. He knows whatsoever is before them and whatsoever is behind them, and they do not intercede except for someone with whom **[209]** He is content. They are wary, for awe of Him. Should any of them say, 'I am a god beneath Him,' such shall We reward with the Gehenna. Thus do We reward the unjust."[260] He thus made it clear, Praised is He, they are servants whom He honoured, do not precede Him in speech – they thus do not speak until He speaks –, act by His command – they thus do not act until He commands them [to do so] –, do not intercede except for someone with whom He is content, and are wary, for awe of Him. Now, this contradicts what these [philosophers] say. According to them, the intelligences or, rather, the whole world, are generated from God through a necessarily concomitant *(lāzim)* generation through which it is impossible that they be afraid or that a command or word happen to come to them from God, or that they have [the possibility] to intercede with Him. The[261] meaning of "intercession" *(shafāʿa)*, according to [these philosophers], is not to invoke God and His Messenger as it is [in] the doctrine of the Muslims. Intercession, according to them, is rather that the heart is attached to [some] means, so much so that on it flows *(fāḍa)*, by the intermediary *(bi-wāsiṭa)* of these means,

---

258 Qur'ān, *Maryam* – xix, 64.

259 See AL-BUKHĀRĪ, *Ṣaḥīḥ*, *Bad' al-khalq*, vol. iv, p. 112–113; *Tafsīr*, vol. vi, p. 94; IBN ḤANBAL, *Musnad*, vol. i, p. 231, 234; AL-TIRMIDHĪ, *Sunan*, *Tafsīr*, vol. iv, p. 377, no 5167.

260 Qur'ān, *al-Anbiyā'* – xxi, 26–29.

261 A translation of the three following pages of Ṣ (p. 209, l. 10 – p. 212, l. 9) was already published in Y. MICHOT, *Reader*, p. 142–144. The footnotes relating to them are given here in an abridged version.

something from which it benefits, just as the rays of the sun flow upon a wall by the intermediary of their flowing on a mirror. Now, this is an intercession of the kind that the associators establish [the existence of] and it is the one which God has rejected in His Book.

Things have got into what Abū Ḥāmid [al-Ghazālī][262] says in *[The Book] to Be Withheld from Those Who are not Worthy of it*,[263] and in others of his books, that are of the genus of what those [philosophers] say about intercession, about prophethood, etc. He even fixes [the number of] properties of the Prophet at three,[264] as mentioned before, and [adopts] other things which they say.

The critique *(nakīr)* of these words by the scholars of Islam was strong, and they said about Abū Ḥāmid and his like things that are well known. **[210]** The companions of Abū l-Maʿālī [al-Juwaynī], such as Abū l-Ḥasan al-Marghīnānī[265] and others, spoke likewise about him. The members of the house of al-Qushayrī[266] and his followers spoke likewise about him; and also the shaykh Abū l-Bayān,[267] Abū l-Ḥasan b. Shukr,[268] Abū ʿAmr b. al-Ṣalāḥ[269] and Abū Zakariyyā'.[270] **[211]** Abū Bakr al-Ṭurṭūshī,[271] Abū ʿAbd Allāh al-Māzarī[272] and Ibn Ḥamdīn al-Qurṭubī[273] spoke likewise about him. Abū Bakr b. al-ʿArabī,[274] his disciple, wrote something about that and even said: "Our shaykh Abū Ḥāmid entered into the belly of the philosophers; he thereafter wanted to come out from among them but was not able [to do so]."[275] **[212]** Abū l-Wafā' b. al-ʿAqīl,[276] Abū l-

262 Abū Ḥāmid Muḥammad al-Ghazālī l-Ṭūsī (d. 505/1111), Ashʿarī theologian and mystic.

263 See AL-GHAZĀLĪ, *Maḍnūn*. On this work, see Y. MICHOT, *Textes N.S. XI*, p. 2; *Reader*, p. 141–147.

264 See M. AFIFI AL-AKITI, *Properties*, p. 189–212; F. GRIFFEL, *Concept*.

265 Probably Ẓahīr al-Dīn ʿAlī b. ʿAbd al-Razzāq Abū Naṣr al-Marghīnānī (d. 506/1112), Ḥanafī ulema from Khurāsān and disciple of al-Ghazālī.

266 ʿAbd al-Karīm b. Hawāzin al-Qushayrī (d. 465/1073), the author of *The Epistle (al-Risāla)*. His two sons are Abū Naṣr ʿAbd al-Raḥīm b. ʿAbd al-Karīm (d. 514/1120), preacher in Baghdād, and Abū l-Fatḥ ʿAbd Allāh b. ʿAbd al-Karīm (d. 521/1127).

267 Naba' b. Muḥammad Abū l-Bayān al-Qurshī (d. 551/1156), known as Ibn al-Ḥawrānī, Shāfiʿī Sufi of Damascus.

268 Abū l-Ḥasan Aḥmad b. ʿAlī b. Muḥammad al-Andalusī (d. in Fayyūm, 640/1242).

269 Taqī l-Dīn Abū ʿAmr ʿUthmān b. ʿAbd al-Raḥmān al-Kurdī l-Shahrazūrī (d. Damascus, 643/1245), known as Ibn al-Ṣalāḥ.

270 Muḥyī l-Dīn Abū Zakariyyā' Yaḥyā b. Sharaf al-Nawawī (d. 676/1277), Shāfiʿī jurist and important traditionist.

271 Abū Bakr Muḥammad b. al-Walīd al-Fihrī l-Ṭurṭūshī (d. Alexandria, 520/1126), Andalusian Mālikī jurist.

272 Abū ʿAbd Allāh Muḥammad b. ʿAlī l-Tamīmī l-Māzarī (d. Mahdiyya, 536/1141), known as al-Imām, Sicilian Mālikī traditionist and jurist.

273 Abū ʿAbd Allāh Muḥammad b. Ḥamdīn al-Qurṭubī (d. 508/1114), Almoravid jurist and Mālikī qāḍī of Cordoba.

274 Abū Bakr Muḥammad b. ʿAbd Allāh b. al-ʿArabī l-Maʿāfirī (d. 543/1148), Mālikī great qāḍī of Seville and one of the major ulema under the Almoravids.

275 On this quote, see E. L. ORMSBY, *Theodicy*, p. 102.

Faraj b. al-Jawzī,[277] Abū Muḥammad al-Maqdisī[278] and others spoke likewise about him. Al-Kardarī[279] and others among the companions of Abū Ḥanīfa spoke likewise about him.

Among the gravest things because of which the imāms of the realizers [of the truth] *(muḥaqqiq)* spoke about [al-Ghazālī] is that about which he was in agreement with those philosophizing Ṣābi'ans. Thereafter, he nevertheless refuted the philosophers and made clear their incoherence *(tahāfut)* and unbelief. He also made it clear, their road *(ṭarīqa)* does not enable [one] to reach the truth. Moreover, he also refuted the *Kalām* theologians and gave his preference to the road of devotion *(riyāḍa)* and Sufism. Thereafter, when he did not obtain, by these roads, what he was in search of, he remained among the people of suspension *(waqf)* and leaned towards the road of the adepts of *ḥadīth*. He died while preoccupying himself with al-Bukhārī and Muslim.

What is aimed at here is [to make clear] that what God has mentioned in His book of the intercession of the Prophets and the angels, by denying and establishing [things], contradicts what these [philosophers] say. [There is] for example this saying of the Most High: "Say: 'Invoke them whom you claim [to be] beneath God! They do not possess [even] a mote's weight in the heavens or in the earth, nor have they any share in either, nor has He a helper among them.' Intercession will benefit none with Him except whomsoever He permits. Yet, when fright is banished from their hearts, they say: 'What did your Lord say?' They say: 'The truth, and He is the Sublime, the Great.'"[280] **[213]** In the authentic *ḥadīth*s, it is established about the Prophet, God bless him and grant him peace, in more than one variant *(wajh)*, that he said: "When God decides some matter in the Heaven, the angels beat with their wings in submission to His words, as if it was a chain [dragged] over a rock, and they are stunned until, when fright is banished from their hearts, they say: 'What did your Lord say?' 'They say: 'The truth, and He is the Sublime, the Great.'" This idea is established about the Prophet, God bless him and grant him peace, in more than one variant *(wajh)*. Al-Bukhārī reported it among the traditions of Abū Hurayra[281] and Muslim reported it from Ibn 'Abbās,[282] on the authority of some men of the Auxiliaries.[283] **[214]** It is also

276 Abū l-Wafā' 'Alī b. 'Aqīl b. Muḥammad b. 'Aqīl al-Baghdādī (d. 512/1119), Ḥanbalī jurist.

277 Abū l-Faraj 'Abd al-Raḥmān b. 'Alī b. al-Jawzī (d. 597/1200), Ḥanbalī ulema.

278 Taqī l-Dīn Abū Muḥammad 'Abd al-Ghanī l-Maqdisī (d. 600/1203), Ḥanbalī ulema and traditionist.

279 Muḥammad b. 'Abd al-Sattār b. Muḥammad, Shams al-a'imma, al-Kardarī (d. 642/1244), Ḥanafī jurist.

280 Qur'ān, *Saba'* – xxxiv, 22–23.

281 See AL-BUKHĀRĪ, *Ṣaḥīḥ*, *Tawḥīd*, vol. ix, p. 141; *Tafsīr*, vol. vi, p. 80, 122; IBN MĀJA, *Sunan*, *Muqaddima*, vol. i, p. 69–70, no 194; AL-TIRMIDHĪ, *Sunan*, *Tafsīr*, vol. v, p. 40, no 3276.

282 'Abd Allāh b. al-'Abbās (d. 68/686–8), great scholar of the first generation; see L. VECCIA VAGLIERI, *EI2*, art. *'Abd Allāh b. al-'Abbās*.

known among the traditions of al-Nawwās b. Sam'ān[284] about the Prophet, God bless him and grant him peace. It is moreover [reported] from Ibn Mas'ūd[285] with a chain going back to a Companion *(mawqūf)* and with one going back to the Prophet *(marfū')*, as well as from Ibn 'Abbās[286] and others.

In this, there is a clear explanation that intercession with God benefits none except whomsoever He permits. The intercessor must inevitably have a permission. Simply turning towards Him does not benefit the person for whom he intercedes. This obligatorily demands *(iqtaḍā)* a renewing of the permission for the intercessors. Now, according to these [philosophers], nothing [coming] from God occurs for the intermediaries. Rather, they are generated from Him by necessarily accompanying *(lāzim)* His essence, eternally and sempiternally.

The angels of the fifth heaven[287]

In this *[ḥadīth]*, it is also [explained] that fright is banished from the hearts of the angels, i.e., that fright disappears from them. In the Qur'ān, the angels are described as awed and afraid. Now, according to these [philosophers], awe and fear of God are not imaginable *(taṣawwara)*. God, Exalted is He, said: "To God prostrates whatever is in the heavens and whatever is on the earth of animals, as well as the angels, and they do not wax arrogant. They fear their Lord above them, and they do whatsoever they are commanded."[288] He also said: "And they are apprehensive, for awe of Him."[289] Concerning intercession, the Most High said:

283 See Muslim, *Ṣaḥīḥ*, vol. vii, p. 36–37; Ibn Ḥanbal, *Musnad*, vol. i, p. 218.

284 Al-Nawwās b. Sam'ān b. Khālid, Companion of Syrian origin; see Ibn al-Athīr, *Usd*, vol. v, p. 45.

285 'Abd Allāh b. Mas'ūd (d. 32/652), famous Companion and reader of the Qur'ān; see J.-C. Vadet, *EI2*, art. *Ibn Mas'ūd*.

286 See Abū Dā'ūd, *Sunan*, *Sunna*, vol. iv, p. 235, no 4738.

287 From Z. al-Qazwīnī, *'Ajā'ib*, p. 94.

288 Qur'ān, *al-Naḥl* – xvi, 49–50.

289 Qur'ān, *al-Anbiyā'* – xxi, 28.

"And how many an angel is there in the heavens whose intercession avails naught, except after God will have granted permission to whomsoever He wills and is content with."[290] His saying "after *(min ba'di an)* God will have granted permission to whomsoever He wills and is content with" obligatorily demands a future permission. This *an* devotes the unaccomplished verb to the future. This excludes that something like that[291] be said about everything which comes up in the Qur'ān on this topic. It is what is said by most *(jumhūr)* of the people of the *ḥadīth* and the *Sunna* and it is what has been transmitted from the imāms of the ancients *(salaf)*. It is also what is proved by the rational *('aqlī)* proofs free from contradiction. [215]

Among the things making the matter manifest on this topic is the fact that God has exempted *(nazzaha)* Himself from [having] an associate and a child in more than one passage. The Most High said for example: "They make the jinns partners unto God, though He created them, and falsely attribute sons and daughters to Him, without any knowledge. Glorified is He and Exalted above that which they ascribe. The Originator of the heavens and the earth! How could He have a child, when He has no female companion, created all things, and He is knowing all things?"[292] God Most High also said: "And say: 'Praise be to God, Who has neither taken any son, nor has He any partner in the sovereignty, nor has He any protector out of lowliness. And magnify Him greatly!'"[293] The Most High also said: "God has not taken any child, nor is there any god with Him; for then each god would go with that which he created."[294] The Most High also said: "Blessed is He Who sent down the Criterion upon His servant, that he may be a warner unto the worlds. He, to Whom belongs the Sovereignty over the heavens and the earth, and Who did not take a child, nor has He any partner in the Sovereignty."[295] The Most High also said: "Look! Is it not out of their mendacity that they say, 'God has begotten,' while indeed they are lying?"[296] The Most High also said: "Say: 'He is God, One. God, the compact! He neither begat, nor was begotten, and there is none equal to Him.'"[297] God has thus exempted Himself from [having] a child and an equal.

Saying such things is found among the associationist Arabs, among the Nazarenes, and others. What is found among these [philosophers] is however

290 Qur'ān, *al-Najm* – liii, 26.

291 I.e., the philosophical view that "nothing [coming] from God occurs for the intermediaries. Rather, they are generated from Him by necessarily accompanying His essence, eternally and sempiternally."

292 Qur'ān, *al-An'ām* – vi, 100–101.

293 Qur'ān, *al-Isrā'* – xvii, 111.

294 Qur'ān, *al-Mu'minūn* – xxiii, 91.

295 Qur'ān, *al-Furqān* – x, 4.

296 Qur'ān, *al-Ṣaffāt* – xxxvii, 151–152.

297 Qur'ān, *al-Ikhlāṣ* – cxii.

worse than all that. This is because the associationist Arabs, the Nazarenes, and their like confess that God is the Creator of all things, its Lord, and its owner, but affirm a generation *(tawallud)* from some points of view, i. e., a generation which occurs [at some moment] as the Nazarenes say it about the Messiah and as the associationist Arabs used to say it about the angels, and similar things. As for these [philosophers], they say that **[216]** the intelligences and the souls are generated from God through a preeternal, eternal, generative process *(tawallud)* necessarily accompanying *(lāzim)* His essence, and that the world is generated from that. The whole world is thus, according to them, generated from God through a preeternal, eternal, generative process necessarily accompanying *(lāzim)* His essence. Though they might not express [this] by the term "child" *(walad)*, they express [it] by the terms "caused" *(ma'lūl)* and "cause" *('illa)*, i. e., the most particular of the [various] species of generation. They also express [it] by the terms 'necessitating" *(mūjib)* and "necessitated" *(mūjab)*.

Now, what God mentions in His book as invalidation *(ibṭāl)* of generation invalidates what they say, rationally and *ex auditu*. The Most High indeed said: "They falsely attribute sons and daughters to Him, without any knowledge"[298] whereas these philosophizers liken the intelligence to the male and the soul to the female. He also said, Praised and Exalted is he: "How could He have a child, when He has no female companion, created all things, and He is knowing all things?"[299] There is indeed no generation except from two principles, not from one. It would be impossible for Him to have a child without a female companion and He, Praised is He, "there is none equal to Him." Now, these [philosophizers] consider Him to be One, consider the world to be caused by Him, and say that from the One nothing emanates except the one, and this is vain. Indeed, from the one alone, the simple, nothing emanates. Or, rather, the one which they suppose [to be] only exists in the minds, not in the concrete *(a'yān)*, and no effect emanates in the world – superior and inferior – except from two or more causes *(sabab)*. When fire is burning it is only burning on the condition that the locus *(maḥall)* receives its burning. To be burning thus results from two causes, not from one cause. Similarly for rays, and similarly for all affairs.

God, Exalted is He, said: "And of all things We have created pairs, that haply you may remember."[300] Some ulema said: "…[that haply] you may know that the Creator of the pairs is One." [God] also said: "Glory be to Him Who created the pairs, all of them, from what the earth grows, and from themselves, and from what they do not know!"[301] **[217]** In the creatures, there is no one from whom

298 Qur'ān, *al-An'ām* – vi, 100.
299 Qur'ān, *al-An'ām* – vi, 101.
300 Qur'ān, *al-Dhāriyāt* – li, 49.
301 Qur'ān, *Yā-Sīn* – xxxvi, 36.

alone something emanates, nor a cause causing its effect independently *(mustaqill bi-maʿlūli-hi)*, with fundamentally no partner – what a group of the *Kalām* theologians mention about the knowledge *(ʿilm)* being the cause of [someone's] being knowledgeable *(ʿālimiyya)* has no reality according to most of them. Being knowledgeable is indeed not adding to the knowledge, and the partisans of the states *(ḥāl)*[302] who affirmed that it adds to the knower said that it is not [something] existential *(wujūdī)*. So, in the existence, there is no cause causing its effect independently, without having a partner. It is thus clear that what these [philosophizers] have mentioned about the Necessary [Existent] being a cause causing its effect independently goes against what existence is like *(ʿalay-hi)*, and their claim that the one, simple, is a complete cause causing independently its effect is an affair going against what existence is like. It is unknown to reason or, rather, it is vain for it. But what is rationally known is that from the One nothing emanates [as] caused, generated from it, except by something else being connected to it. If the world was caused, generated from God, [God] would have [something] connected to Him *(muqārin)*, the generation emanating from both of them together. Indeed, there is no generation except from two principles. To affirm causation and generation obligatorily demands *(iqtaḍā)* to affirm [that God has] an associate in originating *(ibdāʿ)* the world.

They must also necessarily *(lāzim)* [affirm] that, unavoidably, from another point of view. It is indeed not possible for the things that occur *(ḥādith)* [and then] exist in the world to emanate from a complete, eternal, cause, as what such [a cause] causes necessarily accompanies *(lazima)* it, is thus preeternal with it, and is therefore not made to occur *(muḥdath)*. It is thus necessary *(wajaba)* for the occurring things to have another agent, different from the complete, eternal, cause, and that also makes it necessary *(awjaba)* to establish [the existence of] an associate of God that makes the occurring things occur. This is also vain. If indeed that thing which has been assumed to make the occurring things occur is [itself] made to occur, it belongs to the ensemble of occurring things that need an agent making them occur; whereas, if it is preeternal, the occurring things emanate from something preeternal! If it is thus a complete, eternal, cause, it it impossible for the occurring things to occur from it. And if it is an agent by whose choice the occurring things occur from it, what these [philosophizers] say is vain, whether it is said that it comes to make the occurring things occur, after it was not not making them occur, without an occurring reason, or it is said that it has not ceased being an agent, capable *(qādir)* of a choice-based *(ikhtiyārī)* action subsisting in itself. **[218]**

It is thus clear that what these people say to establish [the existence of] an associate and a child for God is among the worse things said by whomsoever says

302 Abū Hāshim al-Jubbāʾī (d. 321/933) and his school; see R. Frank, *Theory*.

that, and that everything which is in the Qur'ān as invalidation thereof by rational and information-related *(khabarī)* proofs invalidates what they say. But to understand this requires to understand the real nature of the things said by the [various religious] communities and their degrees [in error], as well as how the Qur'ān deals with them, invalidates them, and distinguishes the truth from what is vain by means of rational, demonstrative *(burhānī)*, proofs, as has been explained elsewhere.

All this is among the things making clear that the Messengers informed [us], concerning the angels, that they are servants of God who are not generated from Him and whose Creator is not a cause making them be necessarily *(mūjib)*, that they do not do anything *(taṣarrafa)* except with His permission, that they do not precede Him in speech, that they inform the Prophets of the unknown, and that they perform, as extraordinary and other phenomena, things in which there is help to victory for the Prophets and a proof for them.

This also makes clear that these philosophers contradict the Messengers concerning what they inform [us] about as to the proclamation of [God's] oneness *(tawḥīd)* and the angels, and as to the miracles of the Prophets. It makes clear that the miracles are outside of the forces *(quwwa)* of the souls of mankind and that what these [philosophers] say about the miracles is something said without proof, i. e., a vain saying based on a vain principle. We nevertheless do not deny that the forces *(quwwa)* that are in the souls and the rest of the bodies have [some] effects in the world commensurate with them, as said previously, but to relate the extraordinary phenomena to that is vain, just as [it would be] if someone was relating them to the forces *(quwwa)* of the bodies and was claiming that they are of the same sort as the operations of white magic *(nīrānjiyyāt)*, which are natural forces *(quwwa)* like the forces *(quwwa)* [existing] in a magnetic stone. It is indeed known from many viewpoints that the miracles of the Prophets are outside of this genus [of phenomena] and outside of that genus [of them]. And if the person saying that the miracles of the Prophets are psychic forces *(quwwa)* **[219]** is of those who pronounce [matters prophetic] to be lies absolutely, we have established that[303] what we have mentioned of the miracles through numerous ways, like abundantly recurrent reports and like the concurring of traditions *(sunan)* with reports, is something[304] on which an agreement would have been impossible without connivance *(tawāṭu')*, etc.

NINTH VIEWPOINT. It is to say that the influence of the souls has for condition their being conscious *(shu'ūr)*. The soul is indeed living, willing, acting by its will. Its action has for condition its will, and a choice-based *(ikhtiyārī)*, voluntary *(irādī)*, action has for condition consciousness. Now, among the extraordinary

303 anna : ba'ḍ Ṣ
304 mim-mā : bi-mā Ṣ

phenomena [linked] to the Prophets, there are some of which the Prophet is not conscious and there are some which he does not will. Such [phenomena] are thus not [resulting] from an action of his soul. Among these [phenomena], there are even some that [appear] before his existence and the existence of his power *(qudra)*, and there are some that [appear] after his death and the separation of his soul from this world. It is well known, for what [appears] before a force *(quwwa)* comes to his soul, etc., it is impossible for that to be related to his force *(quwwa)*. Indeed, what is inexistent has no force *(quwwa)*. An example of this is the story of the masters of the elephant which God sent down: when [these people] came with an elephant to Mecca, "He sent against them flocks of birds pelting them with stones of shale, and made them like chewed-up straw."[305] The people of the elephant were Nazarenes and their religion was better than the religion of the people of Mecca in that time. These were indeed associators and the religion of the Nazarenes is better than the religion of the associators who worship idols. [Destroying the masters of the elephant] was a prodigy of the Prophet, God bless him and grant him peace, sent out [to proclaim] the sacredness *(ḥurma)* of the House.[306] The year of the elephant was the year of his birth, God bless him and grant him peace. [The event took place] before his birth by about fifty nights, and neither did he [then] have a psychic force *(quwwa)* by which to have an influence, nor a consciousness of what happened, nor a will concerning it. Similarly, what happened as events *(ḥādith)* at the moment of his birth, God bless him and grant him peace, the informations [given by] the diviners about his affairs, and what the jinns started to inform them of concerning his prophethood,[307] were [all] affairs outside of his power *(qudra)*, his knowledge, and his will. Similarly also, what the people of the Book were informed of and what is found written with the people **[220]** of the Book as informations [given by] the anterior Prophets about his prophethood,[308] his messengership and the command to follow him [given by God] to mankind, [These] were [all] affairs outside of his power *(qudra)*, his knowledge, and his will, that came to be before his birth.

---

305 See Qur'ān, *al-Fīl* – cv, 3–5.

306 I.e., the Kaʿba.

307 See A. N. al-Iṣfahānī, *Dalā'il*, p. 107–128, nos 56–70. "Jewish rabbis, Christian monks, and Arab soothsayers had spoken about the apostle of God before his mission when his time drew near. As to the rabbis and monks, it was about his description and the description of his time which they found in their scriptures and what the prophets had enjoined upon them. As to the Arab soothsayers they had been visited by satans from the jinn with reports which they had secretly overheard before they were prevented from hearing by being pelted with stars. Male and female soothsayers continued to let fall mention of some of these matters to which the Arabs paid no attention until God sent him and these things which had been mentioned happened and they recognized them" (Ibn Isḥāq, *Sīra*, trans. Guillaume, *Life*, p. 90).

308 On passages of the Bible which Ibn Taymiyya sees as announcing Muḥammad, see Y. Michot, *Roi croisé*, p. 107–112. See also A. N. al-Iṣfahānī, *Dalā'il*, p. 71–94, nos 32–49; M. al-Qurṭubī, *Iʿlām*, p. 263–280.

Similarly still with that whereby God singled out the Kaʿba, the Sacred House, from the moment when Abraham built it and until this time: the veneration and reverence it [commands], and how the hearts are attracted toward it. It is well known, the kings and others build citadels, cities, and castles, with enormous, accurate building instruments; thereafter, however, it does not take long before these [buildings] are destroyed and treated with contempt. As for the Kaʿba, it is a House built from black stones in a valley without agriculture, next to which there is nothing that the souls desire: gardens, water, etc. Neither are there soldiers there to protect it from enemies, nor is there on the way [leading to] it any of the enjoyments which the souls crave. On the contrary, how often there is on the way [leading to] it, in the matter of fear and fatigue, thirst and hunger, things that nobody knows except God! And in spite of that, of the hearts of the humans longing for it God has made something that nobody knows except He! Of might, nobility, and greatness, He has given to [His] House something by which He has subdued the necks of the people of the earth, so that the greatest of the kings and the chiefs of the despots head towards it and stand there in humility and meekness like any one of the humans. Now, [all] this is among the things that, it is obligatorily known, are outside of the power *(qudra)* of mankind and the forces *(quwwa)* of their souls and bodies. And the one who built it died thousands of years ago!

The Kaʿba in Mecca[309]

This is why the affair of the House is among the things that have baffled these philosophers, astrologers, and naturalists *(ṭabāʾiʿī)*, due to its being outside of the

309 Table in E. Wendt, *Bilder-Mappe.*

gauge *(qiyās)* of their intellects and outside of the canons of their sciences. They consequently fabricated, as lies, things that every intelligent, sensible *(labīb)* person knows. Some of them say for example that there is under the Kaʿba a room in which there is an idol of metal[310] which is incensed and turns its face to the four directions so that people come to the pilgrimage. [221] Now this is among the things which everyone knowledgeable of the matter of Mecca knows to be among the clearest lies. [One also knows] that there is nothing of that [kind] under the Kaʿba, that none of the inhabitants of Mecca goes down into what is under the Kaʿba, neither digs it, nor incenses anything there, and that no idol of metal is there, nor anything else.[311] Ibn Sabʿīn and his like among those used to be baffled by that and sometimes said: "We wish we knew what is the talisman that Abraham, the Friend [of God], designed so that the affair became as it is!"[312] They indeed knew that the affairs of talismans do not reach anything like this, that there is nothing close to this on the earth, and that talismans are ordinary affairs, well-known, with well-known causes. This is why a man designs a talisman, and [why] another designs one like it or greater than it. As for this [affair of the Kaʿba], it is outside of the power *(qudra)* of mankind. In the existence, there is indeed neither a talisman overwhelming the inhabitants of the [whole] earth, nor a talisman[313] operating in the hearts of the inhabitants of the three [central]

310 ṣanam : ṣa'm Ṣ

311 Similar myths about the Kaʿba are still circulating today. For example, the English newspaper *Daily Star* published on its front page of 22 December 2015 a report concerning the discovery, "under Mecca's Grand Mosque," of "an ancient apocalyptic weapon" which was subsequently given to Russia; see D. Trayner, *Ark.* The story went viral on the internet and can still be found in a number of variants on YouTube.

312 "The Kaʿba is a House [built] from stones in a valley without agriculture. There is nobody next to it to preserve it from an enemy, nor are there, next to it, gardens and things that people have a desire for. It has nothing to appeal, nor to frighten. And in spite of that, [God] has preserved it by [its] awe-inspiring appearance *(hayba)* and greatness: everyone coming to it comes to it submissive, humble, unpretentious in the most extreme degree. He has also put in it such an appeal that **[511]** people come to it from the [various] countries of the earth out of love, passionately *(shawq)*, without any mundane motive. It has been in this situation for thousands of years and this is among things that, in the world, are not known [to exist] for any other building. Kings build great castles and these last for a period, after which they are destroyed, nobody desiring to rebuild them nor being frightened by their ruin. Similarly for an [edifice] built for acts of worship: its state changes with the passing of time and an enemy might capture it as Jerusalem was captured. As for the Kaʿba, it has something special *(khāṣṣa)* which does not belong to other [buildings], and this is among the things that have baffled the philosophers and their like. They are of the opinion that what has an influence in this world is the movements of the [celestial] sphere and that something which was built and lasted was built with a fortunate ascendant. Now, they are baffled concerning the ascendant of the Kaʿba as, in the configurations of the [celestial] spheres, they have not found anything that would necessitate such a fortune *(saʿāda)*, might, greatness, permanence, triumph, and supremacy" (Ibn Taymiyya, *Nubuwwāt*, p. 510–511).

313 ṭilasm + : wa lā Ṣ

climes, who are the most eminent of humans and the most perfect of them in intellects and religions. The influence of talismans is only strong when the intellect is weak. It has thus more influence in inanimate beings than in living ones, it has more influence in beasts than in humans, and it has more influence in the youth and the mad than in the intellectuals. Similarly for the influence of the demons: everytime the intellects are weak, their influence is strong.

As for the House, the Qur'ān,[314] and prophethood, their influence is only strong among the people who are the most perfect in intellect and the most accomplished in science and knowledge. Also, Islam spread into the orients of the earths and its occidents as the Prophet said, God bless him and grant him peace: "The earth was folded for me and I saw its orients and its occidents. The rule *(mulk)* of my community shall reach what, thereof, was folded for me."[315]

314 "The sign [constituted by] the Qur'ān is still there *(bāqī)* despite the length of time that has passed since when the Messenger brought it, the verses challenging *(taḥaddī)* [people to bring the like of it] being recited. [These] words of [God] are [indeed still] recited: 'Let them bring a discourse like it, if they are truthful' (Q., *al-Ṭūr* – lii, 34), 'Bring ten sūras like it' (Q., *Hūd* – xi, 13), and 'A sūra like it, and invoke whomever you can, beneath God' (Q., *Yūnus* – x, 38). Also recited are His words 'Say: 'If the humans and the jinns get together to bring the like of this Qur'ān, they will not bring the like of it, even if they assisted one another' (Q., *al-Isrā'* – xvii, 88). **[516]** The fact itself that the Messenger informed of this from the beginning, and that he affirmed it forthrightly though he knew the numerousness of the creatures is a proof that he was doing something extraordinary *(khāriq)* which the two species of creatures *(al-thaqalān)* would be unable to oppose. Such a thing does not belong to others than the Prophets. Moreover, despite the fact that a long time has passed and that it was heard by people agreeing with it and by people opposing it, by Arabs and by non-Arabs, there has not been,* in [any of] the nations, anyone producing a book that people read and saying that it is like the [Qur'ān]. Everyone knows this. There is no speech spoken by people, even in the highest class of speech as far as expression and meaning are concerned, that is not such that people have said something similar to it, something that resembles it and is close to it, be it poetry, or a discourse, or a speech concerning the sciences, maxims, a demonstration, an admonition, epistles, etc. None of these things exists without being such that there also exists something which resembles it and is close to it. Now, the Qur'ān is among the things known by people – the Arabs and the non-Arabs – to be such that nothing similar to it exists, despite the desire which the Arabs, and others than the Arabs, have to oppose it. Its wording is thus a sign, its arrangement is a sign, its informing of unknown matters is a sign, its commanding and prohibiting is a sign, its promising and its threatening is a sign, its majesty, its greatness and its power *(sulṭān)* over the hearts are a sign. When it is translated into non-Arabic, **[517]** its meanings are a sign. In the world, there exists nothing similar to any of that. If it is said that the Torah, the Gospel and the Psalms, there also exists nothing similar to them, this will not harm us. We, we indeed say that the signs of the Prophets do not belong to others than them. If a [sign] belongs to the genus of the Prophets, like informing of God's unknown, this is a sign which they have in common. Similarly for reviving the dead, this is [also] a sign of some other Prophets than the Messiah, just as it was a [sign] of Moses and others." * fa-laysa : wa laysa **N** (Ibn Taymiyya, *Nubuwwāt*, p. 515–517).

315 See Muslim, *Ṣaḥīḥ*, *Fitan*, vol. viii, p. 171; Abū Dā'ūd, *Sunan*, *Fitan*, vol. iv, p. 97–98, no 4252; Ibn Ḥanbal, *Musnad*, vol. v, p. 278, 284; Ibn Māja, *Sunan*, *Fitan*, vol. ii, p. 1304, no 3952; al-Tirmidhī, *Sunan*, *Fitan*, vol. iii, p. 319–320, no 2267.

[Islam] spread into the middle climes – the third, **[222]** the fourth and the fifth – whose [inhabitants] are more just and more perfect than others. It is thus clear that the influence of matters prophetic is the opposite of the influence of magic and talismans. The influence of these is strong when the intellect is weak, whereas the influence of [matters prophetic] is perfect when the intellect is strong. It is clear that this is not simply [due to] the influence of the forces *(quwwa)* of humans – neither their souls nor their bodies –, nor of the forces *(quwwa)* of the natural bodies, nor of the astral forces *(quwwa)* mixed with elementary forces *(quwwa)*. It is rather an affair outside of all this.

If it is supposed that some of these [forces] help in some of that, and it is for example said that the sincerity of Abraham in his invocation,[316] the perfection of his capacitation *(tamkīn)*, his knowledge, and his status of Friend of God made it necessary *(awjaba)* for God to answer his invocation, this is a truth which we do not deny. We indeed do not deny that extraordinary phenomena happen by [God] answering invocations, but what is to be denied is saying that it is simply the force *(quwwa)* of the soul which disposes freely of the world, without God being the one who makes occur, through *(bi-)* such an invocation, some divine causes through *(bi-)* which this created being acts. The invocation is a cause and, this has been taught more than once, a cause is not independent. Rather, there are for it associations *(mushāraka)* and impediments *(māniʿ)*. It is not a cause obligatorily demanding *(iqtaḍā)* by itself the effect *(musabbab)* but it is a cause due to which God answers the invocation, just as a righteous action is a cause due to which God rewards His servant in the hereafter, people love Him, and praise Him. It would not be possible to **[223]** say that the force *(quwwa)* of one of the humans or his righteous action is what makes by itself necessary *(awjaba)* the love of the creatures [for God], their praise [of Him], their invocations, or the reward in the abode of the hereafter. Rather, this is a cause of what God does by His will and His power *(qudra)*, and of what[317] He creates in the souls of His servants – the angels, the jinns, and the humans – of what they do by their choice and their power *(qudra)* which He creates. The invocation is the cause of the [divine] answering and the action is the cause of the rewarding. God, Exalted is He, said: "When My servants ask you about Me, truly I am near. I answer the invocation of the invoker when he invokes Me. So let them respond to me and believe in Me, that they may be led aright."[318] He thus commanded them to respond to Him and to believe in Him, [i.e., to believe] that He shall answer their invocation, their response to Him, and their obedience to His command, this being the cause of the rewarding just as the invocation is the cause of [His] answering.

316 See Qur'ān, *Ibrāhīm* – xiv, 35–41.

317 wa mā : mā Ṣ

318 Qur'ān, *al-Baqara* – ii, 186.

The [following facts] are also extraordinary affairs outside of what was in the power *(maqdūr)* of [the Prophet], God bless him and grant him peace: what happened after his death, for example the fact that God preserved the Book which he brought and made it last hundreds of years despite the large size of the community and its dispersion in the orients of the earth and its occidents. The Book was still preserved after that and, likewise, the Law *(sharīʿa)* was also preserved. No Law lasted for a similarly long period except the Law of Moses. In contrast, kings and philosophers have laws *(nāmūs)* which they have instituted and which do not last except for a short period. As for [a Law] lasting for such [long] periods, with the Book being preserved, this does not [happen] for anyone except the Prophets.

There is also what God, generation after generation, has put into the hearts as love and veneration [of the Prophet] and as knowledge of his august status and high degree, without anyone compelling the hearts to know and to acknowledge [these], and with the intellects of those looking into this being perfect! Every person knowledgeable of the situations of [religious] communities indeed knows that the community of Muḥammad is the most perfect of the nations **[224]** in intellect and knowledge, morality and religion, and knows that whosoever has more knowledge and intellect is more knowledgeable of the august worth of the Messenger. These knowledge, veneration, and love subsisting in the hearts of the creatures [concerning the Prophet] are among the greatest of the extraordinary phenomena, and they are affairs outside of the forces *(quwwa)* of mankind.

Likewise for what there is in the hearts for Abraham, Moses, Jesus, Noah and others, just as the Most High said: "So, when he had withdrawn from them and that which they were worshipping beneath God, We gave him Isaac and Jacob, and each of them We made a Prophet. And we gave them out of Our mercy, and assigned to them a high, faithful renown."[319] The Most Hight also said, to Moses: "And I cast upon you a love from Me, and that you might be reared under My eyes."[320] He also said: "Indeed those who believe and do righteous deeds, the Beneficent will endear them [to His creation]."[321] He also said: "We left [a blessing] upon him among posterity: 'Peace be upon Noah, throughout the worlds!'"[322] He also said: "We left [a blessing] upon him among posterity: 'Peace be upon Abraham!'"[323] He also said: "We left [a blessing] upon both of them among posterity: 'Peace be upon Moses and Aaron!'"[324] He also said: "We left [a

319 Qur'ān, *Maryam* – xix, 49–50.
320 Qur'ān, *Ṭā-Hā* – xx, 39.
321 Qur'ān, *Maryam* – xix, 96.
322 Qur'ān, *al-Ṣaffāt* – xxxvii, 78–79.
323 Qur'ān, *al-Ṣaffāt* – xxxvii, 108–109.
324 Qur'ān, *al-Ṣaffāt* – xxxvii, 119–120.

blessing] upon him among posterity: 'Peace be upon Elias!'"[325] Etc. These praise and love, invocations and veneration existing toward the Prophets and their followers are outside the forces *(quwwa)* of the souls of the Prophets.

Likewise, the cursing and hatred which God has put in the hearts of the believers toward the unbelievers and their followers are **[225]** outside the forces *(quwwa)* of the souls of the Prophets, and all this [takes place] after their death. And the affairs similar to this are many.

TENTH VIEWPOINT. It is to say that people had controversies concerning prophethood: is it simply an attribute subsisting in the soul of the Prophet, as said by those of the adepts of *Kalām* and philosophy who say it? Or is it simply the fact that the words addressed *(khiṭāb)* by God (to mankind) are attached to the Prophet as said by those of the adepts of *Kalām* who say it – the Ash'arīs and their like? Or is [prophethood] a sum *(majmū')* of the two affairs as the majority say it – in three manners, just as they differed in these three manners about the Legal rules? If, at that point, someone says that the Prophet is specially distinguished *(khuṣṣa)* by forces *(quwwa)* in his soul by which he stands out from others in his knowledge and action, this is among the things that most *(jumhūr)* confess and there is no doubt that God favours the Prophets with eminent qualities in their souls, nor that whomever God specially distinguishes by eminent qualities, He wills him good. [It is] as Khadīja[326] said to the Prophet, God bless him and grant him peace, when the revelation came unto him and he feared for himself: "Never! By God, God will never dishonour you! You join ties of relationship, you speak the truth, you bear [people's] burden, you assist the destitute, you entertain guests, and you help against the vicissitudes which affect [people]."[327] [Khadīja] inferred by her intellect that someone in whom God had put these beautiful and noble traits which He had made to be among the greatest causes of happiness, it would not be of His way of acting *(sunna)*, of His wisdom, and of His justice, to dishonour him; on the contrary, He would bestow honours upon him and extol him. In what is known of the way God acts toward His servants, of His bestowing honours upon the people of good, and of His abasing the people of evil, **[226]** there is indeed a lesson for those who have insight.

Thanks to the ruins that are found and observed on the earth and thanks to abundantly recurrent reports, people know how Noah, Abraham, Moses, Jesus, and their followers ended up *('āqiba)*, as well as how those who pronounced them to be liars ended up. They know that God bestowed honours upon these and helped them to be victorious, whereas He punished those and abased them. They

325 Qur'ān, *al-Ṣaffāt* – xxxvii, 129–130.

326 Khadīja bint Khuwaylid (d. 620), the first wife of the Prophet; see W. MONTGOMERY WATT, *EI2*, art. Khadīdja.

327 See AL-BUKHĀRĪ, *Ṣaḥīḥ*, *Bad' al-waḥy*, vol. i, p. 7; MUSLIM, *Ṣaḥīḥ*, *Īmān*, vol. i, p. 97; IBN ḤANBAL, *Musnad*, vol. vi, p. 223.

also know how the people of justice and beneficence end up, among the authorities and the subjects, as well as how the people of injustice and evil end up, among these and those. And this is an affair which exists in all the communities, the Arabs and the non-Arabs with the diversity of their types: the Persians and the Byzantines, the Turks and the Indians, the Abyssinians and the Berbers, etc. The Most High indeed said: "If those who disbelieve had fought you, they would have turned their backs. Then they would have found neither protector nor helper. [It is] God's way of acting, which was surely unique before, and you will not find any substitute for God's way of acting."[328] He also said: "If the hypocrites do not cease, and also those in whose hearts is a disease, and the rumour-mongers in the city, We shall surely spur you against them; then they will not be your neighbours therein except for a short while. Accursed, they will be seized wheresoever they are found and utterly slain. [This was] God's way of acting vis-à-vis those who passed before, and you will not find any substitute for God's way of acting."[329] The Most High also said: "And they swore by God their most solemn oaths that if a warner came to them they would be better guided than any of the communities. Yet when a warner came to them, it increased them in nothing except repugnance, behaving arrogantly upon the earth, and devising evil schemes. Now, evil schemes beset none except their authors. So do they expect anything except the way [God] acted vis-à-vis the ancients? Yet you will not find any substitute for God's way of acting, and you will not find any modification in God's way of acting."[330] The Most High also said: [227] "Ways of acting have passed before you. So journey upon the earth and see how those pronouncing [the Prophets] to be liars ended up!"[331]

This is a wide topic and it is why God invited the creatures to consider [things] by the intellect relying on the senses, and made clear that this is consistent with what the Messengers came with of *ex auditu* [proofs]. He said: "We shall show them Our signs in the horizons and in their own souls until it becomes clear to them that it is the truth. Does it not suffice that your Lord is witness to all things?"[332] He thus informed [us] that He would show the creatures, in the matter of horizon-related and psychic signs, things making clear that the Qur'ān is the truth, what is transmitted *ex auditu* and what is known through the intelligized senses being concordant with each other. The Most High also said: "Have they not journeyed upon the earth, so as to have hearts with which to intelligize or ears with which to hear? Indeed it is not the eyes that are blind, but it is the hearts

328 Qur'ān, *al-Fatḥ* – xlviii, 22–23.
329 Qur'ān, *al-Aḥzāb* – xxxiii, 60–62.
330 Qur'ān, *Fāṭir* – xxxv, 42–43.
331 Qur'ān, *Āl 'Imrān* – iii, 137.
332 Qur'ān, *Fuṣṣilat* – xli, 53.

which are in the breasts that are blind."[333] The Most High also said: "How many a generation have We destroyed before them, who were stronger than them? Then they searched about in the lands: 'Is there any escape?' Therein verily is a reminder for whosoever has a heart, or gives ear, and is a witness."[334] He also said, about the companions of the Fire: "They said: 'Had we listened or been intelligent, we would not be among the companions of the Blaze.'"[335] He also said: "Already We have urged unto the Gehenna many of the jinns and humans: they have hearts by which they understand not, they have eyes by which they see not, they have ears by which they hear not. **[228]** These are as the cattle; rather they are more astray! It is these who are the neglectful."[336]

What is aimed at here is [to make clear] that God specially distinguished the Prophets by eminent qualities, beautiful traits, and noble morals, by which He made them stand out from the other [humans]. So, if someone says that God specially distinguished the Prophet by [some] forces *(quwwa)* in his soul and thereby wants to establish that he has special and eminent qualities, this is true. And if he says that these special qualities are causes of extraordinary phenomena by which God honours him[337] and which are miracles and prodigies, or he says that these special and eminent qualities are themselves among the things that, about him,[338] have been made extraordinary, this is something that shall not be denied. It remains however to speak about [a number of] matters.

One is that nobody should be of the opinion that this is the cause of all the extraordinary phenomena. This would indeed be vain, altogether. It is undeniable that God specially distinguishes the Prophets by eminent qualities by which, for them, He makes things be extraordinary. Nor do we deny that such eminent qualities are causing other extraordinary phenomena. Vain, however, is the claim of anyone claiming that it is these forces *(quwwa)* by which [the Prophets] have been given a preeminence over others which necessarily produce *(awjaba)* what they came with: the [various] species of signs and divine informations and the [various] species of miracles, [these] extraordinary phenomena happening in the world – the heavens and the earth, the air and the clouds, the animals, the trees, the mountains, etc. Some of these affairs, it is indeed not possible that the forces *(quwwa)* of the soul be a cause of them, either because of their incapacity to be so or because such a location *(maḥall)* does not receive the influence of the souls. Souls will notably not be necessarily producing

333 Qur'ān, *al-Ḥajj* – xxii, 46.
334 Qur'ān, *Qāf* – l, 36–37.
335 Qur'ān, *al-Mulk* – lxvii, 10.
336 Qur'ān, *al-A'rāf* – vii, 179.
337 yukrimu-hu : yukrimu-hum Ṣ
338 fī-hi : fī-hā Ṣ

(mūjib) the standing still of the sun,[339] the splitting of the moon,[340] the shaking of the Throne,[341] the scattering of the stars,[342] the turning of wood into an enormous snake, the coming out of a she-camel from the ground, the reviving of dead [humans] and animals, **[229]** the reviving of the four birds after tearing them to pieces, the sending down of the table, and other [extraordinary phenomena] which have been pointed out.

The splitting of the moon[343]

A second aspect is that nobody should be of the opinion that this alone *(mujarrad)* constitutes prophethood and that anyone to whom these characteristics *(khaṣla)* which [the philosophers] mention happen becomes a prophet. Indeed, these three [characteristics] – and things that are more perfect than them – happen to many of the exceptional *(āḥād)* believers: a knowledge-related force *(quwwa)* happens to an [exceptional believer] in his soul, as well as a practical force *(quwwa)* in his soul, by which he is influencing [things]. Also, an inward perception happens to him, so that he sees and hears inwardly, as he is one of the exceptional believers. Now, whosoever sets this as the definition *(ḥadd)* of the Prophet and the ultimate point he reaches is a vain talker rejecting the real nature of that by which God has specially distinguished His Prophets.

What is aimed at here is [to make clear] that what [the philosophers] establish as confirmed eminent qualities of the Prophets shall not be denied as it is true. But the fact that they confine themselves to this definition is vain. Their affirmation that this is the cause of the extraordinary [actions] of [the Prophets] is also vain.

---

339 See *Joshua*, 10: 12–13; M. al-Qurṭubī, *I'lām*, p. 350–351.

340 Qur'ān, *al-Qamar* – liv, 1. See also A. N. al-Iṣfahānī, *Dalā'il*, p. 279–281, nos 207–212; M. al-Qurṭubī, *I'lām*, p. 348–350.

341 The Throne of God is reported to have shaken because of the death of the Anṣārī Companion Sa'd b. Mu'ādh; see al-Bukhārī, *Ṣaḥīḥ, Manāqib al-anṣār*, vol. v, p. 35; Muslim, *Ṣaḥīḥ, Faḍā'il al-ṣaḥāba*, vol. vii, p. 150.

342 See Qur'ān, *al-Infiṭār* – lxxxii, 2.

343 Engraving in M. Yāzījī Zādeh, *Muḥammadiyya*, p. 121.

A third aspect consists in knowing that prophethood is not reached by the endeavour *(iktisāb)* of man and his preparedness *(isti'dād)* as the acquirable *(muktasab)* sciences and the acquirable religiousness are reached thereby. Truly, these people "did not value God as He deserved to be valued,"[344] nor did they value the Prophets properly when[345] they were of the opinion that when, in a man, there is preparedness for the perfection of his soul's purification and for its reformation *(iṣlāḥ)*, knowledges flow *(fāḍa)* on it, because of that, from the agent intellect just as the rays flow on a polished mirror when it is cleansed[346] and the sun is faced by it.[347] [They were also wrong when they thought] that the obtaining *(ḥuṣūl)* of prophethood is not something that God makes occur *(aḥdatha)* by His will and His power *(qudra)* but is only the obtaining of this flux *(fayḍ)* on this prepared [soul], similarly to the obtaining of the rays on that polished body. Many of them thus began seeking prophethood, as is related about a group of ancient Greeks, and as this also happened to a group of people during the days of Islam.[348] **[230]**

This is why people seriously criticized the author of *The Alchemy of Happiness* and the author of *The Book to Be Withheld from Those Who are not Worthy of It* and *The Niche of Lights.* There are indeed, in what he says, things that are of the genus of what is said by those heretics *(mulḥid)*. He expressed them in Islamic idioms *('ibāra)* and Sufi pointers *(ishāra)* and, because of that, the author of *The Taking Off of the Two Sandals (Khal' al-na'layn)*,[349] Ibn Sab'īn, Ibn 'Arabī, and their like among those who built [their thinking] upon this corrupt foundation, were misled *(ightarra)*.

On the contrary, for prophethood, there must unavoidably be a divine revelation by which God specially distinguishes whomever He specially distinguishes thereby among His servants, by His will and His power *(qudra)*. He, Praised is He, knows this Prophet and what, in the matter of revelation, He reveals to him. By

---

344 Qur'ān, *al-An'ām* – vi, 91.

345 A translation of the end of this paragraph and of the two following ones (p. 229, l. 16 – p. 230, l. 9) was already published in Y. Michot, *Reader*, p. 145–146. The footnotes relating to them are given here in an abridged version.

346 juliyat: julliyat Ṣ

347 Allusion to the kind of explanation of the process of revelation proposed by Avicenna; see Ibn Taymiyya, *MF*, trans. Michot, *Musique*, p. 193; *Destinée*, p. 127–128. On the assimilation of the soul to a mirror in al-Ghazālī, see H. Lazarus-Yafeh, *Studies*, p. 312–320; more generally, see D. De Smet, M. Sebti, G. de Callataÿ (eds), *Miroir*.

348 See for example what Ibn Taymiyya writes about al-Suhrawardī (d. 587/1191), Ibn Sab'īn and Ibn 'Arabī in *MF*, trans. Michot, *Mamlūk I*, p. 183–184. According to Ibn Kathīr (*Bidāya*, vol. xiii, p. 261), Ibn Sab'īn believed that prophethood could be acquired and "was a flux flowing on the intellect when it becomes pure."

349 *Khal' al-na'layn fī l-wuṣūl ilā ḥaḍrat al-jam'ayn* is the work of Abū l-Qāsim Aḥmad b. Ḥusayn Ibn Qasī (d. 546/1151), Andalusian Sufi and leader of a revolt against the Almoravids (538/1144). It was commented on by Ibn 'Arabī. See D. R. Goodrich, *Revolt.*

His power *(qudra)*, He specially distinguishes him by what, of his prodigies *(karāma)*, He specially distinguishes him by. As for these heretics, they claim that [God's] talking to Moses, son of 'Imrān, was nothing except what happened in Moses' soul of the [divine] inspiration and revelation, that any of the adepts of [spiritual] exercise and purity may be talked to as Moses, son of 'Imrān, was talked to – and even more than that –, and that he may hear the same talking which Moses heard. The author of *The Revival* notably pretended that in some places, even if it is said that he retracted from that. Among these there are also some who say that the talking that occurs to them is more eminent than what happened to Moses and others. This is the doctrine of Ibn al-'Arabī, the author of *The Meccan Revelations*, and of his like among those who claim that what had happened to Moses and Muḥammad only [did so] by the intermediary of the psychic imagination *(khayāl nafsānī)* – which, for them, is Gabriel – whereas what happened to Ibn 'Arabī was above that. He **[231]** was indeed drawing from the pure intellectual source from which the angel – which is for them [some] imagination in the soul of the Prophet – drew, and the rank of the intellect is above the rank of the imagination. As they were believing that the angels who talk to the Prophets are only imaginations subsisting in the soul of the Prophets, they pretended that, as they drew from the pure intellect, they were effectively drawing from the source from which the angels draw, [the same angels] from whom the Prophets draw. They were thus more eminent than the Prophets according to themselves and their followers.

[Ignorants, hypocrites, and God's pardon]

These and similar [ideas] are among the things which are obligatorily known, from the religion of the Messengers, to be unbelief and, from the religion of [these heretics], to be vain. Whoever understands the Qur'ān and understands the words of these must indeed [do] one of these two things: either pronouncing the Qur'ān to be a lie, or pronouncing these to be liars. If [he does] not, what they say and what the Messenger came with contradict one another in a manner which is known by every person understanding their words and the words of the Prophets. It would be unimaginable for anyone to say that this is consistent with that[350] except for one of the [following] two men: either an ignorant [or an hypocrite].

[This ignorant] would not know the true nature of what the Messengers came with, nor the true nature of what these [heretics] say. In his case, there would be a general veneration of the Prophets and of these people, similarly to those who

350 yuwāfiqu hadhā : [wa an] yuwāfiqa ['alā] hadhā [al-kalām] Ṣ. The three words added here between square brackets by the editor of Ṣ are unnecessary.

used to venerate Muḥammad and Musaylima[351] and [232] used to say: "We bear witness that Muḥammad and Musaylima are the two Messengers of God." This type [of approach] is frequent among those who do not know the true natures of a truthful Prophet and of a lying self-made prophet. Many of these are found among those who relate themselves to jurisprudence, *ḥadīth*, Sufism, asceticism, and worship, to kingship, the emirate, the vizierate, secretaryship, judgeship, muftiship, and professorship, as well as among those whose invocations are answered and in whom there is righteousness, asceticism and worship; and this, because of the deficiency of their knowledge of the perfection of prophethood and messengership, as well as of the true nature of the sayings of whosoever contradicts them from some viewpoints, not from others. Truly, God, Exalted is He, said: "O you who believe! Should any of you become a renegade from his religion, God will bring a people whom He loves and who love Him, humble toward the believers, stern toward the unbelievers. They shall strive in the way of God, and shall not fear the blame of any blamer."[352] When renegades appear, there must thus unavoidably also exist lovers [of God], beloved [by Him], just as Abū Bakr[353] the truthful, God be pleased with him, and his brothers rose to fight the renegades after the trespassing of the Seal of the Envoys and what had happened as crisis *(fitna)* concerning the religion.

As for the hypocrite, [it would be] a free-thinker *(zindīq)* who knows that this contradicts that.[354] He would, however, in public *(aẓhara)* speak of accord *(muwāfaqa)* and harmony *(i'tilāf)* [between the two] because of his belief that prophethood is of the [same] genus as the state of those people, and what he would say would deceive those not cognisant of the true natures of things. Among these there are nevertheless some people whose aim is neither free-thinking nor hypocrisy but who do not know the [exceptional] state of the Messenger and the worth of what he came with. They venerate him in a general manner, see that these [philosophers] have spoken about the prophethood and its reality the way they have spoken about it, are incapable of knowing the true nature of the matter, and believe this[355] about prophethood. There are plenty of such people [233] in the places of [religious] lukewarmness *(amākin al-fatarāt)*[356] where the traces of prophethood are weak because there is nobody there standing up for its realities.

351 Musaylima b. Ḥabīb, pseudo-prophet of the Banū Ḥanīfa, killed at the battle of al-'Aqrabā', under the caliphate of Abū Bakr; see W. Montgomery Watt, *EI2*, art. *Musaylima*.

352 Qur'ān, *al-Mā'ida* – v, 54.

353 The first caliph (r. 11/632–13/634), called "the truthful" (*ṣiddīq*); see W. Montgomery Watt, *EI2*, art. *Abū Bakr*.

354 I.e., this that the philosophers say contradicts that which the Prophets say.

355 I.e., what the philosophers say about prophethood.

356 Places and times of religious lukewarmness are a concept developed by Ibn Taymiyya to promote a more merciful approach to the deficient, unsatisfactory, religiousness, in deeds as well as in words, of many of the Muslims; see Y. Michot, *Mamlūks*; *Extremisms*, p. 34–82.

Such people will be [living] in the regimes *(dawla)* of the Age of Ignorance like the regime of the Banū 'Ubayd[357] and the regime of the Tatars and their like. There are some of those whom God will forgive. Indeed, when they are making the effort which they are able [to make] in order to believe in the Messenger and no power *(qudra)* remains to them for more than that which, of the faith in him, has happened to them, God does not "burden a soul except with that which it is able [to carry]."[358] [This is true] even if what they are saying, once the [divine] justification *(ḥujja)* [of things] is notified to them, is unbelief, as [was the case with the man] who said to his family: "When I am dead, reduce me to powder, then scatter me in the sea! By God! If God were indeed to have power *(qadara)* over me, He would torment me in a way in which He assuredly has not tormented anyone in the worlds!" This *ḥadīth* is in the two *Ṣaḥīḥ*s in more than one variant.[359]

This man ignored God's power *(qudra)* to make him come back [to life] and was hoping that He would not make him come back [to life] as he was ignorant of what He has informed [us] of His making [people] come back [to life in the hereafter]. In spite of this, God forgave him as he was believing in God, in His command and His prohibition, in His promise and His threat, and was afraid of His torment. Also, his ignorance of that was an ignorance in which he had not been notified of [God's] justification, which would have necessitated *(awjaba)* considering the like of his [ideas] as unbelief. There are many similar people among the Muslims, and the Prophet, God bless him and grant him peace, used to give informations about the ancients so that they might be a lesson for this community.

[Dreams and Prophethood]

What is aimed at here is to make clear that what these [philosophers] have established about the confirmed eminent qualities of the Prophets is true, but their ignorance and unbelief lay in what they have denied and pronounced to be a lie, as well as in the vain things they have said from these three[360] and other aspects. By the two first vain aspects they have pronounced to be vain [the idea] that God is the Creator of His creatures by His power *(qudra)* and His will. They

---

357 The Fāṭimid dynasty, founded in 297/909 by the Ismāʿīlī 'Ubayd Allāh al-Mahdī in North Africa; see M. Canard, *EI2*, art. *Fāṭimids.*

358 Qur'ān, *al-Baqara* – ii, 286.

359 See notably al-Bukhārī, *Ṣaḥīḥ*, *Anbiyā'*, vol. iv, p. 176; *Riqāq*, vol. viii, p. 101; *Tawḥīd*, vol. ix, p. 145; Muslim, *Ṣaḥīḥ*, *Tawba*, vol. viii, p. 97–98. See also the Taymiyyan texts translated in Y. Michot, *Extremisms*, p. 58, 61–64, 78–82.

360 The three aspects distinguished within the tenth viewpoint; see *supra*, p. 228–231 of the Arabic text.

have also pronounced as vain the things which He created – the angels, the jinns, etc. – and which they do not know. They moreover pronounced to be vain that by which the Prophets stand out from others and they considered the Prophets to be of the [same] genus as the knowers [possessing] a knowledge shared between the Muslims, the Jews, the Nazarenes, the Magi, and the Ṣābi'ans. **[234]** This is why prophethood became acquirable *(muktasab)* according to them, and why many of them started to seek to become Prophets, from among the earlier ones of them and the later ones. Some of them started thinking that they were Prophets and that they would set down a law *(nāmūs)* by which they would abrogate the Laws *(sharī'a)* of the Prophets, as happened with the imāms of the esotericist (*bāṭiniyya*) Ismā'īlīs and their like. Now, what they affirm of the prophethood, as well as things that are higher than that, happens to exceptional people in whom there is [some] knowledge-related and practical eminence. The people of knowledge and faith in the Messengers however know that the relation of [these people] to the Prophets is of the [same] genus *(jins)* as the relation of those who have true dream visions to the Prophets.

The cave of Mont Ḥirā'[361]

"A true dream vision is one of forty-six parts of prophethood," as is established in the authentic *ḥadīths*[362] about the Prophet, God bless him and grant him peace. It is similarly [reported] about him, in the *Sunan*, that he said: "Being righteously

361 Engraving from M. D. Lārī, *Futūḥ*, p. 76.

362 See notably al-Bukhārī, *Ṣaḥīḥ*, *Ta'bīr*, vol. ix, p. 30–31; Muslim, *Ṣaḥīḥ*, *Ru'yā*, vol. vii, p. 52–53; Ibn Ḥanbal, *Musnad*, vol. ii, p. 18, 50; Abū Dā'ūd, *Sunan*, *Adab*, vol. iv, p. 304, no 5018; al-Dārimī, *Sunan*, *Ru'yā*, vol. ii, p. 123; Ibn Māja, *Sunan*, *Ru'yā*, vol. ii, p. 1282, nos 3893–3894; p. 1285–1286, no 3907; al-Tirmidhī, *Sunan*, *Ru'yā*, vol. iii, p. 363, nos 2372–2373; p. 366, no 2381.

guided, faring righteously, and moderation are one of twenty-five parts of prophethood."[363] In the two *Ṣaḥīḥ*s, it is also established about him that he said: "Faith has over seventy branches or over sixty branches, the highest of which is saying 'There is no god but God,' and the lowest of which is removing what is a nuisance from the road; and modesty is a branch of the faith."[364] **[235]** It is thus undoubtable, something might be a part of prophethood or of faith, and be among [their] smallest branches and parts, like removing what is hurting [from the road] in relation to faith or like a dream vision in relation to prophethood. This is why he said, God bless him and grant him peace: "Nothing will remain of prophethood after me except the ones conveying good news *(mubashshir)*, i.e., the right dream vision which the righteous man sees or which is seen about him."[365] This is also why this part [of prophethood] was the first [thing] through which the Messenger of God, God bless him and grant him peace, was initiated, to make him proceed gradually. So is it [reported] about 'Ā'isha, in the *Ṣaḥīḥ*,[366] that she said: "The first [part] of the revelation through which the Messenger of God, God bless him and grant him peace, was initiated was a right dream vision in his sleep. He was seeing no dream vision but that it came like the bright light of the morning. Thereafter, retreat was made lovable to him and he used to retreat in the cave of Ḥirā':[367] he spent a number of nights there, in adoration, i.e., worship" and [the rest of] the *ḥadīth*…[368] **[236]**

As some of the parts of prophethood happen to exceptional believers who are not Prophets, it is clear that what these [philosophers] mention of the truth is one of the parts of prophethood, whereas what they mention in the matter of vain things is to be thrown back at them. It is clear, the miracles of the Prophets are outside of the psychic and natural forces *(quwwa)* [existing] in the world, superior and inferior. It is also clear, God, Praised is He, is the Creator of everything by His will and His power *(qudra)*, and He creates what He wills by the causes which He makes occur, for the wise purpose *(ḥikma)* which He wills.

This is the amount [of writing] which these sheets [of paper] have capacity for to answer this question. It is indeed a serious question on which the principles of knowledge and faith are built.

---

363 See Abū Dā'ūd, *Sunan, Adab*, vol. iv, p. 247, no 4776; Ibn Ḥanbal, *Musnad*, vol. i, p. 296; al-Tirmidhī, *Sunan, Birr*, vol. iii, p. 247, no 2078.

364 See al-Bukhārī, *Ṣaḥīḥ, Īmān*, vol. i, p. 11; Muslim, *Ṣaḥīḥ, Īmān*, vol. i, p. 46.

365 See notably al-Bukhārī, *Ṣaḥīḥ, Ta'bīr*, vol. ix, p. 31; al-Dārimī, *Sunan, Ru'yā*, vol. ii, p. 123; Ibn Māja, *Sunan, Ru'yā*, vol. ii, p. 1283, nos 3896, 3899; al-Tirmidhī, *Sunan, Ru'yā*, vol. iii, p. 364, no 2374.

366 See al-Bukhārī, *Ṣaḥīḥ, Ta'bīr*, vol. ix, p. 29.

367 The Mountain of Light (*jabal al-nūr*), at the north-east of Mecca, where the Prophet received the first revelation of the Qur'ān; see T. Weir & W. Montgomery Watt, *EI2*, art. *Ḥirā'*.

368 See M. M. Khan, *Ṣaḥīḥ*, vol. ix, p. 91–94, no 111.

Bibliography

ABŪ DĀ'ŪD (d. 275/889), *al-Sunan*. Ed. 'ABD AL-ḤAMĪD, 4 vols (Beirut: Dār Iḥyā' al-Sunnat al-Nabawiyya, n.d.). *[Sunan]*

ABŪ MA'SHAR AL-BALKHĪ (d. 272/886), *Kitāb al-Mudkhal al-kabīr ilā 'ilm aḥkām al-nujūm*. Edition and Latin translation in Richard LEMAY, *Abū Ma'shar*. *[Mudkhal]*

–, *al-Kitāb al-kabīr: 1. Mawālīd al-rijāl; 2. Ṭawāli' al-nisā' wa abrāju-hunna* (Singapore – Djedda – Indonesia: Maṭba'at al-Ḥaramayn, [199.?] – Anastatic reprint of a Cairo edition from the beginning of the 20th c.). *[Kitāb]*

AFIFI AL-AKITI, Muhammad, *The Three Properties of Prophethood in Certain Works of Avicenna and al-Ġazālī*, in Jon MCGINNIS (ed., with the assistance of David REISMAN), *Interpreting Avicenna: Science and Philosophy in Medieval Islam. Proceedings of the Second Conference of the Avicenna Study Group* (Leiden – Boston: Brill, "Islamic Philosophy, Theology and Science. Texts and Studies, LVI," 2004). *[Properties]*

AKASOY, Anna, *Philosophie und Mystik in der späten Almohadenzeit: "Die Sizilianischen Fragen" des Ibn Sab'īn* (Leiden: Brill, 2005). *[Philosophie]*

–, *The* Muḥaqqiq *as Mahdī? Ibn Sab'īn and Mahdism among Andalusian Mystics in the 12th/13th Centuries*, in Wolfram BRANDES & Felicitas SCHMIEDER (eds), *Endzeiten: Eschatologie in den monotheistischen Weltreligionen* (Berlin – New York: De Gruyter Mouton, 2008), p. 313–337. *[Muḥaqqiq]*

AL-JAZĀ'IRĪ B. ḤAMDĀN, A., *al-Kawākib al-lammā'a fī taskhīr mulūk al-jinn fī l-waqt wa l-sā'a* (Tunis: al-Shādhlī l-Zāwiq al-Kutubī, [*c.* 1980]). *[Kawākib]*

AL-SHĀMĪ, Rizq Yūsuf, *Ibn Taymiyya: maṣādiru-hu wa manhaju-hu fī taḥlīli-hā*, in *Journal of the Institute of Arabic Manuscripts*, vol. 38 (Cairo, 1415/1994), p. 183–269. *[Maṣādir]*

AMITAI-PREISS, Reuven, *Sufis and Shamans: Some Remarks on the Islamization of the Mongols in the Ilkhanate*, in *Journal of the Economic and Social History of the Orient*, 42 (Leiden: Brill, 1999), p. 27–46. *[Sufis]*

ANAWATI, Georges Chehata, *Essai de bibliographie avicennienne – Mu'allafāt Ibn Sīnā*. Avant-propos d'Ahmed AMIN. Préface d'Ibrahim MADKOUR (Cairo: Al-Maaref, "Millénaire d'Avicenne," 1950). *[Essai]*

ANONYMOUS, *Majmū'a min alf layla wa layla, wa hiya qiṣṣat al-malik Shahriyār…* (Cairo: Maktabat al-Jindī, [*c.* 1970]). *[Majmū'a]*

ASAD, Muhammad, *The Message of the Qur'ān*. Translated and explained (Gibraltar: Dar al-Andalus, 1980). *[Message]*

ATWOOD, Christopher P., *Encyclopedia of Mongolia and the Mongol Empire* (New York: Facts On File, 2004). *[Encyclopedia]*

BA'LABAKKĪ (AL-; d. 734/1333), *Risālat al-Sulūk*. Ed. Arjan POST, *Glimpse*, p. 173–178. *[Sulūk]*

BĀQILLĀNĪ (AL-), Abū Bakr (d. 403/1013), *Kitāb al-bayān*. Ed. Richard J. MCCARTHY (Beirut: al-Maktabat al-Sharqiyya, 1958). *[Bayān]*

BAYHAQĪ (AL-), Abū Bakr (d. 458/1066), *Dalā'il al-nubuwwa wa ma'rifat aḥwāl ṣāḥib al-sharī'a*. Ed. 'Abd al-Mu'ṭī QAL'AJĪ, 7 vols (Beirut: Dār al-Kutub al-'Ilmiyya, 1408/1988). *[Dalā'il]*

BOYLE, John A., *Genghis Khan. The History of the World Conqueror* by 'Ala-ad-Din 'Ata-Malik Juvaini. Translated from the text of Mizra Muhammad QAZWĪNĪ, with a new introduction & bibliography by David O. MORGAN (Manchester: Manchester University Press – Unesco, 1997). *[Genghis Khan]*

BUKHĀRĪ (AL-; d. 256/870), *al-Ṣaḥīḥ*, 9 vols (Bulaq: al-Maṭba'at al-Kubrā l-Amīriyya, 1311/[1893]–1313/[1895]). *[Ṣaḥīḥ]*
See also Muhammad Muhsin KHAN, *Ṣaḥīḥ*.

BURNETT, Charles, *Ṯābit Ibn Qurra the Ḥarrānian on Talismans and the Spirits of the Planets*, in *La Corónica: A Journal of Medieval Hispanic Languages, Literatures and Cultures*, 36/1 (Fall 2007), p. 13–40. *[Ṯābit]*

– & Gideon BOHAK, *A Judaeo-Arabic Version of Ṯābit Ibn Qurra's* De Imaginibus *and Pseudo-Ptolemy's* Opus Imaginum, in Felicitas OPWIS & DAVID REISMAN (eds), *Islamic Philosophy, Science, Culture, and Religion. Studies in Honor of Dimitri Gutas* (Leiden – Boston: Brill, 2012), p. 179–200. *[Version]*

DĀRIMĪ (AL-; d. 255/869), *al-Sunan*, 2 vols (Beirut: Dār al-Fikr, 1398/1978). *[Sunan]*

DE SMET, Daniel, SEBTI, Meryem, DE CALLATAŸ, Godefroid (eds), *Miroir et Savoir : La transmission d'un thème platonicien des Alexandrins à la philosophie arabo-musulmane* (Louvain: Peeters, 2008). *[Miroir]*

DOUTTÉ, Edmond, *Magie et religion dans l'Afrique du Nord. La société musulmane du Maghrib* (Algiers: Typographie Adolphe Jourdan, 1909). – Anastatic reprint: Brussels: ESH-Éditions, 2013. *[Magie]*

ENCYCLOPÆDIA OF ISLAM. New edition: Vol. I (Leiden: E. J. Brill – Paris: Maisonneuve, M. Besson, 1960); vols. ii–xii (Leiden: E. J. Brill – Paris: Maisonneuve & Larose, 1965–2007). *[EI2]*

ENCYCLOPAEDIA OF THE QUR'ĀN. Ed. Jane DAMMEN MCAULIFFE, 6 vols (Leiden: Brill, 2001–2006). *[EQ]*

ENDRESS, Gerhard, *Reading Avicenna in the Madrasa: Intellectual Genealogies and Chains of Transmission of Philosophy and the Sciences in the Islamic East*, in James MONTGOMERY (ed.), *Arabic Philosophy, Arabic Theology: From the Many to the One. Essays in Celebration of Richard M. Frank* (Leuven: Peeters, 2006), p. 371–422. *[Reading]*

FARHAD, Massumeh, with Serpil BAĞCI (eds), *Falnama. The Book of Omens* (Washington: Smithsonian Institution, 2009). *[Falnama]*

FRANK, Richard, *Abū Hāshim's Theory of "states," its structure and function*, in *Actas do Congresso de Estudos Arabes e Islâmicos, Coimbra – Lisboa, 1 a 8 de setembro de 1968* (Leiden: Brill, 1971), p. 85–100. *[Theory]*

GHAZĀLĪ (AL-), Abū Ḥāmid (d. 505/1111), *Faḍā'iḥ al-bāṭiniyya*. Ed. 'Abd al-Raḥmān BADAWĪ (Cairo: Wizārat al-Thaqāfa wa l-Irshād al-Qawmī, "al-Maktabat al-'Arabiyya, 7," 1383/1964). *[Faḍā'iḥ]*

–, *al-Maḍnūn bi-hi 'alā ghayr ahli-hi*, in Muḥammad Muṣṭafā ABŪ L-'ALĀ' (ed.), *al-Quṣūr al-'awālī min rasā'il al-imām al-Ghazālī*, 4 vols (Cairo: Maktabat al-Jindī, 1390/1970); vol. iii, p. 124–169. *[Maḍnūn]*

GIMARET, Daniel, JOLIVET, Jean & MONNOT Guy, *AL-SHAHRASTĀNĪ, Livre des religions et des sectes.* Traduction avec introduction et notes, 2 vols (Louvain: Peeters – Paris: UNESCO, "Collection Unesco d'œuvres représentatives. Série arabe," 1986). *[Religions I & II]*

GOHLMAN, William E., *The Life of Ibn Sina. A Critical Edition and Annotated Translation* (Albany: State University of New York Press, "Studies in Islamic Philosophy and Science," 1974). *[Life]*

GOICHON, Amélie-Marie, *IBN SĪNĀ. Livre des Directives et Remarques.* Traduction avec introduction et notes (Beirut: Commission internationale pour la traduction des chefs-d'œuvre – Paris: J. Vrin, "Collection d'œuvres arabes de l'UNESCO," 1951). *[Directives]*

GOODRICH, David R., *A "Sufi" Revolt in Portugal: Ibn Qasī and his* Kitāb Khal' al-na'layn. Unpublished PhD dissertation (New York: Columbia University, 1978). *[Revolt]*

GRIFFEL, Frank, *Al-Ġazālī's Concept of Prophecy: The Introduction of Avicennan Psychology into Aš'arite Theology*, in *Arabic Sciences and Philosophy*, 14 (2004), p. 101–144. *[Concept]*

GUILLAUME, Alfred, *The Life of Muḥammad. A Translation of Ibn Isḥāq's* Sīrat Rasūl Allāh, with introduction and notes (London: Oxford University Press, 1955). *[Life]*

GUTAS, Dimitri, *Avicenna's* maḏhab. *With an appendix on the question of his date of birth*, in *Atti del XIII Congresso dell'Union Européenne d'Arabisants et d'Islamisants* (*Venezia 29 sett. – 4 ott. 1986*) – *Quaderni di Studi Arabi*, 5–6 (Venise, 1987–1988), p. 323–336. *[Avicenna]*

GUYARD, Stanislas, *Le fetwa d'Ibn Taymiyyah sur les Nosairis.* Publié pour la première fois avec une traduction nouvelle, in *Journal Asiatique*, série VI, t. XVIII (Paris: Imprimerie Nationale, 1871), p. 158–198. *[Fetwa]*

HAMADHĀNĪ (AL-), 'Abd al-Jabbār (d. 415/1025), *Tathbīt dalā'il al-nubuwwa.* Ed. 'Abd al-Karīm 'UTHMĀN (Beirut: Dār al-'Arabiyya li-l-Ṭibā'a wa l-Nashr wa l-Tawzī', 1386/1966). *[Tathbīt]*

IBN AL-ATHĪR (d. 630/1233), *Usd al-ghāba fī ma'rifat al-Ṣaḥāba*, 5 vols (Cairo, 1280[/1863] – Anastatic reprint: Beirut: Dār Iḥyā' al-Turāth al-'Arabī, n.d.). *[Usd]*

IBN BAṬṬŪṬA (d. 779/1378?), *Riḥla*, see Tim MACKINTOSH-SMITH, *Travels. [Riḥla]*

IBN ḤANBAL (d. 241/855), *al-Musnad*, 6 vols (Cairo: al-Bābī l-Ḥalabī, 1313/[1896] – Anastatic reprint: Beirut: al-Maktab al-Islāmī, 1403/1983). *[Musnad]*

IBN ḤAZM (d. 456/1064), *Kitāb al-Fiṣal fī l-milal wa l-ahwā' wa l-niḥal*, 5 vols (Cairo: al-Khānjī, 1317[/1899]–1321[/1902]). *[Fiṣal]*

IBN AL-'IMĀD, Abū l-Falāḥ (d. 1089/1679), *Shadharāt al-dhahab fī akhbār man dhahaba*, 8 vols (Beirut: Dār al-Fikr, 1414/1994). *[Shadharāt]*

IBN ISḤĀQ (d. 150/767?), *Sīrat Rasūl Allāh*, see Alfred GUILLAUME, *Life. [Sīra]*

IBN KATHĪR (d. 774/1373), *al-Bidāya wa l-nihāya*, 14 vols (Beirut: Maktabat al-Ma'ārif, 1977). *[Bidāya]*

–, *Tafsīr*, 4 vols (Beirut: Dār al-Jīl, 1410/1990). *[Tafsīr]*

IBN KHALLIKĀN (d. 681/1282), *Wafayāt al-a'yān wa anbā' abnā' al-zamān.* Ed. Iḥsān 'ABBĀS, 8 vols (Beirut: Dār Ṣādir, 1397/1977). *[Wafayāt]*

IBN MĀJA (d. 273/887), *al-Sunan.* Ed. Muḥammad Fu'ād 'ABD AL-BĀQĪ, 2 vols (Cairo, 1373/1954 – Anastatic reprint: Beirut: Dār al-Kutub al-'Ilmiyya, n.d.). *[Sunan]*

IBN SĪNĀ, *Kitāb al-Ishārāt wa l-tanbīhāt – Le Livre des Théorèmes et des Avertissements.* Publié d'après les mss. de Berlin, de Leyde et d'Oxford et traduit avec éclaircissements par Jules FORGET, 1e partie. – Texte arabe (Leiden: E. J. Brill, 1892). [*Ishārāt*; **F**]

–, *Al-Ishārāt wa l-tanbīhāt, ma'a* Sharḥ *Naṣīr al-Dīn al-Ṭūsī.* Ed. Sulaymān DUNYĀ, 4 vols (Cairo: Dār al-Ma'ārif, 1968–2e ed.). *[Ishārāt]*
See also Amélie-Marie GOICHON, *Directives*; Shams INATI, *Mysticism.*

–, *al-Risālat al-Aḍḥawiyya fī amr al-ma'ād – Epistola sulla vita futura.* A cura di Francesca LUCCHETTA. I. Testo arabo, traduzione e note (Padova: Antenore, 1969). *[Aḍḥawiyya]*

–, *Kitāb al-Mubāḥathāt.* Ed. Muḥsin Bīdārfar (Qom: Intishārāt-e Bīdār, 1413 H. lunar / 1371 H. solar [/1992]). *[Mubāḥathāt]*
–, *al-Ta'līqāt.* Ed. 'Abd al-Raḥmān Badawī (Cairo: G.E.B.O., 1973). *[Ta'līqāt]*
Ibn Taymiyya (d. 728/1328), *Majmū' al-fatāwā.* Ed. 'Abd al-Raḥmān b. Muḥammad Ibn Qāsim, 37 vols (Rabat: Maktabat al-Ma'ārif, 1401/1981). *[MF]*
See also Yahya M. Michot, *Astrology.*
–, *Dar' ta'āruḍ al-'aql wa l-naql aw muwāfaqa ṣaḥīḥ al-manqūl li-ṣarīḥ al-ma'qūl.* Ed. Muḥammad Rashād Sālim, 11 vols (Riyadh: Dār al-Kunūz al-Adabiyya, [1399/1979]). *[Dar']*
–, *al-Istiqāma.* Ed. Muḥammad Rashād Sālim, 2 vols (Riyadh: Dār al-Faḍīla li-l-Nashr wa l-Tawzī' – Beirut: Dār Ibn Ḥazm li-l-Ṭibā'a wa l-Nashr wa l-Tawzī', 1420/2000). [*Istiqāma*; I]
–, *Kitāb al-Nubuwwāt.* Ed. 'Abd al-'Azīz al-Ṭuwayān, 2 vols (Riyadh: Maktabat Aḍwā' al-Salaf, 1420/2000). [*Nubuwwāt*; N]
–, *Kitāb al-Ṣafadiyya.* Ed. Muḥammad Rashād Sālim, 2 vols (Mansoura: Dār al-Hady al-Nabawī – Riyadh: Dār al-Faḍīla, 1421/2000). [*Ṣafadiyya*; Ṣ]
–, *al-Radd 'alā l-manṭiqiyyīn (Refutation of the Logicians).* Ed. 'Abduṣ-Ṣamad Sharafud-Dīn al-Kutubī, with an Introduction by Sayyid Sulaimān Nadvī (Bombay: Qayyimah Press, 1368/1949). *[Radd]*
See also Yahya M. Michot, *Textes XI.*
–, *Qā'ida sharīfa fī l-mu'jizāt wa l-karamāt*, in *MF*, vol. xi, p. 311–362. *[Mu'jizāt]*
–, *Futyā fī l-Nuṣayriyya*, see Stanislas Guyard, *Fetwa. [Nuṣayriyya]*
–, *al-Risālat al-Qubruṣiyya.* French translation by Yahya M. MICHOT, *Roi croisé. [Qubruṣ]*
Inati, Shams, *Ibn Sīnā and Mysticism. Remarks and Admonitions: Part Four* (London – New York: Kegan Paul International, 1996). *[Mysticism]*
Iṣfahānī (al-), Abū Nu'aym (d. 430/1038), *Dalā'il al-nubuwwa.* Ed. Muḥammad Rawwās Qal'ahjī & 'Abd al-Barr 'Abbās (Beirut: Dār al-Nafā'is, 1406/1986). *[Dalā'il]*
Khan, Muhammad Muhsin, *The Translation of the Meanings of Ṣaḥīḥ al-Bukhārī*, 9 vols (Beirut: Dār al-'Arabiyya, 1405/1985, 4th edn). *[Ṣaḥīḥ]*
Lārī, Muḥyī l-Dīn (d. 933/1526), *Hādhā kitāb futūḥ al-Ḥaramayn*, (Iran?, n.d. [XIXe s.]). *[Futūḥ]*
Lazarus-Yafeh, Hava, *Studies in al-Ghazzali* (Jerusalem: The Magnes Press, 1975). *[Studies]*
Lemay, Richard, *Abū Ma'šar al-Balḫī (Albumasar). Kitāb al-Mudkhal al-kabīr ilā 'ilm aḥkām al-nujūm – Liber introductorii maioris ad scientiam judiciorum astrorum.* Critical edition, 9 vols (Naples: Istituto Universitario Orientale, 1995). *[Abū Ma'shar]*
–, *Books of Magic in Translation from the Arabic and the Birth of a Theology of the Sacraments of the Church in the Twelfth Century*, in Rika Gyselen (ed.), *Charmes et sortilèges, magie et magiciens* (Bures-sur-Yvette: Groupe pour l'Étude de la Civilisation du Moyen-Orient, "Res Orientales, XIV," 2002), p. 165–192. *[Books]*
Lessing, Ferdinand D. (ed.), *Mongolian-English Dictionary* (Berkeley – Los Angeles: University of California Press, 1960). *[Dictionary]*
Lucchetta, Francesca, *Avicenna. Epistola sulla Vita Futura – al-Risālat al-Aḍḥawiyya fī l-Ma'ād.* I. Testo arabo, traduzione, introduzione e note (Padova: Antenore, "Università

di Padova. Pubblicazioni dell'Istituto di Storia della Filosofia e del Centro per Ricerche di Filosofia Medioevale, Nuova serie, 5," 1969). *[Epistola]*

MACKINTOSH-SMITH, Tim, *The Travels of Ibn Battutah.* Abridged, introduced and annotated (London: Picador, 2003). *[Travels]*

MADELUNG, Wilferd, *The Fāṭimids and the Qarmaṭīs of Baḥrayn*, in Farhad DAFTARY (ed.), *Mediaeval Isma'ili History and Thought* (Cambridge: Cambridge University Press, 1996), p. 21–73. *[Fāṭimids]*

MAHDAVI, Yahya, *Bibliographie d'Ibn Sina – Fihrist-e Nuskhat-hā-ye Muṣannafāt-e Ibn-e Sīnā* (Tehran: "Tehran University Publications, 206," 1333/1954). *[Bibliographie]*

MĀWARDĪ (AL-), 'Alī (d. 450/1058), *A'lām al-nubuwwa* (Beirut: Dār al-Kutub al-'Ilmiyya, 1406/1986). *[A'lām]*

MICHOT, Yahya M., *La destinée de l'homme selon Avicenne. Le retour à Dieu (*ma'ād*) et l'imagination* (Louvain: Peeters, "Académie Royale de Belgique, Fonds René Draguet, V," 1986). *[Destinée]*

–, *Musique et danse selon Ibn Taymiyya. Le* Livre du *Samā'* et de la danse *(Kitāb al-samā' wa l-raqṣ) compilé par le Shaykh Muḥammad al-Manbijī.* Traduction de l'arabe, présentation, notes et lexique (Paris: J. Vrin, "Études musulmanes, XXXIII," 1991). *[Musique]*

–, *IBN TAYMIYYA. Lettre à un roi croisé (al-Risālat al-Qubruṣiyya).* Traduction de l'arabe, introduction, notes et lexique (Louvain-la-Neuve: Academia – Lyon: Tawhid, "Sagesses musulmanes, 2," 1995). *[Roi croisé]*

–, *AVICENNE. Réfutation de l'astrologie.* Édition et traduction du texte arabe, introduction, notes et lexique. Préface d'Élizabeth TEISSIER (Beirut: Albouraq, "Sagesses musulmanes, 5," 1427/2006). *[Réfutation]*

–, *IBN TAYMIYYA. Against Extremisms.* Texts translated, annotated and introduced. With a foreword by Bruce B. LAWRENCE (Beirut – Paris: Albouraq, 1433/2012). *[Extremisms]*

–, *IBN TAYMIYYA. Le sang et la foi d'al-Ḥallāj. Fetwas, Commentaire du* Credo, *Épître* et autres textes traduits de l'arabe, introduits et annotés (Beirut – Paris : Albouraq, 1439/2017). *[Sang]*

–, *Vanités intellectuelles… L'impasse des rationalismes selon le* Rejet de la contradiction *d'Ibn Taymiyya*, in *Oriente Moderno*, XIX (LXXX), n. s. (Rome, 2000), p. 597–617. *[Vanités]*

–, *A Mamlūk Theologian's Commentary on Avicenna's* Risāla Aḍḥawiyya: *Being a Translation of a Part of the* Dar' al-Ta'āruḍ *of Ibn Taymiyya*, with Introduction, Annotation, and Appendices, in *Journal of Islamic Studies* (Oxford), Part I, 14:2 (May 2003), p. 149–203; Part II, 14:3 (Sept. 2003), p. 309–363. *[Mamlūk I & II]*

–, *Vizir « hérétique » mais philosophe d'entre les plus éminents : al-Ṭūsī vu par Ibn Taymiyya*, in *Farhang*, 15–16, nos 44–45 (Tehran: Institute for Humanities and Cultural Studies, Winter-Spring 2003), p. 195–227. *[Vizir]*

–, *Ibn Taymiyya on Astrology. Annotated Translation of Three Fatwas*, in *Journal of Islamic Studies*, 11.2 (Oxford, 2000), p. 147–208. – Anastatic reprint, with addenda & corrigenda, in Emile SAVAGE-SMITH (ed.), *Magic and Divination in Early Islam* (Aldershot: Ashgate – Variorum, "The Formation of the Classical Islamic World, 42," 2004), p. 276–340. *[Astrology]*

–, *Le riz trop cuit du Kirmānī.* Présentation, édition, traduction et lexique de l'*Épître d'Avicenne contestant l'accusation d'avoir pastiché le Coran*, in Frank DAELEMANS,

Jean-Marie Duvosquel, Robert Halleux, David Juste (eds), *Mélanges offerts à Hossam Elkhadem par ses amis et ses élèves* (Brussels: Archives et Bibliothèques de Belgique, N° spécial 83, 2007), p. 81–129. *[Riz]*
–, *Misled and Misleading... Yet Central in their Influence: Ibn Taymiyya's Views on the Ikhwān al-Ṣafā'*, in Nader El-Bizri (ed.), *The Ikhwān al-Ṣafā' and their* Rasā'il. *An Introduction* (Oxford: Oxford University Press, 2008), p. 139–179. – Corrected version on *www.muslimphilosophy.com. [Misled]*
–, *Textes spirituels d'Ibn Taymiyya (Nouvelle série). XI. Abū Ḥāmid al-Ghazālī & Fakhr al-Dīn al-Rāzī* (July 2011), p. 1–5, on *www.muslimphilosophy.com. [Textes N.S. XI]*
–, *From al-Ma'mūn to Ibn Sab'īn, via Avicenna: Ibn Taymiyya's Historiography of* Falsafa, in Felicitas Opwis & David Reisman (eds), *Islamic Philosophy, Science, Culture, and Religion. Studies in Honor of Dimitri Gutas* (Leiden – Boston: Brill, 2012), p. 453–475. *[Historiography]*
–, *Textes spirituels d'Ibn Taymiyya (Nouvelle série). XIV. Au-delà de la mystique d'Avicenne* (October 2012), p. 1–6, on *www.muslimphilosophy.com. [Textes N.S. XIV]*
–, *An Important Reader of al-Ghazālī: Ibn Taymiyya*, in *The Muslim World*, 103/1 (January 2013), p. 131–160. *[Reader]*
–, *Al-Ghazālī's Esotericism According to Ibn Taymiyya's* Bughyat al-Murtād, in Georges Tamer (ed.), *Islam & Rationality. The Impact of al-Ghazālī. Papers Collected on His 900th Anniversary*, vol. I (Leiden – Boston: Brill, 2015), p. 345–374. *[Esotericism]*
–, *Mamlūks, Qalandars, Rāfidīs, and the "Other" Ibn Taymiyya.* The Thirteenth Annual Victor Danner Memorial Lecture, April 15, 2015 (Bloomington: Indiana University, Department of Near Eastern Languages and Cultures, 2016). *[Mamlūks]*
–, *Textes spirituels d'Ibn Taymiyya (Nouvelle série). XXI. Miracles et prodiges* (February 2017), p. 1–7, on *www.muslimphilosophy.com. [Textes N.S. XXI]*
Muslim (d. 261/875), *al-Jāmi' al-ṣaḥīḥ*, 8 vols (Constantinople, 1334/[1916] – Anastatic reprint: Beirut: al-Maktab al-Tijārī li-l-Ṭibā'a wa l-Nashr wa l-Tawzī', n.d.). *[Ṣaḥīḥ]*
Nasr, Seyyed Hossein (ed.), *The Study Quran.* A New Translation and Commentary (New York: HarperCollins Publishers, 2015). *[Study Quran]*
Ormsby, Eric L., *Theodicy in Islamic Thought. The Dispute over al-Ghazālī's "Best of All Possible Worlds"* (Princeton: Princeton University Press, 1984). *[Theodicy]*
Pines, Shlomo, *La conception de la conscience de soi chez Avicenne et chez Abu'l-Barakāt al-Baghdādī*, in *Studies in Abu'l-Barakāt al-Baghdādī: Physics and Metaphysics* (Jerusalem: The Magnes Press, The Hebrew University – Leiden: Brill, "The Collected Works of Shlomo Pines, Volume I," 1979), p. 181–258. *[Conception]*
Pingree, David, *Abū Ma'shar al-Balkhī*, in *Dictionary of Scientific Biography*, vol. i (New York: Charles Scribner's Sons, 1970), p. 32–39. *[Abū Ma'shar]*
Post, Argan, *A Glimpse of Sufism from the Circle of Ibn Taymiyya. An Edition and Translation of al-Ba'labakkī's (d. 734/1333)* Epistle on the Spiritual Way (Risālat al-Sulūk), in *Journal of Sufi Studies*, 5 (Leiden: Brill, 2016), p. 156–187. *[Glimpse]*
Qazwīnī (al-), Zakariyyā' (d. 682/1283), *'Ajā'ib al-makhlūqāt* (Lucknow: Nawāl Kishawr, 1879). *['Ajā'ib]*
Qurṭubī (al-), Muḥammad (d. 671/1272), *al-I'lām bi-mā fī dīn al-naṣārā min al-fasād wa l-awhām wa iẓhār maḥāsin dīn al-islām wa ithbāt nubuwwa nabiyyi-nā Muḥammad 'alay-hi l-ṣalāt wa l-salām.* Ed. Aḥmad Ḥijāzī al-Saqqā (Cairo: Dār al-Turāth al-'Arabī, 1980). *[I'lām]*

Rāzī (al-), Fakhr al-Dīn (d. 606/1209), *Sirr al-maktūm fī asrār al-nujūm* (Cairo: al-Maṭba' al-Ḥajariyya, [18.. ?]). *[Sirr]*

–, *Sharḥ al-Ishārāt*, in *Hādhā l-Kitāb al-Mawsūm bi-*Sharḥay al-Ishārāt... Ed. 'Umar Ḥusayn al-Khashshāb, 2 vols (Cairo: al-Maṭba'at al-Khayriyya, 1325[/1907]). *[Sharḥ]*

–, *al-Tafsīr al-kabīr*, 32 vols (Cairo: al-Maṭba'at al-Bahiyya, 1357/1938). *[Tafsīr]*

Reisman, David C., *The Making of the Avicennan Tradition. The Transmission, Contents, and Structure of Ibn Sīnā's* al-Mubāḥathāt *(The Discussions)* (Leiden: Brill, "Islamic Philosophy, Theology and Science. Texts and Studies, XLIX," 2002). *[Making]*

Renaudeau, Michel & Strobel, Michèle, *Peinture sous verre du Sénégal* (Paris: Nathan – Dakar: Les Nouvelles Éditions Africaines, 1984). *[Peinture]*

Roux, Jean-Paul, *Histoire de l'empire mongol* (Paris: Fayard, 1993). *[Histoire]*

–, *La religion des Turcs et des Mongols* (Paris: Payot, "Bibliothèque historique," 1984). *[Religion]*

Seif, Hadi, *Persian Painted Tiles* (Tehran: Soroush Press, 1977). *[Tiles]*

Shahrastānī (al-), Abū l-Fatḥ Muḥammad (d. 548/1153), *Kitāb al-Milal wa l-niḥal*, see Daniel Gimaret, Jean Jolivet & Guy Monnot, *Religions I & II. [Milal]*

Stutley, Margaret, *Shamanism. An Introduction* (London – New York: Routledge, 2003). *[Shamanism]*

Talbot Rice, David, *The Illustrations to the "World History" of Rashīd al-Dīn.* Edited by Basil Gray (Edinburgh: Edinburgh University Press, 1976). *[Illustrations]*

Tirmidhī (al-), Abū 'Īsā (d. 279/893), *al-Sunan.* Ed. 'Abd al-Raḥmān Muḥammad 'Uthmān, 5 vols (Beirut: Dār al-Fikr, 1403/1983). *[Sunan]*

Trayner, David, *Ark of Gabriel: Russia "given ancient apocalyptic weapon uncovered in Saudi Arabia,"* in *Daily Star* (London, 22 December 2015). On internet: *http://www.dailystar.co.uk/news/weird-news/482764/ark-of-gabriel-russia-saudi-arbia-mecca-grand-mosque-ancient-weapon-Admiral-Vladimisky. [Ark]*

Ṭumṭum al-Hindī, *al-Ṭalāsim al-hindiyya wa taskhīr al-rūḥāniyyāt wa asrār al-bakhūrāt.* Ed. Abū Zahrā' al-Kūfī (Beirut: Mu'assasat al-Nūr li-l-Maṭbū'āt, 1431/2010). *[Ṭalāsim]*

–, *Ṭelesmāt-e Ṭimṭim-e Hindī. Taskhīr-e rūḥāniyyāt ve 'azā'im-e jinniyyāt ve navāmīs-e Iflāṭūn ve Balīnās...* (Maktabat 'Arabiyya, n.d.). *[Ṭelesmāt]*

Ṭūsī (al-), Naṣīr al-Dīn, *Sharḥ al-Ishārāt*, in *Hādhā l-Kitāb al-Mawsūm bi-*Sharḥay al-Ishārāt... Ed. 'Umar Ḥusayn al-Khashshāb, 2 vols (Cairo: al-Maṭba'at al-Khayriyya, 1325[/1907]). *[Sharḥ]*

Ullmann, Manfred, *Die Natur- und Geheimwissenchaften im Islam* (Leiden – Köln: E. J. Brill, "Handbuch der Orientalistik, Ergänzungsband VI, 2," 1972). *[Natur]*

Wendt, Edmund, *Bilder-Mappe für Länder- und Völkerkunde, mit Einschluss von Geschichte und Naturgeschichte* (Leipzig: Friedrich Dörffling, 1846). *[Bilder-Mappe]*

Yāqūt (d. 626/1229), *Mu'jam al-buldān.* Ed. Farīd 'Abd al-'Azīz al-Jundī, 7 vols (Beirut: Dār al-Kutub al-'Ilmiyya, 1410/1990). *[Mu'jam]*

Yāzījī Zādeh, Meḥmed (d. 855/1451), *Kitāb al-Muḥammadiyya fī l-kamālāt al-Aḥmadiyya* ([Istanbul]: 1284/[1867]). *[Muḥammadiyya]*

Luis Xavier López-Farjeat

Post Avicennian Philosophy in the Muslim West: Ibn Bājja, Ibn Rushd and Ibn Khaldūn on Veridical Dreams and Prophecy

Introduction

The Arabic version of Aristotle's *On Divination in Sleep* is a relevant source for the configuration of the Islamic philosophical doctrines of veridical dreams and prophecy.[1] This treatise was available to Muslim philosophers in a corrupted version that states (1) that the cause of veridical dreams is God (although this does not imply a direct supernatural intervention but the mediation of a universal intellect), and (2) that the human soul needs certain faculties – "spiritual faculties" (*al-quwā al-rūḥāniyya*) – in order to receive veridical dreams. The first issue is presented in a Neoplatonic metaphysical framework where God is the primary or supreme cause who creates every existent which, before coming to be in a material form in the world, exists as an intellectual form in a first intellect called 'universal intellect' (*al-ʿaql al-kullī*). This intellect emanates from God and contains everything He has created. This same process takes place in the case of veridical dreams: God is their ultimate cause, but the universal intellect is their transmitter or proximate cause. This means that God does not act directly in His creation nor does He decide to send veridical dreams to a particular human being in a given moment. The universal intellect distributes veridical dreams, and people with certain psychological capacities are able to receive and interpret them. Therefore, the adaptor of Aristotle's treatise gives an account of the so-called spiritual faculties.

In our regular intellective processes these faculties enable us to grasp the intellectual form (*ṣūra ʿaqliyya*) of a sensible object. However, in the Arabic *On Divination in Sleep* these faculties also grasp in some cases, in particular those of veridical dreams, what in this treatise is called "spiritual form" (*ṣūra rūḥāniyya*). According to the adaptor of Aristotle's treatise, there are some cases in which a

1 See Frank Griffel, "Philosophy and Prophecy," in *The Routledge Companion to Islamic Philosophy*, eds. R. C. Taylor & L. X. López-Farjeat, New York & London: Routledge, 2016, pp. 385–398.

human being is able to attain intelligibles not by means of sensation, but through a universal active intellect which provides intelligibles directly to the internal senses, first to the common sense, which in turn transmits these contents to the productive imagination.

Elements and adaptations of this theory of divination in sleep are found in several Islamic philosophers especially when they deal with a relevant issue in this tradition, namely, prophecy. Elsewhere I have shown the influence of the Arabic *On Divination* in Ibn Sīnā's (d. 1037) *Epistle concerning Dreams* (*al-Risāla al-Manāmiyya*) and in other works.[2] Ibn Bājja (d. 1138) refers to the same Aristotelian source in the *Rule of the Solitary* (*Kitāb Tadbīr al-Mutawaḥḥid*),[3] and in his *Epitome of the Parva Naturalia* (*Talkhīs Kitāb al-Ḥiss wa-l-maḥsūs*)[4] Ibn Rushd (d. 1198) presents a similar doctrine, though more elaborated, to the one that appears in the Arabic version of Aristotle's treatise. Later on, in the 14th century in his *al-Muqaddimah*[5] Ibn Khaldūn (d. 1406) formulates a contrasting explanation of veridical dreams and prophecy, which appears to be relatively different from the conceptions derived from the Arabic *On Divination in Sleep.*

The aim of this paper is to provide an analysis that contrasts psychological approaches of veridical dreams and prophecy in 12th and 14th centuries – those of Ibn Bājja, Ibn Rushd, and Ibn Khaldūn – drawing special attention to the psychological presuppositions in each conception. I will focus exclusively on the analysis of the processes through which someone attains veridical images or prophecies. Therefore, I will leave aside the discussion concerning the interpretation of those images. In what follows, I first make a brief presentation of the metaphysical and psychological process through which the adaptor of the Arabic version of Aristotle's *On Divination in Sleep* explains veridical dreams and prophecy. Afterwards, I shall discuss the impact of this philosophical conception of veridical dreams and prophecy in Ibn Bājja and Ibn Rushd, two inheritors of

2 See Luis Xavier López-Farjeat, "Avicenna and Thomas Aquinas on Natural Philosophy," *American Catholic Philosophical Quarterly* 88/2 (2014): 309–333.

3 See Ibn Bājja (Ibn Bāǧǧa; Avempace), *La conduite de l'isolé et deux autres épîtres*, Arabic texts included, ed. and trans. C. Genequand, Paris: Vrin, 2010, pp. 132–134; Ibn Bāŷŷa (Avempace), *El régimen del solitario*, trans. Joaquín Lomba, Madrid: Trotta, 1997, pp. 111–115.

4 For Averroes's *Epitome of the Parva naturalia* in Arabic see *Corpus commentariorum Averrois in Aristotelem. Versionum arabicorum*, vol. VII, eds. H. A. Wolfson, S. Pines & Z. Stewart, Cambridge Mass.: The Mediaeval Academy of America, 1972; for the Hebrew version see *Corpus commentariorum Averrois in Aristotelem. Versionum hebraicarum*, vol. VII, eds. H. A. Wolfson, D. Baneth & F. H. Fobes, Cambridge Mass.: The Mediaeval Academy of America, 1954; for the Latin version see *Corpus commentariorum Averrois in Aristotelem. Versionum latinarum*, vol. VII, eds. H. A. Wolfson, D. Baneth & F. H. Fobes, Cambridge Mass.: The Mediaeval Academy of America, 1949; for an English translation see *Epitome of Parva Naturalia*, trans. H. Blumberg, Cambridge Mass.: The Mediaeval Academy of America, 1961.

5 See Ibn Khaldūn, *Muqaddimah*, ed. K. Shahada, Beirut: Dar al-fikr, 2001; *The Muqaddimah*, trans. F. Rosenthal, Princeton: Princeton University Press, 1967.

the psychological explanation that appears in Aristotle's corrupted treatise. Finally, I shall analyze Ibn Khaldūn's conception of veridical dreams and prophecy in order to show that though he intends to defend the covert (*al-ghayb*) dimension of these phenomena, he also has a psychological and, in this sense, natural approach that maintains and at the same time challenges and transforms elements that appear in the philosophical approach of his predecessors.

1. The Arabic Version of Aristotle's On Divination

In the original version of *On Divination in Sleep* Aristotle rejects the view according to which it is God who sends veridical dreams and, instead, he holds that this phenomenon can be explained without appealing to a divine origin. He provides three possible causes of divination through dreams: (1) it could be the continuation of a process started in the human body;[6] (2) it could happen because someone who had a dream later unconsciously causes that situation to occur;[7] or (3) because what someone dreams and then happens in reality is due to mere coincidence.[8] In contrast, as mentioned, the Arabic version[9] of the treatise aims

6 Aristotle, *De Divinatione* 463a3–21.

7 Idem, 463a21–23.

8 Idem, 463a31b11.

9 In Arabic, *Parva naturalia* was known under the title *Kitāb al-Ḥiss wa-al-Maḥsūs*, which is actually the title of the first treatise contained in the *Parva Naturalia*, that is, *De sensu et sensibilibus*. Rotraud Elisabeth Hansberger, who has meticulously reviewed the Arabic manuscript – a copy from 1752 found by Hans Daiber in 1985 in Rampur – has noted that it is not a translation but, rather, an adaptation probably available since the ninth century, pervaded by Neoplatonic and Galenic ideas that take a notorious distance from Aristotle's original work (see Hansberger, "*Kitāb al-Ḥiss wa-l-Maḥsūs:* Aristotle's *Parva Naturalia* in Arabic Guise," in *Les Parva naturalia d'Aristote: Fortune antique et médiévale*, eds. C. Grellard & P.-M. Morel, Paris: Publications de la Sorbonne, 2010, p. 143; see also Hans Daiber, "Salient Trends of the Arabic Aristotle," in *The Ancient Tradition in Christian and Islamic Hellenism: Studies on the Transmission of Greek Philosophy and Science*, eds. G. Endress & R. Kruk, Leiden: Brill, 1997, pp. 29–41). Hansberger's doctoral dissertation is devoted precisely to the transmission of the *Parva Naturalia* in the Arabic context, besides presenting the first critical edition of the only extant manuscript (*The Transmission of Aristotle's* Parva Naturalia *in Arabic*, Somerville College, University of Oxford, Faculty of Oriental Studies, 2006). Unfortunately, her work has not been published yet. A part of her research has been published in some articles where she translates and comments on some relevant passages (see "How Aristotle Came to Believe in God-given Dreams: The Arabic Version of *De divinatione per somnum*," in *Dreaming Across Boundaries: The Interpretation of Dreams in Islamic Lands*, ed. Louise Marlow, Washington/Cambridge, Mass.: Ilex Foundation / Center for Hellenic Studies, 2008, pp. 50–77, and "*Kitāb al-Ḥiss wa-l-Maḥsūs:* Aristotle's *Parva Naturalia* in Arabic Guise," 2010, pp. 143–162; "Plotinus Arabus Rides Again," *Arabic Sciences and Philosophy* 21 (2011): 57–84; "The Arabic Adaptation of the *Parva Naturalia* (*Kitāb al-Ḥiss wa-l-maḥsūs*)," *Studia graeco-arabica* 4 (2014): 301–314. Hansberger has resurrected a topic that had been previously discussed by M. Steinschneider (see Moritz Steinschneider, "Die *Parva Naturalia* des Aristoteles bei den Arabern,"

to explain two issues: (1) that the cause of veridical dreams is God, though He transmits this kind of dream through the mediation of a universal intellect, and (2) that the human soul needs specific faculties – "spiritual faculties" (*al-quwā al-rūḥāniyya*) – in order to receive veridical dreams.[10]

Evidently the Arabic text has nothing to do with the Greek original. However, what is noteworthy is how the adaptor formulates a novel explanation on the divine and divinatory character of dreams, one which draws from other medical and philosophical sources – mainly Galen and Neoplatonism – and, as a result, offers a coherent thesis that inspired later Islamic philosophers and theologians.

According to the Arabic *On Divination*, God is the primary cause who creates every existent which, before coming to be in a material form in the world, exists as an intellectual form in a first intellect emanated from God and called, as mentioned, 'universal intellect' (*al-ʿaql al-kullī*). This intellect contains everything that God has created. This account, which has God creating through the mediation of a universal intellect, fits the Neoplatonic notions of primary and secondary causalities.[11] Although God is the ultimate cause of every occurrence in

---

Zeitschrift der Deutschen Morgenlëndischen Gesellschaft 37 (1883): 477–492; *Zeitschrift der Deutschen Morgenlëndischen Gesellschaft* 45 (1891): 447–453) in the late nineteen century, and by S. Pines (see Shlomo Pines, "The Arabic Recension of *Parva Naturalia* and the philosophical doctrine concerning veridical dreams according to al-*Risāla al-Manāmiyya* and other sources," *Israel Oriental Studies* IV (1974): 104–153) in the twentieth century, but which has not been sufficiently explored albeit the great number of aspects that deserve to be analyzed and discussed. Pines had already suggested that the *Epistle concerning Dreams* (*al-Risāla al-Manāmiyya*) could be considered an essential source for the recognition of a version of the *De divinatione per somnum* that would differ from that of Aristotle (see Shlomo Pines 1974, pp. 152–153). It might well be that the lack of a critical edition of the Arabic *Parva Naturalia* and the fact that Rampur's manuscript is incomplete explain the scarce attention given to this treatise. According to Hansberger's contributions, the manuscript is divided into three sections (*maqālas*). *De sensu* can be found in the first section, while the second one is divided into two parts: the first of these is a version of the *De memoria et reminiscentia*, while the second includes the *De somno et vigilia*, the *De insomniis*, and the *De divinatione per somnum*, all of which are gathered under the same title, *al-Nawm wa-al-yaqaẓa* (*De somno et vigilia*); finally, the third section includes the *De longitudine et brevitate vitae* (see Hansberger 2010, p. 143).

10 See Rotraud Hansberger 2008, p. 56; Carla Di Martino, "La Perception Spirituelle. Perspectives de Recherche pour l'Historie des *Parva Naturalia* dans la Tradition Arabo-Latine," *Veritas* 52/3 (2007), 21–35.

11 See Cristina D'Ancona, "La notion de 'cause' dans les textes Néoplatoniciens Arabes," in *Métaphysiques Médiévales. Études en l'honneur d'André de Muralt*, eds. C. Chiesa & L. Freuler, Genève-Lausanne-Neuchâtel: Cahiers de la Revue de Théologie et de Philosophie, 1999, pp. 47–68; *L'influence du vocabulaire arabe:* "Causa Prima est esse tantum," in *L'élaboration du vocabulaire philosophique au Moyen Âge*. Actes du Colloque International de Louvain la-Neuve et Leuven, 12–14 septembre 1998, eds. J. Hamesse & C. Steel, Turnhout: Brepols, 2000, pp. 51–97; "'Causa prima superior est omni narratione'. Il tema delle sifat Allah nel primo neoplatonismo arabo," *Oriente moderno* 19 (2000): 519–555; Richard Taylor, "Primary Causality and *ibdāʿ* (*creare*) in the *Liber de causis*," in *Wahrheit und Geschichte. Die ge-*

the world, the immediate source is not He but the universal intellect. The first cause, namely God, acts through the second or intermediary causes, but this does not mean that it loses its causal agency. The same process takes place in the case of veridical dreams: God or the first cause is their ultimate cause, but the universal intellect is their transmitter or proximate cause. This means that God does not act directly on what He creates, nor does He decide to send veridical dreams to a particular human being at a given moment:

> The cause and reason of true dream-visions (*ru'yā ṣādiqa*) is the true God, may He be exalted, [and this takes place] through the mediation of the Intellect, since all that God, may He be exalted, wanted to become manifest in this world, was represented by Him in the Intellect immediately, and represented its forms in this world immediately, along with its logical manifestations. The Intellect then made them manifest to the soul and to each of the faculties, in the measure in which the soul decided that the faculty could receive them, given that the Supreme Cause, that is, God, may He be exalted, created them in such manner, when He created the Intellect at that moment, to make manifest what is in it; because God moved [the Intellect] to manifest what is in it.[12]

The universal intellect plays a mediating role and is the one that distributes the veridical dreams. Those endowed with certain psychological capacities are able to receive and interpret those dreams. This is why the adaptor of Aristotle's treatise completes the metaphysical explanation with psychological references, that is, the presentation of the so-called spiritual faculties. The account presented by the adaptor of this treatise regarding spiritual faculties is based on Galen and his conception of three mental faculties located in the brain, namely, productive imagination (*mutakhayyila*), the cogitative faculty (*al-fikr*), and memory (*al-dhikr*).[13] These three faculties, according to the adaptor, stay active while we are asleep as receptacles for both ordinary and veridical dreams. During our ordinary dreams, these three faculties act upon the images that had been previously retained by the soul, particularly by the cogitative faculty; however, in veridical dreams the images are not provided by previous sensitive experiences, but by the universal intellect. This is why the adaptor of the Arabic *On Divination* clarifies that the images to which we have access in dreams could have some meaning (*maʿnā*) or could be utterly false:

---

brochene Tradition metaphysischen Denkens. Festschrift zum 70. Geburtstag von Günther Mensching, eds. Mensching-Estakhr & Städtler, Würzburg: Königshausen & Neumann, 2012, pp. 115–136; "Primary and Secondary Causality," in *The Routledge Companion to Islamic Philosophy*, eds. R. C. Taylor & L. X. López-Farjeat, New York & London: Routledge, 2016, pp. 225–235.

12 *al-Nawm wa-al-yaqaẓa*, f. 42r; Arabic fragment taken from Hansberger 2014, p. 307, translation modified.

13 See Hansberger 2010, pp. 145–146.

> For when [the person] is in the realm of sleep he makes that *maʿnā* present together with the form. Hence the sleeper sees forms of things, and their interpretation is given to him through that *maʿnā* which has [already] been in [the cogitative]. Then the person who is having the dream-vision will believe that dream-vision to be veridical, and the thing which he is seeing to be a reality; whereas it is entirely false, and does not have any *maʿnā*. This occurs due to nothing but these spiritual faculties – I mean the imaginative [faculty], [the cogitative] and [the faculty of] memory – as neither the movement, nor the activity of these faculties rest in the realm of sleep. For when the nature rests and is absorbed in the soul, then the body rests; and when the body rests the senses rest, and when the senses rest, the common sense resorts to the imaginative [faculty], and looks with a spiritual gaze at the forms of things which it has seen in the realm of corporeality. [Before], it used to look at them when they were corporeal and in motion, whereas [now] it looks at them being at rest and motionless in the imaginative [faculty], with them being more perfect and excellent when at rest than when they are moving.[14]

The way the spiritual faculties are approached in the Arabic *On Divination* deserves special attention: in the context of our common intellective processes, the role of these faculties, also known as "internal senses"[15] is to assist when the apprehension of the intellectual form (*ṣūra ʿaqliyya*) of an object takes place; however, as the editor of the treatise R. Hansberger notes, in the Arabic *On Divination* these faculties also access, particularly in the case of veridical dreams, what in this treatise is called a "spiritual form" (*ṣūra rūḥāniyya*). This capacity is mentioned when the adaptor discusses why in some cases veridical dreams do not depict future events with accuracy even though they come from the universal intellect. The adaptor explains that sometimes in veridical dreams what is perceived is the spiritual, not the corporeal form (*ṣūra jismāniyya*). For instance, one could dream that something is happening in a particular city, but the place that appears in a dream may not look like that particular city. The images perceived in veridical dreams are not limited to the particular or the corporeal. The spiritual form is only similar to the corporeal form and is an image of the intellectual form. This way of understanding the "spiritual form" is relevant because, in essence, it consists of an image that is not constructed from the data provided by external

14 *al-Nawm wa-al-yaqaẓa*, f. 40v 1–26; Arabic fragment taken from Hansberger 2008, p. 60, translation modified.

15 For a thorough review of the function of the internal senses, see Harry A. Wolfson, "The Internal Senses in Latin, Arabic, and Hebrew Philosophic Texts," *Harvard Theological Review* XXVIII/2 (1935): 69–133; Deborah Black, "Estimation in Avicenna: The Logical and Psychological Dimensions," *Dialogue* 32 (1993): 219–258; "Imagination and Estimation: Arabic Paradigms and Western Transformations," *Topoi* 19/1 (2000): 59–75; Carla di Martino, "Memory and Recollection in Ibn Sīnā's and Ibn Rushd's Philosophical Texts Translated into Latin in the Twelfth and Thirteenth Centuries: A Perspective on the Doctrine of the Internal Senses in Arabic Psychological Science," in *Forming the Mind. Essays on the Internal Senses and the Mind/Body Problem from Avicenna to the Medical Enlightenment*, ed. H. Lagerlund, Dordrecht: Springer, pp. 17–25.

sensation but which, in fact, is similar to a corporeal form; moreover, since the spiritual form is constituted by an image, it is nothing more than a similitude of the intellectual form.

What can be noticed through this approach is an attempt to grant a cognitive role to the dream images just as they are produced in veridical dreams; that is, they do not derive from the sensitive experiences or from the usual intellective process. Although they do not derive from sensation, the three same mental faculties and the common sense receive these images. In other words, in the case of veridical dreams, according to the Arabic version of the *On Divination*, humans are capable of accessing intelligibles without the mediation of sensation, since in this case it is the universal active intellect which directly provides intelligibles to the internal faculties, starting with the common sense which, in turn, transmits these contents to the productive imagination which becomes the leading faculty:

> As for the sound, spiritual dream-vision, it is the one which comes about from intelligibles of the universal intellect, not from intelligibles of the acquired intellect, [i. e. it comes from intelligibles] which are unknown to the common sense and have not been imagined by the formative [faculty]; the *maʿnā* of which [the faculty of] thought does not know, and which are not deposited in [the faculty of] memory. When these forms appear in the realm of dream-vision, and when the common sense, the formative [faculty] and all other faculties look at them, they know that the forms coming to them from corporeal objects of perception are something false.[16]

As can be seen, in the Arabic *On Divination* there is an explanation of a cognitive process that would justify veridical dreams and prophecy through the interaction of a universal intellect and the internal faculties whose main characteristic is that they work with images.[17] In the next section I shall present elements and adap-

16 *al-Nawm wa-al-yaqaẓa,* f. 41r 5–11; Arabic fragment taken from Hansberger 2014, p. 307, translation modified.

17 The Arabic *On Divination* also deals with the interpretation of veridical dreams. Nevertheless, as I pointed out in the introduction, I leave aside this issue. Anyway, the following passages illustrate the opinion of the adaptor of Aristotle's treatise in this respect: "If the cogitative is not able to find a meaning, at that point the person [who has dreamt] will expose [the content of his dream] to the interpreter. Sometimes the intellect flows upon the interpreter with [those] spiritual words, so that his tongue will pronounce them, while he perceives that he is the one who is interpreting the dream-vision correctly. At other times, the intellect will not flow upon the interpreter, and he will make mistakes while not knowing what to say or what he should interpret. The intellect can flow upon the interpreter for one of two reasons: either the interpreter is spiritual and hence the intellect will flow upon him given his spirituality, or it will flow upon him because of signs that become manifest in the world" (*al-Nawm wa-al-yaqaẓa*, f. 42v–43r); "The evidence that confirms what we have said is the dream-vision of king Heracles, in which he saw those columns. [He dreamt] that he saw those miraculous columns while awake; in addition, he also saw those spiritual words, so he kept marveling about them for a long time. Then, he called some interpreters to interpret the dream-vision,

tations of this understanding of divination in two of the major figures of Islamic philosophy in the West, namely Ibn Bājja and Ibn Rushd. We shall take into account that while these two philosophers conserve the same noetic structure that appears in the Arabic *On Divination*, that is, the interaction of a separated intellect with internal faculties, their explanations, especially that of Ibn Rushd, are more sophisticated, and the specific role of the internal faculties is explained differently in the case of both philosophers.

2. Ibn Bājja and Ibn Rushd

One of the main philosophical matters discussed by Ibn Bājja in the *Tadbīr* is precisely the notion of "spiritual form" (*ṣūra rūḥāniyya*), terminology that, as has been shown, is also present in the Arabic *On Divination*. In the final section of the *Tadbīr* Ibn Bājja enumerates the different kinds of spiritual forms in a descending order starting from those forms that are absolutely separated from matter to those that are related to matter in some degree. Ibn Bājja refers to four kinds of "spiritual forms": (1) the forms of celestial bodies, (2) the active intellect and the acquired intellect; (3) material intelligibles (*maʿqūlāt*); (4) forms (*maʿānī*) as they exist in the inner faculties of the soul (common sense, imagination, and memory).[18] In the *Tadbīr* Ibn Bājja leaves aside the first kind of form and explains that spiritual forms are divided into universal forms (those stored in the active intellect), particular corporeal forms (those found in the common sense), and particular spiritual forms (those stored in the inner faculties of the soul and that may be true or false depending on whether they exist or not in a corporeal particular entity). He refers to the *Kitāb al-Ḥiss wa-al-Maḥsūs*, the name by which the Arabs knew Aristotle's *Parva Naturalia*, and states that, according to this treatise, the forms in the common sense constitute the lowest level of spirituality

but none of them were able to interpret it correctly, but gave him an explanation which was contrary to the truth. But when the king slept again, he saw the spiritual words [which corresponded] to the interpretation of his dream-vision, and he saw the forms of that which would take place in the world from those spiritual forms which he had seen before. Hence, when he woke up from his sleep he had no need of the interpreters anymore, and he accepted as true the explanation of the interpretation given to him during his dream, [and he] rejected the false version of the interpreters. He kept [...] that dream-vision, until what he had seen in his dream happened in the world. The interpretation of the dream-vision that he received while he was sleeping was true and correct, whereas the one provided by the interpreters was incorrect" (*al-Nawm wa-al-yaqaẓa*, f. 41v–42r2). This last example where the dream of king Heracles is explained appears also in Ibn Sīnā's *Epistle concerning Dreams* and Ibn Rushd's *Talkhīs*.

18 Ibn Bājja, 2010, pp. 132–133; 1997, p. 112.

followed by the forms in the imagination and then in the memory; and, finally, the highest level pertains to the forms of the rational faculty.[19]

Ibn Bājja makes a distinction between the rational faculty (*nuṭq*) and the intellect (*ʿaql*). Through the rational faculty human beings are able to abstract particular corporeal forms, as well and conceptualize and attain the first principles of particular sciences; syllogizing, deduction, and induction, are due to our rational faculty. Meanwhile, intellection is a higher level of spirituality because it is not about reasoning processes but about the attainment of spiritual universal forms or intelligibles through conjunction with the active intellect. Following al-Fārābī, Ibn Bājja distinguishes between a "material" or "passive intellect" (*ʿaql bi-l-quwah*), an intellect in act (*ʿaql bi'l-fiʿl*), an acquired intellect (*ʿaql al-mustafāḍ*), and a separated active intellect (*ʿaql al-fa ʿāl*).

The active intellect is characterized in several passages within Ibn Bājja's works as immaterial, eternal, unique, and separated, and as the repository of all the universal spiritual forms.[20] This active intellect fulfills the same functions of the so-called "universal intellect" in the Arabic version of *On Divination*, that is, it works both as a repository of forms and as its provider. The role of the active intellect in human cognition, according to Ibn Bājja, is threefold: (1) in our ordinary intellective acts the active intellect illuminates the material or passive intellect in order to become intellect in act, providing for it universal spiritual forms and the first principles of reasoning; (2) the active intellect provides spiritual forms, turning the human intellect into acquired intellect; (3) finally, the active intellect is responsible of the conjunction (*ittiṣāl*) between the human intellect and the last intelligence (presumably God), going beyond the knowledge provided by reason and science, and attaining happiness through a sort of mystical experience.

In the *Tadbīr* Ibn Bājja briefly alludes to veridical visions and divinations, and he describes them as cases in which particular spiritual forms do not pass through

19 Idem, pp. 132–134; 1997, pp. 112–115.

20 See Ibn Bājja, *'Ilm al-Nafs*, trans. Hasan Maʿsumi, Pakistan Historical Society: Karacchi, 1961; *Libro sobre el alma*, trans. J. Lomba, Trotta: Madrid, 2007; *On the Conjoining* see *Tratado sobre la unión del intelecto con el hombre*, trans. Asín Palacios (with Arabic text), *Al-Andalus*, 7: 1–47, Madrid; Granada, 1942; *Tratado de la unión del Intelecto con el hombre* (in *Carta del adiós y otros tratados filosóficos*), trans. J. Lomba, Trotta: Madrid, 2006, 83–104; Ibn Bāğğa, *Discours sur la conjonction de l'intellect avec l'homme adressé à l'un de ses fréres* (in *La conduite de l'isolé et deux autres épîtres*), trans. Charles Genequand (with Arabic text), Vrin: Paris, 2010, 183–203; *Carta del adiós*, trans. Asín Palacios (with Arabic text), *Al-Andalus*, 8: 1–87, Madrid; Granada, 1943; *Carta del adiós* (in *Carta del adiós y otros tratados filosóficos*), trans. J. Lomba, Trotta: Madrid, 2006, 19–72; *Épître de l'adieu*, (in *La conduite de l'isolé et deux autres épîtres*), trans. Charles Genequand (with Arabic text), Vrin: Paris, 2010, 88–121. See also Hasan Maʿsumi, "Ibn Bājjah on the Human Intellect," *Islamic Studies* IV/2 (1965): 121–136; Joaquín Lomba, "La ciencia del alma en Ibn Bāŷŷa (Avempace)," *Veritas* 52/3 (2007): 79–90.

common sense because they are received directly from the active intellect and not from sensation:

> There is another kind [of form] in which neither the individuals nor the names nor something that could designate them have passed through the common sense, because sometimes [these forms] proceed from the active intellect through the rational faculty, particularly when they refer to future events that only exist in potentiality, such as the veridical visions and divinations that are commonly mentioned. This matter has been explained at the end of the second chapter of the *Kitāb al-Ḥiss*. These things do not occur by human choice, and the effects they produce, as they exist, are not the subject of this treatise. [These things] only exist in a few individuals and rarely take place; therefore it is not possible to conceive a discipline dealing with those things and there is no human conduct that concerns them. For this reason they are not part of this treatise.[21]

As can be seen, Ibn Bājja explicitly refers to the Arabic version of the *Parva Naturalia* where the *On Divination* is included. He keeps the essence of this treatise, namely, that the active intellect is the provider of spiritual forms that contains veridical dreams and prophecies. However, it seems that the role of internal faculties is different: Ibn Bājja stresses that the spiritual forms provided by the active intellect do not need to pass through the common sense, but go directly to the rational faculty in the form of dream visions and divinations, and not as universal spiritual forms. These visions and divinations are forms or images (*maʿānī*). In other words, the contents of dream visions cannot be universal spiritual forms, but particular spiritual forms in the imagination. As mentioned, the forms in the imagination constitute a higher level of spirituality than the forms in the common sense and, at the same time, the rational faculty is superior to the imagination. In the case of dream visions and divinations, the contents are provided by the active intellect to the imagination, through the rational faculty, while in our ordinary intellective process, the imagination is the provider of particular spiritual forms that need the intervention of the active intellect to become universal forms or intelligibles.

In sum, although Ibn Bājja briefly suggests that there is a psychological process that explains dream visions and divinations, it seems that he considers this matter – in the previous passage – as a subject philosophy does not have to deal with. Ibn Bājja refers to the *Kitāb al-Ḥiss*, and his explanation certainly seems to be close to the one that appears in this treatise, with the exception of the role of the common sense, which Ibn Bājja drops from the process perhaps because of its close relation to sense knowledge.

Now, the *Talkhīs Kitāb al-Ḥiss* is an early text and the only work where Ibn Rushd discusses prophecy from a psychological perspective. In the rest of his

21 Ibn Bājja, 2010, p. 135; 1997, pp. 116–117. My translation.

psychological works such as the three commentaries on the *De anima*, prophecy is absolutely absent. The section of the *Talkhīs* where Ibn Rushd discusses veridical dreams and prophecy corresponds to Aristotle's *On Dreams.* Ibn Rushd distinguishes between true dreams (*ru'yā*), divination (*kahāna*), and revelation (*waḥy*), suggesting later that sometimes these phenomena are referred to as 'prophecy' (*nubuwwa*).[22] He explains then that dreams may be false or true and thereafter he investigates to which part of the soul each of these two kinds of dream is related, which is their cause, why veridical dreams take place, as well as other questions, such as why some people are able to interpret veridical dreams while others are not.

Concerning the first question, to which part of the soul each kind of dreams is related, Ibn Rushd holds that both are related to the imaginative faculty (*mutakhayyilah*). He argues that during sleep the imagination is the only faculty that keeps functioning, while other faculties, such as the cogitative and memory do not. The imaginative faculty is described as an active faculty that is continuously forming images coming from memory, the common sense, or from the image or impression of an external object formed by the imagination itself.[23] True and false dreams are primarily related to the imaginative faculty. The images we perceive during sleep have been received from external objects or from memory which, in turn, will move the common sense, which in turn will move other faculties, making us perceive as though the images were really present.[24] Ibn Rushd explains, however, that in the case of true dreams – those which plainly concern future events – we attain some knowledge that neither proceeds from previous knowledge nor is the result of thinking or reflecting as happens with rational knowledge.[25]

Echoing the Arabic *On Divination*, Ibn Rushd holds that the agent producing predictions through true dreams is the same that provides the universal first principles in theoretical thoughts, namely, the active intellect.[26] Nevertheless, he immediately deals with two problematic questions: (1) how can particulars be acquired by man from an intellect whose nature is universal and immaterial?; and (2) how did the knowledge of particular things happen to be bestowed upon a particular man?[27] Ibn Rushd's response to the first question recalls his position in the *Short Commentary on the De anima* as follows: given that the contents provided by the active intellect cannot be received as such in the particular human imagination, then they are turned into particulars by the imagination:

22 Averroes, 1972, p. 66; 1961, p. 39.
23 Idem, p. 69; 1961, p. 41.
24 Idem, pp. 69–70; 1961, p. 41.
25 Idem, p. 73; 1961, p. 43.
26 Idem, p. 72; 1961, p. 42.
27 Idem, p. 75; 1961, p. 44.

> (…) it cannot be denied that the separate intellect endows the imaginative soul with the universal nature that the individual that comes into being possesses, that is to say, with a comprehension of its causes, and the imaginative soul will receive it as a particular by virtue of the fact that it is in matter. It may receive the individual of that which has been comprehended, in reality, or it may receive something similar to it. Just as the intellect endows one with the universal perfections of the soul and matter receives them as particulars, so here too the intellect endows the imaginative soul with the final perfection as a universal, and the soul receives it as a particular.[28]

In other words, it seems that what Ibn Rushd holds is that the contents received by the imagination need to be particularized, but they are related to the universal intelligible and actually those particulars or, in Ibn Rushd's terminology – which recalls the Arabic *On Divination* – those particular spiritual forms (*ṣūra rūḥāniyya*) work as a very similar representation of the universal intelligible. Ibn Rushd writes:

> As to the question why the imaginative faculty does not present in most cases the true individual object which comes under the universal endowed by the intellect, but presents only an object similar to it, the answer is that this will occur because the sense object has two forms: a spiritual form, which is the form that is similar to it; and a corporeal form, which is the form of the sense-object itself, not the form that is similar to it. The form that is similar to it is indeed more spiritual because it is closer to the nature of the universal than the form of the real object. The imaginative soul will therefore receive the thing conceived by the intellect with the greatest perfection possible in its nature to receive, from among the spiritual forms. Sometimes, however, it will receive it in a corporeal form, and then the person who sees during sleep will behold the very form itself and not something similar to it.[29]

Notice that in this passage we can find the same distinction between corporeal and spiritual forms that appeared in the Arabic *On Divination* and also in Ibn Bājja and, as in these two cases, Ibn Rushd explains that the imagination receives spiritual forms that are precisely the content of veridical dreams. According to Ibn Rushd, during sleep the imaginative faculty is more perfect and more spiritual because the external senses are not interfering – an idea that is also found in Ibn Khaldūn.

28 Idem, p. 79; 1961, p. 46, translation modified.
29 Averroes, 1972, pp. 81–82; 1961, pp. 47–48.

3. Ibn Khaldūn

In *al-Muqaddimah* Ibn Khaldūn devotes a short section in book six to explain prophetic knowledge. He assumes that this is a kind of covert knowledge.[30] According to his explanation prophets have been created with an innate disposition to exchange their humanity for an angelical condition.[31] Some remarks on the process through which the prophecy is attained appear in chapter twelve where Ibn Khaldūn provides a detailed exploration on the science on dream interpretation, including the role of sensitive and internal faculties in the reception of veridical dreams, which recalls some details of the psychological account in the Arabic version of Aristotle's *On Divination.* Noteworthy here is the way in which Ibn Khaldūn provides a psychological explanation that may suggest that phenomena such as veridical dreams and prophecy are somehow natural. This does not mean, however, that Ibn Khaldūn is entirely continuing what Ibn Bājja, Ibn Rushd, and previously al-Fārābī and Ibn Sīnā, had started. Although Ibn Khaldūn appeals to a psychological explanation, he does distance himself somewhat from his predecessors.

Ibn Khaldūn points out that dreams are natural to human beings and their contents need to be interpreted in order to be understood for their meaning and in order to figure out in which cases they are to be considered as dream visions or as veridical dreams. "A dream vision" writes Ibn Khaldūn, "is a kind of covert perception (*wa-'l-ru'ya mudrakun min madārik al-ghayb*)."[32] Ibn Khaldūn claims there is a connection between dream visions and prophecy, appealing to some sayings of the prophet Muhammad, and immediately stating that the first revelation given to the Prophet started as a dream vision, something Muhammad further constantly experienced to the extent that every time he dreamed, he anxiously tried to find in his dreams a presage of the triumph of Islam.[33]

After the introduction of the relation between dream visions and prophecy, Ibn Khaldūn proceeds to explain how is it possible for humans to experience dream visions, and surprisingly, he starts providing a biological explanation built upon Galen's anatomical works. According to Ibn Khaldūn, the spirit in the heart (*al-rūḥ al-qalbī*), that is, a fine vapor residing in the cavity of the heart, spreads with the blood through the veins to the entire body, completing the actions and sensations of the animal faculties. This spirit is also the vehicle of the rational soul, and in fact "the rational soul perceives and acts only by means of that vaporous spirit."[34] When Ibn Khaldūn refers to what he calls a "real dream

30 Ibn Khaldūn, 1967, p. 338.
31 Idem, p. 81.
32 Idem, p. 367.
33 Idem, p. 368.
34 Idem, p. 368.

vision," he explains that it "is an awareness on the part of the rational soul in its spiritual essence, of glimpses of the forms of events" (*muṭālaʿat al-nafs al-nāṭiqa fī dhātihā al-rūḥāniyya lamḥatun min ṣuwar al-wāqiʿāt*).[35] For Ibn Khaldūn the very essence of the soul is being spiritual (*rūḥāniyyat*), although the human bodily constitution keeps the soul linked to a set of bodily operations and faculties. He describes the regular human process of knowledge and contrasts it with the way dream visions take place. Although in both cases he underlines the intermediary role of the imaginative faculty, each process is quite different: the former starts with the sensible and ends with spiritual-intellectual pictures, while the latter starts with the awareness of the spiritual realm and ends with some sort of sensible perception.

In the case of our regular process of knowledge, the imaginative faculty attains images provided by the external senses, which derive into imaginary pictures, which in turn are handed over to the faculty of memory, which stores and keeps them available for the soul. The soul can deal with these imaginary pictures and by means of speculation, deduction, and abstraction it acquires spiritual-intellectual pictures. As we can see, the imagination here works as an intermediate faculty between the sensible and the intelligible. In contrast, dream visions are generated when the bodily senses cease their perceptive activity while in the sleeping state, thus freeing the soul to the extent that it becomes aware of its spiritual essence. Thus, the spirit forms pictures of its own that are handed over to the imagination, which turns these into imaginary pictures, which in turn are handed over to the common sense. When the common sense receives these imaginary pictures while in the sleeping state, the person sleeping perceives these as though they were being actually perceived by the external senses. As we can see here, the imagination is also working as an intermediate faculty that enables the spirit to perceive its spiritual essence by the end of the process as though they were sensible. This is the process that produces what Ibn Khaldūn calls "true dream visions:"

> The faculties through which the body perceives knowledge are all connected with the brain. The active part among them is the imagination. It derives imaginary pictures from the pictures perceived by the senses and turns them over to the power of memory, which retains them until they are needed in connection with speculation and deduction. From the (imaginary pictures), the soul also abstracts other spiritual-intellectual pictures. In this way, abstraction ascends from the *sensibilia* to the *intelligibilia.* The imagination is the intermediary between them. Also, when the soul has received a certain number of perceptions from its own world, it passes them onto the imagination, which forms them into appropriate pictures and turns those perceptions over to the common sense. As a result, the sleeper sees them as if they were perceived by the senses. Thus, the percep-

35 Idem, p. 80.

tions come down from the rational spirit to the level of sensual perception, with the imagination again being the intermediary. This is what dream visions actually are.[36]

Now, regarding the difference between these true dream visions and what he calls "confused dreams," Ibn Khaldūn states that the latter are derived from imaginary pictures preserved in the memory while the individual is awake.[37] However, when the pictures proceed from the rational spirit, they are dream visions or veridical dreams. At first glance this process is striking, given that in both confused and veridical dreams the imagination is playing an intermediary role and hence we need to distinguish between these two kinds of images. This is why, according to Ibn Khaldūn, we need a science of dream interpretation. The main difference between confused and veridical dreams is that in the case of the latter the soul does not attain the pictures from imagination or memory, but from its own spiritual essence.

Frequently, however, the soul turns to its spiritual essence in concert with the inward powers. It then accomplishes the spiritual kind of perception for which it is fitted by nature. It takes up some of the forms of things that have become inherent in its essence at that time. Imagination seizes on those perceived forms, and pictures them in the customary molds either realistically or allegorically. Pictured allegorically, they require interpretation.[38]

In other words, the soul is able to attain pictures, or going back to the terminology of the Arabic *On Divination*, "spiritual forms" that are not linked to the particular perceptions of the external senses. This process by means of which the soul "perceives spiritually" results in images that can be presented either realistically or allegorically.[39] The science of the interpretation of dreams essentially consists in defining the features of veridical dreams.

Ibn Khaldūn points out some signs that help distinguish true dream visions from confused dreams. In the case of true dream visions, he points out that the person having such vision wakes up quickly, right after perceiving the vision, as if in a hurry to go back to bodily sense perceptions. Other signs of true dream visions are their detailed nature, the clear way they remain pictured in the memory after the person is awake, and how this image is not prone to forgetfulness. This is so because the perception by the soul of its own spiritual essence in true dream visions happens all at once and not following any consecutive order.[40] Now, regarding the trademarks of confused dreams, these will not be as clear, and individuals who experience them will be prone to forgetting

36 Idem, p. 368–369)
37 Idem, p. 369.
38 Idem, pp. 82–83.
39 Idem, p. 83.
40 Idem, pp. 369–371.

them; it might require effort to remember them, since such dreams take place in time and follow a consecutive order (unlike what happens in true dream visions).

Ibn Khaldūn explains some of the elements of dream interpretation. As mentioned, when true visions take place, the perceptions handed over by the rational spirit to the imagination are turned by imagination into imaginary pictures that are related to the original perceptions of the spiritual essence. Thus, for example, a spiritual idea of greatness could be depicted by imagination by means of an image of the ocean. When the dreamer awakens, he only knows the image, but does not know the idea that underlies it. Hence, the interpreter seeks the idea that underlies the dreamt image, as some images appropriately fit some ideas. However, as mentioned in the introduction, in this paper I do not intend to deal with the requirements of the interpreter. I just wish to mention, before moving on to my concluding remarks, the fact that when explaining the process through which veridical dreams and prophecy take place, Ibn Khaldūn does not appeal to an external universal intellect or to secondary causes in order to justify these phenomena. In fact, Ibn Khaldūn rejects the idea of a first intellect as responsible for occurrences in the world,[41] and is committed to a sort of spiritual knowledge consisting in the awareness of the soul.

Concluding Remarks

Aristotle's original *On Divination in Sleep* clearly rejects the mediation of God or a separate intellect when offering an explanation of the origin of veridical dreams. Nevertheless, the Arabic version of this treatise defends their divine origin through the mediation of a universal intellect, as well as the need of a set of spiritual faculties that, according to the adaptor of the Arabic version, stay active while in the sleeping state. The production of ordinary and veridical dreams differ: in ordinary dreams the spiritual faculties act upon images from previous sensible data stored in the spiritual faculties, whereas in veridical dreams these faculties act upon "spiritual forms" provided directly by the universal intellect.

41 "It should be known that the (opinion) the (philosophers) hold is wrong in all its aspects. They refer all *existentia* to the first intellect and are satisfied with (the theory of the first intellect) in their progress toward the Necessary One (the Deity). This means that they disregard all the degrees of divine creation beyond the (first intellect)" (Idem, p. 401). And earlier, "They draw their conclusions with regard to the most high celestial body in the same way they drew their conclusions with regard to the human essence. They (thus) consider it necessary that the (celestial) sphere must have a soul and an intellect, like human beings. Then, they take as a limit for the (whole system), the number of units, which is ten. Nine are derived in essence and pluralistic. One, the tenth, is primary and singular" (Idem, p. 399). Though this last criticism applies mainly to al-Fārābī and Ibn Sīnā, the idea of a first intellect, as has been shown, is common to Ibn Bājja, Ibn Rushd, and certainly to the Arabic *On Divination*.

These spiritual forms do not derive from sensation or from the regular intellective process, and although they are similar to the corporeal sensible forms, they actually are an image of the intellectual forms. According to Aristotle's corrupted treatise, spiritual forms are provided directly by the universal intellect to the common sense, which hands them over to the productive imagination, which has a major role in the generation of the images that constitute veridical dreams. As has been shown, both Ibn Bājja and Ibn Rushd coincide with the main views of the Arabic *On Divination* regarding the need of a separate intellect as well as its interaction with the spiritual or internal faculties, mainly the imagination. They differ, however, on how this framework is assembled.

Ibn Bājja describes veridical dream visions as instances where the spiritual forms are granted directly by the active intellect, bypassing the usual process that involves sensation and common sense. Thus, in the case of veridical dreams, spiritual forms are provided by the active intellect directly to the imaginative faculty by means of the rational faculty in the form of particular spiritual forms. Ibn Rushd also endows imagination with a major role and, in a similar fashion to Ibn Bājja, holds that in the case of veridical dreams during sleep the active intellect endows imagination with universal intelligibles that are in turn transformed into particular spiritual forms by imagination itself and makes them readily available to the internal faculties. Finally, Ibn Khaldūn keeps a psychological explanation, but his approach to veridical dreams and prophecy is not exactly the same as that of his predecessors. Unlike the Arabic *On Divination*, and the account of Ibn Bājja and Ibn Rushd, for Ibn Khaldūn there is no need for the intervention of a separate intellect; rather, the psychological process, he states, leads to an awareness of the soul's spiritual essence. In this process the soul is able to experience spiritual sensations, as is the case with prophets, that is, individuals who have visions beyond the physical world.

The theories here analyzed are sound psychological approaches to an atypical phenomenon. The main difficulty in the case of both Ibn Bājja and Ibn Rushd is how they explain the acquisition of particular forms proceeding from a universal intellect that stores universals. Both philosophers endow imagination with the major role of transforming universal forms into particular forms. In Ibn Khaldūn's account, the spiritual soul itself is the provider of the particular contents of veridical dreams. Although he explains this awareness of the soul as a psychological process, it is reserved only to prophets. Ibn Khaldūn tries to discern the natural and covert dimension of veridical dreams and prophecy,[42] while Ibn Bājja

42 This attempt to harmonize the natural and supernatural dimensions of prophecy has been described by other interpreters as an attempt to reconcile philosophy and theological orthodoxy. See Fazlur Rahman, *Prophecy in Islam*, Routledge: London & New York, 1958, pp. 105–108; Zaid Ahmad, *The Epistemology of Ibn Khaldūn*, Routledge: London & New York, 2003, p. 7, pp. 9–10, pp. 24–25; see also, for the topic of dream interpretation, pp. 70–75.

and Ibn Rushd appear to conceive these experiences as natural phenomena. These three theories represent very appealing medieval Arabic attempts to elucidate the complex nature of veridical dreams and prophecy.

Bibliography

Primary Sources

Aristotle, "On Divination in Sleep", trans. J. I. Beare, in: *The Complete Works of Aristotle*, vol. 1, ed. Jonathan Barnes, Princeton: Princeton University Press 1984.

Averroes, *Epitome of Parva Naturalia [Librorum Aristotelis qui Parva Naturalia Vocantur (Versionum latinarum)* vol. VII, ed. H. Blumberg, Cambridge Mass.: The Mediaeval Academy of America 1949.

–, *Epitome of Parva Naturalia [Librorum Aristotelis qui Parva Naturalia Vocantur (Versionum hebraicarum)*, vol. VII, ed. H. Blumberg, Cambridge Mass.: The Mediaeval Academy of America 1954.

–, *Epitome of Parva Naturalia*, trans. H. Blumberg, Cambridge Mass.: The Mediaeval Academy of America 1961.

–, *Epitome of Parva Naturalia (Talkhīs Kitāb al-Ḥiss wa-al-maḥsūs) [Librorum Aristotelis qui Parva Naturalia Vocantur (Textum Arabicum)]*, ed. H. Blumberg, Cambridge Mass.: The Mediaeval Academy of America 1972.

Ibn Bājja, *Tratado sobre la unión del intelecto con el hombre*, trans. Miguel Asín Palacios, *Al-Andalus* 7 (1942), pp. 1–47.

–, *Carta del adiós*, trans. Miguel Asín Palacios, *Al-Andalus* 8 (1943), pp. 1–87.

–, *'Ilm al-Nafs*, trans. Hasan Maʿsumi, Karacchi: Pakistan Historical Society 1961.

–, *El régimen del solitario*, trans. Joaquín Lomba, Madrid: Trotta 1997.

–, "Carta del adiós," in: *Carta del adiós y otros tratados filosóficos*, trans. Joaquín Lomba, Madrid: Trotta 2006, pp. 19–72.

–, "Tratado de la unión del Intelecto con el hombre," in: *Carta del adiós y otros tratados filosóficos*, trans. Joaquín Lomba, Madrid: Trotta 2006, pp. 83–104.

–, *Libro sobre el alma*, trans. Joaquín Lomba, Madrid: Trotta 2007.

–, "Discours sur la conjonction de l'intellect avec l'homme adressé à l'un de ses fréres," in: *La conduite de l'isolé et deux autres épîtres*, ed. and trans. Charles Genequand, Paris: Vrin 2010, pp. 183–203.

–, "*Épître de l'adieu*," in: *La conduite de l'isolé et deux autres épîtres*, trans. Charles Genequand, Paris: Vrin 2010, pp. 88–121.

Ibn Khaldūn, *The Muqaddimah*, trans. Franz Rosenthal, Princeton: Princeton University Press 1967.

–, *Muqaddimah*, ed. Khalīl Shahada, Beirut: Dar al-fikr 2001.

Secondary Sources

Ahmad, Zaid, *The Epistemology of Ibn Khaldūn*, London & New York: Routledge 2003.

Black, Deborah, "Estimation in Avicenna: The Logical and Psychological Dimensions," *Dialogue* 32 (1993), pp. 219–258.

–, "Imagination and Estimation: Arabic Paradigms and Western Transformations," *Topoi* 19/1 (2000), pp. 59–75.

D'Ancona, Cristina, "La notion de 'cause' dans les textes Néoplatoniciens Arabes," in: *Métaphysiques Médiévales. Études en l'honneur d'André de Muralt*, eds. Curzio Chiesa and Léo Freuler, Genève-Lausanne-Neuchâtel: Cahiers de la Revue de Théologie et de Philosophie 1999, pp. 47–68.

–, "'Causa prima superior est omni narratione'. Il tema delle sifat Allah nel primo neoplatonismo arabo," *Oriente moderno* 19 (2000), pp. 519–555.

–, "*L'influence du vocabulaire arabe:* 'Causa Prima est esse tantum,'" in: *L'élaboration du vocabulaire philosophique au Moyen Âge.* Actes du Colloque International de Louvain la-Neuve et Leuven, 12–14 septembre 1998, eds. Jacqueline Hamesse and Carlos Steel, Turnhout: Brepols 2000, pp. 51–97.

Daiber, Hans, "Salient Trends of the Arabic Aristotle," in: *The Ancient Tradition in Christian and Islamic Hellenism: Studies on the Transmission of Greek Philosophy and Science*, eds. Gerhard Endress and Renke Kruk, Leiden: Brill 1997, pp. 29–41.

di Martino, Carla, "La Perception Spirituelle. Perspectives de Recherche pour l'Historie des *Parva Naturalia* dans la Tradition Arabo-Latine," *Veritas* 52/3 (2007), pp. 21–35.

–, "Memory and Recollection in Ibn Sīnā's and Ibn Rushd's Philosophical Texts Translated into Latin in the Twelfth and Thirteenth Centuries: A Perspective on the Doctrine of the Internal Senses in Arabic Psychological Science," in: *Forming the Mind. Essays on the Internal Senses and the Mind/Body Problem from Avicenna to the Medical Enlightenment*, ed. Henrik Lagerlund, Dordrecht: Springer 2007, pp. 17–25.

Griffel, Frank, "Philosophy and Prophecy," in: *The Routledge Companion to Islamic Philosophy*, eds. Richard C. Taylor and Luis Xavier López-Farjeat, New York & London: Routledge 2016, pp. 385–398.

Hansberger, Rotraud Elisabeth, *The Transmission of Aristotle's* Parva Naturalia *in Arabic*, unpublished Ph.D. dissertation, Somerville College, University of Oxford, Faculty of Oriental Studies 2006.

–, "How Aristotle Came to Believe in God-given Dreams: The Arabic Version of *De divinatione per somnum*," in: *Dreaming Across Boundaries: The Interpretation of Dreams in Islamic Lands*, ed. Louise Marlow, Washington/Cambridge, Mass.: Ilex Foundation / Center for Hellenic Studies 2008, pp. 50–77.

–, "*Kitāb al-Ḥiss wa-l-Maḥsūs:* Aristotle's *Parva Naturalia* in Arabic Guise," in: *Les Parva naturalia d'Aristote: Fortune antique et médiévale*, eds. Christophe Grellard and Pierre-Marie Morel, Paris: Publications de la Sorbonne 2010, pp. 143–162.

–, "Plotinus Arabus Rides Again," *Arabic Sciences and Philosophy* 21 (2011), pp. 57–84.

–, "The Arabic Adaptation of the *Parva Naturalia* (*Kitāb al-Ḥiss wa-l-maḥsūs*)," *Studia graeco-arabica* 4 (2014), pp. 301–314.

Lomba, Joaquín, "La ciencia del alma en Ibn Bāŷŷa (Avempace)," *Veritas* 52/3 (2007), pp. 79–90.

López-Farjeat, Luis Xavier, "Avicenna and Thomas Aquinas on Natural Philosophy," *American Catholic Philosophical Quarterly* 88/2 (2014), pp. 309–333.
Maʿsumi, Hasan, "Ibn Bājjah on the Human Intellect," *Islamic Studies* IV/2 (1965), pp. 121–136.
Pines, Shlomo, "The Arabic Recension of *Parva Naturalia* and the philosophical doctrine concerning veridical dreams according to al-*Risāla al-Manāmiyya* and other sources," *Israel Oriental Studies* IV (1974), pp. 104–153.
Rahman, Fazlur, *Prophecy in Islam*, London & New York: Routledge 1958.
Steinschneider, Moritz, "Die *Parva Naturalia* des Aristoteles bei den Arabern," *Zeitschrift der Deutschen Morgenlëndischen Gesellschaft* 45 (1891), pp. 447–453.
–, "Die *Parva Naturalia* des Aristoteles bei den Arabern," *Zeitschrift der Deutschen Morgenlëndischen Gesellschaft* 37 (1883), pp. 477–492.
Taylor, Richard C., "Primary Causality and *ibdāʿ* (*creare*) in the *Liber de causis*," in: *Wahrheit und Geschichte. Die gebrochene Tradition metaphysischen Denkens. Festschrift zum 70. Geburtstag von Günther Mensching*, eds. Alia Mensching-Estakhr and Würzburg Städtler: Königshausen & Neumann 2012, pp. 115–136.
–, "Primary and Secondary Causality," in: *The Routledge Companion to Islamic Philosophy*, eds. Richard. C. Taylor and Luis Xavier López-Farjeat, New York & London: Routledge 2016, pp. 225–235.
Wolfson, Harry A., "The Internal Senses in Latin, Arabic, and Hebrew Philosophic Texts," *Harvard Theological Review* XXVIII/2 (1935), pp. 69–133.

God, Man and the Physical World

Andreas Lammer

Two Sixth/Twelfth-Century Hardliners on Creation and Divine Eternity: al-Šahrastānī and Abū l-Barakāt al-Baġdādī on God's Priority over the World*

Introduction

If the philosophical discussion about the question whether the world existed from all eternity or was created in time were a story, it would start with some exegetical issues in Plato, introduce the Unmoved Mover of Aristotle, continue with some Neoplatonic ingenuity at the hands of Proclus, and end with even more ingenuity from Philoponus. That story would, then, have become so famous that it was worth translating into Arabic in a revised version by al-Kindī (d. ~ 256/870), to which Avicenna (d. 428/1037) would write a sequel and al-Ġazālī (d. 505/1111) the finale. Today, this trilogy would predominantly be sold with an elaborate, even if somewhat sterile, afterword by Averroes (d. 595/1198) and be celebrated as an epic classic, being reissued again and again in ever cheaper paperbacks.

The story, however, would also have created a spin-off which only recently would have garnered some fame. This spin-off would introduce many new characters – among them Muḥammad ibn ʿAbd al-Karīm al-Šahrastānī (d. 548/1153) and Abū l-Barakāt al-Baġdādī (d. 560/1164–5) – and continue the story after al-Ġazālī with plenty of recurring elements but also with fresh material. Moreover, it would unfold in a new context: the philosophical milieu of the Islamic East, focusing in the first instalments on sixth/twelfth-century Baġdād, the capital city of the ʿAbbāsid caliphate and one of the most vibrant intellectual centres of the Selǧūk empire.

* I would like to express my gratitude to Frank Griffel, Peter Adamson, Fedor Benevich, and Davlat Dadikhuda as well as to the participants of the MUSAΦ research seminar, in particular Christof Rapp, for the helpful comments and remarks I have received. I also wish to thank the German Research Foundation (DFG) for funding this research.

1. Sixth/Twelfth-Century Baġdād

Al-Šahrastānī was most probably born in 469/1076 in a town located at what is today the Turkmen border to Iran. As a young man, he studied religion and theology in Nēšāpūr, a most important intellectual centre of teaching and learning at that time. At the local *madrasa*, well-known figures such as Abū Ḥāmid al-Ġazālī and Abū l-Qāsim Salmān ibn Nāṣir al-Anṣārī (d. 512/1118) were educated by none other than the prominent Ašʿarī theologian ʿAbd al-Malik ibn ʿAbd Allāh al-Ǧuwaynī (d. 478/1085–6). In turn, al-Anṣārī became one of the teachers of al-Šahrastānī. In 510/1117, al-Šahrastānī went on the *ḥaǧǧ* and, on his way back from Mecca, passed by Baġdād, where he stayed for about three years, holding a teaching position at the Niẓāmiyya *madrasa*, before he left (or had to leave) and moved to Marv around 514/1120.[1]

His slightly younger contemporary Abū l-Barakāt was born to a Jewish family around 473/1080 in Balad, a town at the Tigris river in the north-west of Mosul. Having moved to the capital, he studied medicine (and probably also philosophy) with Abū l-Ḥasan Saʿīd ibn Hibat Allāh (d. 495/1101), possibly around 489/1096. It seems that he stayed most of the time before and after his conversion to Islam in Baġdād, serving Sultan Muḥammad Tapar (r. 498/1105–511/1118) and subsequently his son Maḥmūd ibn Muḥammad ibn Malikšāh (r. 511/1118–525/1131) as well as the caliphal court of Abū Manṣūr Afḍal al-Mustaršid bi-Llāh (r. 512/1118–529/1135) and later Muḥammad al-Muqtafī li-Amr Allāh (r. 530/1136–555/1160) in medical matters.[2]

Both al-Šahrastānī and Abū l-Barakāt were thoroughly familiar with the philosophy of Avicenna. Indeed, they are notoriously known as two of his fiercest critics. They belonged to the intellectual elite in the philosophical milieu of Baġdād in the early sixth/twelfth century, each composing works in which they provided their own detailed discussion of God, the world, priority, relation, and eternity; yet, although drawing on the same materials and investigating the same questions, they offered solutions entirely at odds with one another.

1 cf. Monnot, "al-Shahrastānī, Abū 'l-Fatḥ Muḥammad"; van Ess, "Das Geburtsjahr des Šahrastānī."

2 cf. Madelung, "Abu'l-Barakāt Baġdādī"; Griffel, "Between al-Ghazālī and Abū l-Barakāt al-Baghdādī," 64f. This paragraph is partly based on personal communication with Frank Griffel, who is currently working on a book on *The Formation of Post-Classical Philosophy in Islam.*

2. A Sixth Kind of "Priority"

Two of al-Šahrastānī's works are particularly relevant for his discussion of the world's creation and the nature of God's priority to it: his *al-Muṣāraʿa* and his *Nihāyat al-aqdām fī ʿilm al-kalām*. The former is a direct and critical engagement with certain basic tenets of Avicenna's metaphysics.[3] Al-Šahrastānī singles out seven issues (*masāʾil*, sg. *masʾala*) for discussion and introduces them with material derived from Avicenna's *al-Naǧāt*. He usually continues by distinguishing several "inconsistencies" (*tanāquḍāt*, sg. *tanāquḍ*) in Avicenna's reasoning and/or "raising objections against him" (*al-iʿtirāḍ ʿalayhi*), before finally presenting "the correct choice" (*al-muḫtār al-ḥaqq*). Unfortunately, *al-Muṣāraʿa* is incomplete; the last two issues are merely outlined and not fully discussed. According to al-Šahrastānī himself, "the trials of the time and the blows of misfortune" thwarted the completion of the book.[4] The other work is his voluminous theological *summa* in twenty chapters. Like *al-Muṣāraʿa*, *Nihāyat al-aqdām* investigates basic tenets, this time, however, those of *kalām*. In his argumentation, which often follows a question-response-pattern, al-Šahrastānī draws on a wide range of sources, including Avicenna's *al-Naǧāt*, which he, again, quotes occasionally. The discussion of the eternity is the first topic to be introduced and the longest chapter of all.

What is common to the discussion in both works is their emphasis on two primary points: the denial of the reality of any form of an actual infinite (*mā lā yatanāhā* or *mā lā nihāyata lahu*) and a distinction between various meanings of "priority and posteriority" (*al-taqaddum wa-l-taʾaḫḫur*) as well as the corresponding concept of "togetherness" (*maʿiyya*). In *Nihāyat al-aqdām*, al-Šahrastānī even writes that the whole issue of eternity and creation "revolves around" (*madār al-masʾala ʿalā*) the difference between *īǧāb* (necessitating something) and *īǧād* (bringing something into existence) as well as between priority and posteriority.[5] It needs to be understood that the two terms *īǧāb* and *īǧād*, and the corresponding active participles *mūǧib* and *mūǧid*, represent two starkly different conceptions of God. One could conceive of God as a deity who *had* to create the world on account of His immeasurable benevolence and power. This God would have necessitated (*īǧāb*) a world which could not have been otherwise. Any other possible world would have been less perfect and, thus, less appropriate as the creature of a perfect deity. This God creates out of necessity. Moreover, He did not pick a particular moment as the appropriate beginning for His creative

3 An outline of the work is provided in Madelung, "aš-Šahrastānīs Streitschrift."

4 al-Šahrastānī, *al-Muṣāraʿa* 5, 120.3, tr. Madelung/Mayer; cf. the introduction by Madelung and Mayer (12–14) for a brief discussion of the historical background. All translations, unless otherwise stated, are my own.

5 al-Šahrastānī, *Nihāyat al-aqdām* 1, 7.4.

act but, instead, had always been creating during every moment of His existence – and since God has been existent for all eternity, the world has eternally been with Him as His eternal and infinite effect.

Alternatively, however, one may conceive of God as a freely choosing deity who brought the world into existence (*īǧād*) precisely the way He *wanted* it to be, so that every detail, howsoever little, ultimately originated not only from His immeasurable benevolence and power but also from His will and wisdom: this God decided, for example, about the number of stars in the sky, He ordained in which direction the planets are revolving, and He decreed the spatial size of the universe. In addition, He also picked a particular moment (*waqt*) as the appropriate beginning for His creative act, so that before this moment, He existed without the world, whereas after this moment, He existed with the world.

It is a characteristic feature of al-Šahrastānī's style that he presents his own views with quite some confidence and clarity.[6] It is, then, not difficult to determine his preferred position in his works. In *Nihāyat al-aqdām*, he writes:

> Therefore, the specifier (*al-muḫaṣṣiṣ*) [of all the world's contingent features] must be either a [cause] necessitating [its effect] essentially (*mūǧiban bi-l-ḏāt*) and demanding [it] naturally (*muqtaḍiyan bi-l-ṭabʿ*) or [something] bestowing existence through power and choice (*mūǧidan bi-l-qudra wa-l-iḫtiyār*). The first option is false … So, we know decisively (*qatʿan*) and with certainty (*yaqīnan*) that the Maker is not a necessitating being (*ḏātan mūǧiban*) but a powerful and knowledgeable bestower of existence (*mūǧidan ʿāliman qādiran*).[7]

It is evident that according to al-Šahrastānī, God is not such as always to have been creating the world out of the necessity of His own self. Instead, God is a "specifier" (*al-muḫaṣṣiṣ*), a term which, for al-Šahrastānī, denotes a principle capable of making a decision even if all the alternatives are entirely alike. This concept is part of traditional arguments for the existence of God and for the temporal creation of the world.[8] In a way, it is a version of Buridan's ass, where

6 Mayer points out that al-Šahrastānī, having been a "seasoned preacher," was also rhetorically adept ("The Absurdities of Infinite Time," 111).

7 al-Šahrastānī, *Nihāyat al-aqdām* 1, 14.1–8; cf. *al-Muṣāraʿa* 5, 112.1–113.9.

8 Describing God as a *muḫaṣṣiṣ*, i. e., as a "specifying" principle, is similar to describing Him as a *muraǧǧiḥ*, i. e., as a "preponderating" principle. Yet, it should be realised that in their primary form, the two characterisations are systematically distinct. The *muḫaṣṣiṣ* decides about the design of the world by determining various contingent features, whereas the *muraǧǧiḥ* is responsible for the existence of the world by tipping the scale towards existence. In other words, the *muraǧǧiḥ* did not decide about the concrete *moment* of the world's creation. The moment was "specified" by God being a *muḫaṣṣiṣ*. Nonetheless, in that moment God, as a *muraǧǧiḥ*, turned the essentially neutral, purely contingent, and hitherto entirely non-existent world into a created being. So, just as one can ask how God specified the first moment of creation as a *muḫaṣṣiṣ*, one can ask for the concrete reason that made Him preponderate towards existence as a *muraǧǧiḥ*; cf. also Benevich's contribution to this volume.

the philosophical God-donkey would starve to death when confronted with two entirely identical bales of hay, because there is no cause or reason that could make one bale be preferable to the other, whereas al-Šahrastānī's God-donkey would be able simply to pick one through His "power and choice."[9] The driving forces behind God's creative act are, thus, His knowledge, will, and power, enabling Him to decree all the various features of the world, on whom a necessitating cause would not have been able to pass judgement. As already mentioned, one of these features is the specific moment in which the world came into existence, before which the world was non-existent, and after which the world existed somehow together with God.[10]

In casually speaking of "before" and "after," or of the world's being "with" God, we have already hit upon what, for al-Šahrastānī, constitutes the central issue: the question about the precise nature of God's original priority over the world and His current "togetherness" with the world. Is God's priority temporal, as the terminology of a moment (*waqt*) could be seen to suggest? Or is God merely essentially or causally prior to the world, so that He would be temporally with His creation? Or is God prior in rank or rather in nature? Is God comparable to the world at all, so that one could adequately speak of any priority in the first place, let alone speak of any real "togetherness"? Besides, how many kinds of priority are there? It is questions like these which al-Šahrastānī explicitly marks as the core of the entire debate over creation and eternity.

It is also questions like these which he answers decisively:

> Priority (*al-taqaddum*) may be temporal (*zamāniyyan*), like the priority of the parent to the child; it may be spatial (*makāniyyan*), like the priority of the prayer-leader to the led; it may be by nobility (*šarafiyyan*), like the priority of the learned to the ignorant; and it may be essential (*ḏātiyyan*), like the priority of the cause to the effect. And they have added a fifth sense for it, namely, priority by nature (*bi-l-ṭab'*), like the priority of [the number] one to [the number] two.[11]

This list of five kinds of priority comes from Aristotle's *Categories*. In chapter twelve of this treatise, Aristotle states that priority and posteriority is of four kinds (τετραχῶς, *'alā arba'at awǧuh*), only to add a fifth kind and to conclude the

9 The classical study of Buridan's ass is Rescher, "Choice without Preference." Historically prominent references include Aristotle, *Cael.* II.13, 295b25–296a3 and al-Ġazālī, *Tahāfut al-falāsifa* 1, §46, 23.16–24.4.

10 I say "somehow," because one characteristic element of al-Šahrastānī's position is God's absolute transcendence. It is, thus, questionable whether God could really be said to exist "together with" the world in any way. Still, I shall continue to speak of God as, first, being "before" the world and, then, being "with" it in a somewhat loose sense. God's transcendence will be addressed below, 256f.

11 al-Šahrastānī, *al-Muṣāra'a* 5, 96.2–5, tr. Madelung/Mayer; cf. *Nihāyat al-aqdām* 1, 7.10–14 and 8.8f.

chapter by saying that something could be said to be prior to something else in five different senses (κατὰ πέντε τρόπους, *ʿalā ḫamsat awǧuh*).[12] The same list is reproduced and discussed in Avicenna's *al-Maqūlāt*, the "categories" of his most comprehensive collection of works *al-Šifāʾ*. There, in the fourth chapter of the seventh book, we find the priorities "by time" (*bi-l-zamān*), "by nature" (*bi-l-ṭabʿ*), "in order" (*fī l-martaba*), "by nobility" (*bi-l-šaraf*), and "by causality" (*bi-l-ʿilliyya*).[13] There are two differences between the lists of Avicenna and al-Šahrastānī, both of which will become relevant in what follows. The first difference is that what Avicenna calls priorities "in order" (*fī l-martaba*) and "by causality" (*bi-l-ʿilliyya*) are called "spatial" (*makāniyyan*) and "essential" (*ḏātiyyan*) priorities in al-Šahrastānī. The second difference is that al-Šahrastānī adds a sixth kind to these traditional five:

> It is possible to add a sixth sense (*maʿnā sādis*) for it, namely, priority by existence only (*bi-l-wuǧūd faqaṭ*), like the priority of that which brings something into existence (*al-mūǧid*) over that which is brought into existence (*al-mūǧad*).[14]

What al-Šahrastānī has in mind here apparently is the idea that God, first, *existed without* the world, and that He, then, *existed with* the world. That is to say that God's priority means simply that He existed alone all by Himself prior to the existence of the world. This is the very idea which al-Ġazālī has expressed earlier in his *Tahāfut al-falāsifa* as his immediate response to the philosophers' second attempt on proving the eternity of the world:

> We mean by our assertion that God is prior to the world and time that He was and no world (*annahu kāna wa-lā ʿālam*) and, thereupon, He was and with Him the world (*ṯumma kāna wa-maʿahu ʿālam*). What is to be understood of our assertion that "He was and no world" is only the existence of the essence of the Creator and the non-existence of the essence of the world, whereas what is to be understood of our assertion that "He was and with Him the world" is only the existence of the two essences. Thus, by priority (*al-taqaddum*) we mean His solitude by existence only (*infirādahu bi-l-wuǧūd faqaṭ*).[15]

A similar thought was also already present in the writings of al-Ġazālī's teacher al-Ǧuwaynī, who wrote in his *al-Iršād ilā qawāṭiʿ al-adilla fī uṣūl al-iʿtiqād:*

> The Creator (praised be He) was before (*qabla*) the origination of the originating things alone by His existence (*munfarid bi-wuǧūdihi*) and His attributes, and no originating thing was associated with Him.[16]

12 Aristotle, *Categories* 12, 14a26–14b23.

13 Avicenna, *al-Maqūlāt* VII.4, 266.1–269.12; cf. also *al-Išārāt wa-l-tanbīhāt* II.5.7, 151.10–152.6.

14 al-Šahrastānī, *al-Muṣāraʿa* 5, 96.5 f., tr. Madelung/Mayer, modified; cf. *Nihāyat al-aqdām* 1, 8.9–15.

15 al-Ġazālī, *Tahāfut al-falāsifa* 1, §82, 31.13–17.

16 al-Ǧuwaynī, *al-Iršād* V.1, 33.4f.

This passage reappears almost verbatim in a work of al-Ǧuwaynī's other famous student, al-Anṣārī, who later became one of al-Šahrastānī's teachers. In al-Anṣārī's *al-Ġunya fī l-kalām*, we read:

> The Creator (praised and exalted be He) was before (*qabla*) the origination of the originating things alone by existence (*munfarid bi-l-wuǧūd*) and the attributes, and no originating thing was associated with Him.[17]

However, the underlying idea that God's eternity is to be understood as a priority in existence did not originate in the fifth/eleventh century with the circle around al-Ǧuwaynī.[18] Already before them, Abū Bakr Muḥammad ibn al-Ḥasan ibn Fūrak (d. 406/1015), also an active teacher in Nēšāpūr, attributes to Abū l-Ḥasan al-Ašʿarī (d. 324/935–36) the following view:

> When we say that something is "eternal" (*qadīm*), the reality of our assertion is the same as "something which is prior by His existence (*al-mutaqaddim bi-wuǧūdihi*) over the existence of that which originated after it."[19]

Even before Ibn Fūrak and his Ašʿarite peers – and even before al-Ašʿarī himself – we find the Muʿtazilite Abū ʿAlī al-Ǧubbāʾī (d. 303/915–16) who, according to the testimony of Abū l-Ḥasan ʿAbd al-Ǧabbār (d. 415/1025), has defined, in some of his works, "eternal" (*qadīm*) as that which is "even prior in existence" (*mutaqādim fī l-wuǧūd*).[20] A little later, ʿAbd al-Ǧabbār adds that he also explained that the terms *sābiq* ("preceding"), *mutaqaddim* ("prior"), *aqdam* ("more ancient") and *mutaqādim* ("even prior"), when attributed to God, denote "that He is existent before each existent and that His existence has no beginning."[21]

There seems to be a development, though, from the views reported from the late third/early tenth century on behalf of al-Ǧubbāʾī and al-Ašʿarī to those advanced in the fifth/eleventh century by al-Ǧuwaynī and al-Anṣārī. Of these only the latter two explicitly state that their understanding of God's existence alone prior to His first creative act is meant to counter the objection that any prolonged existence requires a temporal framework, for if that were true, then God's eternal existence would give rise to an eternal time which, in turn, would lead to other inacceptable results. In fact, al-Ǧuwaynī even seems to invoke "his master" al-Ašʿarī as a potential source of inspiration for this *objection* without, however, attributing it to him directly.[22]

17 al-Anṣārī, *al-Ġunya fī l-kalām* II.2.1.1, 350.12f.

18 For the following two passages, cf. also Wisnovsky, "One Aspect of the Avicennian Turn in Sunnī Theology," esp. 69f.

19 Ibn Fūrak, *Muǧarrad maqālāt al-Šayḫ Abī l-Ḥasan al-Ašʿarī* 8, 26.19f.

20 ʿAbd al-Ǧabbār, *al-Muġnī*, vol. 5, 233.17f.; cf. 234.6, 15, 235.1.

21 ʿAbd al-Ǧabbār, *al-Muġnī*, vol. 5, 238.3–5.

22 cf. al-Ǧuwaynī, *al-Iršād* V.1, 32.3–33.4; al-Anṣārī, *al-Ġunya fī l-kalām* II.2.1.1, 350.13f.

What all these passages evince is that there was a certain understanding of God's situation prior to or before His creation of the world which was traditionally discussed by theologians in their description of God as the Eternal Being. Some of them even emphasised the non-temporal character of His eternal existence. We can assume that al-Šahrastānī was familiar with this idea at least through the teaching of his teacher al-Anṣārī (and the works of his teacher's teacher al-Ǧuwaynī).[23] Indeed, the terminology of "existence only" (*wuǧūd faqaṭ*) and of God's "solitude by existence only" (*infirādahu bi-l-wuǧūd faqaṭ*) appears to be characteristic of the later formulations, including those by al-Šahrastānī. In addition, we have seen al-Ġazālī already using this view as a means to reject one prominent argument of the philosophers to prove the eternity of the world.[24]

Despite these precursors, though, there is something genuinely new in al-Šahrastānī. In addition to his awareness of the Ašʿarite consensus on how God's priority ought to be conceptualised, he is also familiar with the common examination of the different senses of priority as it was traditionally discussed by philosophers in the course of investigating the categories and postpredicaments of being. Al-Šahrastānī knows all this, at least, from Avicenna's writings. Thus, what al-Šahrastānī is doing here is to combine these two strands explicitly and to integrate the Ašʿarite conviction about God's original solitary existence into his own refutation of the philosophers' claim of the world's eternity by revising the philosophical understanding of "priority," which for him, as we have already seen, was at the very heart of the entire issue.

It is, then, also not surprising at all that in the above passage, al-Šahrastānī links what is now explicitly labelled a "sixth kind of priority" with the notion of *īǧād*, describing it as "the priority of that which brings something into existence" (*al-mūǧid*). In other words, he associates the sixth kind of priority with a particular conception of God as a freely acting deity. For him, priority by existence only is precisely the instrument with which one can once and for all dispel the otherwise imposing arguments of the philosophers, in particular those of Avicenna.

Given the central importance of the idea of priority by existence for al-Šahrastānī's argument, we should try to comprehend more fully what he means by it

23 cf. also Avicenna, *al-Ilāhiyyāt* IV.1, §§5–6, 164.12–165.4; IX.1, §§20–21, 379.7–19 (≈ *al-Naǧāt* IV.2.25, 613.15–614.14 ≈ *al-Mabdaʾ wa-l-maʿād* 32, 44.8–19). I shall reference Avicenna's *al-Ilāhiyyāt* and *al-Samāʿ al-ṭabīʿī* by mentioning book and chapter numbers together with the paragraph numbers from Marmura's and McGinnis' respective translations *alongside* page and line numbers from the Cairo edition of Avicenna's *al-Šifāʾ*.

24 It could be worthwhile to compare these early theological formulations of "existence only" (*wuǧūd faqaṭ*) to even earlier philosophical accounts of the divine principle as "being only" (*anniyya faqaṭ*), as it is frequently encountered in both the *Arabic Plotinus* and the *Arabic Proclus*, or even to Aristotle's claim that "the eternal things are *prior in substance* to the perishable things" (τὰ μὲν γὰρ ἀΐδια πρότερα τῇ οὐσίᾳ τῶν φθαρτῶν) from *Metaphysics* Θ.8, 1050b6 f., emphasis added.

and whether it is more than a simple trick. In other words, while the above quotations from ʿAbd al-Ǧabbār and Ibn Fūrak as well as al-Ǧuwaynī, al-Anṣārī, and al-Ġazālī help to understand the emergence of al-Šahrastānī's idea historically, we still need to explain it systematically. Since al-Šahrastānī himself does not offer much more explanation than what I have already quoted, it could be helpful to examine how later thinkers, most notably Faḫr al-Dīn, expounded the notion of a sixth kind of priority.[25]

First of all, it needs to be noted that Faḫr al-Dīn indeed mentions "another kind of priority" (*nawʿan āḫar min al-taqaddum*) as the explicit "answer" (*al-ǧawāb*) to the philosophers' misgivings (sg. *iškāl*) about the idea of the world's origination. He even writes at the end of his analysis in *al-Arbaʿīn fī uṣūl al-dīn* that with this, the philosophers' misgivings vanish.[26] Like al-Šahrastānī, Faḫr al-Dīn emphasises that this sixth kind of priority is different from the traditionally received five kinds, which means that it cannot be identified with, or in any way be reduced to, any of them.[27]

Prima facie, however, this project of expounding al-Šahrastānī's idea through materials contained in the works of later writers may seem to be doomed to failure, because Faḫr al-Dīn exemplifies the priority by existence with the priority of yesterday over today. Is this supposed to mean that, ultimately, existential priority is nothing other than a priority by time? The answer to this is found in Faḫr al-Dīn's argumentation that yesterday and today are parts of time, and that time (*al-zamān*) is the very succession of these parts. Were it the case that the priority of yesterday over today is an instance of temporal priority, there would have to be a further time over and above the existences of yesterday and of today which accounts for their priority-posteriority-relation. Thus, yesterday and today could not be the parts of which time as such is composed but would themselves be embedded in a second-order temporal reality. According to Faḫr al-Dīn, this is absurd as it gives rise to various impossible consequences, most importantly an actually infinite number of times, each containing the other.[28]

---

25 cf. esp. Faḫr al-Dīn al-Rāzī, *al-Arbaʿīn* I.2, vol. 1, 26.14–27.14; cf. also *al-Maṭālib al-ʿāliya* IV.1.1.2, vol. 4, 15.1–18.16, where Faḫr al-Dīn provides no less than six arguments for existential priority. In the following analysis, I consider Faḫr al-Dīn's conception of existential priority as being tantamount to al-Šahrastānī's original idea, so that I can employ the former's assertions to elucidate the latter's position.

26 Faḫr al-Dīn al-Rāzī, *al-Arbaʿīn* I.2, vol. 1, 26.14, 27.14; cf. *al-Maṭālib al-ʿāliya* IV.1.1.2, 15.1 f.; cf. also İskenderoğlu, *Fakhr al-Dīn al-Razī and Thomas Aquinas*, 66 and fn. 125, 102; Ceylan, *Theology and tafsīr*, 58–60.

27 cf. however Ibn Kammūna's strategy of reducing all kinds or priorities to those by causality and by nature, mentioned below in fn. 34.

28 cf. Faḫr al-Dīn al-Rāzī, *al-Arbaʿīn* I.2, vol. 1, 27.1–12; *al-Maṭālib al-ʿāliya* IV.1.1.2, vol. 4, 17.4–22; IV.1.9, vol. 4, 198.1–199.21; cf. also Adamson and Lammer, "Fakhr al-Dīn al-Rāzī's Platonist Account of the Essence of Time."

What is more, it even emerges that temporal priority could be construed as dependent upon existential priority, because if the parts of time were not existentially prior and posterior to one another, temporal beings could not be temporally prior and posterior by occurring in different parts of time.

So, if priority by existence is different from temporal priority, how is it different from causal priority?[29] Attempting to argue for their difference may seem to be doomed to failure, again, because we have seen al-Šahrastānī writing that priority by existence is "like the priority of that which brings something into existence (*al-mūǧid*) to that which is brought into existence" (*al-mūǧad*) and, surely, the relation of that which brings something into existence to that which is brought into existence is, in one way or another, a relation of causality. However, Faḫr al-Dīn's example of existential priority, viz., the priority of yesterday over today, is clearly not causal, because yesterday is explicitly said to not be the cause of today's existence. Instead, in terms of its existence, yesterday simply preceded today. Moreover, Faḫr al-Dīn writes, cause and effect necessarily co-exist with one another, which is evidently not true of yesterday and today.[30] This last aspect is important, because it builds upon Avicennian convictions. Avicenna has argued in book six of his *al-Ilāhiyyāt* that "true causes" (*al-ʿilal al-ḥaqīqiyya*) or "essential causes" (*al-ʿilal al-ḏātiyya*) necessarily co-exist with their effects.[31] This is a particularly delicate reference, as Avicenna himself contrasts what is essentially or causally prior with "what is prior in existence" (*mutaqaddim fī l-wuǧūd*), which he explains as "a priority where the cessation of [the cause] is together with the origination of the effect." So, in a way, we can link al-Šahrastānī's sixth kind of priority to Avicenna, too, who not only contrasted existential priority with real essential causal priority but also provided an explanation which tallies well with Faḫr al-Dīn's example of yesterday and today: yesterday is prior in existence of today, because it ceases to exist in the very moment in which today came into being.

However, this passage also shows two further things. First, it clarifies how Faḫr al-Dīn and al-Šahrastānī have developed this notion. They argue that the idea behind existential priority does not only differ from causal priority insofar as what is causally prior needs to co-exist with what is causally posterior but also insofar as existential priority is not causal at all, as we have seen. Yesterday is not the cause of today. Secondly, it elucidates that causal priority is really entirely inapt to describe God's relation to the world, because causal priority relies on the

29 cf. Avicenna, *al-Ilāhiyyāt* IV.1, §6, 164.18–165.4, where a priority by existence is explained along the lines of causal priority; q.v. also below fn. 33.

30 Faḫr al-Dīn al-Rāzī, *al-Arbaʿīn* I.2, vol. 1, 26.17–20; *al-Maṭālib al-ʿāliya* IV.1.1.2, vol. 4, 16.17–17.2.

31 Avicenna, *al-Ilāhiyyāt*, VI.2, §5, 265.1–5 and §8, 266.5–8.

necessary co-existence of cause and effect as in the case of the hand's motion being the cause of the pen's motion.

If we transfer this understanding to al-Šahrastānī, it emerges that although his example relies on two entities which are causally related, viz., God as a *mūǧid* and the world as His *mūǧad*, their causal relation is irrelevant for grasping their existential priority-posteriority-relation.[32] Priority by existence simply describes anything whose existence is present before the existence of some other thing is present, regardless of whether or not these two things are related causally or otherwise – and if they are, indeed, causally related, their causal relation is not such that the cause necessarily co-exists with its effect.

The concept of causality excluded here relies on the notion of necessitation. This elucidates why someone like Avicenna would embrace the idea of God's causal priority over the world, because he conceives of God as a *mūǧib*, who is causally prior to its essentially necessitated effect. However, this is precisely what al-Šahrastānī aims to deny. For him, God is a *mūǧid*, who decided to create the world at one particular moment. The existence of the world is emphatically not a necessary entailment of His divine essence. Accordingly, God certainly was prior to the world, but this priority is not temporal (as we have already seen) nor is it causal (because God's relation to the world is not necessary). Consequently, the idea of existential priority is the antithesis of causal priority, just as the concept of God as a *mūǧid* is the antithesis of God as a *mūǧib*.

While this seems to be plausible, it raises the question how existential priority, then, is really different from natural priority. This question is all the more pressing, as Faḫr al-Dīn, for example, argues that the natural priority of the number one over the number two is likewise expressly not causal.[33] In this, he seems to follow al-Šahrastānī who asserted that the one does not essentially bring the two into existence and even mentions the natural priority of the one over the two as being very similar in kind to existential priority.[34]

32 In fact, al-Šahrastānī explicitly writes that "the priority of that which brings something into existence (*al-mūǧid*) over that which is brought into existence is beyond essential causality" (*al-Muṣāraʿa* 5, 115.1f.); cf. *al-Muṣāraʿa* 5, 100.4–15, 110.6–113.5, 115.2f.

33 cf. Faḫr al-Dīn al-Rāzī, *al-Arbaʿīn* I.2, vol. 1, 24.9–13; cf. also Avicenna, *al-Ilāhiyyāt* IV.1, §5, 164.12–17, where numerical priority is treated as an instance of what is called a priority "with regard to existence."

34 cf. al-Šahrastānī, *al-Muṣāraʿa* 5, 114.9–115.1; *Nihāyat al-aqdām* 1, 8.13–15. Commenting on al-Ṭūsī's *Taǧrīd al-iʿtiqād*, the early eighth/fourteenth century theologian ʿAllāmā al-Ḥillī explains in like manner that the existence of the number one is not sufficient for the existence of the number two, whereas the existence of the cause is sufficient for the existence of the effect; this is the difference between natural and causal priority, he states; cf. *Kašf al-murād fī šarḥ Taǧrīd al-iʿtiqād* I.1.33, 41.7f. This is similar to how the seventh/thirteenth century *išrāqī* philosopher Ibn Kammūna understood these two priorities before. In addition, however, Ibn Kammūna also ultimately aims at reducing all other kinds of priorities these two "real" kinds of essential (i.e., causal) and natural priority, which both share in the idea that there is one

Al-Šahrastānī does not provide an answer to this question, and Faḫr al-Dīn merely writes that the argument which shows that existential priority differs from causal priority evinces that it is different from the priorities by nature (which he calls "priority by essence") and nobility, too.[35] So, we know for sure that al-Šahrastānī and Faḫr al-Dīn *want* existential priority to be different from natural priority, but we do not know why this should be so. Maybe the answer is the following: the paradigm case of essential or natural priority is the irreversible relation between the numbers one and two. Here, we are said to be unable to conceive the essence of the two without at the same time also conceiving the essence of the one. The reason for this is that the essence of the two *as such* contains an internal reference to the one, which is its unit and principle. The essence of the one, however, can be conceived without the two, because it lacks any such internal reference. Thus, the one is prior to the two, because its essence lacks any reference to the two, but not *vice versa.*

This, then, seems to be precisely the difference between the case of a natural priority (between one and two) and that of an existential priority (between God and world). Other than the essence of the two, the essence of the world seems to lack an internal reference to God. Of course, insofar as it is conceived as something created, it would be related to its Creator, but considered *as such*, i.e., in itself as world, it does not rely on its Creator. Thus, the relation between God and world cannot be an instance of natural priority, because the essence of the world does not contain any internal reference to God. It is, thus, not posterior to God *because of its essence and nature.* Since the bare essences of God and world do not explain their relation in terms of priority and posteriority, another kind or priority is required, in order to establish their relation, i.e., one which is different from natural priority – and this is existential priority, i.e., the priority simply of the existence of this essence over the existence of that essence.

An indication that this may indeed be how al-Šahrastānī and Faḫr al-Dīn conceived of existential priority can be found in their predecessor al-Ġazālī. As shown above, al-Ġazālī argued that "what is to be understood of our assertion that 'He was and no world' is only the existence of the essence of the Creator (*wuǧūd ḏāt al-bāri'*) and the non-existence of the essence of the world" (*'adam ḏāt al-'ālam faqaṭ*).[36] The important point here is that the actual result of considering their essences only (*faqaṭ*) is not that their priority relation is natural – but that it is a "priority (*al-taqaddum*) … by existence only" (*bi-l-wuǧūd faqaṭ*).

essence (*ḏāt*) that is prior to another, where this priority, then, can be either in causal terms or not; *al-Ǧadīd fī l-ḥikma* II.5, 112.1–4 and 113.1–7.

35 cf. Faḫr al-Dīn al-Rāzī, *al-Arba'īn* I.2, vol. 1, 26.21; *al-Maṭālib al-'āliya* IV.1.1.2, vol. 4, 17.3f. On the terminological differences, q.v. below, 253ff.

36 al-Ġazālī, *Tahāfut al-falāsifa* 1, §82, 31.15.

The reason why this is so is that these two essences lack any reference to one another, for otherwise they would be naturally prior and posterior, respectively.

Therefore, existential priority emerges as an additional sixth kind of priority which is different from the traditional five kinds, including the priorities of causality, time, and nature: God and world are not related by existing or not existing in different periods of time as temporal moments are; they are not related through necessary entailment and co-existence as cause and effect are; and they are not related through essential internal references to one another as the numbers one and two are.

3. What Can and Cannot Be Done

In essence, the argument of al-Šahrastānī's philosophical opponent rests on a simple premise: God undoubtedly is prior to the world in some way. There are five kinds of priority, so we must be able to identify one or more kinds which aptly characterise God's priority over the world. God is undoubtedly prior in nobility; moreover, being the world's cause, God is also prior in essence or causality; and He seems to be prior in nature, too.[37] In addition, it is absurd to claim that He would be prior in order, i. e., in space. The main question, then, is whether He is also prior in time. If He does not precede the world in time, the philosophers argue, He must be *with* the world in time, so that the world would be eternal. In order to make their point, the philosophers dialectically assume that the world has been created at one particular moment and that God actually preceded the world in time. The scenario to be imagined is that God existed together with time for a certain period and that He, then, at one moment in time, began to create the world, henceforth existing together with both time and the world. According to the philosophers, however, time requires for its existence a body in motion, so that in order for God to precede the world in time, there would

37 Avicenna, *al-Ilāhiyyāt* IX.1, §§19–20, 379.4–12 (≈ *al-Naǧāt* IV.2.25, 613.10–614.6 ≈ *al-Mabdaʾ wa-l-maʿād* 32, 44.4–12) asks explicitly how God precedes (*sabaqa*) his created acts. He considers two options, viz., essential and temporal priority. The former is, then, illustrated with two examples: It is like the number one over the number two and like mover over moved. In his discussion of priority in *al-Maqūlāt* VII.4, Avicenna does not mention any priority "by essence" but instead considers natural priority (like the one over the two) as well as causal priority. These differences in terminology will become relevant below, 253 ff. In his *Tahāfut al-falāsifa*, al-Ġazālī similarly mixes the different senses of priority, speaking of an essential priority, exemplified by the natural priority of the one over the two and the causal priority of a moving body over its moving shadow (cf. *Tahāfut al-falāsifa* 1, §79, 30.15–18). Elsewhere, al-Ġazālī attributes to the philosopher the belief that "the Creator's priority over the world is like the priority of cause over effect, which is a priority by essence and order and not by time" (*Tahāfut al-falāsifa* 1, §1, 12.4f.).

already have to be a body in motion, for otherwise there would not be time by which God would precede the world. This result is either absurd and self-contradictory or actually affirms the eternity of the world: if before the world's creation, the world already existed, then the world is not really created but unmasked as eternal.

Al-Šahrastānī has a two-fold strategy to respond to this argument: he, first, denies that God could have preceded the world in time and, secondly, argues that God actually preceded the world in a non-temporal way, viz., in existence only. In arguing for his first point, the other major topic of al-Šahrastānī's discussion in his two works will become relevant: the denial of the reality of any form of an actual infinite.[38]

Looking at his argumentation in *al-Muṣāraʿa*, we see al-Šahrastānī directly engaged with Avicenna in a dialectical discussion, which helps to clarify the underlying rationale of his position. He argues that his opponent is cheating, for when he formulates God's initial idleness from creating the world and His subsequent activity of creating in terms of what was "before" and what is "now," he actually postulates the existence of two times: one devoid of God's activity and another "filled" with it. For al-Šahrastānī, this talk is not only structurally analogous to imagining some space devoid of body and some space filled with it – it is also equally inacceptable: there is no void space outside the world and it would be absurd to assume void space outside the world, in order to account for God's location or to argue for God's spatial priority, for God simply cannot be described in spatial terms. He exists exalted above space, thus being neither prior to nor together with the world in space. The same applies to time, says al-Šahrastānī: there is no time prior to the world which would document God's idleness, for God exists entirely exalted above time, thus not being "temporally prior" either.[39]

Here, al-Šahrastānī's opponent senses a potential triumph and tries to pin al-Šahrastānī down on what he has just said by arguing that if he readily admits that God is not temporally prior to the world – as he just did – then he must accept that God is inevitably together with the world, for what is not prior to something must be together with something. Thus, the world must be eternally with God, because God, in His divine eternity, was never temporally prior to, i.e., was always together with, the world. This is a perfect response – albeit for al-Šahrastānī, as it allows him to scoff at his opponent:

> I say: He listened poorly, and then he replied poorly! Concomitance in existence and time only follows when the existent is susceptible to time, but we have already explained that it is not possible that the world is temporally together with Him (exalted be He), because it would make it necessary that His existence is temporal. So, temporal con-

38 cf. also Mayer, "The Absurdities of Infinite Time."

39 cf. al-Šahrastānī, *al-Muṣāraʿa* 5, 101.1–102.5; *Nihāyat al-aqdām* 1, 10.4–17.

comitance and association are absurd – and temporal precedence and priority are likewise absurd.[40]

For al-Šahrastānī, there is only one time, viz., that belonging to the world. God, on the other hand, is entirely exalted above time; He is "outside" of both time and the world in a non-temporal sense, just as He is "beyond" both space and the world in a non-spatial sense. Time and space just do not apply to God. If the fact that God is not prior to the world in space does not force Him to be together with the world in space, why, then, would the fact that He is not prior to the world in time force Him to be together with the world in time? There is no harm in admitting that God is not temporally prior to the world, for this – far from ultimately entailing the world's eternity – only bears out His divine transcendence.

Of course, his opponent refuses to be defeated by this, but al-Šahrastānī has two further arguments ready with which he seeks to arrest his opponent's dialectical reasoning. It was Avicenna's own idea to contrast God's "idleness from activity" (*tark li-l-fiʿl*) with His "activity" (*al-fiʿl*) of creating and to demand that God's idleness needs to be understood in temporal terms as an idleness *before* He began to create the world, in order to reveal on that basis the alleged absurdities behind this reasoning and to establish God's now eternal activity instead.[41] To this, al-Šahrastānī replies that in its very core, the meaning of "activity" (*al-fiʿl*) requires a beginning (*awwal*), whereas the very meaning of "eternity" (*al-azal*) denies precisely this: any form of a beginning. Consequently, speaking of an "eternal activity" is inherently contradictory – so contradictory that God's failure to have eternally been engaged in creation does not compromise His divine generosity and perfection.[42]

In a second argument, al-Šahrastānī states that someone might try to argue that God, if He really were perfect and perfectly generous, would have created not only a larger but an infinitely large world.[43] This, however, would be a sophism, as an infinitely large world is sheerly impossible, says al-Šahrastānī, because it would entail the existence of an actual infinite. The fact that God did not create such a world, again, does not bankrupt His divine perfection, as it was not due to any deficiency (*al-naqṣ*) *in Him* that an infinitely large world could not come-to-be but to a deficiency *in the receiver* of His action, namely, the world: "The deficiency devolves on the recipient of the generosity – not on the generosity of the

40 al-Šahrastānī, *al-Muṣāraʿa* 5, 102.9–12, tr. Madelung/Mayer, modified; cf. *Nihāyat al-aqdām* 1, 9.3–10.4.

41 cf. al-Šahrastānī, *al-Muṣāraʿa* 5, 103.1–5; cf. also *al-Muṣāraʿa* 5, 98.5–8, quoting and paraphrasing from Avicenna, *al-Naǧāt* IV.2.24, 612.5–9 (≈ *al-Ilāhiyyāt* IX.1, §15, 378.8–12 ≈ *al-Mabdaʾ wa-l-maʿād* 31, 43.11–13).

42 al-Šahrastānī, *al-Muṣāraʿa* 5, 103.12–104.4.

43 cf. al-Šahrastānī, *al-Muṣāraʿa* 5, 104.5–8.

Bestower."[44] Since an infinite world is just as contradictory as an eternal activity, the fact that God created a spatially finite world is no expression of any shortcoming on His divine behalf – it is just following the rules of what can and cannot be done. God surely could have created a *larger* world but He could not have created an *infinitely large* world.[45] Even God is bound to the finitude of His creative act – in its temporal as much as in its spatial dimension – because, as al-Šahrastānī once more emphasises, time and space are structurally analogous:

> The intellectual conceptualisation regarding time is like the intellectual assessment regarding place – entirely alike as a feather to a feather and a shoe to a shoe.[46]

With al-Šahrastānī once more pressing his point about the structural analogy between time and space, we arrive at the discussion of the possibility of the existence of an actual infinite. Aristotle famously argued in his *Physics* that something infinite cannot exist as fully realised in actuality. Thus, no single infinite body and no single infinite number can ever enter existence. Nonetheless, the infinite can exist *potentially*, so that a single body remains infinitely divisible and one can always add one more to any previous number. This also means that the infinite time of an eternal world's existence constitutes no problem at all, as the past is no longer – and the future not yet – existent, whereas the present is just yet another moment which increases the number of past moments by one.[47]

Philoponus equally famously turned this reasoning against Aristotle himself. His most prominent, and his most challenging, argument is that an eternally existing world would already have contained an infinite number of people whose intellective souls have survived the death of their bodies. Thus, there would, indeed, be an already infinite number of souls actually existing in this very moment; and as if that was not already enough, more and more surviving souls would be added to an ever increasing yet already infinite number as more and more people pass away, liberating their intellective souls from their bodies.[48]

Avicenna, in turn, famously responded to Philoponus and revised Aristotle's account of the infinite.[49] He distinguished between two fundamentally different kinds of infinities: ordered infinities and unordered ones. This distinction, which

---

44 al-Šahrastānī, *al-Muṣāraʿa* 5, 104.7f.

45 That al-Šahrastānī allows for the possibility of a larger world – both spatially and temporally – will become relevant in Abū l-Barakāt's argumentation below, 263ff.

46 al-Šahrastānī, *al-Muṣāraʿa* 5, 104.11f.; cf. *Nihāyat al-aqdām* 1, 52.12–15.

47 cf. esp. Aristotle, *Phys.* IV.6; cf. also *Cael.* I.5–7.

48 cf. esp. Philoponus, *Contra Proclum* I.3, 7.25–11.21; XVIII.3, 619.1–620.19; cf. further Sorabji, "Infinity and the Creation."

49 cf. esp. Avicenna, *al-Samāʿ al-ṭabīʿī* III.7–9; *al-Naǧāt* II.2.11; cf. also *al-Ilāhiyyāt* VI.2, §§6–8, 265.6–266.8; *Lettre au vizir Abū Saʿd*, 27.5–36.9; cf. further the detailed and illuminating exposition in McGinnis, "Avicennan Infinity."

has its roots in remarks made by Aristotle in his *Categories* and was elaborated upon in Avicenna's *al-Maqūlāt*, is significant, as only an ordered infinite is actually impossible, while an unordered infinite is entirely acceptable.[50] Avicenna stated that for a magnitude, number, or set of numbered things to be "ordered" (*murattab*) means to have parts of which some are "prior by nature" (*aqdam bi-l-ṭabʿ*) to others.[51] We have already seen that Avicenna exemplified the priority "by nature" (*bi-l-ṭabʿ*) with the priority of the number one over the number two.[52] We have also seen that the crucial point in any natural priority is that it is irreversible. Not only is it entirely absurd that the number two would precede the number one, it is also clear that the one could exist without the two, but the two could not exist without the one.[53] Thus, both numbers have their respective "position," as it were. Accordingly, an "ordered" magnitude or set has a specific structure, where each of its parts has its specific and determinate position next to the other without there being any overlap among them. In other words, the order of such a magnitude's parts would somehow be *essential* - and, indeed, in *al-Naǧāt*, Avicenna speaks precisely of what is "essentially ordered" (*murattab al-ḏāt*).[54] For Avicenna, an ordered infinite is impossible, because, if it were to exist in actuality and if someone would try to add to it or subtract from it, it would necessarily lead to absurdities.[55]

Avicenna shows the impossibility of an essentially ordered actual infinite with an argument akin to one already used by Abū Yaʿqūb ibn Isḥāq al-Kindī. He considers two parallel but otherwise identical beams A and B which extend from a given point infinitely into one direction. If we, now, were to remove some parts from B and compare what is left with A in various ways, we would realise that we inevitably run into intractable absurdities.[56] As is clear, the reason why we run into these absurdities is the very fact that beams are lines and lines are continuous quantities, whose parts have determinate positions which have a certain order, where no part overlaps with another, so that all parts form a structured consecutive whole. In brief, it is the very fact that some quantities are ordered that keeps these quantities from being or becoming infinite.

This is also the reason why Avicenna does not have to worry about Philoponus' famous argument about the infinite number of intellective souls. Souls are in-

50 cf. Aristotle, *Cat.* 6, 4b21f., 5a15–37; Avicenna, *al-Maqūlāt* IV.1, 127.6–130.3.

51 Avicenna, *al-Naǧāt* II.2.11, 244.12–15; cf. *al-Samāʿ al-ṭabīʿī* III.8, §1, 212.6f.

52 Avicenna, *al-Maqūlāt* VII.4, 266.1–6; cf. McGinnis, "Avicennan Infinity," 218.

53 This is commonly accepted in the tradition before and after al-Šahrastānī; cf. Aristotle, *Cat.* 12, 14a29–35; Avicenna, *al-Maqūlāt* VII.4, 266.2–6; al-Sāwi, *al-Baṣāʾir al-naṣīriyya*, I.2.12, 77.11–26; Faḫr al-Dīn al-Rāzī, *al-Arbaʿīn* I.2, vol. 1, 24.9–13.

54 Avicenna, *al-Naǧāt* II.2.11, 244.13f.

55 cf. esp. Avicenna, *al-Naǧāt* II.2.11, 245.10f.

56 For a more detailed analysis of both al-Kindī's and Avicenna's arguments, cf. McGinnis, "Avicennan Infinity," esp. 203–206 and 215–218.

corporeal and immaterial. They do precisely *not* have a distinct position, they are not arranged next to one another, they are not such that they could not overlap with one another. In short, the quantity of their number is not ordered, and so we would not run into absurdities, if we were to add or subtract from their number. Accordingly, it is by no means absurd that an infinite number of intellective souls is existing in this very moment nor should we be worried about the fact that tomorrow there will be even more of them.

Avicenna's arguments were also known to al-Šahrastānī. In both his *al-Muṣāraʿa* and *Nihāyat al-aqdām*, he explicitly relates, and ultimately rejects, Avicenna's account of an actually existing unordered infinite, in order to restore the strength of Philoponus' arguments and to show that the world must have been created at a certain moment in the finite past.[57] At the heart of al-Šahrastānī's argumentation is the claim that Avicenna's distinction between ordered and unordered quantities is irrelevant. Instead, any argument about an ordered infinite is just as permissible and powerful as an argument about an unordered infinite. Once more playing out his rhetorical strengths, al-Šahrastānī exclaims in rhyming mockery: "[This] demonstration is just as [that] demonstration, [neck to neck] like two competing horses" (*wa-l-burhān ka-l-burhān ka-farasay rihān*).[58]

In his attack on Avicenna's contention, al-Šahrastānī, first, singles out the central criterion at work in the distinction between ordered and unordered quantities. He states that the criterion (*al-ḍābiṭ*) why some infinites are impossible, whereas others are not, is that they have "a sensible position (*waḍʿ ḥissī*), as body, or an intelligible position (*waḍʿ ʿaqlī*), as for example cause and effect." By contrast, whatever lacks such a position, as for example human souls do, can supposedly be infinite.[59] Later, after having restated Avicenna's already mentioned argument about two infinite beams of which one is reduced in size and, thereupon, compared to the other, thus giving rise to intractable absurdities, al-Šahrastānī writes:

> Then we transfer (*nanqulu*) this same demonstration to the numbers of human souls and the numbers of circular motions. They distinguish between the two forms only insofar as body has a position … while souls and [circular] motions have no position. It is said [to them]: Mere position and the lack of it have no impact on the distinction (*lā taʾṯīra lahu fī l-farq*) … Thus, hypothesise "Zayd" and think of him as a point, and hypothesise his ancestors as a straight line up to infinity, and hypothesise "ʿAmr" and think of him as a point falling short of Zayd by an ancestor, or two ancestors, or three, and think of his ancestors as a line up to infinity … We have proven before that the kind

57 cf. al-Šahrastānī, *al-Muṣāraʿa* 5, 95.6–10, 104.11–109.10; cf. *Nihāyat al-aqdām* 1, 6.10–7.3, 13.4–14.1, 23.12–29.11.

58 al-Šahrastānī, *al-Muṣāraʿa* 5, 109.10.

59 al-Šahrastānī, *al-Muṣāraʿa* 5, 95.6–10; cf. *Nihāyat al-aqdām* 1, 23.12–24.9.

> of order in respect of individuals is like what there is in respect of causes and effects. The order in respect of causes, souls, and individuals is like the position in respect of bodies and distances.[60]

Just as Avicenna's argument relied on the assumption of two infinite lines or beams, so al-Šahrastānī's counter-argument relies on two lines, too – with the modification that he uses the lines as a continuous medium meant to represent the discontinuous, or: discrete, order of all the souls of Zayd's and ʿAmr's ancestors. Both groups of ancestors are, given an eternal world, infinite in number. So, the first line represents all ancestors of Zayd, beginning with himself, then his parents, then his grandparents, and so on. The second line, in turn, serves as a medium for the successive arrangement of all the souls of ʿAmr's ancestors, which are likewise infinite. Yet, because ʿAmr is supposed to be one or two or three generations older than Zayd, we run into the same absurd difficulties as Avicenna did with his argument, once we start to consider these two lines of ancestors as both infinite but unequally infinite, as one is less infinite than the other.

It seems that with this argument, al-Šahrastānī discovered a way to transform an unordered quantity into an ordered one. If successful, this could seriously question the underlying rationale behind Avicenna's distinction. In fact, the argument seems to unmask that supposedly relevant distinction as purely terminological; "mere position and the lack of it have no impact on the distinction," as al-Šahrastānī states.

It could be objected, however, that al-Šahrastānī neglected an important aspect in Avicenna's reasoning. Avicenna precisely spoke of an *essential* order, and not of what has merely been accidentally ordered. According to him, each part of a body has a position that belongs to it by virtue of its being a part of the whole. Moreover, Avicenna also spoke of what is "prior by nature." As we have already seen, the idea of a natural priority is that it is irreversible insofar as the number two cannot even be thought of preceding the number one and that the number two implies the precedence of the number one but not *vice versa.* Souls, however, do not have individual positions which have been assigned to them by their own selves, they do not have a position as being part of the infinite number of souls which have come-into-being during the eternal history of the world nor is their order irreversible. Though clearly inventive, al-Šahrastānī's counter-argument appears to be fundamentally flawed, having neglected the crucial aspect that Avicenna envisaged an *essentially* ordered quantity.

Having said this, al-Šahrastānī has expected this worry and is prepared to respond to it. He writes that he "has proven before" (*bayyannā qablu*) that the order "in respect of individuals" works just like the order "in respect of causes

60 al-Šahrastānī, *al-Muṣāraʿa* 5, 108.12–109.10, tr. Madelung/Mayer, modified.

and effects." With this, he probably refers to what he has written a few lines earlier, arguing that souls belong to concrete individuals, and the order of individuals is far from being arbitrary. "The existence of this man (and thereby we point to Zayd) has depended on the existence of the sperm from which he was created, and the existence of that sperm depended on the existence of another man from whom it arose."[61] In his *Nihāyat al-aqdām*, the same thought occurs in what appears to be a direct engagement with Avicenna:

> So, when he said: "[Souls] have neither a natural nor a positional order," it is said [to him]: "When the individuals are ordered as begetter and begotten, souls are likewise ordered by that order, because it is one of the individualising accidents[62] and concomitants of souls that they are such that individuals proceed from individuals. So, this relation persists by the persistence of [the souls], and [so] to this kind belongs an order."[63]

This rejoinder has some merit, for, indeed, individual souls are ordered on account of their history. They have been generated at a certain point in time due to a specific cause and could not have been generated earlier or later. This is why al-Šahrastānī did not write that we should simply arrange whatever souls one after another but that we should arrange a specific set of souls, viz., those of Zayd's and ʿAmr's ancestors – and it now emerges also that he asks us to arrange them in the very order in which they have been caused and created. This order of begetter and begotten is far from being arbitrary.[64]

Here, two further things are noteworthy. First, as has already been mentioned, the tradition before and after al-Šahrastānī seems to agree that the central idea of natural priority, to which we have seen Avicenna explicitly referring, is that the

61 al-Šahrastānī, *al-Muṣāraʿa* 5, 107.3–5, tr. Madelung/Mayer, modified; cf. *Nihāyat al-aqdām* 1, 26.17–27.12; cf. also a similar line of argument, developed in a different context, in al-Ġazālī, *Tahāfut al-falāsifa* 4, §§10–14, 80.5–81.8.

62 One might have hoped that al-Šahrastānī would avoid the term "accidents" (*ʿawāriḍ*, sg. *ʿaraḍ*) here, because it is precisely this word and the idea of the accidental which, being the contrary to the essential, invites the very criticism which this passage apparently attempts to brush off. Incautious though it may be, al-Šahrastānī's point is probably that although these admittedly are accidents, they are *necessary* accidents, i.e., "concomitants" (*lawāzim*, sg. *lāzim*) of an "individualising" (*muʿayyina*) kind.

63 al-Šahrastānī, *Nihāyat al-aqdām* 1, 27.9–12.

64 In which sense it really can be termed "essential" is the subject of the following discussion. Other than that, it should be mentioned that, without explicitly mentioning al-Šahrastānī in this context, Marmura argued that, given Avicenna's position on God's knowledge of particulars, it would seem that Avicenna's God knows the particular souls by knowing their causal history and their individuating principles. This, Marmura continues, would entail "the imposition of an order amongst them" in such a way that "[a]n ordered coexisting infinite of the kind Avicenna deems impossible seems the inevitable result" ("Some Aspects of Avicenna's Theory of God's Knowledge of Particulars," 310). According to Marmura, then, al-Šahrastānī's objection was justified.

prior can exist without the posterior but not *vice versa.* This, however, is not only an appropriate account of the relation between the number one and the number two. It is, by the same token, also an apt characterisation of cause and effect. Thus, although the arrangement of the souls may not be an instance of natural priority as such, it nonetheless shares the claim of essential irreversibility which is so characteristic of natural priority.

Secondly, it is conspicuous that until the sixth/twelfth century, the terminology describing the five traditional kinds of priority remains stable, whereas from the second half of the sixth/twelfth century onwards, some ambiguity occurs; and this ambiguity affects precisely the two kinds of priorities at stake here: those by nature and by causality. Aristotle, Avicenna, and ʿUmar ibn Sahlān al-Sāwī (d. c. 540/1145), for example, refer to the priorities of time, nature, order, nobility, and causality. They do not mention essential priority in this context. In al-Šahrastānī, we read about the priorities of time, nature, place, nobility, and essence, with the latter apparently replacing the priority by causality. In Faḫr al-Dīn, we are informed about the priorities of time, essence, order, nobility, and cause and effect, with the "priority of essence" now standing for what used to be natural priority, while the expression of a priority of cause and effect, against al-Šahrastānī's terminological shift, reoccurs. Finally, Naṣīr al-Dīn mentions the priorities of time, nature, place, nobility and essence, thus keeping the original priority by nature (as in Aristotle, Avicenna, al-Sāwī, and al-Šahrastānī but contrary to Faḫr al-Dīn), while calling what used to be the priority of causality the priority by essence (as also al-Šahrastānī did).[65]

Table 1: Shifting vocabulary for the different senses of "priority."

Aristotle, Avicenna, al-Sāwī[66]	al-Šahrastānī[67]	Faḫr al-Dīn al-Rāzī[68]	Naṣīr al-Dīn al-Ṭūsī[69]
time	time	time	time
nature	nature	essence	nature
order	place	order	place
nobility	nobility	nobility and virtue	nobility
causality	essence	causality	essence
—/—	existence	"another kind"	order

65 It should also be noted that both Faḫr al-Dīn and Naṣīr al-Dīn integrate al-Šahrastānī's idea about a sixth kind of priority.

66 cf. Aristotle, *Cat.* 12, 14a29–35; Avicenna, *al-Maqūlāt* VII.4, 266.2–6; al-Sāwī, *al-Baṣāʾir al-naṣīriyya*, I.2.12, 77.11–26.

67 cf. al-Šahrastānī, *al-Muṣāraʿa* 5, 115.4–116.6; *Nihāyat al-aqdām* 1, 7.9–8.15.

68 cf. Faḫr al-Dīn al-Rāzī, *al-Arbaʿīn* I.2, vol. 1, 24.9–13.

69 cf. Naṣīr al-Dīn al-Ṭūsī, *Resāle andar qesmat-e mawǧūdāt* §20, 12.13f.

This may be a coincidence, but it is striking at that, because the very kinds of priority which are relevant in our present discussion are precisely those which generate the most terminological confusion. As a result, when al-Šahrastānī reads in Avicenna that only that kind of infinite is impossible which is ordered (*murattab*), and when Avicenna, then, exemplifies this with what is "prior by nature" (*aqdam bi-l-ṭabʿ*), and when he, in the same context, also refers to what is "essentially ordered" (*murattab al-ḏāt*), then al-Šahrastānī could very well understand this essential order as an order by causality, because essential order is precisely his way to refer to the order by causality. Finally, the confusion is perfect when we also integrate al-Ġazālī, who writes in his *Tahāfut al-falāsifa* in the same context:

> They [sc. the philosophers] claim that whoever asserts that the world is posterior to God and God prior to it must mean either that He is prior by essence (*mutaqaddim bi-l-ḏāt*) and not by time (*lā bi-l-zamān*), like the priority of the one over the two, for it is [a priority] by nature (*bi-l-ṭabʿ*), … and like the priority of the cause over the effect (*taqaddum al-ʿilla ʿalā l-maʿlūl*); [or he must mean that God is prior to the world by time].[70]

Here, the priorities by essence, nature, and causality are all once more tarred with the same brush; they are together in contrast to what is prior by time. Accordingly, we can say that al-Šahrastānī presented an original counter-argument which seems to undermine Avicenna's rationale in distinguishing between an ordered quantity and an unordered quantity by formulating a novel way in which what supposedly has no order can be unmasked as having an essential order after all. Moreover, even if one wanted to object that al-Šahrastānī's counter-argument, in one way or another, disregards – or not fully observes – the fact that Avicenna spoke of an *essential* order, whereas al-Šahrastānī's transformation, at best, results in an *accidental* ordering, one would still have to accept the fact that for al-Šahrastānī, the situation is not as clear as one might think, because the philosophical tradition of the sixth/twelfth century has already started to modify the theory of the five kinds of priority, either by labelling them differently or by mixing them up altogether. This is particularly true of the priorities by cause, time, and essence, as they all seem to share the pivotal characteristic of "natural priority," viz., irreversibility. So, why not rearrange the five kinds of priority into an essential group (containing irreversible priorities such as those by nature, essence, cause, and time) against an accidental group (containing the priorities of space, order, and nobility)?[71] If so, then al-Šahrastānī could truly claim that souls have a history and that their history is not merely accidental but arranges them in

70 al-Ġazālī, *Tahāfut al-falāsifa* 1, §§78–79, 30.14–17, tr. Marmura, modified.

71 cf. also Ibn Kammūna's (different) strategy of reducing all kinds or priorities to those by causality and by nature mentioned above in fn. 34.

an irreversible order, so that they, while not having individual spatial positions (sg. *waḍʿ ḥissī*), still have individual intellectual positions (sg. *waḍʿ ʿaqlī*), which represent their consecutive order.[72]

Ultimately, al-Šahrastānī argues that there is no quantity of whatever kind that could exist as an infinity fully realised in actuality. Consequently, the philosophers' position of an eternally existent world is refuted, as an eternal world would lead to an infinite number of souls existing in actuality. In addition, al-Šahrastānī states that the supposedly infinite motion of the heavenly spheres would have brought about an infinite time, for time is that which numbers motion (*ʿādd li-l-ḥarakāt*). Since this is absurd, time, too, must necessarily be finite (*yaǧibu an yakūna mutanāhiyan*).[73]

As a result, the world must have been created by God at one moment in the distant, though finite, past. With the world being temporally created and necessarily finite in every respect, we are led back to our initial question about the nature of God's priority to the world. However, al-Šahrastānī has already given his answer. We have seen that God cannot precede the world in time, because time is the number of motion and, thus, belongs to the world and its bodies. Before the world came-into-being there was no time. Moreover, we do not need time or any form of a temporal framework, in order to account for God's inactivity prior to the world's creation, at least just as little as we need any space outside the world, in order to grasp the fact that God is not spatially related to the world. Apart from the corporealist Karrāmiyya, to which al-Šahrastānī occasionally refers in disgust, all seem to agree that God transcends space, and that He is neither prior to nor together with the world in spatial terms.[74] The absolute same applies to God and His relation to time:

> Time and place are twins competing in a single womb, sucking from a single breast, and mollified in a single cradle. So, strike down the eternalist with the corporealist and the corporealist with the eternalist, and seek out the religion of God (exalted be He) between the extremist and the shortcomer. The majesty of God (exalted be He) transcends imaginations (*awhām*) and intellects (*ʿuqūl*), let alone place and time.[75]

72 q.v. above, 250.

73 al-Šahrastānī, *al-Muṣāraʿa* 5, 108.1 f.; cf. *Nihāyat al-aqdām* 1, 28.6; q.v. below, 267.

74 cf. al-Šahrastānī, *al-Muṣāraʿa* 5, 101.4, 11; *Nihāyat al-aqdām* 1, 10.6, 39.10. The theological school associated with the third/ninth century theologian Abū ʿAbd Allāh Muḥammad ibn Karrām was notoriously known for its corporeal account of God as a body who is spatially prior to the world, existing in empty space above the world and being seated on His throne; cf. Zysow, "Karrāmiyya."

75 al-Šahrastānī, *al-Muṣāraʿa* 5, 118.9–12, tr. Madelung/Mayer, modified; cf. al-Šahrastānī, *Maǧles-e maktūb-e Šahrastānī monʿaqed dar Ḫwārazm*, 80.12–81.6, 89.12.

In effect, al-Šahrastānī argues that Avicenna's characterisation of God's relation to the world is inaccurate: God cannot be prior in essence to the world but together with it in time, as this would mean that God is, in fact, in time:

> This characterisation is inapplicable in the case of the Creator (exalted be He), for He is sanctified above time, and so He cannot be prior by essence yet associated with time.[76]

The world, then, is finite in time as it is in space. Although one could imagine a temporal duration before (*qabla*) the world and empty space above (*fawqa*) the world – and maybe even infinite space and infinite time – all this "is pure imagination and sheer fancy" (*wahm muǧarrad wa-ḫayāl maḥḍ*).[77] In fact, there is nothing that could actually be infinite, and so, likewise, God could not produce anything that would actually be infinite. Nonetheless, God precedes the world as its creator; His priority or precedence, however, is of a different sort, thus exceeding the traditionally transmitted five kinds of priority: God is prior to the world "by existence only (*bi-l-wuǧūd faqaṭ*), like the priority of that which brings something into existence (*al-mūǧid*) to that which is brought into existence" (*al-mūǧad*). God is, thus, a *mūǧid* and a *muḫaṣṣiṣ*, capable of specifying one moment for the world's creation, even if all moments are entirely alike. Although in His causation, He is not bound to any necessity, He is necessarily restrained by what is impossible.

A final, even though central, aspect of al-Šahrastānī's position needs to be addressed here. As has been noted several times already, al-Šahrastānī argues for God's absolute transcendence over the world. For him, divine transcendence entails that God cannot be compared to the world; there is no common measure that would apply to both. Once this has been understood, it becomes clear why al-Šahrastānī also explains at length that God cannot be "together with" (*maʿa*) the world in any respect. In *al-Muṣāraʿa*, in the section on "the correct choice," he repeats once more that God is neither prior to nor together with the world in time and space, as has already become clear. Yet, he adds to this that God is also not with the world in nobility, essence, or nature, thus exhausting all five traditional senses of togetherness.[78] What about his sixth kind, then? If God is, first, *prior* to the world in existence, is He then, i. e., after the world has been brought into being, *together* with the world in existence, as al-Ġazālī seems to think, when he wrote above that "what is to be understood of our assertion that 'He was and with Him the world' is only the existence of the two essences?"[79] While al-Šahrastānī does not give a definite answer, it is sufficiently clear from his whole position that

76 al-Šahrastānī, *al-Muṣāraʿa* 5, 117.1 f. tr. Madelung/Mayer, modified; *Nihāyat al-aqdām* 1, 9.7–10.

77 al-Šahrastānī, *Nihāyat al-aqdām* 1, 10.4–7 and 14–17

78 cf. al-Šahrastānī, *al-Muṣāraʿa* 5, 115.4–116.6; *Nihāyat al-aqdām* 1, 9.3–7.

79 al-Ġazālī, *Tahāfut al-falāsifa* 1, §82, 31.13–17.

this needs to be denied. God is not even in existence together with the world.[80] First of all, he states that God is not with the world in nobility, essence, or nature, but failed to explicitly deny whether He is prior in these three senses. It seems reasonable to assume that he would, for example, definitely agree that God is prior, at least, in nobility. So, he generally is not opposed to the idea of allowing priority without togetherness. In addition, it is clear that much of his argumentative strategy was concerned with disentangling the all-too-tight relation between priority and togetherness, which was championed by the philosophers. They argued that if God is not prior to the world in time, He must be together with it in time. Al-Šahrastānī, however, seems to say that one cannot reason from any claim about priorities to a further claim about togetherness. The fact that God is not "prior" in one sense, does not necessitate His being "together with" in that sense (or in any other). Likewise, then, the fact that God is prior in some senses, should not be seen as entailing His subsequent togetherness, either. So, God is prior to the world in existence, probably also in nobility, and arguably also in essence and nature (as long as this does not make Him a *mūǧib*). Yet, this does not mean that He is together with the world in any of these senses, because the meaning of divine priority is, precisely, *transcendence*; and so God is prior to the world by being incomparably above, before, and beyond it. Finally, the clearest statement which al-Šahrastānī provides on this question follows immediately upon his above-quoted claim that the Creator "is sanctified above time and He cannot be prior by essence yet associated (*yuqārinu*) with time":

> And not is He associated (*yuqārinu*) with existence, either, for we have already proven that that which brings something into existence (*al-mūǧid*) is prior in existence to that which is brought into existence (*al-mūǧad*).[81]

In terms of existence, God's priority and transcendence is also established in other parts of al-Šahrastānī's works, for example when he argues that "existence" applies to God and to the world in homonymous ways.[82] As a result, God's existence is unlike the existence of His creatures, i.e., His is not to be compared with theirs – but this does not rule out His existential priority; it only rules out His existential togetherness. Nonetheless, God's transcendence remains nowhere as clear, evident, and explicit as in the cases of time and space.

80 cf. also Madelung "aš-Šahrastānīs Streitschrift," 257.

81 al-Šahrastānī, *al-Muṣāraʿa* 5, 117.2f.; cf. al-Šahrastānī, *Nihāyat al-aqdām* 1, 10.15–11.3. Despite this rather clear passage, I just wrote above that "al-Šahrastānī does not give a definite answer," because this passage does not mention the technical terminology of "togetherness" (*al-maʿiyya*) and being "together with" (*maʿa*) which would have made things crystal clear.

82 cf. al-Šahrastānī, *al-Muṣāraʿa* 2, 41.1–7; cf. also Madelung "aš-Šahrastānīs Streitschrift," 252f.

4. A Difficult Question?

In contrast to al-Šahrastānī's conception, Abū l-Barakāt's God is not transcendent. In fact, we shall see how Abū l-Barakāt employs God's immanence in his account of time as what seems to be an essential step towards his preferred conclusion of an eternal world. While both philosophers agree that God is not temporally prior to the world, they disagree entirely about the meaning of this assertion: for al-Šahrastānī, God is not temporally prior to the world, because God is not temporal – for Abū l-Barakāt, God is not temporally prior to the world, because He is not prior.

Before we can engage with Abū l-Barakāt's discussion, a few things need to be mentioned first about its structure and about the earlier scholarship on the subject. The famous *al-Muʿtabar fī l-ḥikma* of Abū l-Barakāt consists of three books: on logic, on natural philosophy, and on metaphysics. The three chapters which are primarily relevant for the concerns of this study are to be found in the first of two parts of the third book (*al-Muʿtabar* III.1.7–9). Creation, then, is a topic to be treated in metaphysics. This, as such, is no surprise – but the following is: while chapter seven is devoted to "recounting the teachings of those asserting origination and eternity" and chapter nine offers "the completion of the investigation about origination and eternity," chapter eight, interspersed between these two, is concerned with a seemingly different topic: "On time in the manner appropriate for this science."[83] This is not only surprising insofar as it seems to disrupt Abū l-Barakāt's discussion of creation and eternity, it is also unexpected, as Abū l-Barakāt has actually already offered an analysis of time in the second book of *al-Muʿtabar*, viz., that concerned with natural philosophy.[84] What complicates the picture further is the fact that, although chapter III.1.9 promised to "complete" the investigation, Abū l-Barakāt offers yet another long discussion at the beginning of the second part of metaphysics, in which he examines "the beginning of creation" (*bidāyat al-ḫalq*).[85]

This, at first glance, rather confusing situation may have contributed to the somewhat hesitant claims offered by contemporary interpreters of Abū l-Barakāt's thought. Shlomo Pines, for example, in his short entry in the second edition of the *Encyclopaedia of Islam* from 1960, stated that Abū l-Barakāt "seems" to affirm the eternity of the world.[86] Subsequently, Mehmet Dag in his doctoral dissertation, which he completed at Durham University in 1970, wrote that Abū l-Barakāt "refrains from giving his personal opinions on the subject"

83 Abū l-Barakāt al-Baġdādī, *al-Muʿtabar* III.1.7–9, 28.2f., 35.14, 41.13.

84 cf. Abū l-Barakāt al-Baġdādī, *al-Muʿtabar* II.1.17–18. On Abū l-Barakāt's discussion of time, cf. Pines, "Nouvelles etudes"; Dag, *The Philosophy of Abū 'l-Barakāt al-Baghdādī.*

85 cf. Abū l-Barakāt al-Baġdādī, *al-Muʿtabar* III.2.1–5.

86 Pines, "Abu 'l-Barakāt Hibat Allāh b. Malkā al-Baghdādī al-Baladī," 113a.

but that there are, nonetheless, five "strong indications that he believed in the eternity of the world."[87] Twenty-two years later, Ǧamāl Raǧab Saydabī asserts in his monograph *Abū l-Barakāt al-Baġdādī wa-falsafatuhu l-ilāhiyya* that Abū l-Barakāt "leaned towards" (*yamīlu ilā*) the eternity of the world and provides four arguments in support of this contention, explicitly referring to Pines.[88] More recently, Frank Griffel argued that regarding the topic of creation and eternity, "Abū l-Barakāt no longer considers that the issue [about eternity and creation] can be settled by demonstrative arguments." Instead, he presented the arguments of the eternalists together with the counter-arguments of the creationists (in *al-Muʿtabar* III.1.7 and 9), before deciding that the issue should be "revisited" again (in *al-Muʿtabar* III.2.1–5), once more "scrutinizing the available arguments." Although Abū l-Barakāt "eventually … sides with the eternalists," it emerges that "[f]or Abū l-Barakāt, philosophy is dialectical," as Griffel wrote, viewing him as being at the forefront of a new dialectical movement.[89]

There are two judgements commonly shared by all these four accounts: first, they all agree that Abū l-Barakāt ultimately believes in the eternity of the world. Secondly, however, they all insinuate that this question about the world's eternity was a difficult question to answer for Abū l-Barakāt, which explains why his discussion is not sufficiently clear, why he refrained from giving his own opinion, and why he reassessed the various arguments for and against either of the two possible positions again and again. So, despite the fact that eventually Abū l-Barakāt "seems" to "incline towards" eternity and to have "sided with" those upholding it, he is presented as someone who may have had serious doubts or was somehow inarticulate in his argumentation. At any rate, his position is not fully clear and, in one way or another, leaves room for doubt; hence, the diffidence.

There is some truth to this: as has been mentioned, Abū l-Barakāt never explicitly stated his own position – but this by itself does not mean that he was unclear in his argument or uncertain in his aim; it does not even mean that he considered the question to be particularly problematic. Instead, the thinker we become acquainted with when we read *al-Muʿtabar* is at least as confident and assertive as we have experienced al-Šahrastānī to be. At times, it even appears that where the latter was eloquent and rhetorically resourceful, Abū l-Barakāt's language is blunt and abusive, as we shall see. At the end of his discussion, in *al-Muʿtabar* III.1.9, Abū l-Barakāt asserts that "he who grasps intellectually what he has heard, contemplates it in his mind, and follows up on it with his reflection, he will have heard the argument (*al-ḥuǧǧa*) and known the destination" (*al-*

87 Dag, *The Philosophy of Abū 'l-Barakāt al-Baghdādī*, 125.

88 Saydabī, *Abū l-Barakāt al-Baġdādī wa-falsafatuhu l-ilāhiyya*, 161.

89 Griffel, "Between al-Ghazālī and Abū l-Barakāt al-Baghdādī," 71 f.

maḥaǧǧa).[90] This does not sound like someone who is vague or hesitant, so that he would merely be inclined towards one position or adopt a dialectical to-and-fro with no conclusion but mere preference. Abū l-Barakāt knew very well what to argue for and presented precisely that kind of argument from which the attentive reader will be able to understand his intention.

This also means that the structure of Abū l-Barakāt's discussion in *al-Muʿtabar* should not be considered to be convoluted and confused; it is clear and determinate. Abū l-Barakāt examines the question whether or not the world was created at a specific point in time in the first of the two parts of the metaphysical section of his *al-Muʿtabar* (chs. III.1.7–9). The upshot of his argument is that the world is the eternal effect of a perfect, benevolent, omnipotent, and (of course) eternal God.[91] Moreover, the chapter on time (ch. III.1.8) does not disrupt his argumentation but is at the heart of it. Finally, the supposed second discussion on "the beginning of creation" in the second part of the metaphysical section (*al-Muʿtabar* III.2.1–5) does not "revisit" the same issue but investigates an entirely different question: *how* does God create the world eternally – and it is on this question that Abū l-Barakāt fundamentally disagrees with the position of eternalists of the likes of Avicenna, who argued that God can be responsible for only *one* effect and, thus, is bound to create by emanation with the help of further intellects and angels, which bring about the required multiplicity to explain the apparent complexity of our sublunary world.[92] In his discussion about creation and eternity, however, he clearly sides with Avicenna and with all the other "eternalists."

As in al-Šahrastānī, the central question of Abū l-Barakāt's investigation is the nature of God's priority over the world and whether God's priority – assuming for the sake of argument that He created the world at one moment – is of a temporal kind. As we have seen, al-Šahrastānī firmly *denied* this, instead introducing a sixth kind of priority as his solution. As we shall see now, Abū l-Barakāt's intention is to *affirm* this: if God really created the world at one specific moment, He inevitably would be temporally prior to the world. God's temporal priority, however, is intrinsically absurd, and so the initial assumption of the world's temporal creation is to be denied. Consequently, God does not precede the world at all but exists eternally together with the world.

90 Abū l-Barakāt al-Baġdādī, *al-Muʿtabar* III.1.9, 17f.

91 This is also affirmed in the later discussion, e.g., in *al-Muʿtabar* III.2.5, 162.17–21.

92 For broad outlines of Abū l-Barakāt's position, cf. Rahman, "The Eternity of the World," 225–227 and Davidson, *Alfarabi, Avicenna, and Averroes, on Intellect*, 154–161.

5. An Infinite Duration

The first conclusion which Abū l-Barakāt draws in his discussion on behalf of the "creationists" (*al-qā'ilūn bi-l-ḥudūṯ*) is the following:

> So, the preceding non-existence [of the world] had been prior (*qad taqaddama*) to the existence of the creation, and together with the existence of the Creator was an infinite duration (*mudda lā nihāyata lahā*). Thus, the Creator, who is prior to His creation of the world, was existent without the creation for a duration with no beginning whose end is the beginning of His act of bringing the world into existence (*īǧād al-'ālam*).[93]

Already in this passage we find several elements familiar from al-Šahrastānī. It is argued that temporal creation needs to be understood in terms of *īǧād* and that the existence of the world is preceded by its non-existence, so that the world had been non-existent for a while – in fact, an infinite while or duration (*mudda*), in which the world was not, but its Creator was, existent. This duration finds its end in the very first moment of God's creative act which also marks the beginning of the world and the beginning of time. Upon comparing these lines of Abū l-Barakāt's chapter with the way in which al-Šahrastānī introduced the issue in his works, it emerges that Abū l-Barakāt picks precisely the same topics which also stirred al-Šahrastānī: the idea of *īǧād* (as opposed to *īǧāb*) and the nature of this duration in which lies God's priority over the world.

It is, therefore, by no means surprising that in their first response, Abū l-Barakāt's "eternalists" (*al-qā'ilūn bi-l-qidam* or *al-qidamiyyūn*) criticise the idea of a duration throughout which God supposedly remained idle. How is God's infinite inactivity to be conceived, when He never lacked power, when He never was stingy or hindered by some contrary or peer, when He never was lacking anything He required or was doubtfully questioning what He was on the verge of doing? "How is it possible," they ask, "to say that He persisted through an infinite duration in which He was not creating – and thereupon began and, thus, created?"[94] For the eternalists, the entire idea of a preceding duration is not only false, as it contravenes God's perfection and benevolence, it is also superfluous, once the real meaning of possibility (*imkān*) has been understood.[95]

Abū l-Barakāt's reference to the concept of possibility supports Robert Wisnovsky's recent analysis of how Avicenna's account of ontological modality shaped the subsequent discussion in theology and philosophy considerably. Wisnovsky showed that the modal language of Avicenna's metaphysics, which characterises reality with terms such as "essence" (*māhiyya*) and "existence"

93 Abū l-Barakāt al-Baġdādī, *al-Mu'tabar* III.1.7, 28.9–11; cf. al-Ġazālī, *Tahāfut al-falāsifa* 1, §80, 31.5–8, who speaks of "time" instead of a "duration."

94 Abū l-Barakāt al-Baġdādī, *al-Mu'tabar* III.1.7, 28.18 f.

95 cf. Abū l-Barakāt al-Baġdādī, *al-Mu'tabar* III.1.7, 29.13–16

(*wuǧūd*) as well as "necessary" (*wāǧib*), "possible" (*mumkin*), and "impossible" (*mumtaniʿ*), effectively superseded the traditional kalām terminology of what is "eternal" (*qadīm*) and "originating" (*ḥādiṯ*).[96] Now, we see Abū l-Barakāt claiming in a similar vein that understanding creation in terms of what is "originating," and to understand "originating" – as is commonly done – in terms of what is preceded by non-existence, instils the incorrect assumption of a duration in which God was strangely inactive and the world not yet existent. However, once one has comprehended what it means to be "possible in itself," and that to be "originating" just means to be "possible in itself," such an understanding becomes obsolete and the assumption of a preceding duration becomes vain – which also solves the issue about God's idleness despite His perfect generosity.[97] There is no duration of non-existence which precedes the world's existence in which God could have been idle. The only way to do justice to God's divine character is to accept an eternal world as both His eternal gift and a demonstration of His complete perfection.[98]

The creationists, however, are dissatisfied and feel that they have been misrepresented. They never meant this duration to be *temporal.* Of course, there was no time in which God was idle, in particular, because there simply was no time prior to the creation:

> Time, they [sc. the creationists] say, is created together with the creation of the world; it is the magnitude of the motions (*miqdār al-ḥarakāt*) and the motions are originated together with the things undergoing motion. Thus, before the creation of the world there was no duration and no time in which one could talk about inactivity (*al-taʿṭīl*) and activity (*al-šuġl*).[99]

96 cf. Wisnovsky, "One Aspect of the Avicennian Turn in Sunnī Theology."

97 It is, thus, no wonder that Abū l-Barakāt has just examined the implications of possibility in the preceding chapter and explicitly refers back to this in his current discussion; cf. *al-Muʿtabar* III.1.7, 29.22 f.

98 Of course, someone like al-Šahrastānī could object now that an eternal world gives rise to actual infinities, such as infinite days, revolutions, and, in particular, intellective souls. While Abū l-Barakāt admits that the denial of an actual infinite is "the strongest way to enforce the judgment about the [world's] origination" (*al-Muʿtabar* III.1.7, 32.19 f.), there are two ways to evade the challenge. The first is to refer to Avicenna's solution that only the actual existence of essentially ordered infinities is prohibited, as Abū l-Barakāt actually does immediately upon raising the issue about actual infinites (cf. *al-Muʿtabar* III.1.7, 32.21–33.4; cf. also III.1.9, 42.9–43.8). This, however, may not be enough to fend off al-Šahrastānī's above discussed improved version about the infinite number of essentially ordered intellective souls. As far as I can see, Abū l-Barakāt nowhere refers to this argument, and so may have been unaware of it. Yet, even if he has had knowledge of al-Šahrastānī's version, Abū l-Barakāt would not have to worry, because – secondly – he explicitly allows for the existence of actual infinities, as Pines has already worked out almost eighty years ago; cf. Pines, "Etudes," 3–31; for Abū l-Barakāt's discussion, cf. *al-Muʿtabar* II.1.19–22.

99 Abū l-Barakāt al-Baġdādī, *al-Muʿtabar* III.1.7, 30.2–4.

In other words, the creationists employ the Aristotelian conception of time, in order to argue for the non-temporal character of the preceding duration and of God's priority. Since time pertains to motion and since motion pertains to corporeal beings, there is no time without corporeal things. Thus, it is impossible for time to exist prior to God's creation of corporeal things, and so His priority over the world cannot be temporal.

To what extent Abū l-Barakāt here directly envisages al-Šahrastānī's concept of existential priority is not clear. It does not seem that he does, because throughout his *al-Muʿtabar*, as far as I can see, he never alludes to a sixth kind of priority but instead mentions the traditional five kinds, which were well known from the philosophical literature.[100] Yet, even so, Abū l-Barakāt clearly addresses the conception of an eternal God who exists alone with His existence prior to His first creative act; and this is nothing other than the very idea which we have already seen expressed in various works composed by earlier Ašʿarites and Muʿtazilites alike and which al-Šahrastānī developed philosophically. So, although Abū l-Barakāt does not directly refer to al-Šahrastānī, he addresses the underlying rationale of al-Šahrastānī's position. This is particularly apparent when Abū l-Barakāt outlines the creationists' position, saying that "the existence of the Creator was not prior to the existence of the world temporally, and so that assertion of ours is what removes the doubt, resolves the objection, and eliminates the obscenity of impairing God's attributes."[101]

So, the creationists are unhappy about the fact that the eternalists have foisted on them the use of the term *mudda* ("duration") along with its temporal implications and argue in response that the priority of God's existence is not temporal. The eternalists, now, react with a well-known argument which Abū l-Barakāt interprets on their behalf in light of recent philosophical developments, in order to debunk this duration as inevitably temporal. They say:

> Would you [sc. the creationists] say … that the world has a temporal beginning which is the first day and moment in which creation [occurred], where prior to that day and moment was no time, and no creation was before it, or would you not say this? … If you say that, [indeed, that] day was the first day and [that] moment the first moment of all the moments of the creation, prior to which was no time and no creation was before it, then we ask you whether or not it was conceptually possible for the powerful and benevolent Creator to create [already] before the instant in which He created?[102]

100 The only passage I could find in which Abū l-Barakāt enumerates various kinds of priority and posteriority is *al-Muʿtabar* II.1.21, 88.11–15. Here, he omits priority by nobility, which he, nonetheless, seems to be aware of, e.g., in *al-Muʿtabar* II.1.25, 104.4 and II.6.20, 389.9f. There is no chapter or passage in the logic of his *al-Muʿtabar* which could be seen as corresponding to Aristotle's or Avicenna's discussions.

101 Abū l-Barakāt al-Baġdādī, *al-Muʿtabar* III.1.7, 30.6–8.

102 Abū l-Barakāt al-Baġdādī, *al-Muʿtabar* III.1.7, 30.8–16; that we need to read *qabla ān* here (l.

So far, this is the "why-not-earlier" argument, well-known from various discussions. If God truly is powerful and if He really chose a moment as the first moment of His creative act, then He surely would have been capable to select also another or an earlier moment as the first moment of His creation. Moreover, if there was a first moment, then before that moment there was no time, because time was created, as we have already seen, along with the bodies in the first moment of creation. In the past, this argument has been discussed *ad nauseam* with the eternalists arguing that mere talking about what was and was not "before" the first moment already affirms that there is something to which this "beforeness" applies which cannot be anything other than time, while the creationists respond by denying precisely this, stressing that there are no grounds for stipulating a third thing over and above the existence of God and the non-existence of the world, to which the eternalists, again, reply that prior to the world's creation, God would have had to be incapable of creating, which would, thus, violate His divine perfection, and so on. In the end, the creationists argue that speaking of what was before the first creative act does not entail the prior existence of time, while the eternalists insist that it does. Until now, no party could substantiate their claim, the discussion having reached an impasse. Abū l-Barakāt continues:

> If they [sc. the creationists] say that this [i. e., creating the world in an earlier moment], indeed, was possible and conceivable, we ask whether it was also possible for Him before the instant in which He created the creation to create bodies in motion which terminate or end their motions on this day in which you have said the beginning of the world [to have occurred]? – If you say "yes," then, we say: Well, if that is not *time*, that in which there is the possibility of motions and rests (*allaḏī fīhi imkān al-ḥarakāt wa-l-sukūnāt*) before the world and in which you assumed that motions have been possible, for time is the duration in which motion and rest is possible and in which creation and act is possible. They, however, have removed and denied these [motions], but they can only be removed through something which can be said to lack power, benevolence, some specifying factor, or something else.[103]

Once more, Abū l-Barakāt uses the concept of possibility in his refutation of the creationists' denial of God's temporal priority. This time, however, he revolutionises – with the help of al-Ġazālī – the well-known "why-not-earlier" argument on the basis of Avicenna's novel account of time which has replaced that of

15) instead of *qabla an* (treating *alif-nūn* is a noun and not as a conjunction) is confirmed three lines later where the same construction can be found, this time with a pronoun (*-hi*) referring back to *ān* ("instant"): *qabla ān ḫalaqa ḫalqan fīhi* (translated below).

103 Abū l-Barakāt al-Baġdādī, *al-Muʿtabar* III.1.7, 30.17–22, emphasis added; I am reading *al-sukūnāt* for *a-l-s-k-n-ā-t*.

Aristotle.[104] His line of argument is as follows: Abū l-Barakāt contends that the creationists, i. e., those who argue for God's non-temporal priority, are compelled to define time along Aristotelian lines as the number, measure, or magnitude of motion.[105] This definition ties the concept of time to physical reality and, thus, to God's creation. Since time is an aspect of created things, it is itself created and could not have existed already prior to the creation.[106] Therefore, God simply cannot be in time or with time or in any way be essentially related to time. However, between Aristotle and Abū l-Barakāt there was Avicenna – and Avicenna's philosophy, although generally regarded as Peripatetic, further developed the Aristotelian doctrine. While time, before Avicenna, was the measure of motion (*miqdār al-ḥaraka*), after Avicenna, it came to be the *magnitude* of motion (*miqdār al-ḥaraka*), i. e., "that in which the possibility for making a change … primarily occurs" (*allaḏī … fīhi imkān al-taġyīrāt*).[107] Thus, Avicenna argued that time is a magnitude which indicates the size or extent not only of actually occurring motions but also of possible ones. This means that although the nominal expression of Aristotle's definition of time was preserved (due to the double meaning of *miqdār* as both "measure" and "magnitude") and was still prevalent even after Avicenna, it had acquired a different meaning, as it now also embraced possible motion. Thus, Avicenna's restructuring of metaphysics around modal terminology also had similar repercussion for his natural philosophy – it is these which Abū l-Barakāt exploits here.[108]

---

104 For a full account of Avicenna's understanding of time, cf. Lammer, *The Elements of Avicenna's Physics*, 429–524.

105 cf. esp. Aristotle, *Phys.* IV.11, 219b1 f.; cf. also 220a24–26.

106 q.v. also the line of reasoning above, 255.

107 Avicenna, *al-Samāʿ al-ṭabīʿī* II.11, §§4–5, 157.15–18.

108 There is still a potential issue here about whether Abū l-Barakāt's use of Avicenna's novel definition of time is justified. For Avicenna, time is, above all, the magnitude of the motion of the outermost sphere. Accordingly, time only exists when that motion exists. Of course, he provides arguments which aim to show why this motion, indeed, exists and why it is eternal, so that, as a result, time can exist and be eternal, too. However, since Abū l-Barakāt's current reasoning does not rely on these arguments but merely employs the idea of time as the magnitude of possible motion within a dialectical setting which actually presupposes both the non-existence and the non-eternality of the heavenly motion, it is not clear to what extent his argument remains valid. This situation shows that we need to investigate further how Avicenna's understanding of time has been received (and transformed?) early on in the post-Avicennian intellectual milieu and whether there are precursors to the way in which Abū l-Barakāt makes use of it here. In this regard, one may also compare the discussion of time in the works of the seventh/thirteenth century theologian and jurist Sayf al-Dīn al-Āmidī, investigated in Lammer, "Time and Mind-Dependence in Sayf al-Dīn al-Āmidī's *Abkār al-afkār*." Al-Āmidī, too, seems to depart in various details from Avicenna's original conception, including the assessment of the significance of the concept of possibility for the definition of time. Finally, it should be noted that Abū l-Barakāt's argument is strikingly similar to how McGinnis interprets a later discussion in Avicenna's *al-Samāʿ al-ṭabīʿī* III.11, effectively attributing to Avicenna the same argument for the eternity of the world on the

So, Abū l-Barakāt argues that as soon as one allows for possible bodies and possible motions prior to the first day of creation, i. e., as soon as one allows for God's ability to have created actual bodies with actual motions earlier, one admits that the first moment of creation does *not* mark the beginning of time. Time inevitably existed before, because bodies and motions possibly existed earlier – and whenever there is the possibility of motion, there is time, because time is just that magnitude (or duration) in which the possibility of motion occurs.

As already noted, there is a prominent precursor to Abū l-Barakāt's argument. Al-Ġazālī has already reformulated the philosophers' "why-not-earlier" argument by asking whether God could have created before this world an earlier world whose heavenly motions stand in certain numerical and measurable relations to one another. In a dense and complex passage, al-Ġazālī's terminology suddenly mentions the "quantifiable and measurable possibility" (*al-imkān al-muqaddar al-mukammam*) which has "no other reality than time" (*lā ḥaqīqata lahu illā l-zamān*).[109] In addition, Avicenna himself had been talking about possible motion to be created prior to the assumed first moment of the world's existence. Undoubtedly, these are the very ingredients which form the backbone of Abū l-Barakāt's argument here, too. However, it is equally clear that what used to be a side-remark within an already dense passage from al-Ġazālī's *Tahāfut al-falāsifa* is now presented as a fully-fledged argument at the very heart of Abū l-Barakāt's reasoning towards the inevitably temporal nature of God's divine priority.[110]

There is one important question we need to ask here before we can proceed: do the creationists really accept the definition of time as the magnitude of motion? At least Abū l-Barakāt is convinced that they do, for he writes in the following chapter on time:

> Those who maintain this, I mean the separation of the Creator's existence from time, are those who maintain that time is the magnitude of motion (*miqdār al-ḥaraka*) and that the Creator is not in motion, so that He is not in time.[111]

---

basis of the possibility of motions prior to the assumed first motion as Abū l-Barakāt offered here in *al-Muʿtabar*; cf. McGinnis, *Avicenna*, 197 f. I am doubtful whether McGinnis' reading can be squared with the passages he is referring to or, ultimately, with Avicenna's actual theory of time, as it relies on a misunderstanding of the relevance of the notion of "possibility" for the definition of time; cf. Lammer, *The Elements of Avicenna's Physics*, 443, esp. fn. 47; cf. also Pines' analysis of a similar argument in "An Arabic Summary of a Lost Work of John Philoponus," 349 f.

109 al-Ġazālī, *Tahāfut al-falāsifa* 1, §97, 37.8–10; cf. §80, 31.8–11.

110 Apparently, al-Ġazālī was drawing on Avicenna's own version of the argument in *al-Ilāhiyyāt* IX.1, §25, 381.1–8 (≈ *al-Naǧāt* IV.2.26, 616.12–617.9 ≈ *al-Mabdaʾ wa-l-maʿād* 34, 46.13–21) cf. Avicenna, *al-Samāʿ al-ṭabīʿī* III.11, §9, 238.15–239.8; cf. also McGinnis, *Avicenna*, 197 f.

111 Abū l-Barakāt al-Baġdādī, *al-Muʿtabar* III.1.8, 41.3 f.; cf. also *al-Muʿtabar* III.1.7, 30.2–4; III.1.9, 48.9–11.

That Abū l-Barakāt's judgment may, indeed, be justified is borne out by the fact that we have already seen al-Šahrastānī saying that time is that which numbers motion (*ʿādd li-l-ḥarakāt*).[112] So, at least people such as al-Šahrastānī accepted Aristotle's definition of time which, after Avicenna, means that he accepts the new Avicennian version of it, and so Abū l-Barakāt is allowed to level his counter-argument against creationists such as al-Šahrastānī, and reject their claim for God's non-temporal priority.

For our assessment of Abū l-Barakāt's overall strategy, it is important to realise that his argument about time preceding the first creative act is not meant to establish the eternity of the world, which is usually the strategy of comparable arguments.[113] Abū l-Barakāt is precisely not arguing that an earlier time requires an earlier motion and an earlier motion requires an earlier body, so that body existed already before the supposed creation of bodies. Instead, he is aiming at demolishing the creationists' appeal to a non-temporal priority as the only proper way to characterise God's precedence over the world. This reading gains support in the way in which he introduces the argument. Above we have seen that he reported that the creationists denied the existence of any duration or time before the creation of the world, in order to evade having to answer potentially embarrassing questions about God's inactivity (*al-taʿṭīl*) in that duration despite His uncontested perfection, benevolence, power, and unity.[114] It is precisely because God's priority over the world was not temporal, the creationists argued, that these questions do not apply in the first place. Abū l-Barakāt's argument from time, now, is the eternalists' answer to this claim; it is their answer to the concept of God's non-temporal priority – and this means, it is their rejection of al-Šahrastānī's sixth kind of priority, viz., the non-temporal priority by existence only. It is in this regard also worth noting that the current argument, which Abū l-Barakāt puts forth on behalf of the eternalists, does not need to establish an *infinite* time prior to the world's assumed temporal creation; already a finite time is enough to bring up the main objection against temporal creation on the basis of God's idleness despite His perfect generosity and power. In other words, this revised argument from time is a serious problem for someone who, like al-Šahrastānī, vehemently criticised the existence of a spatially and temporally infinite world, while explicitly allowing for a larger spatially and temporally *finite* world.[115]

Indeed, the argument about God's idleness despite His benevolence and power is and remains the major rationale behind the eternalists' rejection of temporal

112 al-Šahrastānī, *al-Muṣāraʿa* 5, 108.1f.; *Nihāyat al-aqdām* 1, 28.6; q.v. also above, 255.

113 q.v. above, 245f.

114 cf. Abū l-Barakāt al-Baġdādī, *al-Muʿtabar* III.1.7, 30.2–4.

115 q.v. above, 248.

creation, to which Abū l-Barakāt refers again and again. Towards the end of chapter seven, for example, he, first, ridicules – and insults – the creationists with the following words:

> [The eternalists] say to them [sc. the creationists] that these assertions and their likes are deliberately deceptive and a burden for anyone who hears them by the abundance of words and the scarcity of deceptive meaning, which the minds of those investigating [them] grow dull from examining them and responding to them.[116]

Thereupon, he continues with clarifying what it is the creationists do not, cannot, or do not want to understand – and this is the basic and simple truth that a complete cause cannot be delayed unless there is some impediment:

> In the case of necessitating causes (*al-asbāb al-mūǧiba*), regardless of whether they are by will or not by will, the effect is not [temporally] posterior to the cause, so long as the causality of [cause] was complete; and [the causality] does not arise anew after not having been from the cause [itself], for otherwise it would have been such as to not be in a state of deficiency with regard to the causality for the expected thing, which originates upon generation and is annexed to the necessitating cause. So, the acts of necessitating something and of bringing something into existence are complete from [the cause] (*ʿanhu*), regardless of whether it is a will in the willer, a power or nature in that which has a nature, or a removal of impediments which would have impeded and blocked the bringing into existence of that which is to be originated. The necessitating causes are, for example, knowledge after ignorance, power after capacity, strength after weakness or [the presence of a] will after the [absence] of a will or resolve … So, if there is none of all these things, then the effect is together with its cause (*al-maʿlūl maʿa ʿillatihi wa-l-musabbab maʿa sababihi*), not being posterior to it in time, and that which is brought into existence is together with that which brings it into existence (*al-mūǧad maʿa mūǧidihi*) – it is not possible to be other than this.[117]

Thus, God, who is assumed to have created the world in a specific moment and who already existed prior to the world's creation in a temporal realm, as Abū l-Barakāt's argument has shown, can only have postponed the creation, if there were some impediment, lack of will, incapacity, weakness or deficiency of resolution. None of these could be assumed to apply to God, because He is perfect, omnipotent, and all alone; there is nothing which could impede Him in His activity just as there is nothing that could remove any impediment. If God has created the world – and there is no doubt about this – then He must always have been creating, because He has always been a cause that always has been perfect and complete.

What is remarkable about this passage is that Abū l-Barakāt explicitly refuses to differentiate between the will and any other kind of cause. The will works just

116 Abū l-Barakāt al-Baġdādī, *al-Muʿtabar* III.1.7, 34.12f.
117 Abū l-Barakāt al-Baġdādī, *al-Muʿtabar* III.1.7, 35.17–35.2.

like a nature does or any power would do: it brings about its effect as soon as it is fully realised or requires something to remove the impediment if it is not. The will, human and divine alike, is not an exception among causal principles but is just like any other.[118] As a consequence, there is no distinction between bringing something into existence (*īǧād*) and necessitating the existence of something (*īǧāb*) for Abū l-Barakāt; he treats both along the same lines, thus collapsing the distinction on which the creationists' – and al-Šahrastānī's – account relied. The world must be conceived as the eternal and necessary effect of God's divinity.

6. From Eternity to Creation and Back Again

So far, we have seen how Abū l-Barakāt's eternalists present their central argument against origination on the basis of the conception of time inherent in the creationists' own position. They need to affirm time as the magnitude of motion, if they want to argue for God's non-temporal priority. God stands outside of time only if time is itself created as an intrinsic feature of created things.

Abū l-Barakāt's discussion, then, has so far, indeed, been dialectical, as Griffel remarked, inasmuch as it described a debate between the creationists and the eternalists. Nowhere did Abū l-Barakāt signal his own personal preference for any of the two positions, apart from the occasional verbal assault on the immeasurable stupidity and incompetence of the creationists. At the end of chapter seven, though, he states that an investigation of time is in order, if we want to settle the present discussion fully:

> Since the verifying statement on this question about the two different positions requires a verifying acquaintance of time and what already has previously been mentioned about time in the sections on natural philosophy is perhaps insufficient in this place, it is required to return to our statement about it.[119]

While this is not the place to investigate Abū l-Barakāt's temporal theory in full, the central idea of his account as it is set out in the metaphysical section of *al-Muʿtabar* is that time is not the magnitude of motion as the preceding philosophical tradition had it and as it was accepted even by the theologians in their desperate attempt to save their troubled understanding of the temporal creation of the world. Instead, time is the magnitude of *existence*.[120]

---

118 cf. the creationists' stance outlined by Abū l-Barakāt al-Baġdādī in *al-Muʿtabar* III.1.9, 43.21–44.12 and the response of his eternalists at 47.8–48.14, discussed in what follows.

119 Abū l-Barakāt al-Baġdādī, *al-Muʿtabar* III.1.7, 35.10–12.

120 For earlier studies on Abū l-Barakāt's account of time, cf. Pines, "Nouvelles etudes"; Dag, *The Philosophy of Abū 'l-Barakāt al-Baghdādī.*

On the basis of an interesting argument that apparently imitates the way in which Avicenna began his own discussion of time – and which itself was based on materials from the tradition of reading chapter VI.2 of Aristotle's *Physics* – Abū l-Barakāt emphasises that time must also be the magnitude of rest. Rest, however, is the absence of motion, so the account of time is incomplete if it were only the magnitude of motion and would, as such, not include the time of rest. So, he proposes to go deeper and to root time in the most fundamental concept of the universe, viz., existence:

> Thus, time and what is intellectually grasped by it are prior in existence and in being intellectually grasped than anything which is known through it and with it. What is intellectually grasped of time is almost equivalent (*yuqāribu*) to that which is intellectually grasped of existence and is associated with it in conceptualisation … If it were said that time is the magnitude of existence (*miqdār al-wuǧūd*), then it would be more appropriate than saying that it is the magnitude of motion, for it measures rest, too, and that which rests and that which is in motion both share in existence.[121]

Time, then, is the magnitude of existence, as is also reaffirmed later on in the chapter.[122] Yet, this is not all. If the existence in question, as Abū l-Barakāt's focus on things in motion and things at rest may suggest, were the existence of the created beings of the cosmos, then his account of time would not seem to provide anything the creationists' account did not already provide. Time would belong to the created world and before the world, there would not have been time. It is clear, however, that this is neither what Abū l-Barakāt means nor what his argument requires. He addresses this worry explicitly:

> How is it said that before the origination of the world there was not time? This is among those things which the mindful people (*al-aḏhān*) do not accept. Investigation makes it necessary that it is not eliminated unless through the elimination of existence, but existence does not come-to-be non-existent just as it does not come-to-be existent … The mindful people do not conceptualise existence which does not have duration and time, be that the existence of the Creator or the existence of something created.[123]

With this, Abū l-Barakāt makes it manifest again that prior to the assumed temporal creation of the world, time necessarily and already has been existent. If you are a creationist, then you have to admit that there has been time, because as a creationist you accept the Aristotelian-Avicennian definition of time, so that any possible motion entails the existence of time; and if you are Abū l-Barakāt, your account of time is associated with the notion of existence, and since God is always existent, there always has been existence, and so there always has been time, too. In order to eliminate time, one would have to eliminate existence, and that is: one

121 Abū l-Barakāt al-Baġdādī, *al-Muʿtabar* III.1.8, 39.9–18.
122 cf. Abū l-Barakāt al-Baġdādī, *al-Muʿtabar* III.1.8, 40.11–13.
123 Abū l-Barakāt al-Baġdādī, *al-Muʿtabar* III.1.8, 40.15–41.1.

would have to get rid of God – which is neither possible nor in the interest of all involved.

Therefore, time itself is inevitably eternal. As a consequence, Abū l-Barakāt disregards the often-established distinction between a non-temporal eternity (describing God's existence) and a temporal time (as belonging to the created cosmos), because it turns out that, after all, "His existence *is* Eternity" (*bal wuǧūduhu huwa l-dahr wa-l-sarmad*).[124] This also means that God as a deity is not at all transcendent, as al-Šahrastānī has it, but is part of this world, because He is part of existence.

This concludes the "excursus" on time, which we find interspersed between the two chapters devoted the question about creation and eternity. However, it emerges that this chapter is not really an excursus at all. As already noted above, the chapter on time is at the heart of Abū l-Barakāt's discussion of creation and eternity: first, because it ultimately convinces the creationists that they have to let go of their idea of God's non-temporal priority. This becomes clear when Abū l-Barakāt, shortly after having resumed the investigation of creation in chapter III.1.9, lets the creationists admit their defeat by situating God *within* a temporal eternity, even though they still argue that God, first, existed without anything else and, then, at one moment in time started to create the world.[125] Secondly, the interspersed chapter on time clearly offers Abū l-Barakāt's personal doctrine of time and, thus, also introduces a personal commitment into an otherwise rather dialectical discussion. In a way, one could say that it effectively *ends* the dialectic of his investigation, because it now proceeds on the basis of his own novel account of time. This means that although Abū l-Barakāt continues with providing arguments on behalf of the "creationists" and the "eternalists," the subsequent discussion presupposes an integral aspect of Abū l-Barakāt's own philosophy, thus suggesting that he identifies with the eternalists, who employ his definition of time as the magnitude of existence.

This brings us to what shall be the final question that needs to be addressed in my analysis here. Since the eternalists, including Abū l-Barakāt himself, are still trying to undermine the creationists' claim for temporal creation of the world, it needs to be asked why it is not satisfactory to assume that God created the world temporally at one moment in time and that He preceded this first moment temporally? The answer is that this would lead us back to the already mentioned and well-known question that the creationists cannot explain why God has

124 Abū l-Barakāt al-Baġdādī, *al-Muʿtabar* III.1.8, 41.6f., emphasis added. For the distinction between *sarmad*, *dahr*, and *zamān* in Arabic philosophy in light of the Greek Neoplatonic distinction between αἰών, ἀΐδιος, and χρόνος and the Aristotelian distinction between eternally unmoved, eternally moved, and occasionally moved beings, cf. Lammer, "Time and Mind-Dependence in Sayf al-Dīn al-Āmidī's *Abkār al-afkār*."

125 cf. Abū l-Barakāt al-Baġdādī, *al-Muʿtabar* III.1.9, 41.22–42.2.

chosen *this* very moment as the first moment of creation as opposed to any other, in particular any *earlier*, moment.[126] To this, the creationists reply that the Divine eternal will is simply capable of decreeing a moment even when all moments are entirely alike and indiscernible.[127] The eternalists, of course, deny this and argue that not even God is able to make a distinction (*tamyīz*) before He actually created all distinctions.[128] So it is with this that we reach another famous impasse: the creationists insist that God's will can simply pick a moment and the eternalists deny this. Indeed, Abū l-Barakāt's eternalists are strong in their denial. They complain that the creationists use their theory of God's divine eternal will as an easy way out to "end the discussion" (*intahā kalāmuhu*).[129] The answer to this, however, has already been given: it is not possible for God to discern between indiscernibles nor is it possible for an effect to be delayed after its cause when that cause is complete. Since "the mindful people, through their natural capacity, do not doubt the eternity of time and place" (*al-aḏhān bi-fiṭratihā lā tašukku qidam al-zamān wa-l-makān*) and since God cannot simply pick one moment as the first moment of creation over another, God must have been creating eternally.[130]

This is almost the end of Abū l-Barakāt's discussion. What follows after this is the seemingly non-committal statement, already quoted above, that there is nothing to add and that "he who grasps intellectually what he has heard, contemplates it in his mind, and follows up on it with his reflection, he will have heard the argument (*al-ḥuǧǧa*) and known the destination" (*al-maḥaǧǧa*).[131] – So, what was the argument which we have heard and what is the destination which we have come to know? Abū l-Barakāt has offered an intense battle between creationists and eternalists, in which the latter very clearly exposed the errors of the former, in particular by unmasking the idea of a non-temporal priority as misguided, because the creationists got caught up in their own espoused account of time. Thereupon, Abū l-Barakāt offers a more correct theory of time which effectively reaffirms the eternalists' claim that God's assumed priority over the world is inevitably temporal. The creationists eventually realise their error and now try to defend God's temporal priority, but Abū l-Barakāt shows how this leads to acknowledging their incapacity to account for God's decision about the first moment of creation. In the end, it is clear that it is the creationists who are at a loss for a convincing solution and who have repeatedly been insulted, first, for their foolish idea of a non-temporal priority and, then, for their stubborn insistence on the supposedly special nature of the divine will. If we take Abū l-

126 cf. Abū l-Barakāt al-Baġdādī, *al-Muʿtabar* III.1.9, 43.16–20.
127 cf. Abū l-Barakāt al-Baġdādī, *al-Muʿtabar* III.1.9, 43.21–44.12
128 cf. Abū l-Barakāt al-Baġdādī, *al-Muʿtabar* III.1.9, 44.13–20, 47.8–48.7.
129 Abū l-Barakāt al-Baġdādī, *al-Muʿtabar* III.1.9, 48.8.
130 Abū l-Barakāt al-Baġdādī, *al-Muʿtabar* III.1.9, 48.9.
131 Abū l-Barakāt al-Baġdādī, *al-Muʿtabar* III.1.9, 48.17f.

Barakāt's word seriously that whoever has heard the discussion and understood the arguments will also have understood his position, it is, indeed, very clear where he himself ought to be positioned: Abū l-Barakāt is an eternalist – and a very strict one at that.

As could be seen, the final nail in the creationists' coffin was Abū l-Barakāt's own account of time. There is, however, a potential issue here. His last argument against the creationists was that God would be incapable of selecting a moment among indiscernibles. The creationists, however, could now accept his argument that God's divine priority is temporal (either, because of accepting Abū l-Barakāt's account of time or keeping to their Aristotelian-Avicennian account) and argue further that time itself is intrinsically structured by what is before and what is after, so that temporal moments are distinct and successively ordered one after another even in the absence of created bodies and motions.[132] On this basis, they could bring up the well-known idea of God's eternal will: God always wanted to create the world at one specific and discriminate moment, and once that moment became present, He initiated His creative act. This is a serious challenge for Abū l-Barakāt, especially because the idea of God's eternal will was a well-known and often employed argument.[133]

Of course, Abū l-Barakāt could easily avoid this consequence by denying that time is intrinsically structured by what is before and after, i. e., by saying that time is not essentially successive – but is it really advisable or in the interest of Abū l-Barakāt to do so? The advantage of the Aristotelian and the Avicennian accounts of time was to explain the intuitive experience of time progressing by making time an accident of the essentially progressing nature of motion. If Abū l-Barakāt denies any such temporal order, he loses a very intuitive aspect of our human experience of time, which might actually impoverish his entire position and put the onus on *him* to explain why time should be static. Alternatively, if he agrees that time, despite the fact that it is not related to motion, is internally structured, one could question his final argument and claim that God, then, has no problem in selecting one moment, because the moments are by themselves discernible.

Although Abū l-Barakāt neither raises this issue nor provides an answer, there is a simple way for him to escape his imminent – and, given the course of his discussion in *al-Muʿtabar*, also rather surprising – defeat in the after time of the match. This way of resolving the issue leads back to what has all along been his favourite argument for the eternity of the world – an argument which was always

132 That time being the magnitude of motion is essentially divisible into before and after is perhaps the most important aspect of Avicenna's temporal theory; cf. Avicenna, *al-Samāʿ al-ṭabīʿī* II.11, §5, 157.18–158.1; for a detailed discussion of this aspect, cf. Lammer, *The Elements of Avicenna's Physics*, esp. 469–477.

133 cf. Abū l-Barakāt al-Baġdādī, *al-Muʿtabar* III.1.7, 33.21–24 as well as the famous passage in al-Ġazālī, *Tahāfut al-falāsifa* 1, §13, 15.1–6.

present in the chapters discussed here: the argument that God is perfect, benevolent, generous, and powerful. Perhaps Abū l-Barakāt would even admit that on his account of time God *could* simply choose a later moment over an earlier one, but He *would* not, because this would make Him less generous and, thus, less perfect. Since more is better, more existence displays more generosity. If we recall, it was precisely the fear of God's potential lack in generosity, power, and perfection which led the creationists to adopting a non-temporal priority. Now, since they have admitted that God is inevitably temporally prior, if an origination is assumed, God is again in danger of becoming less perfect as long as He remains idle and abstains from bestowing His gift of existence to His creatures. So, although Abū l-Barakāt may have to admit that the issue about God's choosing a moment could be answered by taking recourse to the intrinsically successive nature of time together with God's eternal will, it would invite the earlier issue about God's generosity and perfection. Consequently, then, a generous God must create eternally, and this is Abū l-Barakāt's firm eternalist position.

Conclusion: Creation or Emanation

It was the intention of this article not only to investigate two discussions of creation and eternity from the sixth/twelfth century but also to provide a critical examination of the thought of two original thinkers. Both al-Šahrastānī and Abū l-Barakāt display their thorough familiarity with the philosophical materials of their own time as well as their capacity to work with earlier opinions and established theories with ease and self-confidence. That their theories – despite being poles apart – originated in the same intellectual milieu is apparent from the fact that both addressed the same questions, dealt with the same issues, and passed their judgement on the same conceptions. What emerges from the investigation of such strikingly different, though at the same time surprisingly similar, discussions is an understanding of the state of the scientific engagement with the crucial topic of the world's creation in this century: it is the nature of God's divine priority over the world which was considered to be at the heart of the issue; it is the contraposition of bringing into existence (*īǧād*) and necessitating (*īǧāb*) which defines the two opposing alternatives; it is the nature of the will as well as its ability to discern, the issue of the infinite, and the concept of time which map out the territory; finally, it is to all these features that al-Šahrastānī and Abū l-Barakāt offer insightful ideas and novel observations, whose reception in the subsequent centuries has yet to be determined.[134]

134 For some related aspects in the discussion of eternity and origination in the subsequent

One final remark needs to be made: although we have now come to an understanding of al-Šahrastānī's and Abū l-Barakāt's positions on the question of *when* the world came into being, we have learned almost nothing of their understandings of *how* it did. The reason for this is a common attitude within the post-Avicennian intellectual milieu to separate both issues from one another. Thus, regardless of whether or not one agrees with Avicenna on the world's eternity, one can still criticise him on the theory of emanation by either rejecting it in its entirety or questioning various details, in particular the role of the celestial intellects. It is precisely this further question regarding the *modus* of creation to which subsequent thinkers – including al-Šahrastānī and Abū l-Barakāt – offer a large number of different and complex answers. This, too, will have to be the subject of future research, which will demonstrate, again, the originality of the philosophical and intellectual milieu in the centuries after Avicenna.

Bibliography

ʿAbd al-Ǧabbār, Abū l-Ḥasan, *al-Muġnī fī abwāb al-tawḥīd wa-l-ʿadl.* Edited by Muḥammad Muṣṭafā al-Ḥilmī. 16 volumes. Cairo: al-Muʾassasa al-Miṣriyya al-ʿĀmma li-l-Taʾlīf wa-l-Anbāʾ wa-l-Našr, 1958–1965.

Adamson, Peter, and Andreas Lammer, "Fakhr al-Dīn al-Rāzī's Platonist Account of the Essence of Time." In: *Philosophical Theology in Medieval Islam: The Later Ashʿarite Tradition.* Edited by Ayman Shihadeh and Jan Thiele. Islamicate Intellectual History. Studies and Texts in the Late Medieval and Early Modern Periods. Leiden and Boston: Brill, forthcoming.

al-Anṣārī, Abū l-Qāsim Salmān ibn Nāṣir, *Ġunya fī ʿilm al-kalām.* Edited, with an introduction, by Muṣṭafā Ḥasanayn ʿAbd al-Hādī. 2 volumes. Cairo: Dār al-Salām, 2010.

Aristotle, *Categoriae et Liber de interpretatione.* Edited by Lorenzo Minio-Paluello. Scriptorum classicorum bibliotheca oxoniensis. Oxford: Clarendon Press, 1949.

–, *De caelo.* Edited, with an introduction, by Donald J. Allan. Oxford Classical Texts. Oxford: Clarendon Press, 1936.

–, *Metaphysics.* Edited and commented, with an introduction, by William David Ross. 2 volumes. Oxford: Clarendon Press, 1924.

–, *al-Naṣṣ al-kāmil li-manṭiq Arisṭū.* Edited, with an introduction, by Farīd Ǧabr. 2 volumes. Beirut: Dār al-Fikr al-Lubnānī, 1999.

–, *Physics.* Edited and commented, with an introduction, by William David Ross. Oxford: Clarendon Press, 1936.

Avicenna, *al-Mabdaʾ wa-l-maʿād.* Edited by ʿAbd Allāh Nūrānī. Selsele-ye Dāneš-e Īrānī 36. Tehran: Institute of Islamic Studies, McGill University, Tehran Branch, 1984.

century, cf. Lammer, "Eternity and Origination in the Works of Sayf al-Dīn al-Āmidī and Athīr al-Dīn al-Abharī."

–, *al-Nağāt min al-ġaraq fī baḥr al-ḍalālāt.* Edited, with an introduction, by Moḥammad Taqī Dānešpažūh. Tehran: Entešārāt-e Dānešgāh-e Tehrān, 1985.

–, *al-Šifāʾ. al-Manṭiq. al-Muğallad 2: al-Maqūlāt.* Edited by Ǧurǧ Šiḥāta Qanawātī, Maḥmūd Muḥammad al-Ḫuḍayrī, Aḥmad Fuʾād al-Ahwānī, and Saʿīd Zāyid. Cairo: al-Hayʾa al-ʿĀmma li-Šuʾūn al-Maṭābiʿ al-Amīriyya, 1959.

–, *al-Šifāʾ. al-Ilāhiyyāt.* Edited by Ǧurǧ Šiḥāta Qanawātī, Saʿīd Zāyid, Muḥammad Yūsuf Mūsā, and Sulaymān Dunyā. 2 volumes. Cairo: al-Hayʾa al-ʿĀmma li-Šuʾūn al-Maṭābiʿ al-Amīriyya, 1960.

–, *al-Šifāʾ. al-Ṭabīʿiyyāt. al-Muğallad 1: al-Samāʿ al-ṭabīʿī.* Edited by Saʿīd Zāyid. Cairo: al-Hayʾa al-Miṣriyya al-ʿĀmma li-l-Kitāb, 1983.

–, *Lettre au vizir Abū Saʿd.* Edited, translated, and annotated, with an introduction, by Yahya Michot. Sagesses musulmanes 4. Beirut: Les Éditions al-Bouraq, 2000.

–, *The Metaphysics of* The Healing. *A Parallel English-Arabic Text.* Edited, translated, and annotated, with an introduction, by Michael E. Marmura. Islamic Translation Series. Provo: Brigham Young University Press, 2005.

–, *The Physics of* The Healing. *A Parallel English-Arabic Text.* Edited, translated, and annotated, with an introduction, by Jon McGinnis. Islamic Translation Series. Provo: Brigham Young University Press, 2009.

Ceylan, Yasin, *Theology and tafsīr in the Major Works of Fakhr al-Dīn al-Rāzī.* Kuala Lumpur: International Institute of Islamic Thought and Civilization, 1996.

Dag, Mehmet, *The Philosophy of Abū ʾl-Barakāt al-Baghdādī with Special Reference to his Concept of Time.* PhD thesis. Durham University, 1970.

Davidson, Herbert A., *Alfarabi, Avicenna, and Averroes, on Intellect. Their Cosmologies, Theories of the Active Intellect, and Theories of Human Intellect.* New York, Oxford: Oxford University Press, 1992.

al-Ġazālī, Abū Ḥāmid, *The Incoherence of the Philosophers. A Parallel English-Arabic Text.* Edited, translated, and annotated, with an introduction, by Michael E. Marmura. 2nd edition. Islamic Translation Series. Provo: Brigham Young University Press, 2000.

Griffel, Frank, "Between al-Ghazālī and Abū l-Barakāt al-Baghdādī. The Dialectical Turn in the Philosophy of Iraq and Iran During the Sixth/Twelfth Century." In: *In the Age of Averroes. Arabic Philosophy in the Sixth/Twelfth Century.* Edited by Peter Adamson. Warburg Institute Colloquia 16. London and Turin: The Warburg Institute and Nino Aragno Editore, 2011, 45–76.

al-Ǧuwaynī, ʿAbd al-Malik ibn ʿAbd Allāh, *Kitāb al-Iršād ilā qawāṭiʿ al-adilla fī uṣūl al-iʿtiqād.* Translated and annotated, with an introduction, by Muḥammad Yūsuf Mūsā and ʿAlī ʿAbd al-Munʿim ʿAbd al-Ḥamīd. Cairo: Maktabat al-Ḫānǧī, 1950.

al-Ḥillī, ʿAllāmā, *Kašf al-murād fī šarḥ Taǧrīd al-iʿtiqād.* Beirut: Muʾassasat al-Aʿlamī li-l-Maṭbūʿāt, 1988.

Ibn Fūrak, Abū Bakr Muḥammad ibn al-Ḥasan, *Muğarrad maqālāt al-Šayḫ Abī l-Ḥasan al-Ašʿarī.* Edited, with an introduction, by Daniel Gimaret. Buḥūṯ wa-Dirāsāt. Silsila Ǧadīda A. al-Luġa al-ʿArabiyya wa-l-Fikr al-Islāmī. Beirut: Dār al-Mašriq, 1987.

İskenderoglu, Muammer, *Fakhr al-Dīn al-Razī and Thomas Aquinas on the Question of the Eternity of the World.* Islamic Philosophy, Theology and Science. Texts and Studies 48. Leiden, Boston, and Köln: Brill, 2002.

Ibn Kammūna, Saʿd ibn Manṣūr, *al-Kāšif (al-Ǧadīd fī l-ḥikma).* Edited, with an introduction, by Ḥāmed Nāǧī Eṣfahānī. Islamic Philosophy and Theology. Texts and

Studies 8. Tehran Iranian Institute of Philosophy and Institute of Islamic Studies of the Free University of Berlin, 2008.

Lammer, Andreas, "Eternity and Origination in the Works of Sayf al-Dīn al-Āmidī and Athīr al-Dīn al-Abharī. Two Discussions from the Seventh/Thirteenth Century." In: *The Muslim World* 107.3 (2017), 432–481.

–, *The Elements of Avicenna's Physics. Greek Sources and Arabic Innovations.* Scientia Graeco-Arabica 20. Berlin and Boston: Walter de Gruyter, 2018.

–, "Time and Mind-Dependence in Sayf al-Dīn al-Āmidī's *Abkār al-afkār*." In: *The Arabic, Hebrew, and Latin Reception of Avicenna's Physics and Cosmology.* Edited by Dag Nikolaus Hasse, and Amos Bertolacci. Scientia Graeco-Arabica 23. Berlin and Boston: Walter de Gruyter, 2018, 101–161.

Madelung, Wilferd, "Abu'l-Barakāt Baġdādī." In: *Encyclopædia Iranica.* Edited by Ehsan Yarshater. Volume I. London and New York: Routledge & Kegan Paul, 1985, 266–268.

–, "aš-Šahrastānīs Streitschrift gegen Avicenna und ihre Widerlegung durch Naṣīr ad-Dīn aṭ-Ṭūsī." In: *Akten des VII. Kongresses für Arabistik und Islamwissenschaft.* Edited by Albert Dietrich. Abhandlungen der Akademie der Wissenschaften in Göttingen. Philologisch-historische Klasse. Dritte Folge 98. Göttingen: Vandenhoeck & Ruprecht, 1976, 250–259.

Mayer, Toby, "The Absurdities of Infinite Time. Shahrastānī's Critique of Ibn Sīnā and Ṭūsī's Defence." In: *Medieval Arabic Thought. Essays in Honour of Fritz Zimmermann.* Edited by Rotraud Hansberger, M. Afifi al-Akiti, and Charles Burnett. Warburg Institute Studies and Texts 4. London and Turin: The Warburg Institute and Nino Aragno Editore, 2012, 103–134.

McGinnis, Jon, *Avicenna.* Great Medieval Thinkers. New York: Oxford University Press, 2010.

–, "Avicennan Infinity. A Select History of the Infinite through Avicenna." In: *Documenti e studi sulla tradizione filosofica medievale* 21 (2010), 199–222.

Monnot, Guy, "al-Shahrastānī, Abū 'l-Fatḥ Muḥammad." In: *The Encyclopaedia of Islam. New Edition.* Volume 9. Leiden: E. J. Brill, 1997, 214–216.

Philoponus, John, *De aeternitate mundi contra Proclum.* Edited by Hugo Rabe. Leipzig: Teubner, 1899.

Pines, Shlomo, "Abu 'l-Barakāt Hibat Allāh b. Malkā al-Baghdādī al-Baladī." In: *The Encyclopaedia of Islam. New Edition.* Volume 1. Leiden: E. J. Brill, 1960, 111–113.

–, "An Arabic Summary of a Lost Work of John Philoponus." In: Israel Oriental Studies 2 (1972).

–, "Etudes sur Aḥwad al-Zamān Abu'l-Barakāt al-Baghdādī. Physics and Metaphysics." In: *Studies in Abu'l-Barakāt al-Baghdādī. Physics and Metaphysics.* The Collected Works of Shlomo Pines. Volume 1. Jerusalem: The Magnes Press, 1979, 1–95.

–, "Nouvelles etudes sur Aḥwad al-Zamān Abu'l-Barakāt al-Baghdādī. Physics and Metaphysics." In: *Studies in Abu'l-Barakāt al-Baghdādī. Physics and Metaphysics.* The Collected Works of Shlomo Pines. Volume 1. Jerusalem: The Magnes Press, 1979, 96–173.

Rahman, Fazlur, "The Eternity of the World and the Heavenly Bodies in Post-Avicennian Philosophy." In: *Essays on Islamic Philosophy and Science.* Edited by George F. Hourani. Studies in Islamic Philosophy and Science. Albany: State University of New York Press, 1975, 222–237.

al-Rāzī, Faḫr al-Dīn, *al-Arbaʿīn fī uṣūl al-dīn.* Edited, with an introduction, by Aḥmad Ḥiǧāzī al-Saqqā. 2 volumes. Min turāṯ al-Rāzī 11. Cairo: Maktabat al-Kulliyyāt al-Azhariyya, 1986.
–, *al-Maṭālib al-ʿāliya min al-ʿilm al-ilāhī.* Edited by Aḥmad Ḥiǧāzī al-Saqqā. 9 volumes. Beirut: Dār al-Kitāb al-ʿArabī, 1987.
Rescher, Nicholas, "Choice without Preference. A Study of the History and of the Logic of the Problem of 'Buridan's Ass'." In: *Kant-Studien. Philosophische Zeitschrift* 51.1–4 (1959/1960), 142–175.
al-Šahrastānī, Muḥammad ibn ʿAbd al-Karīm, *Majlis. Discours sur l'Ordre et la cre´ation (Maǧles-e maktūb-e Šahrastānī monʿaqed dar Ḫwārazm).* Translated and annotated, with an introduction, by Diane Steigerwald. Edited by Moḥammad Reḍā Ǧalālī Nāʾīnī. Saint-Nicolas: Les Presses de l'Universite´ Laval, 1998.
–, *Struggling with the Philosopher. A Refutation of Avicenna's Metaphysics.* Kitāb al-Muṣāraʿa. Edited and translated, with an introduction, by Wilferd Madelung and Toby Mayer. Ismaili Texts and Translations Series 2. London and New York: I.B.Tauris, 2001.
–, *The Summa philosophiae of al-Shahrastānī. Kitāb Nihāyatu 'l-iqdām fī ʿilmi 'l-kalām.* Edited, translated, and annotated, with an introduction, by Alfred Guillaume. 1934th edition. London: Oxford University Press.
al-Sāwī, ʿUmar ibn Sahlān, *al-Baṣāʾir al-naṣīriyya fī ʿilm al-manṭiq.* Edited and annotated, with an introduction, by Rafīq al-ʿAǧam. Silsilat ʿIlm al-Manṭiq. Beirut: Dār al-Fikr al-Lubnānī, 1993.
Saydabī, Ǧamāl Raǧab, *Abū l-Barakāt al-Baġdādī wa-falsafatuhu l-ilāhiyya.* Dirāsa li-mawqifihi l-naqdī min falsafat Ibn Sīnā. Cairo: Maktabat Wahba, 1996.
Sorabji, Richard, "Infinity and the Creation." In: *Philoponus and the Rejection of Aristotelian Science.* Edited by Richard Sorabji. London: Duckworth, 1987, 164–178.
al-Ṭūsī, Naṣīr al-Dīn, *Resāle andar qesmat-e mawǧodāt.* Translated and annotated by Parviz Morewedge. Edited by Moḥammad Taqī Modarres Raḍawī. In: *The Metaphysics of Ṭūsī.* Islamic Philosophy Translation Series. New York: The Society for the Study of Islamic Philosophy and Science, 1992.
van Ess, Josef, "Das Geburtsjahr des Šahrastānī." In: *Der Islam* 89.1–2 (2012), 111–117.
Wisnovsky, Robert, "One Aspect of the Avicennian Turn in Sunnī Theology." In: *Arabic Sciences and Philosophy* 14 (2004), 65–100.
Zysow, Aron, "Karrāmiyya." In: *The Oxford Handbook of Islamic Theology.* Edited by Sabine Schmidtke. Oxford: Oxford University Press, 2016, 252–262.

Davlat Dadikhuda

Not That Simple: Avicenna, Rāzī, and Ṭūsī on the Incorruptibility of the Human Soul at *Ishārāt* VII.6*

There is no doubt that Avicenna's influence on the post-classical 12th century philosophical tradition was ubiquitous and received in sophisticated and critically diverse ways. One area in which this is especially the case is *ʿilm al-nafs* (the study of the soul) – a discipline the *shaykh al-raʾīs* developed in systematic and novel ways. To get a sense of the critical manner in which 12th century philosophers dealt with the Avicennian heritage in this area, I look here at one particular issue which is the subject of the sixth chapter of the seventh *namaṭ* of the shaykh's *Kitāb al-Ishārāt.* I look at that issue as it was engaged with by the two most important commentators on that work, namely, Fakhr al-Dīn Rāzī (d. 606/1210) and Naṣir al-Dīn Ṭūsī (d. 672/1274).[1] *Ishārāt* VII.6 has to do with the post-mortem subsistence of the human soul; the shaykh will argue there for the following thesis:

No human soul can cease to be

On Avicennian principles, this conclusion is based on two properties of the human soul; first, that it is simple, and two, that it is self-subsistent. Below, section (II), we will consider how exactly these properties function in the argument that is supposed to establish the thesis above.

Fakhr al-Dīn will reject, if not the thesis, than at least the Avicennian argument for it, raising two main difficulties for the shaykh. The first objection has to do with the possibility of the soul's being composed in such a way that only one part of it persists, from which it would then follow that the soul as a whole can cease to

* My thanks to Peter Adamson and Amirhossein Zadyousefi for helpful discussion about the content of this paper.

1 In what follows, I will be using the following editions: Avicenna, *al-Ishārāt wa'l-Tanbihāt*, ed. Mojtabā Zāreʿī, (Qom: 1387). From here on out, I refer to this work as *Ishārāt*, followed by *namaṭ*, chapter, and page numbers); Fakhr al-Dīn Rāzī, *Sharḥ al-Ishārāt*, ed. Najafzāde (Tehrān: 1375, vol. 2–3). From here on out, I refer to this work as *Sharḥ al-Ishārāt*, followed by *namaṭ*, chapter, and page number. Naṣīr al-Dīn Ṭūsī, *Sharḥ al-Ishārāt*, ed. Hasanzāde Amolī (Qom: 1391, vol. 2–3). From here on out, I refer to this work as *Ḥall Mushkilāt*, followed by *namaṭ*, chapter, and page numbers. All translations are mine.

exist. This is an objection to the soul's simplicity property. The second difficulty Rāzī raises is more acute, namely, that VII.6's argument has not shown that the consequent of the following conditional (which we will call BC) is false:

> (BC): if the body can serve as a condition for the soul's possible generation, then it can serve as a condition for its possible corruption

This is an objection to the self-subsistence property of the human soul.[2] Naṣīr al-Dīn, on the other hand, will defend, successfully in my view, VII.6's argument against both objections. A key strategy of the defense will be to draw on premises established in earlier parts of the *Ishārāt*, all the while dialectically refining the shaykh's remarks in the process. In doing this, Ṭūsī's engagement with VII.6 is, on the whole, more holistic and consistent with Avicennian principles than is Rāzī's. But I say 'on the whole' and not 'entirely', because, as we will see, in his response to BC, Ṭūsī's analysis presupposes the truth of a crucial premise the shaykh does not treat anywhere prior to VII.6. That premise concerns the temporal origination (*ḥudūth*) of the human soul.[3]

With that said, let me stop and state how we'll proceed. The discussion that follows will be divided into three sections; the first section (I) will introduce VII.6's argument by clarifying the background which it presupposes (but of which it is independent). Section (II) will be about Rāzī's and Ṭūsī's expositions of *Ishārāt* VII.6. Finally, section (III) will be devoted to their critical engagement with it in its own right.

1. Background

As I said, *Ishārāt* VII.6 is meant to justify the thesis that:

> No human soul can cease to be

Now insofar as corruption designates a kind of change, the question about the soul's corruption amounts to the question of whether it is susceptible to a particular sort of change. But change, on the shaykh's view, must be understood on a hylomorphic model. And thus, the claim about the soul's incorruptibility must be understood against the background of Avicenna's broader philosophy of nature

2 The source of this second objection is probably Sharaf al-Dīn Masʿūdī (d. circa 600/1204). See his *al-Mabāḥith wa'l-Shukūk 'alā'l-Ishārāt* ch. 14, pp. 285–286, ed. A. Shihadeh (Leiden; Boston: Brill 2016). Also, see Ayman Shihadeh, *Doubts on Avicenna: a study and edition of Sharaf al-Dīn al-Masʿūdī's commentary on the Ishārāt* (Leiden; Boston: Brill 2016).

3 For an extensive treatment of this particular issue, see Seyed N. Mousavian and Seyed H.S. Mostafavi 'Avicenna on the Origination of the Human Soul' in *Oxford Studies in Medieval Philosophy* 2017, vol. 5, pp. 41–86.

– specifically, his hylomorphic analysis of change. Accordingly, I here first briefly set out the main elements of that account relevant to the issue at hand, and then turn to the argument at *Ishārāt* VII.6.

1.1. Hylomorphic Change

In the Aristo-Avicennian (A-A) system, hylomorphism is, primarily, a view about the constitution of every day material objects.[4] Secondarily, it is general explanation of the changes that these objects undergo. The view states that the changes, no less than the existence of those material objects, presuppose principles.[5]

The principles involved in the existence of a material object are two: form and matter.[6] Consider for illustrative purposes a white robe. On (A-A), the white robe is a composite in two ways. First, it is a composite of flannel, which is what functions as 'matter' here, and what can be called 'robe-ness', which is what functions as the 'form'. The second way the white robe is a composite of the robe and the (accidental) property of whiteness. The first kind of composition is called substantial, the second is accidental.

The principles involved in the changes material objects undergo are three: the former two, plus privation.[7] Consider again the white robe, which becomes black. The robe is what that undergoes the change, and in that sense functions as the 'matter' of the change. Without it, there would be nothing we could say that changed. The blackness that comes to be, which the robe as matter comes to possess, is the 'form'. This form is what the robe as the matter of the change has a potential for before the change. Without it, there would be nothing we could say that something changed *to*. Finally, with the robe's being white is associated a

4 It states that such objects are complex entities and their complexity, in a fundamental way, consists of principles or factors. For Avicenna's general characterization of his hylomorphic doctrine, see *The Healing; Physics* I.2, ed. and tr. Jon McGinnis (Utah: Brigham Young University Press, 2009). From here on out as *Physics*, followed by book, chapter, paragraph, and page number.

5 *Physics* I.2.3, 14.

6 The formal factor is that which explains why the body is *actually* some way; as such, the form itself is of two types: either substantial or accidental. The former explains why the body is actually a given *kind* of body – like the way being a robe explains why some flannel is a robe; and the latter is that which explains why the robe is modified in some way – e.g., why the robe is white or soft, where whiteness and softness are accidental forms. The material factor, on the other hand, is that which explains why something, e.g., the flannel, is potentially a certain, other type of thing, i.e., a robe.

7 Ibid., I.2.12, 18.

privation of the blackness it will come to be characterized by. Without it, there would be nothing we could say something changed *from.*[8]

The above example is a case of accidental change; for the 'form' involved in it is an accidental form. But if suppose that some flannel, when acted on it some way, comes to be a robe, the same principles of matter, form, and privation apply here too, though the form that comes to be in this case i.e., what we've called 'robeness', is a substantial form.[9] On the shaykh's view, neither type of form, *F*, can exist unless they exist in something else, *s*. In general, then, the following theses about the coming-to-be and passing-away of such forms are true:

1. For a form, *F*, to come to be is for something, *s*, to come to be *F*

And correlatively,

2. For a form, *F*, to cease to be is for something, *s*, to cease to be *F*

Finally, there's the form-matter composite itself, which as noted was either substantial or accidental. The former, in our example, the robe, and the latter 'the white-robe'. Clearly, both types of composites also come to be and passes away. But, in their case, it's not true that they can't exist unless in something else. However, even so, the following theses are still true of them due to their being constituted of (hylomorphic) parts:

3. For something, *s*, to come to be is for something, *F*, to come to be for something else, *M*

And correlatively,

4. For something, *s*, to cease to be is for something, *F*, to cease to be for something else, *M*

Now on the (A-A) account, human beings are material substances, though of a special sort, i.e., they are animate bodies. As *bodies*, they are, like all bodies, hylomorphic composites; as *animate*, they differ from other bodies by the possession of soul, where soul is understood as the principle of the activities char-

8 That is to say, it isn't the whiteness of the robe qua whiteness that's relevant in the explanation of change but qua privation of the incoming blackness; in other words, as long as the robe is white, it lacks (and so there's a privation of) blackness. And it is because it lacks blackness (by actually being white) that it can change so as to acquire blackness.

9 Again, not strictly speaking but for purposes of illustration. Changes involving such substantial forms are called generation (*kawn*) or corruption (*fasād*), depending on the perspective taken, i.e., whether we're considering what *comes to be* or what *ceases to be* as a result of the change. For example, suppose the robe is burnt and ashes result. Qua the coming to be of the ashes, the change is a generation, and qua the ceasing to be of the robe, it is a corruption.

10 Avicenna, *The Healing; Psychology* 1.1, 15, ed. H. Amoli (Tehrān: 1386). Recall that the

acteristic of them qua living. This is why, according to the shaykh, one can truly characterize, in a sense, the soul of living beings as a formal principle.[10]

Given all that, we are then in a better position to understand just what the contention about the soul's incorruptibility at VII.6 amounts to. For human beings, as hylomorphic composites, undeniably undergo various sorts of changes – among others, they come to be (generation) and they pass away (corruption) – so the question is whether the soul in their case is the sort of thing that can be subject to such changes. That is, since, on the basis of the above, we see that Avicenna recognizes two conditions for something to be corruptible – namely, that

(a) it consist of something, *F*, that exists in something else, *M*, or that
(b) it itself exist in something else, *M*

where the first way i. e., (a), is true of composites, and the second way i. e., (b), is true of forms, one may legitimately wonder whether any of these two ways is possibly true of the human soul itself. The question is all the more pressing, as we'll see Fakhr al-Dīn insist when raising his objection BC (section III), since the shaykh is committed to the claim that one of the two ways noted above for something *to come to be* i. e., option (3), is actually true of human souls. So the asymmetry, assuming there is one, demands an explanation.

2. Rāzī's and Ṭūsī's Exposition of *Ishārāt* VII.6

Having set out the background, let us now turn to *Ishārāt* VII.6. In this section, I first (in II.1) clarify, basing myself on the two commentators, the presuppositions of VII.6's argument; then (in II.2), I go on to consider how Rāzī and Ṭūsī explicate VII.6's argument.

2.1.

The shaykh labels *Ishārāt* VII.6 a 'complement' (*takmila*) to the pointers immediately preceding it. According to Fakhr al-Dīn, VII.6 is a 'complement' in that it is supposed to fulfill a purpose that Avicenna had set for himself earlier at VII.1, but from which he had to digress. Rāzī explains:

(substantial) form on the hylomorphic model is that which explains why something is actually a given kind of entity; and what accounts for why something is actually a living being – a giraffe, say – is its soul. So 'form' and 'soul' are extensionally equivalent in material animate entities.

He only named this chapter 'a complement to these pointers' because his goal in the first pointer of this *namaṭ* was to show the soul's subsistence. Consequently, for the sake of that goal, there was a need to show its independence from the body. And so after he finished showing that in the earlier chapters, he wished in this chapter to return to that goal of proving the soul's subsistence. Undoubtedly, then, this chapter is like a complement to what has passed.[11]

Ṭūsī is in agreement with Rāzī that in the argument here at VII.6, the shaykh is tying up loose strings in the earlier VII.1 by

[...] coming back to perfecting the argument for [the soul's] subsistence on the basis of its essential perfections after the separation of the body.[12]

So, as far as how the two commentators see things, the line of thought stretching between VII.1 and VII.6 goes something like this: first, at VII.1, the shaykh sets out to prove that the human soul subsists post-mortem. But to do this, he needs to show first why it has an existence of its own, not dependent on the body's existence (we'll see why below). So throughout VII.2–5, he offers arguments for the soul's independence from the body in terms of an activity or perfection that it has per se or of itself. Finally, on the basis of the considerations adduced in VII.2–5, the shaykh returns, in VII.6, to the goal of VII.1 and now supplements (*takmila*) it with an argument to fully secure it.

Let us now look at this argument. As I said, the claim is to establish is:

No human soul can cease to be

However, this is ambiguous between:

I) No human soul can cease to be after the death the body, and
II) No human soul can cease to be at all (*muṭlaqan*)

So is VII.6 supposed to show (I) or (II)? The shaykh for his part recognizes the difference the two claims.[13] I submit that VII.6 is meant to establish the stronger (II), the reason being that it entails I (but not vice versa). So if claim II is established, then I is also established.

Here then is the gist of *Ishārāt* VII.6's argument for II:

[T1] A complement (*takmila*) to these pointers: [1.1] Know from this (*min hādhā*) that it belongs to the intellecting substance in us to cognize of itself (*bi-dhātih*). [1.2] Now

11 Rāzī, *Sharḥ al-Ishārāt* VII.6, 524.
12 Ṭūsī, *Ḥall Mushkilāt* VII.6, 882.
13 When treating the same issue in his longer works e.g., *The Healing*; *Psychology* V.4, he offers two distinct arguments for these two distinct theses. The distinction between (I) and (II) goes back to Plato, at *Phaedo* 86d–88b (in *Plato: Complete Works*, ed. J.M. Cooper, Ind. Hackett: 1997).

> because it is an *aṣl*, it will not be a composite of a potentiality receptive to corruption conjoined (*muqārana*) to a potentiality for subsisting.[14]

And if the human soul is not receptive to corruption, the argument implies, then this is just to say it cannot cease to be. Therefore, the human soul is incorruptible.

The argument, given its conciseness, presupposes a lot. The dependence on earlier parts of the *Ishārāt* is flagged at [1.1]; both Rāzī and Ṭūsī take the referent of the *min hāḏā* ('from this') clause to be the considerations the shaykh had just raised throughout *Ishārāt* VII.2–5 for the soul's intellectual activity being independent of material instruments. Both commentators take it that the claim in [1.1], i.e., that the soul's intellectual activity is an activity it has per se or 'of itself' (*bi-dhātih*), is a conclusion that follows from those considerations.[15]

Then in [1.2] the shaykh calls the soul an '*aṣl*'. This term is crucial in that it serves as the argument's middle term (as we'll see more clearly in a second), so let us unpack what it means. Our commentators explain that for the human soul to be an *aṣl* is for it to have two properties:

i) simplicity (*basāṭa*)

by which is meant an absence of hylomorphic composition, and

ii) self-subsistence (*qiyām bi-nafsih*)

by which is meant non-inherence in something else, where inherence is a type of existential dependence.[16] From here on out, let 'Ṣ' stand for the property of being an *aṣl*, understood as the conjunction of properties (i)-(ii).

There's an immediate relation between the claim in [1.1] and [1.2]'s claim that the soul is Ṣ. As I understand the shaykh, the relation between the two for him is one of entailment; that is, having an activity independent of matter (= to cognize *bi-dhātih*) entails being Ṣ in the above sense. The entailment relation between having an independent activity and being Ṣ is in turn secured by the independence of activity being a consequence of an independent existence for the thing that has the activity. So the inferential relations should be conceived as follows:

independent activity → independent being → Ṣ

14 Avicenna, *Ishārāt* VII.6, 324. The division of the text by numbers in square brackets is my own. In all his major works, Avicenna offers substantially the same argument. The most detailed version is in *The Healing; Psychology* V.4, 295–297. For some of the other versions, see e.g., *Kitāb al-Najāt*; *Physics* VI.9, 383–386, ed. Dānishpazhuh (Tehrān: 1387), and *Al-Mabda' wa'l-Ma'ād* ch.8, 143–144, ed. A. Nūrānī (Tehrān: 1363).

15 Rāzī, *Sharḥ al-Ishārāt* VII.6, 524; Ṭūsī, *Ḥall Mushkilāt* VII.6, 882.

16 *Sharḥ al-Ishārāt* VII.6, 528; *Ḥall Mushkilāt* VII.6, 882.

And to have an independent existence is just to *not* exist in something else i.e., as in an underlying substrate. The thought, then, is: if *x* has an activity of its own i.e., independent from matter, *x* is existentially independent of matter; and if *x* is independent of matter in being, then *x* is simple and self-subsistent i.e., an Ṣ. That the soul satisfies being an Ṣ was, again, the burden of *Ishārāt* VII.2–5 to demonstrate, so we take it as established at VII.6.

2.2.

Granted the above, the shaykh's argument at T1 (let us call it MA from now on) can then more precisely be captured in the following syllogism – First Figure, second mood:

> Every human soul is Ṣ
> Nothing that is Ṣ can cease to be
> Therefore, no human soul can cease to be

MA's universal affirmative (*mawjiba kulliyya*) minor premise, as noted, is derived from *Ishārāt* VII.2–5. And its universal negative (*sāliba kulliyya*) major, or a premise equivalent to it, is presupposed in what is specifically said at [1.2], the claim there being something like the following conditional:

> If the soul is Ṣ, then it cannot cease to be

And the truth of this premise presupposes the truth of:

> Nothing that is Ṣ can cease to be

Which is just the universal negative major of MA's syllogism.

Having shown at T1 that the human soul can't fail to cease to be, the shaykh then regiments the argument. He does this in two ways; first, by claiming (in [1.3] below) that even if we assume, for the sake of argument, that MA's universal affirmative minor is false, its conclusion would still go through. He writes:

> [1.3] If, though, it [i.e., the human soul] is taken not as an [Ṣ], but rather as if a composite of something like matter and something like form, we apply the argument to the [Ṣ] among [the composite soul's] parts.[17]

Rāzī's first objection will be to this move at [1.3]. Whether the argument here goes through will depend on certain other premises of course – premises that Ṭūsī will supply. Below in section III, we shall consider in detail both the Rāzian objection to [1.3] and the Ṭūsian response.

17 Avicenna, *Ishārāt* VII.6, 324

The second way the shaykh regiments T1's MA argument is by resolving a dialectical objection which assumes that simplicity is a sufficient condition for incorruptibility. He writes:

> [1.4] With accidents, their existence is in their subjects, and so their potential for corruption and generation is in their subjects, though there's no composition in them.[18]

The worry addressed here, as Ṭūsī notes, is that since there are things that are simple – in the sense of not being hylomorphic composites – but are nevertheless subject to corruption, e.g., accidental and substantial forms themselves – why can't, one my ask, the soul be like that?[19] The answer to this should by now be clear; namely, the truth of the universal negative major above. For that premise states that incorruptibility requires *both* simplicity and self-subsistence; but though accidental and substantial forms are simple in the required way, they can't exist, as explained above in section I, without existing in something else.

Finally, in [1.5] we get the upshot of the argumentation in the preceding [1.2–4]:

> [1.5] And if that's the case, then things like this [i.e., like the human soul] are not in themselves receptive to corruption after their necessitation by their causes and their subsistence through them.

Let us now go back to VII.6's MA argument and consider how our two commentators parse it. MA stated:

> Every human soul is Ṣ
> Nothing that is Ṣ can cease to be
> Therefore, no human soul can cease to be

Recall that being an Ṣ means being both (i) simple and (ii) self-subsistent. Now clearly, MA's major premise i.e.

> Nothing that is Ṣ can cease to be

is the crucial one. How does the shaykh justify it? According to Fakhr al-Dīn, the pivot of VII.6's MA argument is the following thesis (call it PM):

> PM: Every temporal event (*ḥādith*) has matter that precedes it

PM is a claim the shaykh had established earlier at *Ishārāt* V.6.[20] In saying that the major premise of MA depends on PM, Rāzī means to say that insofar as a thing's coming to be (or generation) and ceasing to be (or corruption) are events, PM

---

18 Ibid., 324
19 Ṭūsī, *Ḥall Mushkilāt* VII.6, 883.
20 Rāzī, *Sharḥ al-Ishārāt* VII.6, 526.

applies i.e., such events must involve something which functions as matter, so that:

If x comes to be, *x* has matter that precedes it

and likewise:

If x ceases to be, *x* has matter that precedes it

And so taking the truth of the PM thesis for granted, and applying it to cases of corruption, we can say that (PM-C):

PM-C: Everything, *x*, which ceases to be has matter that precedes it

Where the expression 'has matter' means:

There exists something, *s*, which is the bearer of the possibility of *x* to cease to be

If so, then, on Rāzī's understanding of the MA argument, the supposition that the human soul can cease to be will entail, as clarified below, that the soul is not an Ṣ.

Rāzī explains:

[T2] So we say that if the soul admits of corruption, then the possibility of the occurrence of that corruption obtains (*ḥāṣil*) prior the occurrence of that corruption. That possibility inevitably has a substrate; and it is impossible that its substrate be the soul itself (*dhāt al-nafs*). For the substrate of the possibility of a thing is such that it necessarily remains with the realization of that thing. However, the soul does not remain with the realization of its corruption. And therefore, the substrate of that possibility is not the soul but rather its matter.[21]

The argument at T2 goes something like this:

Everything that possibly ceases to be has matter
The soul possibly ceases to be (assumption)
Therefore, the soul has matter

The truth of the PM-C premise presupposes that:

Nothing can be the matter, qua bearer, of its own possibility to cease to be

Rāzī appeals to a well-founded Avicennian principle as the reason for this, namely:

[…] what receives something (*al-qābil*) necessarily remains with what is received (*al-maqbūl*).[22]

21 Ibid., 526.
22 Avicenna, *Physics* III.9.3, 339 (tr. J. McGinnis, modified). *The Healing*; *Metaphysics* IV.2.28, 141, ed. and tr. M. Marmura (Utah: Brigham Young University Press, 2005).

But the soul, when it receives corruption i. e., when its possibility to cease to be is actualized, does not remain; for, self-evidently, nothing is such that it remains when it in fact corrupts. Hence, there must then exist something, *s*, which functions as the matter qua bearer of the soul's possibility to cease to be and which remains with the realization of that possibility. Therefore, the soul has matter (in the sense specified above). But if it has matter, then for the duration of the soul's actual existence, the relation of that matter to the soul will be either one of (1) constitution or (2) a subject of inherence. Whatever the case, the soul's property of being an Ṣ is violated; for if (1), human soul will not be simple – being then composed of this matter and something else, *F*. And if (2), the human soul will not be able to exist unless in that subject. Both of these conclusions contradict the result of *Ishārāt* VII.2–5. This is how Rāzī parses *Ishārāt* VII.6's T1 argument.

Ṭūsī's take on the argument at T1 is more perspicuous than Rāzī's. Like the latter, he thinks the claim presupposed there is MA's major premise:

Nothing that is Ṣ can cease to be

The reason for that, Naṣīr al-Dīn explains, is because there's nothing in the Ṣ that would function as the ground or bearer of the potential for something else to come to be – which is, as we've seen in section I, what corruption as a change on (A-A) amounts to. So as Ṭūsī understands VII.6, the goal there is to show the failure of anything that is an Ṣ to consist of two distinct elements or factors that are related as a state (*ḥāl*) to that of which it is the state i. e., its substrate (*maḥall*). So such an entity would lack any potency for corruption and wouldn't be the sort of thing that can possibly cease to be. Ṭūsī comments on T1's argument as follows:

> [T3] Every temporally subsisting existent [e.g., *x*] that is such as to corrupt is, before corruption, actually subsistent and potentially corrupted. Now, the actuality of subsistence is other than the potentiality of corruption. Otherwise, everything that subsists possibly corrupts and everything that possibly corrupts subsists. Therefore, they are due to two different factors [in *x*]. But it is impossible for what is an [Ṣ] to contain two different things; for it is simple.[23]

To actually exist is not the same as to potentially cease to exist. Otherwise, anything characterized by the one would ipso facto be characterized by the other; but that's clearly false. For example, supposing God exists, He, being necessary, isn't the sort of thing that can possibly corrupt. But if it's possible that there be a being that exist but doesn't have the potential to corrupt, then 'actual existence' and 'potential nonexistence' are distinct features of an object. If that's true, then this claim holds:

23 Ṭūsī, *Ḥall Mushkilāt* VII.6, 882–883.

For all *x*, if x exists at *t* and potentially ceases-to-be at *t'*, there's some factor, call it *e*, in virtue of which *x* has actual existence at *t* and some other factor, call it *e'*, in virtue of which *x* is potentially non-existent after *t'*

Thus, because actual existence and potentially nonexistence are really different, their causal factors, *e* and *e'*, are really different. And therefore, *x* would consist of two really distinct factors, *e* and *e'*; as such, *x* wouldn't be an Ṣ.

Here, however, one may object to the Ṭūsian argument at T3; for all that argument shows is that 'actuality of subsistence' and 'potentiality of corruption' are distinct attributes, but it doesn't show that they cannot have a single bearer or subject. Hence, it's possible, the objector may insist, that

[...] the subject of both attributes is a single thing, but the multiplicity of attributes is in terms of potency and actuality – in the sense that a single subject in actuality possesses one attribute and that very same subject in potentiality possesses another.[24]

Applied to the case of the human soul, the objection states: possibly, the soul itself, even though simple, is the bearer of both the attribute of actual subsistence and the attribute of potential corruption.

The answer to this should be clear from the Avicennian principle we saw Rāzī appeal to in his analysis of T1 – namely, the one from *Physics* III.3.9, which stated:

If *x* has a potential, *F*, for *y*, then *x* must subsist with the actualization of *F*

If so, then it's not possible for the human soul to be that which possesses both attributes; for, as already noted, when its potentiality for corruption is realized, it doesn't survive the process, which then means it is not the thing which had the potentiality in the first place.

Ṭūsī then concludes his analysis:

[T4] If it's then established that the soul is either an [Ṣ] or possesses an [Ṣ], then neither it, nor what is similar to it in not having composition in it and not inhering in something else, is such as to admit corruption. And hence, subsistence and the potentiality of corruption cannot both be combined in that which is simple. If the former obtains, then the latter does not. Therefore, it's not possible for the soul to corrupt.[25]

In sum, as a simple, non-inhering entity, there can't possibly be some factor in the soul which accounts for its potential corruption. In other words, to put in terms of the hylomorphic account of change outlined in section I, neither of the two ways for a thing to corrupt apply to the human soul; it neither (a) consists of some factor, *F*, that exists in something else, *M*, nor (b) does it itself exist in something else, *M*. And hence, it will be impossible for the soul, once it exists, to ever fail to exist. This is just to say it would be incorruptible.

24 Ḥassan Malekshāhī, *Tarjume va Sharḥ Ishārāt va Tanbihāt*, p. 379.
25 *Ḥall Mushkilāt* VII.6, 884.

With that said, let me now pause and briefly take stock before turning to section III. Again, the main argument (MA) we extracted from *Ishārāt* VII.6 was:

Every human soul is Ṣ
Nothing that is Ṣ can cease to be
Therefore, no human soul can cease to be

I noted that the universal negative major was its key premise. And we've seen the justification for in terms of the analysis offered by Rāzī and Ṭūsī. We can summarize the result of that in the following argument – stated in the First Figure, second mood:

Everything that can cease to be has matter
Nothing that has matter is Ṣ
Therefore, nothing that can cease to be is Ṣ

The universal affirmative minor of this argument is based on *Ishārāt* V.6. Its universal negative major is true by definition; for, as we've learned above, the simplicity condition for being an Ṣ excludes having matter. The conclusion of the argument converts to:

Nothing that is Ṣ can cease to be

Which is just the major premise of the MA argument of VII.6.

This, then, constitutes the extent of our two commentators' exposition of *Ishārāt* VII.6. I now turn to their assessment of it.

3. Rāzī's and Ṭūsī's Critical Engagement with *Ishārāt* VII.6

Fakhr al-Dīn raises two main objections to VII.6. The first is specific to what Avicenna had said at [1.3] above (in section II.2), arguing that the reasoning implicit there isn't sufficient to get us the soul's survival. The second objection, i.e., BC, is more general:

BC: just as the body, according to Avicenna, grounds the soul's possible origination, it can likewise ground the possibility of its cessation

In his response to the first, Ṭūsī will argue that Rāzī fails to consider premises the shaykh established earlier which anticipate and resolve the objection. In his response to BC, Ṭūsī will argue that the objection betrays a failure to understand the precise sense in which the soul is temporally originated according to the shaykh. Let us now take up the objections and responses.

Recall that at [1.3], the shaykh had argued that even if we, for the sake of argument, grant the opponent that the human soul *is* a kind of composite, and therefore not simple, the conclusion about its incorruptibility would still go through. That argument went as follows:

> [1.3] If, though, [the human soul] is taken not as an [Ṣ], but rather as if a composite of something like matter and something like form, we apply the argument to the [Ṣ] among [the composite soul's] parts.[26]

That is, suppose the human soul is a composite of some formal factor, *F*, joined to some other factor, *M*, where the *M*-factor functions as matter. And suppose further that the soul ceases to be when factor *F* ceases to be conjoined to factor *M*. Rāzī then fleshes out the reasoning implicit in [1.3] like this:

> [T5] [Then] this [factor *M*] is either such that it does not itself have another [*M*-factor] or, even if it does, [we] inevitably end up at a final [M-factor] that itself has no [further *M*-factor]. Hence, it must be that that [*M*-factor] which doesn't have [an *M*-factor] can't possibly corrupt […]. And by 'the soul', we mean nothing except that subsisting [*M*-factor-less] (*mujarrad*) substance.[27]

So T5's argument seems to be: the human soul is, in itself, nothing but an immaterial, i.e., *M*-less, self-subsisting being. Now, assuming that the soul is composed of *F*-*M* factors, if we apply the considerations in [1.2] to the material *M*-factor which partly composes the soul and which, on this assumption, underlies its possible nonexistence, we, in the last analysis, arrive at the conclusion that this *M*-factor itself must be something simple i.e., not further composed from some other *M* and *F* elements. Why is this so? Though not explicit in Rāzī's exposition, there's good reason to think it's because otherwise an infinite regress would threaten.[28] So an ultimately simple *M* factor must be posited in order to avoid such a regress. If so, then given that anything that can cease-to-be is composed, that simple *M* factor won't have the possibility to cease-to-be. If so, then the simple *M*-factor turns out to be a something that is immaterial, i.e., matter-less, and subsisting. But this is just what it is to be a human soul on the Avicennian view; and therefore, the human soul qua being a simple matter-less substance can't possibly cease to be – which is just the conclusion sought.

Or again, as Ṭūsī fleshes out the thought at [1.3], if the soul isn't an Ṣ, then, taken by itself, either it's a composite of some constituent elements *F*-*M*, or it is a state (*ḥāl*) i.e., *F*, in something else i.e., *M*. If the latter, this contradicts the self-subsistence condition for being an Ṣ. If the soul is a composite though, every composite must be composed either partly or wholly of non-inhering simple

26 *Ishārāt* VII.6, 324

27 Rāzī, *Sharḥ al-Ishārāt* VII.6, 527–527.

28 Compare what Rāzī says at *al-Maṭalib al-ʿAliyyah* VII.3.11, 236, ed. A. Alsaqā' (Beirut: 1987, vol. 7). For Avicenna, the infinite regress entailment is explicit in both *The Healing*; *Psychology* V.4, and *al-Najāt*; *Physics* VI.9 versions of the argument. For an argument against an infinity of material causes in general, see *The Healing*; *Metaphysics*, VII.1.9–18.

elements; otherwise, we get an infinite regress. Whatever the case, if we then consider these simple elements, it turns out that:

> [T6] […] on these presuppositions (*ʿalā taqdīrīn*), what is a non-inhering simple [being], I mean, the [Ṣ] existent in a composite, is not itself a composite of the potentiality of corruption and the actuality (*wujūd*) of subsistence (*thubāt*).[29]

And if there's no potentiality for corruption in that simple, self-subsistent being, then it can never fail to exist.

Rāzī's first objection

Contra [1.3], Rāzī argues as follows: If, as [1.3] explicitly allows, the soul were a composite of some simple material factor, *M*, and formal factor, *F*, then, even if its simple *M*-factor, as the Avicennian insists, persists despite *F* perishing, that remaining *M* factor wouldn't be robust enough of an entity to be characterized as a human soul in the way the shaykh himself understands the soul. That is, Rāzī is urging that the soul can be composed in such a way that if only its simple *M* part were to survive, it would not be the case that the soul as such survives. The objection begins as follows:

> [T7] [F]rom the subsistence of the [*M* part] of the soul it doesn't follow that the soul subsists, just as from the subsistence of the prime matter of elemental bodies it doesn't follow that they [i.e., the elements] subsist.[30]

That is, assuming that only the soul's simple *M* factor persists – the *F* factor passing away – entails that the soul qua whole ceases to be, i.e., insofar the *F*-factor is a part of it that contributes to its complete being. And in that sense, the soul would in fact have the potentiality for corruption in the way any hylomorphic composite in general does, i.e., insofar as once that composite's formal part ceases to exist, what survives isn't identical to what we started out with. This is all the more true in the case at hand, Rāzī explains, because on the shaykh's view, the separated human soul is an entity that has various intellectual and ethical features as properties; but the surviving simple *M* element of the (on the present assumption) composite that is the soul would just not be that sort of thing. And so it just wouldn't be a soul without equivocation. Rāzī presses on:

> [T8] What confirms [the truth of the objection raised] is that […] you say: 'the soul subsists after the body's death, cognizing its intelligibles, perceiving its perceptibles, and characterized by the ethical traits which it acquired in its state of embodiment'. In that case, [from] your allowing that the surviving thing, after bodily death, is its [*M* part] only, it's not possible for you to prove any of that. For someone can object: 'why can't

29 Ṭūsī, *Ḥall Mushkilāt* VII.6, 883.
30 Rāzī, *Sharḥ al-Ishārāt* VII.6, 528.

> one say that [the soul's *M* part] being characterized by these cognitions, perceptions, sciences and ethical traits is conditioned on the realization of [the *F* part] in it, and that when in bodily death this [*F* part] corrupts, then assuredly nothing of these sciences and ethical traits remain'. And so it's evident that the amount they mentioned for the subsistence of the soul is insufficient.[31]

How good is this objection? Well, to the extent that on Avicennian principles intellectual and ethical features follow upon a thing's form – they are formal features of a composite – the objection has bite. For if that's so, it's no doubt true that should the formal part of a composite go, all the features that it grounds would likewise have to go. The criticism is especially weighty, as T8 makes clear, because what motivates the thesis about soul's post-mortem subsistence, on the (A-A) view, is a further thesis about the eschatological states of happiness and misery the human soul will experience in that post-mortem state. For this to be possible, however, the soul has to somehow retain said formal features, for they determine such states – and this is precisely what can't be sustained, Rāzī claims, on the assumption that the soul as such remains intact when only one of its parts i. e., the *M*-part, does so. And hence, on this assumption the soul ceases to be just like a composite as such ceases to be when its form perishes.[32] Hence, contra [1.3]'s argument, the *M* part's survival doesn't suffice for the human soul's survival as such.

Ṭūsī's response

How can the Avicennian resist this conclusion? Naṣīr al-Dīn needs to show that the soul's simple *M* part surviving guarantees the survival of those formal features noted above. He has an argument for that which, I think, goes some distance in meeting the Rāzian objection. The argument takes the form of an elaborate disjunction, and it draws on three crucial premises all of which are taken as established by the shaykh in the earlier parts of the *Ishārāt*. Ṭūsī's response has two virtues: first, in its own right, it suffices to show, contra Rāzī, that the surviving simple *M*-part is robust enough of an entity to be characterized as a soul; and second, it's a neat illustration of Avicenna's consistency on the issue in terms of how certain chapters of the *Ishārāt* hang together.

The argument, as I understand it, goes like this:

1. Suppose that only the simple *M*-part of the soul survives
2. That *M*-part then either (1) has position (*waḍ*) or (2) does not have position.
3. If (1), having position would be a part of what the simple *M*-part is in itself
4. But the simple *M*-part has no position in itself [cf., *Ishārāt* I.14, 197–198]

31 Ibid., 528.
32 Ibid., 528.

5. 3 contradicts 4
6. Therefore, ~(1) [by reductio]
7. Therefore, (2) [from 2, 6]
8. If (2), either (2.1) this position-less simple *M*-part subsists on its own (*infirād*) or (2.2) it does not subsist on its own
9. All that is immaterial and subsists on its own cognizes of itself [cf., *Ishārāt* III.19, 250]
10. If (2.1), the simple *M*-part cognizes of itself [from 8, 9]
11. If the simple *M*-part cognizes of itself then it is the whole soul as such
12. Therefore, the simple *M*-part is the whole soul as such [from 10, 11, modus ponens]
13. 12 contradicts 1
14. Therefore, ~(2.1) [by reductio]
15. Therefore, (2.2) [from 8, 14]
16. If (2.2), either the simple *M*-part (2.2.1) subsists through the body's causal influence or (2.2.2) it does not subsist through the body's causal influence
17. If (2.2.1), the soul doesn't have an independent being from the body
18. If the soul depends on the body for its being, it has no activity per se (*bi-dhātih*)
19. But it does have an activity per se [cf., *Ishārāt* VII.2–5, 321–324]
20. Therefore, the soul doesn't depend on the body in its being [18, 19, modus tollens]
21. Therefore, (2.2.2) the simple *M*-part does not subsist by the body's causal influence [16, 20][33]

The upshot of the argument in 1–21, then, is:

> [T9] If [the soul] does not exist on account of the body's causal influence, then it subsists by that which renders it subsistent, even if the body is not existent. This is just the conclusion sought (*maṭlūb*). Moreover, it's not possible that the forms residing in [the soul], and the perfections that follow upon those forms, corrupt and change after its connection from the body is severed; for change does not exist except as depending on a moveable body, as determined according to philosophical principles.[34]

Does Ṭūsī's analysis succeed in resolving Rāzī's objection? Recall that Rāzī censured the Avicennian by objecting that if the soul can be a composite entity only the simple *M*-part of which survives (as in 2.2) – its *F* perishing – then that simple part would on this supposition turn out to be nothing more than a bare, i. e., featureless, entity, hardly worthy of being considered a soul as such i. e., in the way that sort of entity is normally understood by the Avicennian, with all its cognitive and moral perfections available to it. This would amount to a corruption of the soul as a whole. In his response Ṭūsī shows, in three steps, that the soul's remaining or surviving simple *M*-part, on analysis, turns out to be not a part of the soul but rather a fully-fledged soul as such – with its psychological properties intact. Consequently, there's no real sense then in which it corrupts.

33 Ṭūsī, *Ḥall Mushkilāt* VII.6, 884–885.
34 Ibid., 885.

The gist of each step is as follows. In the first, premises 1 to 7, we learn – on the basis of *namaṭ* I.14, where the shaykh establishes that prime matter, the sort of matter that has no further matter of its own, has position only on account of the form that comes to inhere in it – that the surviving simple (i. e., matter-less) *M*-part can't also be something intrinsically located. If by 4 we know that prime matter has position only due to form, then if the simple *M*-part lacks form but intrinsically still has position, we have a contradiction – it *both* doesn't have position of itself and does have position of itself.[35] In the second step, premises 8 to 16, Ṭūsī shows – on the basis of *namaṭ* III.19, where Avicenna establishes that anything that is immaterial (i. e., matter-less) and self-subsistent is an agent of intellection – that if the simple *M*-part, as unlocated, is self-subsistent, then it follows that that *M*-part is an agent of intellection.[36] As such, as 11 states, it would be the human soul as a whole; for the subsistence of a cognitive self-subsisting substance is all that the Avicennian seeks in showing the human soul survives. But if, as in premise 12, the simple *M*-part's persisting amounts, given 9, to the soul as such surviving, then we have a contradiction; 12 runs up against the initial (Rāzian) assumption, i. e., premise 1 – namely, that the *M*-factor is only a *part* and not the whole soul. And from the denial, by a reductio, of the first disjunct (2.1) of 8 we derive its second disjunct (2.2): the intrinsically unlocated simple *M*-part doesn't subsist by itself. In that case, it, per 16, subsists by the body or not, but rather by something else, whatever that thing may be. Finally, in the third step, premises 17 to 20, Ṭūsī shows, on the basis of *Ishārāt* VII.2–5, where Avicenna argues for the independence of intellectual cognition, that the simple *M*-part must then subsist independently of the body since it has an activity (i. e., cognition) of its own i. e., independent of the body.[37] With 21, we have our conclusion: the positionless simple *M*-part subsists independently of the body in virtue of something which will count as a formal feature of it. But why should it be a formal feature that makes it subsist? Precisely because we had assumed – at

35 Perhaps Ṭūsī also has another point in mind in the reasoning from 1–7, namely, that if the simple *M*-part is intrinsically located, then given premise 4, which goes back to *Ishārāt* I.14, it would follow that it is in fact informed, which on the present assumption it is not. And so another contradiction follows – the simple *M*-part is *both* informed i. e., qua possessing position, and not informed, given the present assumption that it's the *only* surviving part of the whole composite that is the human soul.

36 For Rāzī's and Ṭūsī's debate over *Ishārāt* III.19, see Peter Adamson 'Avicenna and his Commentators on Human and Divine Self-Intellection', in *The Arabic, Hebrew, and Latin Reception of Avicenna's Metaphysics*, ed. Dag Nikolaus Hasse and Amos Bertolacci (Berlin: De Gruyter, 2011), pp. 97–123.

37 And this, again, means that the soul wholly, not partly, subsists despite the nonexistence of the body. Premise 18 is self-evident; the conditional in 19 we've already seen the reason for, namely, that activity follows being, so that if *x* depends on *y* for its existence, *x* depends on *y* for its activity. Premise 20 is a denial of the consequent of 19 on the basis of *Ishārāt* VII.2–5, with 21 following by modus tollens.

premise 8, option (2.2) – that the *M*-part doesn't subsist on its own, and – at premise 16, option (2.2.1) – that it also doesn't subsist in virtue of the body's causal influence. Hence, insofar as the *M*-part is like prime matter, which doesn't subsist unless through form, the *M*-part then subsists in virtue of some formal feature, *F*, whatever it may be. And so long as this formal feature, *F*, survives the soul's separation from the body – and it inevitably must since the *M*-factor survives and survives due only to some formal factor – then the perfective properties that *F* is the source of will also remain with it such that the soul will be incapable of losing them post-mortem. For their loss would be a change, and change requires a body at its subject. But, the human soul in our supposed state of separation has no body. Hence, it won't be able to lose them. Hence, contra the Rāzian objection, the soul as a whole (i. e., with its formal perfective features), not just a part of it, survives.[38]

Rāzī's second objection

Supposing the first objection is adequately dealt with, Rāzī then turns to pointing out a more serious difficulty in the shaykh's more general account of the soul. The strategy here will be to exploit an asymmetry between the origination of the

38 One might object here, with Rāzī, that if the Ṭūsian response is correct, then it follows that "the [*M*-part] of a thing would be equivalent to that entire [i. e., composite] thing in every attribute" (*Sharḥ al-Ishārāt* VII.6, 528). This is because, Rāzī explains, insofar as the soul, on the A-A view, falls under the genus of substance, it will consist of a genus and a differentia. And the genus and differentia, in a certain respect, are just matter and form, which are the two essential parts of any composite. Hence, if the soul's genus qua matter, as a matter-less (*mujarrad*) self-subsistent entity is, by *Ishārāt* III.19, an intellect, an agent of intellection, and intelligible – which just is the soul as a whole – then something impossible follows: a part of a thing becomes to be equivalent to the whole of that thing. That is, if it's true that the persistence of the soul's simple *M*-part, given III.19, is a sufficient condition for the persistence of the soul as such, then it would be true that a part of a composite, i. e., its genus qua matter, would suffice for all the properties of the whole of that composite, properties that it has in virtue of having a differentia qua form which, on the present assumption, has ceased to exist. But on A-A, that's manifestly false; genus qua matter is a constitutive part of a composite and as such cannot exhaust or account for the being of the composite as a whole. Ṭūsī responds by noting, rightly, that this objection commits a fallacy of equivocation; that is, it equivocates on the terms matter and form. For the two are said of the parts of a composite body and the genus and differentia only by *tashshabuh* – analogy or similarity (*Ḥall Mushkilāt* VII.6, 885–886). There's a correspondence between the two pairs, to be sure, but they aren't equivalent. Otherwise, as Ṭūsī contends, "all species of accidents would likewise be hylomorphically composed" (ibid., 886), insofar as accidents have a genus/differentia composition, but no corresponding form/matter composition. Basically, then, the absurdity of the part becoming equivalent to the whole, Ṭūsī argues, only results from Rāzī's treating the genus/differentia distinction as equivalent to the form/matter distinction, and not from the conjunction of the thesis established at *Ishārāt* III.19 and the simple *M*-part of the soul being something itself matter-less (*mujarrad*) and self-subsistent.

human soul on the (A-A) view and its possible cessation. This is the objection we've termed BC. It states:

(BC): if the body can serve as a condition for the soul's possible generation, then it can serve as a condition for its possible corruption

The main thrust of BC is that it seems Avicenna has no principled reason why these two possibilities:

1) The possibility of coming-to-be, and
2) The possibility of ceasing-to-be

cannot function in the same way vis-à-vis their relation to a putative bearer or substrate. Rāzī explains:

[T10] Just as corruption is preceded by the possibility of corruption, in the same way coming-to-be is preceded by the possibility of coming-to-be. And so if the possibility of [the human soul's] coming-to-be is independent of a substratum or, if it is dependent on a substratum but the substratum of that possibility is the body, then one must allow for the possibility of corruption that it [too] does not depend on a substratum or, if it is dependent on it, its substratum is the body. And if this is false here, then that's false there; otherwise, what's the difference?[39]

The objection is particularly apropos, Rāzī thinks, since the shaykh grants 1) insofar as he holds that the soul *does* in fact come-to-be at some *t* and so the possibility of its coming-to-be *does* have matter as its bearer at *t*. On the basis of this admission, why then can't someone, Rāzī asks, maintain:

[T11] If the emanation of the soul from the Active Intellect is conditioned (*mashrūṭan*) upon the realization of a mixture (*mizāj*) receptive for [the soul's] management and action, then, when this body is corrupted, the condition of its emanation from [the Active Intellect] has corrupted. And with that, its annihilation becomes necessary on account of the annihilation of its condition.[40]

Simply put: if the body, or more precisely the complex bodily 'mixture', can serve as a condition for the soul's possible coming-to-be, then it can equally serve as a condition for its possible ceasing-to-be. At the very least, an argument hasn't been provided against thinking that if, as the Avicennian concedes, the possibility of the soul's temporal origination is anchored in a substrate, i. e., a suitable bodily mixture, the possibility of its nonexistence is equally anchored in that same bodily mixture. In sum, the dilemma Rāzī saddles the Avicennian with is that the there's no relevant difference between the two possibilities 1) and 2); they run parallel in that either both inhere in some substrate, in which case the soul, contra

39 Rāzī, *Sharḥ al-Ishārāt* VII.6, 528.
40 Ibid., 528.

VII.6, *would* be susceptible to corruption, or neither does, in which case the temporal coming-to-be of the soul, just like its corruption, would be impossible. And the latter consequence contradicts the shaykh's explicit teaching that no soul pre-exists the body of which it is the soul. This objection, I think, is substantive.

Ṭūsī's response

Rāzī's second objection exercises Ṭūsī, forcing him to offer a searching analysis of the Avicennian position on the soul-body relation as it concerns coming-to-be and passing-away. In responding to BC, Ṭūsī first clarifies the precise sense in which something is said, in general, to serve as a substrate for another thing's possible generation and/or corruption. For he thinks Rāzī misunderstands that and thereby misunderstands two further things: first, what it is for the body to be a substrate for specifically the soul's possible coming-to-be; and second, what it is for the body to be a substrate for the soul's possible ceasing-to-be.

As regards the general account, it is that:

> [T12] The meaning (*ma ʿnā*) of the body being a substrate for the possibility of the existence of blackness is its disposition (*tahayyu ʾuhu*) for the existence of blackness in it, so that the state of the existence of blackness is bounded (*muqtaranan*) to it. And the same is the case for the possibility of corruption. For this reason, it's impossible for something to be a substrate for the possibility of corruption itself.[41]

As I understand it, Ṭūsī is claiming that for something, e.g., *F*, to have its possibility of existence grounded in something else, e.g., *x*, is, fundamentally, for that something else, *x*, to have some dispositional property to exist a certain way i.e., in the *F*-way or as *F*. As such, being a substrate for *F* is about a type of existential dependence – in this case of *F* on *x*, where the existence of the one is conjoined or bound to that of the other. Take the example offered in T12: the color black can possibly come to be, and its possible coming to be has some body as its substrate. This means that that body possess as a real property a disposition to be black. Once that disposition is manifested due to the relevant causal factor(s), the body is actually black. For black to possibly come to be, then, is just for the body to have a property in virtue of which it is possibly black; and for black to actually exist is just for the body to actually be black. This, as you'll recall from section I, then amounts to the claim:

> For something, *F*, to come to be, is for something else, *x*, to come to be *F*

Black's actual existence, on this account, is the same as the body's actually being black. In sum, on Ṭūsī's analysis, to say that

41 Ṭūsī, *Ḥall Mushkilāt* VII.6, 886.

'*x* is a substrate for the possibility of *F*'s existence'

is to say that

'*x* has a disposition to be *F*'

where 'disposition' is understood as positive property had by *x* to exist in a certain i. e., *F*, way. It marks out a kind of potentiality possessed by *x* which, when acted on by the relevant causal factor(s), becomes actualized.

If the above is correct, then once we recall the self-subsistence condition for being an Ṣ which the human soul satisfies, the point Naṣīr al-Dīn makes next – against Rāzī's BC objection – is significant. He writes (emphasis mine):

> [T13] The response [to Rāzī] is that for something [e.g., *x*] to be a substrate for the possible existence, or possible corruption, of something else [e.g., *F*] – *the subsistence (qiwām) of which is clearly distinct* (*mubāyin*) from [*x*] – is unintelligible (*ghayr ma ʿqūl*).[42]

That is, for anything, *F*, the persistence conditions of which are distinct from those of something else, *x*, *x* can't serve as the substrate, in the sense specified above, for the possible existence (or corruption) of *F*. The reason, again, is because *x*'s being a substrate for *F* is just for *x* to have a disposition to exist as *F*. That is to say, for *F* to be is just for *x* to exist in an *F*-way. On that account, *F* would not have a distinct being from *x*. But that can't hold if *F* is something with a distinct or independent subsistence of its own. Thus, if it has been established, on independent grounds, that *F* (= the soul) is distinct in being from *x* (= the body), then it follows that *x* can't serve as its substrate in the sense that *x* is something with a disposition to exist in an *F*-state. Or rather, where *F* has an independent being from *x*, it is, as Ṭūsī puts it, incoherent (*ghayr ma ʿqūl*) to claim that *x* serves as the substrate of *F*'s possible existence; for being a substrate denotes existential dependence, and *F*'s being something with existential autonomy (from *x*) is incompatible with that. In sum, the Rāzian claim would amount to a contradiction: *F* both depends on *x* – qua having *x* as its substrate – and does not depend on *x* – qua being something self-subsistent (insofar as it is an Ṣ).[43]

In light of the above analysis, it's clear that Rāzī's BC objection misunderstands the Avicennian view, according to Ṭūsī, insofar it conceives the soul's

42 Ibid., 886.

43 Ṭūsī's parsing of the Avicennian account in this way has the consequence that a thing's bearing the possibility of another thing's corruption has to be fleshed out in positive terms. In other words, that, say, *F*'s possibility for corruption inheres in *x* would mean that *x* has the disposition for the existence of some *F**, i. e., for being *F**. This is, I think, why Ṭūsī concludes T12 with: For that reason, it's impossible for something to be a substrate for the possibility of corruption itself. Possibility qua disposition is a positive feature of thing; as such, it's always for some other positive state of affairs i. e., for some actuality.

coming to be as the body's coming to be in a certain state *F*, e. g., animate or the like, and likewise the soul's ceasing to be as the body's ceasing to be in an *F* state – just as in the blackness and body example. This of course assumes that the soul's persistence conditions are dependent on those of the body and so overlooks a crucial premise established in earlier *anmāṭ*, namely, that

Every human soul is Ṣ

Ṭūsī is denying precisely that assumption in T13 by appealing to the idea that the soul already been shown to have a mode of being independent from that of the body.

Certainly, Ṭūsī is right that BC, first, misunderstands in what sense the body is a substrate for the soul's possible coming to be and, second, fails to see the relevance of Ṣ to the issue. However, the response, so far at least, is largely negative in character; that is, all it tells us is in what sense the body isn't a substrate for the coming-to-be of the soul (and why isn't it in that sense). But what's Ṭūsī's positive account of how the body serves as a bearer of the soul's possible coming-to-be? For the Rāzian might insist: 'granted that the body doesn't serve as a substrate for the soul's possible existence in the sense specified above in T12; but, since the shaykh clearly endorses the claim that the body *is* a condition for the soul's existence, there's a sense in which it *does* serve as a substrate, and you haven't shown that that sense is one on which the soul's ceasing to exist, per BC, doesn't follow. So the BC objection still stands'. That's a fair point; so more needs to be said in order to show that the Avicennian view precludes the consequence the Rāzian is pushing.

Ṭūsī does say more. The positive account consists of clarifying the precise dispositional role of the body qua being related to the soul's origination (*ḥudūth*). Strictly speaking, Ṭūsī states, it's not the body qua a distinct entity (i. e., from the soul) that it serves as the substrate for the origination of the soul:

> [T14] Rather, only as existing with a specific disposition (*hay'a makhṣūṣa*) before the coming-to-be of the soul is it a substrate and disposed for the coming to be of a humanity-form (*ṣūra insānīyyah*) that conjoins to it and constitutes it as a determinate species. And the existence of that form is not possible unless with its proximate essential principle, i. e., the soul.[44]

Two points are noteworthy in T14: first, in relation to the soul's coming into existence, the body functions as a substrate qua having a specific or 'special disposition' (call this DP). This is a standard Avicennian point; DP refers to the body under the ratio (*ma'nā*) of possessing a certain level of material complexity, since on the Avicennian view not just any old body can come to be ensouled, but a

44 Ibid., VII.6, 887.

body of a special sort. And second, the body qua possessing DP is a substrate for the coming-to-be, not of the human soul proper but, as Ṭūsī says, of the 'form of humanity' (call this FH). Once FH is related or joined to that special sort of body, a specific type of living entity comes to exist, e.g., a human being.

Now this second point is highly interesting in its own right, but is it a legitimate interpretation of Avicenna's view? For it seems to entail that there's a distinction between FH and the soul insofar as the latter, as the end of T14 states, is a causal principle (*mabdaʾ*) of the former. So according to T14, then, it seems that when a human being comes to be, two entities come to be: FH and the human soul. And the former can't come to be unless the latter does. That is, the body qua DP serves as substrate for the coming into being of FH and FH only comes to be, not because of the body qua DP, but because the soul itself, as its essential proximate principle, comes to be first.

If we interpret Ṭūsī as distinguishing two entities here – FH and its principle i.e., the human soul – then this is a departure from the shaykh's account of the soul's temporal origination. And so Ṭūsī here, under pressure from Rāzī, would be innovating. But is this what Ṭūsī is really saying?

I don't think so. Ṭūsī goes on to explain the talk of form of humanity, soul, and their relation to DP, as follows (emphasis mine):

> [T15] The coming to be, by way of [the body's] preparedness and disposition, of that principle [i.e., the soul] of the form conjoined to [the body], and constituting it, *is in the sense that ('alā wajh) that principle becomes linked to [the body] by this type of linkage (irtibāṭ).*[45]

That is to say, when there's a sufficiently complex body disposed for the reception of a human soul, it's not the case that two things come to be – an FH and its principle, the human soul. Rather, only a single thing comes to be, but that thing's coming to be can be considered in two ways. In one way, it can be considered in itself; as such, it is the coming to be of the human soul proper. In another way, it can be considered in relation to the body; as such, it is the coming to be of the soul, not in itself, but qua being related to the body. And I take it its aspect of 'coming to be related to the body' is what FH designates. In other words, the coming to be of 'the human form' is not the coming into being of some entity distinct from the soul but rather just the soul's coming to be i.e., related to the body, where this relation, according to the shaykh, is that of management or governance (*tadbīr*).[46]

Taken in this way, it's a perfectly Avicennian move on Ṭūsī's part. For if the human soul is a distinct (*mubāyin*) entity i.e., an Ṣ, then there's the fact of its

45 Ibid., 887.
46 Avicenna, *Ishārāt* III.5, 235–236.

being in itself and then there's the fact of its being related i. e., to some *x*, which is just the soul considered qua FH. The former fact is more fundamental than the latter one, such that if the soul comes-to-be qua coming-to-be related, then it follows that it must have come-to-be qua in itself. But, crucially, this inference doesn't straight-forwardly go through; it only follows provided that the soul doesn't already pre-exist the body and is self-subsistent. And, interestingly, the former is a claim which the shaykh, as far as I can tell, nowhere argues for in the *Ishārāt*.[47] So Ṭūsī's response to BC, if I've got it right, assumes its truth. The core of the response to BC, abstractly stated, then seems to be:

> For some *x* and *y*, if 1) *y* doesn't pre-exist *x* and 2) *y* is an Ṣ, then *y*'s coming to be related to *x* at *t* is other than *y*'s coming to be in itself at *t*

And if these two facts about *y*, i. e., its coming-to-be in itself and its coming-to-be related, are distinct facts, then if *x* serves as an explanation for *y*'s being related to it at *t*, that doesn't entail that *x* is also the explanation for *y*'s being in itself at *t*. When this premise is applied to the soul, it follows that despite the body qua DP serving as a substrate for the coming-to-be of the soul's relation to it qua FH, it doesn't follow that it therefore serves as a substrate for the soul qua the soul's coming-to-be in itself; for, again, we know on independent grounds that in itself the soul has an existence distinct from the body (i. e., it is an Ṣ). In sum, according to Ṭūsī, only the soul's *coming-to-be related* requires a substrate, which here is the body qua DP, but it's *coming to be as such*, i. e., in itself, does not, due to considerations about its independent or distinct (*mubāyin*) subsistence conditions.

Ṭūsī then, mutatis mutandis, applies the above account to what it means for the body to ground, if it grounds at all, the soul's possible non-existence. He states:

> [T16] And so the body remains a substrate for the possibility of the corruption of the form conjoined to it, and only that linkage ceases from it, it being impossible for it to be a substrate for the possibility of the corruption of that principle insofar as it is an entity (*dhāt*) clearly distinct (*mubāyin*) from [the body].[48]

Based on the considerations above, in parsing T16, we can say that the consequent of BC, namely, that:

> I. the body can be a substrate for the possible non-existence of the soul

can mean either:

> I.a: the body can be substrate for the possible non-existence of the soul *simpliciter*, or

47 The absence of a justification of the soul's temporal origination in the *Ishārāt* is surprising, given that Avicenna usually treats the issue at length in his standard works. See e. g., his most detailed discussion of the issue in *The Healing*; *Psychology* V.3, 286–288.

48 *Ḥall Mushkilāt* VII.6, 887.

I.b: the body can be substrate for the possible non-existence of the soul's relation to the body

If I.a is meant, then, as we've already seen, the objection fails to take Ṣ into account, and so the Rāzian objection fails to actually engage the Avicennian argument at VII.6. If, though, I.b is meant, then BC doesn't draw any blood against the Avicennian view, since it does not follow from I.b that the human soul ceases to exist in itself. Thus, given Ṣ, the body qua DP can be substrate only for the ceasing to be of the FH conjoined to it, which is just to say for the ceasing to be of the relation of governance (*tadbīr*) that the soul on the (A-A) view bears to it. And likewise is the case, Ṭūsī infers, with the antecedent of BC:

> [T17] Therefore, the body, together with the specific disposition, is a condition for the coming to be (*ḥudūth*) of the soul insofar as the soul is a form or a principle of a form, not insofar as it is an independent (*mujarrad*) existent. And [the body] is not a condition for its existence (*wujūd*).[49]

The soul's 'being a form' (or its 'formality'), one can say, consists in its relation of management to the body. It's this relation that the DP of the body is the substrate for, both with respect to the soul's origination and cessation. With regards to the latter, DP is a substrate for it insofar as when that DP corrupts, the soul's governing role vis-à-vis the body is thereby severed. And with regards to the former, DP is a substrate for it in the sense that when the soul comes to be related to the body as its governor it obviously also comes to be simpliciter; for relations presuppose their relata.

Importantly, on this analysis, the soul's self-subsistent status, known on independent grounds, is preserved. And thus, though it's true that there's a sense in which the body is a condition, as the Rāzian objection urged, for the coming to be of the soul, that sense is compatible with the soul being an Ṣ. If that's so, then it doesn't necessarily follow that should that condition cease to be, the thing for whose origination it was a condition for should also cease to be. For, in general, there are counter-examples to that claim, as Ṭūsī concludes:

> [T18] A thing, when it comes to be, need not corrupt by the corruption of what is the condition of its coming to be, like e.g., a building; for it persists after the death of the builder who was a condition for its coming to be.[50]

Hence, DP's corruption doesn't entail the human soul's corruption it itself. And BC is resolved.

But you might then wonder: if the coming to be of the body qua DP necessitates the coming to be of FH (= the soul's relation of governance to the body),

49 Ibid., 887.
50 Ibid., 887.

which in turn necessitates the coming to be of the soul simpliciter – why, then, does making the body necessary for the corruption of FH not likewise necessitate the corruption of the soul simpliciter?[51]

Ṭūsī's answer to this is on point:

> [T19] Because what requires the coming to be of some effect (*ma lūl*) precisely requires the existence of all of the causes of that effect as its conditions. But what requires the corruption of an effect does not require the corruption of [such] causes. Rather, it's sufficient for it that some condition corrupts, even if it be a privation.[52]

Compare: for, say, burning to occur, all the necessary conditions (e.g., fire, something burnable, oxygen, etc.) for its existence must be present; but, for it to cease to be, it's not necessary that all the conditions for its occurrence cease to be; it suffices that at least one them does so (e.g., oxygen). The same applies to FH; it's origination requires all its causes, but its corruption does not. In general, the non-existence of the effect does not entail the non-existence of the cause in itself simpliciter (*muṭlaqan*).

The above constitutes Ṭūsī's handling of the two Rāzian objections. There's an exegetical and a philosophical lesson to be taken away from how the two commentators engage the shaykh at *Ishārāt* VII.6. Exegetically, the lesson is that, of the two commentators, Ṭūsī seems to display much more familiarity than does Rāzī with the Avicennian material. He seems to know much better how Avicenna's claims at VII.6 hang together with ones made in other places in the text. This is especially evident in his response to Rāzī's first objection. And I'd say this is true even with regards to the second objection Rāzī raises, despite the fact that, as we've seen, at a crucial stage in his response Ṭūsī appeals to a premise (i.e., the soul's temporal origination) which Avicenna did not previously discuss anywhere in the *Ishārāt*, let alone establish.

Philosophically, I think, Naṣīr al-Dīn gets the better of the argument, insofar he sufficiently answers both objections in a way that is consistent with established Avicennian principles, whereas Rāzī fails to take such established principles into account when offering his critique. Again, this is especially evident in the case of the first Rāzian objection. Admittedly, though, the Ṭūsian response to the second i.e., BC, objection falters in this regard to some extent, insofar it assumes a premise not treated anywhere in the *Ishārāt*. But still, even if we don't grant Ṭūsī that premise, his response would still suffice, on systematic grounds, in resolving the Rāzian doubt – though it wouldn't be adequate as an interpretation of Avicenna's own view. The reason it would suffice philosophically is simply because there's no doubt that the existence of the relation of the soul to the body pre-

51 Ibid., 887.
52 Ibid., VII.6, 888.

supposes the existence of its terms – soul and body. And the reason it wouldn't be adequate as an Avicennian answer is because it would presuppose that the soul pre-exists the body. Moreover, with respect to this last point, important considerations come up given the answers Ṭūsī in fact provides on behalf of the Avicennian view. In particular, in confronting BC, his analysis raises the more general question of the relation between individuation (*tashakhkhus*), origination (*ḥudūth*), and existence over time (*baqā*) i. e., subsisting in existence. The shaykh's account, as well as Ṭūsī's response to BC, would certainly benefit from a clarification of that relation; however, this sort of issue, being more general, also involves a more properly metaphysical investigation. As such, it falls outside *Ishārāt* VII.6's much more specific aim.

Bibliography

Adamson, Peter, "Avicenna and his Commentators on Human and Divine Self-Intellection". In: *The Arabic, Hebrew, and Latin Reception of Avicenna's Metaphysics*, ed. Dag Nikolaus Hasse and Amos Bertolacci (Berlin: De Gruyter, 2011), pp. 97–123.

Avicenna, *Ishārāt wa'l-Tanbihāt* (ed. Mojtabā Zare'i, Qom: 1387).

–, *The Healing; Metaphysics* (ed. and tr. Marmura, Utah: Brigham Young University Press, 2005).

–, *The Healing; Physics* (ed. and tr. Jon McGinnis, Utah: Brigham Young University Press, 2009).

–, *The Healing; Psychology* (ed. H. Amoli, Tehrān: 1386).

–, *Kitāb al-Najāt; Physics* (ed. Dānishpazhuh, Tehrān: 1387).

–, *Al-Mabda ʾwa'l-Ma ʿād* (ed. A. Nūrānī, Tehrān: 1363).

Ayman Shihadeh, *Doubts on Avicenna: a study and edition of Sharaf al-Dīn al-Mas ʿūdī's commentary on the Ishārāt* (Leiden; Boston: Brill 2016).

Fakhr al-Dīn Rāzī, *Sharḥ al-Ishārāt* (ed. Najafzāde, Tehrān: 1375, vol. 2–3).

–, *Kitāb al-Muḥaṣṣal* (ed. H. Zatāi, Cairo: 1991).

–, *Al-Maṭalib al-ʿAlīyyah*, VII.3.11, 236 (ed. A. Alsaqā', Beirut: 1987, vol. 7).

Malekshāhi, Ḥassan, *Tarjume va Sharḥ Ishārāt va Tanbihāt.* (Intesharat-e Soroush, Tehrān: 1392) vol. 1, 8th edition.

Mousavian, Seyyed N. and Mostafavi, S.H, "Avicenna on the Origination of the Human Soul". In: *Oxford Studies in Medieval Philosophy* 2017, vol. 5, pp. 41–86.

Muehlethaler, Lukas, "Revising Avicenna's Ontology of the Soul: Ibn Kammūna on the Soul's Eternity a Parte Ante". *The Muslim World*, 102.3–4 (Oct. 2012): 597–616.

Naṣīr al-Dīn Ṭūsī, *Sharḥ al-Ishārāt* (ed. Hasanzāde Amolī, Qom: 1391, vol. 2–3).

–, *Talkhīs al-Muḥaṣṣal* (ed. A. Nūrānī, Tehrān: 1359).

Plato, *Phaedo* (in *Plato: Complete Works*, ed. J.M. Cooper, Ind. Hackett: 1997).

Sharaf al-Dīn Mas ʿŪdī, *al-Mabāḥith wa'l-Shukūk ʿalā'l-Ishārāt* (ed. A. Shihadeh, Leiden; Boston: Brill 2016).

Peter Adamson

Fakhr al-Dīn al-Rāzī on Void*

Introduction

In the long-running story of antagonism and mutual influence between Aristotelian philosophy and *kalām*, one of the most obvious clashes concerned the question of void. In the fourth book of his *Physics* Aristotle denied that void exists or could exist, and he was followed in this by most Greek thinkers known to the Arabic-speaking world.[1] Standard *kalām* physics, by contrast, postulated atoms moving within empty space.[2] Philosophers went out of their way to emphasize the disagreement, with al-Fārābī (d. 950) writing a short treatise on the issue and Avicenna (d. 1037) devoting a section of the *Physics* of his *Shifāʾ* to the refutation of void's existence.[3] There were exceptions, with at least two philosophers arguing that void is real: Abū Bakr al-Rāzī (d. 925) and Abū Barakāt al-Baghdādī (d. 1160s).[4] They may however be the exceptions that prove the rule, since both were arguably more open to the ideas of the *mutakallimūn* than were such figures as al-Fārābī and Avicenna.

In general, the protean and multi-faceted thought of Fakhr al-Dīn al-Rāzī (d. 1210) cannot be classified as belonging exclusively to the *kalām* or philosophical traditions. But on the question of void, he seems to be far more *mutakallim* than *faylasūf*. He takes up the issue at numerous places in his sprawling corpus, repeatedly drawing on a cluster of arguments for and against the pos-

* I am grateful to Andreas Lammer for helpful discussion and to the DFG for supporting the project "The Heirs of Avicenna: Philosophy in the Islamic East, 12th-13th Centuries," under whose aegis this piece was written.

1 Aristotle's arguments are criticized by John Philoponus in his commentary on the *Physics:* see John Philoponus 1887–88, 675–94, and further Furley 1991. In fact however, he agrees with Aristotle that there can be no *empty* space, either inside or outside the cosmos. Thus in Fakhr al-Dīn's terms, Philoponus is a defender of self-subsistent place but not of "void."

2 Dhanani 1994.

3 al-Fārābī 1951; Avicenna 2009, §2.8 (hereafter *Healing: Physics*). On Avicenna's arguments against void see McGinnis 2007a and 2007b.

4 For the sources of the earlier al-Rāzī's view see Adamson 2014. On Abū Barakāt see Pines 1979.

sibility of void. In almost all cases, he shows himself to be an adherent of the void. The exception is the *Mabāḥith*, which sticks more closely to Avicenna.[5] This fits with the character of the work. Though he by no means always restricts itself to restating the Avicennan position in the *Mabāḥith*, Fakhr al-Dīn is willing to do so on some topics, including the related debates over the definitions of time and place. But in the course of its broadly Avicennan discussion of void, the *Mabāḥith* already introduces most of the arguments that recur in other works by Fakhr al-Dīn. There, he will declare the arguments in favor of void more compelling. Examples include relatively brief parts of his *Mulakhkhaṣ fī l-ḥikma wa-l-manṭiq*,[6] *Sharḥ ʿUyūn al-ḥikma*,[7] and *al-Arbaʿīn fī uṣūl al-dīn*,[8] as well as a lengthy treatment spread across 30 pages of *al-Maṭālib al-ʿāliya min al-ʿilm al-ilāhī*.[9] I will draw especially on this most detailed discussion of void, albeit with frequent allusions to the other, aforementioned works.[10] In an appendix to the article, I provide an outline of the relevant section of the *Maṭālib*. Readers who wish to follow the order of his discussion should turn to that outline. In what follows I instead highlight some particularly crucial and philosophically fruitful moves made by Fakhr al-Dīn in the *Maṭālib* and elsewhere.

1. What Kind of Void?

First of all, what exactly is void (*khalāʾ*)? Fakhr al-Dīn explains it in the *Arbaʿīn* as follows: "for two bodies not to touch, with no body in between them that touches them" (32). In the *Maṭālib*, his explanation is more technical and draws on his immediately preceding discussion of place, which established that place is "space (*faḍāʾ*)" or three-dimensional extension and not, as the Aristotelians claim, the inner boundary of a containing body.[11] He writes:

> *Maṭālib* §5.1, 155: The mind immediately judges that the body that has place is in need of space (*faḍāʾ*), which is place. If space, i. e. place, could not exist together without what is in place, then it would follow that each needs the other, which is circular and hence

5 Void is discussed in the *Mabāḥith* at vol.1, 338–60; the editor notes the unusual position taken in this work in a note at 340.

6 The discussion of void is at 94r–96v.

7 See the highly critical response to Avicenna's refutation of void at vol.2, 83–99. I cite Avicenna's *ʿUyūn al-ḥikma* itself from this same edition.

8 The discussion of void is at vol.2, 32–8.

9 The discussion of void is at vol.5, 155–85. Cited by page number from this volume and section number from the outline offered in the appendix below.

10 Thus this article provides the final installment of a series of studies of time and place in the *Maṭālib*. For the earlier installments see Adamson 2017, Adamson forthcoming, Adamson and Lammer forthcoming.

11 See again Adamson 2017.

> absurd. So it is established that space, in its existence and in its essence, has no need of what is in place. Furthermore, it is not necessitated by the essence of what is in place, except in the sense that what is in place cannot be separate from it. So it is established that place, in its own essence, has no need of the body in place, and is not necessitated by it. What is like this may exist in isolation (*munfakkan*) from [what is in place]. It follows conclusively that the existence of location (*ḥayyiz*) or space is possible in the absence of (*khāliyan*) what is in place; but this is precisely the meaning of void (*khalāʾ*).

According to this passage, the question of void's existence may seem to reduce to the question of whether space or place – understood as three-dimensional extension – exists. But this would be to overlook the idea of space or place existing *in the absence of* what is in place. As the word "void" (or *kenon* in Greek, or *khalāʾ* in Arabic) implies, what we are really interested in here is space that is "empty," that is, space unoccupied by a body.

In fact though, things are rather more complicated. In the third of the sections (*fuṣūl*) devoted to void in the *Maṭālib* (§7, 179–85), Fakhr al-Dīn provides a survey of views that have been adopted on this question. The subsequent discussion shows that we are not dealing with the simple yes-no question whether or not space can be, or ever actually is, empty. For one thing, some proponents of void insist not only that void exists, but also that it exists *necessarily* (§7.1, 179). Their argument for this is that, even if we imagine space or void to be absent, there would still be the possibility of distinguishing between various directions: left and right, up and down. This shows that space would remain despite our attempts to imagine it away. Furthermore, while we can readily imagine a body like a mountain or sea disappearing, we cannot imagine the place where it exists disappearing. Fakhr al-Dīn rejects all this, though. He states that right-thinking scholars (*ahl al-taḥqīq min al-ʿulamāʾ*) insist that void exists only contingently. Only God exists necessarily, besides which void can be divided into parts, which shows that it is contingent (*ad* §7.1, 180). This fits with a subsequent passage that Fakhr al-Dīn appends to his whole discussion of time, place, and void, which cites verses from the Qurʾān (6:12–13) in support of the idea that the whole temporal and spatial realm is subject to God's creation and governance (*Maṭālib* 184; cf. also §7.4, 181, with arguments against God's being in place).[12]

The void asserted by Fakhr al-Dīn is, then, a contingently existing thing. But one may ask further questions: is void homogeneous, with all its parts exactly alike (§7.2, 180)? I will defer consideration of this question for now, because it becomes the basis for one of Avicenna's arguments against void, and Fakhr al-Dīn has a lot to say about it. One might also ask whether an infinite void surrounds our finite cosmos. It has been pointed out previously that in his great commentary on the Qurʾān, *Mafātīḥ al-ghayb*, Fakhr al-Dīn does in fact assert an

12 Cf. *Maṭālib* vol.4, 197–217 for God's relationship to time and place.

infinite void (*khalāʾ lā nihāya lahu*) surrounding the created universe.[13] This fits with his teaching on place in the *Maṭālib*, which has insisted that directions can still be distinguished outside the cosmos.[14] The point relates to Fakhr al-Dīn's rejection of philosophical arguments against the possibility of multiple worlds. If God has the power to create such worlds, there must be an unlimited space within which those worlds could be placed.[15]

Finally, what about void space inside our universe? Fakhr al-Dīn does not seem to consider the possibility of "massed" void – that is, discrete regions of empty space adjoining bodies (realms of empty space between celestial spheres, perhaps). Rather, he raises the question whether there is "dispersed" void, that is, void "mixed" with particles so as to form bodies of different density.[16] He alludes, without mentioning him by name, to the physical theory of Abū Bakr al-Rāzī, according to which the elements are differentiated by the proportion of void to atoms in a given volume:

> *Maṭālib* §7.5, 182: Some people say that the subtle is distinguished from the dense only thanks to admixture of void. When the parts from which a particular body is generated are mixed with parts of void, it will be a subtle body; if it is not mixed with parts of void, it will be a dense body. Furthermore, whenever the admixture of void is great, the subtlety will be greater. Earth has no admixture of parts of void, so it is inevitably as dense as can be. Water does have an admixture of parts of void, so there is inevitably some subtlety in it. As for airy bodies, they have a greater admixture of void in them, so inevitably air is subtler than water, and likewise for fire, then the celestial spheres.[17]

13 Vol.1, 24. See further Setia 2004, 177. My thanks to Alexander Kalbarczyk for the reference.

14 *Maṭālib* vol.5, 152–3.

15 As also noted by Setia 2004, this is a claim found in both the *Mafātīḥ* and the *Maṭālib* (at vol.6, 193–5).

16 For this distinction see Adamson 2014.

17 This is very close in phrasing to the report of Abū Bakr al-Rāzī's view given by Nāṣir-e Khosraw 2014, 78: "We say that Muḥammad Zakariyyāʾ al-Rāzī claims that matter is eternal, and that it consists of extremely small parts without any sort of composition. And he claims that the Creator, great be His praise, has composed the bodies of the world from those parts in five ways, namely earth, water, air, fire and the sphere. He says that among those bodies, what is more dense becomes more dark; and that the composition of all bodies is from the mixture of the parts of matter with parts of void (meaning absolute place). Furthermore the parts of matter in the composition of earth are more numerous (*bīshtar*) than in the composition of water, whereas the parts of void in earth are less numerous, but more numerous in water. For this reason, water becomes more rare than earth, and more subtle and luminous, whereas earth becomes dense and dark. Likewise, next in order the parts of matter in water are more numerous than in air, and the parts of void in air more than those in water, while the parts of matter in air are more numerous than those in fire, and the parts of void in fire more than those in air. The difference found between these bodies, in terms of rarity and density, and light and darkness, is due to the difference in the parts of those two substances [sc. void and matter] in their composition." My thanks to Hanif Amin for help with the Persian text.

Though he does not necessarily accept all the details of this view, we will see that Fakhr al-Dīn also tends to think that various physical phenomena prove the existence of dispersed void.

This theory should be distinguished from the idea that void explains certain physical phenomena, for instance the ability of the "water-thief" to retain fluid (like when the top hole of a straw is blocked to stop the water from flowing out). As Avicenna already noted (*Healing: Physics*, §2.8.25), such cases of so-called *horror vacui* show not that void is possible, but to the contrary, that bodies move or fail to move so as to *prevent* void from forming. Though Fakhr al-Dīn does speak in this context of an "attractive power" of void (§7.6, 182–3), the phenomena in question don't really establish that void has independent existence. Perhaps for this reason, he devotes little space to the question. In fact his most substantial discussion of *horror vacui* is in the *Mabāḥith* (357–60), which is based closely on Avicenna (*Healing: Physics* §2.8.20–5).[18]

2. Proving the Void

Thus the void whose reality is accepted by Fakhr al-Dīn involves an infinite empty space surrounding the cosmos, and the interstitial or dispersed void found in bodies within the cosmos. These are not different in kind: in both cases we are dealing with empty space or place, that is, three-dimensional extension not occupied by a body. Such a void would have to be a real entity, rather than mere "non-existence (*ʿadam*)" as claimed by some *mutakallimūn*.[19] This is shown by the fact that different parts of the void have different sizes, since one pair of bodies could be separated by a smaller void than another pair of bodies. And clearly, sheer non-existence cannot have a determinate size (*Mabāḥith* 341, *Mulakhkhaṣ* 94r-v). But how to settle the question whether void, so conceptualized, really does exist? In some texts, though not in the *Maṭālib*, Fakhr al-Dīn draws a contrast between two kinds of argument: "intellectual proofs (*adilla ʿaqliyya*)," on the other, "physical evidence (*ʿalāmāt ṭabīʿiyya*)" (*Mabāḥith* 343). We might say that the former consist of thought experiments, the latter of real experiments.

Among the "intellectual" arguments in favor of the void, the most basic is one mentioned early on in the *Maṭālib*'s treatment of the issue (§5.3, 57, cf. *Arbaʿīn* 32). When a body moves into a new place, it must be possible for the new place to accommodate that body. Perhaps the new place was previously empty, in which

18 In this case the earlier Rāzī is mentioned: *Mabāḥith* 357–8 names him as a proponent of the idea that void has a power of attraction.

19 Cf. Avicenna *Healing: Physics*, §2.8.1.

case we have admitted that void exists. If it was not empty, then its previous occupant must give way: it cannot still be there, since otherwise the moving body and the previous occupant would "interpenetrate (*tadākhala*)," which is impossible. So the previous occupant needs to find another place to accommodate it; if that other place is not void, then its occupant will also have to give way, and so on. This, as Fakhr al-Dīn nicely puts it, "would imply that the whole cosmos would have to be shoved around (*tutadāfaʿu*) when any motion occurs, and this claim is not credible." He gives the example of a fish swimming in the sea, which just by its motion would make the entire sea move (§5.3.1, 58). Unfortunately this is not actually a very convincing argument. To take his example, the water in front of the fish could be displaced to the space behind the fish, which the fish has just vacated. This one replacement would be enough, and need have no knock-on consequences for the rest of the ocean. Of course, this potential response is not original with me: the idea of "mutual replacement (*antiperistasis*)" is already mentioned by Aristotle, drawing on Plato.[20]

A good thing, then, that Fakhr al-Dīn has a number of other arguments at his disposal. He later singles out as particularly strong (*fī ghāyat al-quwwa*) the consideration that if atomism is true, then there will have to be void between the atoms:

> *Maṭālib* §5.9, 166: We shall later offer certain proof that sensible bodies are composed from parts, each of which is susceptible to division [only] in the imagination (*al-qisma al-wahmiyya*), but totally insusceptible of division by [actual] splitting (*infikāk*). We shall show too that the shape of each part is spherical. Given that the truth of these two premises is established by certain demonstration, we infer that when those spherical parts are touching and in contact, what is between them will turn out to be void. For when spheres are joined one to another, there must result emptiness, gaps and void spaces between them.

Of course in the present context this is just a kind of promissory note. Insofar as the postulation of void presupposes an atomic theory, a convinced continuist like Avicenna will be unmoved by this "particularly strong" line of thought. A decision on the question, as Fakhr al-Dīn himself says, will have to wait until the discussion of atomism later in the *Maṭālib*.[21]

Yet it would be hasty to assume that his positive case for the void rests entirely on the atomic theory. When we turn to the "physical evidence" considered by

20 *Physics* 4.8, 215a14–17, 8.10, 266b25–267a20; Plato, *Timaeus* 79b which explains breath by appealing to mutual replacement, and 80c which explicitly appeals to the phenomenon to exclude void. See also Opsomer 1999.

21 On which see Setia 2006. Fakhr al-Dīn's commitment to atomism goes all the way back to his early work *Uṣūl al-dīn*, which suggests that angels could reach a buried corpse to perform a post-mortem inquisition by moving through the gaps between the atoms in the earth. I take this information from Shihadeh 2012, 472.

Fakhr al-Dīn, we see that if anything, his discussion presupposes for dialectical purposes that bodies are continuous. He describes phenomena involving vessels like wineskins, flasks, and copper pots, which seem to provide evidence that void does exist. These are presented in some detail in the *Maṭālib* (§5.6–8, 163–6). They include, for instance, the fact that it is possible to insert a needle into a fully inflated wineskin, which shows that even when the interior of the wineskin is "full" there must also be empty space to accommodate the point of the needle. Or again, if we suck air out of a flask and then immerse it in water, water moves into the flask – this shows that the suction increased the amount of void in the flask, which leaves room for the water. As Fakhr al-Dīn recognizes, a continuist could avoid concluding that void is involved here by appealing to changes in density. For instance, the air could allow the needle to enter the wineskin by becoming slightly more compressed. But he rules this out, using Avicenna against himself:

> *Maṭālib ad* §5.6.1, 164: The *shaykh al-ra'īs* [i.e. Avicenna] stated that matter has, in the definition of its essence and true nature, neither volume nor extension. So its relation to all sizes is the same, or so he says. We say: if this is so, then one cannot claim that some sizes are "natural" in relation to that matter, and others "forced." For the relation of all sizes to it will be the same. If so, then that volume which results from suction and rarefaction is natural for that matter, so it should remain as it was, and not decrease when the flask is immersed in the water.

Here Fakhr al-Dīn is engaging in sophistry. When Avicenna says that matter has neither volume nor extension in itself, he is referring to prime matter and not matter like air.[22] Nonetheless, it might be regarded as a good question whether air can retain its nature, that is, avoid being destroyed, despite being forced to give up its natural degree of density. Avicenna evidently thinks that it can. He proposes that in the case of a clepsydra, void is prevented from forming by changes in density (*Healing: Physics* §2.9.20). This no more destroys the water than would a change in respect of heat and cold.[23]

It almost goes without saying that real experiments like these could only concern dispersed void, not the infinite void surrounding the cosmos. The same goes for another argument offered in favor of void by Fakhr al-Dīn (*Maṭālib* §5.4, 159). Imagine, he says, that two flat surfaces are in contact, then pulled apart. Since it will take some time – even if only a very little – for the space in between the two surfaces to fill completely with air, there must be void between the two bodies before the air rushes in. It would seem that he finds this to be one of the most

22 For this contrast see *Healing: Physics* §1.9.1. For Avicenna determinate quantity arises at the level of body, not of matter. See on this Lammer 2018, §3.1.

23 It should however be said that these changes would be unnatural. For instance at *Healing: On Generation and Corruption* 129–30, Avicenna explains that the form of an element gives it various "perfections (*kamālāt*)" including quantitative ones that give it a "natural size (*kamm ṭabīʿī*)." My thanks to Andreas Lammer for these references and for discussion of the issue.

compelling arguments in favor of the void. He lavishes attention on its presuppositions, arguing that two surfaces can indeed touch with no air trapped in between (we can tell this from our own experience by touching our fingers together), that the two surfaces do separate "all at once (*duf atan*)" rather than part by part, and that there is no other way that air can get in between the surfaces apart from traveling in from the edges (§5.4.1–3, 159–61).

The argument is also mentioned as an especially strong one in both the *Mabāḥith* (351) and the *Arbaʿīn*, which states:

> *Arbaʿīn* 35: There can be no answer to this proof on the principles [accepted by] the philosophers (*falāsifa*), but only on theological principles (*uṣūl al-islāmiyyīn*), since on that basis one could say that, at the first moment when one surface is taken away from another, the Free Agent creates a body in between. On this reckoning, void would not arise.

In other words, since God can act instantaneously, when the two bodies are separated, He could create new air in between them so that there is no time lapse before the space is filled with air rushing in from the surrounding environment. The *Maṭālib* also recognizes this possibility (§5.4.3.1, 161), and likewise says that it is not one open to the philosophers since they "deny the Free Agent (*al-fāʿil al-mukhtār*)." It is another nice example of Fakhr al-Dīn's "internal critique" of Avicenna, in this case using Avicennan necessitarianism to undermine Avicennan physics.

3. Responding to Objections

This question of whether God is a "Free Agent," capable of intervening directly in the physical cosmos and of making arbitrary decisions, is also at the center of another argument considered by Fakhr al-Dīn. In this case though, the argument is one offered by Avicenna *against* the possibility of void:

> *Physics: Healing* §2.8.10 (McGinnis trans.): There will not be different directions in the void; but when there is no difference of directions and places, then it is impossible that there be some place that is naturally left behind and another that is naturally tended toward. So, then, there will be no natural rest in the void, since within the void there will be no location that is better suited than another to there being natural rest in it.[24]

Or, as Fakhr al-Dīn rephrases the argument:

> *Maṭālib* §6.2, 168: Void is either pure non-existence and sheer non-being, as the *mutakallimūn* say, or it is an extension with homogeneous (*mutashābih*) parts and regions (*jawānib*), according to what was stated by the ancient philosophers. Either way, there is

24 Cf. Aristotle, *Physics* 4.8, 215a1–14.

> no difference at all between its parts and portions. But if this is so, it cannot be that the body is at rest in just one of its parts or regions, because if the body were to remain fixed (*mustaqirr*) in [that part], laying a claim (*ṭālib*) to it and needing (*lāzim*) to remain in it, despite [that part's] being equivalent to all the other regions and directions (*aṭrāf*), then one possibility would be preponderated over others, which is absurd.

Now we are clearly thinking about void as an infinite, undifferentiated extension. The extension must be infinite, since if it had limits then particular parts of void would be distinguished by their position relative to those limits (this is made clear at §6.2.1, 171). For instance a void with spherical shape would have a center, which could be chosen as the appropriate place for earth to come to rest. But in an infinite void, no one region is more apt than any other to be the place of earth, or of any other natural body.

As Fakhr al-Dīn goes on to say (*ad* §6.2.3–4, 172–3), this argument is only compelling if it is impossible for God to preponderate one region of the void over others to be a natural place for a given body, or to be a place for the whole universe. That might seem obvious to Avicenna, who denies that God can act in an arbitrary fashion, but for Fakhr al-Dīn it is worse than non-obvious, it is false. He appeals to the specified, determinate features of sublunary bodies, which have all been preponderated to be as they are even though it is clear to our intellects that they might be different. The same response is made in Fakhr al-Dīn's commentary on Avicenna's *'Uyūn al-ḥikma* (92, 95), not without a bit of gratuitous abuse concerning the repetitive way that Avicenna has insisted on the homogeneity argument: "it's amazing thing is how the *shaykh*, even in this little book, repeats this argument on the same topic three times, for no good reason!" (96).

Fakhr al-Dīn is no more impressed by a second argument against void given by Avicenna, despite its august pedigree. Already Aristotle had argued that motion in a void would be impossible, because the speed of a motion is inversely proportional to the density of the medium.[25] Fakhr al-Dīn's example is that a stone sinks more quickly in water than in oil (*Maṭālib* §6.3.1, 169). Void, however, provides no resistance at all, from which Aristotle inferred that no ratio (*logos*) can be found for determining the speed of a motion through void. Avicenna repeats this argument at *Healing: Physics* 2.8.11–12, and also in the *'Uyūn al-ḥikma*. Fakhr al-Dīn's commentary on that work already provides his basic response:

> *Sharḥ 'Uyūn al-ḥikma* 98: This argument is exceedingly weak. For we say that motion insofar as it is motion, disregarding the resistance of the medium, doubtless requires a determinate amount of time. Proof: the motion as such takes place over a determinate interval, so the motion to the halfway point of that interval precedes the motion from its

25 *Physics* 215a24–216a11.

halfway point to its end. But wherever priority and posteriority occur, time occurs. So it is established that motion as such requires a certain measure of time.[26]

In other words, motions have inherent speed and resistance serves only to impede the motion and reduce this inherent speed. The *Maṭālib* makes the point with great clarity:

Maṭālib ad §6.3, 1, 174–5: If we assume that part of the [required] time is to accommodate the motion in itself, and part of it to accommodate the hindrance, then the motion in pure void will take place in that amount of time that is appropriate to the motion[27] as it is in itself. Motion occurring in a plenum, meanwhile, will occur in that amount of time plus a further amount of time, as rendered appropriate by whatever is in the interval that offers hindrance.

This response is not particularly innovative, but is historically intriguing nonetheless. Here we see him taking over an idea already put forward by Philoponus and Abū l-Barakāt al-Baghdādī: moving bodies will move a certain distance over a certain time because of the force applied to them and their own qualities, and resistance simply modifies the motion.[28] Fakhr al-Dīn repeats a nice point made by Abū l-Barakāt, that in the Aristotelian cosmology the heavenly spheres do manage to move without encountering resistance. He also argues out that motion cannot depend for its existence on the presence of something that hinders it (*ad* §6.3, 1, 173–4).

A related controversy concerns the case of a stone thrown upward from the surface of the earth. The opponent suggests that, if the stone were to encounter no resistance, it would simply keep moving until it reached the vault of the heavens. This shows that there cannot be void between the earth and the heavens (*Maṭālib* §6.4, 170; *Mabāḥith* 344; *Mulakhkhaṣ*, 96r–96v). To this Fakhr al-Dīn makes the eminently reasonable response that the argument shows only that there is in fact air between the earth and the heavens, not that it would be intrinsically impossible for there to be void instead of air (*Maṭālib ad* §6.4, 2). Assuming that he accepts Abū l-Barakāt's theory of inclination (*mayl*),[29] he might have made a more acute response. The forced inclination bestowed upon the stone by the thrower will be counteracted by the stone's natural inclination to fall back towards the earth, so its upward journey would be halted even without resistance. All that the air resistance will do is make it fall back down a bit earlier.

A final argument against the void, or at least the last one I would like to highlight, concerns the question of how a region of void relates to body. Re-

26 There is a close parallel to this passage at *Maṭālib ad* §6.3, 1, 173.

27 Reading *al-ḥaraka*.

28 See Pines 1979, 15.

29 For the contrast see Adamson 2016, 305. See also Hasnawi 1984, Nony 2011, and McGinnis 2010, 79–84.

member that for Fakhr al-Dīn, void is a real entity: spatial extension that can exist independently of body. But what happens when a void space is occupied by a body? Since the void space is not destroyed when the body arrives in it, it would seem that void and the body are both in exactly the same place: they "overlap" or "interpenetrate." This is an unfortunate result for the proponent of void. For, as we saw above, this proponent actually argues for void on the basis that a moving body cannot interpenetrate with another body residing in the location into which it moves. (The fish cannot overlap with the water through which it is swimming.) As Fakhr al-Dīn phrases the problem, if void is "self-subsisting" then its extension must interpenetrate with that of the occupying body, which is absurd (*Maṭālib* §6.1, 167).

This argument is highly reminiscent of, if not identical to, an argument used by Avicenna against the idea of self-subsisting place. But he also uses it against void in *ʿUyūn al-ḥikma* (cf. *Healing: Physics* §2.8.6):

> *ʿUyūn al-ḥikma* 83: If void existed, place would have dimensions (*abʿād*) in every direction (*jiha*), and would admit of distinction (*faṣl*) in directions, like body. In that case, either these dimensions would interpenetrate those of body, or not. If not, then it prevents this from occurring [i. e. the dimensions of void would stop the dimensions of body from entering], but then it would be a plenum; a contradiction. But if they do penetrate, then one dimension overlaps with another so that from the merging of two equivalent dimensions arise a dimension just like only one of them, which is a contradiction.

In his commentary, Fakhr al-Dīn agrees that place or void does have extension, but demands a reason why it is impossible for this sort of extension to overlap with the extension of a body. Proponents of self-subsisting place and void, after all, think it is obvious that there is a self-subsisting extension inside a cup that can be filled alternately by water and then air (*Sharḥ ʿUyūn al-ḥikma*, 86). Avicenna's mistake is to suppose that adding two extensions will cause an increase in quantity, rather than only number (87).[30]

Conclusion

As I have argued elsewhere, the treatments of time and place in the *Maṭālib* are an important milestone in the history of natural philosophy.[31] Fakhr al-Dīn argues that both of these fundamental principles are self-subsisting entities, which are admittedly dependent for their existence upon God's creative act, but are in-

30 As discussed in Adamson 2017, he gives the same response to an argument concerning "overlapping" extensions in Avicenna's treatment of place in the *Healing*.

31 See n. 10 above.

dependent of bodies. This constituted a direct assault on the broadly Aristotelian physics accepted by Avicenna, in favor of an alternative physics whose innovative character was rather understated by Fakhr al-Dīn himself, given that he claimed simply to be following the ideas of Plato on these issues. In truth, his treatment of void is less groundbreaking. It is admirably complete as a survey of both physical and "intellectual" considerations for and against void. But the core ideas defended by Fakhr al-Dīn are already to be found in Abū l-Barakāt and still earlier authors. On the other hand, the discussion of void in the *Maṭālib* and elsewhere gives us an insight into his motivation for defending the aforementioned theory of time and place. As the last argument mentioned reminds us, there is an intimate connection between the idea of a self-subsisting place and the idea of void. After all, if place is really self-subsisting, then it does not need to be occupied by a body to keep existing; and this means that void should be possible, at least in principle. The empirical evidence considered by Fakhr al-Dīn simply confirms that this possibility is in fact realized within our world.

In light of this, it seems clear that a major reason, if not the primary reason, for Fakhr al-Dīn to insist on the independence of place was to render plausible a belief in the void. This is an intriguing finding as concerns his scholarly profile more generally. Throughout this "physical" section of the *Maṭālib*, Fakhr al-Dīn often speaks of *mutakallimūn* as a well-defined group to which he does not belong. For example, they equate void with "pure non-existence," whereas he does not. His approach is also "philosophical" in a structural sense: his decision to investigate time, place, and void in an unbroken stretch of arguments echoes Avicenna's *Healing*, and thus indirectly Aristotle's *Physics*. Nonetheless, Fakhr al-Dīn aims to reject the Avicennan and Aristotelian picture of the physical world. His physics is in its broad outline, if not in its details, essentially that of earlier *kalām*. The Razian universe is not a continuous body that proceeds from God necessarily and is surrounded by nothing whatsoever, not even empty space. It is an arbitrarily created universe, consisting of atoms, and situated within an infinite void.

Appendix

Outline of the discussion of void in *al-Maṭālib al-ʿāliya min al-ʿilm al-ilāhī*

Faṣl 5: Is void possible? [155–66]

5.1: Body needs place. If place also needed body, we would have circular dependence which is absurd.

    5.1.1: But substance and accident do need each other.

ad 5.1.1: Most accidents (e.g. colors) depend on body, and body can exist without them. Some are not like this: location, motion and rest. Motion and rest however presuppose location. Since body in itself cannot exist without location, body is not the cause of the existence of location. The reverse is not true, so the symmetry claimed by the objection fails.

5.2: If location could not exist without body, then it would be impossible for bodies to move since a body needs to leave location behind once it vacates that location.

5.3: When a body moves, it must replace something else; if this is not void, then what is replaced must in turn exchange places with something else, which leads either to a circle (mutual replacement) or to a regress of bodies moving other bodies, forcing everything in the world to shift, which is not credible.

5.3.1: God may remove what is being replaced, and create a new body in the just vacated region. The possibility of this is proven by the case of a fish in water. If there were any void, the water, being fluid, would immediately fill it; yet fish are able to swim without shifting the whole sea around.

ad 5.3.1: For God to create a body in the vacated region, there must first be void there, since bodies cannot interpenetrate. As for the case of water, it is precisely because there is so much void in water that it is fluid.

5.4: If we suppose one surface touching another completely, and then removed all at once, a void must arise between the two at the first moment of its removal.

5.4.1: Such complete contact is possible: claiming otherwise implies void between the two surfaces, and besides if we put the fingers of our two hands together we can tell that they are completely in contact.

5.4.2: The removal of one surface from another all at once is possible: otherwise the surface being removed would have to break, since one part of it would move while the rest did not. Also, "failure to touch" occurs instantaneously.

5.4.3: Proof that a void must arise if one surface is removed from the other all at once: otherwise a body must arise in between the two surfaces. This cannot already have been present before the surfaces were taken apart, since they were touching. Nor can it move into the gap: the body would either have to pass through pores in the surfaces or come from the sides. Against motion through pores, even surfaces with pores have continuous surfaces between the pores and these interstitial surfaces would also have to be able to come apart all at once. Against motion from the sides, the body rushing into the gap would have to first be at the edges of the vacated space and only then in the middle, since the in-rushing body cannot be in two places at once; but then there must at first be a void in the middle.

5.4.3.1: Perhaps one could say that, when the surfaces are taken apart, the Voluntary Agent [i. e. God] creates a body in between. Or, we could say that in between there is a body that loses density.

ad 5.4.3.1: The philosophers deny a Voluntary Agent, and the second proposal presupposes a body already present between the two surfaces. The second idea has already been disproven in the section on motion (*bāb al-ḥaraka*). Besides, even a body changing in density still needs to begin at the edge and move into the middle.

5.5: The possibility of inserting needles into an inflated wineskin shows that there must be void inside, since otherwise the needle would have to interpenetrate the air inside.

5.5.1: Three other explanations are possible, all of which would explain how there is room for the needle: the wineskin may expand slightly when the needle is inserted; or some air might escape through pores of the wineskin; or the air inside may get more dense.

ad 5.5.1: If we suppose that the wineskin is first stretched out and then inflated as far as it will go, it will be clear that further expanding it, or forcing air out through pores, would require great force. But this is not the case: we can insert the needle easily. The third answer presupposes the possibility of changing the air's density which was already refuted in the section on motion.

5.6: If a flask undergoes suction and then inverted into water, water will ascend into it, which shows that it must be less full (i. e. more void) than it was before the suction.

5.6.1: A different explanation is possible: some air has been removed, so that the air expands to a greater volume by force. When the suction ends and the flask is put into the water, the air returns to its natural volume and water ascends because of *horror vacui.*

ad 5.6.1: This is rejected, for three reasons. First, again we don't accept the talk of changes in density. Second, the parts of the air would individually need to contract on this account; when the suction is removed the parts will either vanish (but why should some vanish while others remain?) or all will return to normal, but then they should take up as much room as they did initially. Third, Avicenna states that no given size is more appropriate to matter than any other size, so no size is "natural" for matter as opposed to "force." Thus the new contracted size of the air should be just as natural as its size prior to the suction, and it will not withdraw to let in the water.

5.7: If a hard, copper vessel is filled with water, then sealed tightly and heated over a hot flame, the vessel bursts. This cannot be because anything penetrates in from outside, nor because the volume of the water itself expands (for reasons discussed regarding the previous arguments). The only explanation then is that the void in the water expands, so that the volume of the contents increases.

5.8: If air is blown into a flask and then stopped with a thumb, and the flask is then immersed in water and the thumb removed, the additional air blown in escapes as bubbles. This shows that the flask was not entirely full of air, otherwise it wouldn't be possible to increase the amount of air contained in it. One might reply by appealing to changes in density, but we know that this is an ineffective response.

5.9: The strongest argument in favor of void: we will later show that sensible bodies are composed from indivisible parts, and that these are spherical. This proves there is void, since when spheres are touching void spaces will be left around them.

Faṣl 6: Proofs against void and replies [167–77]

6.1: The theory of void presupposes voids of different sizes. The extension of any given void would have to be self-subsisting and independent, or identical with the extension of a body. If the former, then the two extensions interpenetrate which is absurd. If the latter, the extension is in fact full; as Aristotle says, "the name void is itself void."

6.2: The supposed void would be homogeneous in its parts, so no body could be at rest or move in it: for why should one part of void be preponderated to hold a given body, if all parts are equivalent, and why should body leave one part and go to another?

6.3: Motion through void is impossible, either in time or not in time.

6.3.1: Against its occurring in time: the time needed is inversely proportional to the density of the medium. Suppose that a body moves through ten cubits of void in one hour and ten cubits of water in ten hours. Now, suppose it moving through a medium ten times less dense than water; in that case, it should move through this medium at the same speed as through void. It will move even more quickly through a still less dense medium. Thus a body could move at the same speed, or faster, than it does through void despite the presence of resistance.

6.3.2: Against its occurring without time: all motion occurs in time, since it covers the first half of an interval before it covers the second half.

6.4: When a stone is thrown upward, it is stopped only by the resistance of a medium, so the medium cannot be void.

6.5: Water drains out of a small hole in a vessel only if the mouth of the vessel is not closed. This is to prevent void from forming.

6.6: Water moves up when you suck on a straw, and flesh in a cupping glass. [Implicit: this is to prevent void from forming.]

6.7: If we insert a tube into the neck of a flask and seal them together, then when the tube is pulled out the flask will collapse inward, and when the tube is pushed in, it will shatter outwards. This is to prevent void from forming.

6.8: If void were possible, one could put an empty flask under water and the flask would fill with water, without air escaping in the form of bubbles. But this is not the case.

ad 6.1: The argument presupposes that place is self-subsisting dimensions, which has already been discussed in the previous section.

ad 6.2: Several points are addressed concerning this argument:

ad 6.2, 1: Void need not be infinite but may extend only to the edge of the universe (even though the upholders of void don't typically adopt this position).

ad 6.2, 2: The parts of void are not necessarily homogeneous; after all places in the universe, on the Aristotelian account, are not. Though all parts of void are susceptible to three dimensions, this may be only a shared concomitant of their different essences.

ad 6.2, 3: The void proponent's idea that God could just arbitrarily choose certain regions of void for certain bodies raises the well-known distinction between power and necessitation, which has been explored elsewhere.

ad 6.2, 4: Animals, plants and minerals are distinguished as particulars by determinate form, location and size, which either happens without a preponderator, is preponderated by God, or is prepared by earlier events. Whichever explanation we choose can also be applied to the location of the universe in a determinate region of infinite void – the third option would involve the universe endlessly moving from one region to another.

ad 6.3: Again, several points are raised:

ad 6.3, 1: All motion needs time (three reasons are given for this premise). When something moves through a medium, part of the time needed for the motion is determined by the motion as such – and this is how long that motion would need if it occurred in void – with an additional part of time due to the resisting medium.

ad 6.3, 2: The opponent simply assumes that there will always be some degree of resistance that relates to the resistance offered by water the way that the time for motion in a void relates to that in water. But resistance, unlike size, may not be susceptible to indefinite diminishing: at some point one may go past a minimum and then no resistance is offered anymore at all.

ad 6.3, 3: Perhaps a very small amount of resistance in a medium effectively offers no resistance at all, just like void. Compare to the fact that one person may not move a stone at all, where twenty men could move it.

ad 6.4: Two points are raised:

ad 6.4, 1: The airy and fiery bodies in the atmosphere stop the motion.

ad 6.4, 2: In any case showing that there is no void there does not show that void is impossible.

ad 6.5–8: These experiments support their claim but do not prove it, since they would have to rule out other explanations. And rival experiments can be performed to show that void *is* possible, as already mentioned [sc. in §5].

Faṣl 7: Distinction (*tafārīʿ*) of positions on the subject of void [179–85]

7.1: A first view agrees with the majority of the ancient thinkers in holding that void does not admit non-existence (*ʿadam*). They prove this in two ways.

7.1.1: If void were non-existent, would right be distinguished from left, or above from below? Clearly the answer is yes, which implies that the dimensions do exist, so that we need empty space after all. Thus void's non-existence is inconceivable, and it is necessarily existent in itself.

7.1.2: We can suppose mountains or seas to vanish, but not the locations in which they exist.

ad 7.1: But right-thinking scholars (*ahl al-taḥqīq min al-ʿulamāʾ*) hold that void is contingently existent, and argue for this in two ways:

ad 7.1, 1: The necessary of existence in itself must be unique (*wāḥid*).

ad 7.1, 2: Void is divisible, and whatever is divisible is contingent.

7.2: If space existed before the universe, then there can have been no directions (above and below), because this requires differentiation through the presence of bodies.

7.3: Aristotle and other ancient thinkers have argued that there cannot be infinite void outside the universe.

7.4: God cannot be in place. For:

7.4.1: If He were, His existence would depend on that location and not vice-versa, but He is the Necessary Existent.

7.4.2: If God were everywhere, He would be divisible, and also "mixed" with created things. But if He were in some determinate location, that location would need to be preponderated.

7.4.3: If there is no space outside the universe God could not be there so would have to be enclosed by the universe.

7.5: Some hold that the four elements and celestial sphere differ in terms of the admixture of parts of void in them.

7.6: Some hold that void has the power to attract bodies and that this explains the falling and sinking of bodies. But this cannot be right, since if it were then it would impossible to break up a body, as the force of void would hold it together.

Bibliography

Primary literature

Avicenna, *The Physics of the Healing*, ed. and trans. J. McGinnis, 2 vols (Provo: 2009).

Fakhr al-Dīn al-Rāzī, *Mulakhkhaṣ fī l-ḥikma wa-l-manṭiq*, Ms. or. oct. 623 Berlin Staatsbibliothek.

–, *Sharḥ ʿUyūn al-ḥikma*, A.Ḥ. al-Saqqā, 2 vols (Cairo: 1986).

–, *al-Arbaʿīn fī uṣūl al-dīn*, A.Ḥ. al-Saqqā, 3 vols (Cairo: 1986).

–, *al-Maṭālib al-ʿāliya min al-ʿilm al-ilāhī*, A.Ḥ. al-Saqqā, 9 vols (Beirut: 1987).

–, *al-Mabāḥith al-Mashriqiyya*, ed. M.M. al-Baghdādī, 2 vols (Beirut: 1990).

al-Fārābī, *On Vacuum*, ed. and trans. N. Lugal and A. Sayili (Ankara: 1951).

John Philoponus, *Commentary on Aristotle's Physics*, ed. H. Vitelli (Berlin: 1887–88).

–, *Corollaries on Place and Void*, trans. D. Furley (London: 1991).

Nāṣir-e Khosraw, *Zād al-musāfirīn*, ed. S.M. ʿEmādī Ḥāʾerī (Tehran: 2014).

Secondary literature

P. Adamson, "Galen on Void," in P. Adamson, R. Hansberger and J. Wilberding (eds), *Philosophical Themes in Galen* (London: 2014), 197–211.

–, *A History of Philosophy Without Any Gaps: Philosophy in the Islamic World* (Oxford: 2016).
–, "Fakhr al-Dīn al-Rāzī on Place," *Arabic Sciences and Philosophy* 27 (2017), 205–36.
–, "The Existence of Time in Fakhr al-Dīn al-Rāzī's *Maṭālib al-ʿāliya*," forthcoming.
P. Adamson and A. Lammer, "Fakhr al-Dīn al-Rāzī's Platonist Account of the Essence of Time," forthcoming.
A. Dhanani, *The Physical Theory of Kalām* (Leiden: 1994).
A. Hasnawi, "La dynamique d'Ibn Sīnā (La notion d'inclination *mayl*)," in J. Jolivet and R. Rashed (eds), *Études sur Avicenne* (Paris, 1984), 102–23.
A. Lammer, *The Elements of Avicenna's Physics: Greek Sources and Arabic Innovations* (Berlin: 2018).
J. McGinnis, "Logic and Science: the Role of Genus and Difference in Avicenna's Logic, Science, and Natural Philosophy," *Document e Studi* 18 (2007a), 186–86.
–, "Avoiding the Void: Avicenna on the Impossibility of Circular Motion in a Void," in P. Adamson (ed.), *Classical Arabic Philosophy: Sources and Reception* (London: 2007b), 74–89.
–, *Avicenna* (New York: 2010).
S. Nony, "La dynamique d'Abū l-Barakāt: faire le vide pour penser le changement du changement," in P. Adamson (ed.), *In the Age of Averroes: Arabic Philosophy in the Sixth/Twelfth Century* (London: 2011), 93–116.
J. Opsomer, "*Antiperistasis:* a Platonic Theory," in A. Pérez-Jiménez et al. (eds), *Plutarco, Platón y Aristóteles* (Madrid: 1999), 417–29.
S. Pines, *Studies in Abū l-Barakāt al-Baghdādī: Physics and Metaphysics* (Jerusalem: 1979).
ʿA. Setia, "Fakhr Al-Din Al-Razi on Physics and the Nature of the Physical World: A Preliminary Survey," *Islam and Science* 2 (2004), 161–80.
–, "Atomism versus Hylomorphism in the Kalām of Fakhr al-Dīn al-Rāzī: a Preliminary Survey of the *Maṭālib al-ʿĀliyyah*," *Islam and Science* 4 (2006), 113–40.
A. Shihadeh, "Classical Ashʿarī Anthropology: Body, Life and Spirit," *Muslim World* 102 (2012), 433–77, at 472.

Universals

Fedor Benevich

The Metaphysics of Muḥammad b. ʿAbd al-Karīm al-Šahrastānī (d. 1153): *Aḥwāl* and Universals*

Introduction

In his recent study "Essence and Existence in the Eleventh- and Twelfth-Century" Robert Wisnovsky argues that the famous post-Avicennian dispute regarding whether essence and existence are distinct in reality or only as two concepts in the mind can be fruitfully interpreted in face of another metaphysical debate: whether the entities called *aḥwāl* (states/modes) in the *kalām*-tradition are additional to the essences (*ḏawāt*) of the things they belong to. According to Wisnovsky, the dispute over the reality of the essence-existence distinction may be regarded as a case study within the dispute about *aḥwāl*. For instance those who believe in the reality of *aḥwāl* would accept that existence is such a *ḥāl* which is additional to the essence of a thing.[1]

What are the *aḥwāl?* Several studies have already addressed this notion. To roughly summarize the history and the content of this theory: There was a dispute about the status of God's attributes (such as "knowing" or "powerful") since the early beginnings of the Islamic theology. One group of theologians claimed that they are additional (*zāʾid*) to God's essence (Ašʿarites), the other rejected it (Muʿtazilites). In order to keep the attributes distinct in their meanings but to avoid stating them as real additional objects some Muʿtazilites (Abū Hāšim al-Ǧubbāʾī (d. 933) was the first) introduced a new kind of entity: *aḥwāl*. Next to a knowing subject (*ʿālim*) and its attribute of knowledge (*ʿilm*) there are two more entities: "being knowledgeable" (*kawn ʿāliman*) predicated of the subject and "being knowledge" (*kawn ʿilman*) predicated of the attribute. This distinction

* I am grateful to Peter Adamson, Andreas Lammer, Hanif Amin Beidokhti, and Davlat Dadikhudah, as well as the editor of this volume and other participants of the conference "Islamic Philosophy from the 12th to the 14th Century" for their helpful feedbacks on the first version of this paper. I am also grateful to DFG for the generous support of the "Heirs of Avicenna" project.

1 Wisnovsky, "Essence and Existence." This reconstruction has some flaws that I have discussed in "Essence-Existence Distinction", 250.

gave rise to a metaphysical debate about whether there are such entities at all, i. e. whether we can accept not only in God's case but also in general that in addition to e. g. instances of the accident "black" (*sawād*) there are such generic notions as "being black" (*kawn sawādan*) i. e. "blackness", "being a color" and "being an accident". The greatest problem was the ontological status of these *aḥwāl*, because both the *aḥwāl* proponents and *aḥwāl* opponents agreed that the only really existing items in the world are atoms (*ǧawāhir*) and their accidents (*aʿrāḍ*). Hence, the *aḥwāl* proponents had to describe *aḥwāl* as "neither existent nor non-existent". Thereby they intended to state that *aḥwāl* are entities ontologically dependent on the subjects they are attributed to, i. e. on atoms and accidents, which are really existent. At least this is how a group of Ašʿarites, most prominently ʿAbd al-Malik b. ʿAbdallāh al-Ǧuwaynī (d. 1085), explained the ontological status of *aḥwāl* when accepting their reality. However, the mainstream Ašʿarite view rejected any reality of *aḥwāl*. Instead, they claimed that all the aforementioned attributes like "blackness" or "being a color" are merely names (*asmāʾ*), words (*alfāẓ*) or judgments (*aḥkām*). We find the highpoint of this movement in the works of Salmān b. Nāṣir al-Anṣārī (d.1118), who maintained that there is no metaphysical space for *aḥwāl* nor do we need them to be real. The traditional Ašʿarite anti-*aḥwāl* metaphysical doctrine comes close to what we would nowadays call a theory of bare particulars: there are only unitary extramental objects like "this black" and "that black" which do not share any metaphysically real attribute.[2]

In this paper, I will investigate the approach to the *aḥwāl* theory by the prominent Islamic theologian Muḥammad b. ʿAbd al-Karīm al-Šahrastānī (d. 1153). Although this author is well known for his encyclopedia of sects and religions *al-Milal wa-l-nihal*, little attention has been devoted to his own contribution to the development of philosophical and theological discussions.[3] I will establish his contribution while analyzing his work on the two central questions of the *kalām*-ontology: the ontological status of *aḥwāl* and the question of whether a thing (*šayʾ*) can be non-existent (*maʿdūm*), since Šahrastānī sees them as related. The main source will be Šahrastānī's treatise *Nihāyat al-aqdām fī ʿilm al-kalām*.[4] We will see first that Šahrastānī rejects the mainstream Ašʿarite nominalism. However, he does not accept the Ǧuwaynian realism about *aḥwāl*

2 Frank, "Theory of Modes"; Frank, *Beings and Their Attributes*; Frank, "Ašʿarite Ontology"; Alami, *L'ontologie modal*; Thiele, "*Aḥwāl*"; Benevich, "Juwaynī and his Opponents".

3 Šahrastānī's scholarship recently concentrated on his Ismāʿīlī aspects which are not relevant for the present study (s. e. g. Steigerwald, *La pansée de Shahratsānī*). Related to them are several studies on Šahrastānī's criticism of Avicenna's concept of God (s. Treiger, "Transcendental Modulation", 329–30, Madelung, "Šahrastānī's Streitschrift" and Jolivet, "Critique").

4 Unfortunately, this undoubtedly important text is available only in one old edition by A. Guillaume (1934) which is far from corresponding to the modern editorial norms.

either. His own path is wholly dispersed with Avicenna's metaphysics: he understands the *aḥwāl* theory through Avicenna's theory of universals. He explains the Muʿtazilite doctrine about the non-existent through Avicenna's essence-existence distinction theory. He develops his own solutions to both problems on the basis of Avicenna's theory of universals and that of mental existence. Combining the Ašʿarite and Avicennian elements of ontology, Šahrastānī builds up his own metaphysics which may be called "Avicennian Ašʿarite". In this respect a case study of his metaphysics will reveal the central general developments in post-Avicennian ontology. In order to understand the historical significance of Šahrastānī's analysis, I will draw some parallels between his study of *aḥwāl* and the theories of other important thinkers of 11–12th centuries like ʿUmar Ḫayyām (d. 1123–4), Faḫr al-Dīn al-Rāzī (d. 1210), Abū l-Barakāt al-Baġdādī (d. 1165), Ibn Ġaylān al-Balḫī (d. c. 1194), Šihāb al-Dīn al-Suhrawardī (d. 1191) and Sayf al-Dīn al-Āmidī (d. 1233).

1. The Rejection of Nominalism

Šahrastānī sees himself in *Nihāya* as an umpire between the *aḥwāl* proponents and opponents.[5] He explains what in his opinion is wrong about each position and suggests his own view instead. In this section, we will see how Šahrastānī argues against the *aḥwāl* opponents. He has two main points of disagreement with them. First, they assumed that the notions of similarity and difference between objects are merely verbal. Second, they claimed that accidents and atoms are different and similar due to their "selves" (*ḏawāt*)[6] and their existences (*wuǧūdāt*), which are identical with their "selves". Šahrastānī rejects both main doctrines of the traditional Ašʿarism (I will begin with the second and then return to the first).

The problem of similarity and specificity was the central issue in the discussion about the metaphysical reality of *aḥwāl*. The *aḥwāl* proponents claimed that we necessarily recognize that two atoms (*ǧawāhir*) are similar in terms of their "being an atom" and differ in terms of "being *this* atom" and "being *that* atom". This was the main argument in support of the reality of *aḥwāl* which were posited to correspond to those elements of similarity and difference. The *aḥwāl*

5 Šahrastānī introduces his own arguments saying in all modesty "the sage who watches over the end of the stepping forward of the two parties said…" *(qāla l-ḥākim al-mušraf ʿalā nihāyat aqdām al-farīqayn)*. Cf. the title of the treatise.

6 In what follows I will translate *ḏāt* as "essence" in a purely Avicennian context and as "self" in the pre-Avicennian *kalām*-context. The reason is that the post-Avicennian *kalām* stands under the influence of Avicenna's philosophical terminology and understand *ḏāt* as essence, whereas applying the notion of "essence" to the pre-Avicennian *kalām* is rather anachronistic.

opponents disagreed. They maintained that things differ and resemble through their "selves" (*ḏawāt*), their "specificity" (*ḫāṣṣiya*) or their existence (*wuǧūd*).[7] Šahrastānī takes this to mean that every particular atom (*ǧawhar*) is different from anything else – be it another atom or an accident "white" – in all respects due to its "self". He objects to this position. According to Šahrastānī, *this* particular atom differs from *that* particular atom through its particular space-occupation (*taḥayyuz maḫṣūṣ*). However, this *atom* cannot differ from this *accident* through its particular space-occupation. Rather it differs by the general fact that atoms occupy space whereas accidents do not (*al-ʿaql innamā yumayyizu bi-muṭlaq al-taḥayyuz*).[8] Hence Šahrastānī agrees with the *aḥwāl* proponents that one has to introduce some generic entities that would correspond to e.g. "space-occupation taken absolutely".

Šahrastānī does not agree with the second horn of the traditional Ašʿarite formula that things differ through their existences either. He recognizes that this position is based on the idea that e.g. in the case of atoms the space-occupation is identical to the existence of an atom (*li-anna wuǧūd wa-l-taḥayyuz wāḥid*). Yet he points out that in this case the aspect by which atoms and accidents differ (space-occupation) would be identical with the aspect which they share (existence), which is absurd.[9] This argumentation reveals Šahrastānī's adherence to the Ǧuwaynian idea that existence is something shared (*muštarak*), i.e. that existence is a univocal notion (at least for worldly objects); otherwise his argument would not go through.[10] However, the *aḥwāl* opponents have never accepted this Ǧuwaynian theory. They endorsed a metaphysics of unitary extramental objects: there are not multiple attributes which belong to the accident "this black". Rather, "this black" represents a unity, a bare particular, which does not share anything with any other accidents or atoms. The same applies to existence. For instance, as it has become manifest especially in Rāzī's doxographical accounts of the different theories of existence (*wuǧūd*), a good mainstream Ašʿarite doctrine would insist that existence is an equivocal notion.[11] This means that atoms and accidents do not share a qualitatively identical attribute of "existence" but only the linguistic utterance expressing the fact that they exist. The meaning of the utterance "existence" will be different in each case. This allows the ex-

---

7 See Benevich, "Juwaynī and His Opponents", 163.
8 Šahrastānī, *Nihāya*, 145.5–11.
9 Šahrastānī, *Nihāya*, 145.12–16.
10 Ǧuwaynī makes clear that he endorses *ištirāk al-wuǧūd* with his argument in favor of *aḥwāl*. He says that knowing existence is different from knowing specific features of things, see Ǧuwaynī, *Šāmil*, 630.10–11; *ibid.*, 637.3–639.3 and *Šāmil* (Frank), 52.3–14; as well as paraphrased in Anṣārī, *Ġunya*, 491.10–15. Šahrastānī famously rejects the univocity of existence between God and world in *Muṣāraʿa*, 40–41.
11 See Rāzī, *Mabāḥiṯ* I, 120.17–21; *Nihāyat al-ʿuqūl* I, 437–38; *Arbaʿīn* I, 143; *Maṭālib* I, 291.

istence of atom to be identical with its space-occupation (one could say "to exist" for an atom means "to exist as a space-occupying item") and to differ from the existence of accident (for which it means "to exist as an item which requires space-occupation"). Hence, Šahrastānī's argument simply would not obtain. However, he rules out the theory on which the traditional Ašʿarite assumption of the equivocity of existence is based: that things do not share anything but "names".

The first move that Šahrastānī makes against the *aḥwāl* opponents is to reject the traditional Ašʿarite nominalism. He has two main arguments in support of his view. The first goes as follows:

> [T1] Is not it the case that if the words are eliminated from the clarification, the judgments in the intellect (*al-qaḍāyā al-ʿaqliyya*) are not eliminated as well, since [even] animals (*al-bahāʾim*), which do not possess speech (*nuṭq*) and intellect, do not lack this [kind of] guidance? For they know from the nature (*bi-l-fiṭra*) which grass is healthy for them and they eat [it]. Furthermore, if they see some other grass similar to the first one, they do not hesitate about whether it is edible like the first. Hence, if they could not imagine (*taḫayyalat*) the same judgment (*ʿayn ḥukm*) about the second as they did about the first, that is its being eatable (*kawn maʾkūlan*), then they would not eat, yet they know the genus [of healthy grass] and they like it, and they know its opposite and they flee from it.[12]

In this passage Šahrastānī brings his opponents to attention that animals can distinguish between what is healthy and good for them and what is not. He probably borrows the idea from Avicenna, who tried to explain through the faculty of estimation how and why the sheep flees from the wolf knowing that it is dangerous for it.[13] Thereby Šahrastānī shows that there has to be something beyond the linguistic utterance which combines the one piece of healthy grass with another in the animal perception, since they do not have language, yet still can have this "same judgment" about all the grass that is healthy for them.

Šahrastānī is on dangerous ground. His argumentation suggests that he accepts that animals can make universal judgments. Avicenna would not allow this. If animals were able to conceive of universals, they would have to have immaterial intellects, or even be immortal.[14] The tension is clear already within Šahrastānī's own text. He wants to establish that judgments of similarity are not bound to merely linguistic items. Rather they are "judgments in the intellect". However, when arguing for this on the basis of the case study of animals he recognizes that they do not have intellects (*lā ʿaqla*). This would mean that they cannot possess

12 Šahrastānī, *Nihāya*, 144.3–8.

13 Avicenna, *Šifāʾ*, *Nafs* I.5, 44.2–7. On this see Hasse, *Avicenna's De Anima*, 129–41 and Black, "Estimation."

14 For the connection between immortality of the soul and the conception of universals s. Adamson, "Correcting Plotinus" and Druart, "Soul's Individuation."

"judgments in the intellect" either. Šahrastānī may also allude to the same problem when using the notion of "imagining" (*taḫayyul*). If he thereby follows the notions of Avicenna's philosophy of mind, he avoids ascribing any intellectual activity to animals. Instead they possess the capacity of imagination, a material faculty which does not operate with universals, but only with images.

Perhaps the problematic character of the "animals-argument" was the reason why Šahrastānī introduces another argument which addresses only the human intellectual activities:

> [T2] We say that you cannot help but ascribe the function of perception (*idrāk*) to the intellects and the function of speech (*kalām*) to the languages. For the intellect perceives humanity as a universal, which is common to the whole species of human and is something different from a concrete particular individual (*al-šaḫṣ al-muʿayyan al-mušār ilayhi*). In the same way [the intellect conceives of] accidenthood (*al-ʿaraḍiyya*) as universal, which is common to the whole species of accidents, while "being color" or "blackness" or "this concrete black" do not occur to it. This perception is necessary in terms of the intellect (*hāḏā l-mudrak bi-ḍarūrat al-ʿaql*). It is the sense of the expression (*mafhūm al-ʿibāra*) which is conceived in the intellect, yet it is not the expression itself. For the expression designates the realized meaning in the intellect (*tadullu ʿalā l-maʿnā fī l-ḏihn*), which is designated (*madlūl*) by the expression. As concerns what is expressed, if the expression changed – were it Arabic, or Persian, or Indian or Romaic – the meaning of the designated would not change.[15]

Šahrastānī maintains in this passage that there is a difference between the linguistic expression and the concept, sense, or meaning that it designates. The utterance can change as it is actually different from one language from another (as he indicates mentioning different languages). However, the concept does not change. Thereby Šahrastānī tries to establish the argumentation of the *aḥwāl* proponents again: if one looks for items that would account for the similarities and differences between things, the right objectives are concepts in the mind and not the linguistic expressions.

Šahrastānī's argumentation may have had two sources. The first is the famous discussion about the place of logic and its relation to grammar. It is in this context that the Arabic philosophers elaborated the idea that though the linguistic expressions are different, the concepts remain the same throughout different languages.[16] One finds this position for instance in Avicenna.[17] The other source may have been Ǧuwaynī's criticism of the traditional Ašʿarite nominalism. He already brought up the argument that linguistic expressions change,

15 Šahrastānī, *Nihāya*, 144.11–17.

16 Endress, "Grammatik und Logik" and Adamson, "Philosophy of Language."

17 Avicenna, *Naǧāt*, 17.9–10.

while the meaning remains the same.[18] This connection bespeaks the fact that a couple of lines earlier Šahrastānī agrees with the *aḥwāl* proponents that no definitions and investigation (*naẓar*) are possible without stating some generic notions.[19] This is another argument that one finds in Ǧuwaynī.[20]

Both of Šahrastānī's arguments, but especially the second, reveal that he sees a big difference between the Ašʿarite nominalism and what I henceforth call "conceptualism". For him nominalism means that the only shared item between two black accidents is the word – i. e. literally the phonetic or the written compound – "black". A nominalist would not agree that "black" as applied to one black accident has the same meaning as "black" as applied to another black accident. In Šahrastānī's interpretation the nominalist position amounts to saying that all usage of words is actually equivocal. The equivocity (*ištirāk al-ism*) is precisely defined as two words having the same linguistic form but different meanings. The same applies to two black accidents which we describe as "black". For the object designated by the word "black" is different in each case. In one case, "black" means "this black", in another case, "black" means "that black". One can go one step further towards the foundations of this doctrine: it amounts to saying that all words designate *extramental objects* and – since all objects are unique – no word can have the same designated meaning.[21] Although the theory that all words apply equivocally may sound problematic, it makes perfect sense in Šahrastānī's account of mainstream Ašʿarite metaphysics if one takes into consideration the fact that for them words refer to the unitary and unique extramental objects, bare particulars. By contrast, Šahrastānī opts for a different position. He says that two black accidents share the concept or the meaning (*mafhūm/maʿnā*) of the word "black" that we apply to both of them. This allows him to keep the idea of univocity. For words with generic meaning in his theory do not refer to extramental objects but to the *concepts* in the mind (therefore the term "conceptualism"). These concepts are stable (i. e. they do not vary from one language to another) and can equally be predicated of many extramental objects.

18 Ǧuwaynī, *Šāmil*, 632.4–9. The idea was widespread within the Islamic theology, s. for instance the same thought in the earlier Ibn Kullāb (Van Ess, *Theologie und Gesellschaft* VI, 411).

19 Šahrastānī, *Nihāya*, 144.9–10.

20 Ǧuwaynī, *Šāmil*, 633.11–20.

21 Šahrastānī is not entirely fair in his reconstruction. The *aḥwāl* opponents did not only claim that things differ through their *ḏawāt* but also that they *resemble each other* through them. Frank, "Primary Entities", 184–86 pointed out that for them instances of knowledge still share the *ḏāt* "knowledge". Hence, the referents of "black" are still identical ("black" in *this* black accident and in *that* black accident), which saves univocity, although the referents are not the concept of "black" but the extramental objects "blacks". However, one can understand the reasons behind Šahrastānī's misinterpretation. For it is not clear in the genuine Ašʿarite doctrine, why *this* black is numerically different from *that* black if they resemble each other in all respects; so that Šahrastānī concluded that they actually do not resemble each other at all.

In traditional Aš'arite theory the meanings of words were extramental objects. In Šahrastānī the meanings of words are concepts in the mind.

Šahrastānī's analysis of the traditional Aš'arite nominalism and its rejection is consonant with the mainstream, post-Avicennian approach to nominalism. It has already been mentioned that Rāzī ascribed to Aš'arites the idea that existence is equivocal. This account nicely fits into the alleged Aš'arite framework that actually all generic notions are equivocal. Rāzī himself both generally denies that the only shared aspect between things is the nominal description (*tasmīya*), on the same basis as Ǧuwaynī and Šahrastānī did,[22] and specifically argues for the univocity of existence.[23] One can see why "existence" can be regarded as the best candidate for following the Aš'arite nominalist rules of reference: it is the extramental objects that exist after all, hence the word "existence" has to refer to something extramental. This could have been the source for the later approach to the problem which we find in Āmidī. On the one hand, he generally rejects the traditional Aš'arite nominalism along the same lines as Šahrastānī. It is not only nominal description (*tasmīya*) that is shared by different things but also what is designated by it (*musammā*).[24] Nevertheless, Āmidī argues elsewhere that both existence and a thing's "being itself" (*ḏātiyya*) is common to the existent selves only *qua* nominal description (*tasmīya*), but not *qua* what is designated by it (*musammā*).[25] I suggest that this contradiction may be solved by the hypothesis that both existence and "being itself" have some specific status among other predicates for Āmidī, since they refer to something which quite intuitively applies to things on the extramental level only: existence and being an object (which *ḏātiyya* effectively means). Insofar as the word existence refers to the existing extramental objects, which are different in themselves, "existence" is an equivocal notion.

A good conceptualist theory would not agree to this, since – as is apparent from Šahrastānī's analysis – words (those that have generic meanings, including "existence") refer to concepts and not to extramental objects. This theory was developed at length by Abū l-Barakāt: "in reality names belong only to the mental concepts (*mutaṣawwarāt ḏihnī*) in each case of calling (*fī kull musammin*) and

22 Rāzī, *Muḥaṣṣal*, 61.12–15 reports an argument in favor of *aḥwāl* whereas later (*ibid.*, 63.8–9) he corrects the argument, so that it would rather probe the real existent (*mawǧūd*) shared features (as opposed to "neither existent, nor non-existent" *aḥwāl*). In any case he appears to agree that they cannot just share linguistic expressions.

23 Rāzī, *Mabāḥiṯ* I, 106–11; *Nihāya* I, 346; *Arbaʿīn* I, 82–83; *Maṭālib* I, 291–94. With some exceptions, e.g. *Muḥaṣṣal*, 54.4–5, Rāzī goes beyond Šahrastānī's conceptualist intentions, because he claims that existence is really and not only conceptually distinct from essence.

24 Āmidī, *Ġāya*, 33.10–34.2.

25 Āmidī, *Abkār* I, 260–62. He does not only claim that "existence" always refers to some "specific existence" (*wuǧūd ḫāṣṣ*), but also rejects that there is such thing as "absolute existence" (*wuǧūd muṭlaq*) at all.

through their mediation to the existent [objects]." The argument for this is based on an analysis of the famous problem of vague particulars:[26] if a man sees a horse from a distance but cannot yet distinguish it from a donkey, he would ascribe a name to it due to what he conceptualizes about it in the mind (*bi-ḥasab mā taṣawwara fī ḏihnihī*) and not due to what its essence really is (*lā bi-l-ism al-mawḍūʿ li-ḥaqīqatihī*). Abū l-Barakāt's analysis goes far beyond Šahrastānī's intentions. He ascribes the same situation to the naming of particulars: we cannot immediately recognize whether Zayd exists or not, therefore the name "Zayd" refers to the image (*ḫayāl*) of Zayd primarily.[27] However, the main pillar of conceptualism that generic notions refer primarily to the concepts in the mind and not to the extramental objects is common to Abū l-Barakāt and Šahrastānī.

2. The Rejection of Realism

Šahrastānī agrees with the *aḥwāl* proponents that we need the notions of similarity and difference and that these notions are not merely verbal. However, he has not yet agreed that these notions have real metaphysical correspondents. The only thing we know by now is that there is some *mafhūm* or *maʿnā* in the intellects. Šahrastānī's polemic against the *aḥwāl* proponents leads him to stick to this purely mental status of generic notions.

Šahrastānī has three main arguments against the real extramental status of *aḥwāl*. The first argument apparently goes back to his acquaintance with the debate on universals in Avicenna. For instance, he uses the most famous argument against universal-realism: if universals are real, then one thing has to appear at two different places at the same time.[28] Šahrastānī concludes the same for *aḥwāl*. If a *ḥāl* is common to two substrates, then it is in both (which is absurd). However, if it is specific in each case, then one can no longer claim its universality (which it should have, since *aḥwāl* render similarities).[29] Hence, the common item "blackness", which connects two black objects, has to be in the mind only, since it cannot be present in extramental reality.

Both the second and the third arguments allude to the problem of the ontological status of *aḥwāl*. The *aḥwāl* proponents, Muʿtazilites as well as Ǧuwaynī, claimed for instance that *aḥwāl* are "neither existent nor non-existent". Šah-

26 On Avicenna's theory of vague individuals see Black, "Avicenna's Vague Individual."

27 Abū l-Barakāt, *Muʿtabar* I, 60.9–17. Cf. Avicenna, *Šifāʾ*, *Ilāhiyyāt* I.5, 26.18–19.

28 Avicenna, *Šifāʾ*, *Ilāhīyāt* V.2, 158.16ff. Avicenna escapes the same problem through introducing his notion of "essence *qua* essence", on this see my forthcoming paper on the principle of identity of indiscernibles and the universal realism in Avicenna.

29 Šahrastānī, *Nihāya*, 146.10–14. Remarkably, Šahrastānī ascribes the same logic to the *aḥwāl* opponents when they argue against the idea that *wuǧūd* is a *ḥāl* (*ibid.*, 140.9–15).

rastānī's criticism is not reducible to the claim that this theory violates the law of excluded middle. Instead Šahrastānī proceeds along two lines. First, he attacks the "neither existent nor non-existent" status of the *aḥwāl* by working within the framework of the *aḥwāl* proponents. He reminds them that they introduced the *aḥwāl* in order to establish a metaphysical correspondence to effects (*maʿlūl*) which are grounded by the inherence of an accident in an atom (the inherence of the accident "knowledge" (*ʿilm*) grounds a *ḥāl* "being knowledgeable" (*kawn ʿāliman*)).[30] Šahrastānī argues that in this case the grounded would be "neither existent nor non-existent" so that the notion of grounding loses its sense again as if we did not have any *aḥwāl* at all.[31] Of course, an *aḥwāl* proponent would just bite the bullet and concede that the effect of grounding is "neither existent nor non-existent". However, Šahrastānī develops his argument further and attacks the "neither existent nor non-existent" status in general:

> **[T3]** The third mistake is that we say: all that you, the followers of the proponents [of *aḥwāl*], establish as metaphysically real in existence is a *ḥāl* for you. Show us any existent in the transparent or hidden [reality] which would not be a *ḥāl*, which is not described with either existence or non-existence. For existence, which is the most general [attribute] and is common both to the pre-eternal and the temporary originated, is a *ḥāl* for you. "Being atom" and space-occupation and the reception of accident – all of them are *aḥwāl*. Hence your doctrine entails that there is nothing in existence which would not be a *ḥāl*. If you declare a real a thing and you say that it is not a *ḥāl*, then this thing [still] would encompass the commonness and specificity, whereas the specific and common is a *ḥāl* for you. Thus, [in your theory], everything is no-thing (*lā šayʾa illā lā šayʾ*) and every existence is non-existence (*lā wuǧūda illā lā wuǧūd*), and this is among the most absurd ideas.[32]

In this passage Šahrastānī brings the *aḥwāl* theory to an unfortunate absurd conclusion: everything in this world is "neither existent nor non-existent". *Aḥwāl* were supposed to represent the common and specific features of the existent things. However, everything we say about these things can be analyzed into the common and specific. Hence, everything what we say about the objects in the world is "neither existent nor non-existent". Even if one insists and postulates something that it is not *ḥāl*, Šahrastānī is ready to ask about this object again, whether it shares something with others or not, so that one can somehow "cut down" the object into universal and particular *aḥwāl*. The real objects would be bundles of the "neither existent nor non-existent" *aḥwāl*.

There is however an assumption behind Šahrastānī's argument which reveals the idiosyncrasy of his interpretation of the *aḥwāl* theory. His claim that we can

30 Ǧuwaynī, *Šāmil*, 631.4–21; 632.15–20.
31 Šahrastānī, *Nihāya*, 147.2–4.
32 *Ibid.*, 147.6–13.

analyze the extramental objects into *aḥwāl* amounts to stating that *aḥwāl* are constituent attributes of these objects. *Aḥwāl* become like bricks of which the extramental objects are built: this particular atom consists of "existence", "being atom", "space-occupation" etc. Šahrastānī understands the *aḥwāl* theory as a realist bundle theory of universals. This assumption does not correspond to the actual *aḥwāl* theory as we know it. For *aḥwāl* used to be understood as properties *additional* (*zāʾid*) to the "selves" of the metaphysical objects. This makes it easy to avoid Šahrastānī's counter-argument: there are existent objects in the world, namely *ḏawāt*, and they possess attributes which are "neither existent nor non-existent". One should remember that this ontological status meant in the *aḥwāl* theory precisely the ontological dependency of *aḥwāl* on the subjects to which they are attached, which implies that these subjects are something different from the attributes attached to them.[33]

Although Šahrastānī's argument does not catch the core of the *aḥwāl* theory, it reveals his understanding of the question of what the *aḥwāl* discussion actually concerns. For him it is a dispute about the ontological status of universals. This corresponds perfectly to the fact that he keeps calling them genera (*aǧnās*) and species (*anwāʿ*), already while reporting the arguments of his predecessors.[34] Again, he was not alone in this interpretation. For instance, earlier Ġazālī wrote in *Tahāfut al-falāsifa* that *aḥwāl* are universals;[35] later Āmidī explicitly called them constituents (*muqawwimāt*), which are universals that constitute essences.[36]

The interpretation of *aḥwāl* as features that constitute the essences of the extramental objects is fundamental for another move that Šahrastānī makes in his criticism of the *aḥwāl* realism. He combines the problem of *aḥwāl* with another important topic of the *kalām* ontology: the ontological status of the non-existent (*maʿdūm*). Roughly speaking, some Muʿtazilites believed that the non-existent is something (*šayʾ*), e. g. "black" is "black" even though it does not exist yet. On the contrary, the Ašʿarites claimed that "black" is "black" only insofar as it already exists.[37] Šahrastānī discusses the problem at length in his *Nihāyat al-aqdām*. One of the arguments that he introduces on behalf of those Muʿtazilites goes as follows:

> **[T4]** The secret of their doctrine is that substances and accidents possess essential attributes which pertain to them *per se* yet not due an act of the agent and the power of the powerful. For we can conceive of substance as substance, concrete being (*ʿayn*) and

33 Benevich, "Juwaynī and His Opponents," 172–73.
34 E. g. Šahrastānī, *Nihāya*, 133.7; 133.16–17; 138.18.
35 Ġazālī, *Tahāfut*, 202.3–4. In *Iqtiṣād*, 131.8–10 he rejects that *aḥwāl* are something different from the real attributes they are predicated of (i. e. "knowledge" is identical to "being knowledge").
36 Āmidī, *Ġāya*, 34.3. Cf. also [T5] *infra*.
37 See Frank, "The Non-Existent" and "Ashʿarite Ontology."

> essence, as well as of accident as accident, essence and concrete being, while it does not occur to us that it is something existent created by the power of the powerful. The created or the temporarily originated requires the agent only in respect of its existence if it is in itself contingent of existence and non-existence, and if the preponderance is placed on the side of existence it requires the prepondarator. Hence, the agent has an effect (*aṯar*) from his powerfulness or his power only on existence. So we say: what belongs to [the originated] *per se* preceded existence. That is its substancehood or accidenthood and it is a thing (*šay*ʾ). What belongs to it due to the power of the powerful is its existence and its presence (*ḥuṣūl*) and what follows upon its existence, that is its space-occupation and its receptivity of accidents. This is a necessary intellectual judgment which no intellect can reject.
>
> On this basis, the answer on [the question] about the effect of the act of bestowing existence (*īǧād*) is brought forth. For the effect of the power (*taʾṯīr al-qudra*) is only existence and the powerful gives [the temporarily originated] only existence. The contingent in itself requires the powerful only in respect of existence. Do we not say that contingency of the contingent *qua* contingency is something which pertains to it due to itself and that from this perspective it does not require the agent and it is not up to the agent to make it contingent? Rather it requires the agent in respect of preponderating (*tarǧīḥ*) to one side of contingency. One knows certainly that the essential features are not related to the agent. Rather this is what occurs to [the temporarily originated] in terms of existence and presence. We say that the agent, if he wants to bestow existence upon substance, cannot help but distinguish (*tamayyuz*) substance by its true essence from accident, so that His intention (*qaṣd*) towards [the substance] can be realized. Otherwise, if substance and accident are not distinguished in non-existence by some feature (*amr*) and some true essence, with this feature and true essence not being something metaphysically real (*šayʾan ṯābitan*), then He will not be able to intend substance instead of accident and motion instead of rest and whiteness instead of blackness etc. The specification with existence (*taḫṣīṣ bi-l-wuǧūd*) can be conceptualized only when the specified (*muḫaṣṣaṣ*) is concrete and distinguishable by the specifier (*muḫaṣṣiṣ*), so that substance is not in the place of accident nor motion in the place of rest nor whiteness in the place of blackness. *Thus, know that the true essences of the genera and species do not depend on the act of the agent.* For if they are not distinct things in their essences, then the bestowing of existence and creation (*iḫtirāʿ*) is not conceivable and the presence of the things coming in some different way would be by chance and luck (*ittifāqan wa-baḫtan*).[38]

In this passage Šahrastānī draws a connection between the realism about essential attributes and the idea that the non-existent is something. He ascribes to the Muʿtazilites the following logic: Let us observe what depends on God in this world. Certainly, the fact that there are things, i.e. their existence (*wuǧūd*) or presence (*ḥuṣūl*), does depend on God. However, essences also have their essential attributes. These essential attributes do not depend on the creating act of God. "Black" is distinguished from "white" through "blackness" independently

38 Šahrastānī, *Nihāya*, 155.4–156.13.

from God. Indeed, God has to be able to distinguish between them before He renders the one or the other existent. That is why the non-existent "black" already is "black" and has some metaphysically real status different from existence.

It is clear that this logic is based on Šahrastānī's reading of the *aḥwāl* realism as a theory of real universal constituents. His jump from the idea that the connection between essences and their essential attributes does not depend on God to the idea that these essences are real non-existent things is based on the assumption that these essential attributes make up the essences when being gathered in a bundle. It is only if we regard universals as real constituents that have to make up the essences *before* they come into existence, that one can conclude the *maʿdūm=šayʾ* formula[39] on the basis of the *aḥwāl* realism. If the essence of "black" is constituted by its essential attributes independently from the fact whether "black" exists, "black" is metaphysically real despite being non-existent.

Again, the "constituent-universals" interpretation of the *aḥwāl* realism makes Šahrastānī miss his target. The *aḥwāl* realists actually were not committed to the *maʿdūm=šayʾ* formula. For instance, Ǧuwaynī believed in the reality of *aḥwāl*, yet he rejected the Muʿtazilite doctrine that the non-existent is real. This is, because his *aḥwāl* are ontologically dependent on *already existent* objects, while being "neither existent nor non-existent" themselves. On the contrary, the "neither existent nor non-existent" *aḥwāl* of Muʿtazilites might have been dependent on both existent and non-existent metaphysical objects.[40] In any case, Šahrastānī's interpretation of *aḥwāl* as constituent universals fully changes their status. They used to be "neither existent nor non-existent" in the genuine doctrine of the *aḥwāl* proponent and always remained such. However, in Šahrastānī's report *aḥwāl* have the non-existent yet real status, before God creates them (and this is why one can claim for the "non-existent yet real" status of essences that they constitute), and become actually existent, after God puts the preponderance (*taraǧǧaḥa*) on the side of existence.[41] So, the "neither existent nor non-existent" *aḥwāl* turn out to be non-existent before creation and existent after it. Nevertheless, the logic which could have confused Šahrastānī is not unconceivable: both the non-existent yet real status of the non-existing "things" of the Muʿtazilite doctrine and "neither existing nor non-existing" *aḥwāl* share an idea of an

---

39 Thereby I henceforth mean the theory that the non-existent is something.

40 Cf. Benevich, "Juwaynī and His Opponents," 172, fn. 108.

41 One should admit that Šahrastānī is not very consistent in his criticism. First, he criticized the *aḥwāl* for their "neither existent, nor non-existent status", now, he attacks them as if they were non-existent. The same applies to the general logic of his arguments about the knowability of *aḥwāl*, although previously he reported that *aḥwāl* are not known on their own according to Abū Hāšim (*Nihāya*, 136.5 and *ibid.*, 137.17 or 137.7–8).

unusual metaphysical status, which is being real without being existent. Although their metaphysical reality is of a different kind ("non-existent thing" vs. "neither existent nor non-existent") it has the common feature of lacking existence.

This is how realism about *aḥwāl* leads in Šahrastānī's eyes to believing that the non-existent essences are metaphysically real. However, apart from that realism, the argumentation in [T4] makes use of two other crucial assumptions: that essences do not depend on God in their essential attributes (the main argument) and that essences and existence are distinct, because we can conceive essence without knowing whether they exist (supporting argument). Both these arguments are Avicennian.[42] The first can be found in the logical part of *Dānišnāma*, where Avicenna argues that nothing makes man an animal;[43] the second in the *Išārāt*, where Avicenna argues for the essence-existence distinction, because we can conceive of the triangle without knowing whether it exists.[44] Hence, Šahrastānī (quite anachronistically, one should admit) ascribes to the Muʿtazilites Avicennian arguments in support of the *maʿdūm=šayʾ* formula. Thereby he combines the question about the reality of *aḥwāl* with another famous dispute: whether essence and existence are distinct or not. As I argued elsewhere, the fact that he uses Avicennian arguments for the essence-existence distinction in support of the *maʿdūm=šayʾ* formula signifies that he sees this two theories as clearly connected.[45] The same approach can be found in Ḫayyām, as well as Ibn Ġaylān and Rāzī.[46] The only difference is that it is only Šahrastānī who combines both issues also with the problem of *aḥwāl*. His Muʿtazilites believe that the non-existent is something, in other words that essence and existence are really distinct, because the essential attributes are independent of God (because one can conceive of them independently from their existence) *and because they are real.* This is clear on the basis of how Šahrastānī criticizes the logic of another "Muʿtazilite" argument which is closely bound to the first one:

> **[T5]** Everyone [should] wonder about the proponents of the reality of *aḥwāl* that they made the species like substancehood, corporeity, accidenthood and "being color" something metaphysically real in non-existence (*ašyāʾ ṯābita fī l-ʿadam*), [basing it on

42 The argument that God does not make atom atom and that His task consists in rendering it existent alone was originally used by some Muʿtazilites, cf. Nīsābūrī, *Masāʾil*, 14–16; 23. Nevertheless, Šahrastānī's approach to the argument as well as its connection with Avicenna's argument on the possibility of doubting existence suggests that Šahrastānī takes it from Avicenna rather than from a real Muʿtazlite source, or at least understands Muʿatzilite argument on the basis of a similar idea that he found in Avicenna.

43 Avicenna, *Dānišnāma*, *Manṭiq*, 15–16.

44 Avicenna, *Išārāt*, *nahǧ* I, 47, cf. *Išārāt*, *namaṭ* IV, 266 and *Avicenna*, *Šifāʾ*, *Maqūlāt* II.1, 61.2–62.16.

45 cf. Benevich, "Essence-Existence Distinction", 227–37.

46 Cf. Ḫayyām, *Risāla fī l-wuǧūd*, 110.8–14; Ibn Ġaylān, *Ḥudūṯ al-ʿalam*, 74.12–18; Rāzī, *Muḥaṣṣal*, 55.5–7; 59.2–16.

the idea that] knowledge is connected to them and everything known has to be something, in order that knowledge can lean (*yatawakkaʾu*) against it. Furthermore, the same objects, i. e. substancehood, acccidenthood, "being color" and "blackness" are *aḥwāl* in existence that cannot be known on their own and are not existent alone. What is this that is known in non-existence so that knowledge leans against it, and is not known in existence?

If they went the well-trodden path of intellects in their conception of things with their genera and species, they [sc. Muʿtazilites] would know that the conceptions of intellects are the quiddities of things with their genera and species, which do not entail their realized existence (*mawǧūda muḥaqqiqa*) or their postulating as real extramental things (*ašyāʾ ṯābita ḫāriǧa ʿan al-ʿuqūl*). And what they have in virtue of themselves and of their genera and of species in the mind (*fī l-ḏihn*) in terms of the essential constituents (*al-muqawwimāt al-ḏātiyya*), by which the "selves" are realized, this does not depend on the act of the agent. So that it is possible that they are known, while existence does not occur (*wa-l-wujūd lā yaḫturu bi-bāl*). For the groundings of existence and quiddity are different (*fa-inna asbāb al-wuǧūd ġayr wa-asbāb al-māhiyya ġayr*). And [the Muʿtazilites] would know that the perceptions of senses (*idrākāt al-ḥawāss*) are the "selves" of things in their concrete being. Their ostentation (*iʿlāmuhā*) entails their realized existence and their postulating as real extrasensory things (*ašyāʾ ṯābita ḫāriǧa ʿan al-ḥawāss*). And what they have in virtue of themselves as regards their concrete being and the ostentation by the sense perception of the accidental specifiers (*al-muḫaṣṣiṣāt al-ʿaraḍiyya*), by which their concrete selves are realized, this depends on the act of the agent. So that they cannot exist deprived of these specifiers. For the groundings of existence and quiddity are different.

When the Muʿtazilites heard the difference between two classes from the philosophers, they thought that the conceptions in the intellects are really postulated things (*al-mutaṣawwarāt fī l-aḏhān hiya ašyāʾ ṯābita fī l-aʿyān*) among the concrete beings and they concluded that the non-existent is a thing (*šayʾ*). And they thought that the existence of genera and species in the intellects is the *aḥwāl* that are postulated as real among the concrete beings.[47]

This passage is the high-point of Šahrastānī's analysis of the correlation between three theories: the realism about *aḥwāl*, the *maʿdūm=šayʾ* theory, and the essence-existence distinction. He begins by criticizing the traditional Muʿtazilite argument for the reality of the non-existent: the non-existent is known, everything known has to be metaphysically real, and hence the non-existent is real.[48] Šahrastānī's crucial move is that these are the *aḥwāl* which Muʿtazlites were

47 Šahrastānī, *Nihāya*, 161.17–163.3. This passage is the explanation of an earlier claim (*ibid.*, 159.9–11) that the Muʿtazilites borrowed the idea from the "logicians and metaphysicians" (*aṣḥāb al-manṭiq wa-l-ilāhiyyīn* i. e. Avicenna) of "the difference between the conceptions in the intellects and the existents among the concrete being" (*al-farq bayna l-mutaṣawwarāt fī l-aḏhān wa-l-mawǧūdāt fī l-aʿyān*) but misunderstood it.

48 Frank, "Al-maʿdūm wal-mawjūd," 189; Rāzī, *Mulaḫḫaṣ*, fol. 77.14–16. I discussed this argument in detail in "The Reality of the Non-Existent".

talking about here: substancehood, accidenthood etc. His criticism proceeds along two lines. First, he reminds the reader of another theory about *aḥwāl* which claims that they are "not known on their own". This theory intended to emphasize the ontologically dependent status of *aḥwāl*. Of course, as long as Šahrastānī reinterprets the *aḥwāl* theory as a theory of universals-constituents, the clause "not known on their own" becomes incomprehensible for him: how can one claim that *aḥwāl* are not known on their own while one actually thinks that they are known in non-existence as constituents of essence, i. e. prior to it? One may notice that Šahrastānī is not absolutely fair here again, because the Ašʿarite *aḥwāl* proponents actually conceded that *aḥwāl* can be known on their own.[49] So much the worse for them in Šahrastānī's view, if we look into the general framework of the second line of his criticism.

Šahrastānī combines two arguments: The first claims that the non-existent is something, because we know it. The second goes back to the logic of [T4] and states that the real *aḥwāl* build up some non-existent essences, because we can conceive of these essences and their essential *aḥwāl* without knowing whether they exist. Both arguments share a common feature that Šahrastānī is ready to attack: one infers from knowing something (essence/*aḥwāl*) apart from knowing something else (existence) that the former can have metaphysical reality without the latter. However, Šahrastānī himself draws another conclusion from this argument: the fact that we can conceive of ontologically separate essences and/or *aḥwāl* apart from their existence as concrete objects does not entail that these *aḥwāl* are separate entities that are postulated as metaphysically real in extramental reality (*fī l-aʿyān*). This follows *precisely because* we can conceive of these *aḥwāl* without knowing whether they are extramentally real. There is a slight move in this argument: previously one knew essences apart from existence; now, Šahrastānī states that one can know them apart from their extramental metaphysical *reality* (note hidden sliding from "existence" to "reality"). This gives him the basis for the complete opposite interpretation of the same argument which I identified as Avicennian earlier.

Šahrastānī shows quite explicitly that he is using Avicenna's *Išārāt* here: the puzzling expression "the groundings (*asbāb*) of existence and quiddity are different" (which just stands for the essence-existence distinction) occurs in both texts.[50] Thus, Avicenna's argument becomes a ground both for the problem that Šahrastānī has to solve, namely the metaphysical reality of the non-existent *aḥwāl*, as well as its solution, namely the pure epistemic reality of *aḥwāl*. Šahrastānī takes the argument that he ascribes to the Muʿtazilites, namely that essence can be conceived apart from existence, and turns it against them. If

49 Ǧuwaynī, *Šāmil*, 642–4. Cf. Šahrastānī, *Nihāya*, 136.5 and *ibid.*, 137.17 or 137.7–8.
50 Cf. Avicenna, *Išārāt, nahǧ* I, 47.8.

something can be conceived without an extramental realization in existence, it means that the epistemic analysis does not entail a direct metaphysical correspondence. Therefore, the mentally distinguishable *aḥwāl* do not have to be extramentally real and distinct.

This inference marks a revolutionary move. The idea that the epistemic analysis entails metaphysical correspondence was the main hidden premise behind the arguments of the *aḥwāl* proponents: as long as we can distinguish between concepts of "blackness" and "whiteness" they have to be distinguishable really. A bold rejection of this idea served the *aḥwāl* opponents in establishing their nominalism.[51] However, it is only Šahrastānī who finds philosophical reasons to deny this one-to-one correspondence between the epistemic and metaphysical level. The fact that we can conceive of "black", i. e. of the bundle of the essential attributes that constitute what it is to be "black", without knowing whether this "black" has a metaphysically real instance, does not entail that there is "black" in the state of non-existence. On the contrary, it means that there is no need for such correspondence. It is only the sense-perception of the extramental objects that grants that these objects are metaphysically real. This is precisely the reason why one cannot conceive of them as non-existent, which amounts to the opposite to the Muʿtazilite interpretation of the Avicennian argument in [T4]. They claimed that essences of things (bundles of their *aḥwāl*) are real even without being existent, because one can conceive of them as non-existent. Now Šahrastānī can claim that the extramental objects perceived by senses cannot be postulated as metaphysically real yet non-existent, precisely because one cannot perceive of these objects without knowing whether they exist.[52]

The combination of the *aḥwāl* theory with the problematic of the ontological status of the non-existent gives Šahrastānī an opportunity to make use of another Avicennian theory. We know that Avicenna's own solution to the status of the non-existent was based on the notion of mental existence (*wuǧūd ḏihnī*).[53] For instance, the objects of our knowledge, which do not exist in the extramental reality, like phoenixes and unicorns, still exist in the mind. The same applies to the *aḥwāl* and consequently the essences that they constitute: Šahrastānī's analysis in [T5] amounts to stating that the mental existence of such notions does not entail their extramental presence. We will see in the next section that his solution to the ontological status of the universals, which he again borrows from Avicenna, makes use of the same idea, since the universals possess precisely only this kind of mental existence in Avicenna's metaphysical doctrine.

---

51 Benevich, "Juwaynī and His Opponents," 162.

52 Cf. Ibn al-Malāhimī, *Tuḥfa*, 62.12–15.

53 On the concept of mental existence in Avicenna see Black, "Fictional Beings" and "Mental Existence."

Concluding on Šahrastānī's attempt to combine the *aḥwāl* theory with the problem of the status of the non-existent, one should note that his solution is not rooted in Avicenna alone. For instance, when Šahrastānī reports of the *aḥwāl* opponents' view that similarities and differences are pure aspects (*wuǧūh*) that are "relations and associations" (*al-nisab wa-l-iḍāfāt*), he accurately introduces what will later become his own opinion: "the aspects in the intellect are mentally supposed concepts and this does not entail the attributes that are postulated as real for the 'selves' (*fa-l-wuǧūh al-ʿaqliyya iʿtibārāt ḏihniyya wa-taqdīriyya wa-lā yaqtaḍī ḏālika ṣifāt ṯābita li-ḏawāt*)."[54] This passage reveals Šahrastānī's attempt to describe the traditional Ašʿarite anti-*aḥwāl* position in terms that would make it identical to his own.[55] Šahrastānī obviously goes too far in this attempt, since we know that the view of the *aḥwāl* opponents would reject that *aḥwāl* are concepts in the mind.[56] Nevertheless, if we remember that Šahrastānī also combines the rejection of the real *aḥwāl* with a rejection of real non-existent things, we can understand his logic. A hint of this logic is given by the notion *taqdīriyya* ("supposed"). It is reminiscent of the Ashʿarite discussion on the ontological status of things, which are non-existent (*maʿdūm*). In order to avoid the Muʿtazilite idea that the non-existent is something real despite its non-existence, since it is known (*maʿlūm*), the Ashʿarites maintained that this thing is "known as regards the supposition of existence" (*maʿlūm ʿalā taqdīr al-wuǧūd*).[57] If we remember now that the *aḥwāl* became in Sahrastānī's interpretation also the non-existent things, it follows that the *aḥwāl* are indeed existent in the supposition, which Šahrastānī regards as a synonym for the mental existence. The "blackness", which can be known apart from being existent but is still "something" (*šayʾ*), is "blackness" by supposition (*taqdīr*) of its existence. This supposition takes place in the mind – so that the "blackness" is mentally existent.

3. Conceptualism

If the epistemic analysis does not ground one-to-one correspondence in the extramental reality, one can conclude that whatever the *aḥwāl* proponents claim about *aḥwāl* – the fact that they stand for the similarities and differences between objects as well as that they can be conceived without knowing whether they actually exist – applies only to concepts, yet does not grant that these concepts are real. Given Šahrastānī's different arguments for impossibility of *aḥwāl* being real,

54 Šahrastānī, *Nihāya*, 135.3–5.

55 This is a particular case of a general Šahrastānī's approach to historical reconstruction, cf. Van Ess, *Der Eine und das Andere* II, 83ff.

56 Anṣārī, *Ġunya*, 494.17–21.

57 Anṣārī, *Ġunya*, 488.18–19.

and given the falsehood of nominalism, Šahrastānī establishes a foundation for conceptualism, i. e. that *aḥwāl* or universals are mere concepts. This is his central conclusion:

> [T6] Therefore, the truth on this problem is that a human finds in[58] his soul the conception (*taṣawwur*) of universal common absolute things with no regard to words (*al-alfāẓ*) and concrete objects (*al-aʿyān*). He finds in his soul mental concepts (*iʿtibārāt ʿaqliyya*) for one thing. They can either go back to the words – and we have already rejected it – or they go back to the concrete existents (*al-aʿyān al-mawǧūda*) – and we have already falsified it. It remains to say that they are only meanings (*maʿānin*) that are existent (*mawǧūda*) as realized in human mind (*ḏihn*). Human intellect (*al-ʿaql*) perceives them insofar they are universal and common and are not existent among the concrete beings (*lā wuǧūd la-hā fī l-aʿyān*). So, there is no "existent" in the absolute sense (*mawǧūd muṭlaqan*) in concrete individuals, neither "accident" in the absolute sense, nor "color" in the absolute sense. Rather, they are concrete beings insofar as the intellect conceptualizes a universal common meaning on their basis (*yataṣawwaru minhā*). Hence, an expression (*ʿibāra*) is formed for it which corresponds to it (*taṭābiquhū*) and indicates it (*tanaṣṣu ʿalayhi*) and the intellect derives from it the meaning (*maʿnā*) and the aspect (*waǧhan*). And an expression is formed for it, so that, if the expression perished or changed, the meaning imagined in the mind would not be invalidated, while being conceptualized in the intellect (*al-mutaṣawwar fī l-ʿaql*).
>
> The opponents of *aḥwāl* were wrong when they traced [the concepts] to abstract expressions *(al-ʿibārāt al-muǧarrada*). They were right when they said: whatever really is a concrete existent (*mā ṯubita wuǧūduhū muʿayyanan*) cannot be common and a concept (*lā ʿumūm fīhi wa-lā ʿtibār*). The proponents of *aḥwāl* were wrong when they traced them back to attributes (*ṣifāt*) in concrete beings. They were right when they said that they are mental meanings (*maʿānin maʿqūla*) apart from expressions. It would be right for them to say that [*aḥwāl*] exist as conceptualized in intellects (*mawǧūda mutaṣawwara fī l-aḏhān*), instead of saying "neither existent, nor non-existent". No one reasonable would reject them in his soul, although some talked about them [using the notion of] "conceptualizing in the intellects", others – "supposition in the intellect" (*bi-l-taqdīr fī l-ʿaql*), others – "true essences" (*al-ḥaqāʾiq*) and the "meaning" (*al-maʿānī*), which are designated (*madlūlāt*) by expressions and words, others – "the attributes of genera and species". And let them talk about the meanings, if they appear to the intellects and are clear for them, how ever is easier for them.
>
> Thus, the true essences and meanings have three aspects (*iʿtibārāt*): Their aspect on their own in their "selves" (*fī ḏawātihā wa-anfusihā*), their aspect in the relation to the concrete individuals and their aspect in the relation to the intellects. (1) Insofar as they are existent in concrete individuals, it occurs to them to be concretized and specified. (2) Insofar as they are conceptualized in the minds, it occurs to them to be common and encompassing. (3) And insofar as they are taken by themselves on their own (*bi-ʿtibār*

58 I correct *min* to *fī*.

ḏawātihā fī anfusihā), they are pure true essences (*ḥaqāʾiq maḥḍa*), that do not have neither community nor specificity.[59]

In this passage Šahrastānī finally concludes what he has worked toward all along: that there are concepts in the mind which stand for our recognition of similarities and differences between extramental objects.[60] For describing these concepts he uses such notions as *iʿtibār* (lit. "consideration"), *maʿnā* (meaning), *ḥaqāʾiq* (true essences) and in general the central notion of conception: *taṣawwur*. He does not forget to take into consideration ideas that he developed while criticizing the *aḥwāl* opponents and proponents. From the criticism of nominalism he develops the idea that names signify (*d-l-l*) the concepts, and the difference between concepts (*iʿtibārāt*) and the linguistic expressions (*ʿibārāt*). From the criticism of the *aḥwāl* realism and its identification with the *maʿdūm=šayʾ* theory Šahrastānī inserts in [T6] the notion of "supposition" (*taqdīr*) for the description of the status of the concepts.

Next to rather artificial connection between the traditional Ašʿarite response to the *maʿdūm=šayʾ* problem and the conceptual status of the *aḥwāl*, the main source for Šahrastānī's solution to the problem of the *aḥwāl* status was Avicenna's theory of universals. It is the latter who extensively argues in his writing that there are no universals in the extramental reality.[61] We have seen above that Šahrastānī inherits from Avicenna his main argument: the presence of the universals outside the mind would lead to the presence of one and the same thing ("blackness") in two instances of black at the same time. It is on this basis that Avicenna concluded that "there is no universal thing in the extramental reality of the concrete individuals" (*laysa fī ḫāriǧ al-aʿyān šayʾ wāḥid ʿāmm*)".[62] In any case, the most significant proof for the fact that Šahrastānī's own theory goes back to Avicenna is the tripartite division according to which one may consider essences. Two of them are not anything new: concrete particulars are in the extramental reality, universals are in the mind. However, Šahrastānī also adds "essences *qua* essences" independent from their existence either in or outside the mind. This is a purely Avicennian idea, famously known under the notion of "the neutrality of essences". "Horseness" *qua* "horseness" is neither universal nor particular. This idea served Avicenna establish real immanent features in the extramental and

59 Šahrastānī, *Nihāya*, 147.14–149.2.

60 One can find this theory in Šahrastānī on some quite unexpected occasions like in a Qurʾān commentary Šahrastānī, *Mafātiḥ*, 50.

61 On Avicenna's theory of universals and essences *qua* essences see Marmura, "Avicenna's Critique of Platonists"; Black, "Fictional Beings"; and Benevich, "Die Göttliche Existenz." Avicenna himself borrowed and developed the theory on the basis of the Late Antique theory of universals, see Rashed, "Ibn ʿAdī et Avicenne."

62 Avicenna, *Šifāʾ*, *Madḫal* I.12, 69.14–15.

intramental things that would not be universals properly speaking, yet still would account for the similarity between these things.

Unfortunately, Šahrastānī does not elaborate much on this theory in the *Nihāya*. However, there is a passage in his other treatise, *Muṣāraʿa*, where he invokes this theory again. There he argues against the Avicennian definition of God as "Necessary Existent", stating that it would lead to a composition in God of "necessity" and "existence". In response to his own criticism Šahrastānī dialectically ascribes Avicenna a counter-argument stating that "necessity" and "existence" are distinct only as two concepts (*iʿtibārāt*), although they correspond to one and the same thing.[63] This is indeed a very Šahrastānian thought, since we saw above that he separates the level of epistemic analysis from that of the metaphysical presence. However, in this case Šahrastānī prefers to be more accurate:

> [T7] As for his statement that the distinction between existence and necessity in terms of commonness and specificity is something conceptual (*iʿtibārī*) in the mind, yet not in existence, it obviously has to be conceded to. For the distinction between the generic and specific meaning is in the mind only, and there is no "animal" in existence which would be a genus nor "rational" which would be a differentia. Rather both of them are concepts (*iʿtibārān*) in the mind, yet not in the extramental reality. How anything universal can be present in existence, as long as there is the universal in the mind only? And you know that "being a color" and "whiteness" are intellectually grasped concepts (*iʿtibārāni ʿaqliyyān*) in the mind, not in the extramental reality. Otherwise the "being color" of the white would be distinct (*ġayr*) from its "whiteness". [...]
>
> [However] I said: The meanings (*al-mafhūmāt*) of the generic and specific words (*al-alfāẓ*) are generic and specific in the mind not due to their relation to the words in the language. For[64] the meanings in the mind are true (*ṣaḥīḥa*) only due to their correspondence (*muṭābiqatihā*) to what is outside the mind. By correspondence, I do not mean that the universal in the mind correspond to the universal outside in the extramental reality, since there is no universal in concrete individuals. Rather the universal in the mind corresponds to each particular in the extramental reality like the common humanity in the mind corresponds to each individual that exist and does not exist. Furthermore, the distinction between different species is due to essential differentiae, whereas the distinction between individuals is due to accidental concomitants.[65]

In the beginning of this passage Šahrastānī repeats the logic which we are familiar with: the distinction between the generic notions in the mind (which apply to one and the same particular) does not entail a real distinction between them in the extramental reality. This is why we do not say that "being color" is distinct from "whiteness"; rather they are one and the same object "white". However, Šah-

63 Šahrastānī, *Muṣāraʿa*, 34.7–9.

64 I prefer the reading *fa-l-mafhūmāt* found in the apparatus over *wa-l-mafhūmāt* in the text of the edition.

65 Šahrastānī, *Muṣāraʿa*, 35.11–37.8.

rastānī does not want to acknowledge that this would save Avicenna from the problem of the composition of "necessity" and "existence" in the Necessary Existent. His response mainly focuses on the idea of the correspondence: the meaning of the concepts in the mind are true not due to the words that express them (remember Šahrastānī's rejection of nominalism). Rather they have some real correspondence in the extramental reality. Šahrastānī speaks of the extramental correspondence of universals to particulars. It is not entirely clear how this is supposed to help him with stating an extramental distinction between "necessity" and "existence", since one could argue that they taken together form one particular, the "Necessary Existent". However, one may suggest, remembering Šahrastānī acceptance of the Avicennian "neutral essences" in *Nihāya*, that he thereby means that universals have to correspond to the "essences *qua* essences" immanent in particulars.[66] Therefore, his counter-argument amounts to stating that "necessity" and "existence" though distinct as universals only in the mind still bare some difference in the extramental reality which makes us worry about the composition in God. In his epistle to ʿUmār b. Sahlān al-Sāwī (d. 1145) Šahrastānī explains the problem about this composition: "necessity" and "existence" do not imply each other.[67] In the same epistle one finds further support for my hypothesis that Šahrastānī means a distinction by essence *qua* essence in *Muṣāraʿa*. Introducing the same argument there, he states that the distinction between "necessity" and "existence" is not only *qua* universals in the mind, but also in themselves (*fī l-ḏāt*), which apparently stands for a distinction in terms of essences *qua* essence.[68]

Šahrastānī's way of arguing is clearly reminiscent of famous Latin scholastic division between three kinds of distinction: real, formal and conceptual. He appears to argue that the composition in God despite not being real is not only conceptual but also formal, since there is no necessary connection between "necessity" and "existence". Yet one should not overrate the significance of Šahrastānī's allowance for what one might call "formal distinction" between essences *qua* essences in the extramental reality. In any case it should not be interpreted as any kind of *real distinction*. Šahrastānī is quite clear about the unity of the extramental particulars. This is actually how he begins criticizing the *aḥwāl* realism:

> **[T8]** As for the [first] aspect concerning why the proponents of the real *aḥwāl* are wrong, it is that they established the attributes of the concrete particular existent [objects] which are specific for them and which they share with other [objects] as [something]

66 Cf. McGinnis, "Logic and Science," 167–73 on the correspondence between universal and immanent essences in Avicenna.

67 Sāwī, *Muṣāraʿat al-Muṣāraʿa*, fol. 100r.1–100v.5.

68 *Ibid.*, fol. 101r.6–101v.6.

> among the existent. This is the most absurd. For what is specific for a concrete thing and what it shares with others is *one* in respect of this concrete [object]. Hence, the existence of a concrete accident and its accidenthood and its being color and its blackness are expressions (*ʿibārāt*) of the [same] concrete particular. For when existence is specified (*taḫaṣṣaṣa*) with accidenthood, it is identical (*bi-ʿaynihī*) to the accident, and when the accidenthood is specified with being color, it is identical with color, and in the same way, being color [is specified] with blackness and blackness with "this particular black".[69]

In this passage Šahrastānī clearly subscribes to the traditional Ašʿarite metaphysics which maintained a complete unity of the extramental particulars. One may notice the notion "expressions" (*ʿibārāt*), which immediately reminds us of the nominalist framework. Šahrastānī uses it later again, stating that all generic notions that describe a particular are "expressions of the same expressed" (*ʿibārāt ʿan muʿabbar wāḥid*).[70] Indeed, earlier he reported the doctrine of the *aḥwāl* opponents using the same notions (*ʿibārātān ʿan muʿabbar wāḥid*).[71] Thereby he referred to a doctrine of Isfarāʾīnī reported by Ǧuwaynī in *Šāmil* that the definition of a thing and the defined object are identical.[72] Hence, Šahrastānī intends to present his theory as a continuation of the traditional Ašʿarite metaphysics. However, his presentation is a conceptual ruse, which may be based on a word play (one may notice that he uses both *ʿibārāt* and *iʿtibārāt* in [T6]). His "expressions" (*ʿibārāt*) are not mere expressions, since we saw that he rejected nominalism. Rather they are "conceptions" (*iʿtibārāt*). In any case, it gives Šahrastānī an opportunity to agree with the traditional Ašʿarite "unitarism" of the extramental objects.

In [T8], Šahrastānī explains the way in which a real particular comes to be by using the notion of "specification" (*taḫaṣṣuṣ*). "Existence" is specified with "accidenthood", "accidenthood" with "being color", "being color" with "blackness", "blackness" with "this black": this is why all these attributes form a real unity. We have already encountered the notions of specific attributes through which the extramental particulars are realized (*taḥaqqaqa*) in [T5]. Šahrastānī also uses this notion in his response to the Muʿtazilite theory that God's only task is to put the preponderance (*taraǧǧaḥa*) on the side of existence. On the contrary, Šahrastānī claims that God specifies (*ḫaṣṣaṣa*) the essences that He is going to create. For existence is the most general attribute – says Šahrastānī – and if God's only task would be to render something existent, then all things would be existence alone. Therefore both the existence and essence of the extramental objects depend on God.[73] This latter idea that God "specifies" the objects reveals that

69 Šahrastānī, *Nihāya*, 136.3–9.
70 Šahrastānī, *Nihāya*, 160.10–11.
71 *Ibid.*, 135.15.
72 Ǧuwaynī, *Šāmil* (Frank), 38.14–15.
73 Šahrastānī, *Nihāya*, 161.1–17.

Šahrastānī resorts again to some Aš'arite sources. In this case it is the theory that God acts as "specifier" (*muḫaṣṣiṣ*) when creating the world, which is found in one of the proofs of God's existence.[74] Šahrastānī inherits and develops it in order to support the unity of the extramental objects, so that the distinction between the different predicates that are said of these objects can be reduced to the conceptual level.

Concluding Remarks

When Šahrastānī in the end of the 11th century engaged in establishing his own metaphysical system, he encountered a whole range of schools and metaphysical theories that he could compare and analyze. The most significant influences for the development of his metaphysics were fourfold. First was the traditional Aš'arite metaphysics, which in Šahrastānī eyes maintained that there are only bare particulars in the extramental reality, whereas all generic notions are merely verbal. Second was the Ǧuwaynian Aš'arite metaphysics, which claimed that the notions of similarity and difference render some metaphysically real objects, which they called *aḥwāl* – Šahrastānī understood this theory as a realism about universals. Third was the Mu'tazilite metaphysics, from which Šahrastānī mostly discussed that they also accepted the reality of *aḥwāl* as well as supposed that the non-existent objects are still metaphysically real. Last but not least was the new Avicennian philosophy, which went the middle way in Šahrastānī's eyes between realism and anti-realism about universals, stating that universals are purely mental features, yet there also are certain "essences *qua* essences" which are immanent in the extramental objects; Avicenna solved the issue about the status of the non-existent with a theory of mental existence.

Šahrastānī's decision between these four metaphysical systems can be summarized as follows: he fully accepts the Avicennian metaphysics of universals alongside the theory of mental existence; he accepts the traditional Aš'arite view on the bare particulars (since he apparently thinks that it is compatible with Avicenna's ontology); he mostly rejects the Ǧuwaynian *aḥwāl*-realist metaphysics but accepts his idea that the similarities and differences between things are not only mere words; and he fully rejects the Mu'tazilite ontology. In the end Šahrastānī's system effectively amounts to stating that there are bare particulars in the extramental reality (like this accident "black" and that "black"), about which we form the same concept "blackness" or "being color" in our minds. As for the extramental reality "being color" and "blackness" are in "this black" as

74 Davidson, *Proofs for God*, 154–212; Wolfson, *The Philosophy of Kalām*, 434–44; and Griffel, *Al-Ghazālī's Philosophical Theology*, 170.

"essences *qua* essences", yet they are identical to it. Hence, the distinction between "blackness" and "being color" in "this black" is conceptual, or even formal, but not real. This is how Šahrastānī's conceptualism works. As for the ontological status of essences, Šahrastānī denies the idea that they depend on God in terms of their existence alone. Instead he suggests that God *specifies* the essence of every existent object: He does not only let existence of "black" preponderate over its non-existence, but also makes the "black" black.

In conclusion, one can note that the conceptualism that Šahrastānī argued for became the most wide spread metaphysical system in the post-Avicennian philosophy. Already in the second half of the 11th century ʿUmar Ḫayyām claimed the same as Šahrastānī will later: there are no real *aḥwāl*, attributes like "being color" are merely conceptual (*iʿtibārī*). On this basis he concludes that existence is such an attribute, so that the essence-existence distinction appears conceptual and not real.[75] Ibn Ġaylān followed Ḫayyām's and Šahrastānī's lead faithfully. He claims that there are only bare *ḏawāt* in the extramental reality that differ in their quiddities (*al-ḏawāt al-muḫtalifat al-māhiyyāt*), whereas universals - which stand for more general similarities and differences (cf. the ultimate task of *aḥwāl*) - exist only in the mind. He also compares them to relational attributes (*al-umūr al-nisabiyya wa-l-umūr al-iḍāfiyya*), which do not have real correspondence in existence. Ibn Ġaylān's account as a whole is strongly reminiscent of Šahrastānī's *Nihāya*.[76] Faḫr al-Dīn al-Rāzī appears to know this tradition very well already in his *Mabāḥiṯ*, where he distinguishes between real composita and objects that are analyzed in many only in the mind.[77] Abū l-Barakāt uses the idea of merely conceptual distinction in order to explain how being existent is predicated of existence itself.[78] Āmidī's position and argumentation comes very close to Šahrastānī.[79] Finally, Suhrawardī is most famous for claiming that the essence and existence are distinct only as two concepts yet are identical extramentally.[80] This position is based on the same conceptualist metaphysics that already Šahrastānī defended: the universals or *aḥwāl* exist only as concepts in the mind and are indistinguishable from the objects they belong to extramentally. Still there remains the question how much of the realist side of Šahrastānī's metaphysics

75 Ḫayyām, *Risāla fī l-wuǧūd*, 102–103; 110.15–17.

76 Ibn Ġaylān, *Ḥudūṯ*, 74.4–12.

77 Rāzī, *Mabāḥiṯ*, 147–49. However we should be careful about Rāzī because his view on "essences *qua* essences" is more realist than that of Šahrastānī or Ḫayyām, since he believes in the priority of essences over existence. This is also clear by his skepticism towards the Šahrastānī-Avicenna solution in *Muḥaṣṣal*, 64.1–3, which lacks enough realism for him.

78 Abū l-Barakāt, *Muʿtabar*, 63.14–64.14.

79 Āmidī, *Ġāya*, 29–37.

80 Suhrawardī, *Talwīḥāt*, 192–93.

would be accepted by other aforementioned authors. This question is however matter of another study.

Bibliography

Adamson, Peter. "Correcting Plotinus: Soul's Relationship to Body in Avicenna's Commentary on the Theology of Aristotle." In *Philosophy, Science and Exegesis in Greek. Arabic and Latin Commentators.* Ed. by P. Adamson, H. Baltussen, and M.W.F. Stone. London: Institute of Classical Studies, 2004, 59–75.

Adamson, Peter and Key, Alexander. "Philosophy of Language in the Medieval Arabic Tradition." In *Linguistic Meaning: New Essays in the History of the Philosophy of Language.* Ed. by M. Cameron and R. Stainton. Oxford: Oxford University Press, 2015, 74–99.

Alami, Ahmed. *L'ontologie modale: Étude de la théorie des modes d'Abū Hāshim al-Jubbāʾī.* Paris: Vrin, 2001.

al-Āmidī, Sayf al-Dīn. *Abkār al-afkār fī uṣūl al-dīn.* Ed. by Aḥmad M. al-Mahdī. 3 vols. Cairo: al-Maktabat Dār al-kutub wa-l-waṯāʾiq al-qawmiyya, 2004.

–, *Ġāyat al-marām fī ʿilm al-kalām.* Ed. by. Aḥmad Farīd al-Mazīdī. Beirut: Dār al-kutub al-ʿilmiyya, 2004.

al-Anṣārī, Abū l-Qāsim Salmān b. Nāṣir al-Nīsābūrī. *al-Ġunya fī l-kalām: dirāsa wa-taḥqīq qism al-ilāhīyāt.* Vol. 1. Ed. by ʿAbd al- M. Ḥ. Hādī. Cairo: 2010.

Avicenna, *Dānišnāma-yi ʿAlāʾī. Risāla-yi manṭiq.* Ed. by Muḥammad M. Muʿīn and Muḥammad Miškat. Tehran: Intišārāt-i anǧuman-i āṯār-i millī, 1952.

–, *al-Išārāt wa-l-tanbīhāt.* Ed. by Muǧtabā al-Zārʿī. Qom: Būstān-i kitāb, 2008.

–, *al-Naǧāt min al-ġarq fī baḥr al-dalālāt.* Ed. by Muḥammad Dānišpažūh, Tehran: Dānišgah-i Tihran, 1985.

–, *al-Šifāʾ, al-Ilāhiyyāt.* Ed. by Michael E. Marmura. Provo: Brigham Young University Press, 2005.

–, *al-Šifāʾ, al-Manṭiq, al-Madḫal.* Ed. by Ǧurǧ Š. Qanawatī, Maḥmūd M. al-Ḫudayrī and Aḥmad F. al-Ahwānī. Cairo: al-Maṭbaʿa al-amīriyya, 1952.

–, *al-Šifāʾ, al-Manṭiq, al-Maqūlāt.* Ed. by Ǧurǧ Š. Qanawātī, Maḥmūd M. al-Ḫudayrī, Aḥmad Fūʾad al-Ahwānī, and Saʿīd Zāyid. Cairo: al-Hayʾa al-ʿāmma li-šuʾūn al-maṭābiʿ al-amīriyya, 1959.

–, *al-Šifāʾ, Nafs.* Ed. by Jan Bakoš. Prague: Travaux De l'académie Tchécoslovaque des sciences, 1956.

al-Baġdādī, Abū l-Barakāt. *Kitāb al-Muʿtabar.* Ed. by Şerefeddin Yaltkaya. 3 vols. Hyderabad: Maṭbaʿat ǧamʿiyyat dāʾirat al-maʿārif al-uṯmāniyya, 1938–39.

Benevich, Fedor. "The Classical Ashʿari Theory of *Aḥwāl.* Juwaynī and His Opponents." In *Journal of Islamic Studies* 27:2 (2016): 136–75.

–, "The Essence-Existence Distinction: Four Elements of the Post-Avicennian Metaphysical Dispute." In *Oriens* 45 (2017): 203–58.

–, "Die Göttliche Existenz: Zum ontologischen Status der Essenz *qua* Essenz bei Avicenna." In *Documenti e studi sulla tradizione filosofica medievale* 26 (2015): 103–28.

–, "The Reality of the Non-Existent Object of Thought: The Possible, the Impossible, and Mental Existence in Islamic Philosophy (eleventh–thirteenth centuries)." In *Oxford Studies in Medieval Philosophy* 6 (2018): 31–61.

Black, Deborah. "Estimation in Avicenna: The Logical and Psychological Dimensions." In: *Dialogue* 32 (1993): 219–58.

–, "Avicenna's Vague Individual and its Impact on Medieval Latin Philosophy." In *Vehicles of Transmission, Translation, and Transformation in Medieval Textual Culture.* Ed. by R. Wisnovsky et a.l. Turnhout: Brepols, 2011, 259–92.

–, "Avicenna on the Ontological and Epistemic Status of Fictional Beings." In: *Documenti e studi sulla tradizione filosofica medievale* 8 (1997): 425–53.

–, "Mental Existence in Thomas Aquinas and Avicenna." In *Mediaeval Studies* 61.1 (1999): 45–79.

Davidson, Herbert A. *Proofs for Eternity, Creation and the Existence of God in Medieval Islamic and Jewish Philosophy.* New-York: Oxford University Press, 1987.

Druart, Thérèse-Anne. "The Human Soul's Individuation and Its Survival After The Body's Death: Avicenna On The Causal Relation Between Body and Soul." In *Arabic Sciences and Philosophy* 10 (2000): 259–73.

Endress, Gerhard. "Grammatik und Logik: Arabische Philologie und Griechische Philosophie im Widerstreit." In *Sprachphilosophie in Antike und Mittelalter: Bochumer Kolloquium, 2.–4. Juni 1982.* Ed. by B. Mojsisch. Amsterdam: Verlag B.R. Grüner, 1986, 163–298.

Frank, Richard M. "Abū Hāshim's theory of 'states': its structure and function." In: *Actas do quarto congresso de estudios árabes e islâmicos, Coimbra-Lisboa, 1 a 8 de setembro de 1968.* Leiden: Brill, 1971, 90–99

–, "The Ašʿarite Ontology I: Primary Entities". In *Arabic Sciences and Philosophy* 9 (1999), 163–231.

–, *Beings and their Attributes.* Albany: State University of New York Press, 1978.

–, "*Al-maʿdūm wal-mawjūd:* The non-existent, the existent and the possible in the teaching of Abū Hāshim and his followers." In *MIDEO* 14 (1980):185–209.

al-Ġazālī, Abū Ḥāmid. *Iqtiṣād fī l-iʿtiqād.* Ed. by. Ibrahim Agâh Çubukçu and Hüseyn Atay. Ankara: Nur Matbaası, 1962.

–, *Tahāfut al-falāsifa.* Edited by Michael Marmura. Provo, Utah: Brigham Young University Press, 2000.

Griffel, Frank. *Al-Ghazālī's Philosophical Theology.* Oxford: Oxford University Press, 2009.

al-Suhrawardī, Šihāb al-Din. *al-Talwīḥāt al-lawḥiyya wa-l-ʿaršiyya.* Ed. by Nağafqulī Ḥabībī. Tehran: Muʾassasa-yi pažūhašī-i hikmat-i wa falsafa-yi Irān, 2009.

al-Ğuwaynī, ʿAbd al-Mālik. *al-Šāmil fī uṣūl al-dīn.* Ed. by ʿAlī Sāmī al-Naššār. Alexandria: Maktabat ʿilm al-uṣūl al-dīn, 1969.

–, *al-Šāmil fī ʿuṣūl al-dīn.* Ed. Richard M. Frank. Tehran, Institute of Islamic Studies McGill University, 1981.

Hasse, Dag. *Avicenna's De Anima in the Latin West: The Formation of a Peripatetic Philosophy of the Soul, 1160–1300.* London-Turin: The Warburg Institute, Nino Aragno Editore, 2000.

Ḫayyām, ʿUmar. *Risāla fī l-wuğūd.* Ed. by Nezhad Ğ. Awwal. *Farhang* 29–32 (1999): 101–118.

Ibn Ġaylān, Afḍal al-Dīn al-Balḫī. *Ḥudūṯ al-ʿalam.* Ed. by Mahdi Muhaqqiq. Tehran: Muʾassassa-yi muṭālaʿāt-i islāmī, 1998.

Ibn al-Malāḥimī, Rukūn al-Dīn al-Ḫwārazmī. *Tuḥfat al-mutakallimīn fī l-radd ʿalā l-falāsifa.* Ed. by Hassan Ansārī and Wilfred Madelung. Tehran: Iranian Institute of Philosophy & Institute of Islamic Studies, Free University of Berlin, 2008.

Jolivet, Jean. "Al-Shahrastani critique d' Avicenne dans la lute contre les philosophes". In *Arabic Sciences and Philosophy* 10 (2000): 275–92.

Madelung, Wilfred. "Aš-Šahrastānīs Streitschrift gegen Avicenna und ihre Widerlegung durch Naṣīr al-Dīn aṭ-Ṭūsī". In *Akten des VII. Kongresses für Arabistik und Islamwissenschaften (Göttingen 15–22 August 1974).* Ed. by Albrecht Dietrich. Göttingen: Vandenhoeck und Ruprecht, 1976, 250–59.

Marmura, Michael. "Avicenna's Critique of Platonists in Book VII, Chapter 2 of the Metaphysics of his Healing." *Arabic Theology, Arabic Philosophy, From the Many to the One. Essays in Celebration of Richard M. Frank.* Ed. by James E. Montgomery. Leuven: Peeters, 2006, 359–64.

McGinnis, Jon. "*Logic and Science: The Role of Genus and Difference in Avicenna's Logic, Science and Natural Philosophy.*" In *Documenti e studi sulla tradizione philosophica medievale* 18 (2007), 165–86.

al-Nīsābūrī, Abū Rāšid. *Kitāb al-masāʾil fī l-ḫilāf bayn al-baṣriyyīn wa-l-baġdādiyyīn.* Ed. by Arthur Biram. Berlin: H. Itzkowksi, 1902.

Rashed, Marwan. "Ibn ʿAdī et Avicenne: sur les types d'existant." In *Aristotele e i suoi esegeti neoplatonici.* Ed. by R. Chiaradonna. Napoli: Bibliopolis, 2004, 107–172.

al-Rāzī, Faḫr al-Dīn. *al-Arbaʿīn fī uṣūl al-dīn.* Ed. by Aḥmad al-Ḥ. al-Saqqā. 2 vols. Cairo: Maktabat al-kulliyyāt al-azhariyya, 1986.

–, *al-Mabāḥiṯ al-mašriqiyya fī ʿilm al-ilāhiyyāt wa-l-ṭabīʿiyyāt.* Ed. by Muḥammad al-M. al-Baġdādī. 2 vols. Beirut: Dār al-kitāb al-ʿarabī, 1990.

–, *al-Maṭālib al-ʿāliyya min al-ʿilm al-ilāhī,* ed. by Aḥmad al-Ḥ. al-Saqqā. 9 vols. Beirut: Dār al-kitāb al-ʿarabī, 1987.

–, *Muḥaṣṣal afkār al-mutaqaddimīn wa-l-mutaʾaḫḫirīn min ʿulamāʾ wa-l-ḥukamāʾ wa-l-mutakallimīn.* ed. by Ṭaha ʿAbd al-Ruʿūf Saʿd. Cairo: Maktabat al-kulliyyāt al- azhariyya, 1978.

–, *Nihāyat al-ʿuqūl fī dirāyat al-ʿuṣūl.* Ed. by Saʿīd ʿA. Fūda. 4 vols. Beirut: Dār al-ḏakāʾir, 2015.

al-Šahrastānī, Muḥammad. *al-Muṣāraʿa.* Ed. by Toby Mayer and Wilfred Madelung. London-New-York: Tauris, 2001.

–, *Mafātiḥ al-asrār wa-maṣābiḥ al-abrār.* Ed. by M.A. Adharshab in Toby Mayer. *Keys to the Arcana: Shahrastānī's Esoteric Commentary on the Qurʾān.* Oxford: Oxford University Press, Institute of Islmaili Studies London, 2009.

–, *Nihāyat al-aqdām fī ʿilm al-kalām.* Ed. by Alfred Guillaume. London: Oxford University Press, 1934.

al-Sāwī, ʿUmar b. Sahlān. *Muṣāraʿat al-Muṣāraʿa.* MS Kazan 1125, fol. 99r–136r.

Steigerwald, Diane. *La pansée philosophique et théologique de Shahrastānī (m. 548/1153).* Les presses de l'université Laval, 1997.

Thiele, Jan. "Abū Hāshim al-Jubbāʾī's (d. 321/933) Theory of 'States' (*aḥwāl*) and its Adaptation by Ashʿarite Theologians." In *Oxford Handbook of Islamic Theology.* Ed. by S. Schmidtke. Oxford: Oxford University Press, 2016, 364–83.

Treiger, Alexander. "Avicenna's Notion of Transcendental Modulation of Existence (*taškīk al-wujūd, analogia entis*) and It's Greek and Arabic Sources." In *Islamic Philosophy, Science, Culture, and Religion: Studies in Honor of Dimitri Gutas.* Ed. by F. Opwis and D. Reisman. Leiden: Brill 2012, 327–63.
Van Ess, Josef. *Der Eine und das Andere.* 2 vols. Berlin: De Gruyter, 2011.
–, *Theologie und Gesellschaft im 2. und 3. Jahrhundert Hidschra: eine Geschichte des religiösen Denkens im frühen Islam.* 6 vols. Berlin: De Gruyter, 1991–95.
Wolfson, Harry. *The Philosophy of Kalam.* Cambridge: Harvard University Press, 1976.
Wisnovsky, Robert. "Essence and Existence in the Eleventh- and Twelfth-Century Islamic East (*Mašriq*): A Sketch." In *The Arabic, Hebrew and Latin Receptions of Avicenna's Metaphysics.* Ed. by D. Hasse and A. Bertolacci. Berlin: De Gruyter, 2012, 27–50.

Yuki Nakanishi

Post-Avicennian Controversy over the Problem of Universals: Saʿdaddīn at-Taftāzānī (d. 1389/90) and Šamsaddīn al-Fanārī (d. 1431) on the Reality of Existence*

Introduction

As a part of his elaborate metaphysical discussions, Avicenna (d. 1037) explored the problem of universals. His examination of this issue provided the subsequent generations of scholars with the theoretical framework to address this conundrum, while also provoking a heated debate on various related questions. Of these, the question that was probably most seriously discussed was: "whether or not the universal exists in the external world". While this post-Avicennian phase of the problem is occasionally mentioned by historians, their focus has predominantly been on how the philosophers and theologians took part in this dispute.[1] The role played by the *mystics* belonging to the so-called "Akbarian school" (i.e. the followers of aš-Šayḫ al-*akbar* Ibn al-ʿArabī [d. 1240]), which is characterised by its peculiar concept *waḥdat al-wuǧūd* ("unity of existence"), has not yet been examined.[2]

According to the theory of *waḥdat al-wuǧūd*, "absolute existence" (*al-wuǧūd al-muṭlaq*), i.e. existence considered as such, is identified with the Real (*ḥaqq*),

* I would like to express my sincere gratitude to Professor Heidrun Eichner (Tübingen), Professor Hidemi Takahashi (Tokyo), Junichi Ono (Tokyo) and the discussants in the international conference "Islamic Philosophy from the 12th to the 14th Century" for their valuable comments on the earlier versions of this paper. Needless to say, all the remaining errors are my own.

1 See Izutsu (1974a); id. (1974b). In this regard, on Avicenna's theory of universals, see, for instance, Avicenna: *al-Ilāhiyyāt* V.1, 195–206; Marmura (1979); id. (1992); id. (tr. [2005]) 148–57.

2 Of course, there are several pioneering studies on this topic, such as Heer (1970); id. (ed./tr. [1979]); id. (tr. [1979]), in which the author examines aspects of the reception and criticism by the famous mystic-scholar ʿAbdarraḥmān Ǧāmī (d. 1492) of post-Avicennian philosophy. In this regard, see also Wisnovsky (2013) 206–07, in which the author offers a brief analysis of the ontology of Ibn al-ʿArabī and Šayḫališrāq as-Suhrawardī (d. 1191) in relation to some related theories that Avicenna puts forward in the *al-Ilāhiyyāt* of his *aš-Šifāʾ*.

the entire universe being conceived to be its self-manifestations.[3] In the present study, I will deal with a "controversy" over this Akbarian conception of existence between Saʿdaddīn at-Taftāzānī (d. 1389/90) and Šamsaddīn al-Fanārī (d. 1431). At-Taftāzānī is one of the most influential philosopher-theologians that was active in Iran and Central Asia in the fourteenth century,[4] while al-Fanārī is one of the most prominent theorists of the Akbarian *Weltanschauung* active in fourteenth- and fifteenth-century Anatolia and Egypt.[5] In *ǧuz*ʾ 1, *maqṣad* 2, *faṣl* 1, *mabḥaṯ* 2 of his theological summa *Šarḥ al-Maqāṣid* (hereafter ŠM), at-Taftāzānī criticises the Akbarian theory of existence from various viewpoints; in the opening section (*faṣl* 1, *maqām* 1) of the *at-tamhīd al-ǧumalī* ("omnibus introduction"), viz. of the central part, of his metaphysical masterpiece *Miṣbāḥ al-uns* (hereafter MU), al-Fanārī puts forward many arguments to refute this critique.[6] Of all discussions between the two, the most relevant to our present investigation is their dispute as to whether or not absolute existence exists in the external world. They argue as follows:

Text 1.1.1: at-Taftāzānī: ŠM I 336, 10–12

[i] Absolute existence is [merely] a universal concept that has no realisation in the external world (mafhūm kullī lā taḥaqquq la-hū fī l-ḫāriǧ), and it [i.e. the universal concept] has an almost infinite [number of] multiple individuals.
[ii] The Necessarily Existent (*wāǧib*) is one existent that has no multiplicity in Itself.

الوجود المطلق مفهوم كلي لا تحقق له في الخارج وله أفراد كثيرة لا تكاد تتناهي والواجب موجود واحد لا تكثر فيه.

Text 1.2: al-Fanārī: MU 159–60, 3/303–04

[i] The first doubt (*šubha*) [raised by at-Taftāzānī in his ŠM] is: absolute [existence] has no realisation except in the mind (*lā taḥaqquq la-hū* illā *fī ḏ-ḏihn*), whereas the Necessarily Existent (*wāǧib*) is He whose existence in the external world is necessary.
[ii][1] The answer (*ǧawāb*) to this [doubt] is: that which has been discussed above in the "matrices" (*ummahāt*) [cf. MU 103–09, 3/90–108]: truth is that the natural universal (*al-kullī aṭ-ṭabīʿī*) exists in the external world, because one of its two divisions, i.e.

3 For a concise summary of this theory, see, for example, Izutsu (1971) 35–55; Chittick/Wilson (trs./intrs. [1982]) 6–17; Chittick (2002).

4 On at-Taftāzānī's life and relationship with philosophy, see, for instance, Madelung (2005).

5 On al-Fanārī's life and works, see, for example, Aydın/Görgün (2005) (both on life and works); Gömbeyaz (2010) (on the problem of the authenticity of his works). For an analysis of this Ottoman intellectual's metaphysical discussions, see, for instance, Nakanishi (2009); id. (2011).

6 At the outset of each text, they respectively say as follows: at-Taftāzānī: ŠM I 336, 5–6: قد أشتهر فيما بين جمع من المتفلسفة والمتصوفة أن حقيقة الواجب هو الوجود المطلق ("It is already well-known that it is [insisted] among the pseudo-philosophers and pseudo-mystics that the reality of the Necessarily Existent (*ḥaqīqat al-wāǧib*) is absolute existence"); al-Fanārī: MU 159, 3/302, 1–2: إعلم أن المنكرين أن حقيقة الحق هي الوجود المطلق من أهل النظر والمتكلمين لهم شبه جمعها في شرح المقاصد وإرتضاها ولا بد من دفعها ("Know: those among the people of speculation (*ahl an-naẓar*) and the rational theologians (*mutakallimīn*) who deny that the reality of the Real (*ḥaqīqat al-ḥaqq*) is absolute existence have [announced their] doubts (*šubah*) [scil. about the identity of the Real with absolute existence], which [at-Taftāzānī] collected in his *Šarḥ al-Maqāṣid* and to which he agreed. It is inevitable [for us] to rebut them").

Text 1.1.2: at-Taftāzānī: ŠM I 336, penult.-ult.

… That the existences [subsist as] multiple things (*takaṯṯur al-wuǧūdāt*) whereas absolute existence is [merely] a universal concept that has no realisation except in the mind (*lā taḥaqquq la-hū illā fī ḏ-ḏihn*) is necessary (*ḍarūrī*).

فتكثر الوجودات وكون الوجود المطلق مفهوما كليا لا... تحقق له إلا في الذهن ضروري.

the mixed (*maḫlūṭ*), exists. [2] The suspicions of those who deny it (*šubah munkirī-hī*) [i.e. the existence of the natural universal in the external world] have already been rebutted there.

الشبهة الأولى أن المطلق لا تحقق له إلا في الذهن والواجب من يجب وجوده في الخارج جوابها ما مر في الأمهات أن الحق وجود الكلي الطبيعي في الخارج لوجود أحد قسميه وهو المخلوط وقد إندفع ثمة شبه منكريه.

According to at-Taftāzānī, absolute existence is merely a universal concept that does not exist in the external world ("*mafhūm kullī lā taḥaqquq la-hū fī l-ḫāriǧ*"), while the Real exists necessarily (Texts 1.1.1 [i]/1.1.2/1.2 [i]). Consequently, in his understanding, absolute existence cannot be identified with Him. Al-Fanārī's refutation of this critique consists of two steps: 1) referring to a preceding section entitled *ummahāt* ("matrices") where he had already provided demonstrations that the universal exists in the external world (Text 1.2 [ii]); 2) rebutting at-Taftāzānī's argument more directly. The first step consists of al-Fanārī's rebuttal of the arguments put forward by Naṣīraddīn aṭ-Ṭūsī (d. 1274) and Quṭbaddīn ar-Rāzī (d. 1365) who likewise deny the existence of the universal in the external world; and the second is, at least in part, his mediation of the dispute between ʿAḍudaddīn al-Īǧī (d. 1355) and at-Taftāzānī over the concept of "individuation" (*taʿayyun*).

In the following sections, I will first examine at-Taftāzānī's theory of quiddity (*māhiyya*) insofar as it is related to his argument to deny the existence of the universal in the external world (§2). I will then examine the two arguments by aṭ-Ṭūsī and ar-Rāzī to the same effect insofar as they are cited in al-Fanārī's refutation (§3). This will be followed by an analysis of the latter's refutation of aṭ-Ṭūsī and ar-Rāzī (§4.1), as well as of at-Taftāzānī (after briefly discussing the "Īǧī-Taftāzānī dispute" over individuation) (§4.2). Finally, I will offer some concluding remarks on al-Fanārī's overall method in this controversy (§5).

1. At-Taftāzānī's Theory of Quiddity: Universal as Nonexistent, Existence as Accident

At-Taftāzānī's theory of the universal is clarified in *ǧuzʾ* 1, *maqṣad* 2, *faṣl* 2, *mabḥaṯ* 1 of ŠM. Within the Avicennian framework of the threefold division, he considers quiddity (*māhiyya*) from three aspects: 1) *bi-šarṭ šayʾ* ("conditioned by something"); 2) *bi-šarṭ lā* ("conditioned by nothing"); and 3) *lā bi-šarṭ* ("unconditioned by anything"). He explains as follows.

Text 2.1: at-Taftāzānī: ŠM I 403, penult.–404, 2

[i] The [quiddity] associated with accidents ([*al-māhiyya*] *muqāranat al-ʿawāriḍ*) is called "mixed [quiddity]" ([*al-m.*] *al-maḫlūṭa*) or "quiddity conditioned by something" (*al-m. bi-šarṭ šayʾ*).

[ii] There is no doubt that this [quiddity] exists, just as the individuals of the quiddity "human" (*insān*) like Zayd and ʿAmr [exist].

[iii] It [i. e. quiddity] can also be considered on the condition that none of the accidents is associated with it. This is called "abstract [quiddity]" ([*al-m.*] *al-muǧarrada*) or "quiddity conditioned by nothing" (*al-m. bi-šarṭ lā*).

[iv] There is no doubt that it is impossible for this [quiddity] to exist in the concrete reality [i. e. in the external world], for "existence" is one of the accidents (*ʿawāriḍ*), and "individuation" (*tašaḫḫuṣ*) is as well [i. e. one of the accidents].

مقارنة العوارض وتسمى المخلوطة والماهية بشرط شيء ولا خفاء في وجودها كزيد وعمرو من أفراد ماهية الإنسان وقد تؤخذ بشرط ألا يقارنها شيء من العوارض وتسمى المجردة والماهية بشرط لا ولا خفاء في إمتناع وجودها في الأعيان لأن الوجود من العوارض وكذا التشخص.

Text 2.2: at-Taftāzānī: ŠM I 408, 3–4

"Absolute [quiddity]" ([*al-m.*] *al-muṭlaqa*), i. e. "[quiddity] unconditioned by anything" ([*al-m.*] *al-maʾḫūḏa lā bi-šarṭ šayʾ*), is more general than these two [i. e. than mixed and abstract quiddity]. [This is] because it can rightly be said of the two necessarily in the way that the absolute (*muṭlaq*) can rightly be said of the delimited (*muqayyad*).

وأما المطلقة أعني المأخوذة لا بشرط شيء فأعم منهما لصدقه عليهما ضرورة صدق المطلق على المقيد.

According to at-Taftāzānī, (1) quiddity conditioned by something is associated with accidents (*ʿawāriḍ*) that are external to the quiddity itself (Text 2.1 [i]); (2) quiddity conditioned by nothing is not associated with those accidents (Text 2.1 [iii]); and (3) quiddity unconditioned by anything is more general than these two (Text 2.2), and is neither "associated" nor "not associated" with the accidents.[7] Of these three divisions, the second corresponds to the universal.[8]

For what reason, then, does at-Taftāzānī deny the existence of the universal (= [2]) in the external world? According to him, it must be denied because "'existence' is one of the accidents" from which quiddity of type (2) is to be separated (Text 2.1 [iv]). That is to say, he argues that the universal does not exist in the external world *on the ground that it is an accident.* In the remaining part of this

7 Cf. at-Taftāzānī: ŠM I 409, 6–7: [*sic*] والمأخوذ لا بشرط شيء أعم من أن يعتبر مع هذا العارض أو لا يتعبر ("The [quiddity unconditioned by anything] is more general (*aʿamm*) than considered with this accident [i. e. with universality] and not considered [with it]").

8 Cf. at-Taftāzānī: ŠM I 404, 1–3; 404, 5–405, 8. On this, see also Heer (2006) 80; Izutsu (1974a) 5–6.

section, therefore, I will examine at-Taftāzānī's argument for the accidentality of existence. He argues for this point in *ǧuzʾ* 1, *maqṣad* 2, *faṣl* 1, *mabḥaṯ* 2 of ŠM by demonstrating that quiddity should be separated in intellection from existence.

Text 2.3: at-Taftāzānī: ŠM I 311, 8–11

[i] The reason why [quiddity], when being intellected, is separated [from existence] (*al-infikāk fī t-taʿaqqul*) is as follows:

[ii] We can conceptualise the quiddity of a thing (*qad nataṣawwaru l-māhiyya*) without considering its existence (*wa-lā nataṣawwaru kawna-hā* [i.e. *kawn al-māhiyya*]) [scil. both in the external world and in the mind].

[iii] As to [the fact that the quiddity of a thing can be conceptualised regardless of whether that thing exists] *in the external world*, it is self-evident [i.e. we need not discuss it here].

[iv] As to [the fact that the quiddity of a thing can be conceptualised regardless of whether that thing exists] *in the mind*, the reason [for it] is as follows: [1] we do not know [i.e. do not accept] (*lā naʿlamu*) that "concept" (*taṣawwur*) is [synonymous with] "existence in intellect" (*al-wuǧūd fī l-ʿaql*). [2] Were it correct, [these two] would be interchangeable (*badīl*). [3] Were it correct, the conceptualisation of a thing (*taṣawwur aš-šayʾ*) would not necessarily require the intellection of its concept [i.e. of that thing] (*taʿaqqul taṣawwuri-hī*). [4] Were it correct, however, it would be possible for what we cannot intellect at all (*mā lā naʿqilu-hū aṣlan*) to exist in the external world, [which is evidently false].

الإنفكاك في التعقل فإنا قد نتصور الماهية ولا نتصور كونها أما في الخارج فظاهر وأما في الذهن فلأنا لا نعلم أن التصور هو الوجود في العقل ولو سلم فلبديل ولو سلم فتصور الشيء لا يستلزم تعقل تصوره ولو سلم فيجوز أن يوجد في الخارج ما لا نعقله أصلا.

According to at-Taftāzānī, we can conceptualise (*nataṣawwaru*) the quiddity of a thing without considering that thing's existence (Text 2.3 [ii]), whether it be "existence in the external world" or "existence in the mind". The fact that we can conceptualise the quiddity of a thing without considering that thing's existence *in the external world* is self-evident to him, and therefore he provides no demonstration for it (Text 2.3 [iii]). But the fact that we can conceptualise the quiddity of a thing without considering that thing's existence *in the mind* is not self-evident to him, and therefore he provides a demonstration for it.

At-Taftāzānī writes that "concept" (*taṣawwur*) is not synonymous with "existence in intellect" (*al-wuǧūd fī l-ʿaql*) (Text 2.3 [iv][1]). Otherwise, these two would be interchangeable (*badīl*) (Text 2.3 [iv][2]). This would, however, require that the "*concept* of a thing being intellected" be replaced with the "*existence* of that thing *in intellect* (i.e. that thing's mental existence) being intellected". On this assumption, even though the concept of a thing is conceptualised, its *mental existence* (i.e. not that concept itself) could be intellected (Text 2.3 [iv][3]). Then, everything existing in the external world would necessarily be something that we cannot think about (Text 2.3 [iv][4]) – or more precisely, something whose mental existence alone we can think about. This is evidently false. Thus, according to at-Taftāzānī, existence is an accident, which means, in turn, that the universal does not exist in the external world.[9]

2. Al-Fanārī's Citation of Two Arguments: Aṭ-Ṭūsī and ar-Rāzī against the Existence of the Universal in the External World

In the *ummahāt*, al-Fanārī provides a detailed argument that the "universal and one self-manifestation" (*taǧallin kullī aḥadī*) of the Real exists in the external world separately from the individual (cf. MU 101–09, 3/83–108); in his system, the Real's "universal and one self-manifestation" corresponds to the universal in question. It must be noted here that he considers this position to be the "orthodox" one that had been taken by most philosophers (*ḥukamāʾ*) as well. He states:

Text 3.1: al-Fanārī: MU 105, 3/97, 1–3 [cf. Appendix: Text 6][10]

Most of the philosophers (*ḥukamāʾ*) hold that the natural universal (*al-kullī aṭ-ṭabīʿī*) exists in it [i. e. in the external world], for one of its [?] two divisions – namely, the mixed [quiddity] or quiddity conditioned by something – exists. [In fact] al-Ḫunaǧī, al-Urmawī, al-Kātibī and the others have already stated definitely that common quiddity (*al-māhiyya al-muštaraka*) exists.

فقد ذهب أكثر الحكماء إلى أن الكلي الطبيعي موجود فيه لوجود أحد قسميه وهو المخلوط والماهية بشرط شيء وقد صرح الخنجي والأرموي والكاتبي وغيرهم بوجود الماهية المشتركة.

According to al-Fanārī, Afḍaladdīn al-Ḫunaǧī (d. 1249), Sirāǧaddīn al-Urmawī (d. 1283) and Naǧmaddīn al-Kātibī (d. ca. 1276) hold that the universal exists in the external world (Text 3.1), in opposition to the view held by at-Taftāzānī (§2).[11] After thus pointing out the "orthodoxy", as it were, of his own theory, al-Fanārī cites two further "exceptions", namely the arguments by aṭ-Ṭūsī and ar-Rāzī, in order to refute these arguments more directly later. Al-Fanārī argues as follows:

9 Through four additional discussions on this topic (cf. ŠM I 310, 14–311, 16), in effect, at-Taftāzānī argues for the accidentality or "superaddition" (*ziyāda*) of existence to quiddity. On the post-Avicennian background of this discussion, see, for example, Eichner (2012); Wisnovsky (2012).

10 The *Vorlage* of the arguments originally advanced by al-Ḫunaǧī and al-Urmawī could not yet be identified.

11 More precisely, in Text 3.1, al-Fanārī uses the following two terms to signify the universal or the "universal and one self-manifestation" of the Real: 1) "common quiddity" (*al-māhiyya al-muštaraka*) (Text 3.2); 2) "reality" (*ḥaqīqa*) (Text 3.3).

Text 3.2: al-Fanārī: MU 105, 3/97, 3-ult. [cf. Appendix: Text 5.1]

[i] The Verifier aṭ-Ṭūsī, however, refuses it [i.e. the most philosophers' argument that the common quiddity (i.e. the universal) exists in the external world] with the following [argument]:

[ii][1] Were it [i.e. common quiddity; cf. Text 5.1 (i)] realised in every one of its individuals (*fī kull afrādi-hā*), it would not be one thing in itself (*bi-ʿayni-hī*); [2] were it realised in the whole [of its individuals] insofar as it is a "whole" (*fī l-kull min ḥayṯu huwa kull*), then the whole [considered] from this perspective (*ḥayṯiyya*) would be one thing, and [the quiddity] could not occur to [multiple] things; [3] were it realised in the whole insofar as [it is] divided [internally into parts] (*fī l-kull min ḥayṯu maʿnā t-tafarruq*), there would [merely] be its "part" (*ǧuzʾa-hū*), not itself (*lā nafsa-hū*), in every one [of those parts].

ومنعه المحقق الطوسي بأنها أن تحققت في كل أفرادها لم يكن شيئا واحدا بعينه وإن تحققت في الكل من حيث هو كل فالكل من تلك الحيثية شيء واحد فلم يقع على أشياء وإن تحققت في الكل من حيث معنى التفرق كان في كل واحد جزئه لا نفسه.

According to aṭ-Ṭūsī, if common quiddity (*al-māhiyya al-muštaraka*), i.e. the universal, were to exist in the external world, it could only do so in individual things – or more specifically, only in the following three ways: 1) "in every one of its individuals" (*fī kull afrādi-hā*) (Text 3.2 [ii][1]); 2) "in the whole [of its individuals] insofar as it is a "whole" (*fī l-kull min ḥayṯu huwa kull*) (Text 3.2 [ii][2]); 3) "in the whole insofar as [it is] divided [internally into parts]" (*fī l-kull min ḥayṯu maʿnā t-tafarruq*) (Text 3.2 [ii][3]).

According to aṭ-Ṭūsī, the first way is impossible, because the universal would then exist so many as its individuals which share it; however, such a thing "would not be *one* thing in itself" (*lam yakun šayʾan wāḥidan bi-ʿayni-hī*) anymore (Text 3.2 [ii][1]), but rather *multiple* things. The second way is also impossible, because there would then be merely one "whole" that has the quiddity; and the universal, in this case, "could not occur to [multiple] things" (*lam yaqaʿ ʿalā ašyāʾ*) (Text 3.2 [ii][2]) – that is, could not be *common* to anything. The third way is likewise impossible, because every one of those internal divisions of a whole which share the universal would then have merely "its part, not itself" (*ǧuzʾa-hū lā nafsa-hū*) (Text 3.2 [ii][2]). Thus, according to aṭ-Ṭūsī, the universal cannot exist in the external world. Next, we will examine ar-Rāzī's argument. He states:

Text 3.3: al-Fanārī: MU 105, 3/99[12]

[i] Quṭbaddīn ar-Rāzī, too, refuses it [i.e. the most philosophers' argument that the universal exists in the external world] with the following [argument]:

12 According to Heer, this passage is taken from ar-Rāzī's *Lawāmiʿ al-asrār* and *Risālat taḥqīq al-kulliyyāt*; but with regard to the former work, I was unable to find out any corresponding passage, and with regard to the latter, I was unable to obtain a copy of the manuscript (Ms. Warner Or. 958 [21]). Cf. Heer (tr. [1979]) 77, par. 15, note 1.

[ii] A number of the realities such as genus (*ǧins*), differentia (*faṣl*) and species (*nawʿ*) are realised in an individual.

[iii] However, were it [i.e. the common quiddity] to exist [within its individuals in the external world], it would be impossible that [the common quiddity] be predicated of one another, [which is evidently false].

ومنعه قطب الدين الرازي أيضا بأن عدة من الحقائق كالجنس والفصل والنوع تتحقق في فرد فلو وجدت إمتنع الحمل بينها.

According to ar-Rāzī, various universals such as genus (*ǧins*), differentia (*faṣl*) and species (*nawʿ*) are realised in their individuals (Text 3.3 [ii]). This, however, does not mean that these universals exist in the external world together with their existing individuals; for if such universals were to exist within the individuals in the external world, they could not be predicated of one another, just as the individual things existing in the external world cannot be predicated of one another (Text 3.3 [iii]). In his view, that is to say, if the universals were to exist in the external world, the predication "human is an animal" would necessarily fall under the same category as the predication "Zayd is ʿAmr", which is evidently false. Thus, ar-Rāzī also belives that the universal cannot exist in the external world.

3. Al-Fanārī's Refutation: Reference to and Modification of the Tradition

3.1. Refutation of aṭ-Ṭūsī and ar-Rāzī

Al-Fanārī begins by refuting these two arguments by aṭ-Ṭūsī and ar-Rāzī. He argues:

Text 4.1: al-Fanārī: MU 106–08, 3/104, 1–6 [i.e. 106, 10-ult.]

[i] If you say: how can something that is one in itself (*al-wāḥid bi-ḏ-ḏāt*) be qualified (*yattaṣifu*) through mutually contradictory attributes (*al-awṣāf al-mutaḍādda*), just like "east-ness" (*mašriqiyya*) and "west-ness" (*maġribiyya*), "knowledge" (*ʿilm*) and "ignorance" (*ǧahl*), etc.?

[ii] I say: the judgement [of aṭ-Ṭūsī and ar-Rāzī] that it is impossible (*istibʿād*) results from [their] analogising the universal from the particular and the invisible from the visible (*qiyās al-kullī ʿalā l-ǧuzʾī wa-l-ġāʾib ʿalā š-šāhid*).

[iii] There is, however, no demonstration to prove that this [i.e. something being qualified through mutually contradictory attributes] would [likewise] be impossible with regard to the universal; for [a universal] not being entified absolutely (*ʿadam at-taʿayyun muṭlaqan*) does not follow from [that universal] not being entified individually (*ʿadam at-taʿayyun aš-šaḫṣī*).

[iv][1] [This is] because it is possible for a universal to be entified through one of the individual entifications (*aḥad at-taʿayyunāt aš-šaḫṣiyya*), not through itself, as long as they [i. e. the individual entifications] are related to [that] universal – that is, [through] a generic or specific entification (*at-taʿayyun an-nawʿī aw al-ǧinsī*); [2] this is a substantial entification (*taʿayyunan ḏātiyyan*), not a notional (*lā ʿilmiyyan*), just like [the entification of] the Universal Spirit (*ar-rūḥ al-kullī*) [i. e. the Sublime Pen or the First Intellect].

[v] Furthermore, [this] judgement that it is impossible will disappear through the following remarks that I cite from the Verifier aṭ-Ṭūsī: "The relation (*nisba*) of all the *loci* (*amkina*) and *tempora* (*azmina*) with what is neither local nor temporal (*mā lā yakūnu makāniyyan wa-lā zamāniyyan*) is uniform (*ʿalā s-sawiyya*), for neither of the two can be considered in it [i. e. in what is neither local nor temporal]". [cf. Appendix: Text 5.2]

فإن قلت كيف يتصف الواحد بالذات بالأوصاف المتضادة كالمشرقية والمغربية والعلم والجهل وغيرها؟ قلت الإستبعاد حاصل من قياس الكلي على الجزئي والغائب على الشاهد ولا برهان على إمتناعه في الكلي إذ لا يلزم من عدم التعين الشخصي عدم التعين مطلقا لجواز أن يتعين بأحد التعينات الشخصية لا بعينه ما دامت منسوبة إلى الكلي وهو التعين النوعي أو الجنسي ويكون تعينا ذاتيا لا علميا كتعين الروح الكلي والإستبعاد يزول بما نقلناه عن المحقق الطوسي أن ما لا يكون مكانيا ولا زمانيا يكون نسبة جميع الأمكنة والأزمنة إليه على السوية فلا يعتبر شيء منهما في نفسه.

According to al-Fanārī, the critics claim that the universal does not exist in the external world (§3), *because they believe that something that is essentially one cannot be qualified through the mutually contradictory many* (Text 4.1 [i]); and this belief results from their "analogising the universal from the particular and the invisible from the visible" (*qiyās al-kullī ʿalā l-ǧuzʾī wa-l-ġāʾib ʿalā š-šāhid*) (Text 4.1 [ii]). In his view, however, this is false, for "[a universal] not being entified *individually*" (*ʿadam at-taʿayyun aš-šaḫṣī*) does not require "[that universal] not being entified *absolutely*" (*ʿadam at-taʿayyun muṭlaqan*) (Text 4.1 [iii]). Here he expands the use of the term "entification/individuation" (*taʿayyun*) even into the realm of genera and species, namely of the universals (Text 4.1 [iv][1]).

The decisive evidence for this claim is, according to al-Fanārī, the very fact that the "*Universal* Spirit" (*ar-rūḥ al-kullī*) exists in the external world (Text 4.1 [iv][2]); for as is obvious from its name, the Universal Spirit is also a universal. What needs to be taken into consideration is that this term is widely used in the Akbarian (or perhaps more generally, Arabic Neoplatonic) tradition to signify the Sublime Pen (*al-qalam al-aʿlā*) and the First Intellect (*al-ʿaql al-awwal*).[13]

13 On the use of this term in the Akbarian school, see, for instance, Ebstein (2014) 152, note 89 & 206; Todd (2014) 65–80, esp. 65–66. Cf. al-Fanārī: MU 271, 3/753, 1–3: مبدأ تعين أعلى الأرواح درجة أعني أوراح الكمل أم الكتاب ومبدأ تعين بعضها علما ووجودا متوحدا ذات القلم الأعلى المسمى بالعقل الأول والروح الكلي ("The principle of the entification [pertaining to] the highest of those spirits with regard to grade (*daraǧatan*), namely of the spirits of the perfect men (*arwāḥ al-kummal*), is the 'Matrix of the Book' (*umm al-kitāb*), and the principle of the individuation [pertaining to] some of them [i. e. of the spirits of the perfect men] – both in [divine] knowledge and in existence [i. e. in the external world] – is the essence of the Sublime Pen, which is [also] called the First

Therefore, al-Fanārī most likely refers to this term here in order to justify his own claim with recourse to this tradition.

Furthermore, al-Fanārī refers here to aṭ-Ṭūsī's argument elsewhere which serves as the theoretical basis for the existence of the universal in the external world. According to aṭ-Ṭūsī, what is neither local nor temporal (*mā lā yakūnu makāniyyan wa-lā zamāniyyan*) is uniformly related (*ʿalā s-sawiyya*) to all the *loci* (*amkina*) und *tempora* (*azmina*), for it has neither of the two in itself (Text 4.1 [v]). Obviously, al-Fanārī interprets here "what is neither local nor temporal" as the universal, "all the *loci* and *tempora*" as the individual things, and "being related" as "being qualified". By his reckoning, that is to say, this remark by aṭ-Ṭūsī asserts that the universal can be qualified through its various individuals because of its separation from them all.

3.2. Refutation of at-Taftāzānī

After rebutting the two arguments of aṭ-Ṭūsī and ar-Rāzī, al-Fanārī now returns to the refutation of at-Taftāzānī's critique itself in the opening section of the *at-tamhīd al-ǧumalī.* Indeed, his refutation just examined (§4.1) is theoretically also directed towards at-Taftāzānī's argument, for it is referred to exactly in the course of his refutation of at-Taftāzānī's critique. But in al-Fanārī's view, at-Taftāzānī will nevertheless counter this refutation by repeating his claim that what in fact exists in the external world is not the universal quiddities (*al-māhiyyāt al-kulliyya*) but the ipseity (*huwiyya*), i. e. the individuals. Al-Fanārī refutes this claim now afresh with recourse to his own theory of "entification/individuation" (*taʿayyun*). As stated above (§1), al-Fanārī's argument here is based on at-Taftāzānī's theory of individuation – or more precisely, his rebuttal of ʿAḍudaddīn al-Īǧī's (d. 1355) discussion. In *ǧuzʾ* 1, *maqṣad* 2, *faṣl* 3, *mabḥaṯ* 2 of ŠM, at-Taftāzānī addresses the issue of whether or not individuation exists as follows:

Text 4.2: at-Taftāzānī: ŠM I 442, 18–443, 12

[i] He who insists that individuation (*taʿayyun*) is existential (*wuǧūdī*) [i. e. exists in the external world] [argues for this claim] with the [following] reasons (*wuǧūh*).

Intellect and the Universal Spirit"); 391, 4/342, 1–2: لما علم الحق سبحانه من مرتبة الإمكان بما حوته ما يقتضي البروز في الرتبة الأولى الإيجادية كالقلم الأعلى المسمى بالعقل الأول والعقل الكل والروح الأعظم أبرزه ("When the Real – praise be to Him – knows what that rank of contingency (*martabat al-imkān*) encompasses, which requires [His] manifestation (*burūz*) into the first existential rank (*ar-rutba al-ūlā l-īǧādiyya*) such as the Sublime Pen that is [also] called the First Intellect, the Universal Intellect (*al-ʿaql al-kull*) and the Greatest Spirit (*ar-rūh al-aʿẓam*), [then He] manifests it [i. e. the first existential rank]").

[ii] The first [reason] is: it [i.e. individuation] is a part (*ǧuz'*) of the individuated (*muta'ayyin*), because it [i.e. the individuated] is tantamount to quiddity accompanied by individuation (*al-māhiyya ma'a t-ta'ayyun*). And it [i.e. quiddity accompanied by individuation] exists.

[iii] I answer to this with the [following] argument: [1] if "something qualified through individuation" (*al-mawṣūf bi-t-ta'ayyun*) is meant by the "individuated", it is evident that individuation occurs to it and is not a part of it [i.e. of the individual]. [2] If the compound composed of the two (*al-maǧmū' al-murakkab min-humā*) is meant [scil. by the "individuated"], then we cannot accept that it exists; for even if the attribute [i.e. individuation] were one of the sensible accidents (*al-a'rāḍ al-maḥsūsa*) [i.e. were to exist], as in the case of "white body" (*al-ǧism al-abyaḍ*), the compound is [always] nothing other than a mentally composed thing (*murakkaban i'tibāriyyan*). How, then, could [the compound] belong to that whose existence is nothing but a conflict (*mā wuǧūdu-hū nafs al-mutanāzi'*)?

[iv] The author of the *al-Mawāqif* [i.e. 'Aḍudaddīn al-Īǧī], however, raises an objection [to this as follows]: what is meant by the "individuated" is that individual whose existence is to be known necessarily (*ḏālika š-šaḫṣ al-ma'lūm wuǧūdu-hū bi-ḍ-ḍarūra*), such as Zayd, for example. His concept [i.e. the concept obtained by Zayd], however, is not only "human" – otherwise, he [i.e. Zayd] would rightly be said of 'Amr [too]; rather, he [i.e. he who insists that individuation is existential; cf. (i)] names the human accompanied by another thing (*al-insān ma'a šay' āḫar*) "individuation". Thus, it [i.e. individuation] is a part of Zayd who exists, and therefore [likewise] exists. [cf. Appendix: Text 7]

[v] The answer [to this objection] is: we accept that his concept [i.e. the concept obtained by Zayd] is not [only] the universal human that can rightly be said of another. But why is it not possible that he is a human delimited through [his] proper individual accidents which cannot rightly be said of another [such as 'Amr] [= (iii)(1)], and is not the compound [made up of the quiddity "human" and his individuation] (*dūna l-maǧmū'*) [= (iii)(2)]? Even if this were true [i.e. this were impossible], it would not necessarily follow that a part of [Zayd's] concept exists in the external world. If this were true [i.e. a part of Zayd's concept were to exist in the external world], this [existing part of Zayd's concept] would be the quantity (*kamm*), quality (*kayfa*) and place (*ayna*) that particularise him; and things like that (*naḥw ḏālika*) belong to that whose existence is to be known necessarily without disputation [i.e. unanimously], because most of them are sensible things. They [i.e. philosophers?] do not, however, name such things "individuation", but "that through which individuation [is realised]".

القائل بكون التعين وحوجيا بوجوه الأول أنه جزء المتعين لكونه عبارة عن الماهية مع التعين وهو موجود وجزء الموجود موجود بالضرورة وأجيبه بانه إن أريد بالمتعين الموصوف بالتعين فظاهر أن التعين عارض له لا جزء منه وإن أريد المجموع المركب منهما فلا نسلم أنه موجود فإن الوصف إذا كان من الأعراض المحسوسة كما في الجسم الأبيض لم يكن المجموع إلا مركبا إعتباريا فكيف إذا كان مما وجوده نفس المتنازع وإعترض صاحب المواقف بأن المراد بالمتعين هو ذلك الشخص المعلوم وجوده بالضرورة كزيد مثلا وليس مفهومه مجرد مفهوم الإنسان وإلا لصدق على عمرو بل الإنسان مع شيء آخر يسميه التعين فيكون جزءا من زيد الموجود فيكون موجودا والجواب أنا سلمنا أن ليس مفهومه مفهوم الإنسان الكلي الصادق على عمرو ولكن لم لا يجوز أن يكون هو الإنسان المقيد بالعوارض المخصوصة المشخصة التي لا تصدق على غيره دون المجموع ولو سلم فجزء المفهوم لا يلزم أن يكون موجودا في الخارج ولو سلم

فذلك الشيء هو ما يخصه من الكم والكيف والأين ونحو ذلك مما يعلم وجوده بالضرورة من غير نزاع لكون أكثرها من المحسوسات وهم لا يسمونها التعين بل ما به التعين.

According to at-Taftāzānī, individuation cannot exist in the external world; for in his view, what in fact exists is the "individuated" (*muta'ayyin*) (Text 4.2 [iii]). By contrast, according to al-Īǧī, individuation exists; for in his understanding, it is a part of the individuated which exists; therefore, given that the whole exists, the part should likewise exist together (Text 4.2 [iv]). In rebutting this argument, at-Taftāzānī argues that the individuated is not the compound (*maǧmū'/inḍimām*) made up of quiddity and individuation, since individuation occurs as an accident to quiddity. Thus, he concludes that since it does not constitute the individuated as one of its parts, individuation cannot exist in the external world together (Text 4.2 [v]).

It is on the basis of this dispute that al-Fanārī refutes at-Taftāzānī's critique. He seems to refute it by steering the middle course between these two post-Avicennian theories of individuation.

Text 4.3: al-Fanārī: MU 160, 3/306, 1–3/308, 2

[i] We say: [1] ipseity (*huwiyya*) [i. e. the individual] is quiddity accompanied by individuation (*al-māhiyya ma'a t-tašaḫḫuṣ*). [2] Individuation is a mental relation (*nisba i'tibāriyya*). [3] Consequently, [nothing] other than its substrate (*ma'rūḍu-hū*) [i. e. the quiddity] will remain as something realised (*mutaḥaqqiqan*).

[ii] It cannot be said [in answer to this]: what in fact exists is that through which individuation [is realised] (*mā bi-hī t-tašaḫḫuṣ*) [i. e. the individual], for existing ipseity (*al-huwiyya al-mawǧūda*) is compounded [scil. of quiddity and individuation] (*inḍimāmāt*).

[iii] [The reason why this cannot be said is] because we say: that through which individuation [is realised] has a quiddity. [Even] on the assumption that it [i. e. the quiddity] does not exist, its individuation remains [always] to be [a mental relation]. Consequently, the compounds [made up of quiddity and individuation] would [necessarily] be mental relations (*nisab i'tibāriyya*).

قلنا الهوية هي الماهية مع التشخص والتشخص نسبة إعتبارية فلم يبق متحققا إلا معروضه لا يقال الموجود ما به التشخص إذ الهوية الموجودة هي الإنضمامات لأنا نقول ما به التشخص له ماهية والفرض أنها غير موجودة فبقي تشخصه والإنضمامات نسب إعتبارية.

While, similar to al-Īǧī, considering individuation to be a part of the individuated (Text 4.3 [i][1]; cf. *supra* Text 4.2 [ii]/[iv]), al-Fanārī recognises it as nonexistent in the external world, just as at-Taftāzānī does (Text 4.3 [i][2]; cf. *supra* Text 4.2 [iii]/[v]). Thus, al-Fanārī is now able to argue that existent consists of quiddity and individuation; but individuation does not exist in the external world, because it is a "mental relation" (*nisba i'tibāriyya*) for him; consequently, quiddity must exist so that existent can exist in the external world (Text 4.3 [i][3]), for non-existents alone cannot constitute any existent (Text 4.3 [iii]).

Concluding Remarks

Al-Fanārī refutes the critiques directed against the theory of *waḥdat al-wuǧūd* by referring to preceding traditions. On the one hand, he refers to the existence of the "Universal Spirit" (*ar-rūḥ al-kullī*) in the external world (Text 4.1 [iii]); as indicated above, this term is widely used in the Akbarian (or perhaps more generally, Arabic Neoplatonic) tradition to signify the Sublime Pen and the First Intellect. On the other hand (and this aspect is more relevant to the present context), he refers to those post-Avicennian philosophical arguments advanced elsewhere by the critics, namely by aṭ-Ṭūsī and at-Taftāzānī themselves – sometimes without alteration, sometimes with modifications (Texts 4.1 [iv]/4.3). Through such argumentation, al-Fanārī most likely aims to rebut the critiques by using the very arguments endorsed by the critics themselves. That is to say, his refutation of the critiques is based largely on his reception of preceding philosophical discussions, at least as far as the problem of universals is concerned.

It is true that, judging from his simplified way of using the related terms (e.g. he regards "quiddity" or "reality" as a sort of the universal), al-Fanārī does not distinguish what at-Taftāzānī calls "quiddity conditioned by nothing" (i.e. the universal) and "quiddity unconditioned by anything" (Texts 2.1/2.2). In this sense, his interpretation of the history of philosophy, which is based on his understanding of such related terms, as is exhibited in Text 3.1, may be far from objective. Nevertheless, we must not overlook the fact that al-Fanārī attempts to justify his own theory *with reference to the philosophical tradition.* In order to elucidate exactly the way how philosophy was received in the post-Avicennian period as well as the extent to which it was modified in the course of this reception, the arguments advanced by the Akbarian mystics should also be taken into full consideration.

Appendix: *Vorlage* of the Texts Cited

1. Naṣīraddīn aṭ-Ṭūsī (d. 1274): *al-Aǧwiba* (answers to *masāʾil* 3 & 4 raised by al-Qūnawī)

Text 5.1: aṭ-Ṭūsī: *al-Aǧwiba* 107, ult.–108, 7 [*ǧawāb* to *masʾala* 3; cf. Text 3.2][14]

[i] I say: general common existence (*al-wuǧūd al-ʿāmm al-muštarak*) [cf. Text 3.2 (ii)(1)] cannot be realised except in intellect (*lā yataḥaqqaqu illā fī l-ʿaql*). [This holds] likewise [true] of everything that is general and common (*kull amr ʿāmm muštarak*). That is to say, no concrete thing cannot occur to multiple things (*aš-šayʾ al-ʿaynī lā yaqaʿu ʿalā ašyāʾ mutaʿaddida*).

[ii] The reason is [as follows]: [1] were it [i.e. something that is general and common] [realised] in every one of such [multiple] things, it would not be one thing in itself (*bi-ʿayni-hī*), but multiple things; [2] were it [realised] in the whole [of the multiple things] insofar as it is a "whole" (*fī l-kull min ḥayṯu huwa kull*) – the whole [considered] from such a perspective (*ḥayṯiyya*) is one thing –, then it could not occur to [multiple] things; [3] were it [realised] in the whole insofar as [it is] divided internally into its parts (*fī l-kull bi-maʿnā t-tafarruq fī āḥādi-hī*), there would [merely] be a "part" of that thing (*ǧuzʾ min ḏālika š-šayʾ*), not that thing itself (*lā nafs ḏālika š-šayʾ*), in every one [of those parts].

[iii] If it is neither [realised] in any one of [these] parts nor in the whole, it cannot occur to them.

أقول الوجود العام المشترك لا يتحقق إلا في العقل وكذلك في كل أمر عام مشترك وذلك أن الشيء العيني لا يقع على أشياء متعددة فإنه إن كان في كل واحد من تلك الأشياء لم يكن شيئا بعينه بل كان أشياء وإن كان في الكل من حيث هو كل والكل من تلك الحيثية شيء واحد فلم يقع على أشياء وإن كان في الكل بمعنى التفرق في أحاده كان في كل واحد جزء من ذلك الشيء لا نفس ذلك الشيء وإن لم يكن في شيء من الأحاد ولا في الكل لم يكن واقعا عليها.

Text 5.2: aṭ-Ṭūsī: *al-Aǧwiba* 113, 9–114, 8 [*ǧawāb* to *masʾala* 4; cf. Text 4.1 (v)][15]

[i] The "denial of the Real's agency on the existents" (*nafy taʾṯīr al-ḥaqq fī l-mawǧūdāt*) as well as the "denial of His relationship with the particular things" (*nafy taʿalluqi-hī bi-l-ǧuzʾiyyāt*) belong to those [theories] which [the people] who could not understand their arguments [i.e. of the philosophers] (*man lam yafham kalāma-hum*) ascribe to them. How can they [i.e. the people who could not understand the philosophers' arguments] deny His agency on the existents after setting Him as the principle of everything (*mabdaʾan li-l-kull*)? How can they deny His relationship with the particular things, though according to them [i.e. to the philosophers], they [i.e. the particular things] emanate from Him and He intellects by virtue of Himself?

[ii] Their view [i.e. of the philosophers] is that knowledge of the cause (*ʿilm bi-l-ʿilla*) necessitates knowledge of the effect (*ʿilm bi-l-maʿlūl*). Rather, since they exclude the "being-in-a-*locus*" (*al-kawn fī l-makān*) from Him, they regard the relation of all *loci*

14 Cf. Schubert (ed./intr. [1995]) 31 [German].
15 Cf. Schubert (ed./intr. [1995]) 32 [German].

with Him as one equal relation (*nisbatan wāḥidatan mutasāwiyyatan*); and since they exclude the "being-in-a-*tempus*" (*al-kawn fī z-zamān*) from Him, they regard the relation of all *tempora* – [including] the past, the future and the present – with Him as one relation.

[iii] Therefore, they [i.e. the philosophers] say: if someone who knows the *loci* is not local (*lam yakun makāniyyan*), he knows [1] that Zayd [stands] in every aspect belonging to ʿAmr (*anna Zaydan fī ayy ǧiha min ǧihāt ʿAmr*); [2] how the indication [moves] from him to him [i.e. from Zayd to ʿAmr] (*kayfa l-išāra min-hū ilay-hī*); [3] how much distance [there is] between the two (*kam bayna-humā min al-masāfa*); and [4] likewise all particles [constituting] the world (*fī ǧamīʿ ḏarrāt al-ʿālam*), although he does not relate any one of them [i.e. of the particles constituting the world] to himself, because he is, [as is assumed], not local (*ġayr makānī*).

[iv] Similarly (*ka-mā … ka-ḏālika*), if someone who knows the *tempora* is not temporal, he knows: [1] that Zayd can be born in any time and ʿAmr [can also be born] in any time (*anna Zaydan fī ayy zamān yūladu wa-ʿAmran fī ayy zamān*); [2] how much period of time [there is] between them two (*kam yakūnu bayna-humā min al-mudda*); and [3] likewise all the temporally-originated things that are connected to *tempora* (*fī ǧamīʿ al-ḥawādiṯ al-murtabiṭa bi-l-azmina*), though he does not relate any one of them [i.e. of the temporally originated things] to the *tempus* that is present to him.

أما نفي تأثير الحق في الموجودات ونفي تعلقه بالجزئيات فما أحال عليهم من لم يفهم كلامهم وكيف ينفون تأثيره في الموجودات بعد أن جعلوه مبدأ للكل وكيف ينفون تعلقه بالجزئيات وهي صادرة عنه وهو عاقل لذاته عندهم ومذهبهم أن العلم بالعلة يوجب العلم بالمعلول بل لما نفوا عنه الكون في المكان جعلوا نسبة جميع الأماكن إليه نسبة واحدة متساوية ولما نفوا عنه الكون في الزمان جعلوا نسبة جميع الأزمنة ماضيها ومستقبلها وحالها إليه نسبة واحدة فقالوا كما يكون العالم بالأمكنة إذا لم يكن مكانيا يكون عالما بأن زيدا في أي جهة من جهات عمرو وكيف تكون الإشارة منه إليه وكم بينهما من المسافة وكذلك في جميع ذرات العالم ولا يجعل نسبة شيء منها إلى نفسه لكونه غير مكاني كذلك العالم بالأزمنة إذا لم يكن زمانيا يكون عالما بأن زيدا في أي زمان يولد وعمروا في أي ومان وكم يكون بينهما من المدة وكذلك في جميع الحوادث المرتبطة بالأزمنة ولا يجعل نسبة شيء منها إلى زمان يكون حاضرا له.

2. Naǧmaddīn al-Kātibī (d. ca. 1276): *ar-Risāla aš-Šamsiyya* (*maqāla* 1, *faṣl* 3, *mabḥaṯ* 2)

Text 6: al-Kātibī: *ar-Risāla aš-Šamsiyya* 57, 11–15 [cf. Text 3.1]

[i] If we say about "animal" (*ḥayawān*), for instance, that it is universal (*kullī*), then here [we have] three elements: [1] the animal insofar as it is what it is (*al-ḥayawān min ḥayṯu huwa huwa*); [2] that it is universal (*kawnu-hū kulliyyan*); and [3] the compound made up of them two (*al-murakkab min-humā*).

[ii] The first is called "natural universal" (*kulliyyan ṭabīʿiyyan*), the second is called "logical universal" (*kulliyyan manṭiqiyyan*) and the third is called "mental universal" (*kulliyyan ʿaqliyyan*).

[iii] The natural universal exists in the external world, because it is a part of "this [individual] animal" that exists in the external world; and a part of something that exists [likewise] exists in the external world. As for the latter two universals, there is a contradiction in their existence [i.e. both logical universal and mental universal cannot

exist in the external world]. The examination of this [theme], however, is beyond the scope of logic (*ḫāriǧ ʿan al-manṭiq*).

إذا قلنا للحيوان مثلا بأنه كلي فهناك أمور ثلاثة الحيوان من حيث هو هو وكونه كليا والمركب منهما والأول يسمى كليا طبيعيا والثاني يسمى كليا منطقيا والثالث يسمى كليا عقليا والكلي الطبيعي موجود في الخارج لأنه جزء من هذا الحيوان الموجود في الخارج وجزء الموجود موجود في الخارج وأما الكليان الآخران ففي وجودهما خلاف والنظر فيه خارج عن المنطق.

3. ʿAḍudaddīn al-Īǧī (d. 1355): *al-Mawāqif* (*mawqif* 2, *marṣad* 2, *maqṣad* 11)

Text 7: al-Īǧī: *al-Mawāqif* 66, 1–7 [cf. Text 4.2 (iv)]

[i] With regard to individuation, it is disputed whether it is existential (*wuǧūdī*) [i.e. exists] or not. The verifiers (*muḥaqqiqūn*) hold that it is existential, because it is a part (*ǧuzʾ*) of the individuated (*muʿayyan*) that exists; and a part of something that exists [likewise] exists.

[ii] Some of them [i.e. people other than the verifiers], however, say: [1] if "something to which individuation occurs [as an accident]" (*maʿrūḍ at-taʿayyun*) is meant by the individuated, then we do not know [i.e. do not accept] that individuation is a part of it [i.e. of the individuated]; rather, it is an accident of it [i.e. do.]; and [2] if the "compound" (*maǧmūʿ*) [made up of quiddity and individuation] is meant [by the "individuated"], then we do not know that it exists.

[iii] The answer [to this claim] is: what is meant by the individuated is the individual (*šaḫṣ*), such as Zayd, for example. There is no doubt (*rība*) of his existence [i.e. as to the fact that the individual thing like Zayd exists]. But his concept is by no means the concept of "human" (*insān*); otherwise, it would rightly be said about ʿAmr that he is Zayd. Then, he is to be the human accompanied by something else that we call "individuation". Consequently, this "[something] else" [must] be a part of Zayd, [which means that] it [i.e. individuation] exists.

وقد إختلف في التعين هل هو وجودي أم لا؟ فذهب المحققون إلى أنه وجودي لأنه جزء المعين الموجود وجزء الموجود موجود وقد قال بعضهم أن أردت بالمعين معروض التعين فلا نعلم أن التعين جزؤه بل هو عارضه أو المجموع فلا نعلم أنه موجود والجواب أن المراد بالمعين هو الشخص مثل زيد ولا ريبة في وجوده وليس مفهومه مفهوم الإنسان قطعا وإلا لصدق على عمرو أنه زيد فإذا هو الإنسان مع شيء آخر نسميه التعين فيكون ذلك الآخر جزء زيد فيوجد.

Bibliography

Primary Sources

Avicenna, aš-Šifāʾ. al-Ilāhiyyāt. Ed. G. C. Anawati/S. Zāyid. 2 vols. al-Qāhira: al-Hayʾa al-ʿāmma li-šuʾūn al-muṭābiʿ al-amīriyya 1380 [1960].

Fanārī, Šamsaddīn al-, Miṣbāḥ al-uns bayna l-maʿqūl wa-l-mašhūd. In: Miftāḥ al-ġayb li-Abī l-Maʿālī Ṣadraddīn Muḥammad b. Isḥāq al-Qūnawī wa-šarḥu-hū Miṣbāḥ al-uns li-Muḥammad b. Ḥamza al-Fanārī. Ed. M. Ḫwāǧawī. 2nd ed. Tihrān: Mawlā 1384 [2005/6].

Īǧī, ʿAḍudaddīn al-, al-Mawāqif fī ʿilm al-kalām. Bayrūt: ʿĀlam al-kutub [n.d.].

Kātibī, Nağmaddīn al-Qazwīnī al-, Risālat aš-Šamsiyya fī l-qawā'id al-manṭiqiyya. In: Šarḥ al-Imām as-Sa'd at-Taftāzānī 'alā š-Šamsiyya fī l-manṭiq li-l-Imām al-Kātibī. Ed. Ğ. B. Ṣāliḥ. 'Ammān: Dār an-nūr 1432 [2011] 50–83.
Taftāzānī, Sa'daddīn at-, Šarḥ al-Maqāṣid fī 'ilm al-kalām. Ed. 'A. 'Umayra. 2nd ed. 5 vols. Bayrūt: 'Ālam al-kutub 1998.
Ṭūsī, Naṣīraddīn aṭ-, al-Ağwiba. In: Schubert (ed. [1995]).

Secondary Sources

Adamson, P. (ed. [2013]), Interpreting Avicenna: Critical Essays. Cambridge: Cambridge UP.
Amīn, 'U. (ed. [1974]), Dirāsāt falsafiyya muhdāt ilā d-duktūr Ibrāhīm Madkūr [Études philosophiques offertes au Dr. Ibrahim Madkour]. al-Qāhira: al-Hay'a al-miṣriyya al-'āmma li-l-kitāb.
Aydın, I. H./T. Görgün (2005), "Molla Fenârî". In: TDVİA, vol. 30, 245–48.
Chittick, W. C. (2002), "Waḥdat al-Shuhūd [& Waḥdat al-Wudjūd]". In: EI2, vol. 11, 37–39.
Chittick, W. C./P. L. Wilson (trs./intrs. [1982]), Fakhruddin 'Iraqi: Divine Flashes. New York: Paulist Press.
Ebstein, M. (2014), Mysticism and Philosophy in al-Andalus: Ibn Masarra, Ibn al-'Arabī and the Ismā'īlī Tradition (IHC 103). Leiden: Brill.
EI2 = P. J. Bearman, et al. (eds. [1986–2004]), Encyclopaedia of Islam: New Edition [2nd ed.]. 12 vols. Leiden: Brill.
Eichner, H. (2012), "Essence and Existence: Thirteetnth-Century Perspectives in Arabic-Islamic Philosophy and Theology: Faḫr al-Dīn al-Rāzī's al-Mulaḫḫaṣ fī al-ḥikma and the Arabic Reception of Avicennian Philosophy". In: Hasse/Bertolacci (eds. [2012]) 123–51.
Gömbeyaz, K. (2010), "Molla Fenârî'ye nispet edilen eserlerde aidiyet problemi ve Molla Fenârî bibliyografyası". In: Yücedoğru/Koloğlu/Kılavuz/Gömbeyaz (eds. [2010]) 467–524.
Hasse, D. N./A. Bertolacci (eds. [2012]), The Arabic, Hebrew and Latin Reception of Avicenna's Metaphysics (SGA 7). Berlin: de Gruyter.
Heer, N. L. (ed./tr. [1979]), "Al-Jāmī's Treatise on Existence". In: Morewedge (ed. [1979]) 223–56.
– (tr. [1979]), The Precious Pearl: Al-Jāmī's Al-Durrah al-Fākhirah together with His Glosses and the Commentary of 'Abd al-Ghafūr al-Lārī. Albany: SUNY Press.
– (2006), "The Sufi Position with Respect to the Problem of Universals" [Paper read at the 1970 annual meeting of the American Oriental Society and updated in Dec. 2006]. In: id. (ed. [2009]) 80–84.
– (ed. [2009]), Papers on Islamic Philosophy, Theology and Mysticism. Seattle. [URL: https://digital.lib.washington.edu/researchworks/bitstream/handle/1773/4883/papers.pdf?sequence=1&isAllowed=y] (viewed on 23 Nov. 2016)
Izutsu, T. (1971), The Concept and Reality of Existence. Tokyo: Keio Institute of Cultural and Linguistic Studies.
– (1974a), "Basic Problems of 'Abstract Quiddity'". In: Muḥaqqiq/Izutsu (eds. [1974]) 1–25.

- (1974b), "The Problem of Quiddity and Natural Universal in Islamic Metaphysics". In: Amīn (ed. [1974]) 131–77.

Kobayashi, H./M. Akutsu/T. Nigo/Sh. Nomoto (eds. [2011]), Isurāmu ni okeru chi no kōzō to henyō: Shisōshi, kagakushi, shakaishi no shiten kara [Structure and Transformation of Knowledge in Islam: Thought, Science, Society and Their Interactions]. Tokyo: Waseda daigaku Isrāmu chiiki kenkyū kikō.

Madelung, W. (2005), "At-Taftāzānī und die Philosophie". In: Perler/Rudolph (eds. [2005]) 227–35.

Marmura, M. E. (1979), "Avicenna's Chapter on Universals in the Isagoge of His Shifāʾ". In: Welch/Cachia (eds. [1979]) 34–56.

- (1992), "Quiddity and Universality in Avicenna". In: Morewedge (ed. [1992]) 77–87.
- (tr. [2005]), The Metaphysics of the Healing: A Parallel English-Arabic Text. Provo, UT: Brigham Young UP.

Morewedge, P. (ed. [1979]), Islamic Philosophical Theology. Albany: SUNY Press.

- (ed. [1992]), Neoplatonism and Islamic Thought. Albany: SUNY Press.

Muḥaqqiq, M./T. Izutsu (eds. [1974]), Manṭiq wa-mabāḥiṯ-i alfāẓ: Maǧmūʿa-i mutūn wa-maqālāt-i taḥqīqī [Collected Texts and Papers on Logic and Language]. Tehran: McGill Univ., Institute of Islamic Studies, Tehran Branch.

Nakanishi, Y. (2009), "Fanārī sonzairon ni okeru kankei: Sonzai no hitsuzensei no shōmei o megutte [Demonstrating the Necessity of Existence: The Concept of Relation (nisba) in the Metaphysics of Šamsaddīn al-Fanārī]". In: Oriento [Bulletin of the Society for Near Eastern Studies in Japan] 52/2, 76–92.

- (2011), "Fanārī sonzairon ni okeru sonzai to hisonzaisha: Sonzai no sonzai shōmei to hitsuzensei no shōmei o megutte [Demonstrating the Existence and Necessity of Existence: The Concepts of Existence and Nonexistent in the Metaphysics of Šamsaddīn al-Fanārī]". In: Kobayashi/Akutsu/Nigo/Nomoto (eds. [2011]) 337–62.

Perler, D./U. Rudolph (eds. [2005]), Logik und Theologie: Das Organon im arabischen und im lateinischen Mittelalter (ST GM 84). Leiden: Brill.

Schubert (ed./intr. [1995]), Annäherungen: Der mystisch-philosophische Briefwechsel zwischen Ṣadr ud-Dīn-i Qōnawī und Naṣīrud-Dīn-i Ṭūsī. Beirut: Steiner.

TDVİA = K. Güran (ed.), Türkiye diyanet vakfı İslâm ansiklopedisi. 43 ciltler. İstanbul: Türkiye diyanet vakfı. 1988–2013.

Todd, R. (2014), The Sufi Doctrine of Man: Ṣadr al-Dīn al-Qūnawī's Metaphysical Anthropology (IPTS 90). Leiden: Brill.

Welch, A. T./P. Cachia (eds. [1979]), Islam: Past Influence and Present Challenge. Edinburgh: Edinburgh UP.

Wisnovsky, R. (2013), "Avicenna's Islamic Reception". In: Adamson (ed. [2013]) 190–213.

Yücedoğru, T./O. Ş. Koloğlu/U. M. Kılavuz/K. Gömbeyaz (eds. [2010]), Uluslararası Molla Fenârî sempozyumu (4–6 Aralık 2009 Bursa): Bildiriler. Bursa: Bursa büyük şehir belediyesi.

Logic and Intellect

Hanif Amin Beidokhti

Suhrawardī on Division of Aristotelian Categories*

Introduction

Aristotle's *Categories* was one of the earliest philosophical treatises translated into Syriac and Arabic. Ibn Muqaffaʿ (d. 757) was the earliest figure who translated a work under this title attributed to Aristotle in the 8th century A.D.[1], and this is probably the oldest work in Arabic on this topic.[2] However, Ibn Muqaffaʿ failed to enjoy the vast attention of later scholars, since the terminology utilized by him was regarded as idiosyncratic and unusual,[3] especially after the complete translation by Isḥāq ibn Ḥunayn (d. 990) in the 9th century. Isḥāq used a Syriac translation provided by his father from Greek. Since then this text, along with Ḥasan ibn Suwār's (d. after 1017) critical notes,[4] became the standard text for studying the *Categories* in the eastern tradition. In both the Hellenistic and Arabic worlds, this text together with Porphyry's *Isagoge* was considered as the introduction to Aristotle's philosophy, with substantial implications for all fields

* I would like to express my thanks to Peter Adamson, Fedor Benevich, Davlat Dadikhuda and Andreas Lammer for valuable comments on earlier drafts of this paper. All translations are mine, unless otherwise indicated.

1 It is controversial whether this work is a translation of a Middle Persian or Syriac or Greek paraphrase. For the text, see: Ibn Muqaffaʿ and Ibn Bihrīz, *al-Mantiq li-Ibn Muqaffaʿ*, *Ḥudūd al-mantiq li-Ibn Bihrīz*, ed. by Dāneš-Pažūh, Mohammad Taqī (Tehran, 1979). For discussion about the authenticity of this attribution, see: Kraus, Paul, "Zu Ibn al-Muqaffaʿ," RSO XIV/1 (1933): 1–5 and Dāneš-Pažūh's introduction to his edition, especially pp. 62–69, rejecting Kraus' theory.

2 The Syriac commentary tradition on the *Categories* began earlier in the 5th century A.D., though, except for few references to Theon's commentary, we have no access to this considerable tradition. See: Peters, F. E., *Aristoteles Arabus: The oriental translations and commentaries on the Aristotelian Corpus* (Leiden, 1968): 7; King, Daniel, *The Earliest Syriac Translation of Aristotle's Categories, Text, Translation and Commentary* (Leiden, Boston, 2010): 3ff; Ferrari, Cleophea, *Der Kategorienkommentar von Abū l-Farağ ʿAbdallāh ibn aṭ-Ṭayyib, Text und Untersuchungen* (Leiden, Boston, 2006): 7–9.

3 See for example: Ḫwārazmī, Muḥammad, *Mafātiḥ al-ʿulūm*, ed. by Ibrāhīm al-Abyārī (Beirut, 1989): 167.

4 Peters, *Aristoteles Arabus*, 1968, p. 8.

of philosophy including logic, physics and metaphysics. As to the Greek commentaries on *Categories*, Ibn Nadīm (d. 990) informs us about works written by Theophrastus, Ammonius, Porphyry, Themistius, Simplicius, Philoponus etc., although none of these commentaries are now extant in Arabic.[5]

In addition to the Arabic translations, Kindī wrote the first Arabic commentary on *Categories* in the 9th century.[6] Thereafter, numerous treatises were composed around this work (including different genres from paraphrases to the commentaries) both by logicians such as Abū Bišr Mattā (d. 940)[7], Ibn Zurʿa (d. 1008) and Ibn Ṭayyib (d. 1043) as well as by philosopher-metaphysicians like Fārābī (d. 950), Ibn Bāǧǧa (d. 1138) and Averroes (d. 1198). Following the Greco-Arabic commentary tradition, in the 11th century, Avicenna (d. 1037), having inherited this vast tradition, instead of commenting on the Alexandrian logic curriculum, wrote his own logical treatises covering materials surrounding Aristotle's *Categories* and Porphyry's *Isagoge*, as two parts of his voluminous *summa*, *Kitāb al-Šifāʾ* (*The Book of the Healing*). *Kitāb al-Šifāʾ* as the key source for the later eastern Peripateticism enjoyed wide scholarly attention, so that many scholars speak of a replacement of Aristotle's works with those of Avicenna. The philosophers, however, did not absorb this novel composition of philosophical sciences uncritically. Even Avicenna's immediate students allowed themselves to modify the master's philosophical inheritance,[8] just as Avicenna had done with the philosophical heritage he received. Besides, Avicenna's philosophy being a prominent representative of Peripatetic philosophy has come under radical criticisms by philosophers and theologians after him, such as Faḫr al-Dīn Rāzī (d. 1210), and was defended by others, such as Naṣīr al-Dīn Ṭūsī (d. 1274), against these critiques.

Of the critics, one of the most prominent was Šihāb al-Dīn Yaḥyā Suhrawardī (d. 1191), who inherited not only the wealthy commentary tradition on *Categories*, but also the works of Avicenna and later thinkers such as ʿUmar ibn Sahlān Sāwī (d. 1058) and Abū l-Barakāt Baġdādī (d. 1152), both of whom were likewise critics of Avicenna as an eminent Aristotelian philosopher. Discussing

5 See: Ibn Nadīm, *al-Fihrist*, ed. by Sayyid, Ayman Fuʾād, vol. 2 (London, 2014): 161–2.

6 Ibid. 2014, vol. 2. p. 162; Ibn Abī Uṣaybīʿa, *ʿUyūn al-anbāʾ fī Ṭabaqāt al-Aṭibbāʾ*, ed. by Nizār Riḍā (Beirut, 1995): 289. This work of Kindī is unfortunately lost. For the importance of *Categories* in Kindī's thought, see: Adamson, Peter, *Al-Kindī* (Oxford; New York, 2008): 25–38.

7 Ḥasan ibn Suwār used Abū Bišr Mattā's commentary for commenting on Isḥāq's translation. See: Ferrari, *Der Kategorienkommentar*, 2006, p. 10.

8 An example of the living philosophical debates between Avicenna and his pupils is *Kitāb al-Mubāḥaṯāt*. For further information, see: Gutas, Dimitri, *Avicenna and the Aristotelian Tradition* (Leiden; Boston, 2013): 159–160. For a detailed study of the text, see: Reisman, David C., *The Making of the Avicennan Tradition: The transmission, Contents, and Structure of Ibn Sīnā's al-Mubāḥaṯāt (The Discussions)* (Leiden et al., 2002). For the text, see: Ibn Sīnā, *al-Mubāḥaṯāt*, ed. by Mohsen Bīdārfar (Qom, 1992).

and analyzing categories was a recurrent motif in all of Suhrawardī's so-called "didactic, Peripatetic" works.[9]

Suhrawardī's discussion of the categories covers almost all aspects of the Peripatetic doctrine including the deduction method for attaining the final list of the categories. This paper will discuss Suhrawardī's critical point of view on the Aristotelian list of the categories. For this purpose, I shall first discuss a long lasting debate on the subject matter of the *Categories* and the proper science for studying its topics and the way it relates to Suhrawardī's treatment of the categories. Then, I shall discuss briefly the historical route of arguments for establishing the tenfold list of the categories probably available to Suhrawardī; after that, I shall introduce Suhrawardī's own reductionist division, as well as the level of certainty that he associates with his fivefold division. This might provide us with a clue for ordering Suhrawardī's works and depict the development of his discussion.

1. Categories Discussion in Suhrawardī's Writings

Suhrawardī's critical engagement with the Aristotelian theory of the categories is evident in all of his main philosophical works, and despite the lengths of discussions, he does not hesitate to reveal his negative attitude towards this doctrine. Although he does not clearly state why he is attacking this doctrine, and while he eventually condemns it as useless, his determinateness in criticizing not only the list but also various aspects of the categories at length shows that he considers the categories to be one of the most prominent components of the Peripatetic tradition. Since Suhrawardī is aware of Avicenna's uncertainties about different aspects of this doctrine – a fact that will be discussed in some detail in the following – I do not believe that his critique of the categories' doctrine should be understood as a direct attack on Avicennan philosophy. In contrast, as Suhrawardī himself claims, it is a critique aimed at a whole tradition, namely at the Peripatetic school (*maššā'*) including Aristotle and Avicenna and post-Avicennan Peripatetics. Criticizing the list in terms of casting doubts on its originality, exhaustiveness, and its method of deduction are only parts of a broader project, which consists in undermining "the backbone of Aristotle's philosophical" project of classifying the whole reality.[10]

9 Just in terms of quantitative extension, almost twenty-five percent of the metaphysics of Suhrawardī in his four didactic-Peripatetic works is dedicated to a discussion of the Aristotelian categories.

10 Studtmann, Paul, "Aristotle's Categories," in *The Stanford Encyclopedia of Philosophy* (Summer 2014 Edition), Ed by Edward N. Zalta, URL = <https://plato.stanford.edu/archives/sum2014/entries/aristotle-categories/>.

2. Avicenna and the Arguments for Enumeration of Categories

As it is well known, Aristotle not only is not consistent about the number of the categories[11], but he also nowhere gives any argument for an exhaustive list of them.[12] Instead, these were the Aristotelian commentators in late antiquity who pondered over providing such arguments indicative of the demonstrative and exhaustive status of the list of the categories. In the eastern tradition, Kindī and Avicenna take over the same enterprise. Avicenna establishes in the *Categories* of *the Healing* [*al-Maqūlāt min Kitāb al-Šifā'*] that categories "are the ten *summa genera* (*al-ağnās al-ʿāliyya*)" and "these ten do not fall under any genus more general than them, nor are they reducible to each other, nor is there any genus beyond them."[13] Although, he provides the most significant argument for establishing them in *Maqūlāt* II.5, he still seems not to be entirely content with his argument,[14] since he manifestly expresses his dissatisfaction in the *Physics* of *the Healing* by saying:

> We ourselves are not that obstinate about preserving the received canon – namely, that the genera are ten, and that each one of them is truly generic and that there is nothing beyond them. (*Šifā', al-Samāʿ al-ṭabīʿī* II.2, 135.8, trans. by Jon McGinnis, *modified*)

After Avicenna, however, a critical approach towards the list was born which consisted in trying to reduce Aristotelian categories (or even to increase them).[15] This approach finds its motivation, in my opinion, in Avicenna's dissatisfaction with providing a demonstrative ground for such a list. The most prominent representative of this novel trend was Suhrawardī. Considering these controversial attempts, he accuses the Peripatetics of lacking demonstration for the number and division of the categories and having made up their list based on inductions, none of them complete and sufficiently convincing. Thus, Avicenna's dissatisfaction with his argument for the division of the categories paves the way for Suhrawardī's radical criticism of the division and even of the benefit of the categories' doctrine in his so-called "didactic-Peripatetic" works. This in turn

11 In *Categories* IV, 1b25–2a4 and *Topics* I.9, 103b20–104a3, Aristotle lists the categories under ten, whereas in *Physics* V.1, 225a37–225b9, *Posterior Analytics* I.22, 83b11–83b17 and *Metaphysics* IV.7, 1017a25 he mentions only eight categories omitting Being-in-a-position and Having.

12 This is also confirmed by Ackrill; See: Ackrill, J.L., *Aristotle's Categories and De Interpretatione* (Oxford: 1963); 104.

13 *Šifā', Manṭiq, Maqūlāt* II.1, 55.5–7.

14 *Šifā', Manṭiq, Maqūlāt* II.5, 86.13–17.

15 See ʿAllāma Ḥillī's commentary on Ṭūsī's *Tağrīd al-iʿtiqād* where he says that some theologians tried to extend the list of the categories to twenty-one categories; Hillī, Abū Manṣūr, *Kašf al-murād fī šarḥ Tağrīd al-iʿtiqād*, ed. by Ḥasan Ḥasan-Zādē Āmolī (Qom: 2011/2012): II.5, 299.

ends with the removal of the discussion of categories from his most prominent work *Ḥikmat al-išrāq* or at least its reduction to a general discussion of substance and accident.

3. The Subject Matter of Logic and the Proper Place for the Study of Categories

Before delving into Suhrawardī's fivefold list, I think it is important to mention that Suhrawardī does not treat the main topics discussed in Aristotle's *Categories* (*Maqūlāt* or *Qāṭīġūriyās* in Arabic), i. e. the ten categories, in the logic parts of his *summae* at all. In his most extensive book, *al-Mašāriʿ wa-l-muṭāraḥāt (*hereafter: *Mašāriʿ*), Suhrawardī covers all sections of the traditional Aristotelian *Organon* in the same late antique fashion, except for the *Categories.* Instead, here and everywhere he considers the categories as belonging to the metaphysics and to some extent to physics, somewhat resembling the Stoic treatment of the categories.[16] Although, as Hossein Ziai has shown, Suhrawardī's general conception of the subject matter of logic is similar to what Avicenna presented in the *Madḫal* of *Šifāʾ*, in the final analysis, he rearticulates logic in a "new structure."[17] Hence, I shall try to justify historically why Suhrawardī does not discuss the categories in his logic and shifts it into the metaphysics.

The discussion about the proper science for treating the *Categories* and its scientific profile exercised some philosophers in late antiquity, although the general agreement was on treating the *Categories* in logic. In his commentary on Aristotle's *Categories*, Simplicius addresses the issue of the goal (*skopos*) of the *Categories* stating that it is about "some ten simple things," which "are most universal" (*holikôtata*), and therefore are called genera (*gene*).[18] Then he distinguishes between four approaches each of them bringing forth Aristotle as a witness: (1) that which studies the categories as simple words (*phônai*) as parts of propositions, i. e. qua logical terms, not qua grammatical entities, and so places

16 For a detailed discussion of Stoic doctrine of the categories and its relation to Aristotle's and Plotinus' criticism of the Stoics, see: Menn, Stephen, "The Stoic Theory of Categories," in *Oxford Studies in Ancient Philosophy* XVII (1999): 215–247. Bocheński writes that the Stoic categories belong to the Stoic physics, see: Bocheński, I. M., *Ancient Formal Logic* (Amsterdam, 1951), p. 87. Suhrawardī, just as Avicenna and Aristotle, needs to discuss some of the notions related to categories, such as motion, in physics, too, since motion is one of the states (*aḥwāl*) belonging to a body inasmuch as it is subject to change, which is the subject-matter of natural philosophy.

17 Ziai, Hossein, *Knowledge and illumination: A study of Suhrawardi's Ḥikmat al-Ishrāq* (Atlanta; Georgia, 1990), pp. 42–45.

18 Simplicius, *On Aristotle's "Categories* 1–4", trans. by Chase, Michael (Ithaca; New York, 2003): 9, 5–10.

the *Categories* as the first book of logic.[19] (2) According to the second view, the goal of the *Categories* is to approach "the very beings, which are signified by words; and that these are what is said (*to legomenon*)," and so the *Categories* deals with "existent substance and the other beings."[20] (3) The third position supports the idea that the goal of the *Categories* concerns neither "significant words" nor "signified realities," but rather concerns "simple notions (*noêmata*)." For the *Categories*' discussion (*logos*) is about the ten genera that are posterior and conceptual. Besides, Aristotle has written, "that it is about things said," which must be notions.[21] Finally, (4) the position upheld by Alexander of Aphrodisias, Porphyry and Simplicius himself, as a synthesis of the former three views, maintains, "This book is the principle *(arkhê)* of the study of logic". Because "speech *(logos)* signifies by virtue of the fact that its primary parts are significant." Since "Aristotle wanted to indicate what these notions *(noêmata)* were which are signified by the primary and simple parts of speech, he carries out a division *(diairesis)* of being, not into individuals," but into these ten genera. Thus, the goal of the *Categories* is to study "the simple and *most generic parts of speech*, *signifying simple realities*, and *the simple notions*, which exist in conjunction with these simple realities".[22]

Although the old Arabic translation of Simplicius's commentary has not come to us, we may believe that it was translated into Arabic and was influential among the commentators of *Categories* in the eastern tradition.[23] Considering the issue of the proper context for studying the categories, one can distinguish between two main philosophical approaches in the eastern tradition: namely, those who consider *Categories* as a logical text, maintaining loyalty to the commentary tradition, such as Kindī,[24] and those who have an ontological interpretation of *Categories* such as Avicenna.[25] Thus, we may find the reason and the background for Suhrawardī's rearrangement in this long lasting discussion as well as in

19 Ibid. 9, 10–15.
20 Ibid. 9.20–25.
21 Ibid. 10.1–5.
22 Ibid. 10.5–20.
23 Ferrari, *Der Kategorienkommentar*, 12–13. Whether this text was still available at Suhrawardī's time is not clear. However, there are some points in Suhrawardī treatment which might suggest that he was acquainted with this text, or reports of it; for example, the claim that the founder of the categories doctrine was the Pythagorean [Ps.-] Archytas, rather than Aristotle is a remark that exists also in Simplicius' commentary. See: Simplicius, *On Aristotle's "Categories* 1–4", 2, 15–20. If so, however, it is not clear why the other philosophers and commentators did not mention it or did not take it seriously.
24 See: Ighbariah, Ahamd, *Between Logic and Mathematics: Al-Kindī's Approach to the Aristotelian Categories*, in *Arabic Sciences and Philosophy* (2012: 22): 51–68.
25 These two approaches stem in fact from the way Aristotle himself treats the categories doctrine, namely that he deals with them in both logic and metaphysics as well as to some extent in physics.

Avicenna's treatment of *Categories* and in the heritage of the Avicennan school, which in brief will be outlined in the following.

Following the above-mentioned late ancient discussion, Avicenna also poses a question concerning the proper place for studying and discussing the categories. In *Madḫal* I.2, he speaks about the subject matter and purpose of each science including logic; there he makes it clear that "logic has its own subject matter which it does not share with any other science."[26] This subject matter consists of "properties acquired by concepts when organized for the purpose of attaining or transmitting knowledge."[27] Thus, logic is according to Avicenna "the inquiry into these aforementioned things [concepts and their properties], inasmuch as [the inquiry] leads from them to knowledge of the unknown, and what applies to them in this respect, nothing else."[28] However, Avicenna does not mention this subject matter in *Madḫal* by name; rather he does it in *Ilāhiyyāt* I.2:

> The subject matter of logic [...] was the secondary intelligible ideas (*al-maʿānī al-maʿqūla al-ṯāniyya*) that depend on the primary intelligible ideas, with respect to the manner by which one arrives through them from the known (*maʿlūm*) to the unknown (*mağhūl*), not with respect to their being intelligibles having [the] intellectual existence that either is not at all attached to matter, or attached to non-corporeal matter. (Avicenna, *Metaphysics of the Healing* I.2, 7.4, trans. Marmura 2005, *modified*)

Taking into account another of Avicenna's clarifications on the subject matter of logic, we may conclude that according to Avicenna the proper place for discussing categories is not logic, but is metaphysics. In *Madḫal*, I.4, after bringing forth examples regarding the categories, he emphasizes again the proper subject matter of logic:

> The art of logic [...] does not inquire about the individuals of these things [e.g. house, its components like wood, brick, earth and their qualities, position etc.], as they exist either in the mind or among the things (*fī l-aʿyān*). It does not also [inquire] about the essences of the things, inasmuch as they are essences, but rather inasmuch as they are predicates, subjects, universals, particulars, and other things that occur to these ideas, regarding what we said before [i.e. as they are helpful for arriving through them from the known to the unknown]" (*Madḫal*, I.4, 22.7–12).

Thus, the categories considered separately, which is the way they are treated in Aristotle's *Categories*, are not logical objects and their discussion does not belong to the science of logic properly. Therefore, Avicenna concludes in the *Maqūlāt* that the categories are adopted from outside into (*daḫīl*) the science of logic and he posits them here not by way of instruction (*taʿlīm*), but by way of imitation

---

26 Sabra, A. I., *Avicenna on the Subject Matter of Logic*, in *The Journal of Philosophy* 77/11 (Nov. 1980): 746–764.

27 Ibid.

28 Ibn Sīnā, *Šifāʾ*, *Madḫal*, ed. by George Anawātī et al. (Cairo, 1959): I.2, 16.10–12.

(*taqlīd*) and postulation (*waḍ*ʿ).[29] Moreover, there is no proper explanation (*al-bayān al-munāsib*) for it in a logical framework; and their features – such as their number and that they do not overlap with each other – are imported to it from other arts (*ṣināʿāt uḫrā*). There is no way to attain knowledge of them other than by minute [empirical] investigation (*istiqṣāʾ*), and this is only after acquiring the level of proficiency in first philosophy. Thus, the student of philosophy just has to accept them without having them demonstrated (*min ġayr an yubarhana*).[30]

It is worth mentioning that there is no other "book" under the same title, namely the *Categories*, in *Naǧāt* and *Dānešnāmeh-ye ʿAlāyī* (hereafter: *Dānešnāmeh*). Instead, Avicenna discusses the ten genera (*al-aǧnās al- ʿašara*) in that part of the logic of *Naǧāt,* which deals with the topics discussed in the *Burhān*[31] of *Šifāʾ*, after introducing the dichotomous division and inasmuch as the categories relate to the essential definition (*ḥadd*).[32] Then, in the *Ilāhiyyāt* of the same book, he briefly introduces substance and accidents among divisions of existents and defines them in the same aforementioned way.[33] In *Dānešnāmeh* the whole discussion is shifted to *Ilāhiyyāt*, there he again defines substance and accident as the modes of existence (*hastī*) or as the highest genera (*ǧenshā-ye barīn*), leading to divisions of the categories after a detailed discussion of divisions of substance.[34] Additionally, in *al-Ishārāt wa-l-tanbīhāt,* Avicenna does not discuss the topic at all, neither in logic nor in metaphysics.[35] Thus, considering Dimitri Gutas' chronology of Avicenna's major philosophical works,[36] we may observe a kind of changing strategy concerning the treatment of the categories in Avicenna's philosophy. That is to say, we observe a development from discussing the categories in a book at the beginning of the logic of *Šifāʾ*, by way of postulation, and as a topic in its metaphysics, to treating them in *Naǧāt* after discussing

29 On the notion of postulation (*waḍ*ʿ) in Avicenna, see: Ibn Sīnā, *Šifāʾ*, *Burhān*, ed. by Abū l-ʿAlā ʿAfīfī (Cairo, 1956), I.12.

30 Ibn Sīnā, *Šifāʾ*, *Maqūlāt*, ed. by George Anawātī et al. (Cairo, 1959), I.1, 6.10–20.

31 Avicenna's treatise reflecting on the topics discussed by Aristotle in *Posterior Analytics.* Following M. T. Dāneš-Pažūh, I hesitate to call this part of *Naǧāt* as the *Burhān* book, although Māǧid Faḫrī does it in his edition; Cf. Ibn Sīnā, *Naǧāt, Mantiq,* ed. by Māǧid Faḫrī (Beirut, 1982).

32 Ibn Sīnā, *Naǧāt, Mantiq,* ed. by Mohammad Taqī Dāneš-Pažūh (Tehran, 1985): 153.10ff.

33 Ibid., *Ilāhiyyāt,* 495.5ff.

34 Ibn Sīnā, *Dānešnāmeh-ye ʿAlāyī, Ilāhiyyāt,* ed. by Mohammad Moʿīn (Tehran, 1952), 8–11, 28–39.

35 See: Ṭūsī's commentary on *Ishārāt* I.2.2, where he emphasizes that treating categories in logic is by way of postulation, since logic is not the appropriate science for studying categories etc. Cf. 58 I.2, Ṭūsī, Naṣīr al-Dīn, *Šarḥ al-Ishārāt wa-l-tanbīhāt, Manṭiq,* ed. by Solaymān Donyā (Cairo, 1983): 2.2, 190. For Avicenna's text, see: Ibn Sīnā, *al-Ishārāt wa-l-tanbīhāt, Manṭiq*, ed. by Moǧtabā Zāreʿī (Qom, 2008): 2.2, 58.

36 Gutas, Dimitri, *Avicenna and the Aristotelian Tradition*, p. 165.

demonstration (*burhān*) and before essential definition, to discussing them in the *Ilāhiyyāt* of *Dānešnāmeh.*[37]

Avicenna still needs to justify why none of the other theoretical sciences, except for metaphysics, can be the proper place for discussing the categories. Looking into the *Šifāʾ*, one finds that there is still another aspect confirming that even when Avicenna was writing the *Šifāʾ*, he believed that metaphysics is the proper place for discussing categories. In the *Ilāhiyyāt* of *Šifāʾ*, as he comes to the discussion on substance, he writes:

> We must know, in this art, the state of the relation of the thing and the existent to the categories …. [We must also] examine the state of substance and [the number] of divisions it has. Because, for an existent [in order] to be an existing substance, it does not need to become natural or mathematical; for they [already exist as] substances, apart from [being specified as] these two division (Avicenna, *Metaphysics of the Healing*, p. 19.14–23, trans. by Marmura 2005, *modified*).

Here, Avicenna is justifying why the discussion of substance and its division is more appropriate for metaphysics than for any other theoretical science. The reason for it, according to this passage is that being substance as an existent is, due to its description, an ontological level before being specified as a natural or mathematical existent. Moreover, substance has also other divisions that are separate and therefore do not belong to mathematics or natural philosophy as their subject matters. The same line of argument can also be valid regarding the accidents: in order to be an existing accident, an accident does not need to become quality or quantity etc.; for they already exist as accidents, i. e. as not in a subject, apart from being specified as these divisions. Hence, the study of accidents as beings belongs to the science of being, i. e. metaphysics. Moreover, one may argue that every existent is necessarily either substance or accident, which means substance and accident are the essential accidentals (*ʿawāriḍ*) of existence. And as we know from the *Kitāb al-Burhān* of *Šifāʾ*, the science that is in charge of studying a subject matter, is also in charge of studying its concomitants (*lawāḥiq*)

37 According to Gutas, Avicenna wrote *Maqūlāt* of *Šifāʾ* in 414/1024, whereas *Naǧāt* has been compiled in 417/1026 or 418/1027. According to Gutas, following Alexander Kalbarczyk, and him following Ǧurǧānī's testimony in Avicenna's biography, the logical part of *Naǧāt* is copied from *al-Muḫtaṣar al-aṣġar fī l-manṭiq* composed in about 1013–1014. For *Dānešnāmeh*, he suggests a composing date around 418/1027, since it "resembles closely to" *Naǧāt* "in both scope and execution." However, he thinks "a more precise relative" dating requires a close study of "its doctrinal points" for detecting possible shifts in emphasis, and so it may be dated later than 418/1027 until Avicenna's death in 428/1037. I would like to suggest the discussion of the categories and the aforementioned shift, between *Naǧāt* and *Dānešnāmeh*, as an evidence for a later composition date for *Dānešnāmeh.* See: Gutas, Dimitri, *Avicenna and the Aristotelian Tradition*, esp. p. 115ff & 434; Kalbarczyk, Alexander, "The Kitāb al-Maqūlāt of the Muḫtaṣar al-awsaṭ fī l-manṭiq: A Hitherto Unknown Source for Studying Ibn Sīnā's Reception of Aristotle's Categories," In *Oriens* 40 (2012): 305–354.

and essential accidentals, namely the study of accidents and substances, especially before being specified as this or that accident. Hence, the study of accidents as beings belongs primarily to the science of being qua being; same as to the most general divisions of accidents, i. e. the accidental categories. Consequently, the accidental categories as the most general accidents should be studied and established in metaphysics.[38] Thus, Avicenna has provided his reader with a well-established argument for the proper science for studying the categories, namely metaphysics.

As to the post-Avicennan tradition, the way that leads to Suhrawardī goes through Avicenna's students. Avicenna's immediate disciple, Bahmanyār ibn Marzbān (d. 1066), devotes a chapter (*al-bāb al-ṯānī*) to Aristotle's *Categories* in the logical book of his *summa*, *al-Taḥṣīl*[39], where he briefly introduces the ten categories. He refers, however, his reader for the discussion about the important characteristics of the categories – such as the reason why accident is not a genus for the accidental categories – to the proper place for studying them (*nuḏkiruhū fī mawḍiʿihī*).[40] As expected, this proper place turns out to be the second book of the same *summa*, i. e. the *Ilāhiyyāt*, which comprises a long chapter on substance and a detailed discussion concerning accidental categories in a quiet long treatise.[41] In the same vein, Bahmanyār's student, Lawkarī (d. 1123), follows his master's method in elaborating the categories in metaphysics and includes it in the first part of his metaphysical book, *Bayān al-ḥaqq bi ḍimān al-ṣidq*[42], which he considers as dedicated to *metaphysica generalis*[43]. Lawkarī also mentions in the

38 However, the study of their specific considerations or specific features should belong to other sciences, for example the study of the quantity in itself apart from matter, or being inasmuch as it is quantifiable, i. e. its attributes (*aḥwāl*) qua quantifiable belongs to mathematics. See: Ibn Sīnā, *Šifāʾ*, *Ilāhiyyāt*, ed. by George Anawātī et al. (Cairo, 1959), I.1, 4–11–13; Ibn Sīnā, *Šifāʾ*, *Madḫal*, I.2, 13; *Dānešnāmeh-ye ʿAlāyī*, *Ilāhiyyāt*, 1, 5.9–12.

39 Considering the order of discussion and structure, Bahmanyār's *Taḥṣīl* is based on Avicenna's *Dānešnāmeh*; See: Bahmanyār Ibn Marzbān, *al-Taḥṣīl*, ed. by Mortaḍā Moṭahharī (Tehran, 1996), preface, p. 1.

40 Bahmanyār Ibn Marzbān, *Taḥṣīl*, I.1.2, 35.

41 Interestingly, the structure of Suhrawardī's discussion regarding the categories in his *Mašāriʿ* is very similar to the structure of *Bahmanyār*'s discussion: both of them discuss substance and accident in the last chapter of first treatise (*Mašāriʿ* I.3; *Taḥṣīl* I.3) and then discuss the other categories in the next coming treatise. However, Suhrawardī precedes the second treatise of *Mašāriʿ* with another discussion on substance and, after critically introducing all categories in a Peripatetic way, criticizes the Peripatetic doctrine of the categories within the same treatise (*Mašāriʿ* II; *Taḥṣīl* II).

42 Lawkarī, Abū l-ʿAbbās Faḍl Ibn Muḥammad, *Bayān al-Ḥaqq bi-Ḍimān al-Ṣidq*, ed. by Dībāǧī, Seyyed Ebrāhīm (Tehran, 1995). *Bayān al-Ḥaqq* I, chapters 7 ff on substance and 14–21 on the accidental categories.

43 See author's preface to the first book of *Bayān al-Ḥaqq* I, p. 4; the Arabic *termini* used by *Lawkarī* are *ʿilm mā baʿd al-ṭabīʿa*, that is *al-ʿilm al-kullī*, *al-ʿilm al-rubūbī* and *al-ʿilm al- Ilāhī al-ʿāmm*, which seems to comprise both parts of *Ilāhiyyāt*.

chapter seven that this discussion has its roots in Aristotle's *Categories* (*Qāṭīġūriyās*, as he writes).[44]

In the second half of the 11th century, we find Ġazālī (d. 1111) proceeding in the same way. In his *Maqāṣid al-falāsafa*, he states that the subject matter of metaphysics is the most general thing, namely absolute existence, and the sought thing (*maṭlūb*) in this science consists in concomitants of existence (*lawāḥiq al-wuǧūd*) inasmuch as it is only existence, such as its being a substance and an accident.[45] After Ġazālī, the same attitude as Avicenna's view in *Naǧāt* appears in Faḫr al-Dīn Razī's (d. 1209) *al-Risāla al-Kamāliyya.* There he writes, "The accustomed tradition is such that the categories are explained in the science of logic, but it [i. e. logic] does not have any connection to them [i. e. the categories], so inevitably, we bring them at the end of logic and the beginning of metaphysics".[46] In his *al-Mabāḥiṯ al-mašriqiyya*, Rāzī includes the discussion on substance and accidents in its metaphysical part.[47]

Modern scholarship considers Abū l-Barakāt Baġdādī as a relevant source for Suhrawardī, too. Although Abū l-Barakāt was critical towards Avicenna, it seems that concerning the proper place for discussing the categories as well as their importance, he was heavily influenced by Avicenna's approach, since in his *al-Mu'tabar fī l-ḥikma* he deals with them in *al-'ilm al-ilāhī*, and does so very briefly.[48] Abū l-Barakāt also accords with Avicenna in believing that the categories' doctrine plays no important role in philosophy.[49] Moreover, he discusses the categories at the beginning of his metaphysics where he speaks about the content of this science (*fī mā yaštamil 'alayhī 'ilm mā ba'd al-ṭabī'a*)[50] together with the chapter where he discusses the genera of substances and accidents, and although he refers to Aristotle's *Categories* as the root of this discussion, he does not call his treatment a discussion on categories, just as Avicenna in *Dānešnāmeh* did not. By contrast, the Avicennan philosophers before him, such as Bahmanyār, devote a separate chapter to the categories under this title in their logic, and refer

44 *Bayān al-Ḥaqq* I.7, p. 37.

45 Ġazālī, Abū Ḥāmid, *Maqāṣid al-falāsafa*, ed. by Maḥmūd Bīǧū (Damascus, 2000): 64. It is a commonplace that Ġazālī's *Maqāṣid al-falāsafa* is based on Avicenna's *Dānešnāmeh* and a great portion of it is a free translation of the latter into Arabic. On this, see: Janssens, Jules, "Le Danesh-Nameh d'Ibn Sina: un texte a revoir?" and "Al-Gazzali, and his use of Avicennian texts," in *Ibn Sīnā and his Influence on the Arabic and Latin World* (Aldershot, 2006): chapters VII and XI.

46 Razī, Faḫr al-Dīn, *al-Risāla al-Kamāliyya fī ḥaqāyiq al-ilāhiyya*, ed. by Ḫālid Abd al-Karīm al-Ṭarzī (Beirut, 2002): 33.

47 Idem., *al-Mabāḥiṯ al-mašriqiyya*, ed. by Muḥammad al-Mu'taṣim bi-l-lāh al-Baġdādī, 2 vols (Qom: 2008).

48 Baġdādī, Abū l-Barakāt, *al-Mu'tabar fī l-ḥikma, ǧuz' ṯāliṯ: fī l-ḥikma al-ilāḥiyya* (2nd Repr. Isfahan: 1994): I.4–5, 14–20.

49 Ibid., I.5, 18.18–21.

50 Ibid., I.4, 12.10.

their reader to the proper place for studying the categories, namely to metaphysic.[51]

This was the route leading up to Suhrawardī, who treated the categories in his metaphysical treatises instead of logic, and did not even call it a discussion related to the book of *Categories*. This may show that this approach leads in fact back to Avicenna who found the logical framework inappropriate for discussing categories and moved this discussion in his *Dānešnāmeh* to metaphysics. Thus, Suhrawardī does not feel the need for more discussion about the topic of the appropriate place for the categories, and confines himself to drop the categories from logic and to place it in metaphysics, within the framework of a general discussion of existence qua existence or *metaphysica generalis*.

4. Three Aspects of Suhrawardī's Treatment of Aristotelian Categories

As to the general order of his discussion, Suhrawardī's study of the categories in its most extensive fashion consists in the following steps: he first introduces the notions of substance and accident by means of a dichotomous division. Then, he claims that the "original" description of substance and accident, proposed even "prior" to Aristotle, is slightly different from what the Peripatetics used to propose. After that, he introduces the traditional descriptions of the accidental categories and does his best in elaborating on them and spelling out the weaknesses of these descriptions by relying on the so-called Peripatetic rules. After doing this, he introduces his novel division and enumeration of the categories. Then, he shows how some of the Peripatetic accidental categories essentially depend on other ones as to their conceptualization. If so, then these dependent categories cease to be the highest or primary *genera* and so fail to be categories properly. Afterwards, he comes back to the forms and tries to criticize the substantiality of the forms based on their Peripatetic properties and descriptions. By means of these critiques, he wants to persuade his reader that the Peripatetic theory of substance, claiming substantiality for the forms, is insufficient and inconsistent. Relying on the allegedly "original" description of substance and accidents, he concludes that the forms have to be accidents too. Finally, he briefly discusses the benefit of the categories' doctrine. In what follows, I shall concentrate on three aspects of this radical project: the enumeration of the categories; the level of certainty of the enumeration; and eventually, the benefit of the categories' doctrine according to *Šayḫ al-Išrāq*, Suhrawardī.

51 Razī has the same approach in *al-Risāla al-Kamāliyya.*

5. Enumeration of Categories

As mentioned before, Suhrawardī introduces all ten Peripatetic categories according to the Peripatetic tenets (*nusāmiḥu fī l-ḥikaya ʿan al-qawm*, "we treat the account of these people with indulgence," by whom he means the Peripatetics)[52] and then tries to hint at their vulnerabilities relying on Peripatetic principles. The main principle he relies on in his critique is that the categories have to be the highest genera of being, namely they have to be such that no other quiddity could be found to be more general than they are, and neither can a general quiddity belong to them as an essential or constitutive part. Thus, if one can find a more general concept within one or more of the categories, as Suhrawardī indeed does, then these alleged categories fail to be fundamental, in terms of the highest genera, for an ontological classification of being.

In this fashion, Suhrawardī paves the way towards his criticism of both the division and the notion of the categories. In the metaphysics of *Mašāriʿ* he informs his reader that in his *Talwīḥāt al-lawḥiyya wa-l-ʿaršiyya* (hereafter: *Talwīḥāt*) he has listed the categories into five. According to his own testimony, the reason why Suhrawardī allows himself to modify the list of the categories is that neither Aristotle nor other Peripatetics have provided any *demonstrative* argument for their list. On the contrary, their list of the highest genera is based on incomplete induction, whereas the assured way of deducing the most general concepts, and in general any conceptual list, is by way of division. The impetus behind this conviction of Suhrawardī might be found, *inter alia*, in Aristotle's *Organon*, especially in his *Posterior Analytics*,[53] where Aristotle in accordance with Plato and many of his contemporaries states that the right way to formulate definitions is by means of dividing the more general kinds into more specific kinds by attaching distinguishing features to the former.[54] Both Plato and Aristotle shared the view that a properly conducted method of division would reveal the essence of the defined object. Thus, Suhrawardī qualifies this division in a unique passage of *Talwīḥāt*, written in the form of questions and answers, in such a way that we can deduce the two following criteria out of it. The division must be (1) a dichotomous division, which is (2) based on negation and affirmation (*al-qisma ḥāṣira bi l-nafy wa-l-iṯbāt*)[55], namely based on the presence and absence of

---

52 Suhrawardī, *al-Mašāriʿ wa-l-muṭāraḥāt, Ilāhiyyāt*, ed. by Henry Corbin (Tehran: 1993), II.1, 221.(17).15–17. [The numbers between parentheses within the page number shall indicate paragraph numbers.]

53 Aristotle, *Posterior Analytics* II.13, 96b27–97a6.

54 Deslauriers, Marguerite, Aristotle on Definition (Leiden, Boston: 2007): 11, 20–21.

55 Suhrawardī, *Talwīḥāt al-lawḥiyya wa-l-ʿaršiyya, al-ʿilm al-ṯāliṯ: al-ilāhī* [*Ilāhiyyāt*], ed. by Naǧafqolī Ḥabībī (Tehran: 2009): I, 182.18–19; Corbin's edition includes only the metaphysics part (*al-ʿilm al-ṯāliṯ*), for the parallel passage see: Suhrawardī, *Talwīḥāt al-lawḥiyya wa-l-*

an attribute relying on the principle of excluded middle. For example, animal divides into rational and irrational concerning the attribute of rationality in it. In the vein of another Aristotelian conviction, Suhrawardī is also careful not to continue the division from the privative branch, since "privative terms in their character of privatives admit of no subdivision. For there can be no specific forms of a negation".[56] Moreover, he is aware that he still needs to prove the comprehensiveness of his list and therefore he needs to justify why the division has to terminate at a certain stage, how each of his categories is completely distinct from other ones, and how they cover the whole of reality. Suhrawardī's answer to this question is that, on the one hand, his criteria of division guarantee the exclusiveness and exhaustiveness of division.[57] On the other hand, after this certain stage every other subdivision falls under these categories (*wa-mā yanqasimu yaqiʿu aqsamuhū taḥtahū*),[58] that is to say, these further subdivisions will not be the highest genera any more, rather they will be species of their highest genus; thus, only these five kinds are the irreducible, not overlapping genera of being. I shall discuss Suhrawardī's answer to the question how each of his categories is fully distinct from other ones after introducing the full scheme of his *diairesis.*

Suhrawardī claims that his division is more complete (*atamm*) than any other division provided by philosophers other than him (*min kulli ḥaṣrin li-ġayrinā*).[59] The question might be raised regarding these other divisions of the categories to which Suhrawardī is referring in his *Mašāriʿ*. Suhrawardī might be referring to two significant attempts towards providing arguments in favor of the comprehensiveness of the list of the categories.[60] These similar attempts in favor of Aristotelian categories were taken up by some Neoplatonist commentators, probably translated into Arabic, as well as by Kindī and Avicenna, before Suhrawardī, though according to Suhrawardī they are not fully demonstrative. Ac-

---

ʿaršiyya, al-ʿilm al-ṯāliṯ, ed. by Henry Corbin (Tehran: 1993): I, 11.(3).7–8. The passage is unique, since, as far as I know it is the only place, where Suhrawardī introduces these two criteria together. In other works, he picks up the example of Quality and shows how his division is complete and results in a definition of Quality; Cf. Suhrawardī, *al-Muqawamāt, Fī l-ʿilm al-ṯāliṯ [Ilāhiyyāt]*, ed. by Henry Corbin (Tehran: 1993): II.1, 147.(23).10–13; *al-Mašāriʿ wa-l-muṭāraḥāt, Ilāhiyyāt*, ed. by Henry Corbin (Tehran: 1993): II.1, 279.(17).2–7.

56 Aristotle, *Parts of Animals* I.3, 642b22–643a6. I should mention that I do not claim that *Parts of Animals* was Suhrawardī's direct source in this regard, rather I am neutral to this. Nevertheless, considering his special interest in *diairesis*, he could find interesting instances for his vision in *Parts of Animals.*

57 Suhrawardī, *Talwīḥāt al-lawḥiyya wa-l-ʿaršiyya*, al-*ʿilm al-ṯāliṯ: al-ilāhī* [*Ilāhiyyāt*], (Tehran: 2009): I, 182.19.

58 Ibid.

59 Suhrawardī, *al-Mašāriʿ wa-l-muṭāraḥāt, Ilāhiyyāt*, ed. by Henry Corbin (Tehran: 1993): II.1, 284.(56).2–3.

60 Thom, Paul, "The division of the Categories according to Avicenna," in *Aristotle and the Arabic Tradition*, ed. by Ahmed Alwishah and Josh Hayes (Cambridge: 2015): 30–49.

cordingly, it would be beneficial if we consider these divisions before looking into Suhrawardī's, and try to elaborate and evaluate them on the basis of the Suhrawardian approach to division.[61]

In the Arabic tradition, Kindī was one of the earliest philosophers who tried to provide an argument for the list of Aristotelian categories. Nearly at the beginning of his work *On the Quantity of Aristotle's Books*, Kindī introduces Aristotle's *Categories* (*Qāṭūġūriyās*) as dealing with the terms or predicables (*maqūlāt*, literally: *things that are said of*). Then he explains that the terms are either subjects[62] or predicates (*maḥmūl*), and adds, the subject (*ḥāmil*) is what is called a substance and the predicates is what is called an "accident" predicated of the substance, that does not give the substance its name and definition.[63] Afterwards, he mentions the nine accidental categories as the kinds of accident.[64] Some pages later, he comes back to this distinction, and divides the predicates of substance into primary and individual (*al-awlā al-mufrada*) and compound (*murakkaba*). Each of these two divides in turn into two further kinds: the former includes "quantity" – due to being equal and unequal –, on the one hand, and "quality" – due to being like or unlike –, on the other hand. The later divides into those existing without matter (*ṭīna*), which is "relation," on the one side, and into those existing with matter, on the other side. Those existing with matter are either combination of quantity with substance (Where and When), or combination of quality with substance (Acting and Being-Acted-Upon) or combination of substance with substance (Having and Position)[65]. The following diagram depicts this division.[66]

Thus, Kindī, relying on both his own intellectual innovation and Greek sources,[67] provides a division of the terms (*maqūlāt*) for deducing the categories. However, he does not explain, for example, based on which criterion the primary

61 I shall emphasize again that what follows is a Suhrawardian analysis and not a report of what Suhrawardī writes about the two mentioned divisions. In fact, Suhrawardī does not speak about any of these two divisions at all.

62 The term used by Kindī for subject is *ḥāmil* that means literally the *holding term* or the *bearer*.

63 Kindī, *Fī Kammiyyat kutub Arisṭū*, in *Rasā'il al-Kindī al-falsafiyya*, ed. Abū Rīda, Muḥammad ʿAbd al-Hādī, p. 365; For translation, see: Kindī, *The Philosophical Works of al-Kindī*, trans. Adamson, Peter; Pormann, Peter E. (Karachi, 2012); Cf. his definition of substance in *Fī Ḥudūd al-ašyāʾ wa-rusūmihā*, in *Rasā'il al-Kindī al-falsafiyya*, p. 166.

64 Kindī, *Kammiyyat*, p. 366.

65 Ibid, pp. 370–372.

66 The diagram is my own. Similar diagrams are to be found in: Ighbariah, Ahmad, "Between Logic and Mathematics: Al-Kindī's Approach to the Aristotelian Categories" and Thom, Paul, "The division of the Categories according to Avicenna". Thom and Ighbariah disagree about Kindī's understanding of the nature of the categories, that is, whereas according to Ighbariah Kindī has a logical understanding of the categories, Thom sets "beings" as the umbrella term for Kindī's division which might imply an ontological understanding of the categories.

67 Thom, *The division of the Categories according to Avicenna*, p. 32.

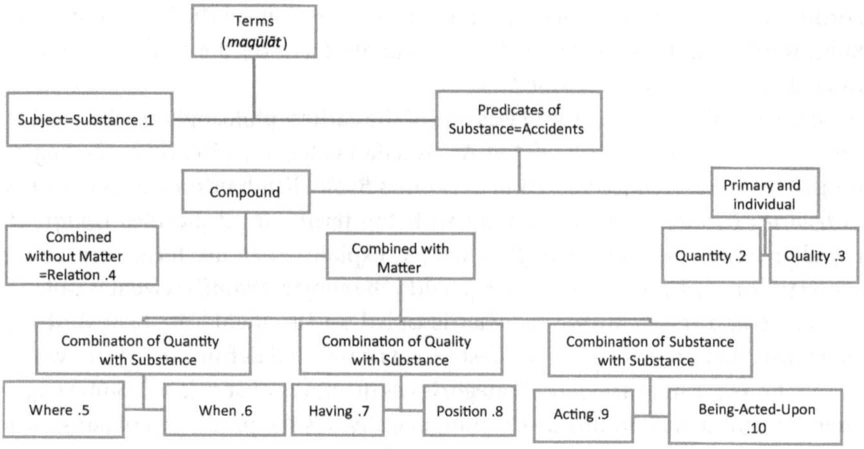

Diagram 1: Kindī's Division of the Categories

and individual accidents are divided into Quantity and Quality. He mentions equality-inequality as characteristics of quantity and likeness-unlikeness as characteristic of quality, but equality-inequality versus likeness-unlikeness does not form a comprehensive cut, according to my reading of Suhrawardī, since they do not make a criterion based on affirmation and negation or based on the presence and absence of an attribute; in other words, they are not contraries. Moreover, the dichotomous nature of division has not been preserved, and whenever that happens, there exists the danger of forming a non-comprehensive cut. Besides, as Fārābī objects[68], the six so-called compound accidents are not based on combination of substance with primary and individual accidents nor with substance[69], since in that case, they must have substance and the primary and individual accidents as their essential parts and so they fail to be the highest genera anymore; a consequence also granted by Suhrawardī.

Avicenna is the other philosopher who took up the task of deducing the categories in *Maqūlāt* II.5 of *Šifāʾ*. He also, along with Fārābī, holds that there could be no compound categories, since all categories must be simple and irreducible, for they are the highest genera. Therefore, they do not have genus nor *differentiae*, and so "no specific division can arrive at them. They can be arrived at, if at all, only by a process of non-specific partition."[70] Thus, it seems that

68 Fārābī, *Kitāb Qāṭāġūriyās ayy al-Maqālāt*, in *Al-Manṭiqiyyāt li-Fārābī*, 3 vol., ed. Dāneš-Pažūh, Moḥammad Taqī (Qom, 1985): 41–82.

69 Ibid., p. 60. Fārābi writes: "When is the relation between the thing (*al-šayʾ*) and the limited time whose existence is coextensive with its existence … The meaning of When is not time nor a compound thing from substance and time".

70 Thom, *The division of the Categories according to Avicenna*, p. 34.

according to Avicenna the project of deducing the categories according to a logical demonstrative way is condemned to failure from the very beginning, although he burdens himself to provide his reader with, in his opinion, the most appropriate (*aqrab*) division. Avicenna calls this division an approximation (*taqrīb*) when he states that he will not guarantee its truth or whether it fulfils being examined by philosophical rules.[71] The following diagram depicts Avicenna's division:

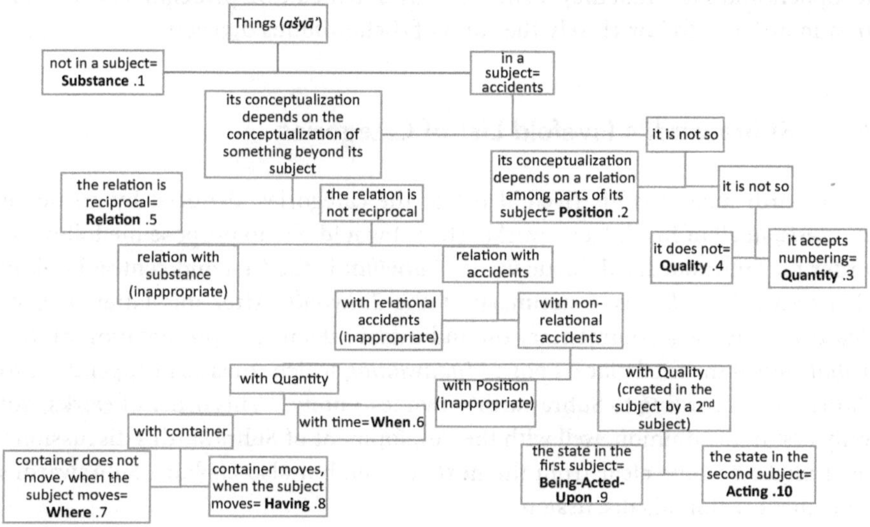

Diagram 2: Avicenna's Division of Categories in Maqūlāt II.5

As we can observe in this diagram, Avicenna is more cautious to preserve the criterion assumed for a dichotomous division: in each step, he tries to produce the division based on affirmation and negation or presence and absence of an attribute. He is also careful not to continue the division from the side of negation or absence of an attribute, such as his cut of things into those, which are not-in-a-subject (*lā fī mawḍūʿin*). However, he does not manage to preserve the dichotomous cuts until the end of the division. For instance, he divides those accidents, whose conceptualization depend on the conceptualization of a non-relational accident beyond them, into three subdivisions, though announcing one of these subdivisions as inappropriate, still doing so, he deviates from the basic rules of dichotomous division, and so his division stands in danger of being incomprehensive and unexclusive. Moreover, from a Suhrawardian point of view, dividing quantitative non-reciprocal relational accidents based on being asso-

71 Ibn Sīnā, *Šifāʾ*, *Manṭiq*, *Maqūlāt*, ed. by Qanawatī et al. (Cairo: 1959), II.5, 86.13.

ciated with container or time is again a cut that is not on the basis of affirmation and negation or based on the presence and absence of an attribute.[72]

Suhrawardī attacks the Peripatetics for lacking *demonstrative* arguments and deviating from the logical rules of divisions to which they should had committed themselves, and therefore he considers himself justified in introducing a new division and consequently a novel list of the highest genera. Since one of his goals in this regard, probably the most important one, is to criticize Peripatetic philosophers and show that they do not stay loyal to their own principles, he does his best in order to follow closely the rules of dichotomous division.

6. Suhrawardī's Fivefold List of Categories

Suhrawardī mentions his fivefold list of the categories, deduced by means of *diairesis*, in all of his didactic works. Here, I would like to propose the following order for Suhrawardī's didactic works: *Talwīḥāt* is the first and central book in this series, *Lamaḥāt* is a summary of the *Talwīḥāt*. After this latter, I place *Mašāriʿ*, which is a commentary on and a more detailed representation of *Talwīḥāt*; and at the final place, I posit *Muqāwamāt*, which consists in appendices to *Talwīḥāt*,[73] according to Suhrawardī's own testimony.[74] This order of works, not only fits, in my opinion, well with the development of Suhrawardī's discussions, as it might become clear from the next section, but also explains Suhrawardī's references within his discussion.

Following this order, I shall begin with *Talwīḥāt*,[75] in which, at the final step of his argument, Suhrawardī provides his reader with a summary of his dichotomous division for the list of the categories:

> When existence is the predicate of it,[76] then either it is existent not in a subject, and it is *Substance*, or it is existent in it [=subject]. [The latter] is either of no stationary (*ġayr*

72 For a study of Avicenna's division of the categories in *Maqūlāt* of *Šifāʾ* as well as their treatment in *Dānešnāmeh*, see: Thom, *The division of the Categories according to Avicenna.* Thom treats Avicenna's discussion in *Maqūlāt* II.5 as a commentary on Aristotle's *Categories*, and so not as Avicenna's own view. In contrast, he regards Avicenna's brief discussion in *Dānešnāmeh* as Avicenna's own division of the categories.

73 In *Mašāriʿ*, Suhrawardī suggests his addressee to study *Mašāriʿ* before *Ḥikmat al-išrāq* and after *Talwīḥāt*; see: *al-Mašāriʿ wa-l-muṭāraḥāt*, *Ilāhiyyāt*, preface, 194.6–8. In *Ḥikmat al-išrāq*, he also mentions *Lamaḥāt*, but does not speak about any didactic or chronological order of works; see: *Ḥikmat al-išrāq*, *al-muqaddama il-l-muṣannif*, 10.(3).4–7.

74 Suhrawardī, *Muqāwamāt*, *Fī l-ʿilm al-ṯāliṯ* [*Ilāhiyyāt*], 124.1–2.

75 In *Mašāriʿ*, Suhrawardī informs his reader that in *Talwīḥāt* he had listed the categories into five; see: *al-Mašāriʿ wa-l-muṭāraḥāt*, *Ilāhiyyāt*, II.5, 278.(55).5. It is worth emphasizing that this proposed order does not exclude the possibility of simultaneous revisions of these works.

76 This restriction aims at preventing the inclusion of the necessary existent, whose existence is

qārr al-ḏāt) essence like *Motion*, or it is stationary (*qārr*) but will not be intellectually grasped (*lā yuʿqalu*) unless together with another thing (*maʿa al-ġayr*), and it is *Relation*. The stationary and non-relational (al-*qārr al-ġayr al-iḍāfiyy*) is either such that division and proportion is necessary (*w-ǧ-b*) to its essence, and it is *Quantity*, or those two are not necessary to its essence, and it is *Quality*. Thus, the original categories are restricted to five (*Talwīḥāt* III, 182).[77]

Suhrawardī explains in the following why he drops the six remaining categories from the list in words different from *Talwīḥāt*, although still here his criticism aims at denying that these categories are the highest genera (*aǧnās ʿāliyya*) of being. According to him, Where, When, Position and Having will not be intellectually grasped unless through relation (*illā bi l-iḍāfa*) and what is "constituted by a thing more general than it" is not a highest genus. Concerning Action and Being-Acted-Upon, Suhrawardī states that they are nothing but motion that is attributed once to the agent of motion and once again to its object.[78]

In *Mašāriʿ* for the first time, Suhrawardī mentions that after having accomplished *Talwīḥāt*, he has found in one of Ibn Sahlān Sāwī's work, unfortunately unknown to us,[79] that Sāwī had listed the categories into the four categories of Substance, Quantity, Quality, and *Nisba* (a different term for Relation).[80] Suhrawardī, then, embarks on a criticism of Sāwī's division of the categories, which leads him to his own list. His main critique of Sāwī's division is that it does not include motion. Motion is neither substance, since it is an accident due to its subsistence in a substrate, nor quantity, although it is measurable. It is not also a quality, for quality is stable, whereas motion is not. It is not to be included under the category of *nisba*, for although motion has a relation to its substrate (*maḥal*), just like other accidental categories, it cannot be considered as a *nisba per se*.[81]

---

same as its essence and therefore cannot be predicated of its essence, in the list. Cf. Suhrawardī, *Talwīḥāt al-lawḥiyya wa-l-ʿaršiyya*, al-*ʿilm al-ṯāliṯ: al-ilāhī* [*Ilāhiyyāt*], (Tehran: 2009), III.2 [*mawrid awwal*].1, 209.10. Ibn Kammūna also confirms this in his commentary on the quoted fragment. See: Ibn Kammūna 2009, p. 50.

77 Suhrawardī proposes the same dichotomous argument for this reductionist list in *Lamaḥāt* III.4, p. 214.102.

78 *Lamaḥāt*, ed. by Naǧafqulī Ḥabībī (Tehran: 2001), III.4, p. 214.102.

79 Surprisingly, Suhrawardī introducing Sāwī as the author (*ṣāḥib*) of *al-Baṣāʾir* might lead us to assume that Sāwī provides this list in the extant logical part of *Baṣāʾir*. However, Sāwī discusses there the ten categories in its traditional fashion revealing no trace of any critical approach. Therefore, we may assume that Suhrawardī has found the aforementioned list in another work, whose title he does not mention, and here, he is simply introducing Sāwī with his most famous work. The other possibility is that Suhrawardī has found this list in in the metaphysics of *Baṣāʾir*, which is lost, thereby assuming that Sāwī treats the categories in the metaphysics of *Baṣāʾir* differently from its treatment in logic.

80 *al-Mašāriʿ wa-l-muṭāraḥāt*, *Ilāhiyyāt*, II.5, 278.(55).5–7.

81 Ibid., 278.(54).5–12.

Thus, Suhrawardī continues, "it is more appropriate (*aqrab*) to establish the list of the categories under five: Substance, Quantity, Quality, Relation (*iḍāfa*) and Motion." His argument here is also almost the same as in the previous works, although it involves some refinements:

That essence which is beyond (*warā'*) existence[82] is either such that it is a *Substance* or it is other than substance. What is not a *Substance*, we call it here a feature (*hay'a*; Suhrawardian accident). Every feature is either such that its stability (*ṯubāt*) is conceptualized or its stability is not conceptualized (*lā yataṣawwar*). If its stability is not conceptualized, then it is *Motion.* But if its stability is conceptualized: either it is such that it is not intellectually grasped (*lā tuʿqalu*) unless in comparison (*qiyās*) to a thing other than it, or it is intellectually grasped without comparison (*dūn al-qiyās*) to a thing other than it. What is not intellectually grasped unless in comparison (*qiyās*) to a thing other than it is *Relation* (*al-iḍāfa*). What is intellectually grasped without comparison (*qiyās*) to a thing other than it is either such that equality or differentiation (*al-tafāwut*) and division are necessary to its essence, or they are not necessary. If these are necessary [to its essence], then it is *Quantity*, and if these are not necessary [to its essence], then it is *Quality.* Thus, the *Quality* occurs at the end of the division and it possesses distinguishing marks (*mummayizāt*) from each side of the division. Inasmuch as it is a feature, it is distinct from the *Substance.* Inasmuch as it is stationary, it is distinct from *Motion.* Inasmuch as it does not need (*lā yaḥtāğu*) anything beyond it and its subject in its conceptualization, it is distinct from *Relation.* And inasmuch as it does not have any need (*lā yaḥwağu*) for considering division, it is distinct from *Quantity.* Thus, its description includes all things that differentiate it from its four counterparts (*Mašāriʿ*, II.5, (55) 278.14–279.7).[83]

The following diagram portrays this division.

As we see in this dichotomous division, Suhrawardī remains faithful to the three aforementioned conditions of *diairesis*; namely that a *diairesis* (i) should always remain dichotomous. (ii) Its cuts should be based on affirmation and negation, that is on the basis of the presence and absence of an attribute. Finally, (iii) there should be no further cut on the negative side of the division.[84]

Now, as we read in the quoted text and see in the diagram, Suhrawardī deduces the category of Quality in all of his *summae* as the last category and negatively, namely by means of negating positive characteristics of other four categories. In

82 See the footnote 76 on the text quoted from *Talwīḥāt.*

83 Prior to this division in the metaphysics of *Mašāriʿ* – and in the corresponding place of *Muqāwamāt*, as well –, Suhrawardī has introduced his modified definitions of substance and accident that are of significant ontological consequences for his later discussions about hylomorphic compounds as well as substantiality of corporeal and specific forms. However, discussing these aspects is beyond the aims and questions of this article.

84 In his commentary on Aristotle's *Categories*, Simplicius writes that Aristotle "carries out a division *(diairesis)* of being" in order to obtain the ten categories; Cf: Simplicius, *On Aristotle's "Categories 1–4"*, trans. by Michael Chase (Ithaca, New York: 2003), 10.10–15. This might be one of the motivations behind Suhrawardī's concentration on *diairesis.*

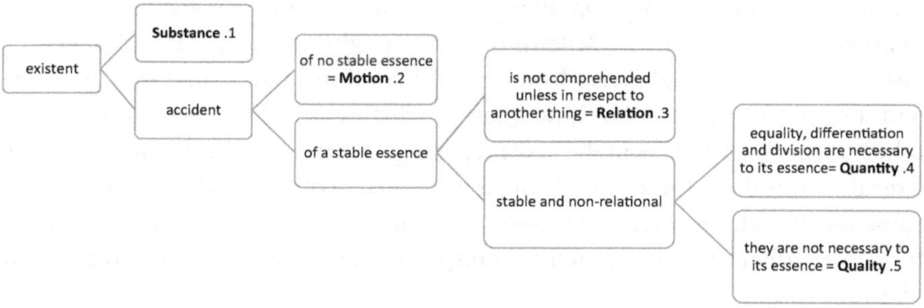

Diagram 3: Division of Categories in Kitāb al-Mašāriʿ wa-l-muṭāraḥāt

other words, according to his division, the category of Quality consists in a genus that is neither substance, nor is it non-stable [=of no motion], nor is it relational, and nor does it accept equality, differentiation and division. However, since he seems to be aware that mere privation cannot describe a thing,[85] therefore he tries to show how this description can endow the reader a positive notion: first in *Talwīḥāt*, he emphasizes that he is using a dichotomous division based on negation and affirmation whose result has to be of certainty.[86] In *Mašāriʿ*, then, he explains how Quality is distinct from other categories, as we read at the end of above-mentioned text, but he is still not completely satisfied with his justification.[87] Therefore, in *Muqāwamāt* he again emphasizes that the description of Quality, as a result of this dichotomous division, is complete and then elaborates the characteristics of Quality using a more affirmative expression:

> The description of Quality is complete, due to the sides of the formulated division: from the division into substance [and feature] there is for it [the distinction of being] feature (*hay'a*). From the division into Motion [and non-moving sides results that] it is of stable essence. From the division into Relation [and non-relational sides results that] it is in no need of (*lā yaḥtāǧ*)[88] anything beyond itself for its conceptualization. From the division into Quantity [and non-quantitative sides results that] equality and division and other [characteristics of Quantity] are not necessary for its essence. (*Muqāwamāt, Ilāhiyyāt*, 147.(23).10–13)

85 In the logic of *Mašāriʿ*, Suhrawardī shows the same awareness and worry about the description of Quality; see: Suhrawardī, *al-Mašāriʿ wa l-muṭāraḥāt, al-ʿilm al-awwal: al-Manṭiq*. Ed. by Maqṣūd Moḥammadī and Ašraf ʿAlīpūr (Tehran: 2006): 92–93.

86 Suhrawardī, *Talwīḥāt al-lawḥiyya wa-l-ʿaršiyya*, al-*ʿilm al-ṯāliṯ: al-ilāhī* [*Ilāhiyyāt*], (Tehran: 2009), I, 182.19.

87 *al-Mašāriʿ wa-l-muṭāraḥāt, Ilāhiyyāt*, II.5, 278.(55).5–7.

88 It might be objected that *lā yaḥtāǧ* is still negative. A possible answer to this objection could be that the grammatical from is negative, but the semantical connotation is completely affirmative, since *to be in need of* is in fact "the absence of an attribute" and thereby the "*lā yaḥtāǧ*" consists in the "presence" of that attribute. Thus, only the last factor remains negative.

Thus, comparing these two parallel passages, namely the passage in *Mašāriʿ* as opposed to the passage in *Muqāwamāt*, we might see no great difference or development, at first glance. However, we may think that in the first passage, Suhrawardī has tried to show how Quality is distinguished (*amtāza, m-y-z*) from other categories, whereas in the second passage he tries to justify how Quality, as a result of this dichotomous division, is what it is. In other words, how it acquires some positive characteristics by means of being deprived of the natural characteristics of other categories, such as being not-a-substance and being stable, be it plausible or not.

Yet Suhrawardī, being aware of possible disagreements against his idiosyncratic list of the categories, regards it as necessary to justify his division in at least three aspects, also identified by his commentator Ibn Kammūna: 1. why the division has to stop after these five categories. 2. How the categories in Aristotelian list relate to these fivefold list. 3. Why he is opposing the first teacher, namely Aristotle.[89]

The answer to the first probable objection is that since the division is based on negation and affirmation, then it covers all possible subdivisions and as the categories are meant to be the highest genera, then all other subdivisions fall under these and so fail to be the *summa genera* any more.[90] Here, Suhrawardī accepts the Peripatetic rule according to which the accident is not a genus for the accidental categories, but it is one of their concomitants (*lawāzim*).[91] Thus, *hayʾa* itself is not a genus, since what is found in the external world is not accident, but quantity or quality etc.; and besides, accident is predicated of them not univocally, but equivocally, namely it is predicated once in the sense of quantity, then, quality and so on. The term "*hayʾa*" is nothing but an umbrella term describing the things that are not substances.[92]

The answer to the second question is related to the previous discussions on the correct description of the accidental categories. Here Suhrawardī tries to show again how, on the one hand, the conceptualization of the four categories of

89 Ibn Kammūna, *Šarḥ Talwīḥāt al-lawḥiyya wa-l-ʿaršiyya, Ilāhiyyāt*, ed. by Naǧafqulī Ḥabībī (Tehran: 2009), I, 52–55.

90 "It was normally held that a *diairesis* could not result in innumerable members." Michael Chase's note in: Simplicius, *On Aristotle's "Categories 1–4"*, p. 106, note 140. Cf. Moraux, Paul, *Der Aristotelismus bei den Griechen von Andronikos bis Alexander von Aphrodisias*, vol. I (Berlin, New York: 1973): 130ff.

91 For instance, see: Suhrawardī, *al-Mašāriʿ wa-l-muṭāraḥāt, Ilāhiyyāt*, II.2, 233.(23).8–10.

92 It is noteworthy that in his illuminationist works such as *Ḥikmat al-išrāq* and *Partaw Nāmē* Suhrawardī speaks of quiddities or existents in terms of substance and feature/disposition (*hayʾa*) and he does not divide the feature into its genera. It does not mean, however, that he has changed his mind and considers feature as a genus, but that he does not believe in the benefit of this further division for his own philosophical project. He also announces this at the final stage of his criticism of the categories doctrine in *Mašāriʿ*. See: *al-Mašāriʿ wa-l-muṭāraḥāt, Ilāhiyyāt*, II.5, 284.(74).5.

Where, When, Position and Having depends on the prior conceptualization of the category of Relation and how, on the other hand, the conceptualization of the two categories of Acting and Being-Acted-Upon depends on the prior conceptualization of the category of Motion.[93] Suhrawardī's general strategy in this regard is as follows: first, he refers to the original description of these categories and shows that these categories fail to be conceptualized unless in "relation" to another thing. Subsequently, he explains that if something fails to be conceptualized unless in "relation", then the "relation" is an essential part of it and is prior to it. This essential part of a genus is either its highest genus or part of it, but a highest genus was supposed to be simple and have no constitutive parts, this is then a contradiction. Therefore, the former ceases to be the highest genus. What ceases to be the highest genus ceases accordingly to be a category. For instance, in the case of the category of Where, he says, "Where consists in 'the being of a substance in place' (*kawn al-ǧawhar fi-l-makān*)."[94] This being (*kawn*) cannot be intellectually grasped, unless the Relation is intellectually grasped prior to it. The argument for this is as follows:

> When the body is in a place, no feature has been realized for it other than its Relation to the place and this relation is a special Relation (*iḍāfa ḫāṣṣa*); its being in the place is not an existence for it, rather it is the existence of a Relation (*bal wuǧūd iḍāfa*). Thus, if the Relation is essential to the whole, whereas every general essential (*ḏātī ʿamm*) is either a genus or part of a genus, then the Relation is general to these things; then, they are not the most general genera. (*Talwīḥāt, Ilāhiyyāt*, III, 183.8–11)

In other words, when a body exists, it exists with certain accidents. One of them is its being in a place. This *being in a place*, namely *being associated with place* is what Suhrawardī calls peculiar or special Relation (*iḍāfa ḫāṣṣa*) for the category of Where, namely that relation which is characteristic for Where, just as *being in time*, namely *being associated with time* is the peculiar or special Relation for the category of When. Where and When are surely accidental features for an existing body, however, they are not accidents in the sense of the highest genera, since the conceptualization of the special Relation is prior to them, and this latter in itself depends on the prior conceptualization of the absolute Relation. That is to say,

93 In his article on Suhrawardī's notion of body as extension, John Walbridge writes, "the remaining Aristotelian categories – place, time, possession, position, action and passion – can be reduced to relation." A close reading of Suhrawardī's texts show that this statement is not free from negligence, since, as mentioned before, according to Suhrawardī the two categories of Acting and Being-Acted-Upon have been reduced to Motion and not Relation. Cf. Walbridge, John: "Al-Suhrawardī on Body as Extension: An Alternative to Hylomorphism from Plato to Leibnitz." In *Reason and Inspiration in Islam.* Ed. by Todd Lawson. London, New York, I. B. Tauris & The Institute of Ismaili Studies, 2005, 235–247.

94 Suhrawardī, *Talwīḥāt al-lawḥiyya wa-l-ʿaršiyya*, al-ʿ*ilm al-ṯāliṯ: al-ilāhī* [*Ilāhiyyāt*], III, 182.20–183.1.

Relation is essential to it, and so to those categories, whereas a *summum genus* has no essential part. Besides, when a body is in a place or in a time, it does not mean that its *existence is* in this or that place and time, but rather that there is a Relation between the body and time or place. In his commentary on this passage, Ibn Kammūna, admitting these two points, adds a further remark: if those four relational accidents (When, Where, Having, Position) were not relations, but generic accidents, they would be "existences," since the categories are the divisions of existent. Then, whenever the body, i.e. the substance, were to move from one place to another place or from one time to another time, it would become necessary for it to receive multiple existences, which is according to him absurd.[95] Consequently, the absolute Relation is a more general essentiality beyond these four categories that results in denial of their being *summa genera.* The same line of argumentation can be provided in case of the dependence of the categories of Acting and Being-Acted-Upon on the Motion.

Concerning the third objection, namely challenging the authority of Aristotle, Suhrawardī surprisingly casts doubt on the Aristotle's pioneering status, and ascribes the doctrine of the categories to the Pythagorean Archytas who was supposed to be Plato's close friend and Aristotle's predecessor in this regard, which was a prevailing idea in late antiquity. He also adds that Archytas does not propose any demonstration for his doctrine.[96]

7. Suhrawardī on the Degree of Certainty of his Division

Although it may seem to run against the commonly accepted picture of Suhrawardī's philosophy as a kind of philosophical mysticism or mystical wisdom, Suhrawardī shows himself as a serious metaphysician paying particular attention to intellectual demonstration. His main critique against the Peripatetics is that their philosophical tenets are not demonstrative. Nearly at the end of the metaphysics of *Talwīḥāt*, he invites his addressee not to imitate him [=Suhrawardī], nor the others (*lā tuqallidnī wa-ġayrī*), but just to consider the demonstration (*burhān*) as the only criterion (*miʿyār*) for truth.[97] He also shares the same

95 Ibn Kammūna, *Šarḥ Talwīḥāt al-lawḥiyya wa-l-ʿaršiyya*, *Ilāhiyyāt*, I, 54.1–4.

96 Suhrawardī, *Talwīḥāt al-lawḥiyya wa-l-ʿaršiyya*, al-*ʿilm al-ṯāliṯ: al-ilāhī* [*Ilāhiyyāt*], III, 183.14–17. For the two Pseudo-Archytasian texts on the categories, see: Szlezák, Thomas Alexander, *Pseudo-Archytas über die Kategorien, Texte zur griechischen Aristoteles-Exegese* (Berlin, New York, 1972). For more information about the relationship between Archytas and pseudo-Archytas, see: Huffman, Carl, *Archytas of Tarentum. Pythagorean, Philosopher and Mathematician King* (Cambridge: 2005): 91 ff, 595 ff.

97 Suhrawardī, *Talwīḥāt al-lawḥiyya wa-l-ʿaršiyya*, *al-ʿilm al-ṯāliṯ: al-ilāhī* [*Ilāhiyyāt*], V.16, 287.16.

concern at the last paragraph of metaphysics of *Muqāwamāt*, as he requests his reader not to be content with the illusion of imitation (*lam yaqniʿ bi-wahm al-taqlīd*).[98] Thus, in my opinion, in the case of the categories Suhrawardī strongly believes that the Peripatetics have failed to offer any *demonstrative* argument for their tenfold list of the categories. He even spells out this conviction in *Mašāriʿ*, after establishing his list and reducing the six remaining categories into Relation and Motion. There he states that the most learned Peripatetic scholars (*al-fuḍalāʾ min šīʿat al-maššāʾīn*) "confess that they do not have any demonstration for their list" (*muʿtarifūn bi-annahū lā burhān lahum ʿala l-ḥaṣr*) and what is mentioned in this regard is nothing but merely "a weak [intellectual] exertion" (*laysa illā takalluf ḍaʿīf*).[99]

In spite of this, Suhrawardī's rhetoric in this regard might remind us of Avicenna's discussion in *Maqūlāt*, where he speaks about the purpose of studying the categories. In my opinion, Suhrawardī is right if he thinks that the Peripatetics, especially Avicenna, are aware that their arguments are not fully established, though he misinterprets Avicenna's point. Avicenna, in *Maqūlāt* I.1 writes that the student of logic has to learn the doctrine of the categories by way of postulation and imitation (*ʿalā sabīl al-waḍʿ wa-l-taqlīd*)[100] and then some lines later he explains the reason for it:

> Since there is no way to the knowledge of this, unless by way of *empirical investigation* (*istiqṣāʾ*, also fact-finding or induction); and there is no way to empirical investigation unless after reaching the level [of mastery] in the science which is called the first philosophy (*Maqūlāt* I.1, 6.15–16).

Significant here is the use of the term *istiqṣāʾ* (also *taqrīb* and *q-r-b* in other places) which I translate as "empirical investigation", although it might be translated as induction, as well, namely as a synonym of the more technical term *istiqrāʾ*.[101] In the rest, Avicenna uses the verb "demonstration" a couple of times saying that it is not possible to demonstrate the categories at the beginning of logic, although he himself provides an argument for the number of the categories in *Maqūlāt* II.5.

Thus, in Avicenna's opinion, the aim of the *Categories* is to accept the ten categories as the highest genera under which the existents are included and take it for granted that the simple words (*al-alfāẓ al-mufrada*) fall upon these things. He

98 Idem., *Muqāwamāt*, *Ilāhiyyāt*, 192.(61).6.

99 Idem., *al-Mašāriʿ wa-l-muṭāraḥāt*, *Ilāhiyyāt*, II.5, (56).283.17–284.2. Corbin's vocalization of *takalluf ḍaʿīf* is confusing. I read it as *takallufun ḍaʿīfun*.

100 *Šifāʾ*, *Manṭiq*, *Maqūlāt* I.1, 6.10.

101 In the later tradition, the scholars understood Suhrawardī's criticism as accusing the Peripatetics of building the list of the categories based on induction. Ṭūsī in *Asās al-iqtibās* expresses the same conviction without mentioning Suhrawardī; see: Ṭūsī, Naṣīr al-Dīn, *Asās al-iqtibās*, ed by Moḥammad Taqī Modarres Raḍawī (Tehran: 1982): 35.1–2.

also adds that the student has to know that one of them is substance and the rest nine are accidents, without demanding any demonstration, rather it is necessary just to accept it.[102] Avicenna even accuses the other commentators who "occupied themselves" with demonstrating the categories in the logic saying, "they burdened themselves with something that is beyond their capacity" (*faqad takallafa mā lā yafī bihī wusʿihī*).[103] The reason for this judgment is that such a demonstration has been abandoned in that book, which is the origin of this discussion (*anna hāḏihī l-mabāhiṯ qad turikat fī kitāb al-laḏī huwa l-aṣl*).[104] I take this book as Aristotle's *Categories*, and thus, Avicenna interprets, in my opinion, the absence of any demonstration in Aristotle's logical corpus as a result of lacking the scientific facilities for it. Thus, Avicenna's point concerns the possibility of providing a demonstration for categories within a logical framework, and not its impossibility in general. He even alludes here to metaphysics,[105] as mentioned before, as the more appropriate context for such a demonstration. His remark about those who tried to demonstrate the categories in their writings on *Categories* means consequently that they lack the philosophical apparatus for such an enterprise, and he is not criticizing their personal capacities.

Suhrawardī, in contrast, seems to have generalized Avicenna's dissatisfaction concluding that "the most virtuous Peripatetic scholars" admit that they fail to provide a demonstrative argument for the enumeration and deduction of the categories. Moreover, there is the additional consideration that this doctrine is not a genuine Aristotelian doctrine, but rather of Pythagorean origins, according to Suhrawardī. In this context, Suhrawardī even uses the word *takalluf* that echoes the same verb used by Avicenna for criticizing the other commentators. He acknowledges, then, his own demonstration as the best and most certain demonstration for the categories.

If my proposed order of Suhrawardī's didactic works is correct, then we can observe a decreasing process in Suhrawardī's opinion concerning the degree of certainty of his fivefold division of the categories. In the first book, *Talwīḥāt*, he claims that his argument for enumeration of the categories is demonstrative (*al-burhān huwa l-laḏī nattabiʿu*)[106]. In another passage of the same book, he even goes further and states that God has provided him with the "demonstration" for the enumeration of the categories (*iḏ yassara l-lāh lanā burhān ḥaṣr al-maqūlāt fīmā ḏakarnā*).[107] In *Mašāriʿ*, he shows less certainty about his division, never-

102 Idem., I.1, 6.16–20.
103 Idem., I.1, 7.6.
104 Idem., I.1, 7.8–9.
105 Idem., I.1, 6.15–16.
106 Suhrawardī, *Talwīḥāt al-lawḥiyya wa-l-ʿaršiyya*, al-*ʿilm al-ṯāliṯ: al-ilāhī* [*Ilāhiyyāt*], I, 183.16–17.
107 Idem., III.2[*mawrid awwal*].1, 209.10.

theless says before proposing his dichotomous division "it is more appropriate (*aqrab*) for the one, who wishes to establish the categories, to list them under five."[108] Then he claims that his own division and list is more complete (*atamm*) than other proposed lists (*ḥaṣr*), nonetheless he does not want to impose the authority of this enumeration upon the reader as well as the authority of the categories' doctrine in general.[109] In *Muqāwamāt*, he even shows more uncertainty and writes, "This enumeration cannot also be considered as free from negligence" (*ṯumma hāḏā l-ḥaṣr ayḍan laysa mimmā lā yaḫlū ʿan musāhila*).[110] Thus, we observe that he modifies his level of certitude regarding the comprehensiveness of his division from demonstrative certainty to the best possible justification as he moves from *Talwīḥāt* through *Mašāriʿ* to the *Muqāwamāt.*[111] It is also noteworthy that in *Mašāriʿ* and *Muqāwamāt*, after spelling out his dissatisfaction and uncertainty regarding his novel division, he says equivocally and surprisingly that there is no such great benefit in studying the categories, and occupying oneself less with this topic is not such a great loss.[112] Thus, Suhrawardī regards even his own long and detailed analysis of the categories as wasting time, or with less harsh words, it is of mere didactic benefits.

However, Avicenna may have inspired Suhrawardī's judgement regarding the benefit of studying the categories. Since at the end of *Maqūlāt* I.1, Avicenna spells out again his dissatisfaction with the inclusion of the doctrine of the categories in logic and writes:

> As to us, we believe in what we said. We follow then the approach of the Peripatetic folk [who traditionally wrote about this topic] and their customs, whether we like it or not.[113] We say: [here you are], this is the book and its preface, although it is not of such a great benefit and advantage; possibly, it may even be harmful and disadvantageous [when it is] at the very beginning [of this science] (*Maqūlāt* I.1, 8.9–10).

Thus, we see how heavily in this context, namely on the purpose and subject matter of the categories, Suhrawardī draws on Avicenna for undermining the validity and advantage of the categories' doctrine that consequently leads to dismissing the study of the categories from *Ḥikmat al-išrāq.*[114] Although, Avi-

108 Suhrawardī, *al-Mašāriʿ wa-l-muṭāraḥāt, Ilāhiyyāt*, II.5, 278.(55).12–13.

109 Ibid., (56).283.17–284.4.

110 Suhrawardī, *Muqāwamāt* III, 147.(23), 13–14.

111 In *Talwīḥāt*, Suhrawardī does not mention any of his other works within this discussion; whereas in *Mašāriʿ* he mentions that in his *Talwīḥāt* he has listed the categories in five (*Mašāriʿ*, p. 278.55.5). In *Muqāwamāt* he mentions both aforementioned works as backgrounds of his discussion on the categories by saying that he has elaborated this idea in the former and discussed it in details in the later (*Muqāwamāt* III, 146.(23).4–5).

112 Suhrawardī, *Mašāriʿ*, II.5, (56).284.4–5; *Muqāwamāt*, III, (23).147.14-(24).148.2.

113 Read as *šiʾnā am abīnā* following the Ms. Leiden Or. 4, fol. 18v.

114 Comparable with Avicenna's *al-Ishārāt wa-l-tanbīhāt.*

cenna's dissatisfaction, as far as I understand, reflects his critical approach concerning the proper science for studying categories, which is more or less a methodological concern.

Concluding Remarks

Suhrawardī's attitude towards the categories, as a metaphysical and not a logical topic, was a result of the philosophical debates concerning the proper science for studying the categories in 10th–12th centuries, having its roots in Avicenna's critical approach. This was not, however, the only aspect of Suhrawardī's enterprise that had its roots in Avicenna. In fact, the critical engagement with the categories' doctrine, initiated by Avicenna, became a common trend in the 11th–12th centuries' philosophizing in the eastern world that continued even until 13th century. Relying on Suhrawardī's testimony, on the one hand, and Ṭūsī's report, on the other hand, some philosophers engaged with the categories and tried to correct its catalog, either with reducing their numbers, in case of Sāwi and Suhrawardī, or with increasing them, in case of some theologians. Interestingly, Rāzī rejects in both *Mabāḥiṯ* and *Risāla kamāliyya* a list provided by a group of people (*qawm*) similar to what Suhrawardī ascribes to Sāwī,[115] which insinuates that Rāzī and Suhrawardī are drawing on a common source.

Suhrawardī attacks the entire doctrine from different aspects. I have focused only on three aspects: the enumeration of the categories, the level of certainty pertaining to this enumeration, and eventually the philosophical benefit of the categories' doctrine. We saw that Suhrawardī, following the late ancient Neoplatonists, casted doubt on the authenticity of the categories' doctrine, and relying on established Peripatetic principles, argued that, contrary to these presuppositions, not all of the categories may considered as the highest genera. Thus, he showed that not only the doctrine of the categories was not originally Aristotelian, but also it was inconsistent and incomplete. Suhrawardī introduced not only the proper method for deducing the categories, i. e. the *diairesis*, but also his novel fivefold list, and argued for its exhaustiveness and elaborated on the relationship between his categories and the Aristotelian catalog. Yet Suhrawardī himself remained in the end doubtful about the level of certainty associated to his novel fivefold list. This is for him a sign of the untrustworthiness of the doctrine. Hence, in *Mašāriʿ*, he concludes that "it is enough to divide the essences into substance and feature" (*hayʾa*)[116], which is what he does in his illuminationist

115 Rāzī, *Risāla kamāliyya*, 35; *Mabāḥiṯ al-mašriqiyya*, vol 1: 270–271.
116 Suhrawardī, *al-Mašāriʿ wa-l-muṭāraḥāt*, *IlāhIyāt*, II.5, (56).284.5.

works, especially in *Ḥikmat al-išrāq*.[117] This, however, does not mean that Suhrawardī abandons his whole analysis of the categories. On the contrary, his conceptions of substance and feature and their subdivisions as well as his understanding of features such as relation in his illuminationist philosophy, each of them having wide range of metaphysical and epistemological consequences, result from this very analysis of the categories. Besides, according to Suhrawardī, the incompleteness and inconsistency of the categories' doctrine shows the failure of the whole enterprise of the categories, since it does not cover all of reality. Consequently, Suhrawardī at the final stage of his categories' discussion in *Muqāwmāt* criticizes the Peripatetics for being forgetful about the highest intelligible beings or the lights.[118]

Bibliography

Manuscripts

Avicenna, *al-Šifā'*, Ms. Leiden Or. 4.

Published Works

Adamson, Peter, *Al-Kindī*. Oxford, New York: Oxford University Press, 2008.
–, *The Philosophical Works of al-Kindī*. Trans. by Peter Adamson; Pormann, Peter E. Karachi: Oxford University Press, 2012.
Aristotle, *Categories* and *De Interpretatione*. Trans. by J.L. Ackrill. Oxford: Clarendon Press, 1963.
–, *The Complete Works of Aristotle. The Revised Oxford Translation*, vols 1–2. Ed. by Jonathan Barnes. Princeton: Princeton University Press, 1991.
Avicenna, *al-Šifā', al-Ilāhiyyāt*. Ed. by Georges Anawati and Sa'īd Zāyid. Cairo: Wizārat al-Ṯaqāfa wa-l-Iršād al-Qawmī, 1960.
–, *al-Šifā', al-Manṭiq, al-Maqūlāt*. Ed. by George Anawati et. al. Cairo: Wizārat al-Ṯaqāfa wa l-iršād al-Qawmī, 1959.
–, *al-Šifā', al-Manṭiq, al-Madḫal*. Ed. by George Anawati et. al. Cairo: al-Idāra al-'Āmma li-l-Ṯaqāfa, 1952.
–, *al-Mubāḥaṯāt*. Ed. by Moḥsen Bīdārfar. Qom: Entešārāt-e Bīdār, 1992.
–, *Naǧāt min al-ġarq fī baḥr al-ḍalālāt*. Ed. by Mohammad Taqī Dāneš-Pažūh. Tehran: Entešārāt-e Dānešgāh-e Tehrān, 1985.
–, *Kitāb al-Naǧāt*. Ed. by Māǧid Faḫrī. Beirut: Dār al-Āfāq al-Ǧadīda, 1982.

117 Idem., *Ḥikmat al-išrāq* I.3, 61.(52).12–15.
118 Idem., *Muqāwamāt, Ilāhlyāt*, 147.(24).15–148.2.

–, *Dānešnāmeh-ye ʿAlāyī, Ilāhiyyāt*. Ed. by Mohammad Moʿīn. Tehran: Anǧoman-e Āṯār-o Mafāẖer-e Farhangī, Dānešgāh-e Būʿalī Sīnā, 1952.
–, *al-Ishārāt wa l-tanbīhāt*. Ed. by Moǧtabā Zāreʿī. Qom: Moʾassese-ye Būstān-e Ketāb, 2013.
Āyatī, Moḥammad Ebrāhīm, *Maqūlāt-o Ārā-ye Marbūṭ be ān*. Tehran: Entešārāt-e Dānešgāh-e Tehrān, 1964.
Bahmanyār ibn Marzbān, *al-Taḥṣīl*. Ed. by Mortaḍā Moṭahharī. Tehran: Entešārāt-e Dānešgāh-e Tehrān, 1996.
al-Baġdādī, Abū l-Barakāt, *al-Muʿtabar fī l-ḥikma*. Ed. by ʿAbdallāh al-ʿAlawī al-Ḥaḍramī et al., 3 vols. Isfahan: Entešārāt-e Dānešgāh-e Isfahan, 1994 [2nd Repr of Hyderabad: 1939].
Bocheński, Innocentius Marie, *Ancient Formal Logic*. Amsterdam: North-Holland Publishing Company, 1951.
Deslauriers, Marguerite, *Aristotle on Definition*. Leiden, Boston: Brill, 2007.
Ferrari, Cleophea, Der Kategorienkommentar von Abū l-Faraǧ ʿAbdallāh ibn aṭ-Ṭayyib, Text und Untersuchungen. Leiden and Boston: Brill, 2006.
Fārābī, *Kitāb Qāṭāġūriyās ayy al-Maqālāt*. In *Al-Manṭiqiyyāt li-Fārābī*. Ed. by Moḥammad Taqī Dāneš-Pažūh, 3 vols. Qom: Manšūrāt Maktabat Āyat Allāh al-ʿUẓmā Marʿašī al-Naǧafī, 1985, 41–82.
Ġazālī, Abū Ḥāmid, *Maqāṣid al-Falāsafa*. Ed. by Maḥmūd Bīǧū. Damascus: Maṭbaʿa al-Ṣabāḥ, 2000.
Gutas, Dimitri, *Avicenna and the Aristotelian Tradition*. Leiden; Boston: Brill, 2013.
Ḥillī, Abū Manṣūr, *Kašf al-murād fī šarḥ Taǧrīd al-iʿtiqād*. Ed. by Ḥasan Ḥasan-Zādeh Āmolī. Qom: Muʾassisat al-Našr al-Islāmī, 2011/2012.
Huffman, Carl A., *Archytas of Tarentum. Pythagorean, Philosopher and Mathematician King*. Cambridge: Cambridge University Press, 2005.
Ḫwārazmī, Muḥammad b. Aḥmad b. Yūsuf, *Mafātiḥ al-ʿulūm*. Ed. by Ibrāhīm al-Abyārī. Beirut: Dār al-Kitab al-ʿArabī, 1989.
Ibn Abī Uṣaybīʿa., *ʿUyūn al-anbāʾ fī Ṭabaqāt al-Aṭibbā*. Ed. by Nizār Riḍā. Beirut: Dār Maktabat al-Ḥayāt, 1995.
Ibn Kammūna, Šarḥ, *Talwīḥāt al-lawḥiyya wa l-ʿaršiyya*. Ed. by Naǧafqolī Ḥabībī, 3 vols. Tehran: Markaz-e Pažūhešī-ye Mīrāṯ-e Maktūb, 2009.
Ibn Muqaffa; Ibn Bihrīz, *ʻAl-Mantiqʾ li-Ibn Muqaffaʿ wa-ʻḤudūd al-mantiqʾ li-Ibn Bihrīz*. Ed. by Mohammad Taqī Dāneš-Pažūh. Tehran: Anǧoman-e Falsafeh-ye Iran, 1979.
Ibn Nadīm, Abū l-Faraǧ Muḥammad b. Ishāq, *Kitāb al-Fihrist*. Ed. by Ayman Fuʾād Sayyid, 4 vols. London: Al-Furqān Islamic Heritage Foundation, 2014.
Ighbariah, Ahamd, "Between Logic and Mathematics: Al-Kindī's Approach to the Aristotelian Categories." In *Arabic Sciences and Philosophy* 22 (2012): 51–68.
Janssens, Jules, "Le Danesh-Nameh d'Ibn Sina: un texte a revoir?" In *Ibn Sīnā and his Influence on the Arabic and Latin World*. Aldershot: Ashgate Variorum, 2006, chapter VII.
–, "Al-Gazzali, and his use of Avicennian texts." In *Ibn Sīnā and his Influence on the Arabic and Latin World*. Aldershot: Ashgate Variorum, 2006, chapter XI.
Kalbarczyk, Alexander, "The Kitāb al-Maqūlāt of the Muḫtaṣar al-awsaṭ fī l-manṭiq: A Hitherto Unknown Source for Studying Ibn Sīnā's Reception of Aristotle's Categories." In *Oriens* 40 (2012): 305–354.

Kindī, *Fī Kammiyyat kutub Arisṭū.* In *Rasā'il al-Kindī al-falsafiyya.* Ed. by Muḥammad ʿAbd al-Hādī Abū Rīda. Egypt: Dār al-Fikr al-ʿArabī, 1950.

King, Daniel, *The Earliest Syriac Translation of Aristotle's Categories, Text, Translation and Commentary.* Leiden, Boston, 2010.

Kraus, Paul, "Zu Ibn al-Muqaffaʿ." In *Rivista degli Studi Orientali* 14 /1 (1933): 1–20.

Lawkarī, Abū l-ʿAbbās Faḍl b. Muḥammad, *Bayān al-ḥaqq bi-ḍimān al-ṣidq.* Ed. by Seyyed Ebrāhīm Dībāǧī. Kuala Lumpur, Tehran: The International Institute of Islamic Thought and Civilization (ISTAC), 1995.

Menn, Stephen, "The Stoic Theory of Categories." In *Oxford Studies in Ancient Philosophy* XVII (1999): 215–247.

Marmura, Michael E., *Avicenna, The Metaphysics of the Healing* [*al-Šifāʾ: al-Ilāhiyyāt*], A parallel English-Arabic text. Trans. by Michael Marmura. Provo, Utah: Brigham Young University Press, 2005.

McGinnis, Jon, *The Physics of the Healing* [*al-Šifāʾ: al-Samāʿ al-ṭabīʿī*]. A parallel English-Arabic text translated, introduced, and annotated by Jon McGinnis. Provo, Utah: Brigham Young University Press, 2009.

Moraux, Paul, *Der Aristotelismus bei den Griechen von Andronikos bis Alexander von Aphrodisias I, Die Renaissance des Aristotelismus im 1. Jh. v. Chr.* Berlin, New York: Walter De Gruyter, 1973.

Peters, Francis Edward, Aristoteles Arabus, The oriental translations and commentaries on the Aristotelian Corpus. Leiden: Brill, 1968.

Razī, Faḫr al-Dīn, *Risāla al-Kamāliyya fī Ḥaqāyiq al-Ilāhiyya.* Ed. by ʿAlī Muḥyī al-Dīn. Beirut: Dār al-Kutub al-ʿIlmiyya, 2002.

–, *al-Mabāḥiṯ al-mašriqiyya.* Ed. by Muḥammad al-Muʿtaṣim bi-l-lāh al-Baġdādī, 2 vols. Qom: Manšūrāt Ḏawī al-Qurbā, 2008.

Reisman, David C., *The Making of the Avicennan Tradition: TheTransmission, Contents, and Structure of Ibn Sīnā's al-Mubāḥaṯāt (The Discussions).* Leiden et. al.: Brill, 2002.

Sabra, Abdelhamid Ibrahim, "Avicenna on the Subject Matter of Logic." In *The Journal of Philosophy* 77/11 (Nov. 1980): 746–764.

Sāwī, ʿUmar ibn Sahlān, *Baṣāʾir al-naṣīriyya fī ʿilm al-manṭiq.* With glosses of Muḥammad ʿAbduh. Ed. by Rafīq al-ʿAǧam. Beirut: Dār al-Fikr al-Lubnānī, 1993.

Simplicius, *On Aristotle's "Categories* 1–4." Trans. by Michael Chase. Ithaca; New York: Cornell University Press, 2003.

–, *On Aristotle Categories* 5–6. Trans. by Frans A.J. de Haas and Barrie Fleet. London: Bloomsbury, 2001.

–, *On Aristotle Categories* 7–8. Trans. by Barrie Fleet. London: Bloomsbury, 2014.

Studtmann, Paul, "Aristotle's Categories." In *The Stanford Encyclopedia of Philosophy* (Summer 2014 Edition). Ed. by Edward N. Zalta, URL=<https://plato.stanford.edu/archives/sum2014/entries/aristotle-categories/>.

–, "Aristotle's Categorial Scheme." In *The Oxford Handbook of Aristotle.* Ed. by Christopher Shields. Oxford, New York: Oxford University Press, 2012, 63–80.

Suhrawardī, Šihāb al-Dīn Yaḥyā, *Ḥikmat al-išrāq.* In *Opera metaphysica et mystica* II. Ed. by Henry Corbin. Tehran: Pažūhešgāh-e ʿOlūm-e Ensānī wa Moṭāleʿāt-e Farhangī, 1993. 1–260.

Suhrawardī, Šihāb al-Dīn Yaḥyā, *Lamaḥāt.* In *Opera metaphysica et mystica* IV. Ed. by Nağafqulī Ḥabībī. Tehran: Pažūhešgāh-e ʿOlūm-e Ensānī wa Moṭāleʿāt-e Farhangī, 2001, 141–241.

–, *al-Mašāriʿ wa l-muṭāraḥāt, al-ʿilm al-ṯāliṯ: al-ilāhī* [*Ilāhiyyāt*]. In *Opera metaphysica et mystica* I. Ed. by Henry Corbin. Tehran: Moʾasseseh-ye Moṭāleʿāt-o Taḥqīqāt-e Farhangī, 1993. 193–506.

–, *al-Mašāriʿ wa l-muṭāraḥāt, al-ʿilm al-awwal: al-Manṭiq.* Ed. by Maqṣūd Moḥammadī and Ašraf ʿAlīpūr. Tehran: Ḥaq Yāwarān, 2006.

–, *al-Muqawamāt, al-ʿilm al-ṯāliṯ: al-ilāhī* [*Ilāhiyyāt*]. In *Opera metaphysica et mystica* I. Ed. by Henry Corbin. Tehran: Moʾasseseh-ye Moṭāleʿāt-o Taḥqīqāt-e Farhangī, 1993, 123–192.

–, *Talwīḥāt al-lawḥiyya wa l-ʿaršiyya.* Ed. by Nağafqolī Ḥabībī. Tehran: Moʾasseseh-ye Pažūhešī-ye Ḥekmat-o Falsafeh-ye Iran [Iranian Institute of Philosophy], 2009.

–, *Talwīḥāt al-lawḥiyya wa l-ʿaršiyya, al-ʿilm al-ṯāliṯ: al-ilāhī* [*Ilāhiyyāt*]. In *Opera metaphysica et mystica* I. Ed. by Henry Corbin. Tehran: Moʾasseseh-ye Moṭāleʿāt-o Taḥqīqāt-e Farhangī, 1993, 1–121.

Szlezák, Thomas Alexander, *Pseudo-Archytas über die Kategorien, Texte zur griechischen Aristoteles-Exegese.* Berlin, New York: Brill, 1972.

Thom, Paul, "The division of the categories according to Avicenna." In *Aristotle and the Arabic Tradition.* Ed. by Ahmed Alwishah and Josh Hayes. Cambridge: Cambridge University Press, 2015, 30–49.

Tūsī, Naṣīr al-Dīn, *Šarḥ al-Ishārāt wa l-tanbīhāt.* Ed. by Solaymān Donyā, 3 vols. Cairo: Dār al-Maʿārif, 1983.

–, *Asās al-iqtibās.* Ed by Moḥammad Taqī Modarres Raḍawī. Tehran: Tehran University Press, 1982.

Walbridge, John and Ziai, Hosein, The Philosophy of Illumination. A New Critical Edition of the Hikmat al-ishrāq, with English Translation, Notes, Commentary and Introduction. Provo, Utah: Brigham Young University Press, 1999.

–, "Al-Suhrawardī on Body as Extension: An Alternative to Hylomorphism from Plato to Leibnitz." In: *Reason and Inspiration in Islam. Theology, Philosophy and Mysticism in Muslim Thought. Essays in Honour of Hermann Landolt.* Ed. by Todd Lawson. London, New York: I. B. Tauris and The Institute of Ismaili Studies, 2005, 235–247.

Ziai, Hossein, *Knowledge and Illumination: A Study of Suhrawardi's Ḥikmat al-Ishrāq.* Atlanta, Georgia: Scholars Press, 1990.

–, The Book of Radiance [Partaw-Nāmeh]. A Parallel English-Persian Text, edited and translated with an introduction by Hossein Ziai. Costa Mesa, California: Mazda Publishers, 1998.

Nariman Aavani

Afḍal al-Dīn Kāshānī on the Unification of the Intellect, Intellector, and Intelligible

One can situate the question of the unification of intellect, intelligible and intellector[1] as a branch of theory of knowledge in Islamic philosophy. To state the problem briefly, in a cognitive event, when one knows an object either something is added to the human being or not. Some theologians consider knowledge to belong to the category of 'relation' (*iḍāfah*) and therefore in the process of knowledge nothing is added to the knower.[2] However, if one holds that in knowledge something is acquired then the question remains of the relationship between the knower and that which is known. Some philosophers have tried to explain this question through theories such as 'formal-representation' (*irtisām*), which involves the appearance of an impression of the object known in the knower.[3] Another response that has been provided is through the principle of unification[4]. According to this principle, when the immaterial substances know

1 I am aware that intellector is not strictly speaking a proper English word. However, I did not refrain from using it as it conveys the linguistic and morphological connection between *ʿāqil* and *maʿqūl* in Arabic.

2 In *Taḥṣīl al-muḥaṣṣal*, Ṭūsī ascribes this view to Abu'l-Ḥasan al-Ashʿarī. See also, Fakhr al-Dīn al-Rāzī's *al-Mabāḥith al-mashriqiyyah*, Dār al-Kutub al-ʿArabī, Beirut, 1410 [AH lunar], pp. 446–450, and W. Hutchins' "Fakhr al-Dīn al-Rāzī on Knowledge." 1971, ProQuest Dissertations and Theses, pp. 73–96. In my view, the case of Rāzī is peculiar since despite his judgment in certain texts that knowledge is of the nature of relation, he defends mental existence in his other works, which implies the existence of the form of the intelligible in the perceiver's mind. Therefore, a thorough study of Fakhr al-Dīn Rāzī's epistemology is yet to be carried out before we can conclude with certainty that he advocated the theory of "knowledge as a relation". It is also noteworthy that many philosophers after Fakhr Rāzī attribute this view to him. For a critique of knowledge as a relation between the knower and the known, see Ṭūsī's *Ajwibah al-masāʾil al-naṣīriyyah*, Pajūhishgāh-i ʿUlūm-i Insānī wa Muṭāliʿāt-i Farhangī, Tehran, 1381[AH solar], pp. 85–90.

3 Ibrahim Kalın. *Knowledge in Later Islamic Philosophy : Mulla Sadra on Existence, Intellect, and Intuition.* New York ; Oxford, Oxford University Press, 2010, pp. 30–35. See also, *Sharḥ al-Ishārāt*, Maṭbaʿat al-Ḥaydarī edition, Vol. III, pp. 298–307.

4 For an excellent study of knowledge as unification, see Kalın's. *Knowledge in Later Islamic Philosophy : Mulla Sadra on Existence, Intellect, and Intuition.* New York; Oxford, Oxford University Press.

an intelligible the relationship between this intellect and the intelligible is one of unification.

The principle of the unification of the intellect, intelligible and intellector (which from now on we will refer to as 'the principle of unification'), has appeared in two forms during the history of Islamic philosophy: 1. the self-intellection of immaterial substances; 2. The intellection of entities outside the knower. The first branch of the principle of unification has a long history in Greek philosophy, and some scholars consider its root to be in the pre-Socratic philosopher Parmenides (d. mid 5th century B.C.)[5]; but so far as is directly related to Islamic philosophy, it is Aristotle (d. 322 B.C.) who in chapters 3.4 and 3.5 of *De Anima* raises a question about the possibility of the intellect being its own object of intellection.[6] Self-intellection was criticized by Sextus Empiricus[7] (d.c. 210 C.E.) and later redefined and reaffirmed by Plotinus (d. 270 C.E.)[8], whose ideas, including those on self-intellection, were transmitted to the Islamic world in the redaction of the so-called *Theology of Aristotle*, including the following famous passage:

One should also mention the theory of configuration (*shabaḥ*). According to this view, when an individual perceives an object, not the thing itself but rather its configuration or similitude (*mithl*) appears in the mind. Shams al-Dīn Iṣfahānī in *Maṭāriḥ al-anẓār* and Ibn Mubārakshāh al-Bukhārī in his commentary on *Ḥikmat al-ʿayn* argue for this view. Lāhījī in *Shawāriq al-ilhām* discusses this position and sees no difference between this view and the one held by the philosophers, i. e. the view that in a perception the quiddity of the thing known and the form that appears in the mind are one.

5 See, Ian M. Crystal, *Self-Intellection and Its Epistemological Origins in Ancient Greek Thought.* Hampshire, England; Burlington, VT, Ashgate, 2002 pp. 21–48; A. A. Long, "Parmenides on Thinking Being." *Proceedings of the Boston Area Colloquium of Ancient Philosophy*, vol. 12, no. 1, 1996, pp. 125–151; A. H. Coxon, *Fragments of Parmenides : A Critical Text with Introduction and Translation, the Ancient Testimonia and a Commentary.* Las Vegas, Parmenides Publishing, 2009, pp. 20–23; 296–297; 340.

6 See I. Crystal, *Self-Intellection and Its Epistemological Origins in Ancient Greek Thought.* Hampshire, England; Burlington, VT, Ashgate, 2002 pp. 115–152. In my brief survey, I do not discuss Plato's role in the development of this issue. For a survey of this principle in Plato and its influence on Neoplatonism, see, J. Pépin,"Éléments pour une histoire de la relation entre l'Intelligence et l'Intelligible chez Platon et dans le Néoplatonisme." *Revue Philosophique De La France Et De l'Étranger*, vol. 146, 1956, pp. 39–64.

7 See I. Crystal, *Self-Intellection and Its Epistemological Origins in Ancient Greek Thought.* Hampshire, England ; Burlington, VT, Ashgate, 2002, pp. 155–177.

8 I. Crystal, "Plotinus on the Structure of Self-Intellection." *Phronesis*, vol. 43, no. 3, 1998, pp. 264–286.
E.K. Emilsson, "Plotinus on the Objects of Thought." *Archiv für Geschichte Der Philosophie*, vol. 77, no. 1, 1995, pp. 32–36; idem, "Cognition and its Objects," *The Cambridge Companion to Plotinus* (Cambridge: Cambridge University Press, 1996), pp. 217–49 and Sarah Rappe, "Self-knowledge and Subjectivity in the Enneads," *The Cambridge Companion to Plotinus* (Cambridge: Cambridge University Press, 1996), pp. 250–74.

> Verily, often it happened to me that I withdrew unto myself and I set aside my body, and I became as it were a purely immaterial substance without body, and I go into my essence, returning to it, beyond things other than myself. Then I am utterly knowledge, knower and that which is known. Then, I saw in my essence things from beauty, magnificence and light which leave me astounded.[9]

Following their Greek predecessors, Islamic philosophers dealt with this issue and tentatively one can divide a history of the principle of unification in Islamic philosophy into four periods [though I solely focus on Persia in my discussion of the post-classical period and therefore I do not consider this survey exhaustive]. The first period starts from the beginning of Islamic philosophy and the translation of philosophical texts of the likes of Aristotle and Plotinus from Greek and Syriac into Arabic. This period includes Islamic philosophers such as al-Kindī (d. 256/870), al-Fārābī (d. 339/950) and Abū'l-Ḥasan al-'Āmirī (d. 381/992), ending in the last quarter of 10th century and the beginning of 11th century with the appearance of Ibn Sīnā (d. 416/1037).

The second period starts with the emergence of Ibn Sīnā and ends with the rise of the school of Mullā Ṣadrā (d. 1050/1640). Philosophers such as Ibn Sīnā, Suhrawardī (d. 578/1191), Fakhr al-Dīn al-Rāzī (d. 606/1209), Khwājah Naṣīr al-Dīn al-Ṭūsī (d. 672/1274) and Bābā Afḍal al-Dīn Kāshānī (Bābā Afḍal') (d. 610/1214) belong to this period.

The third period starts with Mullā Ṣadrā and lasts until the appearance of Ḥājī Mullā Hādī Sabziwārī (d. 1289/1873). Mullā Ṣadrā, Mullā Rajab'alī Tabrīzī (d. 1080/1669–70), Āqā Ḥusayn Khwānsārī (d. 1098/1687), Mawlā Muḥsin Fayḍ Kāshānī (d. 1091/1680), Mullā 'Alī Nūrī (d. 1246/1830–31), Mullā Muḥammad Ja'far Lāhījī,[10] Shaykh Aḥmad al-Aḥsā'ī (d. 1242/1826), and Mullā Ismā'īl Iṣfahānī Wāḥid al-'Ayn (d. 1242/1826) among others belong to this period.

The fourth and final period starts with Mullā Hādī Sabziwārī (d. 1289/1873) and continues to the present day. Mullā Hādī Sabziwārī, Mīrzā Abū'l-Ḥasan Jilwah (d. 1314/1896), Mīrzā Mahdī Āshtiyānī (d. 1332 *[11]/1953), Muḥammad Taqī Āmulī (d. 1350*/1971), Abū'l-Ḥasan Sha'rānī (d. 1352*/1973) , Mahdī Ilāhī

9 Plotinus, *Enneads (Theology) The Arabic translation of Ibn Nā'imah al-Ḥimṣī*, edited by Sayyid Jalāl al-Dīn Āshtiyānī, Imperial Iranian Academy of Philosophy, Tehran, 1976, p. 34. See also, Qāḍī Sa'īd al-Qummī's commentary on the same issue, ibid. pp. 144–145. This fragment in the Original Greek text appears in *Enneads* IV.8.1 which slightly differs from the Arabic text. See also Peter Adamson, *The Arabic Plotinus: A Philosophical Study of the 'Theology of Aristotle'*, Duckworth Publishers, 2003 and Dimitri Gutas, *Greek Thought, Arabic Culture: The Graeco-Arabic Translation Movement in Baghdad and Early Abbasaid Society*, Routledge, 1998.

10 We do not have any information about his exact date of death, but Jalāl al-Dīn Humā'ī argues in his introductory remarks on *Sharḥ al-mashā'ir* of Mullā Muḥammad Ja'far Lāhījī that it must be no later than 1294 A.H/1877 A.D.

11 All the dates with the mark (*) are according to the *Shamsī* (solar hijrī) calendar.

Qumsha'ī (d. 1352*/1973) Sayyid Abu'l-Ḥasan Rafī'ī Qazwīnī (d. 1353*/1974), 'Allāmah Ṭabāṭabā'ī (d. 1360*/1981), Murtaḍā Muṭahharī (d. 1358*/1979) , Mahdī Ḥā'irī Yazdī (d. 1378*/1999), Sayyid Jalāl al-Dīn Āshtiyānī (d. 1384*/2005), Ḥasan Ḥasan Zādah Āmulī (b. 1307*/1928) , Ghulāmḥusayn Ibrāhīmī Dīnānī (b. 1313*/1934), Muḥammad Taqī Miṣbāḥ Yazdī (b. 1313*/1934), Sayyid Kamāl Ḥaydarī (b. 1335*/1956) and Ḥasan Zādah Āmulī among others belong to this period.

In the first period, by and large, we observe a general approval and acceptance of this principle among Muslim philosophers. In the writings of al-Kindī, and explicitly in *A Treatise On Intellect* (*Risālah fī'l-'aql*), we find an acceptance of the principle, with al-Kindī stating that the form that has no potential and matter (*hayūlā*), which does not belong to the realm of imagination (*fanṭāsiyā*), namely the intellectual form, becomes unified with the soul such that the form and the intellect become identically one. As such "Intellect and intelligible are identically one in the human souls."[12] al-Fārābī also discusses this principle in different treatises including *Ārā' ahl al-madīnah al-fāḍilah* (*The Views of the People of the Virtuous City*) and *Risālah fī ma'ānī al-'aql* (*A Treatise On the Meanings of Intellect*). In the latter text he avers that the One is intellect, intelligible and intellector at once, and a reality without any actual multiplicity; for that which prevents an entity from reaching this state is its being material, and the One is beyond matter and its attributes.[13] Regarding the human soul he states that "the meaning of the statement 'it [i.e. the soul] is intellector (*'āqil*)' is nothing but saying that the intelligibles have become forms for the soul, in the sense that it [the soul] has become one with those forms. Therefore, it is intellector *in actu*, intellect *in actu*, and intelligible *in actu* in the same meaning (*'alā ma'nā wāḥid bi-'aynih*)."[14]

Abū'l-Ḥasan al-'Āmirī, in chapter thirteen of his *al-Fuṣūl fī al-ma'ālim al-ilāhiyyah* (*Chapters on Metaphysical Teachings*), likewise affirms that any in-

12 Al-Kindī, *Risālah fī'l-'aql*, published in Y. Qamīr, *Al-Kindī*, Dār al-Mashriq, Beirut, 1993, pp. 84–85. However, Al-Kindī does not accept this principle in case of the first intellect. According to him, there is no unification of intellect, intellector and intelligible on the level of the First intellect. See ibid, p. 85.

13 For a discussion of this principle and its application to the Divine in Al-Fārābī's writings , see, Al-Fārābī, *Ārā' ahl al-madīnat al-fāḍilah*, edited by A.N. Nādir, Dār al-Mashriq, Beirut, 1986, pp. 47–49. See also, Y. Qamīr, *al-Fārābī*, Dār Al-Mashriq, Beirut, 1986, pp. 59–60. See also Ibrahim Kalin, *Knowledge In Later Islamic Philosophy*, Oxford University Press, 2010, pp. 37–46. For a study of the meaning of intellect in Al-Fārābī see, H.A. Davidson, *Al-Farabi, Avicenna and Averroes on Intellect*, Oxford University Press, 1992, pp. 44–73.

14 See, Al-Fārābī, *Majmū'at falsafah Abī Naṣr al-Fārābī*, edited by Nājī Aḥmad Al-Jamālī, Maṭba'at al-Sa'ādah, Cairo, 1907, pp. 49–51. For a discussion of the unification of the human soul with the Active Intellect in his writings see, Al-Fārābī, *Ārā' ahl al-madīnah al-fāḍilah*, edited by A.N. Nādir, Dār Al-Mashriq, Beirut, 1986, pp. 47–49.

tellect *in actu* (*bi'l-fi'l*) knows itself and knows that it has knowledge of itself, and thus is at once intellect, intellector and intelligible.[15]

In contrast to the first period, the second period of the history of Islamic philosophy can arguably be characterized by the rejection of the principle of unification. This period in a sense starts with Ibn Sīnā criticizing and refuting the principle in the *Ishārāt*[16] and *Shifā'*.[17] Although Avicenna accepted the principle of unification in the case of God's self-intellection, he considered it impossible in the case of our knowledge of external objects. In fact, in *al-Ishārāt wa 'l-tanbīhāt* he ridicules Porphyry (d. 305 C.E.) for making nonsensical statements on the matter. For Avicenna it is impossible for two distinct things to become one, for after unification the resulting entity is either one of the original entities alone, both of them, or neither (i. e. a third entity). In none of these cases is unification conceivable.

Fakhr al-Dīn al-Rāzī,[18] Suhrawardī[19] and Khwājah Naṣīr al-Dīn al-Ṭūsī[20] follow Ibn Sīnā in refuting the principle of unification, both in rejecting any kind of unification and in refuting the unification of intellector, intelligible and intellect. They generally repeat arguments presented by Ibn Sīnā. The only exception in this period is Afḍal al-Dīn Kāshānī who supports the idea of unification as a metaphysical basis for self-realization, to whose ideas we will return shortly.[21]

The third period starts with the emergence of Mullā Ṣadrā and his school with his redefinition of problems of Islamic philosophy and his integration of all the previous schools on the basis of the idea of 'being' and its dynamics, facilitated

15 Abū'l-Ḥasan al-'Āmirī, *Rasā'il Abī'l-Ḥasan al-'Āmirī wa shadharātih al-falsafiyyah*, edited by Saḥbān Khalīfāt, University of Jordan Press, Amman, 1988, pp. 372–373.

16 See, Ibn Sīnā, *al-Ishārāt wa al-tanbīhāt*, al-Nashr al-Balāghah, Qum, 1383 [A.H. solar], Vol. III, pp. 292–301.

17 See, Ibn Sīnā, *Kitāb al-shifā'*, edited by I. Madkūr, Sulaymānzādah Publication, Qum, 1430, Vol. VI, pp. 212–220.

18 For a discussion of Fakhr al-Dīn Rāzī's views on the principle of unification, see Fakhr al-Dīn al-Rāzī, *Lubāb al-ishārāt wa al-tanbīhāt*, edited by A. Ḥijāzī , Maktabat al-Kulliyyāt al-Azhariyyah, Cairo, 1986, pp. 176–177.

19 See, Suhrawardī, *Majmū'ah-yi muṣannafāt-i Shaykh-i Ishrāq*, edited by H.Corbin and S.H. Nasr, Mu'assisah-yi Muṭāli'āt-i 'Ulūm-i Insānī, Tehran, 1976, Vol. I, (*al-Muṭāriḥāt*), pp. 474–475. See also, Y. Yazdān Panāh, *Ḥikmat-i ishrāq*, Pajūhishgāh-i Ḥawzah wa Dānishgāh, Qum, 1389 [A.H. solar], Vol. II, pp. 320–329.

20 See Khwājah Naṣīr's commentary on the corresponding chapter in *Ishārāt* in Ibn Sīnā, *Ishārāt wa al-tanbīhāt*, al-Nashr al-Balāghah, Qum, 1383 [A.H. solar], Vol. III, pp. 292–301. He also discusses this issue in his treatise *Fuṣūl al-naṣīriyyah*, edited by Muḥammad Taqī Dānish Pajūh, Intishārāt-i Danishgāh-i Tehrān, 1355 [A.H. solar], p. 14.

21 See, Afḍal al-Dīn Kāshānī, *Muṣannafāt*, edited by Y. Mahdawī and M. Mīnuwī, Intishārāt-i Khwārazmī, 1366 [A.H. Solar] Vol. II, 1366, p. 638. Mawlā Muḥsīn Fayḍ in his *'Ayn al-yaqīn* also discusses a proof for this principle and ascribes it to Bābā Afḍal. See, Fayḍ Kāshānī, *'Ayn al-yaqīn*, edited by S.R. 'Ayyāsh, Dār al-Mahajjat al-Bayḍā', Beirut, 2011, p. 51. See also, Ḥasan Zādah Āmulī's *Ittiḥād-i 'āqil bi ma'qūl*, Būstān-i Kitāb, Qum, 1386 [A.H. solar], pp. 325–334.

through the introduction of principles such as the "primacy of being"(*aṣālat al-wujūd*) and the "gradation of being" (*tashkīk fi'l-wujūd*). His treatment of the principle of unification is no exception in this regard in the sense that he reformulates and reintroduces this principle on the basis of his philosophy of being. There are many important premises upon which Mullā Ṣadrā's understanding of the principle of unification is based, among which two are of utmost importance, one being his idea of trans-substantial motion (*al-ḥarakat al-jawhariyyah*) and the other his understanding of the human soul as "material in origin and spiritual in subsistence" (*jismāniyyat al-ḥudūth wa rūḥāniyyat al-baqā'*).

The principle of the 'material origination of the soul' along with the principle of gradation allow Mullā Ṣadrā to argue that matter and spirit are not two separate, and distinct realities. Rather, he states there is a continuity between them, since they are each particular modes of being. Furthermore, the soul comes into being with matter [not to be mistaken with the statement that it is *from* matter] and as a continuity of matter. Therefore, the soul in its early stages of coming into being is not immaterial to the highest of its capacities. This is in stark contrast to the view of Peripatetic philosophers according to which the soul is immaterial and spiritual by origin (*rūḥāniyyat al-ḥudūth wa'l-baqā'*).

The principle of trans-substantial motion enables Mullā Ṣadrā to justify the gradual and gradational perfection of the soul. According to this perspective, change and movement does not happen only in the accidents – as held by the Peripatetic philosophers – but can also occur in substances. Accidents are dependent on substances and any change in the accidents must have its origin in the substance.

On the basis of principles such as these, Mullā Ṣadrā discusses and defines various types of unification, eventually identifying the type of unification that occurs in the unification of the intellect, intellector and intelligible with the unification that exists between matter and form. Thus, the soul is like the matter which accepts different intelligibles and becomes unified with them. One can say that there are two stages (or 'arcs' *qaws*) in the exposition of the principle of the unification in Mullā Ṣadrā. In the first stage (or 'arc of ascent'), the soul receives the intelligible forms from the Active Intellect. This stage consists of the gradual perfection and ascent of the soul to reach the level of the "Acquired Intellect"(*al-'aql al-mustafād*), which is the highest level of the unification of the individual intellect with the Active Intellect.

Whereas in the first stage the soul is passive and receives the forms from the Active Intellect, in the second stage (or 'arc of descent') the soul, having reached the level of complete unification with the active intellect and thus possessing all the intelligibles *in actu*, actively creates and produces the intelligible forms. This is what Mullā Ṣadrā means by the idea of the soul "existentiating the intelligible forms" *(inshā' al-ṣūwar).*

As for the development of the principle of unification in the third period, we can distinguish two main trends among Muslim philosophers. The first approach is held by those who are Ṣadrean philosophers themselves. They both elaborate on and illustrate the teachings of Mullā Ṣadrā on the principle of unification on the one hand and respond to the criticisms made by the opponents of Ṣadrean philosophy on the other. Mullā Muḥsin Fayḍ Kāshānī,[22] Mullā 'Alī Nūrī,[23] Mullā Muḥammad Ja'far Lāhījī,[24] and Mullā Ismā'īl Iṣfahānī[25] among others belong to this group. In contrast to these figures, there are those who either attack directly the principle of the unification of the intellect, intellector an intelligible, or attack premises necessary for proving the principle, such as the "primacy of being" or the principle of "the simple reality" (*basīṭat al-ḥaqīqah*). Rajab 'Alī Tabrīzī,[26] Qāḍī Sa'īd Qumī,[27] Āqā Ḥusayn Khwānsārī[28] and Shaykh Aḥmad Aḥsā'ī[29] belong to this group. Probably, the most severe attacks on the principle of unification in this period come from Shaykh Aḥmad Aḥsā'ī, who in his commentaries on Mullā

22 See, Fayḍ Kāshānī, *'Ayn al-yaqīn*, edited by S.R. 'Ayyāsh, Dār al-Mahajjat al-Bayḍā', Beirut, 2011, pp. 50–54.

23 See his glosses on the Principle of Unification in *Ḥikmat al-'arshiyyah of* Mullā Ṣadrā, published in Mullā Ismā'īl Wāḥid al-'Ayn', *Sharḥ ḥikmat al-'arshiyyah ma'a ta'līqāt al-ḥakīm al-ilāhī al-Mullā 'Alī al-Nūrī*, edited by M.M. Khudāwirdī, The Iranian Institute of Philosophy, Tehran, 1391 [A.H. solar], p. 21. Though it seems that the part of his commentary in which he comments on the principle in details is lost.

24 See, Muḥammad Ja'far Lāhījī, *Sharḥ risālat al-mashā'ir*, edited by Sayyid Jalāl al-Dīn Āshtiyānī, Intishārāt-i Amīr Kabīr, Tehran, 1376 [A.H. solar], pp. 237–249.

25 See, Mullā Ismā'īl Wāḥid al-'Ayn, *Sharḥ ḥikmat al-'arshiyyah ma'a ta'līqāt al-ḥakīm al-ilāhī al-Mullā 'Alī al-Nūrī*, edited by M.M. Khudāwirdī, The Iranian Institute of Philosophy, Tehran, 1391 [A.H. solar], pp. 536–541. For his proof of the principle of unification, see Ḥasan Zādah Āmulī's *Ittiḥād-i 'āqil bi ma'qūl*, Būstān-i Kitāb, Qum, 1386 [A.H. solar], p. 235. Ḥasan Zādah in this chapter quotes from Mullā Ismā'īl's glosses on *Mashā'ir* which still remain in the manuscript form and have not been published so far.

26 See, Jalāl al-Dīn Humā'ī, *Daw risālah dar falsafah-yi islāmī*, Mu'assisah-yi 'Ulūm-i Insānī Wa Muṭāli'āt-i Farhangī, Tehran, 1375 [A.H. solar], p. 26.

27 See, Gh. Ibrāhīmī Dīnānī, *Mājarā-yi fikr-i falsafī dar islām*, Intishārāt-i Ṭarḥ-i Naw, Tehran, 1385, Vol. III, pp. 236–259, where he discusses Qāḍī Sa'īd's criticisms of the "primacy of being", "the univocity of being" (*al-ishtirāk al-ma'nawī*) in his works such as his commentary on *Tawḥīd* of *Shaykh al-Ṣadūq*, *Sharḥ al-arba'īn* and his *Kilīd-i bihisht.* Dīnānī also discusses Qāḍī Sa'īd's theory of knowledge, which is incompatible with the Principle of Unification.

28 See, Jalāl al-Dīn Humā'ī, *op.cit.*, p. 27.

29 For his criticism of the Principle of Unification, see, Aḥsā'ī, *Sharḥ al-'arshiyyah*, edited by S.A. al-Dabāb, Mu'assisat Shams Hijr, Beirut, 2005, Vol. I, pp. 320–343. See also, Aḥsā'ī, *Sharḥ al-mashā'ir*, edited by T.N. al-Bū'alī, Muassisat al-Balāgh, Beirut, 2007, Vol. I, pp. 224–233. He also has an extensive discussion against the Principle of the Simple Reality (*qā'idat basīṭat al-ḥaqīqah*), which plays an important role in Mullā Ṣadrā's proof of the principle of unification. See, Aḥsā'ī, *Ma'nā basīṭ al-ḥaqīqah kull al-ashiyā'*, edited by S.A. al-Dabāb, Dār al-Maḥajjat al-Bayḍā', Beirut, 2009.

Ṣadrā's *Kītāb al-mashā'ir* (*Metaphysical Penetrations*) and *Kitāb al-'arshiyyah* (*The Wisdom of The Throne*) criticizes the principle of unification along with the other principles underlying it. These criticism were then refuted by Mullā Ismā'īl Iṣfahānī in his commentaries on the same works in a mode of response that resembles the role played by Naṣīr al-Dīn Ṭūsī addressing the criticisms of Fakhr al-Dīn Rāzī.

The fourth and the last period is mostly concerned with one issue, that is, with the validity of one of the most central proofs for the principle of unification, namely the proof by way of "correlation" (*taḍāyuf*). Probably the most important thinker in this period is Hājī Mullā Hādī Sabziwārī, considered by many as the greatest exponent of the school of Mullā Ṣadrā since Mullā Ṣadrā's death, whose teachings have played the most central role in spreading the latter's teachings in Persia, particularly, through his book *Sharḥ al-manẓūmah* (*The Commentary on Manẓūmah*). This work is in a sense a summary of the *Asfār*, and until recently was the most popular text in the philosophy curriculum in Iran. Ḥājī Mullā Hadī discussed and affirmed the principle of unification in several of his works, including his commentary on the *Mathnawī* of Jalāl al-Dīn Rūmī,[30] his glosses on Mullā Ṣadrā's *Asfār*[31] and *Shawāhid al-rubūbiyyah* (*The Divine Witnesses*),[32] and in his theological work in Persian, the *Asrār al-ḥikam* (*The Secrets of Wisdom*).[33] However, in his commentary on the *Manẓūmah*[34] he criticizes the Mullā Ṣadrā's proof of correlation (*taḍāyuf*) for the principle of unification. Although he answers his own criticisms later on, because of his status in philosophy and his role as one of the main exponents of Ṣadrean philosophy, his criticism has left an indelible mark on the philosophers who came after him. The influence of his writings was such that it would not be inaccurate to say that from the time he wrote to the present, the principle of unification has been discussed in Iran mainly in the context of the proof of correlation, involving responses given to questions raised by him. Of course, there are exceptions to this rule, such as in the case of Mīrzā Abū'l-Ḥasan Jilwah, who in his glosses on *Asfār*[35] criticizes the

30 Mullā Hādī Sabziwārī, *Sharḥ-i mathnawī*, edited by M. Burūjirdī, Sāzmān-i Chāp wa Intishārāt, Tehran, 1374, Vol. I, pp. 241–242.

31 See, Mullā Ṣadrā, *al-Ḥikmat al-muta'āliyah*, edited by Muḥammad Riḍā Muẓaffar, Intishārāt-i Sulaymānzādah, Qum, 1430 [A.H. lunar], Vol. III, pp. 247–320, where Sabziwārī's glosses are published as footnotes.

32 See, Sabziwārī's glosses in, Mullā Ṣadrā, *Shawāhid al-rubūbiyyah bā ḥawāshī Ḥājī Mullā Hādī Sabziwārī*, edited by Sayyid Jalāl al-Dīn Āshtiyānī, Būstān-i Kitāb, Qum, 1388 [A.H. solar], p. 717.

33 Sabziwārī, *Asrār al-ḥikam*, edited by Karīm Fayḍī, Intishārāt-i Maṭbū'āt-i Dīnī, Tehran, 1383 [A.H. solar], p. 150.

34 Sabziwārī, *Sharḥ ghurar al-farā'id*, edited by M. Muḥaqqiq and T. Izutsu, Anjuman-i Āthār wa Mafākhir-i Millī, Tehran, 1384, p. 66.

35 M.A. Jilwah, *Majmū'a-yi āthār*, edited by Ḥasan Riḍāzādah, Intishārāt-i Ḥikmat, Tehran, 1385 [A.H. solar], pp. 225–236.

principle of the unification purely on the basis of Peripatetic philosophy, or Muḥyī al-Dīn Mahdī Ilāhī Qumsha'ī, who in his commentary on the *Fuṣūṣ al-ḥikam* (*Bezeles of Wisdom*) of al-Fārābī, dedicates a chapter to this principle and interprets it on the basis of Mullā Ṣadrā's philosophy, more or less without regard for the issues related to the proof of correlation.[36] Abūl-Ḥasan Sha'rānī should be added to this list, since he discusses this principle mainly on the basis of the saying of the Shi'ite Imāms, particularly the *Nahj al-balāghah* (*The Path of Eloquence*), along with some philosophical remarks on the articulation of this principle in *Asrār al-ḥikam* of Ḥājī Mullā Hādī Sabziwārī.[37]

Correlation (*taḍāyuf*)[38] is a relation between two entities in which consideration of one side necessarily implies consideration of the other. Two things are correlative (*mutaḍāyif*) when they have the same stance in potentiality, actuality, being or non-being etc. For instance, the classic example of two correlative things is the relationship that exists between a father and a child. It is impossible to fully understand the meaning of the word "father" without taking into consideration the concept "child", since it is only in relation to this word that fatherhood gains its meaning.

According to Mullā Ṣadrā, the intellector and intelligible are correlatives in the sense that it is impossible for an entity to be an intellector *in actu* without being unified with the intelligibles; if the intellector is not actually unified with the intelligibles it is not in fact an intellector *in actu.*[39]

Sabziwārī criticizes this statement by pointing out that we cannot come to the conclusion that two things are unified in being (*muttaḥid wujūdan*) merely from the fact that they are correlative. Rather we may only come to the conclusion that they co-exist. This is clear from the example of father and child, where the two are correlative realities but are clearly not unified in being, but merely co-exist. Correlation as such is therefore insufficient to prove unification.[40]

---

36 M.M. Ilāhī Qumsha'ī, *Sharḥ-i fuṣūṣ al-ḥikam-i Fārābī*, Intishārāt-i Hirmis, Tehran, 1388 [A.H. solar], pp. 429–437.

37 See Sha'rānī's treatises on the principle of unification, published in Ḥasan Zādah Āmulī's *Ittiḥād-i 'āqil bi ma'qūl*, Būstān-i Kitāb, Qum, 1386 [A.H. solar], pp. 342–351.

38 For a discussion of this concept see, Muẓaffar, *al-Manṭiq*, Dār Al-Ta'āruf, Qum, 2006, pp. 41–57.

39 For a discussion of the proof of correlation and the role that it plays in understanding the principle of unification in Mullā Ṣadrā, see, Mullā Ṣadrā, *al-Ḥikmat al-muta'āliyah*, edited by Muḥammad Riḍā Muẓaffar, Intishārāt-i Sulaymānzādah, Qum, 1430 [A.H. lunar], Vol. III, p. 307.

40 Sabziwārī, *Sharḥ ghurar al-farā'id*, edited by M. Muḥaqqiq and T. Izutsu, Anjuman-i Āthār wa Mafākhir-i Millī, Tehran, 1384, p. 66 and, Mullā Ṣadrā, *al-Ḥikmat al-muta'āliyah*, edited by Muḥammad Riḍā Muẓaffar, Intishārāt-i Sulaymānzādah, Qum, 1430 [A.H. lunar], Vol. III, p. 307–308.

Mīrzā Mahdī Āshtiyānī[41] and Muḥammad Taqī Āmulī[42] are significant examples of philosophers in the fourth period of Islamic philosophy who in their respective glosses on the *Sharḥ al-manẓūmah* respond to the criticisms of Sabziwārī whilst pointing out that Sabziwārī himself changed his mind and finally affirmed this principle.

Turning to the approaches of other thinkers, 'Allamah Rafī'ī Qazwīnī[43] in his short treatise on the principle of unification, having explained different types of unification between two things, considers the unification that exists between the intellector and the intelligible as a unification between two hierarchical realities, one being *in actu* (i. e. the intelligible forms) and the other being *in potential* (i. e. the intellect). In this manner, he defends the proof by correlation of the unification of the intellector and intelligible.

'Allāmah Ṭabāṭabā'ī, in his glosses on Mullā Ṣadrā's *Asfār*,[44] considers Mullā Ṣadrā's proof of the principle of unification unconvincing and thus discusses his own proof in the eleventh chapter of *Nihāyat al-ḥikmah* (*The End of Wisdom*),[45] which has the principle of unification as its main theme. Sayyid Kamāl Ḥaydarī,[46] one of the most prominent students of Javādī Āmulī and a Shi'ite *marja'*, has written an extensive commentary upon this chapter.

Murtaḍā Muṭahharī in his commentaries on *Sharḥ al-manẓūmah*[47] accepts that the proof of correlation is incomplete but attempts to provide possible completioning steps to the argument. Sayyid Jalāl al-Dīn Āshtiyānī[48] on the other hand disagrees with proof of correlation, and furthermore argues that, in every step in the process of perception the soul is not passively receiving the forms, rather it is active and it existentiates the forms (*inshā' al-ṣuwar*).[49] As he sees it, through consideration of this point the issue of correlation can be resolved.

41 M.M. Āshtiyānī, *Ta'līqāt-i Mīrzā Mahdī Mudarris-i Āshtiyānī bar sharḥ-i manẓūmah-yi Sabziwārī*, edited by A. Falāṭūrī and M. Muḥaqqiq, Markaz-i A'lām-i Islām, Tehran, 1424 [A.H. lunar], pp. 95–101.

42 M.T. Āmulī, *Durar al-fawā'id*, edited by Ḥasan Muṣṭafawī, Chāpkhānah-yi Muṣṭafawī, Tehran, 1377 [A.H. lunar], pp. 123–131.

43 A. Rafī'ī Qazwīnī, *Rasā'il*, edited by Ḥ. Riḍānijād, Mu'assisah-yi Pajūhishī-yi Ḥikmat Wa Falsafa-yi Irān, Tehran, 1387 [A.H. solar], pp. 27–32.

44 Mullā Ṣadrā, *al-Ḥikmat al-muta'āliyah*, edited by Muḥammad Riḍā Muẓaffar, Intishārāt-i Sulaymānzādah, Qum, 1430 [A.H. lunar], Vol. III, p. 248.

45 'Allāmah Ṭabāṭabā'ī, *Nihāyat al-ḥikmah*, edited by 'Alī Zāri'ī, Muassasat al-Nashr al-Islāmī, Qum, 1417 [A.H. lunar], pp. 291–320.

46 S.K. Ḥaydarī, *Sharḥ nihāyat al-ḥikmah: 'aql wa'l-'āqil wa'l-ma'qūl*, Nashr-i Sitārah, Qum, 2010.

47 M. Muṭahharī, *Majmū'ah-yi āthār*, Intishārāt-i Ṣadrā, Tehran, 1391 [A.H. solar], Vol. IX (*Sharḥ-i mabsūṭ-i manẓūmah*), pp. 355–399.

48 S.J. Āshtiyānī, *Sharḥ-i ḥāl wa ārā-yi falsafī-yi Mullā Ṣadrā*, Būstān-i Kitāb, Qum, 1387 [A.H. solar], pp. 129–169.

49 See, Mullā Ṣadrā, *Shawāhid al-rubūbiyyah bā ḥawāshī-yi Ḥājī Mullā Hādī Sabziwārī*, edited by Sayyid Jalāl al-Dīn Āshtiyānī, Būstān-i Kitāb, Qum, 1388 [A.H. solar], pp. 156–158.

Ibrāhīmī Dīnānī[50] also discusses the proof of correlation and considers it to be problematic. He explains that the relationship between intellector and the intelligible is that of an illuminative relation (*iḍāfah-yi ishrāqī*).[51]

What is missing in our short depiction of this history is on the one hand the full elucidation of the development of this principle from the time of Avicenna to Mullā Ṣadrā, in particular in figures such as Dawānī (d. 1502/1503 C.E.) and Mīr Dāmād (d. 1631/1632 C.E.), and on the other hand the genealogy of the sources upon which Mullā Ṣadrā draws in order to substantiate his proof for the principle of unification. This article aims to add one brick to this unfinished wall by explaining the 12th century philosopher Afḍal al-Dīn Kāshānī's view of this principle and its role within his philosophy, and also thus to clarify one of the sources for the later development of this principle.

1. Introducing Bābā Afḍal

We know very little about the life of Afḍal al-Dīn Muḥammad Ibn Ḥasan Kāshānī also known as Bābā Afḍal. He was born in Maraq, a village in northwest of Kāshān, Iran; most probably died in 610 AH/1213–1214 AD; and the biographies mention that Naṣīr al-Dīn Ṭūsī (d. 627/1274) was related to him. Indeed, in *Sayr wa Sulūk*, Ṭūsī states that as a young man he studied with Kamāl al-Dīn Muḥammad Ḥāsib, a student of Bābā Afḍal.

From his works it appears that he wrote mainly for a small group of disciples, many of whom may not have known Arabic or had significant training in the intellectual sciences, and Bābā Afḍal almost never mentions previous philosophers by name, with the exception of Aristotle. Each of Bābā Afḍal's books dealing with ontology, epistemology and self-knowledge, namely the *Madārij al-kamāl* (*The Rungs of Perfection*), the *Rah-anjām-nāmah* (*The Book of the Road's End*), the *'Arḍ-nāmah* (*The Book of Displays*), the *Jāwidān-nāmah* (*The Book of the Everlasting*), and the *al-Minhāj al-Mubīn* (*The Clarifying Method*) begin from first principles and definitions, leading even the reader with little training through the stages of their argument to their final conclusions. As such each of these works is more a single philosophical journey than a collection of discussions on particular philosophical fields. These works, in addition to the book of ethics, the *Sāz u pīrāyah-yi shāhān-i purmāyah* (*The Makings and Ornaments of Well-Provisioned Kings*), several translations of Arabic Neoplatonic works and numerous philosophical treatises are all in Persian (though there is an un-

50 Gh. Dīnānī, *Qawā'id-i kullī dar falsafah-yi islāmī*, Pajūhishgāh-i 'Ulūm-i Insānī, Tehran, 1372 [A.H. solar], pp. 411–415.
51 Ibid.

published Arabic version of the *Madārij al-kamāl*, making Bābā Afḍal one of the most important contributors to Islamic philosophy in Persian.

Bābā Afḍal has received relatively little scholarly attention in the West: to begin with, the importance of 'autology' as the basis of his thought was presented by Seyyed Hossein Nasr in an article on Bābā Afḍal in 1984, in which the significance of the issue of unification is also mentioned[52]. Fortunately, however, William Chittick translated around two thirds of Bābā Afḍal's works into English, accompanied by notes and an extensive introduction in 2001 in *The Heart of Islamic Philosophy*, which is the most thorough study of Bābā Afḍal in any European language. This scholarship prepares the ground for the more detailed examination of the specific issue of unification, that I am engaged in here. I have benefitted from Chittick's translations in my presentation here where it proved useful, though both of the arguments I will consider for the principle of unification are taken from sections of the *ʿArḍ-nāmah* that are not translated by him.

2. Bābā Afḍal's Philosophical Project

In order to understand Bābā Afḍal's arguments for the unification of the intellect, intellector and intelligible we need to first understand how this doctrine fits into his wider philosophical project. Like the Islamic philosophers who preceded him, Bābā Afḍal presents his philosophical vision using a collection of concepts drawn from diverse sources, which in his case include not only Peripatetic philosophy but also material from the Qurʾan and hadith, hermeticism, and diverse Islamic intellectual traditions. However, both Bābā Afḍal's philosophy and the language he uses to present it are in many ways *sui generis*, involving insights and modes of expression that appear quite unique, conveyed (generally) in a philosophical Persian that he has crafted precisely for its content.

His various philosophical writings, including six major books and numerous treatises, each take a different approach but lead towards a single goal, the understanding of 'general being' and the nature of the self. We are therefore left with many options of where to begin in presenting his philosophical project, with each possible starting point holding unique insights and yet leading towards a single end. For the purpose of this paper, I have decided to focus on the *Madārij al-kamāl* (*The Rungs of Perfection*), both because of the clarity of Bābā Afḍal's exposition here, and because of the pertinence of this text for the more specific

52 S.H. Nasr, Afdal al-Din Kashani and the Philosophical World of Khwaja Nasir al-Din Tusi," in Michael E. Marmura, ed., *Islamic Theology and Philosophy: Studies in Honor of George F. Hourani*, Albany 1984, pp. 249–64.

topic of the unification of intellect, intellector and intelligible, but I will also benefit from his other writings where necessary.

Let us begin with a passage in which Bābā Afḍal uses the Aristotelian conception of *telos* (*ghāyat*) to alert his reader to the importance of self-knowledge, which will play such an important role in his philosophical project.

> And with respect to the telos of every creature there is another telos that is nobler and worthy, except for the telos of the creation and cultivation of you, which is the utmost of every telos and the accomplishment of every intention. And that being includes (*ʿāmm*) all beings, for it is not one and not many, not little and not much, not perfection and not deficiency, not nature and not choice, not lasting and not transient. Nothing is outside of it and it is transcendent (*farāz*) and encompassing with respect to everything; all are collected under its encompassing. So, I remain in wonderment of a seeker of such a base as this, and one who has awoken to such news, as to why he should be negligent and how he should be asleep.[53]

By phrasing his equation of the end of human existence and all-encompassing being in the language of *telos* Bābā Afḍal here emphasizes the fact that our true nature is something we must travel towards and attain. In this sense, we are like all beings, which must traverse a particular course in order to attain the fullness of their forms, but whereas other beings, including plants and animals, travel towards a particular formal perfection, the perfection humans are travelling towards is the encompassing perfection of being itself, which includes all of the *teloi* of other beings whilst at the same time transcending all differentiation.

Already in this dense passage we see Bābā Afḍal combining several philosophical topics, including epistemology, ontology and psychology, an approach that is characteristic of his methods. We have no other option to engage with each of these topics one by one in order to get a well-rounded sense of his philosophical project.

In Bābā Afḍal's writings it becomes clear that the movement towards the *telos* described here is in fact the motivating force behind his philosophy; the journey towards the human *telos*, the encompassing being, is deeply intertwined with the philosophical process, as he explains in the following passage from the *Madārij al-kamāl:*

> And the coming and going from the Origin and its return to it is not by corporeal motion and transition from one place to another, but rather is a spiritual journey and motion of which the name is 'thought' (*fikr*). It has many stages and waystations, and of those stages some are corporeal and some are spiritual, and it is with 'thought' that one can pass over them all.[54]

---

53 *Madārij al-kamāl* in Bābā Afḍal, *Muṣannafāt*, edited by Yahya Mahdavi and Mojtaba Minovi, Khwarazmi Press, 1366 [A.H. solar], Tehran, p. 4.

54 *Madārij al-kamāl* in *Muṣannafāt*, pp. 26–7.

Philosophical discourse, which is the cultivation of 'thought', therefore has a crucial place in human development towards perfection; the spiritual journey and the philosophical journey are one and the same. In order to understand how the intellectual journey brings about the perfection of the human, we will need to understand Bābā Afḍal's epistemology, and particularly his doctrine of the unification of the intellect, intellector and intelligible. However, this can only be clarified once we have a sense of his ontology, from which his epistemology is inseparable.

One of Bābā Afḍal's presentations of his ontology, which is particularly helpful for understanding the meaning of the statement that the human *telos* is "a being that includes all beings," is found in, *The Book of the Road's End* (*Rah-anjām-nāmah*). There he divides 'the existent' (*mawjūd*) into two types: "being" and "finding". "Being" refers to the existence of those entities that do not possess awareness, such as material things, the most important quality of which is their particularity. "Finding" refers to things that are found and known by the soul, and is further divided into particular finding, meaning sensation and imagination, and universal, which entails intellection. Amongst these levels Bābā Afḍal establishes a hierarchy, of which the criterion is the level of dependence on the external world and instruments of knowing, moving from the particulars and culminating in the intellected universals. In this hierarchy, that which is less dependent on instruments of knowing and is more immaterial is both higher and more encompassing. That which is most immaterial, universal and encompassing, which will thus be the being that encompasses all other beings, is the human self.

The ontology presented in *The Book of the Road's End* (*Rah-Anjām-Nāmah*) is complemented and clarified by another approach to dividing up being, presented in the *Madārij al-kamāl* (*The Rungs of Perfection*). Here the criterion for distinguishing between the various levels of existence is 'apparentness' versus 'concealedness'. The most concealed entities are those that exist only *in potentia*, such as a tree existing within a seed. The next level, consisting of corporeal objects, is classified as that which is 'concealed to itself but apparent to another' – that is to say, physical objects – are not self-aware, but self-aware beings can perceive them. The third and final degree belongs to beings that are self-aware and to which self-awareness is identical, namely intellects. Although we may expect that the human soul belongs to this class, Bābā Afḍal explains that the soul only potentially possesses this characteristic, and it is only when it actualizes its intellectuality that it can truly be considered self-aware. On the basis of this distinction we can see that the soul is only potentially intellecting, and requires a process of actualization in order to reach the highest stage of being according to this categorization.

Bābā Afḍal takes several approaches to explaining how the soul actualizes this potential. In one passage in the *Madārij al-kamāl* he states, "That which increases knowledge and awareness is the souls looking at the lasting things through the selfhood of self without the tool of sensation and the intermediary of imagination and sense-intuition, and its seeking the knowledge of certainty without doubt."[55] Hence, it is the contemplation of the intelligibles that increases the soul's awareness, bringing it towards actuality in intellection.

He then compares this process to the process of nutrition, in which the 'nourishment-seeking bodies' actualize their potential for growth through taking in food. Crucially, just as the body gains no benefit from food until it has assimilated it and hence becomes unified with it, "Until the known thing joins with the soul's reality, potency, and substance and becomes like its substance, the soul has no share of the profit and benefit of that knowledge."[56] In the process of intellection, the reality (or essence) of the known object is separated from the accidents, which gradually fade from the imagination and memory of the knower, while the reality is unified with the soul, giving certainty.

In the light of Bābā Afḍal's presentation of ontology and the human *telos* that we have discussed, it is clear that this process of the assimilation of intelligible realities implies the soul's movement to higher levels of being and the attainment of the goal for which it was created. Crucially, this movement towards universality is described as self-knowledge, for as Bābā Afḍal explains:

> the one aware of and knowing the universal of the universals is not a universal below it and less than it in generality and compass…Rather, the knower of the universal of universals is nothing other that the universal of universals. He who is aware of it is not aware of something belonging to self, but rather, he is aware of self…This is the perfection of perfections and the final goal of all final goals…he perfection of the act of perception and intellection is in the unification of the intellector, the intellect, and the intellected. It is this that is complete being, perpetual joy…[57]

Here we see Bābā Afḍal again combining the domains of ontology, epistemology and the perfection of the human soul in a single discussion. Most importantly for the topic of this paper, Bābā Afḍal describes this process of perfection and the attainment of the goal in the philosophical language of the unification of intellector, the intellect, and the intellected. This doctrine therefore plays a central role in his philosophical project, describing not only the manner by which human perfection is attained but also clarifying the nature of that perfection.

---

55 W.C. Chittick, *The Heart of Islamic Philosophy,* Oxford University Press, 2001, p. 264; *Muṣannafāt*, p. 41.

56 Chittick, pp. 264–5, *Muṣannafāt,* p. 41.

57 Chittick, p. 270; *Muṣannafāt*, p. 51.

3. Arguments for Unification

Argument 1

In the *ʿArḍ-Nāmah* (*Book of Displays*), Bābā Afḍal explains that the relationship between the knower or intellector and the known entities as being a relationship between universal and particulars, such that the knower encompasses the known entity, explaining that just as a universal has many instantiations a single knower can know many entities. Going to some length to explain the nature of this encompassing, he argues that there must be no separation between knower and known, that is to say they are unified. His argument takes the form of a *reductio ad absurdum:*

> Either: a) the knower and known are united and the known is within the essence of the knower, which is the point to be proved,
> Or, b) the known is outside the knower.
> If b) then either, i) the knower has no relation to the known,
> Or, ii) "the knower must go out of itself/essence in order to join it, for it is outside its essence"
> Or, iii) the known is "brought into the essence and joined to itself."

However, i), ii) and iii) are all absurd: if there is no relation between the knower and the known then no knowledge has taken place, which is contrary to our initial supposition. Likewise it is meaningless to speak of something 'going outside its essence' to join another object and it is similarly impossible for an external object to be joined to an essence. As such, all possible ways in which the known could be outside the knower are absurd, and therefore the knower and known must be united, such that the known is within the knower.[58][59]

58 See, *Muṣannafāt*, p. 232.

59 One might ask how (iii) would be any different from the unification principle since it declares that the known is brought to the self and becomes one with it. The response to this question is that for Bābā Afḍal any entity that is other than the self lies outside the self and therefore is distinct from it. Anything that is other than the self can never become one with the self since it would require a unification of the essence with something that is non-essence, a unification that Bābā Afḍal considers impossible and meaningless. Therefore, an intelligible is not something that comes to the soul from the outside world but rather the intelligible's very existence is through the soul's act of intellection. This is what Bābā Afḍal means by the principle of the unification and it is distinct from the claim(iii). See also his *Muṣannafāt* pp. 25; 37.

Argument 2

In another passage in the *ʿArḍ-Nāmah* (*Book of Displays*), Bābā Afḍal explains the unification of the intellector and intelligible, or knower and known, by considering the relationship between the knowledge of the knower and the being of the known. Considering the difference between potential knowledge and actual knowledge, we can note that in potential knowledge the known entity is only potentially known, whereas in actual knowledge the known entity is actually known. There is thus a correlation between the state of knowledge and the state of the known. From another point of view, something that exists within the soul is known and likewise something that is known exists within the soul. That is to say, what it means for something to be known is for it to exist within the soul – being known and existence within the soul mean the same thing. As such, Bābā Afḍal states that "as for the essentially known, its being is not separate from its being known, and its existence *is* its being known, and knowing it is for it to exist."[60]

Taking this passage in the *ʿArḍ-nāmah* as a basis, a more complete argument can be constructed using material taken from other passages in Bābā Afḍal's works, which would have the following form:

1. The Intellect in actus is an immaterial substance.
2. The intellect and the intelligible are correlated in potentiality in the sense that if one is *in actu*, the other is *in actu* and vice versa in terms of potentiality.
3. The intelligible is immaterial but it is not a substance to itself, so it needs a locus of existence in order to exist.
4. The soul is the locus of existence of the intelligible, in the sense that they exist in the intellect or actualized soul.
5. Anything that exists in the actualized soul (intellect) is one with it since it is an immaterial substance that has not parts or measure.
6. Therefore, the intelligible and intellector are unified.

Concluding Remarks: The Wider Significance of Bābā Afḍal's Discussion of Unification

Bābā Afḍal – perhaps accompanied by his contemporary Suhrawardī- was the first philosopher after Ibn Sīnā's influential attack on unification to advocate the principle of unification. He presents substantial philosophical arguments for the principle, which takes a vitally important place in his philosophical project, allowing him to explain philosophically the spiritual movement of the soul through the levels of being towards its *telos*, all-encompassing being.

60 *Muṣannafāt*, p. 202.

However, in addition to the intrinsic philosophical interest of Bābā Afḍal's arguments for the principle of unification as components in his philosophical project, these arguments also possess historical importance, allowing us to gain a clearer idea of Mullā Ṣadrā's influences in his formulation of his much debated 'proof by correlation', for we know that Mullā Ṣadrā was a close reader of Bābā Afḍal's works and even translated large sections of the *Jāwīdān-nāmah* into Arabic in his *Iksīr al-ʿārifīn*. Studying Bābā Afḍal and the principle of unification thus allows us to appreciate one of the most important formulations of this principle in the Islamic tradition, while also clarifying the genealogy of epistemology in Islamic philosophy.

Bibliography

Adamson, P., *The Arabic Plotinus: A Philosophical Study of the 'Theology of Aristotle'*, Duckworth Publishers, 2003.

Aḥsāʾī, *Sharḥ al-ʿarshiyyah*, edited by S.A. al-Dabāb, Muʾassisat Shams Hijr, Beirut, 2005.

–, *Sharḥ al-mashāʿir*, edited by T.N. al-Būʿalī, Muʾassisat al-Balāgh, Beirut, 2007.

–, *Maʿnā basīṭ al-ḥaqīqah kull al-ashiyāʾ*, edited by S.A. al-Dabāb, Dār al-Maḥajjat al-Bayḍāʾ, Beirut, 2009.

ʿĀmirī, *Rasāʾil Abīʾl-Ḥasan al-ʿĀmirī wa shadharātih al-falsafiyyah*, edited by Saḥbān Khalīfāt, University of Jordan Press, Amman, 1988.

Āmulī, M.T., *Durar al-fawāʾid*, edited by Ḥasan Muṣṭafawī, Chāpkhānah-yi Muṣṭafawī, Tehran, 1377 [A.H. lunar].

Āshtiyānī, M., *Taʿlīqāt-i Mīrzā Mahdī Mudarris-i Āshtiyānī bar sharḥ-i manẓūmah-yi Sabziwārī*, edited by A. Falāṭūrī and M. Muḥaqqiq, Markaz-i Aʿlām-i Islām, Tehran, 1424 [A.H. lunar].

Āshtiyānī, S.J., *Sharḥ-i ḥāl wa āra-yi falsafī-yi Mullā Ṣadrā*, Bustān-i Kitāb, Qum, 1387 [A.H. solar].

Chittick, W., *The Heart of Islamic Philosophy,* Oxford University Press, 2001.

Coxon, A. H., *Fragments of Parmenides : A Critical Text with Introduction and Translation, the Ancient Testimonia and a Commentary.* Las Vegas, Parmenides Publishing, 2009.

Crystal, I.M., *Self-Intellection and Its Epistemological Origins in Ancient Greek Thought.* Hampshire, England; Burlington, VT, Ashgate, 2002.

Davidson, H.A., *Al-Farabi, Avicenna and Averroes on Intellect*, Oxford University Press, 1992.

Dīnānī, Gh., *Mājarā-yi fikr-i falsafī dar islām*, Intishārāt-i Ṭarḥ-i Naw, Tehran, 1385 [A.H. solar].

–, *Qawāʿid-i kullī dar falsafah-yi islāmī*, Pajūhishgāh-i ʿUlūm-i Insānī, Tehran, 1372 [A.H. solar].

Emilsson, E.K., "Plotinus on the Objects of Thought." *Archiv für Geschichte Der Philosophie*, vol. 77, no. 1, 1995, pp. 32–36.

–, "Cognition and its Objects," *The Cambridge Companion to Plotinus,* Cambridge University Press, Cambridge, 1996, pp. 217–49.

Fārābī, *Ārā' ahl al-madīnat al-fāḍilah*, edited by A.N. Nādir, Dār al-Mashriq, Beirut, 1986.

Fayḍ Kāshānī, *'Ayn al-yaqīn*, edited by S.R. 'Ayyāsh, Dār al-Mahajjat al-Bayḍā', Beirut, 2011.

Gutas, D., *Greek Thought, Arabic Culture: The Graeco-Arabic Translation Movement in Baghdad and Early Abbasaid Society*, Routledge, 1998.

Ḥasan Zādah Āmulī, *Ittiḥād-i 'āqil bi ma'qūl,* Bustān-i Kitāb, Qum, 1386 [A.H. solar].

Humā'ī, J., *Daw risālah dar falsafah-yi islāmī*, Mu'assisah-yi 'Ulūm-i Insānī Wa Muṭāli'āt-i Farhangī, Tehran, 1375.

Hutchins, W., "Fakhr al-Dīn al-Rāzī on Knowledge." 1971, ProQuest Dissertations and Theses.

Ibn Sīnā, *Sharḥ al-Ishārāt*, Maṭba'at al-Ḥaydarī, Qum, 1377 [A.H. lunar].

–, *Kitāb al-shifā'*, edited by I. Madkūr, Sulaymānzādah Publication, Qum, 1430.

Ilāhī Qumsha'ī, M., *Sharḥ-i fuṣūṣ al-ḥikam-i Fārābī*, Intishārāt-i Hirmis, Tehran, 1388 [A.H. solar].

Jilwah, A., *Majmū'a-yi āthār*, edited by Ḥasan Riḍāzādah, Intishārāt-i Ḥikmat, Tehran, [A.H. solar].

Kalın, I., *Knowledge in Later Islamic Philosophy : Mulla Sadra on Existence, Intellect, and Intuition*, Oxford University Press, Oxford, 2010.

Kāshānī, A., *Muṣannafāt*, edited by Y. Mahdawī and M. Mīnuwī, Intishārāt-i Khwārazmī, 1366 [A.H. solar].

Kindī, *Risālah fī'l-'aql*, published in Y. Qamīr, *Al-Kindī*, Dār al-Mashriq, Beirut, 1993.

Lāhījī, *Sharḥ risālat al-mashā'ir*, edited by Sayyid Jalāl al-Dīn Āshtiyānī, Intishārāt-i Amīr Kabīr, Tehran, 1376 [A.H. solar].

Long, A. A., "Parmenides on Thinking Being." *Proceedings of the Boston Area Colloquium of Ancient Philosophy*, vol. 12, no. 1, 1996, pp. 125–151.

Mullā Ṣadrā, *Shawāhid al-rubūbiyyah bā ḥawāshī Ḥājī Mullā Hādī Sabziwārī*, edited by Sayyid Jalāl al-Dīn Āshtiyānī, Būstān-i kitāb, Qum, 1388 [A.H. solar].

–, *al-Ḥikmat al-muta'āliyah*, edited by Muḥammad Riḍā Muẓaffar, Intishārāt-i Sulaymānzādah, Qum, 1430 [A.H. lunar]

Muṭahharī, M., *Majmū'ah-yi āthār*, Intishārāt-i Ṣadrā, Tehran, 1391 [A.H. solar].

Nasr, S.H., Afdal al-Din Kashani and the Philosophical World of Khwaja Nasir al-Din Tusi," in Michael E. Marmura, ed., *Islamic Theology and Philosophy: Studies in Honor of George F. Hourani*, Albany 1984, pp. 249–64.

Nasr, S.H. and Leaman, O. (eds.), *History of Islamic Philosophy*, Routledge, 1996.

Pépin, J., "Éléments pour une histoire de la relation entre l'Intelligence et l'Intelligible chez Platon et dans le Néoplatonisme." *Revue Philosophique De La France Et De l'Étranger*, vol. 146, 1956, pp. 39–64.

Plotinus, *Enneads,* translated by A. H. Armstrong et al. Harvard University Press, Cambridge, 1966.

–, *Enneads (Theology) The Arabic translation of Ibn Nā'imah al-Ḥimṣī*, edited by Sayyid Jalāl al-Dīn Āshtiyānī, Imperial Iranian Academy of Philosophy, Tehran, 1976.

Qamīr,Y., *al-Fārābī*, Dār Al-Mashriq, Beirut, 1986.

Rafī'ī Qazwīnī, *Rasā'il*, edited by Ḥ. Riḍānijād, Mu'assisah-yi Pajuhishī-yi Ḥikmat wa Falsafa-yi Irān, Tehran, 1387 [A.H. solar].

Rappe, S., "Self-knowledge and Subjectivity in the Enneads," *The Cambridge Companion to Plotinus* (Cambridge: Cambridge University Press, 1996), pp. 250–74.

Rāzī, *al-Mabāḥith al-mashriqiyyah*, Dār al-Kutub al-ʿArabī, Beirut, 1410 [AH lunar].
–, *Lubāb al-ishārāt wa al-tanbīhāt*, edited by A. Ḥijāzī, Maktabat al-Kulliyyāt al-Azhariyyah, Cairo, 1986.
Sabziwārī, *Sharḥ-i mathnawī*, edited by M. Burūjirdī, Sāzmān-i Chāp wa Intishārāt, Tehran, 1374 [A.H. solar].
–, *Asrār al-ḥikam*, edited by Karīm Fayḍī, Intishārāt-i Maṭbūʿāt-i Dīnī, Tehran, 1383 [A.H. solar].
–, *Sharḥ ghurar al-farāʾid*, edited by M. Muḥaqqiq and T. Izutsu, Anjuman-i Āthār Wa Mafākhir-i Millī, Tehran, 1384[A.H. solar].
Ṣadūqī Suhā, M., *Tārīkh-i ḥukamā' wa 'urafā-yi muta'akhkhir*, Intishārāt-i Ḥikmat, 1381 [A.H. solar].
Suhrawardī, *Majmūʿah-yi muṣannafāt-i Shaykh-i Ishrāq*, edited by H.Corbin and S.H. Nasr, Muʾassisah-yi Muṭāliʿāt-i ʿŪlūm-i Insānī, Tehran, 1976.
Ṭabāṭabāʾī, *Nihāyat al-ḥikmah*, edited by ʿAlī Zāriʿī, Muassasat al-Nashr al-Islāmī, Qum, 1417 [A.H. lunar].
Ṭūsī, *Ajwibah al-masāʾil al-naṣīriyyah*, Pajūhishgāh-i ʿUlūm-i Insānī wa Muṭāliʿāt-i Farhangī, Tehran, 1381[AH solar].
–, *Fuṣūl al-naṣīriyyah*, edited by Muḥammad Taqī Dānish Pajūh, Intishārāt-i Danishgāh-i Tehrān, 1355 [A.H. solar]
Wāḥid al-ʿAyn, *Sharḥ ḥikmat al-ʿarshiyyah maʿa taʿlīqāt al-ḥakīm al-ilāhī al-Mullā ʿAlī al-Nūrī*, edited by M.M. Khudāwirdī, The Iranian Institute of Philosophy, Tehran, 1391 [A.H. solar].
Yazdān Panāh, Y., *Ḥikmat-i ishrāq*, Pajūhishgāh-i ḥawzah wa Dānishgāh, Qum, 1389 [A.H. solar].

Anthropomorphism and Incorporealism

Livnat Holtzman

The Bedouin Who Asked Questions: The Later Ḥanbalites and the Revival of the Myth of Abū Razīn al-ʿUqaylī*

Introduction

One of the many merits of the influential Ḥanbalite scholar and activist Taqī al-Dīn Aḥmad ibn Taymiyya (d. 728/1328) was his accessibility. The many literary sources about his life report that people from all over the Mamluk sultanate and beyond it, whether educated or lay, had easily accessed *shaykh al-islām* (Ibn Taymiyya's honorific title) to seek his learned opinion in matters of practice and dogma. The educated sent him letters (later recorded, so we believe, in *Majmūʿ al-Fatāwā*, the massive collection of his responsa) and attended his *majālis* (study-sessions). In contrast, the laymen or commoners (*al-ʿāmma*) approached him directly asking for his opinion on miscellaneous matters of ritual, daily conduct and dogma. Some of these communications were preserved in the *fatāwā* that Ibn Taymiyya authored for the sake of the many who eagerly embraced his advice and learned opinion. In addition, Ibn Taymiyya's disciples and contemporaries documented part of the oral and written exchange between him and his admirers. However, it is likely that most of these dynamic everyday exchanges that lasted for decades were never recorded.

Ibn Taymiyya's accessibility and more so, his tolerance towards the questions of the public stood in contrast to the approach that prevailed among the members of the religious establishment (henceforth, the *ʿulamāʾ*) in Damascus and Cairo.[1] Both Ibn Taymiyya and the other *ʿulamāʾ* answered questions on matters of

* This research was supported by THE ISRAEL SCIENCE FOUNDATION (grant ISF 79/10). This article stems from my presentation at the international conference entitled 'Islamic Philosophy from the 12th to the 14th Centuries' that was held in the Annemarie Schimmel Kolleg, Universität Bonn, 24–26 February 2016. I wish to thank the participants of the conference for their illuminating remarks that helped improve this article. The article is a follow-up of Chapter Two and Chapter Five in my recently-published monograph *Anthropomorphism in Islam: the challenge of traditionalism (700–1350)*. Edinburgh, 2018. My thanks are extended to Abdelkader Al Ghouz for his helpful insights and suggestions.

1 For the definition of *ʿulamāʾ* in the Mamluk state, see the definitive discussion of Yaacov Lev in: Lev 2009, pp. 3–10.

practice. However, unlike the other *ʿulamāʾ* who refrained from addressing theological issues, Ibn Taymiyya also answered theological questions. In this respect he stood out among his contemporaries. The traditionalistic *ʿulamāʾ* were either indifferent to or uninformed of speculative theology (*kalām*) and philosophy. The rationalistic *ʿulamāʾ*, those who were well read in Ashʿarite *kalām*, believed that the domain of theology and philosophy should remain inaccessible to the public, whether laymen or the more educated elite. The Shāfiʿite-Ashʿarite contemporaries of Ibn Taymiyya severely criticized him for his tolerant approach towards theology and philosophy, an approach which he transmitted to his foremost disciple, Ibn Qayyim al-Jawziyya (d. 750/1350).[2]

We claim that the approach of both master and disciple to theological questions is associated with the revival of the myth of Abū Razīn al-ʿUqaylī, the Bedouin who dared ask the Prophet questions on various theological matters. Both Ibn Taymiyya and Ibn Qayyim al-Jawziyya (henceforth, the later Ḥanbalites) presented Abū Razīn as a symbol of piety in their polemic with the Ashʿarites. In the following pages, we argue that the myth of Abū Razīn served two purposes: first, this myth justified Ibn Taymiyya's enthusiasm to educate the public by answering their questions on theological matters; second, by recounting this myth the later Ḥanbalites conveyed the message that asking theological questions was a welcome and desired activity that complied with the spirit of the authentic Islam of the Prophet and *al-salaf al-ṣāliḥ* (the pious and worthy ancestors of Sunnite Islam). Consequently, prohibiting the public from asking such questions contradicted the Prophetic ethos.

Ibn Taymiyya's unique approach of never shying away from answering people's theological questions and providing them with answers is the core of the present article. This article comprises four parts: the first part presents the textual roots of the intolerant approach towards questions later to be embodied in the theological formula of *bi-lā kayfa* (literally, 'without asking how'). This formula that was habitually added to every anthropomorphic description of God in the

2 Anke von Kügelgen and Georges Tamer observe that Ibn Taymiyya was harshly criticized by his contemporaries for his excessive occupation in philosophy and *kalām*. Both Tamer and von Kügelgen highlight the famous accusation that the ultra-traditionalistic Hadith scholar and historian Shams al-Dīn al-Dhahabī (d. 748/1348) directed against Ibn Taymiyya. According to al-Dhahabī's avowal, he participated in some of Ibn Taymiyya's study sessions, where he was appalled to discover that Ibn Taymiyya delved in philosophical questions. In a letter addressed to Ibn Taymiyya, al-Dhahabī accused him for having 'repeatedly swallowed the poison of the philosophers (*sumūm al-falāsifa*)': Von Kügelgen 2013, p. 257; Tamer 2013, p. 331. The Ḥanbalite Ibn Rajab (d. 795/1393), the author of one of the most important biographies on Ibn Taymiyya indeed confirmed that 'some of Ibn Taymiyya's learned and pious admirers disapproved of his preoccupation with (*tawaghghul maʿa*) the *kalām* theologians and the philosophers': Von Kügelgen 2013, p. 258. See von Kügelgen's summary of the relevant literature about these two anecdotes: idem, pp. 257–8, footnotes 15–18.

Quran and the Hadith, denied the possibility of inquiring about the modality of the divine attributes (*ṣifāt Allāh*). Used by both the traditionalists and the Ashʿarites with a slight difference in meaning, the *bi-lā kayfa* had its roots in *aḥādīth* which recorded the Prophet's intolerance to questions. In addition, this formula was sourced in anecdotes describing the first generations of traditionalistic scholars practicing the same intolerance towards questions. The second part of the article presents the *ḥadīth* of Abū Razīn al-ʿUqaylī as a dramatic contrast to the *bi-lā kayfa* approach and Ibn Qayyim al-Jawziyya's efforts to insert this *ḥadīth* in the traditionalistic curriculum. The third part examines the myth of Abū Razīn as reflected in the polemic between the Ashʿarites and the later Ḥanbalites. The fourth part concludes this article with two questions that were directed at Ibn Taymiyya. This concluding part examines Ibn Taymiyya's methodological approach to questions of both lay and educated men.

The later Ḥanbalites presented Abū Razīn as a role model, using the material attributed to him precisely against the Ashʿarite version of the *bi-lā kayfa* formula. The theological questions that this article considers pertain to the much discussed topic of anthropomorphism (*tashbīh*) in Islam as reflected in several problematic texts in the Quran and the Hadith. Ibn Taymiyya dedicated the lion's share of his theological oeuvre to this topic.

1. "Do not ask questions" (Q. 5:101) and the *bi-lā kayfa* Formula

The Quran displays a wide range of theological and metaphysical topics in a group of verses which the scholars, following the Quran itself, defined as the *mutashābihāt*, the ambiguous verses. In verse 7 of sura 3 (*sūrat Āl ʿImrān*), the Quran subtly and indirectly suggests that delving in the meaning of the *mutashābihāt* is undesirable. Accordingly, the Quran describes those who 'observe the ambiguous part' of the scripture as people 'whose hearts are infected with disbelief', and warns that these people wish to create dissension, *fitna* (Q. 3:7). On the other hand, asking questions about the *muḥkamāt*, the verses which are precise in their meaning, is not perceived as problematic in the Quran.[3] The classical interpretations of Q. 3:7, backed by the history of the politico-theological schisms in the early Muslim community, accentuated the status of theological matters in comparison to legal and normative matters. The inter-

3 'It is He who revealed to you the Book. Some of its verses are precise in meaning – they are the foundations of the Book – and other ambiguous. Those whose hearts are infected with disbelief observe the ambiguous part, so as to create dissension by seeking to explain it. But no one knows its meaning except God. Those who are well-grounded in knowledge say: "We believe in it: it is all from our Lord". But only the wise take heed'. (Quran 3: 7, as translated by N. J. Dawood).

preters of Q. 3:7 were unanimous that theological issues were generally an unfavorable topic for discussion; whereas, legal and normative issues were constantly examined and questioned.[4] Another Quranic verse that discourages the believers from asking questions is Q. 5:101, which states: 'Believers, do not ask questions about things which, if made known to you, would only pain you'.

As a natural continuation of the concept articulated by these two Quranic verses, the Hadith literature adopted the line that rejected asking questions. Although the dominant image of *al-umma*, the early Muslim community, as reflected in the Hadith literature is that of a learning society which directed questions to the Prophet and other dominant figures,[5] the Hadith literature mainly articulates an unequivocal prohibition to ask questions, a prohibition that followed the wording of Q. 5:101. *Ṣaḥīḥ al-Bukhārī* which contains a chapter entitled 'Dislike of asking too many questions about certain topics and dislike of asking questions that are not one's concern'[6] is one such example. The *aḥādīth* and historical anecdotes in this chapter correspond with Q. 5:101. Muḥammad ibn Ismāʿīl al-Bukhārī (d. 256/870), for instance, quotes a letter that the influential *ṣaḥābī* al-Mughīra ibn Shuʿba (death date is placed between 48–51/ 668–71) sent to the caliph Muʿāwiya (d. 60/680). In this letter al-Mughīra testified: 'The Prophet used to forbid *qīla wa-qāla* (idle talk, gossip) and the habit of asking too many questions'.[7] Less selective Hadith compilations, like Aḥmad ibn Ḥanbal's (d. 241/855) *Musnad*, and Abū Dāwūd's (d. 275/889) *Sunan* included a marginal and 'weak' *ḥadīth* in which an anonymous *ṣaḥābī* (*rajulun min aṣḥāb al-nabī*) declared: 'The Messenger of God prohibited asking the *ghalūṭāt*'.[8] The Syrian traditionalist al-Awzāʿī (d. 157/774; one of four prominent *muḥaddithūn*, Hadith scholars, of his generation) explained that the *ghalūṭāt* (also: *ghulūṭāt* or *ughlūṭāt*) were evil questions which were difficult to answer.[9]

The prohibition to ask questions was a conspicuous trend in the Hadith literature. Accordingly, the corpus of *aḥādīth* that described the Prophet's disdain from idle questions inspired the most prominent feature of the traditionalistic ethos: the condemnation of questions on theological topics and especially on the anthropomorphic descriptions of God in the Quran and the Hadith. This ethos

4 The discussion of the Mālikite Quran exegete, Abū ʿAbd Allāh al-Qurṭubī (d. 671/1272) of Q. 3:7 is extremely comprehensive, and serves as a defining introduction to the topic of *al-muḥkamāt* and *al-mutashābihāt.* Al-Qurṭubī, *Jāmiʿ*, vol. 4, pp. 7–14 (commentary of Q. 3:7).

5 Dozens of questions that the Prophet was asked appear in the form of *fatāwā* in the last section of Ibn Qayyim al-Jawziyya's *Iʿlām al-Muwaqqiʿīn*, vol. 6, pp. 209–603. For the structure of 'question and answer' in the Hadith, see: Speight, 'Narrative Structures', pp. 266–7.

6 Al-Bukhārī, *Ṣaḥiḥ*, vol. 4, pp. 361–3 (*Kitāb al-Iʿtiṣām bi'l-Sunna, bāb mā yukrahu min kathrat al-suʾāl*).

7 Al-Bukhārī, *idem*, vol. 4, p. 362, *ḥadīth* 7292.

8 Abū Dāwūd, *Sunan*, p. 404, *ḥadīth* 3656 (*Kitāb al-ʿIlm, bāb al-kalām fī kitāb Allāh bi-ghayr ʿilm*)

9 Ibn Ḥanbal, *Musnad*, vol. 39, p. 92, *ḥadīth* 23687 (*musnad al-anṣār*).

took the form of the traditionalistic *bi-lā kayfa* formula, the most prominent manifestation of intolerance towards theological questions. In its earliest phase, in the 2nd/8th century, this formula meant 'without asking further questions'. Inspired by the corpus of *aḥādīth* that we presented above, this formula started circulating among the scholarly circles of traditionalists in various learning centres. Thus, when the leading *muḥaddithūn* al-Awzāʿī, Sufyān al-Thawrī (d. 161/778), al-Layth ibn Saʿd (d. 175/791), and Mālik ibn Anas (d. 179/796) taught the problematic texts of *aḥādīth al-ṣifāt*, i. e. the Hadith material that describes God in anthropomorphic language, they used to add the phrase *bi-lā kayfa* at the end of the transmission process, thus signalling their disciples not to ask questions about the meaning of the anthropomorphic descriptions. These scholars are also quoted as saying that *aḥādīth al-ṣifāt* should be transmitted verbatim, and that the scholars who teach these texts should refrain from interpreting them.[10] Similarly, the *muḥaddith* Sufyān ibn ʿUyayna (d. 198/813) from Mecca declared: 'The only possible way to interpret the Quranic verses in which God describes Himself is by reciting these verses verbatim and then by uttering nothing additional about them'.[11]

The early version of the *bi-lā kayfa* formula probably emerged from sayings like 'I have never seen more virtuous people than the Companions of Muḥammad; they asked him only twelve (in a different version, thirteen) questions until the day he died, all of which appeared in the Quran'.[12] Similar sayings that supported the traditionalistic *bi-lā kayfa* formula reinforced the image of the traditionalists as an unquestioning community, a community whose thirst for knowing the divine was self-suppressed. However, this image was inaccurate. We find frequent mention in the historical sources of *muḥaddithūn* who forbade their disciples to ask questions using the *bi-lā kayfa* formula. This finding in itself indicates that both students of Hadith and lay people were inclined to ask questions about the divine, and that *aḥādīth al-ṣifāt* provoked such questions. The reaction of the *muḥaddithūn* to these forbidden questions – as recorded in the sources – was intense and highly dramatic. For example, a man once asked Mālik ibn Anas how exactly God sat on the throne. Mālik did not respond. He bowed his head in silence and perspired profusely – a sign of his dissatisfaction and fury. After providing his formulaic answer ('the sitting [of God on the Throne] is undeniably known. The way it is actually done is incomprehensible.

10 Abū Bakr al-Ājurrī, *Kitāb al-Sharīʿa*, p. 327, *ḥadīth* 720.

11 Al-Bayhaqī, *Al-Asmāʾ wa'l-Ṣifāt*, vol. 2, p. 307, *ḥadīth* 869.

12 The first saying attributed to Ibn ʿAbbās (d. 68/687–8), appears in the early Hadith compilation of the *muḥaddith* ʿAbd Allāh al-Dārimī from Samarqand (d. 255/869, not Abū Saʿīd al-Dārimī, the Baghdadian *muḥaddith*). Al-Dārimī, *Sunan*, vol. 1, p. 63, *ḥadīth* 125. Accordingly, this *ḥadīth* also appears in al-Ṭabarānī, *Al-Muʿjam al-Kabīr*, vol. 11, p. 454, *ḥadīth* 12288, and Ibn Rajab, *Rawāʾiʿ al-Tafsir*, vol. 1, p. 452 (interpretation of Q. 5:101).

Believing it is obligatory, and questioning it is an undesirable innovation'), he accused the inquirer of heresy and had him expelled from his study-session.[13] In another version of this anecdote, a man from Iraq asked Mālik the same question. Malik was furious: he called the man vicious, and ordered his disciples to remove the man from his presence. The disciples grabbed the man by his arms and legs and threw him out.[14] A less dramatic reaction – albeit equally disapproving – was the reaction of Sufyān ibn ʿUyayna. He was asked to explain how God carried the sky on one finger, as one *ḥadīth* claimed, while another *ḥadīth* claimed that He held the hearts of the believers between two of His fingers.[15] Sufyān evaded the question, but the disciple who asked him was persistent. 'Leave me be!' cried Sufyān, however the disciple continued to ask more and more questions. Finally, Sufyān provided the disciple with the traditionalistic *bi-lā kayfa* formula. This formula apparently put an end to the disciple's questions.[16]

The connection between the *bi-lā kayfa* and the Hadith material was made even clearer in the 3rd–4th/9th–10th centuries when hardcore traditionalists quoted *ḥadīth al-ghalūṭāt.* This text declared that the Prophet prohibited asking 'evil questions'. Ignoring this *ḥadīth*'s dubious origin, the traditionalists quoted it in the course of their on-going polemics with the Muʿtazilites and other rationalistic sects. For example, the traditionalistic theologian Abū Saʿīd al-Dārimī (d. between 280–2/893–5) connected the *ghalūṭāt* with the sophistic argumentations of the speculative theologians, the *mutakallimūn.* According to al-Dārimī, *ghalūṭāt* are questions that cause one to make grave mistakes.[17] Abū Bakr al-Ājurrī's (d. 360/935) *Kitāb al-Sharīʿa*, an important source of Ḥanbalite traditionalism, expressed the same position: 'The *ʿulamā*' of the past and present hated when people presented difficult questions to them, and they refused to answer them, because they dreaded the quarrels and dispute that the Hadith forbade.'[18]

With the emergence of Ashʿarism in the 4th/10th century, a dramatic transformation occurred in the *bi-lā kayfa* formula. The original *bi-lā kayfa* formula prevented any possibility for an intellectual dialogue or a speculative theological contemplation. Based on this restrictive device, the Ashʿarites developed a her-

13 Al-Bayhaqī, *Al-Asmāʾ wa'l-Ṣifāt*, vol. 2, pp. 305–6, anecdote 867.

14 Ibn ʿAbd al-Barr, *Tamhīd*, vol. 7, p. 151.

15 These two *aḥādīth* have numerous versions and variations. For the *ḥadīth* about God holding the believers' hearts between two of His fingers, see: Abū Bakr al-Ājurrī, *Kitāb al-Sharīʿa*, p. 330–2, *ḥadīth* 729. For *ḥadīth aṣābiʿ al-raḥmān* (the *ḥadīth* about the Merciful's fingers) in which God carries the sky on one finger, the earth on another finger and so on, see: Abū Bakr al-Ājurrī, *Kitāb al-Sharīʿa*, p. 332, *ḥadīth* 736.

16 Al-Dhahabī, *Siyar Aʿlām al-Nubalāʾ*, vol. 8, pp. 465–6 (the biography of Sufyān ibn ʿUyayna).

17 Al-Dārimī, *Radd*, p. 7. Abū Saʿid al-Dārimī is mentioned in Ibn Abī Yaʿlā's *Ṭabaqāt al-Ḥanābila* as one of the early Ḥanbalites; however, it is more likely that he was not associated with them. Ibn Abī Yaʿlā, *Ṭabaqāt al-Ḥanābila*, vol. 1, p. 312, biographical entry 298.

18 Abū Bakr al-Ājurrī, *Kitāb al-Sharīʿa*, pp. 80–1.

meneutical device which corroborated their more advanced and pensive version of the *bi-lā kayfa* formula.[19] Their version of the *bi-lā kayfa* formula meant 'without attributing physical characteristics' to God; however, this formula covered much more than a mere prohibition to attribute a hand, a leg, or a face to God. The Ashʿarite *bi-lā kayfa* was divided into two parts: The first part was identical to the traditionalistic *bi-lā kayfa*. The Ashʿarites called this part *tafwīḍ*, which means 'entrusting power or authority to someone else'. Practically, by this term the Ashʿarites conveyed their reluctance to investigate, discuss, or interpret the anthropomorphic expressions in the Quran and the Hadith. They therefore 'entrusted' the authority of explaining or interpreting the anthropomorphic expressions to God and His Prophet.[20] The second part of the Ashʿarite *bi-lā kayfa* was quite the opposite. The Ashʿarites in fact adopted the hermeneutical device that the Muʿtazilites applied on the anthropomorphic verses in the Quran; the device known as *ta'wīl*, namely figurative interpretation. Unlike the Muʿtazilites who rejected *aḥādīth al-ṣifāt*, the Ashʿarites largely accepted this material and also interpreted most of it figuratively.[21]

Unlike the traditionalistic *bi-lā kayfa*, the Ashʿarite *bi-lā kayfa* was not a strict ban on asking questions about the anthropomorphic descriptions in the Quran and the Hadith. This dual approach of the Ashʿarites towards the anthropomorphic descriptions supposedly reverted to the eponymous founder of the Ashʿarite school, Abū 'l-Ḥasan al-Ashʿarī (d. 324/935). In his traditionalistic creed *al-Ibāna*, al-Ashʿarī declared:

> [We confirm] that God sits enthroned on high, based on what He said: 'The Merciful who sits enthroned on high' [Q. 20:5]. [We confirm] that He has a face without asking how (*bi-lā kayfa*), based on what He said: 'But the face of your Lord will abide forever' [Q. 55:27]. [We confirm] without asking how that He has two hands, based on what He said 'My own hands have made' [Q. 38:75]. [We confirm] without asking how that He has an eye, according to what He said 'under Our watchful eyes' [Q. 11:37].[22]

The above quoted text demonstrates the *tafwīḍ* part of the Ashʿarite *bi-lā kayfa* approach which is identical to the traditionalistic *bi-lā kayfa*. However, elsewhere al-Ashʿarī is quoted as saying that one should apply intellectual effort (*ʿaql*) in order to explain the anthropomorphic expressions.[23] The subsequent generations of Ashʿarite theologians embraced this recommendation. Thus, the Ashʿarite theologian Muḥammad ibn al-Ḥasan ibn Fūrak (d. 406/1015) who

19 Abrahamov 1995, pp. 368–9.

20 Makdisi 1963, p. 51. For the most comprehensive discussion of this term in the writings of anti-Taymiyyan Ashʿarites, see: El-Rouayheb 2010, pp. 275–87, 301–2.

21 Frank 1991, p. 141ff.

22 Al-Ashʿarī, *Al-Ibāna*, p. 9; Frank 1991, pp. 175–6, 178.

23 Ibn Fūrāk, *Mujarrad*, p. 41.

attributed this saying to al-Ashʿarī in *Mujarrad Maqālāt al-Ashʿarī* (A Summary of al-Ashʿarī's Doctrines), systematically applied the hermeneutical device of *ta'wīl* on the anthropomorphic Hadith material in his treatise *Mushkil al-Ḥadīth aw Ta'wīl al-Akhbār al-Mutashābiha* (The Figurative Interpretation of the Ambiguous Hadith Material), a work which presents a systematic figurative reading of *aḥādīth al-ṣifāt.*[24]

As far as the Ashʿarites were concerned, the prerogative of inquiring into the meaning of the anthropomorphic descriptions in the Quran and the Hadith was strictly reserved for the scholarly elite, while the lay public was banned from questioning the modality (*kayfiyya*) of the divine attributes. This approach is expressed forcefully in *Iljām al-ʿAwāmm ʿan ʿIlm al-Kalām* (Restraining the Lay Public from Approaching Speculative Theology) authored by the polymath Abū Ḥāmid al-Ghazālī (d. 505/1111). In this work, al-Ghazālī specifies that laymen (*al-ʿawāmm*) should never ask questions (*al-sukūt ʿan al-su'āl*) about the anthropomorphic texts, because this topic is beyond their limited intellectual capacity.[25] Al-Ghazālī further claims that there is no point in answering the questions of the laymen about the anthropomorphic texts because such answers are likely to confuse them and increase their ignorance. 'Whoever allows a suckling baby to eat bread and meat will cause his death – explains al-Ghazālī – the same goes for the laymen. If they ask about the meaning [of the anthropomorphic expressions], you must rebuke them, and prevent them from asking further by lashing them with a whip'. Al-Ghazālī rationalizes this harsh approach with two perfect anecdotes. The first anecdote recounts that the caliph ʿUmar ibn al-Khaṭṭāb (d. 23/644) severely lashed a man for having the audacity to polemicize about the ambiguous verses in the Quran. The other anecdote presented the Prophet himself, who once heard a group of people arguing about predetermination (*qadar*), a question that attracted the attention of both scholars and laymen.[26] The laymen asked the Prophet to share his understanding of predetermination. The Prophet refused to answer them and said that they were obliged to believe in predetermination and not argue about the topic. He further added: 'Your predecessors perished because they asked too many questions'.[27]

24 See Daniel Gimaret's introduction. Ibn Fūrak, *Muškil al-Ḥadīṯ*, pp. 11m–14 m (of the introduction).

25 Al-Ghazālī, *Majmūʿat Rasā'il*, p. 324. Al-Ghazālī included the ultra-traditionalistic scholars in the category of *al-ʿawāmm*. Frank 1994, p. 80; Griffel 2009, p. 267.

26 The major discussions about *qadar* in fact started in the Umayyad period. Watt 1948 remains to-date the definitive most accessible work about the early discussions about predetermination.

27 Al-Ghazālī, *Majmūʿat Rasā'il*, p. 324. The anecdote about ʿUmar appears frequently in the theological literature. See, for example, al-Ājurrī, *Al-Sharīʿa*, p. 79, *ḥadīth* 153. The Prophetic *ḥadīth* which al-Ghazālī paraphrases appears in: al-Bukhārī, *Ṣaḥīḥ*, vol. 4, p. 361, *ḥadīth* 7288 (*Kitāb al-Iʿtiṣām bi'l-Kitāb wa'l-Sunna, bāb al-iqtidā' bi-sunan Rasūl Allāh*).

Al-Ghazālī's condescending approach towards the lay public was duplicated by the following generations of Ashʿarite scholars and *ʿulamāʾ* who affiliated themselves with Ashʿarism. Thus, for example, we find the following passage in an Ashʿarite refutation of Ibn Taymiyya written by the Damascene *muḥaddith* and jurist (and not a theologian) Shihāb al-Dīn Aḥmad ibn Yaḥyā ibn Ismāʿīl ibn Jahbal (d. 733/1333). This passage is copied from al-Ghazālī's *Iljām al-ʿAwāmm*, with several juicy rhetorical ornaments that Ibn Jahbal added to the original text:

> Silence is the religious duty of the layman, because by asking questions he is exposed to matters which are beyond his capacity. If he asks an ignorant, his ignorance will increase. If he asks a scholar, the latter will not be able to make him understand. It is as if a mature man tries to teach a child about the pleasures of sex, the importance of domestic duties, or the benefits of going to school, and fails. Therefore, if a layman asks you about these matters (i.e., the anthropomorphic descriptions in *aḥādīth al-ṣifāt*), rebuke him and prevent him from asking. Tell him: 'You bird, this is not your nest, so fly away!' Mālik [ibn Anas] ordered to throw out the man who asked him [about God's sitting on a throne], did he not? He said: 'You are a vicious man' while perspiring profusely. Did he not? ʿUmar did the same to whoever asked him about the ambiguous verses. Did he not? The Prophet said: 'Your predecessors perished because they asked too many questions'. Did he not? Keeping silent about the question of predetermination and more so, about the divine attributes is obligatory.[28]

In the Mamluk period, the corpus of *aḥādīth* and historical anecdotes that articulated the prohibition to ask questions on theological issues was shared by all the trends of Islamic Sunnism. The Shāfiʿite-Ashʿarites used this corpus as textual evidence for the validity of their elitist worldview. The later Ḥanbalites were familiar with this corpus; however, they extracted a different message from the texts. They believed that asking questions about theology is a welcome activity when the questions are presented in a proper venue and in good faith. The Ḥanbalite Ibn Rajab (d. 795/1392; Ibn Rajab is generally assumed to be Ibn Qayyim al-Jawziyya's disciple, although he was not)[29] who quoted the same corpus of *aḥādīth* and anecdotes in his interpretation of Q. 5: 101 mentioned the prohibition to ask questions (*masāʾil*, sing. *masʾala*) on subtle and difficult issues 'that God has deliberately concealed from His servants'.[30] One may think that Ibn

28 Al-Subkī, *Ṭabaqāt al-Shāfiʿiyya*, vol. 9, pp. 82–3 (the biography of Ibn Jahbal).

29 Ibn Rajab was merely a young participant in Ibn Qayyim al-Jawziyya's sessions. He wrote the best and most comprehensive biographical entry on Ibn Qayyim al-Jawziyya in his monumental *Dhayl Ṭabaqāt al-Ḥanābila*. In fact, after a period of time in which he gave responsa in the Taymiyyan style, Ibn Rajab abandoned this method, and refrained from giving *fatāwā* altogether. Because he took this position, he was rejected by the adherents of Ibn Taymiyya (*al-taymiyyūn*). In addition, he was equally rejected by the majority of the traditionalists in Damascus (although he was the teacher of all the Ḥanbalites of his time). Ibn Ḥajar, *Inbāʾ al-Ghumr*, vol. 1, pp. 460–1.

30 Ibn Rajab *Rawāʾiʿ al-Tafsīr*, vol. 1, p. 450 (interpretation of Q. 5:101).

Rajab's overall stance would follow the prohibition to ask questions on theological matters; however, this is not the case. In his magnum opus *Laṭā'if al-Maʿārif*, which surveys the Islamic calendar, its special dates, celebrations, fasts, and prayers, Ibn Rajab dedicated the opening chapter to *majālis al-waʿẓ* (hortatory preaching assemblies). Ibn Rajab chose to open the chapter with a marginal *ḥadīth* in which Abū Hurayra (d. circa 58/678) asked the Prophet two questions: 'What was the material from which the entire creation was made of?' and 'What was the material from which paradise was built?' The Prophet's answer was detailed, indicating his tolerance to Abū Hurayra's questions.[31] By quoting this *ḥadīth*, Ibn Rajab signaled to his readers that the *majlis al-waʿẓ* is a place in which questions on such delicate matters can be raised, and that the participants may expect elaborate answers to their questions. Since the visitors of the preaching assemblies were people from all echelons of society, Ibn Rajab here in fact welcomes theological questions from the public. This approach, which is opposed to the Shāfiʿite-Ashʿarite approach, also had its roots in the Hadith literature.

2. The *ḥadīth* of Abū Razīn al-ʿUqaylī

The anecdote of Abū Hurayra asking the Prophet theological questions is the tip of the iceberg. According to Ibn Rajab in his interpretation of Q. 5: 101, the Prophet welcomed questions from the members of the Bedouin delegations who arrived in Medina to pledge their allegiance to him. Being newly converts, the Bedouins' questions about practice and faith were tolerated, 'while the *muhājirūn* and the *anṣār*, whose faith was solidly fixed in their hearts, were forbidden to ask subtle questions'.[32] This prerogative of asking questions was granted to the Bedouin converts because they presented their questions in good faith. Unlike the hypocrites of Medina (*al-munāfiqūn*) and 'the People of the Book' (*ahl al-kitāb*) who presented questions to undermine the Prophet's authority and doubt the veracity of his mission,[33] the Bedouins lacked finesse and sophistication. Their questions, therefore, could not cause any harm by casting doubts in the hearts of the believers or belittling the Prophet. The *ṣaḥābī* Anas ibn Mālik (d. 93/711) testified: 'We were forbidden to ask questions, and this prohibition was

31 Ibn Rajab, *Laṭā'if al-Maʿārif*, vol. 1, p. 45. The *ḥadīth* appears in al-Bayhaqī, *Al-Asmā' wa'l-Ṣifāt*, vol. 2, p. 265; Al-Ḥākim al-Nīsābūrī, *Mustadrak*, vol. 2, p. 490 (*Kitāb al-Tafsīr*, interpretation of Q. 45: 13) ; al-Tirmidhī, *Sunan*, vol. 4, p. 672; Ibn ʿAsākir, *Tārīkh Dimashq*, vol. 41, p. 338 (includes different versions of this *ḥadīth*).

32 Ibn Rajab, *Rawāʾiʿ al-Tafsīr*, vol. 1, p. 451 (interpretation of Q. 5:101).

33 Ibn Rajab, *idem*, vol. 1, pp. 448–9 (interpretation of Q. 5:101).

articulated in the Quran. We were therefore pleased each time when an intelligent man from the people of the desert came and asked the Prophet questions'.[34]

Several new converts are presented in the sources as asking the Prophet questions that were accepted with grace.[35] One of these converts was a Bedouin by the name of Abū Razīn al-ʿUqaylī (death date unknown) who inquired exactly on topics one should not inquire, but he still received respectful and elucidating answers from the Prophet. For example, assuming that God has an actual location in the physical world, Abū Razīn asked the Prophet where God had been before He created the heaven and earth:

> Abū Razīn said: I asked: 'Oh, Messenger of God! Where was our Lord before He created the sky and the earth? He answered: 'He was in lofty clouds (*ʿamāʾ*), beneath which was a vacuity (*hawāʾ*), and above which was a vacuity. Then He created the throne above the water (*māʾ*)'.[36]

Abū Razīn's questions were recognized by later scholars as the almost exclusive source for Prophetic dicta on God's attributes and actions. The Persian Hadith scholar (and an expert on Sufism), Abū Nuʿaym al-Iṣfahānī (d. 430/1038), observed that all the *aḥādīth* transmitted on Abū Razīn's behalf were based on the questions that he directed to the Prophet on matters of faith (*al-tawḥīd wa'l-uṣūl*).[37] The questions that Abū Razīn asked the Prophet were documented in a cluster of short *aḥādīth* and in one extremely lengthy *ḥadīth.* This corpus in its entirety was preserved in Aḥmad ibn Ḥanbal's *Musnad.* Some of the material was also preserved in the early Hadith compilation of the *muḥaddith* Sulaymān ibn Dāwūd al-Ṭayālisī (d. 204/819 or 820).[38] As we analyzed elsewhere, the Abū Razīn corpus originated from the tales of Abū Razīn's closest relatives and acquaintances, all of whom were members of Abū Razīn's tribe, the Banū al-Muntafiq. In the 8th century, this material was transmitted by a handful of *muḥaddithūn* in Medina and Damascus. During the 3rd/9th century the material started circulating in Baghdad, where it was adopted by the Ḥanbalites and other ultra-traditionalistic *muḥaddithūn.*[39] The case of the extremely lengthy *ḥadīth* from the Abū

---

34 Al-Dāraquṭnī, *Kitāb al-Ruʾya*, p. 255, anecdote 157.

35 See for example the story of 'a group of people from Yemen' (*nafar min ahl 'l-yaman*) who asked the Prophet about the beginning of creation (*awwal hādhā 'l-amr*). The Prophet's answer was: 'In the beginning there was nothing but God. Thereafter there was His throne on the water. Thereafter He wrote everything in the heavenly book. Thereafter He created the heaven and earth'. Al-Bukhārī, *Ṣaḥīḥ*, p. 789, *ḥadīth* 3191 (*Kitāb Badʾ 'l-Khalq, bāb mā jāʾa fī qawl Allāh taʿālā wa-huwa 'lladhī yabdaʾu 'l-khalq*). For further references to Hadith material, see al-Bayhaqī, *Al-Iʿtiqād*, pp. 92–3.

36 Al-Ṭayālisī, *Musnad*, vol. 2, p. 418, *ḥadīth* 1189; Ibn Ḥanbal, *Musnad*, vol. 26, p. 108, *ḥadīth* 16188, p. 117–8, *ḥadīth* 16200.

37 Al-Iṣbahānī, *Maʿrifat al-Ṣaḥāba* vol. 5, p. 2418.

38 Al-Ṭayālīsī, *Musnad*, vol. 2, pp.414–9; Ibn Ḥanbal, *Musnad*, vol. 26, pp. 100–20.

39 Holtzman 2018, pp. 84–5.

Razīn corpus (henceforth, the lengthy *ḥadīth*)[40] illustrates the circulation and the proliferation of this corpus among the ultra-traditionalistic circles. Let us first consider the form and content of the lengthy *ḥadīth*.

The lengthy *ḥadīth* is a patchwork of *aḥādīth* recounted by members of the Banū al-Muntafiq. Originally from al-Yamāma, this powerful tribe settled in the marshes of Kufa and Basra during the Arab conquest of Iraq in the 1st/7th century.[41] The lengthy *ḥadīth* in fact provides an indirect explanation for their sole domination in the marshes: The Prophet predicted that this tribe would live far from any civilization, without any neighbours to harass them.[42] According to ʿAbd Allāh ibn Aḥmad ibn Ḥanbal (d. 290/903), who compiled Ibn Ḥanbal's *Musnad*, the Medinese *muḥaddith* Ibrāhīm ibn Ḥamza al-Zubayrī (d. 230/845) sent ʿAbd Allāh a letter in which he included this lengthy *ḥadīth*. Ibrāhīm, a lineal descendant of the anti-caliph ʿAbd Allāh ibn Zubayr (d. 72/692)[43] claimed to have recorded the lengthy *ḥadīth* faithfully from one of his teachers.[44] In his letter, Ibrāhīm asked ʿAbd Allāh to transmit this *ḥadīth* to his disciples on Ibrāhīm's behalf, granting him written permission to teach the material. The chain of transmitters as quoted by ʿAbd Allāh indicates that in the 2nd/8th and 3rd/9th centuries the lengthy *ḥadīth* circulated in Medina, and Ibrāhīm's letter to ʿAbd Allāh widened the circulation of this *ḥadīth* to include Baghdad.[45]

With the complete absence of any corroborative textual evidence about Abū Razīn and the event that he describes in the lengthy *ḥadīth*, we are compelled to accept this *ḥadīth*'s narrative at face value. According to the narrative of the lengthy *ḥadīth*, Abū Razīn al-ʿUqaylī[46] was sent by his tribesmen to negotiate with the Prophet. Accompanied by his friend (who remained unnamed), Abū Razīn arrived in Medina at the end of month of Rajab, supposedly in the *Hijrī* year 9 (approx. November 15th, 630).[47] The two friends entered the Prophet's mosque

40 For a full translation of the lengthy *ḥadīth*, see: Holtzman 2018, pp. 376–82.

41 Al-Qalqashandī, *Nihāyat al-Arab*, p. 75; Levi Della Vida, 'al-Muntafiḳ', *EI*^{2}, vol. 7, p. 582.

42 Ibn Ḥanbal, *Musnad*, vol. 26, p. 127, *ḥadīth* 16206.

43 Al-Dhahabī, *Siyar*, vol. 11, pp. 60–1; al-Bukhārī, *Al-Tārīkh al-Kabīr*, vol. 1, p. 283.

44 The teacher is the Medinese *muḥaddith* ʿAbd al-Raḥmān ibn al-Mughīra al-Ḥizāmī (death date unknown). Al-Bukhārī, *idem*, vol. 5, p. 354.

45 For a thorough analysis of Abū Razīn's lengthy *ḥadīth* (its circulation, transmitters, literary devices etc.): Holtzman 2018, pp. 69–87, 383.

46 There was much dispute among scholars about Abū Razīn's identity, because he was identified as either Laqīṭ ibn ʿĀmir or Laqīṭ ibn Ṣabira (or Ṣabara). Al-Nawawī, *Tahdhīb*, vol. 2, p. 72. See also Ibn al-Athīr, *Usd al-Ghāba*, vol. 5, p. 253, biography 5100.

47 Ibn Kathīr, whose only source about the encounter between Abū Razīn and the Prophet is the lengthy *ḥadīth* inserted the text in the chapter of the *Hijrī* year 9 (630–1 A.D.) in his *Al-Bidāya wa'l-Nihāya* simply because all the tribal delegations came to the Prophet in the year 9. This year is called therefore 'the year of the delegations'. Ibn Kathīr, *Al-Bidāya wa'l-Nihāya*, vol. 7, p. 231.

shortly after the Morning Prayer and heard the Prophet preach to the crowd.[48] After his address, the Prophet ordered the people, who probably wanted to pursue their daily routine, to stay in their places. Everyone obeyed. Abū Razīn testified: 'The people sat down, and I and my friend stood there, until his (i. e. the Prophet's) mind opened to us and his eyes fell on us.'[49] The bold Abū Razīn, having noticed that he drew the Prophet's attention, commenced his series of questions. Abū Razīn asked ten questions about the divine and the hereafter, and the Prophet answered each question patiently. Abū Razīn then asked the eleventh question, which reflected his complete submission to the Prophet and his conversion to Islam.[50] The Prophet's answers to Abū Razīn's questions included several anthropomorphic and corporealistic descriptions of God on the Day of Judgement. With each answer provided by the Prophet, Abū Razīn gradually shifted from his initial position as a bold infidel and became a believer, who finally pledges allegiance to the Prophet. One of the questions that Abū Razīn asked was the following:

> I said: 'Oh Messenger of God, how is it possible that on the Day of Resurrection we will look at Him and He will look at us, and there will be so many of us in the land while He is but one person (*shakhṣ wāḥid*)?' The Prophet] answered: 'I will tell you about it, by using a similar example from God's blessings. The sun and the moon are both signs from Him, and they are small. You see both of them and they see all of you at the same time, and you do not differ one from the other in seeing them. By your Eternal God! There is no doubt that He has more power to make you all see Him and see all of you than the sun and the moon have, and all the same, you see both of them and they see all of you at the same time, and you do not differ one from the other in seeing them.'[51]

Further in the dialogue, Abū Razīn asked the Prophet: 'And with what will we see [our Lord]?' The Prophet answered: 'With the same [organ] you use today in order to see.'[52] The lengthy *ḥadīth* presents two protagonists: the inquisitive Abū Razīn and the Prophet who obligingly answers his questions. The depiction of the Prophet in the lengthy *ḥadīth* does not resemble the depiction of the Prophet in the Hadith material quoted by the Ashʿarites al-Ghazālī and Ibn Jahbal: As presented in the previous section, the Prophet in these anecdotes was intolerant to theological questions. In the lengthy *ḥadīth*, the Prophet does not tire from answering Abū Razīn's questions in great detail. Thus, for example, when Abū Razīn asks the Prophet about the Resurrection, the Prophet's answer is detailed:

48 Ibn Ḥanbal, *Musnad*, vol. 26, pp. 121–2, *ḥadīth* 16206.

49 Ibn Ḥanbal, *idem*, vol. 26, p. 122, *ḥadīth* 16206.

50 Ibn Ḥanbal, *idem*, vol. 26, p. 127, *ḥadīth* 16206.

51 Ibn Ḥanbal, *idem*, vol. 26, p. 124, *ḥadīth* 16206.

52 Ibn Ḥanbal, *idem*, vol. 26, p. 125, *ḥadīth* 16206. For a concise presentation of the different views regarding the beatific vision, including the traditionalistic stance of seeing God with one's eyes, see: Gimaret, 'Ru'yat Allāh', *EI*[2].

> I asked: 'Oh Messenger of God! How will He be able to assemble us when our decaying corpses will be torn out by the winds and the wild beasts?' The Prophet answered: 'I will tell you by using a similar example from God's blessings. Sometimes you look at the face of the earth that was worn out and shabby with its dry clods, and say: "This earth will never live again". Thereafter your Lord sends rain to this earth. Within a few days you will look at the face of the earth again, and suddenly you will see it soft and moist, covered with greenery. By God! Is He not the most capable to summon the dead from the water like He summoned the plants of the earth to appear? And so they will come out from beneath the stones and from their resting places, they will look at Him, and He will look at them'.[53]

Apart from the lengthy *ḥadīth*, the Abū Razīn corpus included indications to the close friendship that supposedly evolved between Abū Razīn and the Prophet. Thus, for instance, an anecdote which was preserved in the *Musnad* of Aḥmad ibn Ḥanbal recounts a feast of a male-lamb in the private chambers of ʿĀʾisha, the Prophet's favoured wife. Abū Razīn attended this feast at the specific invitation of the Prophet. During this feast, Abū Razīn consulted the Prophet about his wife's tongue-lashing. The Prophet advised him either to divorce her or educate her.[54]

Parts of the Abū Razīn corpus were preserved in Hadith compilations and theological treatises that were composed in Khurāsān and further east. Thus, for example, we find some of the material attributed to Abū Razīn in the Hadith compilations of Ibn Māja (d. 273/887) and al-Tirmidhī (d. 279/892).[55] The ultra-traditionalistic scholar Ibn Khuzayma (d. 311/924) included this corpus in his *Kitāb al-Tawḥīd*, a Hadith compilation and theological treatise which promotes a literal reading of the anthropomorphic expressions in the Hadith.[56] Ibn Taymiyya who warmly embraced *Kitāb al-Tawḥīd* accepted the Abū Razīn corpus after reading Ibn Khuzayma's testimony that he only used the most reliable Hadith accounts as textual proof in his *Kitāb al-Tawḥīd.*[57] In other scholarly circles, the Abū Razīn corpus was regarded problematic. For example, the traditionalistic theologian (with rationalistic tendencies) and Hadith scholar Ibn Qutayba (d. 276/889) observed that the material attributed to Abū Razīn was controversial (*mukhtalaf fīhi*). Ibn Qutayba presented several arguments against the inclusion of this material in the traditionalistic curriculum. All of these arguments relied on the Bedouin origin of the transmitters. According to Ibn Qutayba, some of the *aḥādīth* that were attributed to Abū Razīn were 'reprehensible versions' (*alfāẓ tustashnaʿu*) of widely accepted Hadith material. Ibn Qutayba no doubt referred

53 Ibn Ḥanbal, *idem*, vol. 26, pp. 123–4, *ḥadīth* 16206.

54 Ibn Ḥanbal, *idem*, vol. 26, p. 309, *ḥadīth* 16384.

55 Al-Tirmidhī, *Sunan*, vol. 5, p. 288, *ḥadīth* 3109 (*Kitāb tafsīr al-qurʾān, bāb wa-min sūrat Hūd*); Ibn Māja, *Sunan*, p. 48, *ḥadīth* 182 (*bāb ma ankarathu al-jahmiyya*).

56 Ibn Khuzayma, *Tawḥīd*, pp. 437–41, 460–76.

57 Ibn Taymiyya, *Bayān Talbīs al-Jahmiyya*, vol. 7, p. 46.

to the lengthy *ḥadīth* when he mentioned those reprehensible versions.[58] Another example is evident in the thematic compilation of *aḥādīth al-ṣifāt* by the illustrious *muḥaddith* and Shāfiʿite lawyer Abū Bakr al-Bayhaqī (d. 458/1066). Al-Bayhaqī, who was also an Ashʿarite theologian, cited several *aḥādīth* from the Abū Razīn corpus,[59] but ignored the lengthy *ḥadīth.*

While prominent Hadith authorities from Iraq and Khurasan like Sulaymān ibn Aḥmad al-Ṭabarānī (d. 360/971) transmitted the lengthy *ḥadīth* and included it in their writings, other Hadith authorities chose to ignore it.[60] Al-Bukhārī, for instance, studied Hadith from Ibrāhīm ibn Ḥamza al-Zubayrī, the *muḥaddith* who introduced this lengthy *ḥadīth* to ʿAbd Allāh ibn Aḥmad ibn Ḥanbal.[61] Even so, al-Bukhārī did not include this lengthy *ḥadīth* or any other *ḥadīth* attributed to Abū Razīn in his *Ṣaḥīḥ.* The great *muḥaddith* from Isfahan, Abū ʿAbd Allāh ibn Manda (d. 301/914) mentioned that this *ḥadīth* was read publicly in a gathering of the scholars of Iraq, among whom were ʿAbd Allāh ibn Aḥmad ibn Ḥanbal and the Baghdadian Hadith scholar Muḥammad ibn Iṣḥāq al-Sāghānī (d. 270/883), 'and none of the scholars rejected it or argued about its authenticity'.[62] Ibn Manda fiercely defended the authenticity of this *ḥadīth:*

> No one dared to reject this *ḥadīth* or argue about [the credibility of] its transmitters. On the contrary, they (i.e. the Iraqi and Persian *muḥaddithūn*) transmitted it while accepting it wholeheartedly. Only a heretic or an ignoramus or a transgressor of the Quran and the Sunna, rejects it.[63]

This ardent declaration, preceded by a list of the distinguished Iraqi and Persian scholars who taught this *ḥadīth*, indicates that Abū Razīn's lengthy *ḥadīth* was rejected in certain circles; otherwise, such a statement in its favour would have not been required.

The scholar who in particular strove to retrieve the lengthy *ḥadīth* from Aḥmad ibn Ḥanbal's *Musnad* and include it in the traditionalistic curriculum was Ibn Qayyim al-Jawziyya. We find that Ibn Qayyim al-Jawziyya copied this *ḥadīth* verbatim from Aḥmad ibn Ḥanbal's *Musnad* and discussed its content in three different works: his treatise on the divine attributes, *Al-Ṣawāʿiq al-Mursala ʿalā al-Jahmiyya wa'l-Muʿaṭṭila* (Thunderbolts Directed against the Jahmiyya and

58 Ibn Qutayba, *Ta'wīl Mukhtalif al-Ḥadīth*, p. 323.
59 Al-Bayhaqī, *Al-Asmā' wa'l-Ṣifāt*, vol. 2, pp. 235–6 (*ḥadīth* 801), pp. 304–5 (*ḥadīth* 864), p. 485 (*ḥadīth* 1069), p. 486 (*ḥadīth* 1070).
60 Al-Ṭabarānī, *Al-Muʿjam al-Kabīr*, vol. 19, pp. 211–14 (*ḥadīth* 477). For a list of scholars from Iraq and Khurāsān who taught this *ḥadīth* between the 3rd/9th to the 5th/11th centuries, see: Ibn Qayyim al-Jawziyya, *Zād al-Maʿād*, vol. 3, p. 51. Ibn al-Qayyim relied heavily on an unknown text by Ibn Manda.
61 Al-Bayhaqī, *Al-Asmā' wa'l-Ṣifāt*, vol. 2, p. 223.
62 Ibn Qayyim al-Jawziyya, *Ḥādī al-Arwāḥ*, p. 536.
63 Ibn Qayyim al-Jawziyya, *Zād al-Maʿād*, vol. 3, p. 51.

Muʿattila),[64] his elaborate treatise on the hereafter, *Ḥādī al-Arwāḥ ilā Bilād al-Afrāḥ* (The Leader of the Souls to the Land of Joy), and his sophisticated biography of the Prophet, *Zād al-Maʿād fī Hady Khayr al-ʿIbād* (Provisions for the Afterlife, on the Teachings of the Best of All People).[65] In *Ḥādī al-Arwāḥ*, Ibn al-Qayyim decided to include this *ḥadīth* 'to decorate our book with it, because its majesty, awe and the light of prophethood that it contains attest to its veracity'.[66] Ibn Qayyim al-Jawziyya set this *ḥadīth* in a chapter that describes a controversy between the traditionalists whether sexual intercourse between the believers and their spouses in the hereafter would entail pregnancy. Since one of Abū Razīn's questions touched the exact same topic, and the Prophet's answer assured Abū Razīn that there would be no pregnancies in the hereafter, Ibn Qayyim al-Jawziyya thusly justified the inclusion of this *ḥadīth* in *Ḥādī al-Arwāḥ*.[67] In *Zād al-Maʿād* this *ḥadīth* appears in a chapter entitled 'the arrival of the delegation of the Banū al-Muntafiq' to the Prophet. Here, Ibn Qayyim al-Jawziyya used the *ḥadīth* as a historical source.

Ibn Qayyim al-Jawziyya was eager to prove that this rather dubious *ḥadīth* was wide-spread (*mashhūr*) and hence acceptable to the traditionalists. In his eagerness, he quoted a conversation he had with the great *muḥaddith* of Damascus, Abu'l-Ḥajjāj al-Mizzī (d. 742/1341). Ibn Qayyim al-Jawziyya testified: 'When I asked him about this *ḥadīth*, he said that the majesty of prophethood rests upon it (*ʿalayhi jalālatu 'n-nubuwwati*)'.[68] Al-Mizzī was being polite: In his *Tuḥfat al-Ashrāf bi-Maʿrifat al-Aṭrāf* (The Gem of the Notables, about the Knowledge of the Abbreviated Content of the Hadith),[69] al-Mizzī quoted the beginning of the lengthy *ḥadīth*, and expressed his doubts about this *ḥadīth*. According to al-Mizzī, he found a shorter version – in fact, a version of one sentence of this *ḥadīth* in a distorted copy of the *Sunan* of Abū Dāwūd al-Sijistānī (d. 276/889). Al-Mizzī, who was not a Ḥanbalite, was afraid that this particular tradition was added to the copy of the *Sunan* by the Sufi *muḥaddith* Abū Saʿīd ibn al-Aʿrābī (d. 340/952).[70] Al-Mizzī's concern regarding the authenticity of the lengthy *ḥadīth* is further

64 The *ḥadīth* appears in the abridgement of the *Ṣawāʿiq*. Ibn Qayyim al-Jawziyya and Muḥammad ibn al-Mawṣilī, *Mukhtaṣar al-Ṣawāʿiq al-Mursala*, pp. 1170–86.

65 Ibn Qayyim al-Jawziyya, *Ḥādī al-Arwāḥ*, pp. 530–7; Ibn Qayyim al-Jawziyya, *Zād al-Maʿād*, vol. 3, pp. 48–56.

66 Ibn Qayyim al-Jawziyya, *Ḥādī al-Arwāḥ*, p. 536.

67 Ibn Qayyim al-Jawziyya, *idem*, p. 537. For Abū Razīn's tenth question, see: Ibn Ḥanbal, *Musnad*, vol. 26, p. 126, *ḥadīth* 16206.

68 Ibn Qayyim al-Jawziyya, *Ḥādī al-Arwāḥ*, p. 536.

69 *Tuḥfat al-Ashrāf* is an index to the six canonical Hadith compilations arranged in *aṭrāf*, namely abbreviated content of the *aḥādīth*. Regarding the arrangement and importance of this work, see: Juynboll 2007, pp. xvii–xviii.

70 Al-Mizzī, *Tuḥfat al-Ashrāf*, vol. 7, pp. 583–4. For the full text of this one line *ḥadīth* see, Abū Dāwūd, *Sunan*, p. 368, *ḥadīth* 3266 (*Kitāb al-Aymān wa'l-Nudhūr, bāb fī 'l-qasam hal yakūnu yamīnan*).

evidence that this *ḥadīth* was a part of the Ḥanbalite and ultra-traditionalistic curriculum, and that the other trends of Islamic traditionalism did not use or cite it.

3. Abū Razīn in the Polemic between the Ashʿarites and the Later Ḥanbalites

Ibn Qayyim al-Jawziyya's efforts to include the lengthy *ḥadīth* of Abū Razīn in the traditionalistic curriculum by rehabilitating its credibility drew inspiration from the teachings of his much-admired mentor. Ibn Taymiyya mentioned Abū Razn in several of his works as a role model of healthy instincts and firm belief in God. For example, Ibn Taymiyya briefly referred to Abū Razīn and his encounter with the Prophet in a central passage which appears in *Al-Risāla al-Akmaliyya* (The Epistle on the Absolute Perfection of the Divine Attributes). In this passage, Ibn Taymiyya addresses Abū Razīn's question about divine laughter (*al-ḍaḥk*). This question is recorded both in the lengthy *ḥadīth* and in one of the brief anecdotes that comprise the Abū Razīn corpus. The following brief anecdote presents the best exposition of Abū Razīn's question to the Prophet:

> Wakīʿ ibn ʿUdus (Abū Razīn's nephew whose death date is unknown) recounted this story which he heard from his uncle, Abū Razīn: The Messenger of God said: 'Our Lord laughs because of the despair of His servants, and because He knows that the time for Him to change things is near'. I asked: 'Oh Messenger of God, does God really laugh?' And he answered: 'Yes'. I said: 'A Lord who laughs benevolently will never deprive us of His bounty'.[71]

In *Al-Akmaliyya*, Ibn Taymiyya presents God's laughter as one of the divine attributes of perfection (*ṣifāt al-kamāl*), and determines:

> Laughter in its proper place is a praiseworthy and perfect attribute. Let us take for instance two living creatures, one which laughs from whatever makes it laugh and the other which does not laugh at all. Surely the first creature is more complete and closer to perfection than the other creature.[72]

Thereafter Ibn Taymiyya observes that laughter is a trait which differentiates the human being from other creatures, and explains why God's perfection necessitates attributing laughter to Him.[73] In the course of Ibn Taymiyya's proof, which

71 Ibn Ḥanbal, *Musnad*, vol. 26, p. 106, *ḥadīth* 16187.

72 Ibn Taymiyya, *Al-Risāla al-Akmaliyya*, p. 55. The *Akmaliyya* is also included in *Majmūʿ al-Fatāwā*, however in this compilation it is untitled. The quoted passage is found in: *Majmūʿ al-Fatāwā*, vol. 6, pp. 71–2.

73 Ibn Taymiyya, *Al-Risāla al-Akmaliyya*, p. 56. For Ibn Taymiyya's proof of God's laughter, see: Holtzman 2010, pp. 194–9.

relies entirely on an advanced reading of the above quoted anecdote, Ibn Taymiyya refers to Abū Razīn as 'this intelligent Bedouin' (*al-aʿrābī al-ʿāqil*) who did not hesitate to inquire the Prophet about divine laughter. Moreover, Ibn Taymiyya claimed that by virtue of Abū Razīn's healthy instincts (*ṣiḥḥat fiṭratihi*) Abū Razīn deduced that God's laughter proved the existence of His praiseworthy benevolence (*al-iḥsān al-maḥmūd*). Abū Razīn also deduced that 'this attribute is one of the attributes of perfection'. This is of course an anachronistic description as Abū Razīn lived in the 1st/7th century when the term *ṣifāt al-kamāl* was not part of the religious discourse. Ibn Taymiyya's analysis emphasizes a unique feature of Abū Razīn: his ability to instinctively construct a rationalistic proof (*dalīl*) based on the above mentioned Prophetic dictum. According to Ibn Taymiyya, Abū Razīn came to the conclusion that he could interpret God's laughter as a sign of the divine beneficence based on the assumption that laughter is a praiseworthy attribute, 'whereas the gloomy person who never laughs is dispraised for never laughing'.[74] Abū Razīn of course never expressed this idea explicitly. We have here Ibn Taymiyya speculating on Abū Razīn's train of thought based on his understanding of Abū Razīn's psyche.

Ibn Taymiyya's discussion represents the Ḥanbalite affirmation of laughter as one of the divine attributes.[75] The Ashʿarites, on the other hand, were less certain about this attribute. The Ashʿarites as a rule included divine laughter among the lesser group of anthropomorphic attributes which are mentioned in the *aḥādīth* with few transmitters (*akhbār al-āḥād*). A saying ascribed to Abū 'l-Ḥasan al-Ashʿārī determines that attributes which are mentioned in *akhbār al-āḥād* may or may not exist. In other words, these *aḥādīth* provide information which is probable but not evident or conclusive.[76] Accordingly, the Ashʿarites accepted most of the *aḥādīth* about divine laughter with the reservation that the laughter mentioned in these *aḥādīth* was metaphorical. Thus, the Ashʿarite theologian Ibn Fūrak included the above quoted brief anecdote in his *Mushkil al-Ḥadīth*.[77] Ibn Fūrak believed that by his response to the Prophet ('A Lord who laughs benevolently will never deprive us of His bounty') Abū Razīn provided a figurative interpretation of divine laughter, because he understood laughter as a symbol of bounty. Based on textual evidence from Arabic poetry, Ibn Fūrak determined that one of the meanings of *ḍaḥk* is 'revealing what lies behind a certain act'.[78] Accordingly, Ibn Fūrak believed that Abū Razīn interpreted the words of the

74 Ibn Taymiyya, *idem*, p. 55.
75 Holtzman 2010, p. 184; Watt 1994, p. 37.
76 Ibn Fūrak, *Mujarrad Maqālāt al-Shaykh Abī 'l-Ḥasan al-Ashʿarī*, p. 41.
77 Ibn Fūrak, *Mushkil al-Ḥadīth*, pp. 66, 69.
78 Ibn Fūrak, *idem*, p. 69.

Prophet about divine laughter thusly: 'God reveals His grace and unveils His benevolence'.[79]

The Ashʿarite theologian and *muḥaddith* Abū Bakr al-Bayhaqī dedicated an entire chapter on *aḥādīth* that mention divine laughter in his *Al-Asmāʾ wa'l-Ṣifāt* (The Names and the Attributes), which is a massive compilation of anthropomorphic traditions. The chapter about divine laughter includes the above quoted anecdote from the Abū Razīn corpus.[80] Al-Bayhaqī added that the laughter in this anecdote should be interpreted as 'revealing' or 'uncovering': 'The Bedouins say "the earth laughs (*ḍaḥakat 'l-arḍ*) when the plants grow", because the earth reveals the beauty of the plants and uncovers the flowers'.[81] Accordingly, God did not laugh but revealed His benevolence.[82]

We note that both Ibn Fūrak and al-Bayhaqī addressed the Abū Razīn anecdote about divine laughter. The Ashʿarite theologian Fakhr al-Dīn al-Rāzī (d. 606/1209), however, ignored the anecdote completely. In his *Asās al-Taqdīs* (The Foundation of Veneration), a treatise whose purpose was to fight the literal understanding of the divine attributes, al-Rāzī dedicated a brief chapter to divine laughter. In this chapter, al-Rāzī did not quote the Abū Razīn anecdote, but other *aḥādīth* which mention divine laughter. Al-Rāzī explained that he had found these texts in the Hadith compilation of the Shāfiʿite *muḥaddith* Muḥyī al-Sunna al-Baghawī (d. 510/1117, or 516/1121–2).[83] Presumably, al-Rāzī rejected the Abū Razīn corpus because it was included in the extremely popular *Kitāb al-Tawḥīd* by the ultra-traditionalistic scholar Ibn Khuzayma, a book which al-Rāzī forcefully refuted.[84]

Al-Rāzī's reading of the *aḥādīth* which mention that God laughs was far more radical than the figurative interpretation suggested by his predecessors Ibn Fūrak and al-Bayhaqī. He was more interested in presenting well-rationalized argumentations against the literal reading of these *aḥādīth* than providing the ready-made solution of *taʾwīl*. Al-Rāzī's argumentation in *Asās al-Taqdīs* contains four stages. Al-Rāzī clarifies that an actual laughter (*ḥaqīqat 'l-ḍaḥk*) cannot be included among the divine attributes because: (a) according to the Quran, God makes people laugh and cry ('He who moves men to laughter and to tears', Q. 53:43), but does not laugh and cry Himself; (b) the verbal noun *ḍaḥk* means 'the shrinking of the facial skin when one's heart is joyous', a description which one cannot attribute to God; (c) the assumption that God laughs entails the as-

79 Ibn Fūrak, *idem*, p. 69.
80 Al-Bayhaqī, *Al-Asmāʾ wa'l-Ṣifāt*, vol. 2, p. 411.
81 Al-Bayhaqī, *idem*, vol. 2, p. 412.
82 Al-Bayhaqī, *idem*, vol. 2, p. 413.
83 Al-Rāzī, *Asās al-Taqdīs*, p. 188. Cf. al-Baghawī, *Sharḥ al-Sunna*, vol. 8, pp. 186–8 (*Kitāb al-fitan, bāb ākhir man yakhruju min 'l-nār*).
84 Holtzman 2018, pp. 301–13.

sumption that God cries, but only the profoundly stupid can attribute crying to God; (d) laughter is generated from astonishment, which is only ascribed to humans who are astonished when something unexpected occurs. One cannot assume that God, who knows both the hidden and the revealed, would be astonished by anything.[85]

Ibn Taymiyya refuted *Asās al-Taqdīs* in several of his works, the most prominent of which is *Bayān Talbīs al-Jahmiyya fī Taʾsīs Bidaʿihim al-Kalāmiyya* (Clarifying the Deception of the Jahmiyya Regarding the Foundation of Their Kalāmic Innovations). In this work, Ibn Taymiyya included a full version of the lengthy *ḥadīth* of Abū Razīn[86] while adding his implied criticism against the authors of some Hadith compilations who abbreviated this lengthy text to meet their stylistic standards.[87] In addition, Ibn Taymiyya criticized al-Rāzī for not using the most reliable *aḥādīth* available about divine laughter.[88]

Although Ibn Taymiyya's presentation of Abū Razīn was scanty and fragmentary, it inspired Ibn Qayyim al-Jawziyya. Following Ibn Taymiyya, Ibn Qayyim al-Jawziyya emphasized Abū Razīn's role in enriching the Prophetic discourse and clarifying theological issues by presenting his questions to the Prophet. Ibn Qayyim al-Jawziyya even broadened Abū Razīn's activity to encompass the entire early Islamic community. He claimed that:

> They used to ask him (i.e. the Prophet) questions about the ambiguous texts which describe the divine attributes that they were having trouble to grasp. And he (i.e. the Prophet) used to answer by confirming (*bi-taqrīrihā*) these texts not by using metaphors (*bi'l-majāz*) and false figurative interpretation (*al-taʾwīl al-bāṭil*). For example, Abū Razīn al-ʿUqaylī asked him about divine laughter, because the Prophet said: 'He will look at you and you will be worried and fearful. He will keep on laughing because He knows that your relief is approaching and will come soon'. Abū Razīn was amazed from the mentioning of divine laughter, and he asked: 'Oh Messenger of God, does God really laugh?' and the Messenger of God answered: 'Yes'. And so Abū Razīn responded: 'A god who laughs benevolently will never deprive us of his bounty'. Were the Jahmite (the Ashʿarite) being asked about this matter, he would have said: 'It is inconceivable to attribute laughter to God, just as it is inconceivable to attribute to Him such attributes as sitting on the throne, descending, and coming and arriving'.[89]

Ibn Qayyim al-Jawziyya offers a mocking presentation of the Ashʿarite discourse: their restrictions on the religious discourse prevent them from providing straightforward answers to simple questions such as 'Does God really laugh?' By

85 Al-Rāzī, *Asās al-Taqdīs*, pp. 188–9. For a systematic refutation of al-Rāzī's argument about divine laughter, see: Ibn Taymiyya, *Bayān Talbīs al-Jahmiyya*, vol. 6, pp. 323–32.
86 Ibn Taymiyya, *idem*, vol. 7 pp. 46–57.
87 Ibn Taymiyya, *idem*, vol. 7 pp. 45–6.
88 Ibn Taymiyya, *idem*, vol. 7, p. 327.
89 Ibn Qayyim al-Jawziyya, *Mukhtaṣar al-Ṣawāʿiq al-Mursala*, p. 1430.

using the example of Abū Razīn's questions, Ibn Qayyim al-Jawziyya leads his readers to an understanding that simple innocent questions deserve straightforward answers. Ibn Qayyim al-Jawziyya claims that Abū Razīn and the Prophet's Companions understood the attributes literally, as denoting an actual reality: when the Prophet described the beatific vision, the *ṣaḥāba* understood that it would be an actual seeing with their own eyes (*ru'yat al-ʿiyān*). Here Ibn Qayyim al-Jawziyya presents Abū Razīn as the prototype of the inquiring *ṣaḥābī* who asked difficult questions and received clear answers. The Abū Razīn case, argues Ibn Qayyim al-Jawziyya, proved that the Prophet led the *ṣaḥāba* to understand and affirm the concepts of God's laughter and the beatific vision by using two devices: the words (*khiṭāb*) that described these concepts (laughter, seeing), and the explanations that the Prophet provided. Abū Razīn asked the Prophet about the possibility of seeing God, and the Prophet answered by giving the example of the sun and the moon (as quoted above). This answer was an affirmation of the actuality (*taqrīran li-ḥaqīqat 'l-ṣifa*) of the beatific vision. Moreover, the Prophet made the concept of the beatific vision accessible to the *ṣaḥāba* by using examples and arithmetic measurements (*al-amthāl wa'l-maqāyīs al-ʿaqliyya*).[90] The dialogue between the Prophet and Abū Razīn therefore validated the discourse that both Ibn Taymiyya and Ibn Qayyim al-Jawziyya wished to promote, in which discussing the divine attributes in an informative and respectful way was desirable.

4. Ibn Taymiyya and the Questions of the Public

The myth of Abū Razīn represented one of the fundamental principles in Ibn Taymiyya's worldview, that everyone was entitled to ask theological questions and receive elucidating responses which were similar to the Prophet's responses to Abū Razīn. In this section, we examine two case studies which reflect Ibn Taymiyya's approach towards questions. Ibn Qayyim al-Jawziyya's practice of answering theological questions will be examined in another opportunity.

Ibn Taymiyya's career as a certified *muftī* started in 678/1279 when he was seventeen years old. From that point until his death forty-nine years later, Ibn Taymiyya issued hundreds of *fatāwā*. He continued to issue *fatāwā* even during his two-year stay in the Citadel of Damascus, where he was imprisoned for his views about the visitation of the graves of venerated and pious men and women (*ziyārat al-qubūr*). In Jumādā al-Ūlā of the *Hijrī* year 728 (April 1328) and by the order of the sultan, his books, papers, ink, and pens were confiscated. He died on

90 Ibn Qayyim al-Jawziyya, *idem*, p. 1431.

20th Dhū 'l-Qaʿda 728 (25th September 1328).[91] Although his disciples strove to collect his dispersed writings, their Promethean efforts could not have rescued the entire oeuvre of Ibn Taymiyya. As Caterina Bori described in her illuminating 2009 article, Ibn Taymiyya's daily production of *fatāwā* and epistles was overwhelming. His writing was circumstantial and dependent on the questions that people asked him. In addition, he generously distributed his writings among his disciples and clientele. Last but not least, his travels and change of residence also contributed to the loss of an unknown quantity of his work.[92] Still, the surviving works of Ibn Taymiyya comprise an inconceivably gigantic corpus, which even today – almost eighty years after the inauguration of the first scientific effort to study his legacy[93] – is far from being thoroughly studied and exhausted.

Ibn Taymiyya's disciples admired his insistence on answering every question that was addressed to him. This insistence was part of Ibn Taymiyya's passion for teaching. The biographical sources depict Ibn Taymiyya as a natural teacher who never missed an opportunity to convey his doctrines to any audience. His biographer and close friend Sirāj al-Dīn al-Bazzār (d. 749/1349) reported on a doctrinal dispute among Ibn Taymiyya's disciples in which al-Bazzār himself participated. In the heat of the long-drawn-out discussion, the disciples decided to go to Ibn Taymiyya and ask for his opinion. However, Ibn Taymiyya surprised them when he showed up unexpectedly in the place where they were assembled. Before they even had the opportunity to ask Ibn Taymiyya about his view on the issue in dispute, he began lecturing them methodically and leading them to the correct answer. According to al-Bazzār, this event represented the elegance of the Taymiyyan methodology: First, Ibn Taymiyya examined the disciples' arguments, then he elaborated on the stances of the *ʿulamāʾ* of previous generations by fully citing their opinions which he knew by heart, and finally he gave his verdict on the issue in question. The astonished disciplines held their breath in awe as Ibn Taymiyya displayed his intellectual and pedagogical talent. When the lecture was over, the disciples' admiration to Ibn Taymiyya grew even further.[94]

Ibn Taymiyya's natural inclination towards teaching is a plausible explanation of his insistence to quench people's thirst for knowledge. Another explanation is ideological. Bori emphasizes in her article that Ibn Taymiyya's profound conviction that no one should be denied the access of knowledge emanated from the Prophetic ethos: just as the Prophet 'never refused to fulfill the wishes of any

91 See the most useful chronology of Ibn Taymiyya's life in Michot 2006, pp. 150, 169.

92 Bori 2009, pp. 54–6.

93 The monumental *Essai sur les doctrines sociales et politiques de Taḳī-d-Dīn Aḥmad b. Taimīya, canoniste ḥanbalite né à Ḥarrān en 661/1262, mort à Damas en 728/1328* (Cairo: Imprimerie de l'institut français d'archéologie orientale, 1939) by Henri Laoust is the first meaningful step in Taymiyyan studies in Western scholarship.

94 Al-Bazzār, *Al-Aʿlām al-ʿAliyya*, p. 605.

person who approached him',[95] so did Ibn Taymiyya hate the idea that he would deny any of his books (either his own writings or the writings of others that his personal library held) from anyone who needed it.[96] Ibn Qayyim al-Jawziyya also testified that Ibn Taymiyya followed the Prophetic ethos of instructing the people between right and wrong: 'In my opinion, our sheikh, may God sanctify his soul, was very dedicated to teaching in his *fatāwā* whenever he could. Whoever reads his *fatāwā* finds that this feature is very conspicuous'.[97] To Bori's observation that Ibn Taymiyya was generous with his books and writings we would like to add that this generosity was also manifested in his tolerant attitude to questions addressed to him. The myth of Abū Razīn, as we have shown in the previous section, was one of the key-elements in Ibn Taymiyya's understanding of the Prophetic ethos. This myth inspired Ibn Taymiyya to answer theological questions.

The elegies which were written after Ibn Taymiyya's demise by the leading scholars (not necessarily Ḥanbalites) of his times highlight Ibn Taymiyya's natural inclination to share his knowledge with others, and his tolerance of the questions he was asked. A friend of Ibn Taymiyya, ʿAbd Allāh ibn Khiḍr ibn ʿAbd al-Raḥmān (d. 731/1331)[98] declared in his poem: 'Whenever an applicant (*sā'il*) came to ask him something, he was received by immense generosity and amiable behavior'.[99] The verb *sa'ala* in Arabic denotes both asking a question and asking for something (either a material object or a service). Therefore, the applicant or inquirer, *al-sā'il*, in this poem could have been after one of Ibn Taymiyya's books or his learned opinion. In another poem, the Baghdadian Ḥanbalite scholar Ṣafī al-Dīn ʿAbd al-Mu'min ibn ʿAbd al-Ḥaqq (d. 739/1338) lamented in reference to Ibn Taymiyya: 'Where are these branches of knowledge and piercing mind that we were used to see whenever a question was asked and a legal opinion was given in response? Where did the pleasant disposition and welcoming attitude to all visitors disappear?'[100]

Nearly all the responsa in Ibn Taymiyya's *Majmūʿat al-Fatāwā* are prefaced with questions. The same goes for his independent monographs in which he further developed topics that were succinctly discussed in his responsa. Thus, for example, in the opening statement of his nine-volume-monograph *Minhāj al-Sunna al-Nabawiyya* (The Way of the Prophetic Sunna), Ibn Taymiyya remarked

95 Al-Bazzār, *idem*, p. 608.
96 Al-Bazzār, *idem*, p. 609; Bori 2009, p. 55.
97 Ibn Qayyim al-Jawziyya, *Iʿlam al-Muwaqqiʿīn*, vol. 6, p. 47.
98 All that is known about ʿAbd Allāh ibn Khiḍr ibn ʿAbd al-Raḥmān is that he came from 'the Lands of the Greeks' (*bilād al-rūm*), died at the age of ninety, and was buried in al-Bāb al-Saghīr, the cemetery of the Sufis in Damascus. Ibn ʿAbd al-Hādī, *Al-ʿUqūd al-Durriyya*, p. 287.
99 Ibn ʿAbd al-Hādī, *idem*, p. 286.
100 Ibn ʿAbd al-Hādī, *idem*, p. 298.

that he decided to compose this massive book when a group of people asked his opinion on a book authored by one of the scholars of the Twelver Shīʿa. They also brought the book for his consideration.[101] The book that Ibn Taymiyya received was *Minhāj al-Karāma* (The Way of Miracle Performance) authored by his contemporary the Shīʿite Ibn al-Muṭahhar al-ʿAllāma al-Ḥillī (d. 726/1325). *Minhāj al-Sunna* was Ibn Taymiyya's opportunity to refute the Shīʿite doctrines and to thoroughly develop his own theology which he attributed to *al-salaf al-ṣāliḥ*.

We cannot assume that the questions that were recorded in the surviving works of Ibn Taymiyya are indeed faithful reflections of the original questions addressed to him. Ibn Taymiyya probably styled some of these questions for the sake of clarity. Other questions were added by the later editors of Ibn Taymiyya's works in their attempt to organize the massive amount of his writings that were discovered in a state of complete chaos after Ibn Taymiyya's demise.[102] In addition, Ibn Taymiyya himself composed questions which he attributed to anonymous inquirers. After all, opening theological treatises with questions was a conventional literary device in the didactic and religious writings of different cultures from antiquity until Ibn Taymiyya's times and beyond. Whether authentic or not, Ibn Taymiyya systematically presented these questions as the incentive for writing the lion's share of his magnificent literary oeuvre. Furthermore, these questions, some of which evolved around metaphysical themes, reflect the genuine interests and concerns of people who lived in the Mamluk Sultanate and in other areas of the Muslim world.

The authenticity of a question can be easily verified when we have collaborative evidence from other sources. In the beginning of December 1298 (Rabīʿ Awwal of *Hijrī* year 698),[103] Ibn Taymiyya received the following question that arrived with a representative of the people of the Syrian town of Hamat:

> What do you, the most prominent scholar, the leader of religion, think of the anthropomorphic verses (*āyāt al-ṣifāt*; literally, the verses on the divine attributes) such as "The Merciful who sits enthroned on high" (Q. 20:5), "and then ascended on the throne"(7:54, 10:3), "Then, turning to the sky, which was but a cloud of vapour" (Q. 41:11) and so forth? [What do you think of] the anthropomorphic traditions *(aḥādīth al-ṣifāt)* such as "The hearts of the human beings are [held] between two of the All-

101 For the historical background of *Minhāj al-Sunna al-Nabawiyya*, see al-Jamil 2010, p. 229–31.

102 Holtzman 2009, p. 48ff; Holtzman 2016, pp. 576–7.

103 Ibn Taymiyya, *Al-Fatwā al-Ḥamawiyya al-Kubrā* (al-Tuwayjirī's edition), p. 193. The year is not indicated in any of the manuscripts that formed the basis for the preparation of al-Tuwajirī's edition; nonetheless, the year was added by al-Tuwayjirī based on an indication in several historical and biographical sources. See, for example, Ibn ʿAbd al-Ḥādī, *Al-ʿUqūd al-Durriyya*, p. 148.

> Merciful's fingers", and "The Almighty placed His foot in hellfire" and so on? What did other scholars say about these [texts]? Please clarify the matter, may you be rewarded by God, if God wills.[104]

Ibn Taymiyya initially refused to answer this question and referred the inquirer to other Damascene scholars. However, the man insisted that the people that he represented (most probably, the town's sheikhs and local leaders) sought only Ibn Taymiyya's opinion.[105] His insistence persuaded Ibn Taymiyya to answer this question with great consideration. On December 10th 1298 (the 5th of Rabīʿ Awwal 698), Ibn Taymiyya dictated his lengthy response (70 printed pages). The proliferation of this response, entitled *Al-Ḥamawiyya al-Kubrā* (the Grand [Response Written] for the People of Hamat), was the outset of a series of events known as Ibn Taymiyya's ordeals (*miḥan*).[106] Several years after the composing of *Al-Ḥamawiyya al-Kubrā*, Ibn Taymiyya used the same question attributed to the people of Hamat as the starting point of his much larger work, the eight-volume *Bayān Talbīs al-Jahmiyya.*[107]

The reason that led the people of Hamat to address their question about *āyāt al-ṣifāt* and *aḥādīth al-ṣifāt* to Ibn Taymiyya is not explicitly articulated in the sources. However, given the theological tendencies of the local *ʿulamā'* it is understandable why the people of Hamat believed that Ibn Taymiyya was their only recourse. The Chief Judge of Hamat at the time *Al-Ḥamawiyya al-Kubrā* was composed was the Shāfiʿite Sharaf al-Dīn ibn al-Bārizī al-Juhanī (d. 738/1338). His father, Najm al-Dīn al-Bārizī al-Juhanī (d. 683/1285), who was the Chief Judge of Hamat before him, was an expert in rationalistic argumentations (*al-ʿaqliyyāt*) of Ashʿarite *kalām.*[108] As a scholar with a strong Ashʿarite background,[109] Sharaf al-Dīn was intolerant of theological questions. His father Ibn al-Bārizī thought that one 'should stop delving in the topic of the divine attributes' (*al-kaff ʿan al-khawḍ fī 'l-ṣifāt*).[110] We may assume that Sharaf al-Dīn

104 Ibn Taymiyya, '[Al-Ḥamawiyya al-Kubrā]', *Majmūʿat al-Fatāwā*, vol. 5, p. 7. Ibn Taymiyya did not cite the *aḥādīth* verbatim. For the most complete version of the first *ḥadīth*, see: Muslim, *Ṣaḥīḥ*, p. 1065 (*Kitāb al-Qadar, bāb taṣrīf Allāh taʿālā al-qulūb*), *ḥadīth* 2654; for the second *ḥadīth*, see: Muslim, *Ṣaḥīḥ*, pp. 1142–3 (*Kitāb al-Janna, bāb al-nār yadkhuluhā al-jabbārūn, ḥadīth* 2846).

105 Ibn Taymiyya, *Bayān Talbīs al-Jahmiyya*, vol. 1, p. 4.

106 These *miḥan* were already treated in previous researches, therefore we refrain from describing them here. The basic literature on the ordeals includes: Murad, 1979, pp. 1–32; Jackson 1994, pp. 41–56; Michot 2006, pp. 156–60; Hoover 2012; Holtzman 2016, p. 567.

107 Based on the historical sources, the editorial team of *Bayān Talbīs al-Jahmiyya fī Taʾsīs Bidaʿihim al-Kalāmiyya* determined that this work was composed while Ibn Taymiyya was in detention in the Citadel of Cairo between April 1306 (Ramaḍān 705) and September 1307 (Rabīʿ Awwal 707). Ibn Taymiyya, *Bayān Talbīs al-Jahmiyya*, *qism al-dirāsa*, p. 25.

108 Al-Subkī, *Ṭabaqāt al-Shāfiʿiyya*, vol. 8, pp. 189–90.

109 Al-Subkī, *idem*, vol. 10, pp. 387–91.

110 Al-Ṣafadī, *Aʿyān al-ʿAṣr*, vol. 5, p. 332.

followed his father's footsteps in prohibiting the laymen to delve in theology, and that his view was adopted by the local *'ulamā'* in Hamat.

Had Ibn Taymiyya followed the traditionalistic *bi-lā kayfa* formula, he would have answered the people of Hamat bluntly: 'Accept the anthropomorphic descriptions in the Quran and the Hadith and refrain from asking questions about them'. However, although his response contained several such citations from the mouth of his predecessors, the traditionalists,[111] Ibn Taymiyya produced a rich and elaborate treatise that examined various aspects of the question that the people of Hamat presented. In this respect, he was not a faithful representative of Islamic traditionalism. In *Al-Ḥamawiyya al-Kubrā*, Ibn Taymiyya professed his unequivocal acceptance of the entire corpus of anthropomorphic texts. Moreover, the reading method of the anthropomorphic texts that Ibn Taymniyya offered in *Al-Ḥamawiyya al-Kubrā* was interpreted by his Ashʿarite rivals as extreme literalism. While the anonymous inquirer wondered how to understand the descriptions of God in *āyāt al-ṣifāt* and *aḥādīth al-ṣifāt*, Ibn Taymiyya clarified in his response that understanding these descriptions as metaphors (*majāz*) by applying a figurative reading (*ta'wīl*) was unacceptable. According to Ibn Taymiyya, the anthropomorphic descriptions denoted an actual reality (*ḥaqīqa*) and were not merely metaphors (*majāz*) as the Ashʿarites claimed.[112] In Ibn Taymiyya's times, the proponents of *ta'wīl* were the senior *'ulamā'*, namely the holders of official posts in the religious establishment. These *'ulamā'* who received salaries from the Mamluks, held the posts of qadis and muftis. They belonged to all four Sunnite schools of law, but their theological affiliation was the Ashʿarite school of theology. As professed Ashʿarites, these *'ulamā'* were profoundly influenced by the writings of Fakhr al-Dīn al-Rāzī, and accordingly they promoted al-Rāzī's figurative reading of the anthropomorphic texts.

Al-Ḥamawiyya al-Kubrā also highlights a more practical aspect of the dispute over the divine attributes, namely, the issue of raising of hands (*rafʿ al-yadayn*) during *du'ā'* (the invocation of God) or pointing with the index finger (*al-ishāra bi'l-sabbāba*) to indicate God's aboveness (*al-fawqiyya*). This issue was another bone of contention between Ibn Taymiyya and the *'ulamā'* of his time. The Ashʿarite *'ulamā'* of the Mamluk period prohibited these two practices based on al-Rāzī's argumentations as presented in his popular treatise *Asās al-Taqdīs*. The rationale behind this prohibition, as articulated in *Asās al-Taqdīs* was that God was not confined to a specific place, and therefore one could claim that He was above. As a result, raising one's hands or pointing one's finger to the sky while

111 Ibn Taymiyya, [Al-Ḥamawiyya al-Kubrā], *Majmū'at al-Fatāwā*, vol. 5, p. 41, the opinion of Abū Nuʿaym al-Iṣbahānī (d. 420/1038).

112 Ibn Taymiyya, idem, *Majmū'at al-Fatāwā*, vol. 5, p. 20.

invoking God's name was abominable.[113] In *Al-Ḥamawiyya al-Kubrā*, Ibn Taymiyya encouraged the people of Hamat to raise their gaze and hands towards the sky during *du'ā'*. Ibn Taymiyya's profound conviction that God was indeed above was corroborated by numerous textual references from the Quran and the Hadith. Ibn Taymiyya further argued that the natural human inclination (*fiṭra*) directed the believers to raise their hands in prayer. He also accused the Ash'arites of being detached from their *fiṭra*, and that this detachment led them to deny God's aboveness.[114] Ibn Taymiyya's directives and admonishments to the people of Hamat therefore implied censuring al-Rāzī's argumentations and reprimanding the *'ulamā'* who blindly followed al-Rāzī's discourse. This criticism actually meant that Ibn Taymiyya considered these *'ulamā'* enemies of the Prophetic Sunna. *Al-Ḥamawiyya al-Kubrā* was therefore a political text calling for a silent opposition to the Ash'arite-leaning religious establishment.[115]

There is no doubt that the question of the people of Hamat is authentic: The question ignited a chain of actual events that were extensively recorded in various sources.[116] We still do not know (and will probably never know) whether the inquirer from Hamat carried with him a written question to Ibn Taymiyya, or whether he delivered an oral message to the Damascene scholar. We also cannot determine whether the text in the opening paragraph of *Al-Ḥamawiyya al-Kubrā* bears the exact wording of the original question or was paraphrased by either Ibn Taymiyya himself or his disciples who edited his writings posthumously. However, it is highly likely that the original rendition of the people of Hamat was preserved in *Al-Ḥamawiyya al-Kubrā*. First, the original rendition merely contains a request for Ibn Taymiyya's guidance in the matter in dispute, and does not present any previous knowledge or prepossession of the inquirers. Second, the rendition of the question is simple and unsophisticated. Third, the rendition presents the theological issue in a straightforward and even in a shallow manner. All these factors lead us to believe in the authenticity of the question.

Majmū'at al-Fatāwā also contains more elaborate and sophisticated questions the authenticity of which is impossible to determine. Thus, we find in the sixth volume of *Majmū'at al-Fatāwā* the following series of questions:

> What is your opinion about the divine throne (*al-'arsh*)? Is it ball-shaped, or not? If it is indeed ball-shaped, and God is beyond it, encompasses it (*muḥīṭ bihi*) and is separated from it (*bā'in 'anhu*), what is the point in directing our gazes and hands upwards during the invocation of God's name (*du'ā'*) instead of lowering them? Surely, there is no difference between this direction and the other directions that encompass us when we

113 Holtzman 2018, pp. 313–16.
114 Ibn Taymiyya, [Al-Ḥamawiyya al-Kubrā], *Majmū'at al-Fatāwā*, vol. 5, p. 20.
115 Holtzman 2018, pp. 316–33.
116 Holtzman 2018, pp. 324–8.

> pray *duʿā*ʾ, is it not? Nevertheless, we find in our hearts the inclination to direct our gazes and hands upwards and not to direct them either right or left. Please educate us about this urge to look upwards that we find in our hearts, because this is the natural disposition with which we were created (*fuṭirnā*). Please give us an answer which is both simple and healing, an answer which will dispel any doubt and confirm the truth, if God wills. May God enable us to benefit from your wisdom and knowledge for many years to come! Amen.[117]

The editors of *Majmūʿat al-Fatāwā* (in both widely used editions) designated Ibn Taymiyya's response as *Al-Risāla al-ʿArshiyya* (The Epistle about the Divine Throne).[118] This work comprises six different epistles that were written in response to questions supposedly directed at Ibn Taymiyya by anonymous inquirers. The above quoted passage which is the opening paragraph of *Al-Risāla al-ʿArshiyya* presents a question of an educated person. The inquirer was not a professional religious scholar (hence, not one of the *ʿulamā*ʾ), because he did not wish to argue with Ibn Taymiyya and refute his doctrines. In addition, his question imparted humility towards Ibn Taymiyya's genius. A Damascene or a Cairene notable, the anonymous inquirer was well-informed about the controversy between Ibn Taymiyya and the Shāfiʿite-Ashʿarites about *al-Ḥamawiyya al-Kubrā*. He was also well-informed of Fakhr al-Dīn al-Rāzī's argumentation against raising one's hands during *duʿā*ʾ. As opposed to the question of the people of Hamat, the inquirer presented a detailed and sophisticated question. However, on second observation, the anonymous inquirer was too biased to Ibn Taymiyya's approach as made known in *Al-Ḥamawiyya al-Kubrā*. In fact, it seems that the inquirer did not seek a response that would rescue him from his supposedly bewildered state – as reflected in his question – but suggested what the response to his question might be: to be attentive to the *fiṭra*, namely the natural inner 'compass' that leads the people to raise their hands while praying to God. This suggestion correlates the question of the anonymous inquirer to Ibn Taymiyya's response to the people of Hamat.

The anonymous inquirer revealed the traditionalistic dimension of his personality only after presenting himself as an educated and updated man. The first part of his question illustrates the praying man standing on earth which is encompassed by different directions and by the globular throne. His remark that

117 Ibn Taymiyya, [*Al-Risāla al-ʿArshiyya aw al-Iḥāṭa*], *Majmūʿat al-Fatāwā*, vol. 6, p. 326.

118 Ibn Taymiyya, [*Al-Risāla al-ʿArshiyya aw al-Iḥāṭa*], *Majmūʿat al-Fatāwā* eds. ʿĀmir al-Jazzār and Anwar al-Bāz (Al-Mansura and Riyadh: Dār al-Wafāʾ li'l-Ṭibāʿa wa'l-Nashr wa'l-Tawzīʿ and Maktabat al-ʿAbīkān, 1419/1998), vol. 6, pp. 326–60. This is the edition which we used for this article. The second edition is: Ibn Taymiyya, [*Al-Risāla al-ʿArshiyya*], *Majmūʿ Fatāwā Shaykh al-Islām Aḥmad ibn Taymiyya*, eds. ʿAbd al-Raḥmān ibn Muḥammad ibn Qāsim and Muḥammad ibn ʿAbd al-Raḥmān ibn Muḥammad ibn Qāsim (Riyadh: Maṭābiʿ al-Riyāḍ, 1381–8/1961–67), vol. 6, pp. 545–601. This edition is frequently cited in scholarship.

there is no point in directing one's gaze and hands upwards implies that the earth is spherical in its shape, and that it forms the center of the universe. This is the core of the Ptolemaic geocentric cosmology.[119] According to the anonymous inquirer, the throne which is part of that universe is also spherical, and it 'wraps' the spherical earth. This part of the question suggests familiarity with theories that prevailed in the Mamluk period about the divine throne as the ninth sphere (*al-falak al-tāsiʿ*). This concept is briefly mentioned *in Rasāʾil Ikhwān al-Ṣafā* (The Epistles of the Brethren of Purity), the 4th/10th century work of Ismaʿilite doctrine.[120] Ibn Taymiyya mentioned Ikhwān al-Ṣafā as the source of this idea in his response to the anonymous inquirer.[121] Another likely source to inspire the anonymous inquirer is a brief passage from a pseudo-Avicennan treatise entitled *Fī Ithbāt al-Nubuwwāt wa-Taʾwīl Rumūzihim wa-Amthālihim* (Affirming the Prophecies of the Prophets, and Interpreting Their Symbolic Language and Parables) that came into circulation in the 7th/13th century.[122] In this passage, the earth is encompassed by nine spheres: eight of them carry the ninth sphere which is also called 'the sphere of the spheres' (*falak al-aflāk*). This passage came to verify Q. 69: 17 '...and the angels will stand on all its sides with eight of them carrying the throne of your Lord on their heads'. According to this interpretation, the eight angels are therefore the eight spheres.[123]

In his response to the anonymous inquirer, Ibn Taymiyya does not mention Avicenna but rather 'the leaders of the philosophers' (*aʾimmat al-falāsifa*). Ibn Taymiyya challenges the theory of the throne as the ninth sphere and determines

---

119 Siddiqi 1995, pp. 9–10; Gidley 2006, pp. 32–2.

120 *Rasāʾil Ikhwān al-Ṣafā*, vol. 2, p. 26; vol. 4, p. 224. I thank Michael Ebstein for providing me these references.

121 Ibn Taymiyya, [*Al-Risāla al-ʿArshiyya aw al-Iḥāṭa*], *Majmūʿat al-Fatāwā*, vol. 6, p. 327.

122 For the controversy about the authenticity of *Fī Ithbāt al-Nubuwwāt*, see: Gutas 2014, pp. 485–6; Marmura 2008, pp. 133–4, fn. 49; Davidson 1992, pp. 87, fn. 56 , 91–2 fn. 74. Michael Marmura who edited *Fī Ithbāt al-Nubuwwāt* strongly believed in its authenticity and elaborated on his position in the English preface of this treatise. Ibn Sīna, *Fī Ithbāt al-Nubuwwāt*, vii–xi. Apart from an analysis of the treatise's content and style which supposedly led to Avicenna's authorship of this treatise, Marmura discovered that 'a treatise about the affirmation of prophecy' (*risāla fī ithbāt al-nubuwwa*, in the singular undefined form) was mentioned in the list of Avicenna's writings in the biographical supplement written by the Persian scholar Ẓahīr al-Dīn al-Bayhaqī (d. 565/1169–70). This inclusion means that *Fī Ithbāt al-Nubuwwāt* came into circulation during the lifetime of al-Bayhaqī, namely in the middle of the 6th/12th century. Al-Bayhaqī, *Tatimmat Ṣiwān al-Ḥikma*, p. 187. As opposed to Marmura's position, Gutas determined that the treatise was inauthentic. Based on 'its muddling account of the faculties of the soul and the absence of any mention of Guessing Correctly middle terms', Gutas inferred that *Fī Ithbāt al-Nubuwwāt* was authored by the disciples of Abū Ḥāmid al-Ghazālī after his death. This assumption places the date of the treatise in the end of the 6th/12th century, and its circulation by the middle of the 7th/13th century. Gutas 2014, p. 489.

123 Ibn Sīna, *Ithbāt al-Nubūwwāt*, pp. 53–4.

that the astronomers, the philosophers, and the mystics have no actual proof that there is nothing beyond the ninth sphere. In fact, the philosophers had no satisfactory explanation why there are only nine spheres and not ten or twelve.[124] Ibn Taymiyya refutes other aspects of the philosophers' theory, for example the idea that the ninth sphere (or the divine throne) is the cause of the circular movement of the other spheres. His refutation is a mix of textual evidence and logical argumentations. Ibn Taymiyya declares that the Quranic verses and *aḥādīth* which characterize the throne as 'glorious' (*majīd*, Q. 85:15),[125] 'magnificent' (*ʿaẓīm*, Q. 23:86–7), and 'noble' (*karīm*, Q. 23:113), 'prove that the divine throne is completely separated from all which is created' (*wa-amā 'l-ʿarsh fa'l-akhbār tadullu ʿalā mubāyanatihi li-ghayrihi*).[126] The throne therefore cannot be 'a kind of a sphere' (*min jins al-aflāk*) otherwise 'its relationship to what lies beneath it would be similar to the relationship of [any other body] to what lies beneath it'.[127] Ibn Taymiyya also explains that the philosophers' argumentations relied entirely on what they had witnessed and what they had grasped through their senses. In this respect, their methodology was superior to that of the speculative theologians, the *mutakallimūn* who tried to refute the philosophers without any substantial proof at their disposal. However, the philosophers' argumentations were limited in topics related to the divine. The ultimate source of knowledge about this topic is the revelation. 'However, if we investigate this matter closely – concludes Ibn Taymiyya – we realize that what we know through reliable arithmetic calculations does not negate what is written in the Quran and the Hadith. The reliable sciences of the Quran and the Hadith do not negate any reliable conclusion which is based on reason and calculation'.[128]

In a formidable display of his analytical skills combined with massive citations from the Hadith literature, Ibn Taymiyya presents his worldview which is as follows: The throne is not globular; the throne is above the globular spheres and does not 'wrap' them; the only possible direction of the throne is above.[129] In *Al-Risāla al-ʿArshiyya* Ibn Taymiyya examines every one of these possibilities[130] and comes to the conclusion that God's encompassment (*al-iḥāṭa*) of the world,

124 Ibn Taymiyya, [*Al-Risāla al-ʿArshiyya aw al-Iḥāṭa*], *Majmūʿat al-Fatāwā*, vol. 6, pp. 327–8.

125 The verse reads *dhū 'l-ʿarsh 'l-majīd* (Q. 85:15). Ibn Taymiyya remarks: 'You can read the word *majīd* in this verse as a nominative, in which case *majīd* is an attribute of God (He is the glorious Lord of the throne), and you can read the word *majīd* as a genitive, in which case *majīd* is an attribute of the throne (He is the Lord of the glorious throne)'. Ibn Taymiyya, [*Al-Risāla al-ʿArshiyya aw al-Iḥāṭa*], *Majmūʿat al-Fatāwā*, vol. 6, p. 329. Obviously, Ibn Taymiyya preferred the second reading.

126 Ibn Taymiyya, *idem*, *Majmūʿat al-Fatāwā*, vol. 6, p. 329.

127 Ibn Taymiyya, *idem*, *Majmūʿat al-Fatāwā*, vol. 6, p. 330.

128 Ibn Taymiyya, *idem*, *Majmūʿat al-Fatāwā*, vol. 6, pp. 333–4.

129 Ibn Taymiyya, *idem*, *Majmūʿat al-Fatāwā*, vol. 6, pp. 339.

130 Ibn Taymiyya, *idem*, *Majmūʿat al-Fatāwā*, vol. 6, pp. 339–48.

which is a concept that attributes all directions to God, can clarify God's aboveness. To illustrate the meaning of the encompassing, Ibn Taymiyya quotes a rare *ḥadīth* in which one of the Prophet's Companions, Abū Dharr al-Ghifārī (d. circa 32/652) testified that the Prophet said: 'If you would send down a man tied in a rope to the lower earth, he would have landed on God (*la-habaṭa ʿalā Allāh*)'.[131] After examining the possibility of sending a man to the center of earth, Ibn Taymiyya comes to the conclusion that this idea is impractical.[132] His conclusion is therefore that the Prophet did not convey a feasible possibility (*ḥaqīqiyyan*):

> There are things which lie beneath our feet, meaning that they are below, and things which exist above our heads, meaning that they are above. When we throw something from the above downwards in the direction of our legs, we only imagine that this thing lands down. Let us assume that one of us, tied is a rope, is sent down through a hole in the ground and lands on whatever is there. This is but an assumption, and it is impractical for us to perform anyhow. The purpose of this *ḥadīth* was to clarify the concept of the Creator's encompassment (*al-iḥāṭa*) of the creation.[133]

According to Ibn Taymiyya, the Muʿtazilites read this *ḥadīth* as a sophisticated parable illustrating God's all-encompassing knowledge, while the incarnationists (*al-ḥulūliyya*) and the pantheists (*al-ittiḥādiyya*) read this *ḥadīth* as proof that God was physically everywhere.[134] Ibn Taymiyya read the text as a hypothesis that the Prophet presented to the Companions. This hypothesis, that God was under the lowest earth, was meant to illustrate the concept of God's encompassment in theory, and not in practice:

> This *ḥadīth* teaches us that God is capable of encompassing the creation. But it is well-known from the Quran and the Hadith that this encompassment will take place in the Day of Resurrection. Approving the encompassment as a rule does not contradict reason and revelation. However, we discuss only what we know, and we abstain from discussing what we do not know.[135]

In contrast to this *ḥadīth* which presents a possibility of God being under the lowest earth, there are numerous Quranic verses and *aḥādīth* that encourage the believer to direct his gaze upwards when invoking God. One of these texts is the

---

131 In this rather peculiar *ḥadīth*, the Prophet described to the Companions the structure of the earth which is comprised of seven earths. Al-Tirmidhī who quoted this *ḥadīth* remarked that there were *muḥaddithūn* who interpreted this *ḥadīth* thus: the man 'would have landed on the knowledge of God'. Al-Tirmidhī rejected this interpretation because God's knowledge, power and sovereignty were everywhere, not merely in the lowest earth. Al-Tirmidhī, *Sunan*, vol. 5, pp. 403–4 (*Kitāb Tafsīr al-Qur'an*, interpretation of Q. 57).

132 Ibn Taymiyya, [*al-Risāla al-ʿArshiyya aw al-Iḥāṭa*], *Majmūʿat al-Fatāwā*, vol. 6, p. 342.

133 Ibn Taymiyya, idem, *Majmūʿat al-Fatāwā*, vol. 6, p. 343.

134 Ibn Taymiyya, idem, *Majmūʿat al-Fatāwā*, vol. 6, p. 343.

135 Ibn Taymiyya, idem, *Majmūʿat al-Fatāwā*, vol. 6, p. 343.

ḥadīth in which Abū Razīn asks the Prophet how will God be able to see the Muslims on the Day of Resurrection 'when there will be so many of us in the land while He is but one person'. For Ibn Taymiyya, the Prophet's answer that the moon above sees all the people is proof that one should gaze upwards during *duʿā'*.[136]

To summarize his argumentations, Ibn Taymiyya says that two false premises that came from the philosophical discourse confused the inquirer. According to the first premise, if the throne was globular, then God who was above it should have been globular as well. According to the second premise, if the throne was the ninth sphere, then all directions were applicable to it, since it 'wrapped' the earth, which was globular as well. These premises were false because:

> The notion that God resembled the spheres is inconceivable. It is an absurd to describe Him as similar in size and shape to the spheres. As clarified before [in the scriptures], He is so great and big that it is impossible to describe Him on the same scale as the spheres. For Him, the spheres are smaller than a chick-pea or a peppercorn that we hold in our palms. For Him, the spheres are smaller than a coin or a ball that the children play with. We grab the ball and make it jump. But no reasonable man will say: 'Since I am taller than the ball, I encompass the ball like a sphere'. God is far greater than that. These people 'underrate the might of God. But on the Day of Resurrection He will hold the entire earth in His grasp and fold up the heavens in His right hand. Glory be to Him! Exalted be He above their idols!' (Q. 39: 67). As for the second premise, that you face the sphere when you look in each of the six directions, this is a false premise even according to the logicians who are knowledgeable in astronomy. Even the speculative theologians understand that you turn only to the direction which it possible to turn to. I have therefore clarified that the two premises that you presented were incorrect both in terms of logic and reason. In addition, they contradicted the Quran and the Hadith. The hearts must turn upwards when praying to Him, and not to any other direction as we proved here. It is irrelevant whether the throne is the ninth sphere or not, whether it encompasses the ninth sphere and is a globular object or not, whether it is above the ninth sphere and is not a globular object or not. It is irrelevant whether the Creator encompasses the entire creation in His grasp or whether He is above the creation, upwards, above our heads, and not in another direction. Therefore, and after taking into consideration every hypothesis in this regard, both premises of your question are false. When we invoke God, we invoke Him gazing upwards and not to any other direction. This is the way in which we were created.[137]

Were the series of questions that the anonymous inquirer presented in *Al-Risāla al-ʿArshiyya* authored by Ibn Taymiyya himself as a literary device? The other questions that open the shortest epistles in *Al-Risāla al-ʿArshiyya* are less elaborative than the question that we discussed but no less sophisticated. For example, another inquirer asked: 'Do the divine throne and the divine pedestal exist

136 Ibn Taymiyya, idem, *Majmūʿat al-Fatāwā*, vol. 6, p. 345.
137 Ibn Taymiyya, idem, *Majmūʿat al-Fatāwā*, vol. 6, pp. 348–9.

or are they merely a metaphor (*majāz*)?'[138] This question again indicates that the inquirer was well-familiar with the Ashʿarite terminology. Another inquirer asked Ibn Taymiyya: 'Two men argued about the nature of the sky and the earth. One of them claimed that the sky and the earth are globular, while the other rejected this idea claiming that there was no textual evidence to substantiate it. Which of the two claims is true?'[139] These questions seem to come from the mouth of an educated audience who was familiar with the premises and conventions of Ashʿarite *kalām*.

Whether these questions were authored by Ibn Taymiyya for didactic purposes or were authentic questions, Ibn Taymiyya used them to present his worldview which includes two aspects, as specified in *Al-Risāla al-ʿArshiyya*. The first aspect is that asking questions about God is an acceptable behavior. Abū Razīn al-ʿUqaylī who is briefly mentioned in *Al-Risāla al-ʿArshiyya* is the literary device cited to illustrate this idea. The second aspect is that the answer conveys the idea of *bi-lā kayfa*, but without actually saying *bi-lā kayfa*. Ibn Taymiyya was willing to educate his audience, examine every puzzle and analyze every question. His learned and rich responsa informed his audience about every aspect of a given issue, while leading the audience to the recognition that 'we discuss only what we know, and we abstain from discussing what we do not know'.[140]

Bibliography

Primary Sources

Abū Dāwūd, Sulaymān ibn al-Ashʿath al-Sijistānī, *Sunan Abī Dāwud*, edited by a team of the editorial house (Riyadh: Bayt al-Afkār al-Dawliyya, 1420/1999).

Anonymous authors, *Rasā'il Ikhwān al-Ṣafā wa-Khullān al-Wafā'*, no editor mentioned (Qom: Markaz al-Nashr, Maktab al-Iʿlām al-Islāmī, 1984–5).

Al-Ājurrī, Abū Bakr Muḥammad ibn al-Ḥusayn ibn ʿAbd Allāh, *Kitāb al-Sharīʿa*, edited by the editorial board of Mu'assasat al-Rayyān (Beirut: Mu'assast al-Rayyān, 1421/2000).

Al-Ashʿarī, Abu 'l-Ḥasan ʿAlī ibn Ismāʿīl, *Al-Ibāna ʿan Uṣūl al-Diyāna*, no editor mentioned (Beirut: Dār Ibn Zaydūn, n.d.).

Al-Baghawī, al-Ḥusayn ibn Masʿūd, *Sharḥ al-Sunna*, ed. Shuʿayb al-Arnā'ūṭ (Damascus-Beirut: al-Maktab al-Islāmī, 1403/1983, 2nd edition).

Al-Bayhaqī, Abū Bakr Aḥmad ibn al-Ḥusayn, *Al-Iʿtiqād wa'l-Hidāya ilā Sabīl al-Irshād*, eds. Abū ʿAbd Allāh Aḥmad ibn Ibrāhīm Abū al-ʿAynayn et al. (Riyadh : Dār sal-Faḍīla, 1420/1999).

138 Ibn Taymiyya, idem, *Majmūʿat al-Fatāwā*, vol. 6, p. 350.
139 Ibn Taymiyya, idem, *Majmūʿat al-Fatāwā*, vol. 6, p. 351.
140 Ibn Taymiyya, idem, *Majmūʿat al-Fatāwā*, vol. 6, p. 343.

–, *Kitāb al-Asmā' wa'l-Ṣifāt*, ed. ʿAbd Allāh ibn Muḥammad al-Ḥāshidī (Jedda: Maktabat al-Sawādī li'l-Tawzīʿ, 1413/1993).

Al-Bayhaqī, Ẓahīr al-Dīn Abū 'l-Ḥasan ʿAlī ibn Abi 'l-Qāsim, *Kitāb Tatimmat Ṣiwān al-Ḥikma*, ed. Muḥammad Shafīʿ (Lahore: L. Ishwar Das, 1351/1935).

Al-Bazzār, ʿUmar ibn ʿAlī, *Al-Aʿlām al-ʿAliyya fī Manāqib Ibn Taymiyya*, in: *al-Qawl al-Jalī*, ed. Yaḥyā Murād, Beirut: Dār al-Kutub al-ʿIlmiyya, 1426/2005.

Al-Bukhārī, Abū ʿAbd Allāh Muḥammad ibn Ismāʿīl, *Al-Jāmiʿ al-Ṣaḥīḥ*, eds. Muḥibb al-Dīn al-Khaṭīb, Muḥammad Fu'ād ʿAbd al-Bāqī and Quṣayy Muḥibb al-Dīn al-Khaṭīb (Cairo: al-Maktaba al-Salafiyya, 1400/ [1980]).

–, *Kitāb al-Tārīkh al-Kabīr*, ed. Muḥammad ʿAbd al-Muʿīd Khān (Hyderabad-Deccan: The Dairatu'l-Maʿarif-I Osmania, 1375/1955).

Al-Dāraquṭnī, Abu 'l-Ḥasan ʿAli ibn ʿUmar, *Kitāb al-Ru'ya*, eds. Ibrāhīm Muḥammad al-ʿAlī and Aḥmad Fakhrī al-Rifāʿī (Zarqa: Maktabat al-Manār, 1411/1990).

Al-Dārimī, ʿAbd Allāh ibn ʿAbd al-Raḥmān al-Samarqandī, *Sunan al-Dārimī*, eds. Fawāz Aḥmad Zimrlī and Khālid al-Sabʿ al-ʿAlamī (Karachi: Qadīmī Kutubkhāne, 1407/ [1986]).

Al-Dhahabī, Shams al-Dīn Abū ʿAbd Allāh Muḥammad ibn Aḥmad ibn ʿUthmān, *Siyar Aʿlām al-Nubalā'*, eds. Shuʿayb al-Arna'ūṭ and Ḥusayn al-Asad (Beirut: Mu'assasat al-Risāla, 1405/1985, 3rd edition).

Al-Ghazālī, Abū Ḥāmid, *Majmūʿat Rasā'il al-Imām al-Ghazālī*, ed. Ibrāhīm Amīn Muḥammad (Cairo: al-Maktaba al-Tawqīfiyya, n.d.).

Al-Ḥākim al-Nīsabūrī, Abū ʿAbd Allāh Muḥammad ibn ʿAbd Allāh, *Al-Mustadrak ʿalā 'l-Ṣaḥīḥayn*, ed. Muṣṭafā ʿAbd al-Qādir ʿAṭā (Beirut: Dār al-Kutub al-ʿIlmiyya, [1408/ 1988]).

Ibn ʿAbd al-Barr, Abū ʿUmar Yūsuf ibn ʿAbd Allāh ibn Muḥammad al-Namarī al-Andalūsī, *Al-Tamhīd li-mā fī 'l-Muwaṭṭa' mina 'l-Maʿānī wa'l-Asānīd*, eds. Muṣṭafā ibn Aḥmad al-ʿAlawī and Muḥammad ʿAbd al-Kabīr al-Bakrī (Morocco: Wizārat ʿUmūm al-Awqāf wa'l-Shu'ūn al-Islāmiyya, 1387/1967).

Ibn ʿAbd al-Hādī, Abū ʿAbd Allāh Muḥammad ibn Aḥmad al-Dimashqī al-Ṣāliḥī, *Al-ʿUqūd al-Durriyya fī Manāqib Shaykh al-Islām Ibn Taymiyya*, in: *al-Qawl al-Jalī*, ed. Yaḥyā Murād (Beirut: Dār alKutub al-ʿIlmiyya, 1426/2005).

Ibn Abī Yaʿlā, Abu 'l-Ḥusayn Muḥammad, *Ṭabaqāt al-Fuqahā' al-Ḥanābila*, ed. ʿAlī Muḥammad ʿUmar (Cairo: Maktabat al-Thaqāfa al-Dīniyya, 1419/1998).

Ibn ʿAsākir, Abu 'l-Qāsim ʿAlī ibn al-Ḥasan ibn Hibat Allāh ibn ʿAbd Allāh, *Tārīkh Madīnat Dimashq*, ed. ʿUmar ibn Gharāma al-ʿUmrawī et al. (Beirut: Dār al-Fikr, 1995–2001).

Ibn al-Athīr, ʿIzz al-Dīn Abu 'l-Ḥasan ʿAlī ibn Muḥammad al-Jazarī, *Usd al-Ghāba fī Maʿrifat al-Ṣaḥāba*, ed. ʿAlī Muḥammad Muʿawwaḍ and ʿĀdil Aḥmad ʿAbd al-Mawjūd (Beirut: Dār al-Kutub al-ʿIlmiyya, 1417/1996).

Ibn Fūrak, Abū Bakr Muḥammad ibn al-Ḥasan al-Iṣbahānī al-Ašʿarī, *Kitāb Muškil al-Ḥadīṯ aw Ta'wīl al-Aḫbār al-Mutašābiha*, ed. Daniel Gimaret (Damascus: Institut Français d'Études Arabes de Damas, 2003).

–, *Mujarrad Maqālāt al-Shaykh Abī 'l-Ḥasan al-Ashʿarī*, ed. Daniel Gimaret (Beirut: Dār al-Mashriq, 1987).

Ibn Ḥajar al-ʿAsqalānī, Abu 'l-Faḍl Aḥmad ibn ʿAlī Shihāb al-Dīn, *Inbā' al-Gumr bi-Abnā' al-ʿUmr*, ed. Ḥasan Ḥabashī (Cairo: Lajnat Iḥyā' al-Turāth al-Islāmī, 1389/1969).

Ibn Ḥanbal, Aḥmad ibn Muḥammad, *Musnad al-Imām Aḥmad*, eds. Shuʿayb al-Arnāʾūṭ et al. (Beirut: Muʾassasat al-Risāla, 1416/1995).

Ibn Kathīr, ʿImād al-Dīn Abu ʾl-Fidāʾ Ismaʿīl ibn ʿUmar, *Al-Bidāya waʾl-Nihāya fī al-Tārīkh*. ed. ʿAbd Allah ibn ʿAbd al-Muḥsin al-Turkī ([Cairo]: Dār Hajar liʾl-Ṭibāʿa waʾl-Nashr waʾl-Tawzīʿ waʾl-Iʿlān, 1424/2003).

Ibn Khuzayma, Abū Bakr Muḥammad ibn Isḥāq, *Kitāb al-Tawḥīd wa-Ithbāt Ṣifāt al-Rabb ʿAzza wa-Jalla*, ed. ʿAbd al-ʿAzīz ibn Ibrāhīm al-Shahwān (Riyadh: Dār al-Rushd, 1408/1988).

Ibn Māja, Abū ʿAbd Allāh Muḥammad ibn Yazīd al-Qazwīnī, *Sunan Ibn Māja*, ed. Muḥammad Nāṣir al-Dīn al-Albānī (Riyadh: Maktabat al-Maʿārif liʾl-Nashr waʾl-Tawzīʿ, 1417/[1996]).

Ibn Qayyim al-Jawziyya, Abū ʿAbd Allāh Muḥammad ibn Abī ibn Ayyūb, *Ḥādī al-Arwāḥ ilā Bilād al-Afrāḥ*, ed. Zāʾid ibn Aḥmad al-Nushayrī (Mecca: Dār ʿĀlim al-Fawāʾid, 1428/[2007]).

–, *Iʿlām al-Muwaqqiʿīn ʿan Rabb al-ʿĀlamīn*, ed. Abū ʿUbayda Mashhūr ibn Ḥasan Āl Salmān (Dammam: Dār Ibn al-Jawzī, 1423/[2002–3]).

–, *Zād al-Maʿād fī Hady Khayr al-ʿIbād*, no editor mentioned (Cairo: Dār al-Fajr liʾl-Turāth, 1425/2004).

Ibn Qayyim al-Jawziyya and Muḥammad ibn al-Mawṣilī, *Mukhtaṣar al-Ṣawāʿiq al-Mursala*, ed. al-Ḥasan ibn ʿAbd al-Raḥmān al-ʿAlawī (Riyadh: Maktabat Aḍwāʾ al-Salaf, 1425/2004).

Ibn Qutayba, Abū Muḥammad ʿAbd Allāh ibn Muslim, *Taʾwīl Mukhtalif al-Ḥadīth*, ed. Muḥammad Muḥyī al-Dīn al-Aṣfar (Beirut and Doha: al-Maktab al-Islāmī and Muʾassasat al-Ishrāq, 1419/1999).

Ibn Rajab, ʿAbd al-Raḥmān ibn Aḥmad, *Al-Dhayl ʿalā Ṭabaqāt al-Ḥanābila*, ed. ʿAbd al-Raḥmān ibn Sulaymān al-ʿUthaymin (Mecca: Maktabat al-ʿAbīkān 1425/2005).

–, *Laṭāʾif al-Maʿārif fīmā li-Mawāsim al-ʿĀm mina ʾl-Waẓāʾif*, ed. Yāsīn Muḥammad al-Sawwās (Beirut: Dār Ibn Kathīr, 1420/1999).

–, *Rawāʾiʿ al-Tafsīr: Tafsīr Ibn Rajab al-Ḥanbalī*, ed. Abū Maʿādh Ṭāriq ibn ʿAwḍ Allāh ibn Muḥammad (Riyadh: Dār al-ʿĀṣima liʾl-Nashr waʾl-Tawzīʿ, 1422/2001).

Ibn Sīna, *Fī Ithbāt al-Nubuwwāt (Proof of Prophecies)*, ed. Michael Marmura (Beirut: Dār al-Nahār, 1968).

Ibn Taymiyya, Taqī al-Dīn Aḥmad ibn ʿAbd al-Ḥalīm, *Bayān Talbīs al-Jahmiyya fī Taʾsīs Bidaʿihim al-Kalāmiyya*, edited by a team of editors under the supervision of sheikh ʿAbd al-ʿAzīz al-Rājiḥī (Medina: Majmaʿ al-Malik Fahd li-Ṭibāʿat al-Muṣḥaf al-Sharīf, 1426/2005).

–, *Al-Fatwā al-Ḥamawiyya al-Kubrā*, ed. Ḥamd ibn ʿAbd al-Muḥsin al-Tuwayjirī, Riyadh: Dār al-Ṣumayʿī liʾl-Nashr waʾl-Tawzīʿ, 1419/1998.

–, *Al-Risāla al-Akmaliyya*, ed. Aḥmad Ḥamdī Imām (Cairo: Maṭbaʿat al-Madanī, 1403/1983).

–, *Majmūʿat al-Fatāwā*, eds. ʿĀmir al-Jazzār and Anwar al-Bāz (Al-Mansura and Riyadh: Dār al-Wafāʾ liʾl-Ṭibāʿa waʾl-Nashr waʾl-Tawzīʿ and Maktabat al-ʿAbīkān, 1998).

Al-Iṣbahānī, Abū Nuʿaym Aḥmad ibn ʿAbd Allāh, *Maʿrifat al-Ṣaḥāba*, ed. ʿĀdil ibn Yūsuf al-ʿAzāzī (Riyadh: Dār al-Waṭan liʾl-Nashr, 1419/1998).

Al-Mizzī, Jamāl al-Dīn ibn al-Ḥajjāj Yūsuf, *Tuḥfat al-Ashrāf wa-Maʿrifat al-Aṭrāf*, ed. Bashār ʿAwwād Maʿrūf (Beirut: Dār al-Gharb al-Islāmī, 1999).

Muslim ibn Ḥajjāj, Abu 'l-Ḥusayn al-Qushayrī al-Nīsābūrī, *Ṣaḥīḥ Muslim*, ed. Abū Ṣuhayb al-Karmī (Riyadh: Bayt al-Afkār al-Duwaliyya, 1419/1998).

Al-Nawawī, Muḥyī al-Dīn Abū Zakariyyā' Yaḥyā ibn Sharaf, *Tahdhīb al-Asmā' wa'l-Lughāt*, no editor mentioned (Beirut: Dār al-Kutub al-ʿIlmiyya, n.d.; repr. of the 1927 edition of Idārat al-Ṭibāʿa al-Munīriyya, Cairo).

Al-Qalqashandī, Abu 'l-ʿAbbās Aḥmad, *Nihāyat al-Arab fī Maʿrifat Ansāb al-ʿArab*, ed. Ibrāhīm al-Abyārī (Beirut: Dār al-Kitāb al-Lubnānī, 1400/1980).

Al-Qurṭubī, Abū ʿAbd Allāh Muḥammad ibn Aḥmad al-Anṣārī, *Al-Jāmiʿ li-Aḥkām al-Qur'ān*, ed. Sālim Muṣṭafā al-Badrī (Beirut: Dār al-Kutub al-ʿIlmiyya, 1420/2000).

Al-Rāzī, Fakhr al-Dīn Muḥammad Ḍiyā' al-Dīn ʿUmar ibn al-Khaṭīb, *Asās al-Taqdīs*, ed. Aḥmad Ḥijāzī al-Saqā (Cairo: Maktaba Kulliyyāt al-Azhariyya, 1406/1989).

Al-Ṣafadī, Ṣalāḥ al-Dīn Khalīl Aybak, *Aʿyān al-ʿAṣr wa-Aʿwān al-Naṣr*, ed. ʿAmr Muḥammad ʿAbd al-Ḥamīd, Beirut: Dār al-Kutub al-ʿIlmiyya, 1430/2009.

Al-Subkī, Tāj al-Dīn Abū Naṣr 'Abd al-Wahhāb ibn 'Alī, *Ṭabaqāt al-Shāfiʿiyya al-Kubrā*, eds. Maḥmūd Muḥammad al-Ṭināḥī and 'Abd al-Fattāḥ Muḥammad al-Ḥilw (Cairo: Dār Iḥyā' al-Kutub al-'Arabiyya, [1992]).

Al-Ṭabarānī, Abū al-Qāsim Sulaymān ibn Aḥmad, *Al-Muʿjam al-Kabīr*, ed. Ḥamdī ʿAbd al-Majīd al-Salafī (Cairo: Maktabat Ibn Taymiyya, 1984).

Al-Ṭayālisī, Sulaymān ibn Dāwūd ibn al-Jārūd, *Musnad Abī Dāwūd al-Ṭayālisī*, ed. Muḥammad ibn ʿAbd al-Muḥsin al-Turkī (Giza: Dār Hajar, 1419/1999).

Al-Tirmidhī, Muḥammad ibn ʿĪsā ibn Sawra, *Sunan al-Tirmidhī*, ed. Muḥammad Nāṣir al-Albānī (Riyadh: Maktabat al-Maʿārif li'l-Nashr wa'l-Tawzīʿ, 1417/[1996–7]).

Secondary Sources

Abrahamov, B. (1995), 'The *Bi-lā Kayfa* Doctrine and Its Foundations in Islamic Theology', *Arabica* 42, pp. 365–79.

al-Jamil, T. (2010), 'Ibn Taymiyya and Ibn al-Muṭahhar al-Ḥillī: Shiʿi Polemics and the Struggle for Religious Authority in Medieval Islam', in: *Ibn Taymiyya and His Times.* Edited by Yossef Rapoport and Shahab Ahmed, Karachi: Oxford University Press, pp. 229–246.

Bori, C. (2009), 'The Collection and Edition of Ibn Taymīyah's Works: Concerns of a Disciple', *Mamlūk Studies Review* 13.2, pp. 47–67.

Davidson, H. A. (1992), *Alfarabi, Avicenna, and Averroes, On Intellect*, New York and Oxford: Oxford University Press.

Dawood, N. J., trans., (2000 [1956]), *The Koran with a Parallel Arabic Text*, London: Penguin Classics.

El-Rouayheb, Kh. (2010), 'From Ibn Ḥajar al-Haytamī (d. 1566) to Khayr al-Dīn al-Ālūsī (d. 1899): Changing Views of In Taymiyya among Non-Ḥanbalī Sunni Scholars', In: Y. Rapoport and Sh. Ahmed (eds.), *Ibn Taymiyya and His Times*, Karachi: Oxford University Press, pp. 269–318.

Frank, R. M. (1991), 'Elements in the Development of the Teaching of al-Ashʿari', *Le Museon: Revue d'Etudes Orientales* 104, pp. 141–90.

Frank, R. M. (1994), *Al-Ghazālī and the Ash'arite School*, Durham-London: Duke University Press.

Gidley, J. (2006), 'Spiritual Epistemologies and Integral Cosmologies: Transforming Thinking and Culture', in: S. Awbrey et al., *Integral Learning and Action: A Call to Wholeness*, New York: Peter Lang Publishing, pp. 29–55.

Gimaret, D. (1995), 'Ru'yat Allāh', In P. Bearman, Th. Bianquis, C.E. Bosworth et al. (eds.) *The Encyclopaedia of Islam, Second Edition (EI2)*, vol. 8, p. 649 (Leiden: Brill); Available on Brillonline.com.

Griffel, F. (2009), *Al-Ghazālī's Philosophical Theology*, Oxford: Oxford University Press.

Gutas, D. (2014), *Avicenna and the Aristotelian Tradition*, Leiden and Boston: Brill.

Holtzman, L. (2010), 'Does God Really Laugh?: Appropriate and Inappropriate Descriptions of God in Islamic Traditionalist Theology', in: A. Classen (ed), *Laughter in the Middle Ages and Early Modern Times*, Berlin: de Gruyter, pp. 165–200.

Holtzman, L. (2016), 'Accused of Anthropomorphism: Ibn Taymiyya's *Miḥan* as Reflected in Ibn Qayyim al-Jawziyya's al-Kafiyah al-Shafiyah', *The Muslim World* 106.3, pp. 561–87.

Holtzman, L. (2018), *Anthropomorphism in Islam: The Challenge of Traditionalism (700–1350)*, Edinburgh: Edinburgh University Press.

Hoover, J. (2012), 'Ibn Taymiyya', *Oxford Bibliographies- Islamic Studies*, DOI: 10.1093/OBO/97801953901550150.

Jackson, Sh. A. (1994), 'Ibn Taymiyyah on Trial in Damascus', *Journal of Semitic Studies* 39.1, pp. 41–85.

Juynboll, G. H. A. (2007), *Encyclopedia of Canonical Ḥadīth*, Leiden-Boston: Brill.

von Kügelgen, A. (2013), 'The Poison of Philosophy: Ibn Taymiyya's Struggle For and Against Reason', in: B. Krawietz and G. Tamer (eds), *Islamic Theology, Philosophy and Law: Debating Ibn Taymiyya and Ibn Qayyim al-Jawziyya*, Berlin and Boston: de Gruyter, pp. 253–328.

Lev, Y. (2009), 'Symbiotic Relations: Ulama and the Mamluk Sultans', *Mamlūk Studies Review* 19.1, pp. 1–26.

Levi Della Vida, G., 'al-Muntafiḳ', in P. Bearman, Th. Bianquis, C.E. Bosworth et al. (eds.) *The Encyclopaedia of Islam, Second Edition (EI2)*, vol. 7 (1993), pp. 582–3 (Leiden:Brill). Available on Brillonline.com.

Makdisi, G. (1963), 'Ash'arī and the Ash'arites in Islamic Religious History II', *Studia Islamica* 18, pp. 19–39.

Marmura, M. (2008), 'Some Questions Regarding Avicenna's Theory of the Temporal Origination of the Human Rational Soul', *Arabic Sciences and Philosophy* 18, pp. 121–138.

Michot, Y. (2006). *Muslims under Non Muslim Rule: Ibn Taymiyya* , Oxford: Interface.

Murad, H. Q. (1979), 'Ibn Taymiya on Trial: A Narrative Account of His Miḥan', *Islamic Studies 18*, pp. 1–32.

Siddiqi, A. H. (1995), 'Muslim Geographic Thought and the Influence of Greek Philosophy', *GeoJournal* 37.1, pp. 9–15.

Speight, M. R. (2000), 'Narrative Structures in the Ḥadīth', *Journal of Near Eastern Studies* 59.4, pp. 265–71.

Tamer, G. (2013), 'The Curse of Philosophy: Ibn Taymiyya as a Philosopher in Contemporary Islamic Thought', in: B. Krawietz and G. Tamer (eds), *Islamic Theology,*

Philosophy and Law: Debating Ibn Taymiyya and Ibn Qayyim al-Jawziyya, Berlin and Boston: de Gruyter, pp. 329–74.
Watt, W. M. (1948), *Free Will and Predestination in Early Islam*, London: Luzac and Company.
Watt, W. M. (1994), *Islamic Creeds: A Selection*, Edinburgh: Edinburgh University Press.

Jon Hoover

Ibn Taymiyya's Use of Ibn Rushd to Refute the Incorporealism of Fakhr al-Dīn al-Rāzī*

Introduction

Ernest Renan famously declared that Ibn Rushd/Averroes (d. 595/1198) was the "last representative" of philosophy in the Arab and Islamic world.[1] We now know that Ibn Rushd was by no means the last. Instead, the philosophy of Ibn Sīnā/Avicenna (d. 428/1037) triggered an "Avicennan pandemic" that spread throughout the lands of medieval Islam and profoundly shaped Islamic thought down to the nineteenth century.[2] Ibn Rushd did not enjoy a comparable fortune. While he stirred debate in medieval Europe, his influence in the Islamic world appears to have been minimal. Peter Adamson in the introduction to the 2011 edited volume *In the Age of Averroes* briefly surveys possible reasons for this. One is that Ibn Rushd lived in Andalusia, far from the central lands of Islam. Adamson does not think this sufficient to explain his lack of impact. Instead, Adamson argues, it likely has to do with Ibn Rushd's links to the ruling Almohads, who many opponents took to be heretics, and even more so with the fact that Ibn Rushd did not engage the prevailing philosophy of Ibn Sīnā directly. He circumvented it by calling for a return to Aristotle.[3] Yet, even if the Islamic world

* The research for this publication was funded by a Leverhulme Trust Fellowship. All translations from the Qur'ān and other Arabic texts are my own.

1 This statement is found in both the first and last editions of Ernest Renan, *Averroès et l'averroïsme: essai historique*, 1st ed. (Paris, A. Durand, 1852), 1; and 4th ed. (Paris: Calmann Lévy, 1882), 2.

2 Jean R. Michot, "La pandémie avicennienne au VIe/XIIe siècle: présentation, *editio princeps* et traduction de l'introduction du *Livre de l'advenue du monde* (*Kitāb ḥudūth al-ʿālam*) d'Ibn Ghaylān Al-Balkhī," *Arabica* 40 (1993): 287–344. As examples of the literature on Ibn Sīnā's influence on medieval and early modern Islamic thought, see Robert Wisnovsky, "Avicenna's Islamic Reception," in: *Interpreting Avicenna: Critical Essays*, ed. Peter Adamson (Cambridge, UK: Cambridge University Press, 2013), 190–213; and Heidrun Eichner, "Handbooks in the Tradition of Later Eastern Ashʿarism," in: *The Oxford Handbook of Islamic Theology*, ed. Sabine Schmidtke (Oxford, UK: Oxford University Press, 2016), 494–514.

3 Peter Adamson, "Introduction," in: *In the Age of Averroes: Arabic Philosophy in the Sixth/Twelfth Century*, ed. Peter Adamson (London: The Warburg Institute, 2011), 1–7 (3, 7). Oliver

took far more interest in Ibn Sīnā than Ibn Rushd, the Andalusian philosopher was not ignored entirely. The Damascene traditionalist theologian Ibn Taymiyya (d. 728/1328) has much to say about Ibn Rushd and quotes him extensively. This attention to Ibn Rushd is extraordinary, especially when no one else in the medieval Islamic east seems to have shown much concern for him.[4] This, too, requires explanation. Why was Ibn Rushd of interest to Ibn Taymiyya and not to others?

Before addressing this question, attention must first be given to the relevant texts and recent research. Ibn Taymiyya refers to Ibn Rushd in several of his books,[5] and he quotes him extensively in his two long works *Bayān talbīs al-jahmiyya* [hereafter *Bayān*] and *Dar' taʿāruḍ al-ʿaql wa al-naql* [hereafter *Dar'*]. *Bayān* – eight volumes in the 2005 Medina edition – is a refutation of the Ashʿarī theologian Fakhr al-Dīn al-Rāzī's (d. 606/1210) *Ta'sīs al-taqdīs*, which is in turn a rebuttal of Karrāmī and Ḥanbalī anthropomorphism.[6] Ibn Taymiyya wrote *Bayān* between Ramaḍān 705/April 1306 and Dhū al-Ḥijja 706/June 1307 while imprisoned in Cairo on charges of corporealism.[7] In *Bayān* Ibn Taymiyya quotes

Leaman, *Averroes and his Philosophy*, rev. ed. (Richmond, UK: Curzon Press, 1998), 176–177, lists further reasons suggested by earlier scholars for Ibn Rushd's lack of influence.

4 Henry Corbin, "En Orient, après Averroès," in: *Multiple Averroès: Actes du Colloque International organisé à l'occasion du 850e anniversaire de la naissance d'Averroès. Paris 20–23 septembre 1976*, ed. Jean Jolivet (Paris: Les belles lettres, 1978), 323–332. Corbin claims that he had not found even one reference to Ibn Rushd in the Islamic east before the seventeenth century (323–324). Ibn Rushd did apparently receive some attention in the medieval Islamic west; see Yamina Adouhane, "Al-Miklātī, A Twelfth Century Ašʿarite," *Arabic Sciences and Philosophy* 22.2 (2012): 155–197 (155–156). Adouhane argues that the Maghribī Ashʿarī theologian Abū al-Hajjāj al-Miklātī (d. 626/1228–1229) drew on Ibn Rushd, albeit without acknowledgement, in his work *Kitāb lubāb al-ʿuqūl fī al-radd ʿalā al-falāsifa fī ʿilm al-usūl.*

5 See for example *Al-Jawāb al-ṣaḥīḥ li-man baddala dīn al-Masīḥ*, ed. ʿAlī ibn Ḥasan ibn Nāṣir, ʿAbd al-ʿAzīz ibn Ibrāhīm al-ʿAskar, and Ḥamdān ibn Muḥammad al-Ḥamdān, 7 vols. (Riyadh: Dār al-ʿāṣima, 1993–1999), 5:19, 31; *Kitāb al-radd ʿalā al-manṭiqiyyīn*, ed. ʿAbd al-Ṣamad Sharaf al-Dīn al-Kutubī (Bombay: Al-Maṭbaʿa al-qayyima, 1368/1949), 148; *Kitāb al-ṣafadiyya*, ed. Muḥammad Rashād Sālim, 2 parts in 1 vol. (Manṣūra, Egypt: Dār al-hudā al-nabawiyya, 1421/2000), 1:149, 2:186; *Kitāb al-nubuwwāt*, ed. ʿAbd al-ʿAzīz ibn Ṣāliḥ al-Ṭuwayyān, 3 vols. (Medina: al-Jāmiʿa al-Islāmiyya bi-l-Madīna al-Munawwara, ʿImādat al-baḥth al-ʿilmī, 1420/2000), 1:364, 459, 2:760; and *Minhāj al-sunna al-nabawiyya fī naqḍ kalām al-Shīʿa al-Qadariyya*, ed. Muḥammad Rashād Sālim, 9 vols. (Riyadh: Jāmiʿat al-Imām Muḥammad ibn Saʿūd al-Islāmiyya, 1986), 1:199, 236, 246, 323, 348, 356, 357, 374, 375, 399, 402, 2:281.

6 Ibn Taymiyya, *Bayān talbīs al-Jahmiyya fī ta'sīs bidaʿihim al-kalāmiyya*, ed. Yaḥyā ibn Muḥammad al-Hunaydī, et al., 10 vols. 2d printing (Medina: Majmaʿ al-Malik Fahd li-tibāʿat al-muṣḥaf al-sharīf, 1426/2005); volumes 1–8 contain the edited text; volume 9 comprises studies on the text; and volume 10 is indexes. Fakhr al-Dīn al-Rāzī, *Ta'sīs al-taqdīs*, ed. Anas Muḥammad ʿAdnān al-Sharafāwī and Aḥmad Muḥammad Khayr al-Khaṭīb (Damascus: Dār nūr al-ṣabāḥ, 2011); also known as *Asās al-taqdīs* as in Fakhr al-Dīn al-Rāzī, *Asās al-taqdīs*, ed. Aḥmad Ḥijāzī al-Saqqā (Cairo: Al-Maktaba al-azhariyya, 1406/1986).

7 For the dating and circumstances of Ibn Taymiyya's writing of *Bayān*, see Jon Hoover, "Early

at length from Ibn Rushd's *al-Kashf ʿan manāhij al-adilla* [hereafter *Kashf*], which outlines what the general public should believe, and also selections from Ibn Rushd's *Faṣl al-maqāl*, which explicates the religious obligation to engage in philosophy.[8] Ibn Taymiyya's second tome *Darʾ* comes to ten volumes in the edition of Rashād Sālim and dates to 713/1313 or later.[9] In *Darʾ* Ibn Taymiyya argues that there is no contradiction between reason and revelation, and he quotes several selections from Ibn Rushd's *Kashf* and the latter's *Tahāfut al-tahāfut*[10] refuting the *Tahāfut al-falāsifa*[11] of al-Ghazālī (d. 505/1111), as well as nearly the whole of his short *Ḍamīma*.[12]

There is furthermore the question of which text of *Kashf* Ibn Taymiyya quotes. In a 2005 study, Marc Geoffroy explains that Ibn Rushd wrote two distinct versions of *Kashf*. The first version was composed in 575/1179–1180. At the outset, Ibn Rushd divides human beings into the general public (*jumhūr*) and the learned elite (*ʿulamāʾ*), and he explains that the treatise is devoted to explaining what the general public should believe. Whereas the elite for example know that God is incorporeal, the general public should not deny that God has a body so as not to sow confusion concerning the affirmations of revelation. Then, Ibn Rushd carefully sidelines Ashʿarī theological positions dominant among the Almohads ruling Andalusia and North Africa at the time in favor of views more amenable to

---

Mamlūk Ashʿarīs against Ibn Taymiyya on the nonliteral reinterpretation of God's attributes (*taʾwīl*)," in: *Philosophical Theology in Islam: The Later Ashʿarite Tradition*, ed. Jan Thiele and Ayman Shihadeh (Leiden: Brill, forthcoming).

8 Editions of Ibn Rushd's *al-Kashf ʿan manāhij al-adilla* will be discussed below. Further reference to *Faṣl al-maqāl* will be to Averroës, *Decisive Treatise & Epistle Dedicatory* [Arabic and English], trans. Charles E. Butterworth (Provo, UT: Brigham Young University Press, 2001), 1–33; an earlier English translation is found in Ibn Rushd (Averroes), *On the Harmony of Religion and Philosophy: A Translation, with Introduction and Notes, of Ibn Rushd's* Kitāb faṣl al-maqāl, *with Its Appendix (*Ḍamīma*) and an Extract from* Kitāb al-kashf ʿan manāhij al-adilla (London: Luzac, 1961). For a recent analysis of *Faṣl al-maqāl*, see Caterina Belo, *Averroes and Hegel on Philosophy and Religion* (Farnham, UK: Ashgate, 2013), 21–47. For references to and quotations from Ibn Rushd in Ibn Taymiyya's *Bayān*, see the index entries in *Bayān*, 10:210 (Muḥammad ibn Aḥmad ibn Muḥammad Ibn Rushd), 10:256–257 (*Faṣl al-maqāl*), and 10:260 ([*al-Kashf ʿan*] *manāhij al-adilla*).

9 Ibn Taymiyya, *Darʾ taʿāruḍ al-ʿaql wa al-naql*, ed. Muḥammad Rashād Sālim, 11 vols. (Riyadh: Jāmiʿat al-Imām Muḥammad ibn Saʿūd al-Islāmiyya, 1979–1983). On the dating of *Darʾ*, see Jon Hoover, *Ibn Taymiyya's Theodicy of Perpetual Optimism* (Leiden: Brill, 2007), 10–11.

10 Averroès, *Tahafot at-Tahafot*, ed. Maurice Bouyges (Beirut: Imprimerie Catholique, 1930); trans. Simon van den Bergh, *Averroes' Tahafut al-tahafut*, 2 vols. (London: Luzac, 1954).

11 Al-Ghazālī, *The Incoherence of the Philosophers*, ed. and trans. Michael E. Marmura (Provo, UT: Brigham Young University, 1997).

12 The Arabic of *al-Ḍamīma* (*Risālat al-ihdāʾ*) is printed with an English translation in Averroës, *Decisive Treatise & Epistle Dedicatory*, 38–42. For references to and quotations from Ibn Rushd in *Darʾ*, see the index entries in *Darʾ*, 11:77–78 (Ibn Rushd), 11:329–330 (*Tahāfut al-tahāfut*), and 11:345–346 ([*al-Kashf ʿan*] *manāhij al-adilla*). Ibn Taymiyya's quotes Ibn Rushd's *Ḍamīma* in *Darʾ* 9:383–390.

Aristotelianism. Geoffroy suggests that Ibn Rushd's aim in doing this is to offer an alternative expression of Almohad orthodoxy. This effort failed, and Geoffroy shows that Ibn Rushd, apparently under duress, rewrote the section in *Kashf* on God and body to conform to the teaching of Almohad founder Ibn Tūmart (d. 524/1130) that everyone – even the general public – must affirm God's incorporeality. Ibn Rushd justifies his new view not from the texts of revelation but as required by the needs of the time to ward off corporealist error.[13]

The first version of *Kashf* is preserved in MS Escurial 632, fols. 20v–74r, which is the sole source for the first modern edition, by Müller in 1859,[14] and the primary source for the later editions of Qāsim (1964)[15] and al-Jābirī (1998).[16] Qāsim also consulted MS Taymūriyya, *ḥikma* 129 located in Dār al-kutub in Cairo and noted that it contained various additions, but he did not include these in his edition, nor recognize the significance of the revised text. Geoffroy has now identified MS Istanbul, Köprülü 1601, fols. 117v–194v, as a better witness to this same revised text. This manuscript contains additions mentioning Ibn Tūmart and affirming Almohad doctrines and deletions of material offending orthodox Almohad sensibilities. Geoffroy provides an edition of the chapter on God and body from the later version of *Kashf* and translates key passages to illustrate Ibn Rushd's retraction of his earlier views.[17]

---

13 Marc Geoffroy, "À Propos de l'almodhadisme d'Averroès: L'anthropomorphisme (*taǧsīm*) dans la seconde version du *Kitāb al-kašf ʿan manāhiǧ al-adilla*," in: *Los Almohades: problemas y perspectivas*, ed. Patrice Cressier, Maribel Fierro, and Luis Molina, 2 vols. (Madrid: Consejo superior de investigaciones científicas, 2005), 2:853–894. On Ibn Rushd's rewriting of *Kashf*, see also Maribel Fierro, "The Religious Policy of the Almohads," in: *The Oxford Handbook of Islamic Theology*, ed. Sabine Schmidtke (Oxford, UK: Oxford University Press, 2016), 679–692 (681–683).

14 Marcus Joseph Müller, *Philosophie und Theologie von Averroes* (Munich: G. Franz, 1859), 27–127 (Arabic), 26–118 (German).

15 Ibn Rushd, *Manāhij al-adilla fī ʿaqāʾid al-milla*, ed. Maḥmūd Qāsim, 2d ed. (Cairo: Maktabat al-anjlū al-Miṣriyya, 1964. Qāsim also published an earlier edition with the same press in 1955 based on MS Taymūriyya, *ḥikma* 133, which, unbeknownst to Qāsim, was a copy of Müller's edition; for details see Geoffroy, "À Propos de l'almodhadisme d'Averroès," 856–857. Qāsim's 1964 edition of *Kashf* is translated as Averroes, *Faith and Reason in Islam: Averroes' Exposition of Religious Arguments*, trans. Ibrahim Najjar (Oxford: Oneworld, 2001). A nearly full translation of *Kashf* from a 1910 Cairo printing is found in J. Windrow Sweetman, *Islam and Christian Theology*, 2 parts in 2 vols. each (London: Lutterworth, 1945–1967), 2.2.82–180, and there is also a Spanish translation of *Kashf* in Manuel Alonso, *Teología de Averroës: estudios y documentos* (Madrid: Consejo Superior de Investigagiones Científicas, Instituto Miguel Asin, 1947), 203–355.

16 Ibn Rushd, *Al-Kashf ʿan manāhij al-adilla fī ʿaqāʾid al-milla*, ed. Muḥammad ʿĀbid al-Jābirī (Beirut: Markaz dirāsāt al-waḥda ʿarabiyya, 1998); subsequent references to *Kashf* in this study will be to this edition.

17 Geoffroy, "À Propos de l'almodhadisme d'Averroès," 886–894 (Arabic text); the Arabic text indicates additions in bold and places deletions between two short vertical lines in a smaller font. Marc Geoffroy, "Ibn Rušd et la théologie almohadist: une version inconnue du *Kitāb al-*

Geoffroy observes that Ibn Taymiyya copies parts of Ibn Rushd's second Arabic version of the chapter on God and body into his *Darʾ*.[18] From this, Geoffroy surmises that it was only this last version that circulated in eastern Islamic lands.[19] However, Ibn Taymiyya in fact copies the first version of the *Kashf* discussion on God and body into *Bayān*. None of the revisions found in the later version are included.[20] It is thus apparent that Ibn Taymiyya had access to both Arabic versions of Ibn Rushd's *Kashf*, at least by the time he wrote *Darʾ*. It may be that he knew only the first version when writing *Bayān*, but it is also possible that he was by then already acquainted with both versions but chose not to use the latter because, as we will see below, its call for even the general public to affirm God's incorporeality did not serve his purposes.

As is evident from Geoffroy's remarks, knowledge of Ibn Taymiyya's interest in Ibn Rushd is not new to modern scholarship. When Ibn Rushd's *Kashf* and *Faṣl al-maqāl* were published together in Cairo in the early twentieth century, Ibn Taymiyya's comments in *Darʾ* on the first two chapters of *Kashf* and a brief part of the third chapter were compiled and added as an appendix.[21] Additionally, a

---

kašf ʿan manāhiǧ al-adilla dans deux manuscrits d'Istanbul," *Medioevo* 26 (2001): 327–356, provides a detailed introduction to MS Istanbul, Köprülü 1601 and a later Istanbul witness to the second version of *Kashf*. Extending the work of Geoffroy, Silvia Di Donato, "Le *Kitāb al-kašf ʿan manāhiǧ al-adilla* d'Averroès: Les phases de la rédaction dans les discours sur l'existence de Dieu et sur la direction, d'après l'original arabe et la traduction hébraïque," *Arabic Sciences and Philosophy* 25 (2015): 105–133, studies an anonymous Hebrew translation of *Kashf* that includes additions to the first Arabic version, especially in the early part of the treatise on the existence of God. These additions are then for the most part included in the second Arabic version along with further additions and modifications. The Hebrew translation does not include revisions of passages undermining Almohad doctrine, and Di Donato argues that it probably derives from a lost revision of the first Arabic text that was then further revised as the second Arabic version to placate Almohad orthodoxy.

18 Ibn Taymiyya, *Darʾ*, 10:248–300; Frank Griffel, "Ibn Tūmart's Rational Proof for God's Existence and Unity, and His Connection to the Niẓāmiyya Madrasa in Baghdad," in: *Los Almohades: problemas y perspectivas*, 2:753–813 (795 n 127), also notes Ibn Taymiyya's inclusion of a revised version of the *Kashf* chapter on God and corporeality into *Darʾ* and translates two of its key additions (797, 800).

19 Geoffroy, "À Propos de l'almodhadisme d'Averroès," 861.

20 Going beyond the chapter on God and body in *Kashf* studied by Geoffroy, Di Donato, "Le *Kitāb al-kašf*," 128–130, examines an addition to the chapter on God and location (*jiha*) mentioning Ibn Tūmart. Ibn Taymiyya's quotation of this passage in *Bayān*, 1:162, does not include this addition, which further confirms that he is quoting the first version of the Arabic text. He also does not include this addition when quoting the same passage in *Darʾ* 6:216, which means that he quotes from both versions of *Kashf* within *Darʾ*.

21 Ibn Rushd, *Kitāb falsafat al-qāḍī al-fāḍil Muḥammad ibn Aḥmad Ibn Rushd al-Andalusī al-mushtamil ʿalā kitābayn jalīlayn, al-awwal* Faṣl al-maqāl fī-mā bayna al-sharīʿa wa al-ḥikma min al-ittiṣāl *wa* Dhaylihi, *wa al-thānī* al-Kashf ʿan manāhij al-adilla fī ʿaqāʾid al-milla *[wa-yalīhimā]* al-Radd *ʿalā falsafat Ibn Rushd al-ḥafīd taʾlīf Taqī al-Dīn ibn Taymiyya*, 2d printing (Cairo: al-Maṭbaʿa al-jammāliyya, 1328/1910); Ibn Taymiyya's quoted comments on the first chapter of *Kashf* dealing with God's existence are from *Darʾ* 9:72–73, 78, 79–80, 80–81, 82–84,

number of studies, mostly in Arabic, have examined Ibn Taymiyya's relation to Ibn Rushd. This research shows that, despite shared interests in reconciling reason and revelation, Ibn Taymiyya is scathingly critical of Ibn Rushd for his division of humanity into the learned elite who can access the truth through logical demonstration (*burhān*) and the general public who are limited to the realm of rhetoric, and for positing revelation as a presentation of religion appropriate to the level of the general public but something different from the rational truth accessible to the elite. Despite this, Ibn Taymiyya and Ibn Rushd concur to a great extent on what the plain senses (*ẓāhir*) of the revealed texts mean. They agree that the texts do not deny corporeality of God, and thus they reject Ashʿarī *kalām* proofs for God's incorporeality. They also agree that the revelation supports God's continuous creation of the world from eternity, and they therefore reject the emanation metaphysics of Ibn Sīnā and *kalām* proofs for the existence of God based on the temporal origination of the world. Yet, while Ibn Taymiyya makes use of Ibn Rushd's arguments to refute the *kalām* theologians and Ibn Sīnā, he insists that the plain sense of the revealed text is true for everyone, not just the general public. For Ibn Taymiyya, Ibn Rushd at the level of the general public treats the revelation as tantamount to falsehood and at the level of the elite posits an incorporeal God stripped of attributes, especially His attributes of action, and so characterizes God as nothing more than an Aristotelian unmoved mover.[22]

89–90, 110–112, 113, 123–124, 126, 128–129, 131, 132–133, 324, 330–331; his comments on the second chapter dealing with God's unity are from *Dar*ʾ 9:338, 348–349, 350–351, 354, 371–373, 382–383; and his brief comment on God's attribute of will in the third chapter is from *Dar*ʾ 10:198–199. Ibn Taymiyya also comments on further parts of *Kashf* in *Dar*ʾ, but these passages are not included in the appendix. Dominque Urvoy, *Averroès: Les ambitions d'un intellectual musulman* (Paris: Flammarion, 1998), 215 n 1, reports two other Cairene editions of *Faṣl al-maqāl* and *Kashf* including Ibn Taymiyya's texts as an appendix, the first printed by al-Maṭbaʿa al-sharqiyya dated 1321/1903, and the second an undated printing by Maḥmūd ʿAlī Subayh. I was not able to inspect these editions, but they were apparently printed under the title *Falsafat Ibn Rushd.* The edition, *Falsafat Ibn Rushd* (Cairo: al-Maktaba al-maḥmūdiyya al-tijāriyya, 1388/1968), includes Ibn Taymiyya's passages from *Dar*ʾ in the footnotes.

22 See especially Anke von Kügelgen, "Dialogpartner im Widerspruch: Ibn Rushd und Ibn Taymīya über die "Einheit der Wahrheit"," in: *In Words, Texts and Concepts Cruising the Mediterranean Sea: Studies on the Sources, Contents and Influences of Islamic Civilization and Arabic Philosophy and Science Dedicated to Gerhard Endress on His Sixty-Fifth Birthday*, ed. R. Arnzen and J. Thielmann (Leuven: Peeters, 2004), 455–481, which examines Ibn Taymiyya's discussion of Ibn Rushd in *Dar*ʾ, focusing especially on his criticism of Ibn Rushd's elitism and the question of divine corporeality; and ʿAbd al-ʿAzīz ʿAmmārī, *Manāḥī naqd Ibn Taymiyya li-Ibn Rushd* (Beirut: Jadāwil li-l-nashr wa al-tawzīʿ, 2013), which provides a systematic exposition of Ibn Taymiyya's views on Ibn Rushd from a wide range of sources apart from *Bayān*. Other studies include ʿAbd al-Majīd al-Ṣaghīr, "Mawāqif rushdiyya li-Taqī al-Dīn Ibn Taymiyya? Mulāḥaẓāt awwaliyya", in: *Dirāsāt maghribiyya muhdāt ilā al-mufakkir al-maghribī Muḥammad ʿAzīz al-Habābī* 1st ed. (Rabat: 1985), 93–117; 2nd ed. (Rabat: Al-Markaz al-thaqīf; al-ʿarabī, 1987), 164–182; al-Ṭablāwī Maḥmūd Saʿd, *Mawqif Ibn Taymiyya*

Research on Ibn Taymiyya's relation to Ibn Rushd to this point has been based on *Dar'* and discussions found in a number of other treatises, but no attention has been given to his interaction with Ibn Rushd in his early tome *Bayān*. This study will focus on Ibn Taymiyya's use of Ibn Rushd's *Kashf* in *Bayān* on the interconnected questions of God's relation to body (*jism*) and direction or location (*jiha*) and God's visibility in the hereafter.[23] This will show that Ibn Taymiyya's attitude toward Ibn Rushd in *Bayān* is much the same as that found by earlier research on his other works. However, this study will also begin asking more forthrightly than previous studies what it is about the philosopher that Ibn Taymiyya finds useful for his own purposes, particularly on the questions of God and corporeality that are here in view. Ibn Taymiyya's discussions of Ibn Rushd in *Bayān* fall within the first two volumes of the eight volume edition, and it here becomes apparent that quoting and commenting on Ibn Rushd is not simply a matter of critiquing the philosopher. Instead, Ibn Taymiyya puts Ibn Rushd to work marginalizing his opponent Fakhr al-Dīn al-Rāzī from his self-proclaimed position as a mainstream rationalist theologian and refuting his arguments. There are in fact points in *Bayān* where Ibn Taymiyya simply lets Ibn Rushd do the hard work of making the rational argument for him, and this suggests that Ibn Taymiyya may have found difficulty defending his views rationally on his own and that he is perhaps learning from Ibn Rushd how to substantiate the argument.

---

min falsafat Ibn Rushd: Fī al-ʿaqīda wa-ʿilm al-kalām wa al-falsafa (Cairo: Maṭbaʿat al-amāna, 1409/1989); and ʿAbd al-Raḥmān Talīlī, "Athar Ibn Rushd fī al-Mashriq al-ʿarabī: Tabīʿat al-radd al-Taymī ʿalā falsafat Ibn Rushd," *Al-Mishkāt* 3 (2005): 55–70 (I am grateful to Nadjet Zouggar for sending me this article). See also Yahya J. Michot, "A Mamlūk Theologian's Commentary on Avicenna's *Risāla Aḍḥawiyya:* Being a Translation of a Part of the *Dar' al-Taʿāruḍ* of Ibn Taymiyya, with Introduction, Annotation, and Appendices," *Journal of Islamic Studies* 14.2 (2003): 149–203 (Part I) and 14.3 (2003): 309–363 (Part II), at pp. 168–172 of Part I, on Ibn Taymiyya's criticism of Ibn Rushd's esotericism; and Jon Hoover, "Perpetual Creativity in the Perfection of God: Ibn Taymiyya's Hadith Commentary on God's Creation of This World," *Journal of Islamic Studies* 15.3 (2004): 287–329 (290–291, 295), for comments on the similarity between Ibn Rushd and Ibn Taymiyya regarding continuous creation. Richard Taylor, "Averroes: God and the Noble Lie," in: *Laudemus Viros Gloriosos: Essays in Honor of Armand Maurer, CSB* (Notre Dame, IN: University of Notre Dame Press, 2007), 38–59, sorts through various western understandings of Ibn Rushd and then provides an analysis of his view of revealed religion as a "noble lie" that parallels Ibn Taymiyya's reading of the Andalusian philosopher as distinguishing demonstrative truth for the elite from rhetoric for the general public.

23 Ibn Taymiyya in *Bayān* also quotes from *Kashf* and *Faṣl al-maqāl* when discussing proofs for God's existence, God's creation of the world, and the interpretation of God's attributes, but these discussions will be left aside in the interest of keeping the study to a manageable size.

1. Invoking Ibn Rushd to Subvert al-Rāzī's Claim to the Rational Mainstream

As noted above, Ibn Taymiyya's *Bayān* is a refutation of Fakhr al-Dīn al-Rāzī's work *Taʾsīs al-taqdīs*, which constitutes in turn al-Rāzī's refutation of theological anthropomorphism. In *Taʾsīs* al-Rāzī argues at length that God is not perceptible to the human senses, that God is independent of space and location, and that God is neither in the world nor distinct from the world in any particular direction. Thus, revealed texts suggesting that God has a body or is located above the heavens may not be interpreted according to their plain senses. Their meanings must be either reinterpreted to mean something else (*taʾwīl*) or delegated to God and given no further investigation (*tafwīḍ*).[24]

To Ibn Taymiyya, a God imperceptible to the senses that exists neither inside nor outside the world does not exist at all. He retorts in *Bayān* that God is in fact perceptible to human senses such as sight and hearing.[25] He refutes al-Rāzī's arguments against qualifying God with body, space, and location, and he defends the plain senses of texts indicating God's aboveness (*fawqiyya*) and overness (*ʿulūw*) and God's sitting on the Throne (*al-istiwāʾ ʿalā al-ʿarsh*). He explains further that God's sitting on the Throne is a report-based attribute (*ṣifa khabariyya*), which is known only by revealed tradition, whereas God's being above the world is also known by reason and the human natural constitution (*fiṭra*).[26] Through extensive rational argumentation, Ibn Taymiyya carves out conceptual space for the corporeality of God, but he does not explicitly affirm that God has a body. However, he does not deny it either, and he asserts that neither affirming nor denying was the view of the early Muslims (*salaf*).[27] Lest he be accused of crass anthropomorphism, Ibn Taymiyya also stresses God's uniqueness: while the plain senses of the revealed texts are known, there is no similarity between God and creatures, and the modality (*kayfiyya*) of God's attributes is not known. This draws Ibn Taymiyya into a theological double perspective. On the one hand, there is no likeness between God and creatures, but, on the other, God is described with names and attributes that carry meanings in human language that are known and must be explained in a way that is fitting and worthy of God.[28] Ibn Taymiyya's arguments discussed in the rest of this study operate within this latter perspective of the linguistic meanings of terms applied to God. The former perspective of God's unlikeness lies in the background.

---

24 Al-Rāzī, *Taʾsīs*, 46 (al-Rāzī's opening propositions), 227–228 (rule of *taʾwīl*).
25 See for example Ibn Taymiyya, *Bayān*, 2:353–355
26 Ibn Taymiyya, *Bayān*, 1:54, 94; 2:454.
27 Ibn Taymiyya, *Bayān*, 1:289–290; 8:536–546.
28 Ibn Taymiyya, *Bayān*, 2:347–350.

Ibn Taymiyya brings Ibn Rushd into play first in *Bayān* to undermine and marginalize al-Rāzī's pretension to speak for the rational mainstream of Islamic theology. Al-Rāzī positions himself as an advocate of prevailing rationality with two claims. Al-Rāzī's first claim, which appears at the very beginning of *Taʾsīs*, is that "the great majority of rational and respectable people" are agreed that God is not spatially extended (*mutaḥayyiz*), that God is not subject to location (*jiha*), and that God neither dwells in the world nor is distinct from it. Al-Rāzī's "great majority" includes the philosophers who "have agreed on affirming existents that are not spatially extended and do not dwell in something spatially extended, like intellects, souls, and matter."[29] The second thing that al-Rāzī claims is that his opponents are the Karrāmīs and the Ḥanbalīs. He argues that they must, contrary to their own doctrine, acknowledge an existent that is not accessible to the senses. Otherwise, God would be divisible and made up of parts.[30]

Ibn Taymiyya uses Ibn Rushd to confound both of al-Rāzī's claims. As for the first, Ibn Taymiyya opposes al-Rāzī's claim to majority belief by citing respected scholarly authorities who affirm that God is located in the direction "above." These include Mālik ibn Anas (d. 179/795), the student of Abū Ḥanīfa (d. 150/767) Abū Muṭīʿ al-Balkhī (d. 199/814), Aḥmad ibn Ḥanbal (d. 241/855), the Ḥanbalī scholars Abū Yaʿlā al-Farrāʾ (d. 458/1066) and Ibn Qudāma (d. 620/1223), and early *kalām* theologians such as Ibn Kullāb (d. ca. 240/855) and al-Ashʿarī (d. 324/935).[31] Along the way, Ibn Taymiyya observes, "The best of the philosophers (*falāsifa*), like Abū Walīd ibn Rushd, report that the doctrine of the philosophers (*ḥukamāʾ*) is affirming [God's] overness above created things (*ithbāt al-ʿulūw fawq al-makhlūqāt*)."[32] A little later, Ibn Taymiyya introduces Ibn Rushd more fully as a commentator on Aristotle and the author of the *Tahāfut al-tahāfut* refuting al-Ghazālī. He criticizes Ibn Rushd for alleging that the elite have superior knowledge through demonstration that is not accessible to the general public. Yet, he is pleased to report that Ibn Rushd "transmitted affirmation of location [for God] from the philosophers and firmly established that by means of their rational methods, which they call demonstrations."[33] Ibn Taymiyya then proceeds to quote the entire section on God and location (*jiha*) from Ibn Rushd's *Kashf*.[34]

29 Al-Rāzī, *Taʾsīs*, 47; Ibn Taymiyya, *Bayān*, 1:59; Ibn Taymiyya also notes al-Rāzī's claim briefly in *Darʾ*, 6:246.

30 Al-Rāzī, *Taʾsīs*, 50; Ibn Taymiyya, *Bayān*, 1:230–231. Ibn Taymiyya also alludes to al-Rāzī's claim briefly in *Darʾ*, 6:245: "...whoever says that the dispute about [God's overness (*ʿuluw*)] is only with the Karrāmīs and the Ḥanbalīs..."

31 Ibn Taymiyya, *Bayān*, 1:61–217.

32 Ibn Taymiyya, *Bayān*, 1:148–149.

33 Ibn Taymiyya, *Bayān*, 1:156.

34 Ibn Taymiyya, *Bayān*, 1:158–166; Ibn Rushd, *Kashf*, 145–149; Averroes, *Faith and Reason*, 62–67.

In this section on *jiha*, Ibn Rushd first reports that the early Muslims affirmed location of God up until the time when the Muʿtazilīs and later Ashʿarīs such as al-Juwaynī (d. 478/1085) and his followers negated it. He then establishes the textual foundation of the doctrine and asserts its universality. He writes, "The plain senses of the whole revelation (*ẓawāhir al-sharʿ kulluhā*) require affirming location," and he supports this with Qurʾānic proof texts such as, "The All-Merciful sat on the Throne" (Q. 20:5), "Eight [angels] will carry the Throne of your Lord above them on that day" (Q. 69:17), and, "The angels and the Spirit will ascend to Him" (Q. 70:4).[35] Ibn Rushd states as well that religious prescriptions are based on God being in heaven because it is from heaven that the revelation descended. Moreover, Ibn Rushd asserts, "All of the philosophers (*ḥukamāʾ*) are agreed that God and the angels are in heaven just as all the revelations are agreed on that."[36]

Ibn Rushd then addresses the Muʿtazilī and later Ashʿarī charge that affirming location of God necessarily implies that God is in a place (*makān*) and thus has a body (*jism*). Ibn Rushd denies this, and to circumvent it, he elaborates an Aristotelian cosmology that breaks the implication between location and place. He explains that the six directions or locations indicated by the outer surfaces of a body do not constitute its place. Only the surface of another body surrounding that body constitutes its place, like the air surrounding a human being is the human being's place, or like the celestial sphere surrounding the air is the place of the air. Then, when it comes to the outermost sphere of the universe, it has no place because there is no body beyond it that encompasses it. There can be no further body or bodies beyond the outermost sphere because that would entail a sequence of bodies without end. The outer surface of the outermost sphere is not a place at all because it cannot contain another body. Moreover, Ibn Rushd in his Aristotelianism denies the possibility of void space and thereby rules out the existence of a void beyond the outermost sphere. Beyond the outermost sphere, there are no dimensions.

Ibn Rushd then explains that the ancients spoke of the outermost sphere as the abode of spirits, that is, the realm of God and the angels, which is outside time and place.[37] Ibn Rushd concludes, "Establishing location is necessary according

35 Ibn Taymiyya, *Bayān*, 1:158–159; Ibn Rushd, *Kashf*, 145; Averroes, *Faith and Reason*, 62–63 (my translations of passages from Ibn Rushd, *Kashf*, do not follow those of Averroes, *Faith and Reason*).

36 Ibn Taymiyya, *Bayān*, 1:159; Ibn Rushd, *Kashf*, 145; Averroes, *Faith and Reason*, 63.

37 For further analysis of Ibn Rushd's argument on location and its thoroughly Aristotelian character, see Barbara Canova, "Aristote et le Coran dans le *Kitāb al-kašf ʿan manāhiǧ al-adilla* d'Averroès," in: *Averroes et la averroïsmes juif et latin: Actes du colloque international (Paris, 16–18 juin 2005)*, ed. Jean-Baptiste Brenet (Turnhout, Belgium: Brepols, 2007), 193–213 (196–208). For clarification of Ibn Rushd's thought on the void, see Miklós Maróth, "Averroes

to revelation and reason,"[38] which is to say that both revelation and reason affirm that God is above the world but is not in a place and is not corporeal. However, Ibn Rushd clarifies, it is difficult to affirm location and deny corporeality together because this has no parallel in the visible world. It is for this reason that revelation does not deny body of God explicitly. The truth of the matter is known only to the elite, the philosophers, while the general public are either forbidden from seeking knowledge about it or they are given some kind of representation of it from the visible world. Ibn Rushd wraps up his section on location in *Kashf* with a discussion of the elite, the general public, and those in between who are subject to doubts, a disparaging reference to *kalām* theologians.[39]

After quoting Ibn Rushd's text, Ibn Taymiyya offers no comment on its Aristotelian character nor any of its other substantive aspects. His purpose is simply to show that philosophers affirm that God is in the location above, contrary to what al-Rāzī claims, and he continues on citing other scholarly authorities to show that al-Rāzī's theological views are marginal. He expresses no embarrassment whatsoever that Ibn Rushd is his one and only example of a philosopher supporting his views against al-Rāzī. Somewhat later in *Bayān*, Ibn Taymiyya invokes the section on location in *Kashf* again and quotes parts of it to remake the point against al-Rāzī that the philosophers uphold location.[40] Ibn Taymiyya is again spare with his comments, but he does highlight Aristotle as Ibn Rushd's unmentioned source for his concept of place: "According to Aristotle, place (*makān*) is the inner surface of the body encompassing and in contact with the outer surface of the body encompassed."[41]

---

on the Void," in: *La lumière de l'intellect: La pensée scientifique et philosophique d'Averroès dans son temps*, ed. Ahmad Hasnawi (Leuven: Peeters, 2011), 11–22.

38 Ibn Taymiyya, *Bayān*, 1:162; Ibn Rushd, *Kashf*, 147; Averroes, *Faith and Reason*, 64.

39 Ibn Taymiyya, *Bayān*, 1:159–166; Ibn Rushd, *Kashf*, 145–149; Averroes, *Faith and Reason*, 63–67.

40 Ibn Taymiyya, *Bayān*, 1:403–406.

41 Ibn Taymiyya, *Bayān*, 1:405. Ibn Taymiyya, *Dar*ʾ 6:5–7:140, discusses God and location at length including critiques of texts by Ibn Sīnā and al-Rāzī. Within this discussion, Ibn Taymiyya, *Dar*ʾ, 6:212–237, quotes Ibn Rushd, *Kashf*, 145–159 (Averroes, *Faith and Reason*, 62–77) on location, textual interpretation, and the vision of God, to again make the point that the philosophers, apart from Ibn Sīnā and his followers, affirm that God is above the universe. Ibn Taymiyya's accompanying discussion here (*Dar*ʾ 6:210–212, 237–249) is much fuller and more lucid than that of *Bayān*, and he again highlights Aristotle as the source of Ibn Rushd's notion of place, but he does not add anything substantially new. Also, Ibn Taymiyya is here quoting from the first Arabic version of *Kashf* identified by Geoffroy and not the second that he quotes later in *Dar*ʾ when discussing God and body. As shown in Di Donato, "Le *Kitāb al-kašf*," 128–130, Ibn Rushd's discussion of location in the second version includes an addition expressing deference to Ibn Tūmart's denial of location even if not complete acceptance. This is of no use to Ibn Taymiyya's argument, and, assuming that he had read this part of the second version of *Kashf*, it is understandable that he preferred to ignore it and keep to the wording of the first version.

Even though Ibn Taymiyya has little to say about Ibn Rushd's Aristotelian notions of place and space at this early point in *Bayān*, he does use them later in the work to build a rational argument against al-Rāzī. Al-Rāzī in *Taʾsīs* conceives of space as self-subsisting. Space exists on its own apart from the objects within it. Al-Rāzī then argues that a spatially extended and located God would be in need of the space and location that He occupies within that wider expanse of self-subsisting space.[42] Ibn Taymiyya is diffident about speaking of God using the non-scriptural term spatial extension (*taḥayyuz*), but he provides a counter argument anyway to preclude al-Rāzī's alleged errors. He denies the existence of any free-standing space that God might be thought to occupy. Space does not exist apart from spatially extended objects. Rather, the space that a spatially extended God might be said to occupy derives from God himself. It does not exist apart from God, and God in no way depends upon it for His existence.[43] For Ibn Taymiyya then, in this argument against al-Rāzī at least, God is tantamount to a vast spatial extension encompassing the world. Put another way, it could perhaps be said that Ibn Taymiyya builds on Ibn Rushd's Aristotelian cosmology by adding another sphere above the outermost sphere, with this additional sphere being God.

Al-Rāzī's second claim about his position within the world of Islamic theology is that the Ḥanbalīs and the Karrāmīs are his opponents, and he assumes that their view that God is accessible to the senses leads to affirming composition and corporeality in God. Ibn Taymiyya denies that this is so. He allows that al-Rāzī's polemic might apply to some Ḥanbalīs in Khurasān, but he says that it does not apply to the best of the Ḥanbalīs, nor to all Karrāmīs. Rather, Ibn Taymiyya argues, it is al-Rāzī who is opposed by all the prophets, the first three generations of the *salaf*, all the great leaders of the Muslim community, *kalām* theologians like al-Ashʿarī and al-Bāqillānī (d. 403/1013), and even by "the intelligent among the philosophers" (*ḥudhdhāq al-falāsifa*). Again, his only example of a philosopher is Ibn Rushd.[44] When introducing Ibn Rushd here, Ibn Taymiyya mentions his *Tahāfut al-tahāfut*, *Faṣl al-maqāl* (called *Taqrīr al-maqāl*), and *Kashf* (identified as *Manāhij al-adilla*), and he turns especially to *Kashf* where Ibn Rushd maintains that it is incorrect to deny God's corporeality at the exoteric level (*fī al-ẓāhir*) of the general public even if the learned elite deny it at the esoteric level (*fī al-bāṭin*). Ibn Taymiyya characterizes *Kashf* as follows:

> This book includes elucidation of the creed (*iʿtiqād*) that the revelation (*sharīʿa*) set forth and the obligation to present it to the general public just as the revelation set it forth, and elucidation of the part of that [creed] which has been furnished with demonstrative proof (*burhān*) for the learned, similar to what is supported by what

42 Al-Rāzī, *Taʾsīs*, 86–89.
43 Ibn Taymiyya, *Bayān*, 3:590–675.
44 Ibn Taymiyya, *Bayān*, 1:231–235 (235).

> compels assent for the general public. In it he mentioned what, according to his method, must not be stated openly to the general public, and in it he mentioned what is necessary among the things that have been furnished with demonstrative proof according to the method of those who employ it. Also, he mentioned that it is not appropriate at the level of revelation to say that God is a body or is not a body, even though he does say that God is not a body at the esoteric level. Despite this, he affirms location esoterically and exoterically, and he mentions that this is the view of the philosophers.[45]

Immediately after this introduction, Ibn Taymiyya quotes Ibn Rushd's entire discussion of God and body (*jism*) from *Kashf* to undermine al-Rāzī's unrelenting incorporealism. The quotation is from the first version of *Kashf* and not the later version in which Ibn Rushd makes concessions to Ibn Tūmart.[46] The essentials of Ibn Rushd's argument are as follows. Revelation is silent on whether God is corporeal. The revelation does mention God's face and hands, but it does not explicitly affirm that God has a body. However, the revelation also does not deny body of God, and the general public, following revelation, should not deny body of God either. This, according to Ibn Rushd, is for three reasons. First, the *kalām* proofs for God's incorporeality are not demonstrative, and the fact that *kalām* theologians describe God as an essence with attributes added to that essence actually entails corporeality in God. Second, the general public cannot imagine something that is beyond sense perception. So, denying that God has a body would lead them to conclude that God does not exist at all. Third, explicitly denying corporeality of God could sow doubts among the general public about what the revelation reports concerning the hereafter and the vision of God. This is to be avoided so as not to undermine religious adherence. Ibn Rushd then compares the revelation's silence on God's corporeality to its reserve in speaking about the soul (*nafs*). Revelation does not define the soul because of "the difficulty in furnishing a demonstrative proof for the general public for the existence of a self-subsisting existent that is not a body."[47] Ibn Rushd then raises the question of how the general public should think of God if body is to be neither affirmed nor denied of Him. He responds that they should think of God as light since the Qur'ān says, "God is the light of the heavens and the earth" (Q. 24:35). Light can also be perceived by the senses, which is important to the general

45 Ibn Taymiyya, *Bayān*, 1:235–236.

46 As noted above, Ibn Taymiyya does quote the later version of Ibn Rushd's *Kashf* discussion of God and body, which includes additions speaking of Ibn Tūmart, into *Dar'*, 10:248–300 (quotations interspersed with Ibn Taymiyya's commentary and refutation). In *Dar'* Ibn Taymiyya's concern in discussing this text is to criticize Ibn Rushd and Ibn Tūmart's views directly, and not to use the text to undermine the likes of al-Rāzī. The later version of *Kashf* thus serves Ibn Taymiyya's purposes in *Dar'* better than the first version which is closer to his own views.

47 Ibn Taymiyya, *Bayān*, 1:241; Ibn Rushd, *Kashf*, 141; Averroes, *Faith and Reason*, 60.

public. Yet, light has no body, which means that people of demonstration should also think of God as light.[48]

After completing the quote from Ibn Rushd's discussion of God and body, Ibn Taymiyya comments,

> It becomes plain in this passage that [Ibn Rushd] on the esoteric level takes the view of the philosophers, which is that the soul is not a body, and the Creator is likewise [not a body]. However, he does not allow the general public to be told about this because it is, to their minds, impossible. Thus, he gave them the best and nearest of similitudes by mentioning the term "light." This is the view of the leaders of the philosophers in matters similar to it like belief in God and the Last Day. He made plain by clear arguments that the denial mentioned by the *kalām* theologians opposes revelation, and he is correct about that at both the esoteric and exoteric levels. He made plain that the *kalām* theologians' denial of body of God is based on weak arguments, and he made the corruption [of those arguments] plain. He mentioned that [God's incorporeality] is known only if it is known that the soul is not a body. Now, it is known that what he and his philosopher colleagues point to [here] is weaker than that for which he faults the *kalām* theologians. In fact, the *kalām* theologians have shown that [the philosophers'] arguments are corrupt. [The *kalām* arguments] are better than [the arguments] that the [philosophers] use to show that the arguments of the *kalām* theologians are corrupt. Analysis of both groups shows that the arguments of both groups for negating body [of God] are invalid. It is apparent that the philosophers' claim that the soul is not a body and that it is qualified with neither motion nor rest and neither entering nor exiting and that it only senses by means of the imagination (*taṣawwur*) is invalid. It is likewise with their view of the angels. The invalidity of the view of these [philosophers] is more apparent than the invalidity of the view of the *kalām* theologians in matters like this regarding the Lord.[49]

Ibn Taymiyya rejects Ibn Rushd's arguments for the incorporeality of God on the esoteric level as even weaker than the arguments of the *kalām* theologians. He is happy to let the *kalām* theologians and the philosophers demolish each other's arguments because it leaves standing his own view – and the view of Ibn Rushd on the exoteric level – that corporeality is neither affirmed nor denied of God. Ibn Taymiyya does not build a rational case of his own for this view. Instead, he allows Ibn Rushd to speak unimpeded, and he leans on the philosopher to make the rational case for the general public's approach to revelation. That aside, Ibn Taymiyya's stated purpose for quoting these passages on body and location from Ibn Rushd's *Kashf* is no more than to refute al-Razi's claims that the philosophers agree with him and that his only opponents are Ḥanbalīs and Karrāmīs. Ibn

48 Ibn Rushd, *Kashf*, 138–145; Averroes, *Faith and Reason*, 56–62.

49 Ibn Taymiyya, *Bayān*, 1:247–248. Following this commentary, Ibn Taymiyya, *Bayān*, 1:248–249, requotes the first portion of Ibn Rushd's discussion of God and location (*Kashf*, 145; Averroes, *Faith and Reason*, 62–63) that immediately follows the section on God and body in *Kashf*.

Taymiyya insists that Ibn Rushd represents the philosophical mainstream and that al-Rāzī faces stiff opposition not only from Ḥanbalīs and Karrāmīs but from the philosophers as well. Ibn Taymiyya's contention is of course disingenuous. Al-Rāzī was not aware of Ibn Rushd so far as we know. The two scholars were twelfth-century contemporaries living at opposite ends of the Islamic world – al-Rāzī in the east and Ibn Rushd in the west.

Despite his audacity and ingenuity in invoking Ibn Rushd to supplant Ibn Sīnā and marginalize al-Rāzī, Ibn Taymiyya does not regard the Andalusian philosopher an unequivocal ally, particularly on the question of God and location. A bit later in *Bayān*, Ibn Taymiyya quotes a passage from *Faṣl al-maqāl* in which Ibn Rushd distinguishes between two categories of plain senses in the revelation with regard to the question of reinterpretation (*taʾwīl*). One category of plain sense may not be reinterpreted by anyone, whereas the second category must be reinterpreted by the elite, the people of demonstration, lest they become unbelievers. Under this latter category fall revealed texts affirming God's sitting and descending. Those capable of demonstration must reinterpret these texts, but those incapable of demonstration may imagine them in their corporeal senses.[50] Ibn Taymiyya takes this to be a straight contradiction with what Ibn Rushd affirms in *Kashf*. In *Kashf*, the plain senses of revealed texts indicating location do not need to be reinterpreted, neither by the general public nor by the elite, since in Ibn Rushd's Aristotelian universe God and the angels are located in the outer sphere, the abode of spiritual entities.[51]

2. Calling on Ibn Rushd to Argue for the Vision of God

Ibn Taymiyya's last use of Ibn Rushd in *Bayān* occurs about one-quarter way into the work. This is a clear instance of Ibn Taymiyya calling on Ibn Rushd to provide the rational argument, in this case against Ashʿarī efforts to affirm the vision of God in the hereafter. Ibn Taymiyya's discussion falls within a long refutation of al-Rāzī's assertion that God is neither inside the world nor outside it.[52] Ibn Taymiyya argues that God must be an existent accessible to the senses because God would otherwise be nothing at all. He asserts, "The People of the Sunna and the Community (*ahl al-sunna wa al-jamāʿa*) confess that God – Exalted is He – is seen, and they are agreed that what cannot be known by any of the senses is

50 Ibn Taymiyya, *Bayān*, 2:90–93; Averroës, *Decisive Treatise*, 19–20.

51 Ibn Taymiyya, *Bayān*, 2:93–94.

52 Ibn Taymiyya, *Bayān*, 2:325–455. For an overview of the vision in the early Islamic tradition, see Claude Gilliot, "La vision de Dieu dans l'au-delà: Exégèse, tradition et théologie en islam," in: *Pensée grecque et sagesse d'orient hommage à Michel Tardieu*, ed. Mohammad Ali Amir-Moezzi, et al. (Turnhout, Belgium: Brepols, 2009), 237–269.

nothing but a non-existent, not an existent."[53] Thus, Ibn Taymiyya explains, al-Rāzī's understanding of God who is inaccessible to the senses is tantamount to a non-existent even though al-Rāzī affirms that God is a self-subsisting reality with properties distinguishing Him from other realities.[54]

Turning to the vision of God in the hereafter, Ibn Taymiyya notes that the Muʿtazilīs and the philosophers deny the vision because it would require God to be a spatially extended body and would situate Him in a particular direction or location (*jiha*) relative to the person who sees Him. Ibn Taymiyya himself affirms that God will indeed be seen in the hereafter and that God will be situated in a location relative to those seeing Him.[55] He notes, however, that some Ashʿarīs and the Ḥanbalī theologian Abū Yaʿlā affirm that God will be seen without location. Moreover, he claims that some later Ashʿarīs like al-Ghazālī and al-Rāzī come close to the Muʿtazilīs by interpreting the vision as an increase in knowledge.[56] Others say that God will be seen but "not above the one seeing [Him], neither to his right nor his left, and not in any of his [other] directions."[57] Ibn Taymiyya condemns these views as denials of the vision, and he claims that such denials are opposed by revelation, reason, and the human natural constitution (*fiṭra*). He then quotes the full discussion of the vision of God from *Kashf* in order to let Ibn Rushd do the difficult work of demolishing the Ashʿarī arguments that an incorporeal God may be seen.[58]

Ibn Rushd first observes that the Muʿtazilīs deny both corporeality and location of God, and thus the vision of God as well, since everything seen is situated in a location relative to the one who sees it. Ibn Rushd then notes that Ashʿarīs have difficulty combining God's incorporeality with the possibility of seeing something that has no body. Thus, Ibn Rushd claims, they resort to sophistic arguments. These are of two kinds: those directed against the Muʿtazilīs and those designed to prove the possibility of the Ashʿarī view.

Concerning the first kind, Ibn Rushd explains that the Ashʿarīs oppose the Muʿtazilīs by arguing that not every object seen needs to be situated in a location relative to the one seeing it because that principle applies only in the visible world, not the invisible. No location is required if the human sees without eyes. Ibn Rushd rejects this as confusing the intellect, which perceives things not situated

53 Ibn Taymiyya, *Bayān*, 2:341.
54 Ibn Taymiyya, *Bayān*, 2:363–365.
55 Ibn Taymiyya, *Bayān*, 2:392–433.
56 For a discussion of al-Rāzī's arguments on the vision of God, see Yasin Ceylan, *Theology and Tafsīr in the Major Works of Fakhr Al-Dīn Al-Rāzī* (Kuala Lumpur: International Institute of Islamic Thought and Civilization, 1996), 146–154. For the views of al-Ashʿarī and other early *kalām* theologians, see Daniel Gimaret, *La doctrine d'al-Ashʿarī* (Paris: Cerf, 1990), 329–344.
57 Ibn Taymiyya, *Bayān*, 2:433–435 (435).
58 Ibn Taymiyya, *Bayān*, 2:436–450; Ibn Rushd, *Kashf*, 185–191; Averroes, *Faith and Reason*, 71–77.

in a location or place, with the power of sight. Sight depends on the object seen being located in a specific place, and it requires light, a transparent intermediary body, and color in the object seen. For Ibn Rushd, only objects that are colored can be seen.

The second kind of argument made by the Ashʿarīs seeks to prove the possibility of seeing a God who has no body. Within this kind, Ibn Rushd reports two arguments. The first proceeds as follows. Something may be seen by virtue of its being either colored, or corporeal, or a color, or an existent. Now difficulties follow from saying that something is seen by virtue of its being colored, corporeal, or simply a color. Thus, the Ashʿarīs argue, a thing is most certainly seen by virtue of its being an existent. Ibn Rushd rejects the possibility of seeing something without color, and he adds that, if something could be seen merely by virtue of being an existent, then sounds could be seen as well. Other such absurdities would also result. The second argument is attributed by Ibn Rushd to the Ashʿarī theologian al-Juwaynī. According to this argument, the senses perceive things in themselves and not by virtue of the states that distinguish one thing from another because those states are not things existing in themselves. Ibn Rushd rejects this as invalid because sight would not be able to distinguish things on the basis of color if things could not be distinguished by their states.

According to Ibn Rushd, the cause of the Ashʿarī difficulties on the vision of God is their open denial of divine corporeality among the general public in direct contravention of revelation. The revelation does not permit denying body of God. This is because the general public has difficulty believing that one can see something incorporeal. The minds of the general public are confined to what they can imagine, and the revelation would have stated clearly that God had no body if it had intended to do so. Instead, as Ibn Rushd noted earlier in his discussion of God and body, the revelation likens God to light, the most highly exalted of existents accessible to the senses and the imagination, and then it indicates as well that people will see God in the hereafter as they see the sun, all of which does not subject the general public to doubt. Such images are also fitting for the learned elite who know by demonstration that the vision is in reality an increase in knowledge. From this, Ibn Rushd concludes that the vision should be taken in its plain sense and without openly denying or affirming that God has a body.

After quoting the entirety of Ibn Rushd's section on the vision in *Kashf*, Ibn Taymiyya provides a vigorous response, which is translated here in full.

> It is known that this man [Ibn Rushd] adopts the view of the philosophers and [the view] that most of the things that the messengers reported concerning belief in God and the Last Day are similitudes (*amthāl*) propounded [for the general public]. This is the most corrupt of views, and it is the view of the clever among the irreligious hypocrites. They might know that it is hypocrisy (*nifāq*) and irreligion (*zandaqa*), but they still consider

it to be the perfection of truth and knowledge just as these philosophers consider it to be that. This is not the place to elucidate this. The point is simply that even though he adopts the view of the philosophers and the Muʿtazilīs concerning the vision [of God] at the esoteric level – that it is an increase in knowledge, as a group of the later Ashʿarīs similarly think – he indeed knows that it is not possible [that the Ashʿarīs] affirm the vision that the lawgiver reported while denying that they say He is a body, and that, on the contrary, affirming it necessarily entails that they say that He is a body and a location. It has become plain that combining these two things opposes what is perceived by reason and the senses. This is what he has made plain by proof, and it is accepted from him.

As for his claim that [the vision] at the esoteric level is an increase in knowledge, he did not mention any argument as proof for it, and it has become plain from the preceding that he has no argument for the principle behind that, which is the denial that He is a body, except to affirm that the rational soul (*al-nafs al-nāṭiqa*) is not a body. He made plain the corruption of the *kalām* theologians' arguments that God is not a body with clear arguments. Now, it is known that the principle upon which he built [his own] denial, that is, the matter of the soul, is weaker by far and that the great majority of rational people laugh at what these [philosophers] say about the soul in regard to the negative attributes [e. g. incorporeality] more than they laugh at those who affirm seeing something that does not – in their terminology – have a body and is not [situated] in a location. We have made this plain elsewhere.

As for his allegation and the allegation of others among the Jahmīs, the Muʿtazilīs, and those who are like them that the vision that the Messenger reported is an increase in knowledge, anyone who pays attention to the texts knows necessarily that the Messenger reported the vision of something that will be seen. Moreover, clear rational proofs permit this vision, even though the methods that he mentions are not to be used to show that. Those weak methods are weak because those who use them only establish the vision of something that is neither in a location, nor spatially extended (*mutaḥayyiz*), nor dwelling in something spatially extended. On account of this, they argue for divesting the vision of the preconditions required for it to take place because they believe that those preconditions are impossible with regard to God.

If it is said that it is correct that everything subsisting in itself is seen, as commonly understood, and if it is made a precondition that what is seen be [situated] in a location relative to the one who sees and that it be spatially extended and subsisting in something spatially extended, then it is not possible for rational people to dispute the possibility of proofs for the possibility of that vision. Those who deny it only deny it because they think that God – Exalted is He – is not above the world and that He – in their terminology – is not a body, not spatially extended, not dwelling in something spatially extended, and such like among the negative attributes that they have innovated, not to mention their opposition to authentic tradition and clear reason.

The point here is that those disputing the author [al-Rāzī] say to him: We affirm that the vision of the Lord is possible by the Book, the Sunna, and consensus, and by clear rational proofs. We affirm by necessity and by rational inquiry that only that which – in their terminology – is in a location, is spatially extended, or dwells in something spatially extended is seen. If it is established that only that which is spatially extended or dwells in something spatially extended is seen, and that what makes this possible is

> existence and its perfection, it has been established that there are no existents that are not spatially extended or not dwelling in something spatially extended. On the contrary, it has been established that it is impossible for that to exist. This preserves this attribute [of visibility] for the soul, for the angels, and for the Lord – Glory be to Him, Exalted is He.[59]

In this discussion of Ibn Rushd's comments on the vision of God in *Kashf*, Ibn Taymiyya first criticizes Ibn Rushd for his esotericism but then gratefully accepts the philosopher's rational arguments against the Ashʿarīs: it is indeed not possible to affirm the vision of God and deny corporeality of God simultaneously. Ibn Taymiyya goes on to reject Ibn Rushd's interpretation of the vision as an increase in knowledge, and he explains that Ibn Rushd's foundation for this is his argument earlier in *Kashf* for the incorporeality of God from the alleged incorporeality of the soul. Ibn Taymiyya dismisses this argument as obviously weaker than the arguments of even the Ashʿarīs. With the field now cleared for his own view, Ibn Taymiyya explains that the vision of God is reported from the Messenger and that it is rationally possible and rationally defensible. Moreover, if one must speak in terms of *kalām* theology, the only existents that actually exist and can be seen are those that involve spatial extension. The implication, which Ibn Taymiyya does not quite draw out explicitly, is that God himself is spatially extended. Otherwise, God could not be seen in the hereafter. The work that Ibn Rushd performs for Ibn Taymiyya on the vision of God is rational refutation of the Ashʿarī position. This paves the way for Ibn Taymiyya to affirm that believers will see God in the hereafter in a particular location. This is the position that Ibn Rushd himself prescribes for the general public.

Conclusion

To conclude, we return to the question with which we began: why was Ibn Rushd of interest to Ibn Taymiyya specifically? It is not just that Ibn Taymiyya and Ibn Rushd often agree on what the plain senses of the theological content of the Qurʾān and the Ḥadīth mean. It is also that Ibn Rushd in *Kashf* supports his interpretations with sophisticated rationalizations and provides rational arguments against opponents. Ibn Taymiyya recognizes this, turns it to his purposes, and perhaps even learns from it as he works out his own theology. Ibn Taymiyya has no sympathy for Ibn Rushd's esotericism and explicit incorporealism at the level of the learned elite, but, as we have seen in this study of *Bayān*, he does welcome the philosopher's Aristotelian rationalization of God's location above the world, his defense of revelation's silence on whether God has a body at the

59 Ibn Taymiyya, *Bayān*, 2:450–453.

level of the general public, and his refutation of Ashʿarī arguments for the possibility of seeing an incorporeal God. Ibn Rushd provides Ibn Taymiyya rational resources to resist and marginalize al-Rāzī's incorporealism and to affirm that God is indeed located above the heavens without resort to incorporealist reinterpretation. It was the incorporealism of the likes of al-Rāzī that predominated in the later Ashʿarī tradition, as well as in the Sunnī and Shīʿī theological traditions more broadly. At this stage of our knowledge, it appears that Ibn Taymiyya was the foremost and perhaps only medieval advocate of Ibn Rushd's ideas, or at least some of them, in the eastern lands of Islam. Ibn Taymiyya was no Averroist philosopher, but he did put Ibn Rushd to use for his own traditionalist ends.

Bibliography

Adamson, Peter, "Introduction." In: *In the Age of Averroes: Arabic Philosophy in the Sixth/ Twelfth Century*, ed. Peter Adamson, 1–7. London: The Warburg Institute, 2011.

Adouhane, Yamina, "Al-Miklātī, A Twelfth Century Ašʿarite." *Arabic Sciences and Philosophy* 22.2 (2012): 155–197.

Al-Ghazālī, *The Incoherence of the Philosophers.* Ed. and trans. Michael E. Marmura. Provo, UT: Brigham Young University, 1997.

Alonso, Manuel, *Teología de Averroës: estudios y documentos.* Madrid: Consejo Superior de Investigagiones Científicas, Instituto Miguel Asin, 1947.

Al-Rāzī, Fakhr al-Dīn, *Asās al-taqdīs.* Ed. Aḥmad Ḥijāzī al-Saqqā. Cairo: Al-Maktaba al-azhariyya, 1406/1986.

–, *Taʾsīs al-taqdīs.* Ed. Anas Muḥammad ʿAdnān al-Sharafāwī and Aḥmad Muḥammad Khayr al-Khaṭīb. Damascus: Dār nūr al-ṣabāḥ, 2011.

Al-Ṣaghīr, ʿAbd al-Majīd, "Mawāqif rushdiyya li-Taqī al-Dīn Ibn Taymiyya? Mulāḥaẓāt awwaliyya." In: *Dirāsāt maghribiyya muhdāt ilā al-mufakkir al-maghribī Muḥammad ʿAzīz al-Habābī*, 1st ed., 93–117. Rabat: 1985. 2nd ed., 164–182. Rabat: Al-Markaz al-thaqīf; al-ʿarabī, 1987.

ʿAmmārī, ʿAbd al-ʿAzīz, *Manāḥī naqd Ibn Taymiyya li-Ibn Rushd.* Beirut: Jadāwil li-l-nashr wa al-tawzīʿ, 2013.

Averroës, *Decisive Treatise & Epistle Dedicatory.* Trans. Charles E. Butterworth. Provo, UT: Brigham Young University Press, 2001.

Averroes, *Faith and Reason in Islam: Averroes' Exposition of Religious Arguments.* Trans. Ibrahim Najjar. Oxford: Oneworld, 2001.

Averroes, *On the Harmony of Religion and Philosophy: A Translation, with Introduction and Notes, of Ibn Rushd's* Kitāb faṣl al-maqāl, *with Its Appendix (*Ḍamīma*) and an Extract from* Kitāb al-kashf ʿan manāhij al-adilla. Trans. George F. Hourani. London: Luzac, 1961.

Averroès, *Tahafot at-Tahafot.* Ed. Maurice Bouyges. Beirut: Imprimerie Catholique, 1930.

Averroes, *Tahafut al-tahafut.* Trans. Simon van den Bergh. 2 vols. London: Luzac, 1954.

Belo, Caterina, *Averroes and Hegel on Philosophy and Religion.* Farnham, UK: Ashgate, 2013.

Canova, Barbara, "Aristote et le Coran dans le *Kitāb al-kašf ʻan manāhiğ al-adilla* d'Averroès." In: *Averroes et la averroïsmes juif et latin: Actes du colloque international (Paris, 16–18 juin 2005)*, ed. Jean-Baptiste Brenet, 193–213. Turnhout, Belgium: Brepols, 2007.

Ceylan, Yasin, *Theology and Tafsīr in the Major Works of Fakhr Al-Dīn Al-Rāzī.* Kuala Lumpur: International Institute of Islamic Thought and Civilization, 1996.

Corbin, Henry, "En Orient, après Averroès." In: *Multiple Averroès: Actes du Colloque International organisé à l'occasion du 850e anniversaire de la naissance d'Averroès. Paris 20–23 septembre 1976*, ed. Jean Jolivet, 323–332. Paris: Les belles lettres, 1978.

Di Donato, Silvia, "Le *Kitāb al-kašf ʻan manāhiğ al-adilla* d'Averroès: Les phases de la rédaction dans les discours sur l'existence de Dieu et sur la direction, d'après l'original arabe et la traduction hébraïque." *Arabic Sciences and Philosophy* 25 (2015): 105–133.

Eichner, Heidrun, "Handbooks in the Tradition of Later Eastern Ashʻarism." In: *The Oxford Handbook of Islamic Theology*, ed. Sabine Schmidtke, 494–514. Oxford, UK: Oxford University Press, 2016.

Fierro, Maribel, "The Religious Policy of the Almohads." In: *The Oxford Handbook of Islamic Theology*, ed. Sabine Schmidtke, 679–692. Oxford, UK: Oxford University Press, 2016.

Geoffroy, Marc, "À Propos de l'almodhadisme d'Averroès: L'anthropomorphisme (*tağsīm*) dans la seconde version du *Kitāb al-kašf ʻan manāhiğ al-adilla.*" In: *Los Almohades: problemas y perspectivas*, ed. Patrice Cressier, Maribel Fierro, and Luis Molina, 2 vols., 2:853–894. Madrid: Consejo superior de investigaciones científicas, 2005.

–, "Ibn Rušd et la théologie almohadist: une version inconnue du *Kitāb al-kašf ʻan manāhiğ al-adilla* dans deux manuscrits d'Istanbul." *Medioevo* 26 (2001): 327–356.

Gilliot, Claude, "La vision de Dieu dans l'au-delà: Exégèse, tradition et théologie en islam." In: *Pensée grecque et sagesse d'orient hommage à Michel Tardieu*, ed. Mohammad Ali Amir-Moezzi, et al., 237–269. Turnhout, Belgium: Brepols, 2009.

Gimaret, Daniel, *La doctrine d'al-Ashʻarī.* Paris: Cerf, 1990.

Griffel, Frank, "Ibn Tūmart's Rational Proof for God's Existence and Unity, and His Connection to the Niẓāmiyya Madrasa in Baghdad." In: *Los Almohades: problemas y perspectivas*, ed. Patrice Cressier, Maribel Fierro, and Luis Molina, 2 vols., 2:753–813. Madrid: Consejo superior de investigaciones científicas, 2005.

Hoover, Jon, "Early Mamlūk Ashʻarīs against Ibn Taymiyya on the nonliteral reinterpretation of God's attributes (*taʼwīl*)." In: *Philosophical Theology in Islam: The Later Ashʻarite Tradition*, ed. Jan Thiele and Ayman Shihadeh. Leiden: Brill, forthcoming.

–, "Perpetual Creativity in the Perfection of God: Ibn Taymiyya's Hadith Commentary on God's Creation of This World." *Journal of Islamic Studies* 15.3 (2004): 287–329.

–, *Ibn Taymiyya's Theodicy of Perpetual Optimism.* Leiden: Brill, 2007.

Ibn Rushd, *Al-Kashf ʻan manāhij al-adilla fī ʻaqāʼid al-milla.* Ed. Muḥammad ʻĀbid al-Jābirī. Beirut: Markaz dirāsāt al-waḥda ʻarabiyya, 1998.

–, *Falsafat Ibn Rushd.* Cairo: al-Maktaba al-maḥmūdiyya al-tijāriyya, 1388/1968.

–, *Kitāb falsafat al-qāḍī al-fāḍil Muḥammad ibn Aḥmad Ibn Rushd al-Andalusī al-mushtamil ʻalā kitābayn jalīlayn, al-awwal* Faṣl al-maqāl fī-mā bayna al-sharīʻa wa al-

ḥikma min al-ittiṣāl *wa* Dhaylihi, *wa al-thānī* al-Kashf ʿan manāhij al-adilla fī ʿaqāʾid al-milla *[wa-yalīhimā]* al-Radd *ʿalā falsafat Ibn Rushd al-ḥafīd taʾlīf Taqī al-Dīn ibn Taymiyya.* 2d printing. Cairo: al-Maṭbaʿa al-jammāliyya, 1328/1910.
–, *Manāhij al-adilla fī ʿaqāʾid al-milla.* Ed. Maḥmūd Qāsim. 2d ed. Cairo: Maktabat al-anjlū al-Miṣriyya, 1964.
Ibn Taymiyya, *Al-Jawāb al-ṣaḥīḥ li-man baddala dīn al-Masīḥ.* Ed. ʿAlī ibn Ḥasan ibn Nāṣir, ʿAbd al-ʿAzīz ibn Ibrāhīm al-ʿAskar, and Ḥamdān ibn Muḥammad al-Ḥamdān. 7 vols. Riyadh: Dār al-ʿāsima, 1993–1999.
–, *Bayān talbīs al-Jahmiyya fī taʾsīs bidaʿihim al-kalāmiyya.* Ed. Yaḥyā ibn Muḥammad al-Hunaydī, et al. 10 vols. 2d printing. Medina: Majmaʿ al-Malik Fahd li-tibāʿat al-muṣḥaf al-sharīf, 1426/2005.
–, *Darʾ taʿāruḍ al-ʿaql wa al-naql.* Ed. Muḥammad Rashād Sālim. 11 vols. Riyadh: Jāmiʿat al-Imām Muḥammad ibn Saʿūd al-Islāmiyya, 1979–1983.
–, *Kitāb al-nubuwwāt.* Ed. ʿAbd al-ʿAzīz ibn Ṣāliḥ al-Ṭuwayyān. 3 vols. Medina: al-Jāmiʿa al-Islāmiyya bi-l-Madīna al-Munawwara, ʿImādat al-baḥth al-ʿilmī, 1420/2000.
–, *Kitāb al-radd ʿalā al-manṭiqiyyīn.* Ed. ʿAbd al-Ṣamad Sharaf al-Dīn al-Kutubī. Bombay: Al-Maṭbaʿa al-qayyima, 1368/1949.
–, *Kitāb al-ṣafadiyya.* Ed. Muḥammad Rashād Sālim. 2 parts in 1 vol. Manṣūra, Egypt: Dār al-hudā al-nabawiyya, 1421/2000.
–, *Minhāj al-sunna al-nabawiyya fī naqḍ kalām al-Shīʿa al-Qadariyya.* Ed. Muḥammad Rashād Sālim. 9 vols. Riyadh: Jāmiʿat al-Imām Muḥammad ibn Saʿūd al-Islāmiyya, 1986.
Maróth, Miklós, "Averroes on the Void." In: *La lumière de l'intellect: La pensée scientifique et philosophique d'Averroès dans son temps*, ed. Ahmad Hasnawi, 11–22. Leuven: Peeters, 2011.
Michot, Jean R., "La pandémie avicennienne au VIe/XIIe siècle: présentation, *editio princeps* et traduction de l'introduction du *Livre de l'advenue du monde* (*Kitāb ḥudūth al-ʿālam*) d'Ibn Ghaylān Al-Balkhī." *Arabica* 40 (1993): 287–344.
Michot, Yahya J., "A Mamlūk Theologian's Commentary on Avicenna's *Risāla Aḍḥawiyya:* Being a Translation of a Part of the *Darʾ al-Taʿāruḍ* of Ibn Taymiyya, with Introduction, Annotation, and Appendices." *Journal of Islamic Studies* 14.2 (2003): 149–203 (Part I) and 14.3 (2003): 309–363 (Part II).
Müller, Marcus Joseph, *Philosophie und Theologie von Averroes.* Munich: G. Franz, 1859.
Renan, Ernest, *Averroès et l'averroïsme: essai historique.* 1st ed. Paris, A. Durand, 1852. 4th ed. Paris: Calmann Lévy, 1882.
Saʿd, al-Ṭablāwī Maḥmūd, *Mawqif Ibn Taymiyya min falsafat Ibn Rushd: Fī al-ʿaqīda wa-ʿilm al-kalām wa al-falsafa.* Cairo: Maṭbaʿat al-amāna, 1409/1989.
Sweetman, J. Windrow, *Islam and Christian Theology.* 2 parts in 2 vols. each. London: Lutterworth, 1945–1967.
Talīlī, ʿAbd al-Raḥmān, "Athar Ibn Rushd fī al-Mashriq al-ʿarabī: Tabīʿat al-radd al-Taymī ʿalā falsafat Ibn Rushd." *Al-Mishkāt* 3 (2005): 55–70.
Taylor, Richard, "Averroes: God and the Noble Lie." In: *Laudemus Viros Gloriosos: Essays in Honor of Armand Maurer, CSB*, 38–59. Notre Dame, IN: University of Notre Dame Press, 2007.
Urvoy, Dominque, *Averroès: Les ambitions d'un intellectual musulman.* Paris: Flammarion, 1998.

von Kügelgen, Anke, "Dialogpartner im Widerspruch: Ibn Rushd und Ibn Taymīya über die "Einheit der Wahrheit"." In: *In Words, Texts and Concepts Cruising the Mediterranean Sea: Studies on the Sources, Contents and Influences of Islamic Civilization and Arabic Philosophy and Science Dedicated to Gerhard Endress on His Sixty-Fifth Birthday*, ed. R. Arnzen and J. Thielmann, 455–481. Leuven: Peeters, 2004.

Wisnovsky, Robert, "Avicenna's Islamic Reception." In: *Interpreting Avicenna: Critical Essays*, ed. Peter Adamson, 190–213. Cambridge, UK: Cambridge University Press, 2013.

Authors

Nariman Aavani is a PhD candidate in the Committee for the Study of Religion at Harvard University. His current research focuses on a cross-cultural study of the notions of selfhood and subjectivity in premodern era (1300–1500AD) in which he investigates the implications of the theories of selfhood for conceptualization of ethics and moral reasoning in this period. His most recent scholarship include the entry on "Qāḍī Sa'īd Qummī" in *Encyclopedia of Philosophy of Religion*, edited by Stewart Goetz and Professor Charles Taliaferro, Wiley-Blackwell, [forthcoming 2019]; "Madhusūdana Sarasvati (d.1640) and Maḥmūd Shabistarī (d.1340) on Self-knowledge: A Reconsideration of the Categories in Philosophy of Religion", a chapter in *A Handbook in Global Critical Philosophy of Religion,* edited by T. Knepper and G. Kopf, Springer, [forthcoming 2018], "Platonism in Safavid Persia: Mīrdāmād and Āqājānī on the Platonic Forms" in *Ishraq: Islamic Philosophy Yearbook*, No. 8: 2017, pp.112–137; and a translation of Jalāl al-Dīn Dawānī's *Risālat al-zawrā'* in *An Anthology of Philosophy in Persia: Vol. 5: From the School of Shiraz to the Twentieth Century.* Edited by Nasr et al. London: I.B. Tauris, 2015.

Peter Adamson is Professor of Late Ancient and Arabic Philosophy at the LMU in Munich. He is the author of two monographs on early Arabic philosophy, the book series *A History of Philosophy Without Any Gaps,* and numerous articles on figures ranging from Plato and Aristotle to Averroes and Fakhr al-Din al-Razi. He has also edited and co-edited numerous books, including *The Cambridge Companion to Arabic Philosophy* (2005) and *Interpreting Avicenna: Critical Essays* (2013).

Hanif Amin Beidokhti is a PhD student of philosophy at Ludwig-Maximilians-Universität München. He studied philosophy and civil engineering in Iran. His interests are mainly in philosophy in the Islamic World, especially the Avicennian and Illuminationist schools, Graeco-Arabic and Islamic Studies. He also teaches classical philosophical Persian at LMU Munich. Currently, he is writing his PhD on Šihāb al-Dīn Suhrawardī's critique of the Peripatetic Doctrines of the Categories and Hylomorphism.

Fedor Benevich has studied philosophy and Islamic studies at EKU Tubingen and LMU Munich. In 2016, he received his PhD at LMU Munich with a thesis on Avicenna's metaphysics and logic. Since 2016, he has worked in the "Heirs of Avicenna" project, funded by DFG at LMU Munich. His research interests include metaphysics and epistemology in late antiquity and the Islamic world. His current research focuses on the post-Avicennian philosophy in the Islamic East. Among his recent publications are *Essentialität und Notwendigkeit: Avicenna und die* Aristotelische *Tradition* (Leiden: Brill, 2018); "The Essence-Existence Distinction: Four Elements of the Post-Avicennian Metaphysical Dispute (11–13th centuries)", Oriens 45.2 (2017): 1–52; "The Reality of the Non-Existent Object of Thought: The Possible, The Impossible, and Mental Existence in Islamic Philosophy (11–13th c.),"*Oxford Studies in Medieval Philosophy* (2018): 31–61.

Davlat Dadikhuda studied medieval and contemporary philosophy at the University of Toronto and Islamic philosophy at McGill University. Currently, he is a doctoral student at the Ludwig-Maximillians-University in Munich, where he works on Avicenna and the Avicennian tradition.

Maribel Fierro (Ph.D. in Semitic Philology, University Complutense of Madrid) is Research Professor at the Institute of Languages and Cultures of the Mediterranean (CSIC – Spain). She has worked and published on the political, religious and intellectual history of al-Andalus and the Islamic West, Islamic law, the construction of orthodoxy and the persecution of heresies, and violence and its representation in Medieval Arabic sources. Her standing research projects are: *Practicing knowledge in Islamic societies and their neighbors* (Anneliese Maier Award 2014, Alexander von Humboldt Foundation) and *Local contexts and global dynamics: al-Andalus and the Maghreb in the Islamic East* (with Mayte Penelas, financed by the Spanish MINECO). Among her publications: *The Almohad revolution. Politics and religion in the Islamic West during the twelfth-thirteenth centuries* (2012), and *Knowledge, heresy and politics in the Medieval Islamic West* (forthcoming). She is the editor of volume 2 (*The Western Islamic world, eleventh-eighteenth centuries*) of *The New Cambridge History of Islam* (2010); *Orthodoxy and heresy in Islam: Critical Concepts in Religious Studies* (2013); with J. Tolan, *The legal status of dimmi-s in the Islamic West* (2013) and with H. Ansari, C. Adang and S. Schmidtke of *Accusations of unbelief in Islam: A diachronic perspective on* takfir (2015).

Dimitri Gutas (Ph.D. 1975, Yale University) is Professor of Arabic at Yale. He has published on the medieval Graeco-Arabic translation movement and its lexicography, the transmission of Greek philosophical texts into Arabic, and Arabic philosophy. Most recently he published the Greek text and medieval Arabic translation of Theophrastus, *On First Principles* (2010), the editio maior of Aristotle's *Poetics* (2012, with Leonardo Tarán), and the revised and enlarged second edition of his foundational *Avicenna and the Aristotelian Tradition* (2014).

Livnat Holtzman is Chair of the Department of Arabic at Bar-Ilan University, Ramat Gan, Israel. Her research fields cover Islamic theology and Islamic traditionalism from the inception of Islam until the 15th century. Her current research focuses on non-textual elements in the process of Hadith transmission. She is co-editor (with Caterina Bori) of *A Scholar in the Shadow: Essays in the Legal and Theological Thought of Ibn Qayyim al-Jawziyya* (*Oriente Moderno* 90/1, 2010). Her most recent publication is *Anthropomorphism in Islam: The Challenge of Traditionalism (700–1350)* (Edinburgh University Press, 2018). This monograph focuses on the discussions on the divine attributes and anthropomorphism (*tashbīh*) among the traditionalistic circles in the major centres of learning in the Islamic world. The monograph also contains the first large-scale analysis of the language of gestures in Islamic theological discourse.

Jon Hoover (Ph.D. University of Birmingham 2002) is Associate Professor of Islamic Studies at the University of Nottingham in the United Kingdom. He has published *Ibn Taymiyya's Theodicy of Perpetual Optimism* (Brill 2007) and historical studies investigating, among other things, Ibn Taymiyya's vision of God's dynamic essence and perpetual creativity, the duration of Hell-Fire according to Ibn Qayyim al-Jawziyya and Ibn al-Wazir, Ibn Taymiyya's defense of theology, and the reception of Ibn Taymiyya. He is editor of the Brill monograph series "The History of Christian-Muslim Relations," and he has written on topics in Christian-Muslim relations and co-edited *The Character of Christian-Muslim Encounter* (Brill 2015). His current research projects focus on Ibn Taymiyya's utilitarianism and his interpretation of God's attributes.

Andreas Lammer is junior professor of Arabic Philosophy, Culture, and History at Trier University in Germany. His primary research interests are in Greek and Arabic natural philosophy in both the Aristotelian and the Avicennian tradition, and more broadly in the transmission of philosophical and scientific literature from Greek into Arabic and from Arabic into Latin. He obtained his PhD in philosophy and Arabic studies from LMU Munich, and published several papers on the notions of time, creation, and nature in Ancient, Late Ancient, and Islamic philosophy as well as a monograph on the history of Greek and Arabic natural philosophy entitled *The Elements of Avicenna's Physics: Greek Sources and Arabic Innovations* (De Gruyter 2018). He is currently working on a translation of al-Ġazālī's masterpiece *The Incoherence of the Philosophers* into German and co-editing a conference volume on doxographical literature in the Greek, Syriac, and Arabic traditions.

Luis Xavier López-Farjeat is associate professor at the Faculty of Philosophy of Universidad Panamericana, Mexico City. He is editor of "Tópicos, Journal of Philosophy" and Associate Director of the "Aquinas and 'the Arabs' International Working Group". He has published on Classical Islamic Philosophy. He has co-edited with Jörg Tellkamp "Philosophical Psychology in Arabic Thought and the Latin Aristotelianism of the 13th Century" (Vrin, Paris, 2013), and with Richard C. Taylor "The Routledge Companion to Islamic Philosophy" (Routledge, New York, 2016).

Yahya Michot (Ph.D. Louvain, 1981) has just retired from Hartford Seminary where he was for ten years Professor of Islamic Thought and editor of *The Muslim World* journal. Before 2008, he taught at Louvain and Oxford. His studies have focused on Avicenna and Ibn Taymiyya. He notably explored Avicenna's influence on later Sunnism and English thought, that of Ibn Taymiyya on pre-Wahhābi puritanism in Turkey and modern Islamism. He has published several books and articles about Islamic thought, drugs in Muslim societies, Ottoman spirituality and European Islam. These publications include *Avicenne: Lettre au vizir Abū Sa'd* (*Editio princeps* & translation, 2000), *al-Aqhisārī: Against Smoking. An Ottoman Manifesto* (2010), *Ibn Taymiyya: Against Extremisms* (2012), and *Ibn Taymiyya: Le sang et la foi d'al-Ḥallāj* (2017). He is currently preparing editions of the pseudo-Ghazālian *Junnat al-asmā'* and of Duncan Black Macdonald's diary of his sabbatical stay in Egypt in 1908.

Yuki Nakanishi is doctoral candidate at the University of Tübingen in Oriental and Islamic Studies (since 2013). His research interest is in Islamicate intellectual history. After receiving his B.A. in Iranian Studies and M.A. in Islamic Studies in Tokyo (2007 and 2009), he worked as a research fellow at the Japan Society for the Promotion of Science (JSPS) (2009–2012) and has been working on his dissertation with the focus on the historical relationship among post-Avicennian intellectual trends, particularly between philosophy, theology (*kalām*) and the so-called "Akbarian mysticism". Among his recent publications are "Demonstrating the Necessity of Existence: The Concept of Relation (*nisbah*) in the Metaphysics of Shams al-Dīn al-Fanārī", in: *Oriento* 52/2 (2009), 76–92; and "Between Critique and Reception of Philosophical Traditions: Ṣā'in al-Dīn ibn

Turka al-Iṣfahānī's (d. 1432) Theory of Science and Existence According to the *Tamhīd al-qawāʿid*", in: *Oriento* 60/1 (2017), 53–63 (both in Japanese).

List of Illustrations, Tables and Diagrams

Index

The index comprises both proper names and key words used in the thirteen articles of this edited volume. The alphabetical order disregards the Arabic definite article (al.). The letter "n" refers to footnotes.